LINUX®
SHELLS BY EXAMPLE

ISBN 0-13-014711-7

PRENTICE HALL PTR
OPEN SOURCE TECHNOLOGY SERIES

- LINUX DESK REFERENCE
  Scott Hawkins

- LINUX ASSEMBLY LANGUAGE PROGRAMMING
  Bob Neveln

- LINUX SHELLS BY EXAMPLE
  Ellie Quigley

LINUX
SHELLS BY EXAMPLE

ELLIE QUIGLEY

Prentice Hall PTR
Upper Saddle River, New Jersey 07458
www.phptr.com

Library of Congress Cataloging in Publication Data

Quigley, Ellie.
Linux shells by example / Ellie Quigley.
p. cm.
ISBN 0-13-014711-7
1. Linux. 2. Operating systems (Computers) I. Title

QA76.76.O63 Q538 2000
005.4'469--dc21

00-024614

Editorial/Production Supervision: *Vanessa Moore*
Cover Design Director: *Jerry Votta*
Cover Designer: *Talar Agasyan*
Manufacturing Manager: *Alexis Heydt*
Marketing Manager: *Kate Hargett*
Acquisitions Editor: *Mark Taub*
Editorial Assistant: *Michael Fredette*
Project Coordinator: *Anne Trowbridge*

Prentice-Hall, Inc.
Upper Saddle River, New Jersey 07458

The publisher offers discounts on this book when ordered in bulk quantities.
For more information, contact:

Corporate Sales Department
Prentice Hall PTR
1 Lake Street
Upper Saddle River, NJ 07458
Phone: 800-382-3419; FAX: 201-236-7141
E-mail: corpsales@prenhall.com

Printed in the United States of America
10 9 8 7 6 5 4 3 2 1

ISBN 0-13-014711-7

Prentice-Hall International (UK) Limited, *London*
Prentice-Hall of Australia Pty. Limited, *Sydney*
Prentice-Hall Canada Inc., *Toronto*
Prentice-Hall Hispanoamericana, S.A., *Mexico*
Prentice-Hall of India Private Limited, *New Delhi*
Prentice-Hall of Japan, Inc., *Tokyo*
Pearson Education Asia Pte. Ltd.
Editora Prentice-Hall do Brasil, Ltda., *Rio de Janeiro*

For Daniel, Christian, Nicky, Jake, Kimby, and Jessie
(the best little kids in the whole wide world!)

TABLE OF CONTENTS

CHAPTER 2

CHAPTER 3

CHAPTER 4

CHAPTER 5

CHAPTER 7

THE GAWK UTILITY: GAWK PROGRAMMING 181

CHAPTER 8

THE INTERACTIVE BASH SHELL . . . 259

CHAPTER 9

CHAPTER 10

CHAPTER 11

APPENDIX A

APPENDIX B

APPENDIX C

PREFACE

Playing the "shell" game has been a lot of fun with UNIX, and now with Linux as well. After publishing my previous book, *UNIX Shells by Example*, Mark Taub (the Prentice Hall acquisitions editor who keeps me writing books) suggested I write a Linux shells book. We both thought it would be "a piece of cake," or at least I did. After all, there shouldn't be much difference between the Bourne and Bourne Again shells, or between C and TC shells; Maybe just a few neat new figures, right? Wrong! This project was like writing a brand new book from scratch.

Although there are many similarities, the UNIX and Gnu tools and shells offer a plethora of new extensions and features. Linux offers not only the Gnu tools, but also a number of fully functional shells. Since I had already covered the Korn shell in detail in *UNIX Shells by Example*, I decided to concentrate on the two most popular Linux shells—Bourne Again shell (*bash*) and TC shell (*tcsh*).

Due to all the new features, enhancements, built-ins, etc., the shell chapters had to be split up, or they would have become unwieldy. What in the previous book consisted of two chapters has now become four. It was a lengthy, tedious process and when I had just about completed the *bash* chapter, I realized I was not using the most up-to-date version, so back to the drawing board I went. Since all of you will not necessarily be using the same version of *bash*, I have tailored this book to cover the old and the new versions.

The first section of this book presents the Gnu tools you will need to write successful shell programs—*gawk*, *grep*, and *sed*. These are the ideal tools for pattern matching, manipulating, text editing, and extracting data from pipes and files.

When learning about the shell, it is presented first as an interactive program where everything can be accomplished at the command line, and then as a programming language where the programming constructs are described and demonstrated in shell scripts.

Having always found that simple examples are easier for quick comprehension, each concept is captured in a small example, followed by the output and an explanation of each line of the program. This method has proven to be very popular with those who learned Perl programming from my first book, *Perl by Example*, and then shell programming from *UNIX Shells by Example*. *Linux Shells by Example* should get you up to speed quickly and before you know it, you will be able to read, write, and maintain shell programs.

The shells are presented in parallel so that if, for example, you want to know how redirection is performed in one shell, there is a parallel discussion of that topic in each of the other shell chapters, and for quick comparison there is a chart in Appendix B of this book.

It is a nuisance to have to go to another book or the Linux man page when all you want is enough information about a particular command to jog your memory on how the command works. To save you time, Appendix A contains a list of useful commands, their syntax, and a definition. Examples and explanations are provided for the more robust and often-used commands.

The comparison chart in Appendix B will help you keep the different shells straight, especially when you port scripts from one shell to another, and as a quick syntax check when all that you need is a reminder of how the construct works. It compares Korn, Borne, Bash, Tcsh, and C shells.

One of the biggest hurdles for shell programmers is using quotes properly. The section on quoting rules in Appendix C presents a step-by-step process for successful quoting in some of the most complex command lines. This procedure has dramatically reduced the amount of time programmers waste when debugging scripts with futile attempts at matching quotes properly.

I think you'll find this book a valuable tutorial and reference. The objective is to explain through example and keep things simple so that you have fun learning and same time. I am confident that you will be a productive shell programmer in a short amount of time. Everything you need is right here at your fingertips. Playing the Linux shell game is fun. You'll see!

Ellie Quigley
www.ellieq.com

ACKNOWLEDGMENTS

My gratitude goes to Elizabeth Stachelin, for her original drawings; Deac Lancaster, for CD creation and editing; Patrick Wilson, for hardware support and proofreading (especially getting Linux up and running on my laptop!); and Melvin Toy, for Linux updates and classroom support.

Thanks also to all the people at Prentice Hall who brought this book into being: production editor Vanessa Moore, the best of the bestest; acquisitions editor, Mark Taub; copy editor, Bernadette Bentley; and proofreader, Miriam O'Neal.

CHAPTER

INTRODUCTION TO LINUX SHELLS

1.1 Why Linux?

In 1991, Linus Torvalds, a Finnish college student, developed a UNIX-compatible operating system kernel at the University of Helsinki, Finland. It was designed to be UNIX on a PC. What started as one man's hobby has become a full-fledged 32-bit operating system installed worldwide on an estimated 10 million computers. And the number of users is growing at a phenomenal rate. At first, Linux appealed to hackers who wanted an operating system that allowed them the freedom to get down to the kernel level, to tweak and probe at the code with the same freedom and enthusiasm shown by the UNIX hackers of the early '80s. Now, as with UNIX, Linux is no longer associated solely with college hackers and "geeks" but has exploded in popularity worldwide for both personal and professional use, often serving systems with large networks of computers. For many, Linux is an alternative to Windows, and a large Linux culture has evolved sponsoring consortiums, conventions, expos, newgroups, and publications in a new revolution to rival Window's dominance in the PC world.

With the help of many system programmers and developers, Linux has grown into today's full-fledged UNIX- and POSIX-compatible operating system. In 1992, the Free Software Foundation added its Gnu software to the Linux kernel to make a complete operating system and licensed the Linux source code under its General Public License. Hundreds of Gnu utilities were provided by the Free Software Foundation, including improvements to the standard UNIX Bourne shell. The Bourne Again shell, the Linux default shell, is an enhanced Bourne shell, not only at the programming level, but also when used interactively, allowing the user to tailor his working environment and create shortcuts to improve efficiency. The Gnu tools, such as *grep*, *sed*, and *gawk*, are similar to their UNIX namesakes, but have also been improved and designed for POSIX[1] compliancy. The combination of the kernel and the Gnu tools and the fact that Linux could run on PCs, made

1. The requirements for shell functionality are defined by the POSIX (Portable Operating System Interface) standard, POSIX 1003.2.

Linux a viable alternative to the proprietary UNIX and Microsoft operating systems, not to mention the fact that Linux is free to anyone who wants it, with all its source code, and a number of office suites and software packages. Whether you download Linux from the Internet, or buy a version distributed on a CD, Linux is portable, stable, and secure. It gives your PC the power of a workstation.

1.1.1 What Is POSIX?

In order to provide software standards for different operating systems and their programs, the POSIX (also referred to as the Open Systems Standards) evolved, consisting of participants from the Institute of Electrical and Electronics Engineering (IEEE) and the International Organization for Standardization (ISO). Their goal was to supply standards that would promote application portability across different platforms, to provide a UNIX-like computing environment; i.e., new software written on one machine that would compile and run on another machine with different hardware. For example, a program written for a BSD UNIX machine will run on Solaris, Linux, and HpUX machines. In 1988 the first standard was adopted, called POSIX 1003.1. Its purpose was to provide a C language standard. In 1992, the POSIX group established standards for the shell and utilities to define the terms for developing portable shell scripts, called the IEEE 1003.2 POSIX shell standard and general utility programs. Although there is no strict enforcement of these standards, most UNIX vendors try to comply with the POSIX standard. The term "POSIX compliancy" when discussing shells and their general UNIX utilities, is an attempt to comply to the standards presented by the POSIX committee, when writing new utilities or adding enhancements to the existing ones. For example, the Bourne Again shell is a shell that is almost 100% compliant and *gawk* is a user utility that can operate in strict POSIX mode.

1.2 Definition and Function of a Shell

The shell is a special program used as an interface between the user and the heart of the operating system, a program called the *kernel*, as shown in Figure 1.1. The kernel is loaded into memory at boot time, and manages the system until shutdown. It creates and controls processes, manages memory, file systems, communications, and so forth. All other programs, including shell programs, reside on the disk. The kernel loads programs from the disk into memory, executes them, and cleans up the system when they terminate. The shell is a utility program that starts up when you log on. It allows users to interact with the kernel by interpreting commands that are typed either at the command line or in a script file.

When you log on, an interactive shell starts up and prompts you for input. After you type a command, it is the responsibility of the shell to: (a) parse the command line; (b) handle wildcards, redirection, pipes, and job control; and (c) search for the command, and if found, execute that command. When you first learn Linux, you spend most of your time executing commands from the prompt. You will be using the shell interactively.

If you type the same set of commands on a regular basis, you may want to automate those tasks. To do so, you place each command in an executable file, called a shell script.

A shell script is much like a batch file. More sophisticated scripts contain programming constructs for making decisions, looping, file testing, and so forth. Writing scripts not only requires learning programming constructs and techniques, but also assumes that you have a good understanding of Linux utilities and how they work. There are some utilities, such as *grep, sed*, and *gawk,* that are extremely powerful when used in scripts for the manipulation of command output and files. After you have become familiar with these tools and the programming constructs for your particular shell, you will be ready to start writing useful scripts. When executing commands from within a script, you will be using the shell as a programming language.

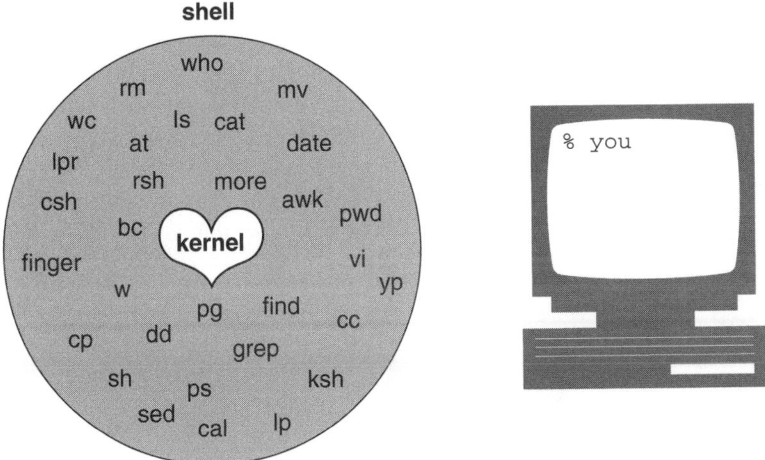

Figure 1.1 The kernel, the shell, and you.

1.2.1 The Three Major UNIX Shells

The three prominent and supported shells on most UNIX systems are the Bourne shell (AT&T shell), the C shell (Berkeley shell), and the Korn shell (superset of the Bourne shell). All three of these shells behave pretty much the same way when running interactively, but have some differences in syntax and efficiency when used as scripting languages.

The Bourne shell is the standard UNIX shell, and the shell used to administer the system. Most of the system administration scripts, such as the *rc start* and *stop* scripts and *shutdown,* are Bourne shell scripts, and when in single-user mode, this is the shell commonly used by the administrator when running as root (superuser). This shell was written at AT&T and is known for being concise, compact, and fast. The default Bourne shell prompt is the dollar sign ($).

The C shell, developed at Berkeley, added a number of features, such as command line history, aliasing, built-in arithmetic, filename completion, and job control. The C shell has been favored over the Bourne shell by users running the shell interactively, but administrators prefer the Bourne shell for scripting, because Bourne shell scripts are simpler and faster than the same scripts written in C shell. The default C shell prompt is the percent sign (%).

The Korn shell is a superset of the Bourne shell written by David Korn at AT&T. A number of features were added to this shell above and beyond the enhancements of the C shell. Korn shell features include an editable history, aliases, functions, regular expression wildcards, built-in arithmetic, job control, coprocessing, and special debugging features. The Bourne shell is almost completely upward-compatible with the Korn shell, so older Bourne shell programs run fine in this shell. The default Korn shell prompt is the dollar sign ($).

1.2.2 The Major Linux Shells

The shells used by Linux do not exclusively belong to the Linux operating system. They are freely available and can be compiled on any UNIX system. But when you install Linux, you will have access to the Gnu shells and tools, not the standard UNIX shells and tools. Although Linux supports a number of shells, the Bourne Again shell (*bash)* and the TC shell (*tcsh)* are by far the most popular. The Z shell is another Linux shell that incorporates a number of features from the Bourne Again shell, the TC shell, and the Korn shell. The Public Domain Korn shell (*pdksh*) a Korn shell clone, is also available, and for a fee you can get AT&T's Korn shell, not to mention a host of other unknown smaller shells.

To see what shells are available under your version of Linux, look in the file, */etc/shell.*

EXAMPLE 1.1

```
$ cat /etc/shell
/bin/bash
/bin/sh
/bin/ash
/bin/bsh
/bin/tcsh
/bin/csh
/bin/ksh
/bin/zsh
```

EXPLANATION

1 The */etc/shell* file contains a list of all shell programs available on your version of Linux. The most popular versions are *bash* (Bourne Again shell)*, tcsh* (TC shell), and *ksh* (Korn shell).

To change to one of the shells listed in */etc/shell*, type the *chsh* command and the name of the shell. For example, to change permanently to the TC shell, use the *chsh* command. At the prompt, type:

```
chsh /bin/tcsh
```

1.2.3 History of the Shells

The first significant, standard UNIX shell was introduced in V7 (seventh edition of AT&T) UNIX in late 1979, and was named after its creator, Stephen Bourne. The Bourne shell as a programming language is based on a language called Algol, and was primarily used to automate system administration tasks. Although popular for its simplicity and speed, it lacks many of the features for interactive use, such as history, aliasing, and job control. Enter *bash*, the Bourne Again shell, which was developed by Brian Fox of the Free Software Foundation under the Gnu copyleft license and is the default shell for the very popular Linux operating system. It was intended to conform to the IEEE POSIX P1003.2/ISO 9945.2 Shell and Tools standard. *Bash* also offers a number of new features (both at the interactive and programming level) missing in the original Bourne shell (yet Bourne shell scripts will still run unmodified). It also incorporates the most useful features of both the C shell and Korn shell. It's big. The improvements over Bourne shell are: command line history and editing, directory stacks, job control, functions, aliases, arrays, integer arithmetic (in any base from 2 to 64), and Korn shell features, such as extended metacharacters, select loops for creating menus, the let command, etc.

The C shell, developed at the University of California at Berkeley in the late 1970s, was released as part of 2BSD UNIX. The shell, written primarily by Bill Joy, offered a number of additional features not provided in the standard Bourne shell. The C shell is based on the C programming language, and when used as a programming language, it shares a similar syntax. It also offers enhancements for interactive use, such as command line history, aliases, and job control. Because the shell was designed on a large machine and a number of additional features were added, the C shell has a tendency to be slow on small machines and sluggish even on large machines when compared to the Bourne shell.

The TC shell is an expanded version of the C shell. Some of the new features are: command line editing (emacs and vi), scrolling the history list, advanced filename, variable, and command completion, spelling correction, scheduling jobs, automatic locking and logout, time stamps in the history list, etc. It's also big.

With both the Bourne shell and the C shell available, the UNIX user now had a choice, and conflicts arose over which was the better shell. David Korn, from AT&T, invented the Korn shell in the mid-1980s. It was released in 1986 and officially became part of the SVR4 distribution of UNIX in 1988. The Korn shell, really a superset of the Bourne shell, runs not only on UNIX systems, but also on OS/2, VMS, and DOS. It provides upward-compatibility with the Bourne shell, adds many of the popular features of the C shell, and is fast and efficient. The Korn shell has gone through a number of revisions. The most widely used version of the Korn shell is the 1988 version, although the 1993 version is gaining popularity. Linux users may find they are running the free version of the Korn shell, called The Public Domain Korn shell, or simply *pdksh*, a clone of David Korn's 1988 shell. It is free and portable and currently work is underway to make it fully compatible with its namesake, Korn shell, and to make it POSIX compliant. Also available is the Z shell (*zsh*), another Korn shell clone with TC shell features, written by Paul Falsted, and freely available at a number of Web sites.

1.2.4 What Shells This Book Covers

Due to the great number of new features provided in the Bourne Again shell and TC shell, this book will concentrate on those two popular shells. The Korn shell, as well as Bourne and C shell, were presented in *UNIX Shells by Example*[2], and will not be covered again here. The Bourne Again shell, as of Release 2.0, is very similar in functionality to the Korn shell as a programming language, with many of the features of the C shell when used interactively. The TC shell, likewise, is almost identical to the C shell when used as a programming language, but has many new features for interactive use.

1.2.5 Uses of a Shell

One of the major uses of a shell is to interpret commands entered at the prompt. The shell parses the command line, breaking it into words (called *tokens*), separated by white space, i.e., tabs, spaces, or a newline. If the words contain special metacharacters, the shell evaluates them. The shell handles file I/O and background processing. After the command line has been processed, the shell searches for the command and starts its execution.

Another important function of the shell is to customize the user's environment, normally done in shell initialization files. These files contain definitions for setting terminal keys and window characteristics; setting variables that define the search path, permissions, prompts, and the terminal type; and setting variables that are required for specific applications such as windows, text-processing programs, and libraries for programming languages. The Bourne Again and the TC shells also provide further customization with the addition of history and aliases, filename and command completion, spell checking, help features, built-in variables set to protect the user from clobbering files, inadvertently logging out, and to notify the user when a job has completed, etc.

The shell can also be used as an interpreted programming language. Shell programs, also called scripts, consist of commands listed in a file. The programs are created in an editor (although online scripting is permitted). They consist of Linux commands interspersed with fundamental programming constructs, such as variable assignment, conditional tests, and loops. You do not have to compile shell scripts. The shell interprets each line of the script as if it had been entered from the keyboard. Because the shell is responsible for interpreting commands, it is necessary for the user to have an understanding of what those commands are. Appendix A of this book contains a list of useful commands and how they work.

1.2.6 Responsibilities of the Shell

The shell is ultimately responsible for making sure that any commands typed at the prompt get properly executed. Included in those responsibilities are:

1. Reading input and parsing the command line.
2. Evaluating special characters.

---

2. Quigley, Ellie. *UNIX Shells by Example, 2nd Edition*. Upper Saddle River, NJ: Prentice Hall, 1999.

3. Setting up pipes, redirection, and background processing.
4. Handling signals.
5. Setting up programs for execution.

Each of these topics is discussed in detail as it pertains to a particular shell.

1.3 System Startup and the Login Shell

When you start up your system, the first process is called *init*. Each process has a process identification number associated with it, called the *PID*. Because *init* is the first process, its PID is 1. The *init* process initializes the system and then starts another process to open terminal lines, and sets up the standard input (*stdin*), standard output (*stdout*), and standard error (*stderr*), which are all associated with the terminal. The standard input normally comes from the keyboard; the standard output and standard error go to the screen. At this point, a login prompt (*Login:*) appears at your console. After you type your login name, you are prompted for a password (you will be given up to 10 chances to enter the correct password). The */bin/login* program then verifies your identity by checking the first field in the /etc/*passwd* file. If your username is there, the next step is to run the password you typed through an encryption program to determine if it is indeed the correct password. Once your password is verified, the *login* program sets up an initial environment consisting of variables that define the working environment that will be passed to the shell. The *HOME, SHELL, USER,* and *LOGNAME* variables are assigned values extracted from information in the */etc/passwd* file. The *HOME* variable is assigned your home directory; the *SHELL* variable is assigned the name of the login shell, the last entry in the *passwd* file. The *USER* and/or *LOGNAME* variables are assigned your login name. A PATH variable to help the shell find commonly used utilities is located in specified directories. It is a colon separated list initially set to: */usr/local/bin:/bin:/usr/bin*. When *login* has finished, it will execute the program found in the last entry of the */etc/passwd* file. Normally, this program is a shell. If the last entry in the */etc/passwd* file is */bin/tcsh* or *bin/csh*, the TC shell program is executed. If the last entry in the */etc/passwd* file is */bin/bash, /bin/sh,* or is null, the Bourne Again shell starts up. If the last entry is */bin/pdksh*, the Public Domain Korn shell is executed. This shell is called the *login shell.*

After the shell starts up, it checks for any systemwide initialization files and then checks your home directory to see if there are any shell-specific initialization files there. If any of these files exist, they are executed. The initialization files are used to further customize the user environment. After the commands in those files have been executed, a shell prompt appears on your console, unless a windowing program, such as X Windows or Gnome is launched, at which point a number of *xterm* or visual shell windows will appear. When you see the shell prompt, either at the console or in an *xterm* or other desktop window, the shell program is now waiting for your input.

1.3.1 Parsing the Command Line

When you type a command at the prompt, the shell reads a line of input and parses the command line, breaking the line into words, called *tokens*. Tokens are separated by spaces or tabs, and the command line is terminated by a newline.[3] The shell then checks to see whether the first word is a built-in command or an executable program stored on disk. If it is built-in, the shell will execute the command internally. Otherwise, the shell will search the directories listed in the *PATH* variable to find out where the program resides. If the program is found, the shell will fork a new process and then execute the program. The shell will sleep (or wait) until the program finishes execution and then, if necessary, will report the status of the exiting program. A prompt will appear and the whole process will start again. The order of processing the command line is as follows:

1. History substitution (if set).
2. Command line is broken up into tokens (words).
3. History is updated.
4. Quotes are processed.
5. Alias substitution and functions are defined (if applicable).
6. Redirection, background, and pipes are set up.
7. Variable substitution (*$user*, *$name*, etc.) is performed.
8. Command substitution (echo for *today is 'date'*) is performed.
9. Filename substitution, called *globbing* (*cat abc.??*, *rm *.c*, etc.) is performed.
10. Program execution.

1.3.2 Types of Commands

When a command is executed, it is an alias, a function, a built-in command, or an executable program on disk. Aliases are abbreviations (nicknames) for existing commands and apply to the C, TC, Bash, and Korn shells. Functions apply to the Bourne (introduced with AT&T System V, Release 2.0), Bash, and Korn shells. They are groups of commands organized as separate routines. Aliases and functions are defined within the shell's memory. Built-in commands are internal routines in the shell, and executable programs reside on disk. The shell uses the path variable to locate the executable programs on disk and forks a child process before the command can be executed. This takes time. When the shell is ready to execute the command, it evaluates command types in the following order:[4]

1. Aliases
2. Keywords
3. Functions (*bash*)
4. Built-in commands
5. Executable programs

---

3. The process of breaking the line up into tokens is called *lexical analysis*.

4. Numbers 3 and 4 are reversed for Bourne and Korn(88) shells. Number 3 does not apply for C and TC shells.

If, for example, the command is "xyz," the shell will check to see if "xyz" is an alias. If not, is it a built-in command or a function? If neither of those, it must be an executable command residing on the disk. The shell then must search the path for the command.

1.4 Processes and the Shell

1.4.1 What Is a Process?

A process is a program in execution and can be identified by its unique PID (process identification) number. The kernel controls and manages processes. A process consists of the executable program, its data and stack, program and stack pointer, registers, and all the information needed for the program to run. When you log in, the process running is normally a shell (*bash*)[5], called the login shell. The shell belongs to a process group identified by the group's PID. Only one process group has control of the terminal at a time and is said to be running in the foreground. When you log on, your shell is in control of the terminal and waits for you to type a command at the prompt. On Linux systems, the shell will normally start up another process, *xinit*, to launch the X Windowing system. After X Windows starts, a window manager process (*twm, fvwm,* etc.) is executed, providing a virtual desktop.[6] Then from a pop-up menu, you can start up a number of other processes, such as *xterm* (gets a terminal), *xman* (provides manual pages), or *emacs* (starts a text editor). Multiple processes are running and monitored by the Linux kernel, allocating each of the processes a little slice of the CPU in a way that is unnoticeable to the user.

1.4.2 What Is a System Call?

The shell can spawn (create) other processes. In fact, when you enter a command at the prompt or from a shell script, the shell has the responsibility of finding the command either in its internal code (built-in) or out on the disk, and then arranging for the command to be executed. This is done with calls to the kernel, called *system calls*. A system call is a request for kernel services and the only way a process can access the system's hardware. There are a number of system calls that allow processes to be created, executed, and terminated. (The shell provides other services from the kernel when it performs redirection and piping, command substitution, and the execution of user commands.) The system calls used by the shell to cause new processes to run are discussed in the following sections. See Figure 1.2.

5. The default Linux shell is *bash*, the Bourne Again shell.
6. A number of desktop environments come with Linux, including Gnome, KDE, X, etc.

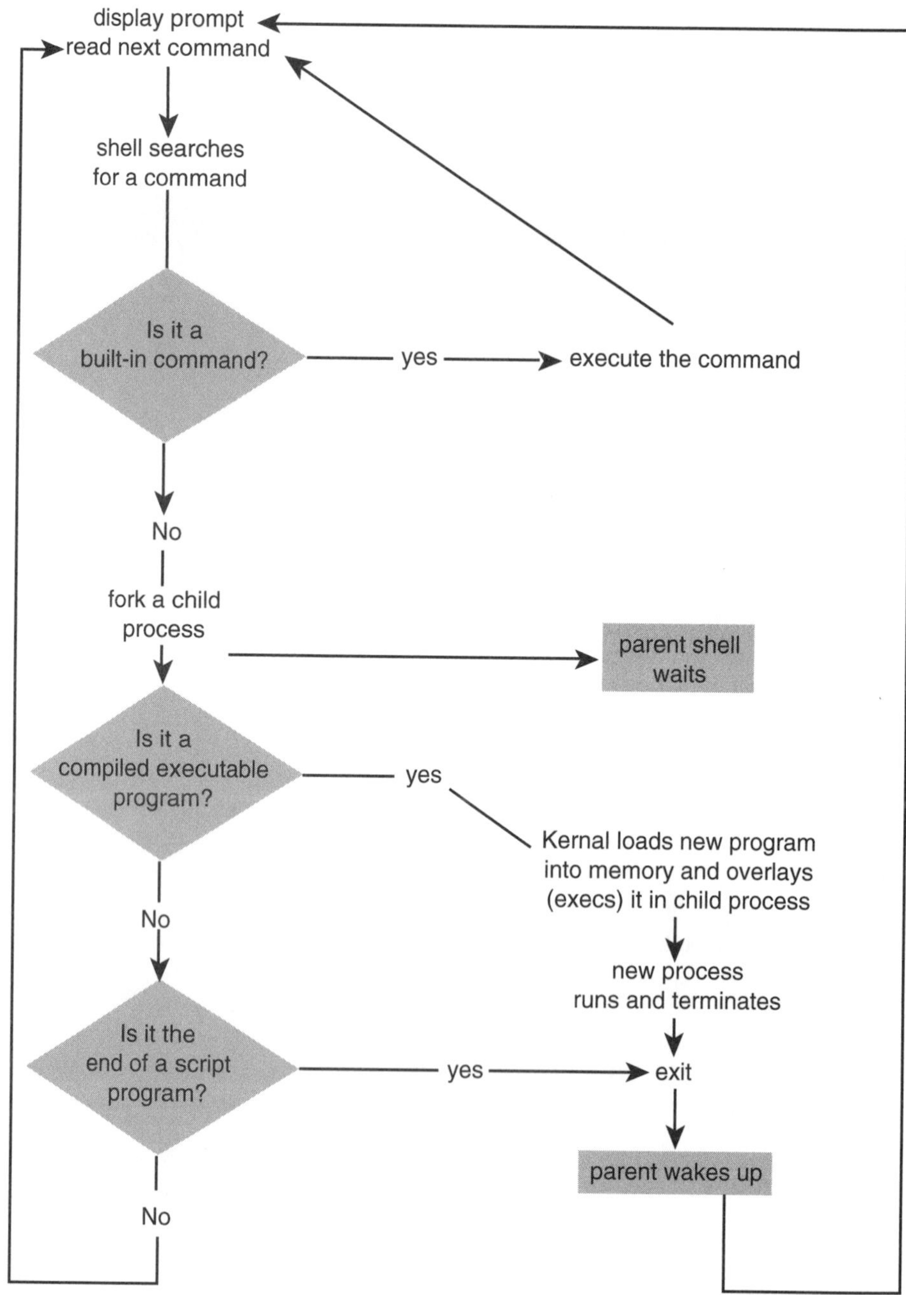

Figure 1.2 The shell and command execution.

1.4.3 What Processes Are Running?

The *ps* Command. The *ps* command with its many options displays a list of the processes currently running in a number of formats. The following example shows all processes that are running by users on a Linux system. (See Appendix A for *ps* and its options.)

EXAMPLE 1.2

```
$ ps au   (Linux ps)
USER        PID %CPU %MEM  SIZE   RSS TTY STAT START   TIME COMMAND
ellie       456  0.0  1.3  1268   840   1 S    13:23   0:00 -bash
ellie       476  0.0  1.0  1200   648   1 S    13:23   0:00 sh
/usr/X11R6/bin/sta
ellie       478  0.0  1.0  2028   676   1 S    13:23   0:00 xinit
/home/ellie/.xi
ellie       480  0.0  1.6  1852  1068   1 S    13:23   0:00 fvwm2
ellie       483  0.0  1.3  1660   856   1 S    13:23   0:00
/usr/X11R6/lib/X11/fv
ellie       484  0.0  1.3  1696   868   1 S    13:23   0:00
/usr/X11R6/lib/X11/fv
ellie       487  0.0  2.0  2348  1304   1 S    13:23   0:00 xclock -bg
#c0c0c0 -p
ellie       488  0.0  1.1  1620   724   1 S    13:23   0:00
/usr/X11R6/lib/X11/fv
ellie       489  0.0  2.0  2364  1344   1 S    13:23   0:00 xload -
nolabel -bg gr
ellie       495  0.0  1.3  1272   848  p0 S    13:24   0:00 -bash
ellie       797  0.0  0.7   852   484  p0 R    14:03   0:00 ps au
root        457  0.0  0.4   724   296   2 S    13:23   0:00
/sbin/mingetty tty2
root        458  0.0  0.4   724   296   3 S    13:23   0:00
/sbin/mingetty tty3
root        459  0.0  0.4   724   296   4 S    13:23   0:00
/sbin/mingetty tty4
root        460  0.0  0.4   724   296   5 S    13:23   0:00
/sbin/mingetty tty5
root        461  0.0  0.4   724   296   6 S    13:23   0:00
/sbin/mingetty tty6
root        479  0.0  4.5 12092  2896   1 S    13:23   0:01 X :0
root        494  0.0  2.5  2768  1632   1 S    13:24   0:00 nxterm
-ls -sb -fn
```

The *pstree* Command. Another way to see what processes are running and what processes are child processes is to use the Linux *pstree* command. The *pstree* command displays all processes as a tree with its root being the first process that runs, called *init*. If a user name is specified, then that user's processes are at the root of the tree. If a process spawns more than one process of the same name, *pstree* visually merges the identical branches by putting them in square brackets and prefixing them with the number of times the processes is repeated. To illustrate, in the following example, the *httpd* server process has started up 10 child processes. (See Appendix A for list of *pstree* options.)

EXAMPLE 1.3

```
pstree
init---4*[getty]
init-+-atd
     |-bash---startx---xinit-+-X
     |                       `-fvwm2-+-FvwmButtons
     |                               |-FvwmPager
     |                               `-FvwmTaskBar
     |-cardmgr
     |-crond
     |-gpm
     |-httpd---10*[httpd]
     |-ifup-ppp---pppd---chat
     |-inetd
     |-kerneld
     |-kflushd
     |-klogd
     |-kswapd
     |-lpd
     |-2*[md_thread]
     |-5*[mingetty]

              |-nmbd
     |-nxterm---bash---tcsh---pstree
     |-portmap
     |-sendmail
     |-smbd
     |-syslogd
     |-update
     |-xclock
     `-xload
```

1.4.4 System Calls for Creating and Terminating Processes

The *fork* System Call. A new process is created with the *fork* system call. The *fork* system call creates a duplicate of the calling process. The new process is called the *child* and the process that created it is called the *parent.* The child process starts running right after the call to *fork*, and both processes initially share the CPU. The child process has a copy of the parent's environment, open files, real and user identifications, umask, current working directory, and signals.

When you type a command, the shell parses the command line and determines whether or not the first word is a built-in command or an executable program. If the command is built-in, the shell handles it, but if not, the shell invokes the *fork* system call to make a copy of itself (see Figure 1.3). Its child will search the path to find the command, as well as set up the file descriptors for redirection, pipes, command substitution, and background processing. While the child shell works, the parent normally sleeps. (See "The *wait* System Call" below.)

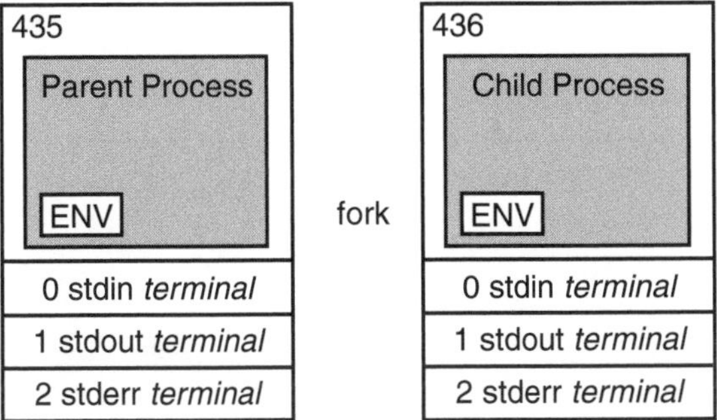

Figure 1.3 The *fork* system call.

The *wait* System Call. The parent shell is programmed to go to sleep (wait) while the child takes care of details such as handling redirection, pipes, and background processing. The *wait* system call causes the parent process to suspend until one of its children terminates. If *wait* is successful, it returns the PID of the child that died and the child's exit status. If the parent does not wait and the child exits, the child is put in a zombie state (suspended animation) and will stay in that state until either the parent calls *wait* or the parent dies.[7] If the parent dies before the child, the *init* process adopts any orphaned zombie process. The *wait* system call, then, is not just used to put a parent to sleep, but to ensure that the process terminates properly.

The *exec* System Call. After you enter a command at the terminal, the shell normally forks off a new shell process: the child process. As mentioned earlier, the child shell is responsible for causing the command you typed to be executed. It does this by calling the *exec* system call. Remember, the user command is really just an executable program. The shell searches the path for the new program. If it is found, the shell calls the *exec* system call with the name of the command as its argument. The kernel loads this new program into memory in place of the shell that called it. The child shell, then, is overlaid with the new program. The new program becomes the child process and starts executing. Although the new process has its own local variables, all environment variables, open files, signals, and the current working directory are passed to the new process. This process exits when it has finished, and the parent shell wakes up.

7. To remove zombie processes, the system must be rebooted.

The *exit* System Call. A program can terminate at any time by executing the *exit* call. When a child process terminates, it sends a signal (*sigchild*) and waits for the parent to accept its exit status. The exit status is a number between 0 and 255.[8] An exit status of zero indicates that the program executed successfully, and a nonzero exit status means that the program failed in some way.

For example, if the command *ls* had been typed at the command line, the parent shell would *fork* a child process and go to sleep. The child shell would then *exec* (overlay) the *ls* program. The *ls* program would run in place of the child, inheriting all the environment variables, open files, user information, and state information. When the process (*ls*) finished execution, it would exit and the parent shell would wake up. A prompt would appear on the screen, and the shell would wait for another command. If you are interested in knowing how a command exited, each shell has a special built-in variable that contains the exit status of the last command that terminated. (All of this will be explained in detail in the individual shell chapters.) See Figure 1.4 on page 15 for an example of process creation and termination.

EXAMPLE 1.4

```
    (C and TC Shell)
1   > cp filex filey
    > echo $status
    0
2   > cp xyz
    Usage: cp [-ip] f1 f2; or: cp [-ipr] f1 ... fn d2
    > echo $status
    1
    (Tcsh, Bourne, Korn, and Bash Shells)
3   $ cp filex filey
    $ echo $?
    0
    $ cp xyz
    Usage: cp [-ip] f1 f2; or: cp [-ipr] f1 ... fn d2
    $ echo $?
    1
```

EXPLANATION

1 The *cp* (copy) command is entered at the TC shell command line prompt (>). After the command has made a copy of *filex* called *filey*, the program exits and the prompt appears. The tcsh *status* variable contains the exit status of the last command that was executed. If the status is zero, the *cp* program exited with success. If the exit status is nonzero, the *cp* program failed in some way.

---

8. If the program is terminated by a signal, its return value is 128 + *n*, where *n* is the signal number.

EXPLANATION (CONTINUED)

2 When entering the *cp* command, the user failed to provide two filenames: the source and destination files. The *cp* program sent an error message to the screen, and exited, with a status of one. That number is stored in the tcsh *status* variable. Any number other than zero indicates that the program failed.

3 The Tcsh, Bourne, Bash, and Korn shells process the *cp* command as the TC shell did in the first two examples. The only difference is that the Bourne and Korn shells store the exit status in the *?* variable, rather than the *status* variable. [a]

a. The TC shell provides both the *status* and *?* variables for holding exit status.

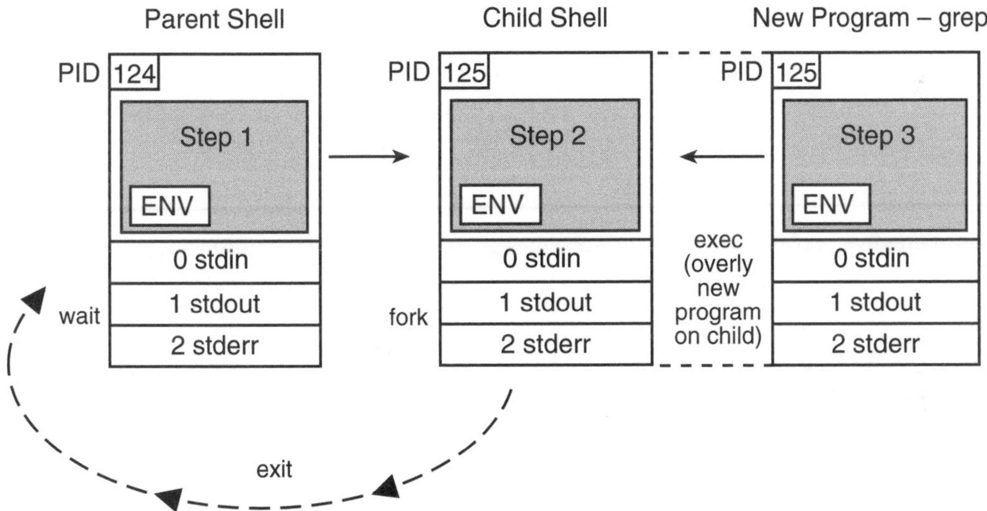

Figure 1.4 The *fork, exec, wait,* and *exit* system calls. See following Explanation.

EXPLANATION

1 The parent shell creates a copy of itself with the *fork* system call. The copy is called the child shell.

2 The child shell has a new PID and is a copy of its parent. It will share the CPU with the parent.

3 The kernel loads the *grep* program into memory and executes (*exec*) it in place of the child shell. The *grep* program inherits the open files and environment from the child.

4 The *grep* program exits, the kernel cleans up, and the parent is awakened.

1.5 The Environment and Inheritance

When you log on, the shell starts up and inherits a number of variables, I/O streams, and process characteristics from the */bin/login* program that started it. In turn, if another shell is spawned (forked) from the login or parent shell, that child shell (subshell) will inherit certain characteristics from its parent. A subshell may be started for a number of reasons: for handling background processing; for handling groups of commands; or for executing scripts. The child shell inherits an environment from its parent. The environment consists of process permissions (who owns the process), the working directory, the file creation mask, special variables, open files, and signals.

1.5.1 Ownership

When you log on, the shell is given an identity. It has a real user identification (*UID*), one or more real group identifications (*GID*), and an effective user identification and effective group identification (*EUID* and *EGID*). The EUID and EGID are initially the same as the real UID and GID. These ID numbers are found in the *passwd* file and are used by the system to identify users and groups. The EUID and EGID determine what permissions a process has access to when reading, writing, or executing files. If the EUID of a process and the real UID of the owner of the file are the same, the process has the owner's access permissions for the file. If the EGID and real GID of a process are the same, the process has the owner's group privileges.

The UID, found in the */etc/passwd* file, is called the real UID. Its value is a positive integer that is associated with your login name. The real UID is the third field in the password file. When you log on, the login shell is assigned the real UID and all processes spawned from the login shell inherit its permissions. Any process running with a UID of zero belongs to root (the superuser) and has root privileges. The real group identification, the GID, associates a group with your login name. It is found in the fourth field of the password file.

The EUID and EGID can be changed to numbers assigned to a different owner. By changing the EUID (or EGID[9]) to another owner, you can become the owner of a process that belongs to someone else. Programs that change the EUID or EGID to another owner are called *setuid* or *setgid* programs. The */bin/passwd* program is an example of a *setuid* program that gives the user root privileges. *Setuid* programs are often sources for security holes. The shell allows you to create *setuid* scripts, and the shell itself may be a *setuid* program.

1.5.2 The File Creation Mask

When a file is created, it is given a set of default permissions. These permissions are determined by the program creating the file. Child processes inherit a default mask from their

9. The *setgid* permission is system-dependent in its use. On some systems, the *setgid* on a directory may cause files created in that directory to belong to the same group that is owned by the directory. On others, the EGID of the process determines the group that can use the file.

parents. The user can change the mask for the shell by issuing the *umask* command at the prompt or by setting it in the shell's initialization files. The *umask* command is used to remove permissions from the existing mask.

Initially, the *umask* is 000, giving a directory 777 (*rwxrwxrwx*) permissions and a file 666 (*rw-rw-rw-*) permissions as the default. On most systems, the *umask* is assigned a value of *022* by the */bin/login* program or the */etc/profile* initialization file.

The *umask* value is subtracted from the default settings for both the directory and file permissions as follows:

```
 777 (Directory)                    666 (File)
-022 (umask value)                 -022 (umask value)
-------                            ---------
 755                                644

Result: drwxr-xr-x                 -rw-r--r--
```

After the *umask* is set, all directories and files created by this process are assigned the new default permissions. In this example, directories will be given read, write, and execute for the owner; read and execute for the group; and read and execute for the rest of the world (others). Any files created will be assigned read and write for the owner, and read for the group and others. To change permissions on individual directories and permissions, the *chmod* command is used.

1.5.3 Changing Ownership and Permissions

The *chmod* Command. The *chmod* command changes permissions on files and directories. Every Linux file has a set of permissions associated with it to control who can read, write, or execute the file. There is one owner for every Linux file and only the owner or the superuser can change the permissions on a file or directory. A group may have a number of members, and the owner of the file may change the group permissions on a file so that the group can enjoy special privileges. To see what permissions a file has, type at the shell prompt:

```
ls -l filename
```

A total of nine bits constitutes the permissions on a file. The first set of three bits controls the permissions of the owner of the file, the second set controls the permissions of the group, and the last set controls the permissions for everyone else. The permissions are stored in the mode field of the file's inode. The user must own the files to change permissions on them.[10]

10. The caller's EUID must match the owner's UID of the file, or the owner must be superuser.

Table 1.1 illustrates the eight possible combinations of numbers used for changing permissions.

Table 1.1 Permission Modes

Decimal	*Binary*	*Permissions*
0	000	none
1	001	--x
2	010	-w-
3	011	-wx
4	100	r--
5	101	r-x
6	110	rw-
7	111	rwx

The symbolic notation for *chmod* is as follows:
r = read; *w* = write; *x* = execute; *u* = user; *g* = group; *o* = others; *a* = all.

EXAMPLE 1.5

```
1  $ chmod 755 file
   $ ls -l file
   -rwxr-xr-x 1 ellie 0 Mar  7 12:52 file
2  $ chmod g+w file
   $ ls -l file
   -rwxrwxr-x  1 ellie 0 Mar 7 12:54 file
3  $ chmod go-rx file
   $ ls -l file
   -rwx-w---- 1 ellie 0 Mar 7 12:56 file
4  $ chmod a=r file
   $ ls -l file
   -r--r--r-- 1 ellie 0 Mar 7 12:59 file
```

EXPLANATION

1. The first argument is the octal value *755*. It turns on *rwx* for the user, *r* and *x* for the group, and others for file.
2. In the symbolic form of *chmod*, write permission is added to the group.
3. In the symbolic form of *chmod*, read and execute permission are subtracted from the group and others.
4. In the symbolic form of *chmod*, all are given only read permission. The = sign causes all permissions to be reset to the new value.

The *chown* Command. The *chown* command changes the owner and group on files and directories. On Linux, only the superuser, *root*, can change ownership. To see the usage and options for *chown*, use the *chown* command with the *--help* option as shown in Example 1.6. Example 1.7 demonstrates how to use *chown*.

EXAMPLE 1.6

```
(The Command Line)
# chown --help
Usage: chown [OPTION]... OWNER[.[GROUP]] FILE...
  or:  chown [OPTION]... .[GROUP] FILE...
Change the owner and/or group of each FILE to OWNER and/or GROUP.

  -c, --changes            be verbose whenever change occurs
  -h, --no-dereference     affect symbolic links instead of any
                           referenced file
                           (available only on systems with lchown
                           system call)
  -f, --silent, --quiet    suppress most error messages
  -R, --recursive          operate on files and directories recursively
  -v, --verbose            explain what is being done
      --help               display this help and exit
      --version            output version information and exit

Owner is unchanged if missing. Group is unchanged if missing, but
changed to login group if implied by a period. A colon may replace
the period.

Report bugs to fileutils-bugs@gnu.ai.mit.edu
```

EXAMPLE 1.7

```
(The Command Line)
1   $ ls -l filetest
    -rw-rw-r--   1 ellie    ellie          0 Jan 10 12:19 filetest
2   $ chown root filetest
    chown: filetest: Operation not permitted
3   $ su root
    Password:
4   # ls -l filetest
   -rw-rw-r--   1 ellie    ellie           0 Jan 10 12:19 filetest
5   # chown root filetest
6   # ls -l filetest
    -rw-rw-r--   1 root     ellie          0 Jan 10 12:19 filetest
7   # chown root:root filetest
8   # ls -l filetest
    -rw-rw-r--   1 root     root           0 Jan 10 12:19 filetest
```

EXPLANATION

1 The user and group ownership of *filetest* is *ellie.*

2 The *chown* command will only work if you are the superuser, i.e., user *root.*

3 The user changes identity to *root* with the *su* command.

4 The listing shows that user and group are *ellie* for *filetest.*

5 Only the superuser can change the ownership of files and directories. Ownership of *filetest* is changed to *root* with the *chown* command. Group ownership is still *ellie.*

6 Output of *ls* shows that *root* now owns *filetest.*

7 The colon (or a dot) is used to indicate that owner *root* will now change the group ownership to *root.* The groupname is listed after the colon. There can be no spaces.

8 The user and group ownership for *filetest* now belongs to *root.*

1.5.4 The Working Directory

When you log on, you are given a working directory within the file system, called the *home directory.* The working directory is inherited by processes spawned from this shell. Any child process of this shell can change its own working directory, but the change will have no effect on the parent shell.

The *cd* command, used to change the working directory, is a shell built-in command. Each shell has its own copy of *cd.* A built-in command is executed directly by the shell as part of the shell's code; the shell does not perform the *fork* and *exec* system calls when executing built-in commands. If another shell (script) is forked from the parent shell, and the *cd* command is issued in the child shell, the directory will be changed in the child shell. When the child exits, the parent shell will be in the same directory it was in before the child started.

1.5.5 Variables

The shell can define two types of variables: local and environment. The variables contain information used for customizing the shell, and information required by other processes so that they will function properly. Local variables are private to the shell in which they are created and not passed on to any processes spawned from that shell. Environment variables, on the other hand, are passed from parent to child process, from child to grandchild, and so on. Some of the environment variables are inherited by the login shell from the */bin/login* program. Others are created in the user initialization files, in scripts, or at the command line. If an environment variable is set in the child shell, it is not passed back to the parent.

EXAMPLE 1.8

```
1   > cd /

2   > pwd
    /

3   > bash

4   $ cd /home

5   $ pwd
    /home

6   $ exit

7   > pwd
    /

    >
```

EXPLANATION

1 The > prompt is a TC shell prompt. The *cd* command changes directory to /. The *cd* command is built into the shell's internal code.

2 The *pwd* command displays the present working directory, /.

3 The Bash shell is started.

4 The *cd* command changes directories to */home*. The dollar sign (*$*) is the Bash prompt.

5 The *pwd* command displays the present working directory, */home*.

6 The Bash shell is exited, returning to the TC shell.

7 In the TC shell, the present working directory is still /. Each shell has its own copy of *cd*.

1.5.6 Redirection and Pipes

File Descriptors. All I/O, including files, pipes, and sockets, are handled by the kernel via a mechanism called the *file descriptor*. A file descriptor is a small unsigned integer, an index into a file-descriptor table maintained by the kernel and used by the kernel to reference open files and I/O streams. Each process inherits its own file-descriptor table from its parent. The first three file descriptors, 0, 1, and 2, are assigned to your terminal. File descriptor 0 is standard input (*stdin*), 1 is standard output (*stdout*), and 2 is standard error (*stderr*). When you open a file, the next available descriptor is 3, and it will be assigned to the new file. If all the available file descriptors are in use,[11] a new file cannot be opened.

Redirection. When a file descriptor is assigned to something other than a terminal, it is called *I/O redirection.* The shell performs redirection of output to a file by closing the standard output file descriptor, 1 (the terminal), and then assigning that descriptor to the file (see Figure 1.5).When redirecting standard input, the shell closes file descriptor 0 (the terminal) and assigns that descriptor to a file (see Figure 1.6). The Bourne and Korn shells handle errors by assigning a file to file descriptor 2 (see Figure 1.7). The TC shell, on the other hand, goes through a more complicated process to do the same thing (see Figure 1.8).

EXAMPLE 1.9

```
1  $ who > file
2  $ cat file1 file2 >> file3
3  $ mail tom < file
4  $ find / -name file -print 2> errors
5  > ( find / -name file -print > /dev/tty) >& errors
```

EXPLANATION

1. The output of the *who* command is redirected from the terminal to *file.* (All shells redirect output in this way.)
2. The output from the *cat* command (concatenate *file1* and *file2*) is appended to *file3.* (All shells redirect and append output in this way.)
3. The input of *file* is redirected to the *mail* program; that is, user *tom* will be sent the contents of *file.* (All shells redirect input in this way.)
4. Any errors from the *find* command are redirected to *errors.* Output goes to the terminal. (The Bourne, Bash, and Korn shells redirect errors this way.)
5. Any errors from the *find* command are redirected to *errors.* Output is sent to the terminal. (The C and TC shells redirect errors this way. > is the TC shell prompt.)

11. See the built-in commands, *limit* and *ulimit*, discussed in Table 8.32 on page 377.

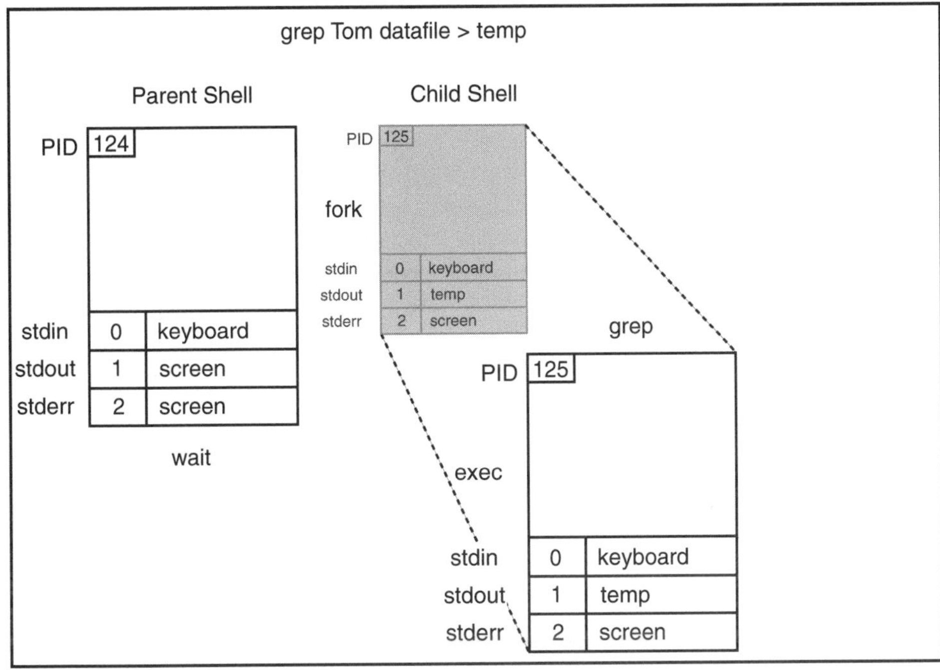

Figure 1.5 Redirection of standard output.

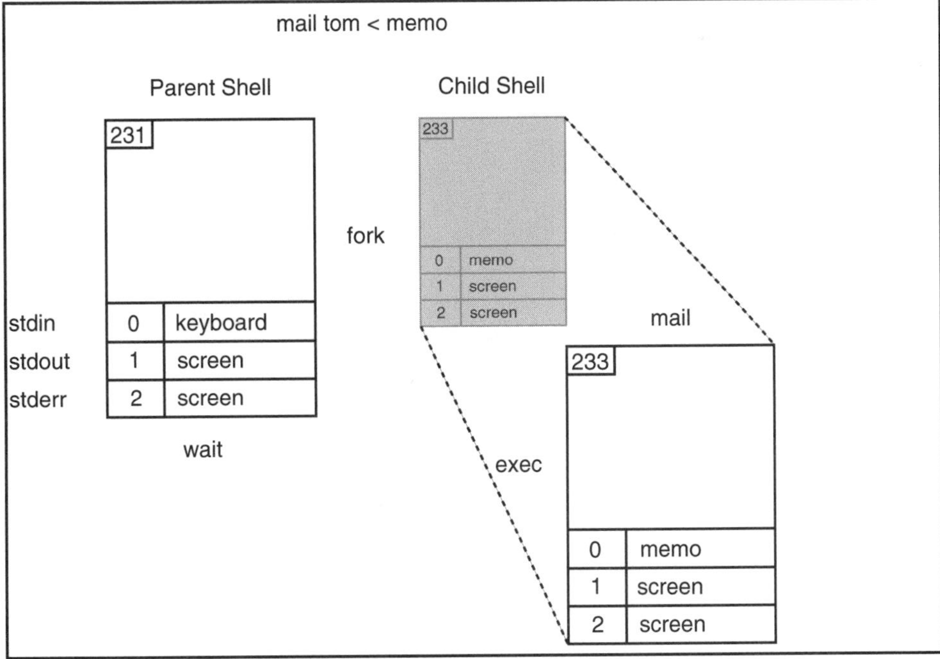

Figure 1.6 Redirection of standard input.

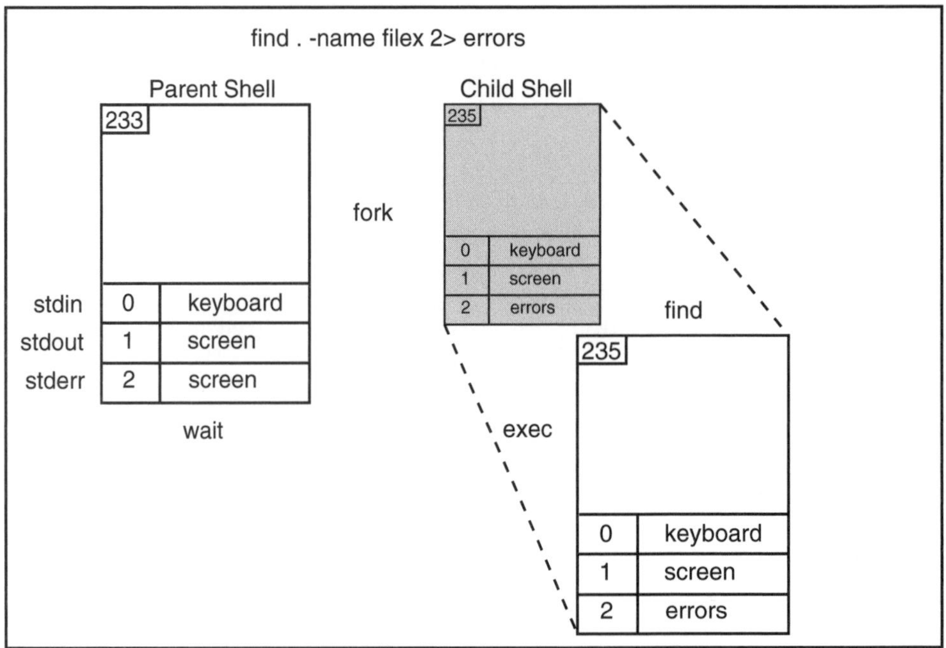

Figure 1.7 Redirection of standard error (Bourne, Bash, and Korn shells).

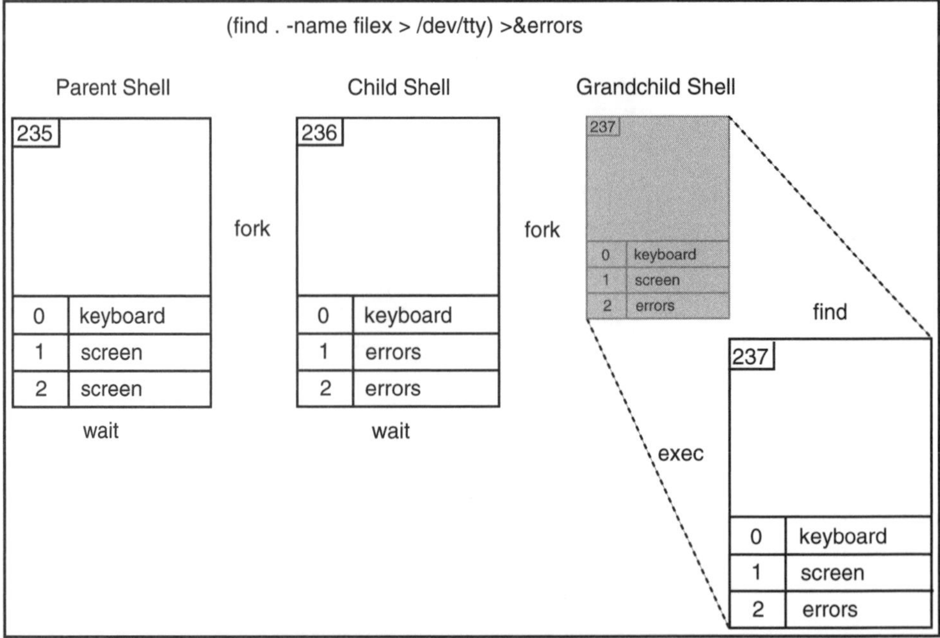

Figure 1.8 Redirection of standard error (C and TC shell).

Pipes. A pipe allows processes to communicate with each other. It is a mechanism whereby the output of one command is sent as input to another command. The shell implements pipes by closing and opening file descriptors; however, instead of assigning the descriptors to a file, it assigns them to a pipe descriptor created with the *pipe* system call. After the parent creates the pipe file descriptors, it forks a child process for each command in the pipeline. By having each process manipulate the pipe descriptors, one will write to the pipe and the other will read from it. The pipe is merely a kernel buffer from which both processes can share data, thus eliminating the need for intermediate temporary files. After the descriptors are set up, the commands are *exec*'ed concurrently. The output of one command is sent to the buffer, and when the buffer is full or the command has terminated, the command on the right-hand side of the pipe reads from the buffer. The kernel synchronizes the activities so that one process waits while the other reads from or writes to the buffer.

The syntax of the *pipe* command is:

```
who | wc
```

In order to accomplish the same thing without a pipe, it would take three steps:

```
who > tempfile
wc tempfil
rm tempfile
```

With the pipe, the shell sends the output of the *who* command as input to the *wc* command; i.e., the command on the left-hand side of the pipe writes to the pipe and the command on the right-hand side of the pipe, reads from it. You can tell if a command is a writer if it normally sends output to the screen when run at the command line. A reader is a command that waits for input from a file or from the keyboard or from a pipe.

Pipes are created with the *pipe* system call. The parent shell calls the *pipe* system call, which creates two pipe descriptors, one for reading from the pipe and one for writing to it. The files associated with the pipe descriptors are kernel-managed I/O buffers used to temporarily store data, thus saving you the trouble of creating temporary files. Figures 1.9 through 1.13 illustrate the steps for implementing the pipe.

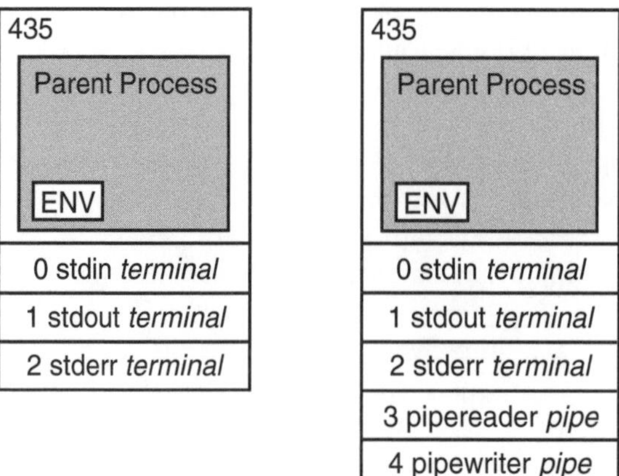

Figure 1.9 The parent calls the *pipe* system call for setting up a pipeline.

(1) The parent shell calls the *pipe* system call. Two file descriptors are returned: one for reading from the pipe and one for writing to the pipe. The file descriptors assigned are the next available descriptors in the file-descriptor (fd) table, *fd 3* and *fd 4*.

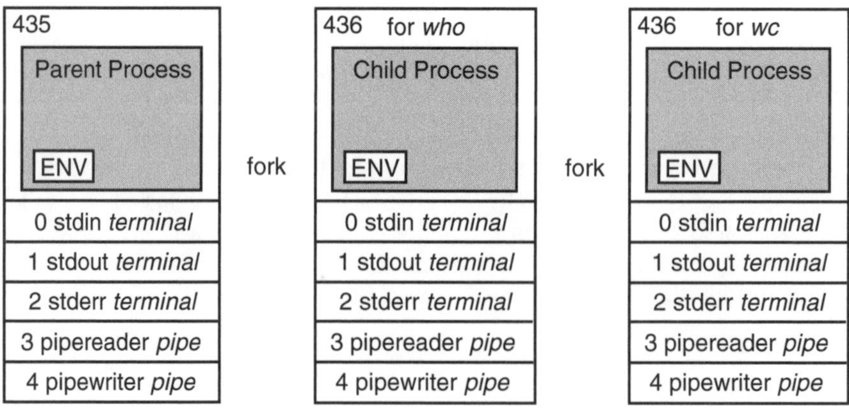

Figure 1.10 The parent forks two child processes, one for each command in the pipeline.

(2) For each command, *who* and *wc*, the parent forks a child process. Both child processes get a copy of the parent's open file descriptors.

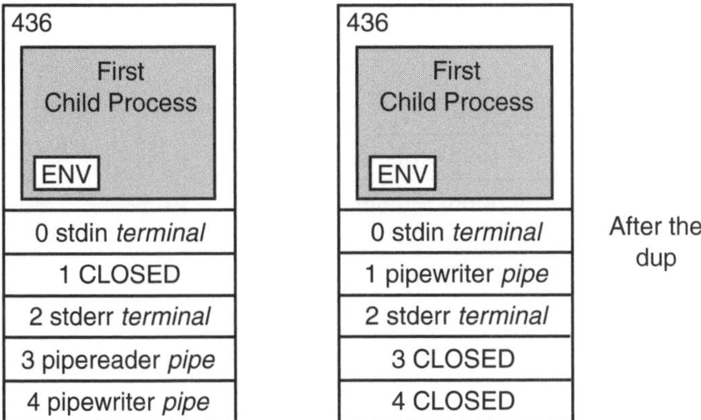

Figure 1.11 The first child is prepared to write to the pipe.

(3) The first child closes its standard output. It then duplicates (the *dup* system call) file descriptor *4*, the one associated with writing to the pipe. The *dup* system call copies *fd 4* and assigns the copy to the lowest available descriptor in the table, *fd 1*. After it makes the copy, the *dup* call closes *fd 4*. The child will now close *fd 3* because it does not need it. This child wants its standard *output* to go to the pipe.

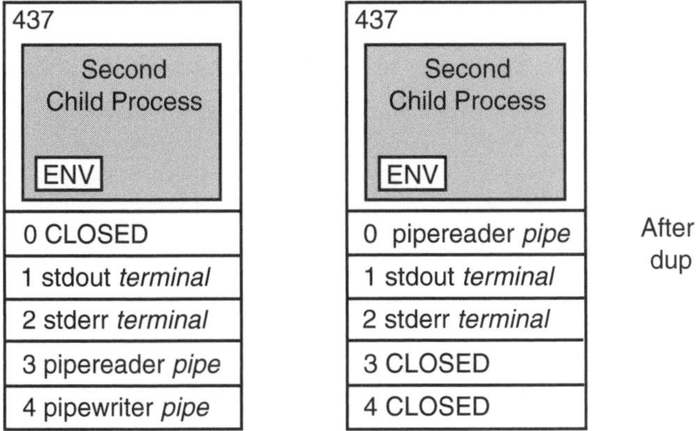

Figure 1.12 The second child is prepared to read input from the pipe.

(4) Child 2 closes its standard input. It then duplicates (*dups*) the *fd 3*, which is associated with reading from the pipe. By using *dup*, a copy of *fd 3* is created and assigned to the lowest available descriptor. Because *fd 0* was closed, it is the lowest available descriptor. *Dup* closes *fd 3*. The child closes *fd 4*. Its standard *input* will come from the pipe.

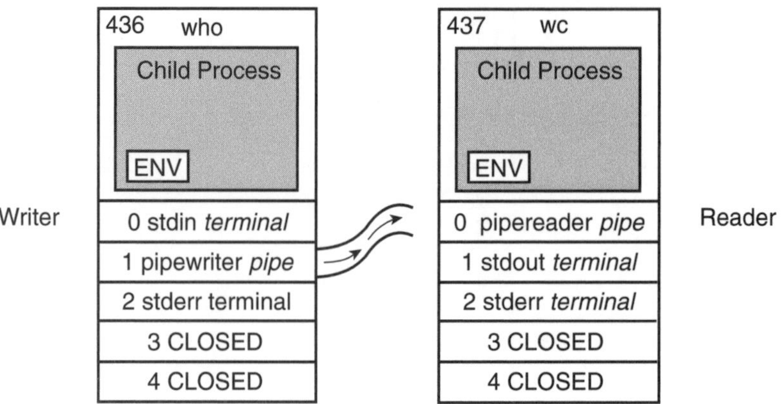

Figure 1.13 The output of *who* is sent to the input of *wc*.

(5) The *who* command is executed in place of Child 1 and the *wc* command is executed to replace Child 2. The output of the *who* command goes into the pipe and is read by the *wc* command from the other end of the pipe. The last command in the pipe (*wc*) sends output to the standard out.

1.5.7 The Shell and Signals

A signal sends a message to a process and normally causes the process to terminate, usually due to some unexpected event such as a hangup, bus error, or power failure, or by a program error such as illegal division by zero or an invalid memory reference. Signals can also be sent to a process by pressing certain key sequences. For example, you can send or deliver signals to a process by pressing the **Break**, **Delete**, **Quit**, or **Stop** keys, and all processes sharing the terminal are affected by the signal sent. You can kill a process with the *kill* command. By default, most signals terminate the program. Each process can take an action in response to a given signal:

1. The signal can be ignored.
2. The process can be stopped.
3. The process can be continued.
4. The signal can be caught by a function defined in the program.

The Bourne, Bash, and Korn shells allow you to handle signals coming into your program, (see “Trapping Signals” on page 459) either by ignoring the signal, by specifying some action to be taken when a specified signal arrives, or by resetting the signal back to its default action. The C and TC shells are limited to handling ^C (Control-C), the interrupt character.

Table 1.2 lists the standard signals which a process can use.

Table 1.2 Standard Signals

Number	*Name*	*Description*	*Action upon Process*
0	EXIT	shell exits	termination
1	SIGHUP	terminal has disconnected	termination
2	SIGINT	user presses Control-C	termination
3	SIGQUIT	user presses Control-\	termination
4	SIGILL	illegal hardware instruction	program error
5	SIGTRAP	produced by debugger	program error
8	SIGFPE	arithmetic error; e.g., division by zero	program error
9	SIGKILL	cannot be caught or ignored	termination
10	SIGUSR1	application-defined signal for user	
11	SIGSEGV	invalid memory references	program error
12	SIGUSR2	application-defined signal for user	
13	SIGPIPE	broken pipe connection	operator error
14	SIGALRM	time-out	alarm sent
15	SIGTERM	termination of a program	termination
17	SIGCHLD	child process has stopped or died	ignored
18	SIGCONT	starts a stopped job; can't be handled or ignored	continue if stopped
19	SIGSTOP	stops a job; can't be handled or ignored	stops the process
20	SIGSTP	interactive stop; user presses Control-z	stops the process
21	SIGTTIN	a background job is trying to read from the controlling terminal	stops the process
22	SIGTTOU	a background job is trying to write to the controlling terminal	stops the process

1.6 Executing Commands from Scripts

When the shell is used as a programming language, commands and shell control constructs are typed in an editor into a file, called a *script*. The lines from the file are read and executed one at a time by the shell. These programs are interpreted, not compiled. Compiled programs must convert the program into machine language for it to be executed. Therefore, shell programs are usually slower than binary executables, but they are easier to write and are used mainly for automating simple tasks. Shell programs can also be written interactively at the command line, and for very simple tasks, this is the quickest way. However, for more complex scripting, it is easier to write scripts in an editor (unless you are a really great typist). The following script can be executed by any shell to output the same results. Figure 1.14 illustrates the creation of a script called "doit" and how it fits in with already existing Linux programs/utilities/commands.

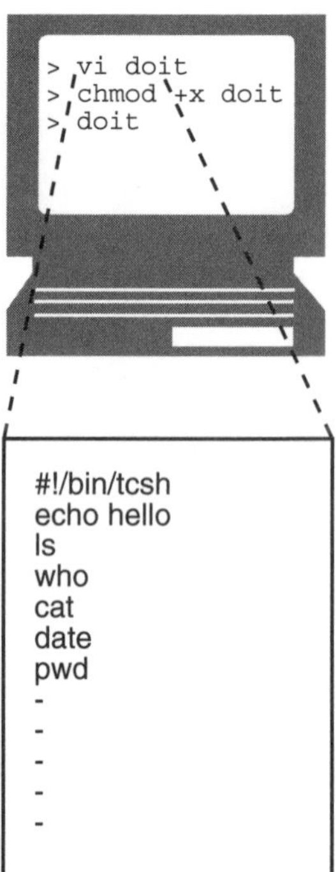

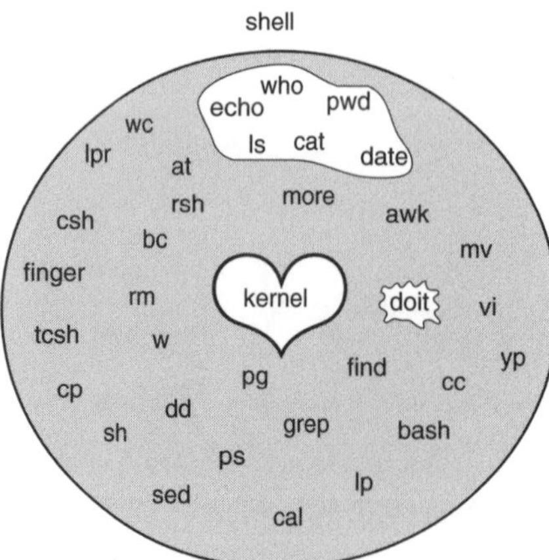

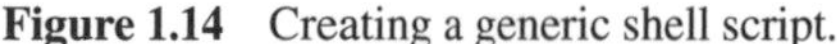

Figure 1.14 Creating a generic shell script.

EXPLANATION

1 Go into your favorite editor and type a set of Linux commands, one per line. Indicate what shell you want by placing the pathname of the shell after the *#!* on the first line. This program is being executed by the TC shell and it is named *doit*.

2 Save your file and turn on the execute permissions so that you can run it.

3 Execute your program just as you would any other Linux command.

1.6.1 Sample Scripts: Comparing Shells

At first glance, the following programs look very similar. They are. And they all do the same thing. The main difference is the syntax. After you have worked with these shells for some time, you will quickly adapt to the differences and start formulating your own opinions about which shell is your favorite. A detailed comparison of differences among the C, TC, Bash, Bourne, and Korn shells is found in Appendix B. Notice that the C and TC shell scripts are identical; and that the Bash and Korn shell scripts are very similar with minor syntax or command changes. The Bourne shell is quite different in syntax but can be run by either the Bash or Korn shells.

The following scripts send a mail message to a list of users, inviting each of them to a party. The place and time of the party are set in variables. The people to be invited are selected from a file called *guests*. A list of foods is stored in a word list, and each person is asked to bring one of the foods from the list. If there are more users than food items, the list is reset so that each user is asked to bring a different food. The only user who is not invited is the user *root*.

1.6.2 The TC Shell Script

EXAMPLE 1.10

```
1   #!/bin/tcsh -f
    # TC shell
2   # The Party Program--Invitations to friends from the "guest" file
3   set guestfile = ~/shell/guests
4   if ( ! -e "$guestfile" ) then
        echo "$guestfile:t non-existent"
        exit 1
    endif
5   setenv PLACE "Sarotini's"
    @ Time = `date +%H` + 1
    set food = ( cheese crackers shrimp drinks "hot dogs" sandwiches )
6   foreach person ( `cat $guestfile` )
        if ( $person =~ root ) continue
         # Start of here document
7       mail -v -s "Party" $person << FINIS
          Hi ${person}! Please join me at $PLACE for a party!
        Meet me at $Time o'clock.
        I'll bring the ice cream. Would you please bring $food[1] and
        anything else you would like to eat? Let me know if you can't
        make it. Hope to see you soon.
             Your pal,
                 ellie@`hostname` # or `uname -n`
    FINIS
```

EXAMPLE 1.10 (CONTINUED)

```
8       shift food
        if ( $#food ==  0 ) then
            set food = ( cheese crackers shrimp drinks "hot dogs"
            sandwiches )
        endif
9   end

    echo "Bye..."
```

EXPLANATION

1 This line lets the kernel know that you are running a TC shell script. The *-f* option is a fast startup. It says, "Do not execute the *.tcshrc* file," an initialization file that is automatically executed every time a new *tcsh* program is started.

2 This is a comment. It is ignored by the shell, but important for anyone trying to understand what the script is doing.

3 The variable *guestfile* is set to the full path name of a file called *guests*.

4 This line reads: If the file *guests* does not exist, then print to the screen "*guests nonexistent*" and exit from the script with an exit status of 1 to indicate that something went wrong in the program.

5 Set variables are assigned the values for the place, time, and list of foods to bring. The *PLACE* variable is an environment variable. The *Time* variable is a local variable. The @ symbol tells the TC shell to perform its built-in arithmetic; that is, add 1 to the *Time* variable after extracting the hour from the *date* command. The *Time* variable is spelled with an uppercase *T* to prevent the TC shell from confusing it with one of its reserved words, *time*.

6 For each person on the guest list, except the user *root*, a mail message will be created inviting the person to a party at a given place and time, and asking him or her to bring one of the foods on the list.

7 The mail message is created in what is called a *here document*. All text from the user-defined word *FINIS* to the final *FINIS* will be sent to the *mail* program. The *foreach* loop shifts through the list of names, performing all of the instructions from the *foreach* to the keyword *end*.

8 After a message has been sent, the food list is shifted so that the next person will get the next food item on the list. If there are more people than food items, the food list will be reset to ensure that each person is instructed to bring a food item.

9 This marks the end of the looping statements.

1.6.3 The C Shell Script

EXAMPLE 1.11

```
1  #!/bin/csh -f
   # Standard Berkeley C Shell
2  # The Party Program--Invitations to friends from the "guest" file
3  set guestfile = ~/shell/guests
4  if ( ! -e "$guestfile" ) then
       echo "$guestfile:t non-existent"
       exit 1
   endif
5  setenv PLACE "Sarotini's"
   @ Time = `date +%H` + 1
   set food = ( cheese crackers shrimp drinks "hot dogs" sandwiches )
6  foreach person ( `cat $guestfile` )
       if ( $person =~ root ) continue
    # Start of here document
7      mail -v -s "Party" $person << FINIS
       Hi ${person}! Please join me at $PLACE for a party!
       Meet me at $Time o'clock.
       I'll bring the ice cream. Would you please bring $food[1] and
       anything else you would like to eat? Let me know if you can't
       make it. Hope to see you soon.
            Your pal,
                ellie@`hostname` # or `uname -n`
   FINIS
8      shift food
       if ( $#food ==  0 ) then
            set food = ( cheese crackers shrimp drinks "hot dogs"
            sandwiches )
       endif
9  end

   echo "Bye..."
```

EXPLANATION

1 This line lets the kernel know that you are running a C shell script. The *-f* option is a fast startup. It says, "Do not execute the *.cshrc* file," an initialization file that is automatically executed every time a new csh program is started.

If you look closely, this is the only line that differs from the TC shell script, shown in Example 1.10; therefore, lines 2 through 9 were already explained in the previous example.

1.6.4 The Bourne Again Shell Script

EXAMPLE 1.12

```
1   #!/bin/bash
    # Gnu bash versions 2.x
2   # The Party Program--Invitations to friends from the
    # "guest" file
3   guestfile=~/shell/guests
4   if [[ ! -e "$guestfile" ]]
    then
        printf "${guestfile##*/} non-existent"
        exit 1
    fi
5   export PLACE="Sarotini's"
    (( Time=$(date +%H) + 1 ))
    set cheese crackers shrimp drinks "hot dogs" sandwiches
6   for person in $(cat $guestfile)
    do
        if  [[ $person = root ]]
        then
             continue
        else
             # Start of here document
7            mail -v -s "Party" $person <<- FINIS
             Hi ${person}! Please join me at $PLACE for a party!
             Meet me at $Time o'clock.
             I'll bring the ice cream. Would you please bring $1
             and anything else you would like to eat? Let me know
             if you can't make it.
                    Hope to see you soon.
                            Your pal,
                            ellie@$(hostname)
             FINIS
8            shift
             if (( $# ==  0 ))
             then
               set cheese crackers shrimp drinks "hot dogs" sandwiches
             fi
        fi
9   done
    printf "Bye..."
```

EXPLANATION

1. This line lets the kernel know that you are running a Bash shell (Bourne Again) script. Any versions prior to 2.x will not support all of this syntax. Older versions of Bash are similar to the standard Bourne shell. All versions are backward compatible.

2. This is a comment. It is ignored by the shell, but important for anyone trying to understand what the script is doing.

3. The variable *guestfile* is set to the full path name of a file called *guests.*

4. This line reads: If the file *guests* does not exist, then print to the screen "*guests nonexistent*" and exit from the script.

5. Variables are assigned the values for the place and time. The list of foods to bring is assigned to special variables (positional parameters) with the *set* command.

6. For each person on the guest list, except the user *root*, a mail message will be created inviting the person to a party at a given place and time, and assigning a food from the list to bring.

7. The mail message is sent. The body of the message is contained in a *here document.*

8. After a message has been sent, the food list is shifted so that the next person will get the next food on the list. If there are more people than foods, the food list will be reset, ensuring that each person is assigned a food.

9. This marks the end of the looping statements.

1.6.5 The Bourne Shell Script

EXAMPLE 1.13

```
1   #!/bin/sh
    # Standard AT&T Bourne Shell
2   # The Party Program--Invitations to friends from the
    # "guest" file
3   guestfile=/home/ellie/shell/guests
4   if [ ! -f "$guestfile" ]
    then
        echo "`basename $guestfile` non-existent"
        exit 1
    fi
5   PLACE="Sarotini's"
    export PLACE
    Time=`date +%H`
    Time=`expr $Time + 1`
    set cheese crackers shrimp drinks "hot dogs" sandwiches
6   for person in `cat $guestfile`
    d
        if  [ $person = root ]
        then
             continue
        else
             # Start of here document
7            mail -v -s "Party" $person <<- FINIS
             Hi $person! Please join me at $PLACE for a party!
             Meet me at $Time o'clock.
             I'll bring the ice cream. Would you please bring $1
             and anything else you would like to eat? Let me know
             if you can't make it.
                    Hope to see you soon.
                            Your pal,
                            ellie@`hostname`
             FINIS
8            shift
             if [ $# -eq  0 ]
             then
               set cheese crackers shrimp drinks "hot dogs" sandwiches
             fi
        fi
9   done
    echo "Bye..."
```

EXPLANATION

1. This line lets the kernel know that you are running a *sh* shell (Bourne) script. This is the Bourne shell distributed with UNIX systems, such as Solaris and HP-UX. It is the last released version from ATT, SVR4. If running Linux, this script will work fine even if the shell is Bash.
2. This is a comment. It is ignored by the shell, but important for anyone trying to understand what the script is doing.
3. The variable *guestfile* is set to the full path name of a file called *guests*. Tilde expansion is not allowed with Bourne shell. See other shell examples.
4. This line reads: If the file *guests* does not exist, then print to the screen "*guests nonexistent*" and exit from the script.
5. Variables are assigned the values for the place and time. The list of foods to bring is assigned to special variables (positional parameters) with the *set* command.
6. For each person on the guest list, except the user *root*, a mail message will be created inviting the person to a party at a given place and time, and assigning a food from the list to bring.
7. The mail message is sent. The body of the message is contained in a *here document.*
8. After a message has been sent, the food list is shifted so that the next person will get the next food on the list. If there are more people than foods, the food list will be reset, ensuring that each person is assigned a food.
9. This marks the end of the looping statements.

1.6.6 The Korn Shell Script

EXAMPLE 1.14

```
1   #!/bin/ksh
    # AT&T Korn Shell
2   # The Party Program--Invitations to friends from the
    # "guest" file
    # AT&T Korn Shell (1988)
3   guestfile=~/shell/guests
4   if [[ ! -a "$guestfile" ]]
    then
       print "${guestfile##*/} non-existent"
       exit 1
    fi
5   export PLACE="Sarotini's"
    (( Time=$(date +%H) + 1 ))
    set cheese crackers shrimp drinks "hot dogs" sandwiches
6   for person in $(< $guestfile)
    do
       if  [[ $person = root ]]
       then
           continue
       else
           # Start of here document
7          mail -v -s "Party" $person <<- FINIS
           Hi ${person}! Please join me at $PLACE for a party!
           Meet me at $Time o'clock.
           I'll bring the ice cream. Would you please bring $1
           and anything else you would like to eat? Let me know
           if you can't make it.
                 Hope to see you soon.
                        Your pal,
                        ellie@$(hostname)
           FINIS
8          shift
           if (( $# ==  0 ))
           then
             set cheese crackers shrimp drinks "hot dogs" sandwiches
           fi
       fi
9   done
    print "Bye..."
```

EXPLANATION

1. This line lets the kernel know that you are running a Korn shell script.
2. This is a comment. It is ignored by the shell, but important for anyone trying to understand what the script is doing.
3. The variable *guestfile* is set to the full path name of a file called *guests*.
4. This line reads: If the file *guests* does not exist, then print to the screen "*guests nonexistent*" and exit from the script. The *-a* switch to test existence of a file is a Korn shell option.
5. Variables are assigned the values for the place and time. The list of foods to bring is assigned to special variables (positional parameters) with the *set* command.
6. For each person on the guest list, except the user *root*, a mail message will be created inviting the person to a party at a given place and time, and assigning a food from the list to bring.
7. The mail message is sent. The body of the message is contained in a *here document.*
8. After a message has been sent, the food list is shifted so that the next person will get the next food on the list. If there are more people than foods, the food list will be reset, ensuring that each person is assigned a food.
9. This marks the end of the looping statements.

CHAPTER

2

THE LINUX TOOL BOX

Just as there are essential tools that a carpenter uses, there are also essential tools (also called utilities) the shell programmer needs to write meaningful and efficient scripts. There are hundreds of Linux tools available, and many of them are everyday commands such as *ls, pwd, who,* and *vi*. These utilities, provided by the Free Software Foundation under the Gnu Public License Agreement, are enhanced versions of their like-named popular UNIX utilities. The three major utilities that will be discussed here are *grep, sed,* and *gawk.*[1] Before you fully appreciate the power of *grep, sed,* and *gawk*, you must have a good foundation in the use of regular expressions and regular expression metacharacters.

2.1 Regular Expressions

2.1.1 Definition and Example

For users already familiar with the concept of regular expression metacharacters, this section may be bypassed. However, this preliminary material is crucial to understanding the variety of ways in which *grep, sed,* and *gawk* are used to display and manipulate data.

What is a regular expression? A regular expression[2] is just a pattern of characters used to match the same characters in a search. In most programs, a regular expression is enclosed in forward slashes; for example, */love/* is a regular expression delimited by forward slashes, and the pattern *love* will be matched any time the same pattern is found in the line being searched. What makes regular expressions interesting is that they can be controlled by special metacharacters. Let us look at an example that will help you understand this concept. Suppose that you are working in the *vi* editor on an email message to your friend. It looks like this:

---

1. A complete list of other useful Linux utilities is found in Appendix A of this book.
2. If you receive an error message that contains the string *RE*, there is a problem with the regular expression you are using in the program.

```
% vi letter
----------------------------------------------------------------
Hi tom,
I think I failed my anatomy test yesterday. I had a terrible
stomach ache. I ate too many fried green tomatoes.
Anyway, Tom, I need your help. I'd like to make the test up
tomorrow, but don't know where to begin studying. Do you
think you could help me? After work, about 7 PM, come to
my place and I'll treat you to pizza in return for your help.
Thanks.
                              Your pal,
                              guy@phantom


~
~
~
~
----------------------------------------------------------------
```

Now, suppose you find out that Tom never took the test either, but David did. You also notice that in the greeting, you spelled *Tom* with a lowercase *t.* So you decide to make a global substitution to replace all occurrences of *tom* with *David,* as follows:

```
 % vi letter
----------------------------------------------------------------
Hi David,
I think I failed my anaDavidy test yeserday. I had a terrible
sDavidachache. I think I ate too many fried green Davidatoes.
Anyway, Tom, I need your help. I'd like to make the test up
Davidorrow, but don't know where to begin studying. Do you
think you could help me? After work, about 7 PM, come to
my place and I'll treat you to pizza in return for your help.
Thanks.
                              Your pal,
                              guy@phanDavid


~
~
~

-->  :1,$s/tom/David/g
----------------------------------------------------------------
```

The regular expression in the search string is *tom.* The replacement string is *David.* The *vi* command reads "for lines 1 to the end of the file ($), substitute *tom* everywhere it is found on each line and replace it with *David.*" Hardly what you want! And one of the occurrences of *Tom* was untouched because you only asked for *tom*, not *Tom*, to be replaced with *David*. So what to do?

Regular expression metacharacters are special characters that allow you to delimit a pattern in some way so that you can control what substitutions will take place. There are metacharacters to anchor a word to the beginning or end of a line. There are metacharacters that allow you to specify a range of characters, or some number of characters, to find both upper and lowercase characters, digits, non-digits, and so forth. For example, to change the name *tom* or *Tom* to *David*, the following *vi* command would have done the job:

```
:1,$s/\<[Tt]om\>/David/g
```

This command reads, "From the first line to the last line of the file (*1,$*), substitute (*s*) the word *Tom* or *tom* with *David*," and the *g* flag says to do this globally (i.e., make the substitution if it occurs more than once on the same line). The regular expression metacharacters are \< and \> for beginning and end of *word*, and the pair of brackets, [*Tt*], match for one of the characters enclosed within them, for either *T* or *t*. There are five basic metacharacters that all Linux/UNIX pattern-matching utilities recognize, and also an extended set of metacharacters that vary from program to program.

2.1.2 Regular Expression Metacharacters

There are two standard sets of regular expression metacharacters, a basic set and an extended set. In addition, there are a set of metacharacters provided by the POSIX[3] standard. Table 2.1 presents basic regular expression metacharacters that can be used in all versions of *vi, ex, grep, egrep, sed,* and *gawk*. Additional metacharacters are described for each of the utilities where applicable.

Table 2.1 Regular Expression Metacharacters

Metacharacter	*Function*	*Example*	*What It Matches*
^	Beginning of line anchor	/^love/	Matches all lines beginning with *love*.
$	End of line anchor	/love$/	Matches all lines ending with *love*.
.	Matches one character	/l..e/	Matches lines containing an *l*, followed by two characters, followed by an *e*.
*	Matches zero or more of the preceding characters	/ *love/	Matches lines with zero or more spaces, followed by the pattern *love*.

3. POSIX stands for the Portable Operating System Interface for Computer Environments.

Table 2.1 Regular Expression Metacharacters (Continued)

Metacharacter	***Function***	***Example***	***What It Matches***
[ ]	Matches one in the set	/[Ll]ove/	Matches lines containing *love* or *Love.*
[x-y]	Matches one character within a range in the set	/[A-Z]ove/	Matches letters from *A* through *Z* followed by *ove.*
[^]	Matches one character not in the set	/[^A–Z]ove/	Matches lines not containing *A* through *Z.* Matches *love* or *dove*,or *:over* but not *Love* or *Dove,* etc.
\	Used to escape a metacharacter	/love\./	Matches lines containing *love*, followed by a literal period. Normally the period matches one of any character.
Additional metacharacters are supported by many UNIX programs that use RE metacharacters.			
\<	Beginning of word anchor	/\<love/	Matches lines containing a word that begins with *love* (supported by *vi* and *grep*).
\>	End of word anchor	/love\>/	Matches lines containing a word that ends with *love* (supported by *vi* and *grep*).
\(..\)	Tags match characters to be used later	/\(love\)able \1rs/	May use up to nine tags, starting with the first tag at the leftmost part of the pattern. For example, the pattern *love* is saved as tag 1, to be referenced later as \1; in this example, the search pattern consists of *loveable* followed by *lovers* (supported by *sed, vi,* and *grep*).
x\{m\} *or* x\{m,\} *or* x\{m,n\}	Repetition of character x, m times, at least m times, at least m and not more than n times[a]	o\{5,10\}	Matches if line contains between *5* and *10* repeating *o*'s (supported by *vi* and *grep*).

a. Not dependable on all versions of UNIX or all pattern-matching utilities; usually works with *vi* and *grep*.

Assuming that you know how the *vi* editor works, each metacharacter is described in terms of the *vi* search string. In the following examples, characters are highlighted to demonstrate what *vi* will find in its search.

EXAMPLE 2.1

```
(A Simple Regular Expression Search)
   % vi picnic
   ---------------------------------------------------------------
   I had a lovely time on our little picnic.
   Lovers were all around us. It is springtime. Oh
   love, how much I adore you. Do you know
   the extent of my love? Oh, by the way, I think
   I lost my gloves somewhere out in that field of
   clover. Did you see them?  I can only hope love
   is forever. I live for you. It's hard to get back in the
   groove.
   ~
   ~
   ~
   /love/
   ---------------------------------------------------------------
```

EXPLANATION

The regular expression is *love*. The pattern *love* is found by itself and as part of other words, such as *lovely*, *gloves*, and *clover*.

EXAMPLE 2.2

```
(The Beginning of Line Anchor (^))
% vi picnic
---------------------------------------------------------------
I had a lovely time on our little picnic.
Lovers were all around us. It is springtime. Oh
love, how much I adore you. Do you know
the extent of my love? Oh, by the way, I think
I lost my gloves somewhere out in that field of
clover. Did you see them? I can only hope love
is forever. I live for you. It's hard to get back in the
groove.
~
~
~
/^love/
---------------------------------------------------------------
```

EXPLANATION

The caret (^) is called the beginning of line anchor. *Vi* will find only those lines where the regular expression *love* is matched at the beginning of the line, i.e., *love* is the first set of characters on the line; it cannot be preceded by even one space.

EXAMPLE 2.3

```
(The End of Line Anchor ($))
% vi picnic
-----------------------------------------------------------------
I had a lovely time on our little picnic.
Lovers were all around us. It is springtime. Oh
love, how much I adore you. Do you know
the extent of my love? Oh, by the way, I think
I lost my gloves somewhere out in that field of
clover. Did you see them?  I can only hope love
is forever. I live for you. It's hard to get back in the
groove.
~
~
~
/love$/
-----------------------------------------------------------------
```

EXPLANATION

The dollar sign ($) is called the end of line anchor. *Vi* will find only those lines where the regular expression *love* is matched at the end of the line, i.e., *love* is the last set of characters on the line and is directly followed by a newline.

EXAMPLE 2.4

```
(Any Single Character ( . ))
% vi picnic
-----------------------------------------------------------------
I had a lovely time on our little picnic.
Lovers were all around us. It is springtime. Oh
love, how much I adore you. Do you know
the extent of my love? Oh, by the way, I think
I lost my gloves somewhere out in that field of
clover. Did you see them?  I can only hope love
is forever. I live for you. It's hard to get back in the
groove.
~
~
~
/l.ve/
-----------------------------------------------------------------
```

EXPLANATION

The dot (.) matches any one character, except the newline. *Vi* will find those lines where the regular expression consists of an *l*, followed by any single character, followed by a *v* and an *e*. It finds combinations of *love* and *live*.

EXAMPLE 2.5

```
(Zero or More of the Preceding Character ( * ))
% vi picnic
-----------------------------------------------------------------
I had a lovely time on our little picnic.
Lovers were all around us. It is springtime. Oh
love, how much I adore you. Do you know
the extent of my love? Oh, by the way, I think
I lost my gloves somewhere out in that field of
clover. Did you see them?  I can only hope love
is forever. I live for you. It's hard to get back in the
groove.
~
~
~
/o*ve/
-----------------------------------------------------------------
```

EXPLANATION

The asterisk (*) matches zero or more of the preceding character.[a] It is as though the asterisk were glued to the character directly before it and controls only that character. In this case, the asterisk is glued to the letter *o*. It matches for only the letter *o* and as many consecutive *o*'s as there are in the pattern, even if there are no *o*'s at all. *Vi* searches for zero or more *o*'s followed by a *v* and an *e*, finding *love, loooove, lve*, and so forth.

a. Do not confuse this metacharacter with the shell wildcard (*). They are totally different. The shell asterisk matches for zero or more of any character, whereas the regular expression asterisk matches for zero or more of the preceding character.

EXAMPLE 2.6

```
(A Set of Characters ( [ ] ))
% vi picnic
-----------------------------------------------------------------
I had a lovely time on our little picnic.
Lovers were all around us. It is springtime. Oh
love, how much I adore you. Do you know
the extent of my love? Oh, by the way, I think
I lost my gloves somewhere out in that field of
clover. Did you see them?  I can only hope love
is forever. I live for you. It's hard to get back in the
groove.
~
~
~
/[Ll]ove/
-----------------------------------------------------------------
```

EXPLANATION

The square brackets match for one of a set of characters. *Vi* will search for the regular expression containing either an uppercase or lowercase *l* followed by an *o*, *v*, and *e*.

EXAMPLE 2.7

```
(A Range of Characters ( [ - ] ))
% vi picnic
-----------------------------------------------------------------
I had a lovely time on our little picnic.
Lovers were all around us. It is springtime. Oh
love, how much I adore you. Do you know
the extent of my love? Oh, by the way, I think
I lost my gloves somewhere out in that field of
clover. Did you see them?  I can only hope love
is forever. I live for you. It's hard to get back in the
groove.
~
~
~
/ove[a-z]/
-----------------------------------------------------------------
```

EXPLANATION

The dash between characters enclosed in square brackets matches one character in a range of characters. *Vi* will search for the regular expression containing an *o*, *v*, and *e*, followed by any character in the ASCII range between *a* and *z*. Because this is an ASCII range, the range cannot be represented as [*z-a*].

EXAMPLE 2.8

```
(Not One of the Characters in the Set ( [^] ))
% vi picnic
---------------------------------------------------------------------
I had a lovely time on our little picnic.
Lovers were all around us. It is springtime. Oh
love, how much I adore you. Do you know
the extent of my love? Oh, by the way, I think
I lost my gloves somewhere out in that field of
clover. Did you see them?  I can only hope love
is forever. I live for you. It's hard to get back in the
groove.
~
~
~
/ove[^a-zA-Z0-9]/
---------------------------------------------------------------------
```

EXPLANATION

The caret inside square brackets is a negation metacharacter. *Vi* will search for the regular expression containing an *o*, *v*, and *e*, followed by any character *not* in the ASCII range between *a* and *z*, *not* in the range between *A* and *Z*, and *not* a digit between 0 and 9. For example, it will find *ove* followed by a comma, a space, a period, and so on, because those characters are *not* in the set.

2.2 Combining Regular Expression Metacharacters

Now that the basic regular expression metacharacters have been explained, they can be combined into more complex expressions. Each of the regular expression examples enclosed in forward slashes is the search string and is matched against each line in the text file.

EXAMPLE 2.9

```
Note: The line numbers are NOT part of the text file. The vertical
bars mark the left and right margins.
   ---------------------------------------------------------------
1  |Christian Scott lives here and will put on a Christmas party.|
2  |There are around 30 to 35 people invited.|
3  |They are: |
4  |                                     Tom|
5  |Dan|
6  |   Rhonda Savage|
7  |Nicky and Kimberly.|
8  |Steve, Suzanne, Ginger and Larry.|
   ---------------------------------------------------------------
```

EXPLANATION

1 **`/^[A-Z]..$/`**
Will find all lines beginning with a capital letter, followed by two of any character, followed by a newline. Will find *Dan* on line 5.

2 **`/^[A-Z][a-z ]*3[0-5]/`**
Will find all lines beginning with an uppercase letter, followed by zero or more lowercase letters or spaces, followed by the number 3 and another number between 0 and 5. Will find line 2.

3 **`/[a-z]*\./`**
Will find lines containing zero or more lowercase letters, followed by a literal period. Will find lines 1, 2, 7, and 8.

4 **`/^ *[A-Z][a-z][a-z]$/`**
Will find a line that begins with zero or more spaces (tabs do not count as spaces), followed by an uppercase letter, two lowercase letters, and a newline. Will find *Tom* on line 4 and *Dan* on line 5.

5 **`/^[A-Za-z]*[^,][A-Za-z]*$/`**
Will find a line that begins with zero or more uppercase and/or lowercase letters, followed by a noncomma, followed by zero or more upper- or lowercase letters and a newline. Will find line 5.

2.2.1 More Regular Expression Metacharacters

The following metacharacters are not necessarily portable across all utilities using regular expressions, but can be used in the *vi* editor and some versions of *sed* and *grep*. There is an extended set of metacharacters available with *egrep* and *awk*, which will be discussed later.

EXAMPLE 2.10

```
(Beginning and End of Word Anchors ( \< \> ))
% vi textfile
----------------------------------------------------------------
    Unusual occurrences happened at the fair.
--> Patty won fourth place in the 50 yard dash square and fair.
    Occurrences like this are rare.
    The winning ticket is 55222.
    The ticket I got is 54333 and Dee got 55544.
    Guy fell down while running around the south bend in his last
    event.
    ~
    ~
    ~
    /\<fourth\>/
----------------------------------------------------------------
```

EXPLANATION

Will find the word *fourth* on each line. The \< is the beginning of word anchor and the \> is the end of word anchor. A word can be separated by spaces, end in punctuation, start at the beginning of a line, end at the end of a line, and so forth.

EXAMPLE 2.11

```
% vi textfile
------------------------------------------------------------------
    Unusual occurrences happened at the fair.
--> Patty won fourth place in the 50 yard dash square and fair.
    Occurrences like this are rare.
    The winning ticket is 55222.
    The ticket I got is 54333 and Dee got 55544.
--> Guy fell down while running around the south bend in his last
    event.
    ~
    ~
    ~
    /\<f.*th\>/
```

EXPLANATION

Will find any word beginning with an *f*, followed by zero or more of any character (.*), and a word ending with *th*.

EXAMPLE 2.12

```
(Remembered Patterns \( \))
% vi textfile (Before Substitution)
    Unusual occurences happened at the fair.
    Patty won fourth place in the 50 yard dash square and fair.
    Occurences like this are rare.
    The winning ticket is 55222.
    The ticket I got is 54333 and Dee got 55544.
    Guy fell down while running around the south bend in his last
    event.
    ~
    ~
    ~
1.  :1,$s/\([Oo]ccur\)ence/\1rence/
--------------------------------------------------
```

EXAMPLE 2.12 (CONTINUED)

```
% vi textfile (After Substitution)
--> Unusual occurrences happened at the fair.
    Patty won fourth place in the 50 yard dash square and fair.
--> Occurrences like this are rare.
    The winning ticket is 55222.
    The ticket I got is 54333 and Dee got 55544.
    Guy fell down while running around the south bend in his last
    event.
       ~
       ~
       ~
```

EXPLANATION

1 The editor searches for the entire string *occurence* or *Occurence* (note: the words are misspelled), and if found, the pattern portion enclosed in parentheses is tagged (i.e., either *occur* or *Occur* is tagged). Since this is the first pattern tagged, it is called tag `1`. The pattern is stored in a memory register called register `1`. On the replacement side, the contents of the register are replaced for `\1` and the rest of the word, *rence,* is appended to it. We started with "occurence" and ended up with "occurrence." See Figure 2.1.

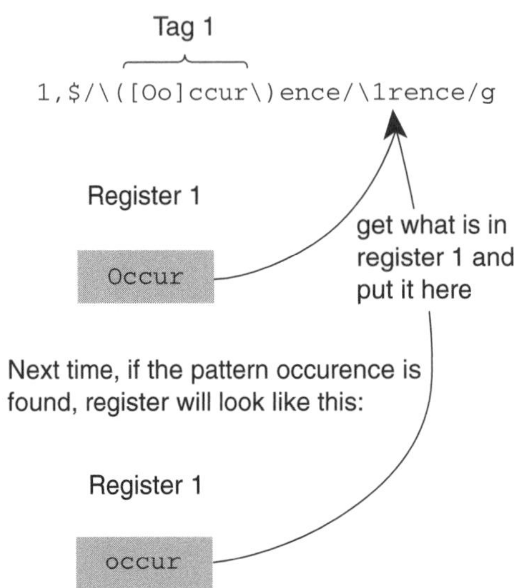

Figure 2.1 Remembered patterns and tags.

EXAMPLE 2.13

```
  % vi textfile (Before Substitution)
  -------------------------------------------
  Unusual occurrences happened at the fair.
  Patty won fourth place in the 50 yard dash square and fair.
  Occurrences like this are rare.
  The winning ticket is 55222.
  The ticket I got is 54333 and Dee got 55544.
  Guy fell down while running around the south bend in his last
  event.
  ~
  ~
  ~
  1. :s/\(square\) and \(fair\)/\2 and \1/
  -------------------------------------------
  % vi textfile (After Substitution)
  -------------------------------------------
  Unusual occurrences happened at the fair.
--> Patty won fourth place in the 50 yard dash fair and square.
  Occurrences like this are rare.
  The winning ticket is 55222.
  The ticket I got is 54333 and Dee got 55544.
  Guy fell down while running around the south bend in his last
  event.
  ~
  ~
  ~
```

EXPLANATION

1 The editor searches for the regular expression *square and fair*, and tags *square* as #1 and *fair* as #2. On the replacement side, the contents of register 2 are substituted for \2 and the contents of register 1 are substituted for \1. See Figure 2.2.

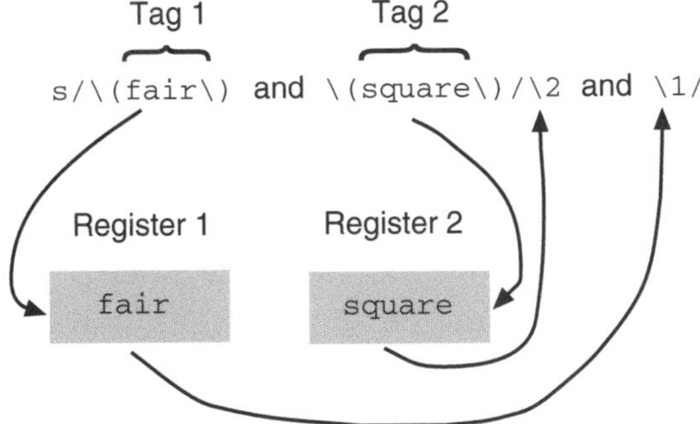

Figure 2.2 Using more than one tag.

EXAMPLE 2.14

```
(Repetition of Patterns ( \{n\} ))
% vi textfile
------------------------------------------
    Unusual occurrences happened at the fair.
    Patty won fourth place in the 50 yard dash square and fair.
    Occurrences like this are rare.
--> The winning ticket is 55222.
    The ticket I got is 54333 and Dee got 55544.
    Guy fell down while running around the south bend in his last
    event.
    ~
    ~
    ~
    ~
1.  /5\{2\}2\{3\}\./
```

EXPLANATION

1 Searches for lines containing two *5*s, followed by three *2*s, followed by a literal period.

CHAPTER

3

THE *GREP* FAMILY (GNU & SONS)

The UNIX *grep* family consists of the commands *grep, egrep*, and *fgrep*. The *grep* command globally searches for regular expressions in files and prints all lines that contain the expression. The *egrep* and *fgrep* commands are simply variants of *grep*. The *egrep* command is an extended *grep*, supporting more RE metacharacters. The *fgrep* command, called *fixed grep,* and sometimes *fast grep*, treats all characters as literals; that is, regular expression metacharacters aren't special—they match themselves.

Linux uses the Gnu version of grep, which in functionality is much the same as *grep*, but better. In addition to POSIX character classes (see Tables 3.1 and 3.2), there are a number of new options, including *-G*, *-E*, and *-F*, which allow you to use regular *grep* for everything, and still get the functionality of both *egrep* and *fgrep*.[1]

3.1 The *grep* Command

3.1.1 The Meaning of *grep*

The name *grep* can be traced back to the *ex* editor. If you invoked that editor and wanted to search for a string, you would type at the *ex* prompt:

```
: /pattern/p
```

The first line containing the string *pattern* would be printed as "*p*" by the *print* command. If you wanted all the lines that contained *pattern* to be printed, you would type:

```
:g/pattern/p
```

When *g* precedes *pattern*, it means "all lines in the file," or "perform a global substitution."

1. To use *grep* recursively, see Appendix A for Gnu *rgrep* and *xargs*.

Because the search pattern is called a *regular expression*, we can substitute *RE* for *pattern* and the command reads:

```
: g/RE/p
```

And there you have it. The meaning of *grep* and the origin of its name. It means "globally search for the *r*egular *e*xpression (RE) and *p*rint out the line." The nice part of using *grep* is that you do not have to invoke an editor to perform a search, and you do not need to enclose the regular expression in forward slashes. It is much faster than using *ex* or *vi*.

3.1.2 How *grep* Works

The *grep* command searches for a pattern of characters in a file or multiple files. If the pattern contains white space, it must be quoted. The pattern is either a quoted string or a single word[2], and all other words following it are treated as filenames. *Grep* sends its output to the screen and does not change or affect the input file in any way.

FORMAT

```
grep word filename filename
```

EXAMPLE 3.1

```
% grep Tom /etc/passwd
```

EXPLANATION

Grep will search for the pattern *Tom* in a file called */etc/passwd*. If successful, the line from the file will appear on the screen; if the pattern is not found, there will be no output at all; and if the file is not a legitimate file, an error will be sent to the screen. If the pattern is found, *grep* returns an exit status of 0, indicating success; if the pattern is not found, the exit status returned is 1; and if the file is not found, the exit status is 2.

The *grep* program can get its input from a standard input or a pipe, as well as from files. If you forget to name a file, *grep* will assume it is getting input from standard input, the keyboard, and will stop until you type something. If coming from a pipe, the output of a command will be piped as input to the *grep* command, and if a desired pattern is matched, *grep* will print the output to the screen.

2. A word is also called a token.

EXAMPLE 3.2

```
% ps aux | grep root
```

EXPLANATION

The output of the *ps* command (*ps aux* displays processes running on this system) is sent to *grep* and all lines containing *root* are printed.

3.1.3 Basic and Extended Regular Expressions

The *grep* command supports a number of regular expression metacharacters (see Table 3.2) to help further define the search pattern. It also provides a number of options (see Table 3.3) to modify the way it does its search or displays lines. For example, you can provide options to turn off case-sensitivity, display line numbers, display filenames, and so on.

There are two versions of regular expression metacharacters: *basic* and *extended*. The regular version of *grep* uses the basic set (Table 3.2), and *egrep* (or *grep -E)* uses the extended set (Table 3.3). With Gnu *grep*, both sets are available. The basic set consists of:

^, $, ., *, [ ], [^], \<, and \>

In addition, Gnu *grep* recognizes: \b, \w, and \W, as well as a new class of POSIX metacharacters. (See Table 3.4.)

With the *-E* option to Gnu *grep*, the extended set are available, but even without the *-E* option, regular *grep*, the default, can use the extended set of metacharacters provided that the metacharacters are preceded with a backslash.[3] For example, the extended set of metacharacters are:

?, +, { }, |, ( )

The extended set of metacharacters have no special meaning to regular *grep*, unless they are backslashed as follows:

\?, \+, \{, \|, \(, \)

The format for using the Gnu *grep* is shown in Table 3.1.

Table 3.1 Gnu *grep*

Format	***What It Understands***
grep 'pattern' filename(s)	Basic RE metacharacters (the default)
grep -G 'pattern' filename(s)	Same as above; the default
grep -E 'pattern' filename(s)	Extended RE metacharacters
grep -F 'pattern' filename	No RE metacharacters

3. In any version of *grep*, a metacharacter can be quoted with a backslash to turn off its special meaning.

Table 3.2 *grep*'s Regular Expression Metacharacters (The Basic Set)

Metacharacter	*Function*	*Example*	*What It Matches*
^	Beginning of line anchor	^love	Matches all lines beginning with *love*.
$	End of line anchor	love$	Matches all lines ending with *love*.
.	Matches one character	l..e	Matches lines containing an *l*, followed by two characters, followed by an *e*.
*	Matches zero or more characters	*love	Matches lines with zero or more spaces, of the preceding characters followed by the pattern *love*.
[ ]	Matches one character in the set	[Ll]ove	Matches lines containing *love* or *Love*.
[^]	Matches one character not in the set	[^A–K]ove	Matches lines not containing *A* through *K* followed by *ove*.
\<[a]	Beginning of word anchor	\<love	Matches lines containing a word that begins with *love*.
\>	End of word anchor	love\>	Matches lines containing a word that ends with *love*.
\(..\)[b]	Tags matched characters	\(love\)able	Tags marked portion in a register to be remembered later as number 1. To reference later, use \1 to repeat the pattern. May use up to nine tags, starting with the first tag at the leftmost part of the pattern. For example, the pattern *love* is saved in register 1 to be referenced later as \1.
x\{m\} x\{m,\} x\{m,n\}[c]	Repetition of character x, m times, at least m times, or between m and n times	o\{5\} o\{5,\} o\{5,10\}	Matches if line has 5 *o*'s, at least 5 *o*'s, or between 5 and 10 *o*'s
\w	alphanumeric word character;[a-zA-Z0-9]	l\w*e	Matches an *l* followed by zero more word characters, and an *e*.
\W	nonalphanumeric word character;[^a-zA-Z0-9]	love\W+	Matches *love* followed by one or more non-word characters, such as a period, question mark, etc.
\b	word boundary	\blove\b	Matches only the word *love*.

a. These metacharacters do not work unless backslashed, even with *grep -E and Gnu egrep*; they don't work with UNIX *egrep* at all.

b. These metacharacters are really part of the extended set, but are placed here because they work with UNIX *grep* and Gnu regular *grep*, if backslashed. They do not work with UNIX *egrep* at all.

c. The \{ \} metacharacters are not supported on all versions of UNIX or all pattern-matching utilities; they usually work with *vi* and *grep*. They don't work with UNIX *egrep* at all.

Table 3.3 The Additional Extended Set (Used with *egrep* and *grep -E*)

<table>
<tr><th>Metacharacter</th><th>Function</th><th>Example</th><th>What It Matches</th></tr>
<tr><td>+</td><td>Matches one or more of the preceding characters</td><td>[a–z]+ove</td><td>Matches one or more lowercase letters, followed by ove. Would find move, approve, love, behoove, etc.</td></tr>
<tr><td>?</td><td>Matches zero or one of the preceding characters</td><td>lo?ve</td><td>Matches for an l followed by either one or not any o's at all. Would find love or lve.</td></tr>
<tr><td>a|b|c</td><td>Matches either a or b or c</td><td>love | hate</td><td>Matches for either expression, love or hate.</td></tr>
<tr><td>()</td><td>Groups characters</td><td>love(able | rs)
(ov)+</td><td>Matches for loveable or lovers. Matches for one or more occurrences of ov.</td></tr>
<tr><td>(..) (...) \1 \2[a]</td><td>Tags matched characters</td><td>\(love\)ing</td><td>Tags marked portion in a register to be remembered later as number 1. To reference later, use \1 to repeat the pattern. May use up to nine tags, starting with the first tag at the leftmost part of the pattern. For example, the pattern love is saved in register 1 to be referenced later as \1.</td></tr>
<tr><td>x{m}
x{m,}
x{m,n}[b]</td><td>Repetition of character x, m times, at least m times, or between m and n times</td><td>o\{5\}
o\{5,\}
o\{5,10\}</td><td>Matches if line has 5 o's, at least 5 o's, or between 5 and 10 o's</td></tr>
</table>

a. Tags and back references do not work with UNIX *egrep*.

b. The \{ \} metacharacters are not supported on all versions of UNIX or all pattern-matching utilities; they usually work with *vi* and *grep*. They do not work with UNIX egrep at all.

The POSIX Character Class. POSIX (the Portable Operating System Interface) is an industry standard to ensure that programs are portable across operating systems. In order to be portable, POSIX recognizes that different countries or locales may differ in the way they encode characters, represent currency, and how times and dates are represented. To handle different types of characters, POSIX added to the basic and extended regular expressions, the bracketed character class of characters shown in Table 3.4.

The class, for example, [:alnum:] is another way of saying *A-Za-z0-9.* To use this class, it must be enclosed in another set of brackets for it to be recognized as a regular expression. For example, *A-Za-z0-9,* by itself, is not a regular expression, but *[A-Za-z0-9]* is. Likewise, *[:alnum:]* should be written *[[:alnum:]].* The difference between using the first form, *[A-Za-z0-9]* and the bracketed form, *[[:alnum:]]* is that the first form is dependent on ASCII character encoding, whereas the second form allows characters from other languages to be represented in the class, such as Swedish rings and German umlauts.

Table 3.4 The Bracketed Character Class

Bracket Class	*Meaning*
[:alnum:]	alphanumeric characters
[:alpha:]	alphabetic characters
[:cntrl:]	control characters
[:digit:]	numeric characters
[:graph:]	nonblank characters (not spaces, control characters, etc.)
[:lower:]	lowercase letters
[:print:]	like [:graph:], but includes the space character
[:punct:]	punctuation characters
[:space:]	all white-space characters (newlines, spaces, tabs)
[:upper:]	uppercase letters
[:xdigit:]	allows digits in a hexadecimal number (0-9a-fA-F)

EXAMPLE 3.3

```
1   % grep '[[:space:]]\.[[:digit:]][[:space:]]' datafile
    southwest   SW     Lewis Dalsass          2.7     .8   2   18
    southeast   SE     Patricia Hemenway      4.0     .7   4   15

2   % grep -E '[[:space:]]\.[[:digit:]][[:space:]]' datafile
    southwest   SW     Lewis Dalsass          2.7     .8   2   18
    southeast   SE     Patricia Hemenway      4.0     .7   4   15

3   % egrep '[[:space:]]\.[[:digit:]][[:space:]]' datafile
    southwest   SW     Lewis Dalsass          2.7     .8   2   18
    southeast   SE     Patricia Hemenway      4.0     .7   4   15
```

EXPLANATION

1,2,3 For all Linux variants of *grep* (other than *fgrep*), the POSIX bracketed class set is supported. In each of these examples, *grep* will search for a space character, a literal period, a digit [0-9] and another space character.

3.1.4 *grep* and Exit Status

The *grep* command is very useful in shell scripts, because it always returns an exit status to indicate whether it was able to locate the pattern or the file you were looking for. If the pattern is found, *grep* returns an exit status of 0, indicating success; if *grep* cannot find the pattern, it returns 1 as its exit status; and if the file cannot be found, *grep* returns an exit status of 2. (Other Linux/UNIX utilities that search for patterns, such as *sed* and *awk*, do not use the exit status to indicate the success or failure of locating a pattern; they report failure only if there is a syntax error in a command.)

In the following example, *john* is not found in the */etc/passwd* file.

EXAMPLE 3.4

```
1   % grep 'john' /etc/passwd
2   % echo $status  (bash/tcsh/csh)
    1
    or
    $ echo $?   (bash/sh/ksh/tcsh)
    1
```

EXPLANATION

1 *Grep* searches for *john* in the */etc/passwd* file, and if successful, *grep* exits with a status of 0. If *john* is not found in the file, *grep* exits with `1`. If the file is not found, an exit status of 2 is returned.

2 The TC/C shell variable, *status*, and the Bourne/Korn shell variable, *?*, are assigned the exit status of the last command that was executed. With the Bourne Again (*bash*) shell you can use either the *?* or *status* variable to check exit status.

3.1.5 Regular *grep* Examples (*grep, grep -G*)

```
% cat datafile
northwest    NW    Charles Main        3.0    .98    3    34
western      WE    Sharon Gray         5.3    .97    5    23
southwest    SW    Lewis Dalsass       2.7    .8     2    18
southern     SO    Suan Chin           5.1    .95    4    15
southeast    SE    Patricia Hemenway   4.0    .7     4    17
eastern      EA    TB Savage           4.4    .84    5    20
northeast    NE    AM Main Jr.         5.1    .94    3    13
north        NO    Margot Weber        4.5    .89    5     9
central      CT    Ann Stephens        5.7    .94    5    13
```

EXAMPLE 3.5

```
grep NW datafile  or grep -G NW datafile
northwest         NW        Charles Main         3.0    .98    3     34
```

EXPLANATION

Prints all lines containing the regular expression *NW* in a file called *datafile*.

EXAMPLE 3.6

```
grep NW d*
datafile: northwest NW     Charles Main         3.0    .98    3     34
db:northwest        NW     Joel Craig           30     40     5     123
```

EXPLANATION

Prints all lines containing the regular expression *NW* in all files starting with a *d*. The shell expands *d** to all files that begin with a *d*; in this case the filenames are *db* and *datafile*.

EXAMPLE 3.7

```
grep '^n' datafile
northwest         NW        Charles Main         3.0    .98    3     34
northeast         NE        AM Main Jr.          5.1    .94    3     13
north             NO        Margot Weber         4.5    .89    5      9
```

EXPLANATION

Prints all lines beginning with an *n*. The caret (^) is the beginning of line anchor.

EXAMPLE 3.8

```
grep '4$' datafile
northwest         NW        Charles Main         3.0    .98    3     34
```

EXPLANATION

Prints all lines ending with a *4*. The dollar sign (*$*) is the end of line anchor.

EXAMPLE 3.9

```
grep TB Savage datafile
grep: Savage: No such file or directory
datafile:eastern    EA      TB Savage            4.4    .84     5    20
```

EXPLANATION

Because the first argument is the pattern and all of the remaining arguments are filenames, *grep* will search for *TB* in a file called *Savage* and a file called *datafile*. To search for *TB Savage*, see the next example.

EXAMPLE 3.10

```
grep 'TB Savage' datafile
eastern          EA         TB Savage           4.4    .84    5     20
```

EXPLANATION

Prints all lines containing the pattern *TB Savage.* Without quotes (in this example, either single or double quotes will do), the white space between *TB* and *Savage* would cause *grep* to search for *TB* in a file called *Savage* and a file called *datafile*, as in the previous example.

```
% cat datafile
northwest     NW     Charles Main         3.0      .98     3      34
western       WE     Sharon Gray          53       .97     5      23
southwest     SW     Lewis Dalsass        2.7      .8      2      18
southern      SO     Suan Chin            5.1      .95     4      15
southeast     SE     Patricia Hemenway    4.0      .7      4      17
eastern       EA     TB Savage            4.4      .84     5      20
northeast     NE     AM Main Jr.          5.1      .94     3      13
north         NO     Margot Weber         4.5      .89     5       9
central       CT     Ann Stephens         5.7      .94     5      13
```

EXAMPLE 3.11

```
grep '5\..' datafile
western       WE    Sharon Gray      5.3   .97   5   23
southern      SO    Suan Chin        5.1   .95   4   15
northeast     NE    AM Main Jr.      5.1   .94   3   13
central       CT    Ann Stephens     5.7   .94   5   13
```

EXPLANATION

Prints a line containing the number 5, followed by a literal period and any single character. The "dot" metacharacter represents a single character, unless it is escaped with a backslash. When escaped, the character is no longer a special metacharacter, but represents itself, a literal period.

EXAMPLE 3.12

```
grep '\.5' datafile
north         NO    Margot Weber     4.5   .89   5   9
```

EXPLANATION

Prints any line containing the expression *.5*.

EXAMPLE 3.13

```
grep '^[we]' datafile
western       WE    Sharon Gray      5.3   .97   5   23
eastern       EA    TB Savage        4.4   .84   5   20
```

EXPLANATION

Prints lines beginning with either a *w* or an *e*. The caret (^) is the beginning of line anchor, and either one of the characters in the brackets will be matched.

EXAMPLE 3.14

```
grep '[^0-9]' datafile
northwest       NW      Charles Main          3.0    .98   3    34
western         WE      Sharon Gray           5.3    .97   5    23
southwest       SW      Lewis Dalsass         2.7    .8    2    18
southern        SO      Suan Chin             5.1    .95   4    15
southeast       SE      Patricia Hemenway     4.0    .7    4    17
eastern         EA      TB Savage             4.4    .84   5    20
northeast       NE      AM Main Jr.           5.1    .94   3    13
north           NO      Margot Weber          4.5    .89   5     9
central         CT      Ann Stephens          5.7    .94   5    13
```

EXPLANATION

Prints all lines containing one nondigit. The caret inside brackets means match one character not in the range. Because all lines have at least one nondigit, all lines are printed. (See the *-v* option.)

EXAMPLE 3.15

```
grep '[A-Z][A-Z] [A-Z]' datafile
eastern         EA      TB Savage         4.4  .84    5    20
northeast       NE      AM Main Jr.       5.1  .94    3    13
```

EXPLANATION

Prints all lines containing two capital letters followed by a space and a capital letter, e.g., *TB Savage* and *AM Main.*

EXAMPLE 3.16

```
grep 'ss* ' datafile
northwest       NW      Charles Main      3.0   .98    3    34
southwest       SW      Lewis Dalsass     2.7   .8     2    18
```

EXPLANATION

Prints all lines containing an *s* followed by zero or more consecutive *s*'s and a space. Finds *Charles* and *Dalsass.*

```
% cat datafile
northwest     NW    Charles Main        3.0    .98    3    34
western       WE    Sharon Gray         53     .97    5    23
southwest     SW    Lewis Dalsass       2.7    .8     2    18
southern      SO    Suan Chin           5.1    .95    4    15
southeast     SE    Patricia Hemenway   4.0    .7     4    17
eastern       EA    TB Savage           4.4    .84    5    20
northeast     NE    AM Main Jr.         5.1    .94    3    13
north         NO    Margot Weber        4.5    .89    5     9
central       CT    Ann Stephens        5.7    .94    5    13
```

EXAMPLE 3.17

```
grep '[a-z]\{9\}' datafile
northwest        NW        Charles Main        3.0    .98    3    34
southwest        SW        Lewis Dalsass       2.7    .8     2    18
southeast        SE        Patricia Hemenway   4.0    .7     4    17
northeast        NE        AM Main Jr.         5.1    .94    3    13
```

EXPLANATION

Prints all lines where there are at least nine repeating lowercase letters, for example, *northwest, southwest, southeast*, and *northeast*.

EXAMPLE 3.18

```
grep '\(3\)\.[0-9].*\1      *\1' datafile
northwest        NW        Charles Main        3.0    .98    3    34
```

EXPLANATION

Prints the line if it contains a *3* followed by a period and another number, followed by any number of characters (.*), another *3* (originally tagged), any number of tabs, and another *3*. Because the *3* was enclosed in parentheses, \(*3*\), it can be later referenced with `\1`. \1 means that this was the first expression to be tagged with the \(\) pair.

EXAMPLE 3.19

```
grep '\<north' datafile
northwest        NW      Charles Main      3.0   .98   3   34
northeast        NE      AM Main Jr.       5.1   .94   3   13
north            NO      Margot Weber      4.5   .89   5    9
```

EXPLANATION

Prints all lines containing a word starting with *north*. The \< is the beginning of word anchor.

EXAMPLE 3.20

```
grep '\<north\>' datafile
north            NO      Margot Weber      4.5   .89   5    9
```

EXPLANATION

Prints the line if it contains the word *north*. The \< is the beginning of word anchor, and the \> is the end of word anchor.

EXAMPLE 3.21

```
grep '\bnorth\b' datafile
north            NO      Margot Weber      4.5   .89   5    9
```

EXPLANATION

Prints the line if it contains the word *north*. The *\b* a word boundary. It can be used instead of the word anchors (see previous example) on all Gnu variants of *grep*.

EXAMPLE 3.22

```
grep '^n\w*\W' datafile
northwest      NW       Charles Main       3.0   .98   3   34
northeast      NE       AM Main Jr.        5.1   .94   3   13
```

EXPLANATION

Prints any line starting with an "n," followed by zero or more alphanumeric word characters, followed by a nonalphanumeric word character. *\w* and *\W* are standard word metacharacters for Gnu variants of *grep*.

EXAMPLE 3.23

```
grep '\<[a-z].*n\>' datafile
northwest      NW       Charles Main       3.0   .98   3   34
western        WE       Sharon Gray        5.3   .97   5   23
southern       SO       Suan Chin          5.1   .95   4   15
eastern        EA       TB Savage          4.4   .84   5   20
northeast      NE       AM Main Jr.        5.1   .94   3   13
central        CT       Ann Stephens       5.7   .94   5   13
```

EXPLANATION

Prints all lines containing a word starting with a lowercase letter, followed by any number of characters, and a word ending in *n*. Watch the **.*** symbol. It means any character, including white space.

3.2 Extended *grep* (*grep -E* or *egrep*)

The main advantage of using extended *grep* is that additional regular expression metacharacters (see Table 3.4) have been added to the basic set. With the *-E* extension, *Gnu grep* allows the use of these new metacharacters.

Table 3.5 *egrep*'s Regular Expression Metacharacters

Metacharacter	*Function*	*Example*	*What It Matches*
^	Beginning of line anchor	^love	Matches all lines beginning with *love*.
$	End of line anchor	love$	Matches all lines ending with *love*.

Table 3.5 *egrep*'s Regular Expression Metacharacters (Continued)

Metacharacter	*Function*	*Example*	*What It Matches*
.	Matches one character	l..e	Matches lines containing an *l*, followed by two characters, followed by an *e*.
*	Matches zero or more characters	*love	Matches lines with zero or more spaces, of the preceding characters followed by the pattern *love*.
[ ]	Matches one character in the set	[Ll]ove	Matches lines containing *love* or *Love*.
[^]	Matches one character not in the set	[^A–KM–Z]ove	Matches lines not containing *A* through *K* or *M* through *Z*, followed by *ove*.
New with *grep -E* or *egrep*			
+	Matches one or more of the preceding characters	[a–z]+ove	Matches one or more lowercase letters, followed by *ove*. Would find *move*, *approve*, *love*, *behoove*, etc.
?	Matches zero or one of the preceding characters	lo?ve	Matches for an *l* followed by either one or not any *o*'s at all. Would find *love* or *lve*.
a|b	Matches either a or b	love|hate	Matches for either expression, *love* or *hate*.
()	Groups characters	love(able|ly) (ov)+	Matches for *loveable* or *lovely*. Matches for one or more occurrences of *ov*.
x{m} x{m,} x{m,n}[a]	Repetition of character x, m times, at least m times, or between m and n times	o\{5} o\{5,} o\{5,10}	Matches if line has 5 *o*'s, at least 5 *o*'s, or between 5 and 10 *o*'s
\w	alphanumeric word character;[a-zA-Z0-9]	l\w*e	Matches an *l* followed by zero more word characters, and an *e*.
\W	nonalphanumeric word character;[^a-zA-Z0-9]		
\b	word boundary	\blove\b	Matches only the word *love*.

a. The { } metacharacters are not supported on all versions of UNIX or all pattern-matching utilities; they usually work with *vi* and *grep*. They don't work with UNIX *egrep* at all.

3.2.1 *Extended grep* Examples (*egrep* and *grep -E*)

The following examples illustrate the way the extended set of regular expression metacharacters are used with *grep -E* and *egrep*. The *grep* examples presented earlier illustrate the use of the standard metacharacters, also recognized by *egrep*. With basic Gnu *grep (grep -G)*, it is possible to use any of the additional metacharacters, provided that each of the special metacharacters is preceded with a backslash.

In the following examples, all three variants of *grep* are shown to accomplish the same task.

```
% cat datafile
northwest     NW     Charles Main          3.0    .98    3    34
western       WE     Sharon Gray           53     .97    5    23
southwest     SW     Lewis Dalsass         2.7    .8     2    18
southern      SO     Suan Chin             5.1    .95    4    15
southeast     SE     Patricia Hemenway     4.0    .7     4    17
eastern       EA     TB Savage             4.4    .84    5    20
northeast     NE     AM Main Jr.           5.1    .94    3    13
north         NO     Margot Weber          4.5    .89    5     9
central       CT     Ann Stephens          5.7    .94    5    13
```

EXAMPLE 3.24

```
1 % egrep 'NW|EA' datafile
  northwest     NW      Charles Main      3.0   .98   3   34
  eastern       EA      TB Savage         4.4   .84   5   20

2 % grep -E 'NW|EA' datafile
  northwest     NW      Charles Main      3.0   .98   3   34
  eastern       EA      TB Savage         4.4   .84   5   20

3 % grep 'NW|EA' datafile
4 % grep 'NW\|EA' datafile
  northwest     NW      Charles Main      3.0   .98   3   34
  eastern       EA      TB Savage         4.4   .84   5   20
```

EXPLANATION

1 Prints the line if it contains either the expression *NW* or the expression *EA*. In this example, *egrep* is used. If you do not have the Gnu version of *grep*, use *egrep*.

EXPLANATION (CONTINUED)

2 In this example, the Gnu *grep* is used with the *-E* option to include the extended metacharacters. Same as *egrep*.

3 Regular *grep* does not normally support extended regular expressions; the vertical bar is an extended regular expression metacharacter used for alternation. Regular *grep* doesn't recognize it and searches for the explicit pattern 'NW|EA.' Nothing matches; nothing prints.

4 With Gnu regular *grep* (*grep -G*), if the metacharacter is preceded with a backslash it will be interpreted as an extended regular expression just as with *egrep* and *grep -E*.

```
% cat datafile
northwest     NW     Charles Main         3.0     .98     3     34
western       WE     Sharon Gray          53      .97     5     23
southwest     SW     Lewis Dalsass        2.7     .8      2     18
southern      SO     Suan Chin            5.1     .95     4     15
southeast     SE     Patricia Hemenway    4.0     .7      4     17
eastern       EA     TB Savage            4.4     .84     5     20
northeast     NE     AM Main Jr.          5.1     .94     3     13
north         NO     Margot Weber         4.5     .89     5      9
central       CT     Ann Stephens         5.7     .94     5     13
```

EXAMPLE 3.25

```
% egrep '3+' datafile
% grep -E '3+' datafile
% grep '3\+' datafile
northwest          NW          Charles Main         3.0    .98    3     34
western            WE          Sharon Gray          5.3    .97    5     23
northeast          NE          AM Main              5.1    .94    3     13
central            CT          Ann Stephens         5.7    .94    5     13
```

EXPLANATION

Prints all lines containing one or more *3*s.

EXAMPLE 3.26

```
% egrep '2\.?[0-9]' datafile
% grep -E '2\.?[0-9]' datafile
% grep '2\.\?[0-9]' datafile
western      WE    Sharon Gray      5.3   .97   5   23
southwest    SW    Lewis Dalsass    2.7   .8    2   18
eastern      EA    TB Savage        4.4   .84   5   20
```

EXPLANATION

Prints all lines containing a *2*, followed by zero or one period, followed by a number in the range between 0 and 9.

EXAMPLE 3.27

```
% egrep '(no)+' datafile
% grep -E '(no)+' datafile
% grep '\(no\)\+' datafile
northwest    NW    Charles Main     3.0   .98   3   34
northeast    NE    AM Main          5.1   .94   3   13
north        NO    Margot Weber     4.5   .89   5    9
```

EXPLANATION

Prints lines containing one or more occurrences of the pattern group *no*.

EXAMPLE 3.28

```
% grep -E '\w+\W+[ABC]' datafile
northwest    NW    Charles Main     3.0   .98   3   34
southern     SO    Suan Chin        5.1   .95   4   15
northeast    NE    AM Main Jr.      5.1   .94   3   13
central      CT    Ann Stephens     5.7   .94   5   13
```

EXPLANATION

Prints all lines containing one or more alphanumeric word characters (*w+*), followed by one or more non-alphanumeric word characters (*W+*), followed by one letter in the set *A, B, C*.

EXAMPLE 3.29

```
% egrep 'S(h|u)' datafile
% grep -E 'S(h|u)' datafile
% grep 'S\(h\|u\)' datafile
western         WE      Sharon Gray         5.3   .97   5   23
southern        SO      Suan Chin           5.1   .95   4   15
```

EXPLANATION

Prints all lines containing *S*, followed by either *h* or *u*; i.e., *Sh* or *Su*.

EXAMPLE 3.30

```
% egrep 'Sh|u' datafile
% grep -E 'Sh|u' datafile
% grep 'Sh\|u' datafile
western         WE      Sharon Gray         5.3   .97   5   23
southern        SO      Suan Chin           5.1   .95   4   15
southwest       SW      Lewis Dalsass       2.7   .8    2   18
southeast       SE      Patricia Hemenway   4.0   .7    4   17
```

EXPLANATION

Prints all lines containing the expression *Sh* or *u*.

3.2.2 Anomalies with Regular and Extended Variants of *grep*

The variants of Gnu *grep,* supported by Linux, are almost, but not the same, as their UNIX namesakes. For example, the version of *egrep,* found in Solaris or BSD UNIX, does not support three metacharacter sets: \{ \}for repetition, \(\) for tagging characters, and \< \>, the word anchors. Under Linux, these metacharacters are available with *grep* and *grep -E*, but *egrep* does not recognize \< \>. The following examples illustrate these differences, just in case you are running *bash* or *tcsh* under a UNIX system other than Linux, and you want to use *grep* and its family in your shell scripts.

```
% cat datafile
northwest    NW    Charles Main         3.0    .98    3    34
western      WE    Sharon Gray          53     .97    5    23
southwest    SW    Lewis Dalsass        2.7    .8     2    18
southern     SO    Suan Chin            5.1    .95    4    15
southeast    SE    Patricia Hemenway    4.0    .7     4    17
eastern      EA    TB Savage            4.4    .84    5    20
northeast    NE    AM Main Jr.          5.1    .94    3    13
north        NO    Margot Weber         4.5    .89    5     9
central      CT    Ann Stephens         5.7    .94    5    13
```

EXAMPLE 3.31

```
  (Linux Gnu grep)
1 % grep '<north>' datafile    Must use backslashes
2 % grep '\<north\>' datafile
  north        NO       Margot Weber       4.5    .89    5    9

3 % grep -E '\<north\>' datafile
  north        NO       Margot Weber       4.5    .89    5    9

4 % egrep '\<north\>' datafile
  north        NO       Margot Weber       4.5    .89    5    9

  (Solaris egrep)
5 % egrep '\<north\>' datafile
  <no output; not recognized>
```

EXPLANATION

1 No matter what variant of *grep* is being used, the word anchor metacharacters, < >, must be preceded with a backslash.

2 This time, *grep* searches for a word that begins and ends with *north*. \< represents the beginning of word anchor and \> represents the end of word anchor.

3 *Grep* with the *-E* option, also recognizes the word anchors.

4 The Gnu form of *egrep* recognizes the word anchors.

5 When using Solaris (SVR4), *egrep* does not recognize word anchors as regular expression metacharacters.

EXAMPLE 3.32

```
   (Linux Gnu grep)
1  % grep 'w(es)t.*\1' datafile
   grep: Invalid back reference

2  % grep 'w\(es\)t.*\1' datafile
   northwest      NW        Charles Main        3.0    .98    3     34

3  % grep -E 'w(es)t.*\1' datafile
   northwest      NW        Charles Main        3.0    .98    3     34

4  % egrep 'w(es)t.*\1' datafile
   northwest      NW        Charles Main        3.0    .98    3     34

   (Solaris egrep)
5  % egrep 'w(es)t.*\1' datafile
   <no output; not recognized>
```

EXPLANATION

1. When using regular *grep*, the ( ) extended metacharacters must be backslashed or an error occurs.
2. If the regular expression, *w\(es\)t,* is matched, the pattern, *es*, is saved and stored in memory register 1. The expression reads: if *west* is found, tag and save ***es***, search for any number of characters (.*) after it, followed by ***es*** (\1) again, and print the line. The ***es*** in *Charles* is matched by the backreference.
3. This is the same as the previous example, except, *grep* with the *-E* switch, does not precede the ( ) with backslashes.
4. The Gnu *egrep* also uses the extended metacharacters, ( ), without backslashes.
5. With Solaris, *egrep* doesn't recognize any form of tagging and backreferencing.

EXAMPLE 3.33

```
   (Linux Gnu grep)
1  % grep '\.[0-9]\{2\}[^0-9]' datafile
   northwest       NW      Charles Main     3.0     .98     3      34
   western         WE      Sharon Gray      5.3     .97     5      23
   southern        SO      Suan Chin        5.1     .95     4      15
   eastern         EA      TB Savage        4.4     .84     5      20
   northeast       NE      AM Main Jr.      5.1     .94     3      13
   north           NO      Margot Weber     4.5     .89     5       9
   central         CT      Ann Stephens     5.7     .94     5      13
```

EXAMPLE 3.33 (CONTINUED)

```
2 % grep -E '\.[0-9]{2}[^0-9]' datafile
  northwest     NW     Charles Main     3.0     .98     3     34
  western       WE     Sharon Gray      5.3     .97     5     23
  southern      SO     Suan Chin        5.1     .95     4     15
  eastern       EA     TB Savage        4.4     .84     5     20
  northeast     NE     AM Main Jr.      5.1     .94     3     13
  north         NO     Margot Weber     4.5     .89     5      9
  central       CT     Ann Stephens     5.7     .94     5     13

3 % egrep  '\.[0-9]{2}[^0-9]' datafile
  northwest     NW     Charles Main     3.0     .98     3     34
  western       WE     Sharon Gray      5.3     .97     5     23
  southern      SO     Suan Chin        5.1     .95     4     15
  eastern       EA     TB Savage        4.4     .84     5     20
  northeast     NE     AM Main Jr.      5.1     .94     3     13
  north         NO     Margot Weber     4.5     .89     5      9
  central       CT     Ann Stephens     5.7     .94     5     13

  (Solaris egrep)
4 % egrep  '\.[0-9]{2}[^0-9]' datafile
  <no output; not recognized with or without backslashes>
```

EXPLANATION

1 The extended metacharacters, { }, are used for repetition. The Gnu and UNIX versions of regular *grep* do not evaluate this extended metacharacter set unless the curly braces are preceded by backslashes. The whole expression reads: search for a literal period \., followed by a number between 0 and 9, *[0-9]*, if the pattern is repeated exactly two times, *\{2\}*, followed by a nondigit *[^0-9]*.

2 With extended *grep*, *grep -E*, the repetition metacharacters, *{2}*, do not need to be preceded with backslashes as in the previous example.

3 Because Gnu *egrep* and *grep -E* are functionally the same, this command produces the same output as the previous example.

4 This is the standard UNIX version of *egrep*. It does not recognize the curly braces as an extended metacharacter set either with or without backslashes.

3.3 Fixed *grep (grep -F* and *fgrep*)

The *fgrep* command behaves like *grep*, but does not recognize any regular expression metacharacters as being special. All characters represent only themselves. A caret is simply a caret, a dollar sign is a dollar sign, and so forth. With the *-F* option, Gnu *grep* behaves exactly the same as *fgrep*.

3.4 Recursive *grep* (*rgrep*)

Unlike the members of the *grep* family, Linux's *rgrep* can recursively descend a directory tree. *Rgrep* has a number of command line options and supports the same metacharacters as regular *grep* (*grep-R*). See page 713 in Appendix A for a complete description of *rgrep*, or type *rgrep-?* for online help. (Not supported on regular versions of UNIX.)

EXAMPLE 3.34

```
% fgrep '[A-Z]****[0-9]..$5.00' file      or
% grep -F '[A-Z]****[0-9]..$5.00' file
```

EXPLANATION

Finds all lines in the file containing the literal string *[A-Z]****[0-9]..$5.00.* All characters are treated as themselves. There are no special characters.

3.5 *grep* with Pipes

Instead of taking its input from a file, *grep* often gets its input from a pipe.

EXAMPLE 3.35

```
%  ls -l
drwxrwxrwx  2  ellie    2441 Jan 6 12:34  dir1
-rw-r--r--  1  ellie    1538 Jan 2 15:50  file1
-rw-r--r--  1  ellie    1539 Jan 3 13:36  file2
drwxrwxrwx  2  ellie    2341 Jan 6 12:34  grades

% ls -l | grep '^d'
drwxrwxrwx  2  ellie    2441 Jan 6 12:34  dir1
drwxrwxrwx  2  ellie    2341 Jan 6 12:34  grades
```

EXPLANATION

The output of the *ls* command is piped to *grep*. All lines of output that begin with a *d* are printed; that is, all directories are printed.

3.6 *grep* with Options

The *grep* command has a number of options that control its behavior. Not all versions of UNIX support exactly the same options, so be sure to check your man pages for a complete list. The Gnu version of *grep* added a number of new options and alternative ways to use the options, shown in Table 3.6. The Gnu *grep* options work with all the different variants of *grep*, including *grep -G*, *-E*, and *-F*, as shown in Table 3.7.

Table 3.6 Gnu *grep* Options

Option	***What It Does***
-b	Precedes each line by the block number on which it was found. This is sometimes useful in locating disk block numbers by context.
-c	Displays a count of matching lines rather than displaying the lines that match.
-h	Does not display filenames.
-i	Ignores the case of letters in making comparisons (i.e., upper- and lowercase are considered identical).
-l	Lists only the names of files with matching lines (once), separated by newline characters.
-n	Precedes each line by its relative line number in the file.
-s	Works silently, that is, displays nothing except error messages. This is useful for checking the exit status.
-v	Inverts the search to display only lines that do not match.
-w	Searches for the expression as a word, as if surrounded by \< and \>. This applies to *grep* only. (Not all versions of *grep* support this feature; e.g., SCO UNIX does not.)

Table 3.7 Gnu *grep* Options for All Variants of Gnu *grep (-G,-E,* and *-F)*

-#	Matches will be printed with # lines of leading and trailing context; i.e., *grep* -2 pattern filename will cause *grep* to print the matched line with the two lines before and after it.
-A #, --after-context=#	Print # lines of trailing context after matching lines; i.e, the matched line and the specified # lines after it.
-B #, --before-context=#	Print # lines of leading context before matching lines: i.e., the matched lines and the specified # lines before it.
-C, --context	Equivalent to -2. Prints the two lines before and after the matched line.
-V, --version	Displays the version information about *grep* which should be included in all bug reports.
-b, --byte-offset	Displays the byte offset before each line of output.
-c, --count	Prints a count of matching lines for each input file. With the *-v* prints a count of nonmatching lines.

Table 3.7 Gnu *grep* Options for All Variants of Gnu *grep* (*-G,-E,* and *-F*) (Continued)

-e PATTERN, --regexp=PATTERN	Use PATTERN literally as the pattern; useful to protect patterns beginning with -.
-f FILE, --file=FILE	Obtain patterns from FILE, one per line. The empty file contains zero patterns, and therefore matches nothing.
-h, --no-filename	Suppress the prefixing of filenames on output when multiple files are searched.
-i, --ignore-case	Ignore case distinctions in both the pattern and the input files.
-L, --files-without-match	Print just the names of all files where the pattern does not match.
-l, --files-with-matches	Print just the names of all files where the pattern does match.
-n, --line-number	Prefix each line of output with the line number where the match occurred.
-q, --quiet	Quiet; suppress normal output. Can be used instead of *-n*.
-s, --silent	Suppress error messages about nonexistent or unreadable files.
-v, --revert-match	Invert the sense of matching, to select nonmatch-in lines.
-w, --word-regexp	Select only those lines containing matches that are words. Matches are for strings containing letters, digits, and the underscore, on word boundaries.
-x, --line-regexp	Select only those matches that exactly match the whole line.
-y	Obsolete synonym for *-i*.
-U, --binary	Treat the file(s) as binary. This option is only supported on MS-DOS and MS-Windows.
-u, --unix-byte-offsets	Report UNIX-style byte offsets. This option has no effect unless *-b* option is also used; it is only supported on MS-DOS and MS-Windows.

```
% cat datafile
northwest    NW   Charles Main        3.0   .98   3   34
western      WE   Sharon Gray         53    .97   5   23
southwest    SW   Lewis Dalsass       2.7   .8    2   18
southern     SO   Suan Chin           5.1   .95   4   15
southeast    SE   Patricia Hemenway   4.0   .7    4   17
eastern      EA   TB Savage           4.4   .84   5   20
northeast    NE   AM Main Jr.         5.1   .94   3   13
north        NO   Margot Weber        4.5   .89   5    9
central      CT   Ann Stephens        5.7   .94   5   13
```

EXAMPLE 3.36

```
% grep -n '^south' datafile
3:southwest       SW        Lewis Dalsass        2.7    .8     2    18
4:southern        SO        Suan Chin            5.1    .95    4    15
5:southeast       SE        Patricia Hemenway    4.0    .7     4    17
```

EXPLANATION

The *-n* option precedes each line with the number of the line where the pattern was found, followed by the line.

EXAMPLE 3.37

```
% grep -i 'pat' datafile
southeast         SE        Patricia Hemenway    4.0    .7     4    17
```

EXPLANATION

The *-i* option turns off case-sensitivity. It does not matter if the expression *pat* contains any combination of upper- or lowercase letters.

EXAMPLE 3.38

```
% grep -v 'Suan Chin' datafile
northwest         NW        Charles Main         3.0    .98    3    34
western           WE        Sharon Gray          5.3    .97    5    23
southwest         SW        Lewis Dalsass        2.7    .8     2    18
southeast         SE        Patricia Hemenway    4.0    .7     4    17
eastern           EA        TB Savage            4.4    .84    5    20
northeast         NE        AM Main Jr.          5.1    .94    3    13
north             NO        Margot Weber         4.5    .89    5     9
central           CT        Ann Stephens         5.7    .94    5    13
```

EXPLANATION

Prints all lines *not* containing the pattern *Suan Chin*. This option is used when deleting a specific entry from the input file. To really remove the entry, you would redirect the output of *grep* to a temporary file, and then change the name of the temporary file back to the name of the original file as shown here:

```
grep -v 'Suan Chin' datafile > temp
mv temp datafile
```

Remember that you must use a temporary file when redirecting the output from *datafile*. If you redirect from *datafile* to *datafile*, the shell will "clobber" the *datafile*. (See "Redirection" on page 22.)

```
% cat datafile
northwest    NW    Charles Main         3.0    .98    3    34
western      WE    Sharon Gray          53     .97    5    23
southwest    SW    Lewis Dalsass        2.7    .8     2    18
southern     SO    Suan Chin            5.1    .95    4    15
southeast    SE    Patricia Hemenway    4.0    .7     4    17
eastern      EA    TB Savage            4.4    .84    5    20
northeast    NE    AM Main Jr.          5.1    .94    3    13
north        NO    Margot Weber         4.5    .89    5     9
central      CT    Ann Stephens         5.7    .94    5    13
```

EXAMPLE 3.39

```
% grep -l 'ss'  *
datafile
datebook
```

EXPLANATION

The *-l* option causes *grep* to print out only the filenames where the pattern is found instead of each line of text.

EXAMPLE 3.40

```
% grep -c 'west' datafile
3
```

EXPLANATION

The *-c* option causes *grep* to print the number of lines where the pattern is found. This does not mean the number of occurrences of the pattern. For example, if *west* is found three times on a line, it only counts the line once.

EXAMPLE 3.41

```
% grep  -w 'north' datafile
north         NO       Margot Weber        4.5   .89   5    9
```

EXPLANATION

The *-w* option causes *grep* to find the pattern only if it is a word,[a] not part of a word. Only the line containing the word *north* is printed, not *northwest*, *northeast*, and so forth.

a. A word is a sequence of alphanumeric characters starting at the beginning of a line or preceded by white space and ending in white space, punctuation, or a newline.

EXAMPLE 3.42

```
% echo $LOGNAME
lewis
% grep -i "$LOGNAME" datafile
southwest         SW         Lewis Dalsass        2.7    .8     2     18
```

EXPLANATION

The value of the shell *ENV* variable, *LOGNAME*, is printed. It contains the user's login name. If the variable is enclosed in double quotes, it will still be expanded by the shell, and in case there is more than one word assigned to the variable, white space is shielded from shell interpretation. If single quotes are used, variable substitution does not take place; that is, *$LOGNAME* is printed.

3.6.1 Gnu *grep* Options Examples

EXAMPLE 3.43

```
% grep -V
grep (GNU grep) 2.2

Copyright (C) 1988, 92, 93, 94, 95, 96, 97 Free Software Foundation,
Inc. This is free software; see the source for copying conditions.
There is NO warranty; not even for MERCHANTABILITY or FITNESS FOR A
PARTICULAR PURPOSE.
```

EXPLANATION

With the *-V* option, *grep's* version and copyright information are listed. The version information should be included with any bug reports sent to the Gnu Foundation.

```
% cat datafile
northwest    NW    Charles Main         3.0    .98    3    34
western      WE    Sharon Gray          53     .97    5    23
southwest    SW    Lewis Dalsass        2.7    .8     2    18
southern     SO    Suan Chin            5.1    .95    4    15
southeast    SE    Patricia Hemenway    4.0    .7     4    17
eastern      EA    TB Savage            4.4    .84    5    20
northeast    NE    AM Main Jr.          5.1    .94    3    13
north        NO    Margot Weber         4.5    .89    5     9
central      CT    Ann Stephens         5.7    .94    5    13
```

EXAMPLE 3.44

```
1 % grep -2 Patricia datafile
  southwest     SW       Lewis Dalsass        2.7   .8    2    18
  southern      SO       Suan Chin            5.1   .95   4    15
  southeast     SE       Patricia Hemenway    4.0   .7    4    15
  eastern       EA       TB Savage            4.4   .84   5    20
  northeast     NE       AM Main Jr.          5.1   .94   3    13

2 % grep -C Patricia datafile
  southwest     SW       Lewis Dalsass        2.7   .8    2    18
  southern      SO       Suan Chin            5.1   .95   4    15
  southeast     SE       Patricia Hemenway    4.0   .7    4    15
  eastern       EA       TB Savage            4.4   .84   5    20
  northeast     NE       AM Main Jr.          5.1   .94   3    13
```

EXPLANATION

1. After a line matching *Patricia* is found, *grep* displays that line and the two lines before and after it.
2. The *-C* option is the same as *-2*.

EXAMPLE 3.45

```
% grep -A 2 Patricia datafile
southeast     SE       Patricia Hemenway    4.0   .7    4    15
eastern       EA       TB Savage            4.4   .84   5    20
northeast     NE       AM Main Jr.          5.1   .94   3    13
```

EXPLANATION

After a line matching *Patricia* is found, *grep* displays that line and the two lines after it.

EXAMPLE 3.46

```
% grep -B 2 Patricia datafile
southwest       SW        Lewis Dalsass       2.7   .8    2   18
southern        SO        Suan Chin           5.1   .95   4   15
southeast       SE        Patricia Hemenway   4.0   .7    4   15
```

EXPLANATION

After a line matching *Patricia* is found, *grep* displays that line and the two lines before (preceding it).

EXAMPLE 3.47

```
% grep -b '[abc]' datafile
0:northwest       NW        Charles Main        3.0   .98   3   34
39:western        WE        Sharon Gray         5.3   .97   5   23
76:southwest      SW        Lewis Dalsass       2.7   .8    2   18
115:southern      SO        Suan Chin           5.1   .95   4   15
150:southeast     SE        Patricia Hemenway   4.0   .7    4   15
193:eastern       EA        TB Savage           4.4   .84   5   20
228:northeast     NE        AM Main Jr.         5.1   .94   3   13
266:north         NO        Margot Weber        4.5   .89   5    9
301:central       CT        Ann Stephens        5.7   .94   5   13
```

EXPLANATION

With the *-b* option, *grep* prints the byte offset from the input file before each line of output.

Instead of using the datafile for this example, we'll use a file called negative to demonstrate the *-e* and *-x* options.

```
% cat negative
-40 is cold.
This is line 1.
This is line 2.5
-alF are options to the ls command
```

EXAMPLE 3.48

```
1   % grep -e '-alF' negative
    -alF are options to the ls command

2   % grep --regexp=-40 negative
    -40 is cold.
```

EXPLANATION

1 With the *-e* option, *grep* treats all characters in the pattern equally, so that leading dashes are not mistaken for options.

2 The alternate way to represent *-e* is *--regexp=pattern*, where pattern is the regular expression; in this example the regular expression is *-40*.

EXAMPLE 3.49

```
% grep -x -e '-40 is cold.' negative
-40 is cold.
```

EXPLANATION

With the *-x* option, *grep* will not match a line unless the search pattern is identical to the entire line. The *-e* is used to allow a dash as the first character in the search string.

```
% cat datafile
northwest    NW    Charles Main        3.0    .98    3    34
western      WE    Sharon Gray         53     .97    5    23
southwest    SW    Lewis Dalsass       2.7    .8     2    18
southern     SO    Suan Chin           5.1    .95    4    15
southeast    SE    Patricia Hemenway   4.0    .7     4    17
eastern      EA    TB Savage           4.4    .84    5    20
northeast    NE    AM Main Jr.         5.1    .94    3    13
north        NO    Margot Weber        4.5    .89    5     9
central      CT    Ann Stephens        5.7    .94    5    13
```

EXAMPLE 3.50

```
1 % cat repatterns
  western
  north

2 % grep -f repatterns datafile
  northwest     NW     Charles Main     3.0     .98     3     34
  western       WE     Sharon Gray      5.3     .97     5     23
  northeast     NE     AM Main Jr.      5.1     .94     3     13
  north         NO     Margot Weber     4.5     .89     5      9
```

EXPLANATION

1 The file *repatterns* is displayed. It contains *grep*'s search patterns that will be matched against lines in an input file. *Western* and *north* are the patterns *grep* will use in its search.

2 With the *-f* option followed by a filename (in this example, *repatterns*), *grep* will get its search patterns from that file and match them against lines in *datafile*. *Grep* searched for and printed all lines containing patterns *western* and *north*.

```
% cat datafile
northwest    NW   Charles Main        3.0    .98    3    34
western      WE   Sharon Gray         53     .97    5    23
southwest    SW   Lewis Dalsass       2.7    .8     2    18
southern     SO   Suan Chin           5.1    .95    4    15
southeast    SE   Patricia Hemenway   4.0    .7     4    17
eastern      EA   TB Savage           4.4    .84    5    20
northeast    NE   AM Main Jr.         5.1    .94    3    13
north        NO   Margot Weber        4.5    .89    5     9
central      CT   Ann Stephens        5.7    .94    5    13
```

EXAMPLE 3.51

```
1 % grep  '[0-9]' datafile db
  datafile:northwest NW     Charles Main       3.0   .98    3    34
  datafile:western   WE     Sharon Gray        5.3   .97    5    23
  datafile:southwest SW     Lewis Dalsass      2.7   .8     2    18
  datafile:southern  SO     Suan Chin          5.1   .95    4    15
  datafile:southeast SE     Patricia Hemenway 4.0   .7     4    15
  datafile:eastern   EA     TB Savage          4.4   .84    5    20
  datafile:northeast NE     AM Main Jr.        5.1   .94    3    13
  datafile:north     NO     Margot Weber       4.5   .89    5     9
  datafile:central   CT     Ann Stephens       5.7   .94    5    13
  db:123

2 % grep -h '[0-9]' datafle db
  northwest          NW     Charles Main       3.0   .98    3    34
  western            WE     Sharon Gray        5.3   .97    5    23
  southwest          SW     Lewis Dalsass      2.7   .8     2    18
  southern           SO     Suan Chin          5.1   .95    4    15
  southeast          SE     Patricia Hemenway 4.0   .7     4    15
  eastern            EA     TB Savage          4.4   .84    5    20
  northeast          NE     AM Main Jr.        5.1   .94    3    13
  north              NO     Margot Weber       4.5   .89    5     9
  central            CT     Ann Stephens       5.7   .94    5    13
  123
```

EXPLANATION

1. If more than one file is listed, *grep* prepends each line of its output with the filename. Filenames are *datafile* and *db.*
2. With the *-h* option, *grep* suppresses the header information; i.e, does not print the filenames.

EXAMPLE 3.52

```
% grep -q Charles datafile or grep --quiet Charles datafile
% echo $status
0
```

EXPLANATION

The *quiet* option suppresses any output from grep. It is used when the exit status is all that is needed. If the exit status is zero, *grep* found the pattern.

3.6.2 *Regular grep* Review (*grep -G*)

Table 3.8 contains examples of *grep* commands and what they do.

Table 3.8 Review of *grep*

grep ***Command***	***What It Does***
`grep '\<Tom\>' file`	Prints lines containing the word *Tom.*
`grep 'Tom Savage' file`	Prints lines containing *Tom Savage.*
`grep '^Tommy' file`	Prints lines if *Tommy* is at the beginning of the line.
`grep '\.bak$' file`	Prints lines ending in *.bak.* Single quotes protect the dollar sign ($) from interpretation.
`grep '[Pp]yramid' *`	Prints lines from all files containing *pyramid* or *Pyramid* in the current working directory.
`grep '[A-Z]' file`	Prints lines containing at least one capital letter.
`grep '[0-9]' file`	Prints lines containing at least one number.
`grep '[A-Z]...[0-9]' file`	Prints lines containing five-character patterns starting with a capital letter and ending with a number.
`grep -w '[tT]est' files`	Prints lines with the word *Test* and/or *test.*
`grep -s "Mark Todd" file`	Finds lines containing *Mark Todd*, but does not print the line. Can be used when checking *grep*'s exit status.
`grep -v 'Mary' file`	Prints all lines NOT containing *Mary.*
`grep -i 'sam' file`	Prints all lines containing *sam*, regardless of case (e.g., *SAM, sam, SaM, sAm*).
`grep -l 'Dear Boss' *`	Lists all filenames containing *Dear Boss.*
`grep -n 'Tom' file`	Precedes matching lines with line numbers.
`grep "$name" file`	Expands the value of variable *name* and prints lines containing that value. Must use double quotes.
`grep '$5' file`	Prints lines containing literal *$5.* Must use single quotes.
`ps -ef| grep "^ *user1"`	Pipes output of *ps -ef* to *grep*, searching for *user1* at the beginning of a line, even if it is preceded by zero or more spaces.

3.6.3 *egrep* and *grep -E* Review

Table 3.9 contains examples of *egrep* commands and what they do.

Table 3.9 Review of *egrep*[a]

egrep ***Command***	***What It Does***
`egrep '^ +' filefg`	Prints lines beginning with one or more spaces.
* `egrep '^ *' file`	Prints lines beginning with zero or more spaces.
`egrep '(Tom | Dan) Savage' file`	Prints lines containing *Tom Savage* or *Dan Savage*.
`egrep '(ab)+' file`	Prints lines with one or more *ab*'s.
`egrep '^X[0-9]?' file`	Prints lines beginning with *X* followed by zero or one single digit.
* `egrep 'fun\.$' *`	Prints lines ending in *fun.* from all files.
`egrep '[A-Z]+' file`	Prints lines containing one or more capital letters.
* `egrep '[0-9]' file`	Prints lines containing a number.
* `egrep '[A-Z]...[0-9]' file`	Prints lines containing five-character patterns starting with a capital letter, followed by three of any character, and ending with a number.
* `egrep '[tT]est' files`	Prints lines with *Test* and/or *test*.
* `egrep "Susan Jean" file`	Prints lines containing *Susan Jean*.
* `egrep -v 'Mary' file`	Prints all lines NOT containing *Mary*.
* `egrep -i 'sam' file`	Prints all lines containing *sam*, regardless of case (e.g., *SAM, sam, SaM, sAm,* etc.).
* `egrep -l 'Dear Boss' *`	Lists all filenames containing *Dear Boss*.
* `egrep -n 'Tom' file`	Precedes matching lines with line numbers.
* `egrep -s "$name" file`	Expands variable name, finds it, but prints nothing. Can be used to check the exit status of *egrep*.

a. The asterisk preceding the command indicates that both *egrep* and *grep* handle the pattern in the same way.

LINUX TOOLS LAB 1

grep/egrep Exercise

Steve Blenheim:238-923-7366:95 Latham Lane, Easton, PA 83755:11/12/56:20300
Betty Boop:245-836-8357:635 Cutesy Lane, Hollywood, CA 91464:6/23/23:14500
Igor Chevsky:385-375-8395:3567 Populus Place, Caldwell, NJ 23875:6/18/68:23400
Norma Corder:397-857-2735:74 Pine Street, Dearborn, MI 23874:3/28/45:245700
Jennifer Cowan:548-834-2348:583 Laurel Ave., Kingsville, TX 83745:10/1/35:58900
Jon DeLoach:408-253-3122:123 Park St., San Jose, CA 04086:7/25/53:85100
Karen Evich:284-758-2857:23 Edgecliff Place, Lincoln, NB 92743:7/25/53:85100
Karen Evich:284-758-2867:23 Edgecliff Place, Lincoln, NB 92743:11/3/35:58200
Karen Evich:284-758-2867:23 Edgecliff Place, Lincoln, NB 92743:11/3/35:58200
Fred Fardbarkle:674-843-1385:20 Parak Lane, DeLuth, MN 23850:4/12/23:780900
Fred Fardbarkle:674-843-1385:20 Parak Lane, DeLuth, MN 23850:4/12/23:780900
Lori Gortz:327-832-5728:3465 Mirlo Street, Peabody, MA 34756:10/2/65:35200
Paco Gutierrez:835-365-1284:454 Easy Street, Decatur, IL 75732:2/28/53:123500
Ephram Hardy:293-259-5395:235 CarltonLane, Joliet, IL 73858:8/12/20:56700
James Ikeda:834-938-8376:23445 Aster Ave., Allentown, NJ 83745:12/1/38:45000
Barbara Kertz:385-573-8326:832 Ponce Drive, Gary, IN 83756:12/1/46:268500
Lesley Kirstin:408-456-1234:4 Harvard Square, Boston, MA 02133:4/22/62:52600
William Kopf:846-836-2837:6937 Ware Road, Milton, PA 93756:9/21/46:43500
Sir Lancelot:837-835-8257:474 Camelot Boulevard, Bath, WY 28356:5/13/69:24500
Jesse Neal:408-233-8971:45 Rose Terrace, San Francisco, CA 92303:2/3/36:25000
Zippy Pinhead:834-823-8319:2356 Bizarro Ave., Farmount, IL 84357:1/1/67:89500
Arthur Putie:923-835-8745:23 Wimp Lane, Kensington, DL 38758:8/31/69:126000
Popeye Sailor:156-454-3322:945 Bluto Street, Anywhere, USA 29358:3/19/35:22350
Jose Santiago:385-898-8357:38 Fife Way, Abilene, TX 39673:1/5/58:95600
Tommy Savage:408-724-0140:1222 Oxbow Court, Sunnyvale, CA 94087:5/19/66:34200
Yukio Takeshida:387-827-1095:13 Uno Lane, Ashville, NC 23556:7/1/29:57000
Vinh Tranh:438-910-7449:8235 Maple Street, Wilmington, VM 29085:9/23/63:68900

(Refer to the database called datebook *on the CD.)*

1. Print the version of *grep* you are using.
2. Print all lines containing the string *San*.
3. Print all lines either *CA* or *ca*.
4. Print all lines where the person's first name starts with *J*.
5. Print all lines ending in *700* and the two lines before and after each of the lines matched.
6. Print all lines that don't contain *834*.
7. Print all lines where birthdays are in *December*.
8. Print all lines where the phone number is in the *408* area code.

9. Print all lines containing an uppercase letter, followed by four lowercase letters, a comma, a space, and one uppercase letter.
10. Print lines where the last name begins with *K* or *k*.
11. Print lines preceded by a line number where the salary is six figures.
12. Print lines containing *Lincoln* or *lincoln* (*grep* is insensitive to case).
13. Print lines containing a 3 followed by a single dash, and at least one other digit.
14. Print the line containing *Jesse* and the two lines preceding it.
15. Print lines containing either the patterns *Yukio* or *Vinh* found at the beginning of the line.
16. Put *grep*'s search patterns *San Francisco* and *Sir Lancelot* in a file. *Grep* will use the file to match lines in the *datebook* file.

CHAPTER 4

THE STREAMLINED EDITOR

4.1 What Is *sed*?

The *sed* command is a streamlined, noninteractive editor. It allows you to perform the same kind of editing tasks used in the *vi* and *ex* editors. Instead of working interactively with the editor, the *sed* program lets you type your editing commands at the command line, name the file, and then see the output of the editing command on the screen. The *sed* editor is nondestructive. It does not change your file unless you save the output with shell redirection. All lines are printed to the screen by default.

The *sed* editor is useful in shell scripts where using interactive editors such as *vi* or *ex* would require the user of the script to have familiarity with the editor and allow the user to make unwanted modifications to the open file. You can also put *sed* commands in a file called a *sed* script, if you need to perform multiple edits or do not like worrying about quoting the *sed* commands at the shell command line.[1]

4.2 Versions of *sed*

Linux uses the Gnu version of *sed,* copyrighted by the Free Software Foundation. This version is almost identical to the *sed* provided by standard UNIX distributions.

1. Remember, the shell will try to evaluate any metacharacters or white space when a command is typed at the command line; any characters in the *sed* command that could be interpreted by the shell must be quoted.

EXAMPLE 4.1

```
% sed -V    or   sed --version
GNU sed version 3.02

Copyright (C) 1998 Free Software Foundation, Inc.
This is free software; see the source for copying conditions.
There is NO warranty; not even for MERCHANTABILITY or FITNESS FOR A
PARTICULAR PURPOSE, to the extent permitted by law.
```

4.3 How Does *sed* Work?

The *sed* editor processes a file (or input) one line at a time and sends its output to the screen. Its commands are those you may recognize from the *vi* and *ed/ex* editors. *Sed* stores the line it is currently processing in a temporary buffer, called a *pattern space*. Once *sed* is finished processing the line in the pattern space (i.e., executing *sed* commands on that line), the line in the pattern space is sent to the screen (unless the command was to delete the line or suppress its printing). After the line has been processed, it is removed from the pattern space and the next line is then read into the pattern space, processed, and displayed. *Sed* ends when the last line of the input file has been processed. By storing each line in a temporary buffer and performing edits on that line, the original file is never altered or destroyed.

4.4 Addressing

You can use addressing to decide which lines you want to edit. The addresses can be in the form of numbers or regular expressions, or a combination of both. Without specifying an address, *sed* processes all lines of the input file.

When an address consists of a number, the number represents a line number. A dollar sign can be used to represent the last line of the input file. If a comma separates two line numbers, the addresses that will be processed are within that range of lines, including the first and last line in the range. The range may be numbers, regular expressions, or a combination of numbers and regular expressions.

S*ed* commands tell *sed* what to do with the line: print it, remove it, change it, and so forth.

FORMAT

```
sed 'command' filename(s)
```

EXAMPLE 4.2

```
1 % sed '1,3d' myfile

2 % sed -n '/[Jj]ohn/p' datafile
```

EXPLANATION

1 All lines of *myfile* are printed, except lines 1, 2, and 3 or delete lines 1, 2, and 3.

2 Only lines matching the pattern *John* or *john* in *myfile* are printed.

4.5 Commands and Options

Sed commands tell *sed* how to process each line of input specified by an address. If an address is not given, *sed* processes every line of input. If a *sed* command is preceded by an exclamation point (!), the negation operator, the command affects every line not selected by the address(es) The % is the shell prompt. See Table 4.1 for a list of *sed* commands and what they do, and see Table 4.2 for a list of options and how they control *sed*'s behavior. With the *-h* option, *sed* displays a list of its command line options and a short description of what each one does.

EXAMPLE 4.3

```
% sed -h
Usage: sed [OPTION]... {script-only-if-no-other-script} [input-file]...

    -n, --quiet, --silent
                    suppress automatic printing of pattern space
    -e script, --expression=script
                    add the script to the commands to be executed
    -f script-file, --file=script-file
                    add the contents of script-file to the commands to
                    be executed
    --help          display this help and exit
    -V, --version output version information and exit
```

EXPLANATION

If an *-e*, *--expression*, *-f*, or *--file* option is not given, then the first nonoption argument is taken as a *sed* script to be interpreted. All remaining arguments are names of input files; if no input files are specified, then the standard input is read.

Table 4.1 *sed* Commands

Command	*Function*
a\	Appends one or more lines of text to the current line.
b label	Branches to the : command bearing the label. Without a label, branches to the end of the script.
c\	Changes (replaces) text in the current line with new text.
d	Deletes a line(s) from the pattern space.
D	Deletes the first line of the pattern space.
i\	Inserts text above the current line.
h	Copies the contents of the pattern space to a holding buffer.
H	Appends the contents of the pattern space to a holding buffer.
g	Gets what is in the holding buffer and copies it into the pattern buffer, overwriting what was there.
G	Gets what is in the holding buffer and copies it into the pattern buffer, appending to what was there.
l	Lists nonprinting characters.
n	Reads the next input line and starts processing the new line with the next command rather than the first command.
N	Appends the next line of input to the current pattern space, inserting an embedded newline between the two. Changes the current line number.
p	Prints lines in the pattern space.
P	Prints the first line from the pattern space.
q	Quits or exits *sed.*
r file	Reads lines from *file*.
t label	Branch-if-test, i.e., if any substitutions have been made since last input line or t or T command, branches to the : command with the *label* or to the end of file if no *label.*
T label	Branch-on-error, i.e., if no substitutions have succeeded since last input line or t or T command, branches to the : command with the *label* and to the end of file if no *labe*l.
w file	Writes and appends the pattern space to *file*.
W file	Writes and appends first line of the pattern space to *file*.
!	Applies the command to all lines *except* the selected ones.

Table 4.1 *sed* Commands (Continued)

Command	*Function*
s/re/string/	Substitutes regular expression, *re,* with *string*.
=	Prints the current line number.
# comment	The comment extends until the next newline (or the end of an *-e* script expression).
Substitution Flags	
g	Globally substitutes on a line.
p	Prints lines.
w	Writes lines out to a file.
x	Exchanges contents of the holding buffer with the pattern space.
y	Translates one character to another (cannot use regular expression metacharacters with *y*).

Table 4.2 *sed* Options

Options	*Function*
-e command, *--expression=command*	Allows multiple edits. Same as above.
-h, --help	Prints a message summarizing the command line options and the address for reporting bugs.
-n, --quiet, --silent	Suppresses default output.
-f, *--file=script-file*	Precedes a *sed* script filename. Same as above (*script-file* is file containing *sed* commands.)
-V, --version	Prints version and copyright information.

When multiple commands are used or addresses need to be nested within a range of addresses, the commands are enclosed in curly braces and each command is either on a separate line or terminated with semicolons.

The exclamation point (!) can be used to negate a command. For example,

```
% sed '/Tom/d' file
```

tells *sed* to delete all lines containing the pattern *Tom*, whereas,

```
% sed '/Tom/!d' file
```

tells *sed* to delete lines NOT containing *Tom.*

The *sed* options are *-e, -f,* and *-n.* The *-e* is used for multiple edits at the command line, the *-f* precedes a *sed* script filename, and the *-n* suppresses printing output.

4.6 Error Messages and Exit Status

When *sed* encounters a syntax error, it sends a pretty straightforward error message to standard error; but if it cannot figure out what you did wrong, *sed* gets "garbled," which you could guess means confused. The exit status that *sed* returns to the shell, if its syntax is error-free, is a zero for success and a nonzero integer for failure.[2]

EXAMPLE 4.4

```
1   % sed '1,3v ' file
    sed: -e expression #1, char 4: Unknown command: ''v''

    % echo $status (echo $?  if using sh or ksh shells)
    2

2   % sed '/John' file
    sed: -e expression #1, char 5: Unterminated address regex

3   % sed 's/1235/g' file
    sed: -e expression #1, char 7: Unterminated 's' command
```

EXPLANATION

1 The *v* command is unrecognized by *sed.* The exit status was 2, indicating that *sed* exited with a syntax problem.

2 The pattern */^John* is missing the closing forward slash.

3 The substitution command, *s,* contains the search string but not the replacement string.

---

2. For a complete list of diagnostics, see the UNIX man page for *sed.*

4.6.1 Metacharacters

Like *grep*, *sed* supports a number of special metacharacters to control pattern searching. See Table 4.3.

Table 4.3 *sed*'s Regular Expression Metacharacters

Metacharacter	*Function*	*Example*	*What It Matches*
^	Beginning of line anchor	/^love/	Matches all lines beginning with *love*.
$	End of line anchor	/love$/	Matches all lines ending with *love*.
.	Matches one character, but not the newline character	/l..e/	Matches lines containing an *l*, followed by two characters, followed by an *e*.
*	Matches zero or more characters	/ *love/	Matches lines with zero or more spaces, followed by the pattern *love*.
[ ]	Matches one character in the set	/[Ll]ove/	Matches lines containing *love* or *Love*.
[^]	Matches one character not in the set	/[^A–KM–Z]ove/	Matches lines not containing *A* through *K* or *M* through *Z* followed by *ove*.
\(..\)	Saves matched characters	s/\(love\)able/\1rs/	Tags marked portion and saves it as tag number 1. To reference later, use \1. \1 will be replaced with tagged pattern. May use up to nine tags, starting with the first tag at the leftmost part of the pattern. For example, *love* is saved in register 1 and remembered in the replacement string. *loveable* is replaced with *lovers*.
&	Saves search string so it can be remembered in the replacement string	s/love/**&**/	The ampersand represents the search string. The string *love* will be replaced with itself surrounded by asterisks; i.e., *love* will become ***love***.
\<	Beginning of word anchor	/\<love/	Matches lines containing a word beginning with *love*.
\>	End of word anchor	/love\>/	Matches lines containing a word that ends with *love*.
x\{m\} x\{m,\} x\{m,n\} [a]	Repetition of character x, m times at least m times at least m and not more than n times	/o\{5\}/	Matches if line has 5 *o*'s, at least 5 *o*'s, or between 5 and 10 *o*'s.

a. Not dependable on all versions of UNIX or all pattern-matching utilities; usually works with *vi* and *grep*.

4.7 *sed* Examples

```
% cat datafile
northwest     NW    Charles Main        3.0    .98    3     34
western       WE    Sharon Gray         5.3    .97    5     23
southwest     SW    Lewis Dalsass       2.7    .8     2     18
southern      SO    Suan Chin           5.1    .95    4     15
southeast     SE    Patricia Hemenway   4.0    .7     4     17
eastern       EA    TB Savage           4.4    .84    5     20
northeast     NE    AM Main Jr.         5.1    .94    3     13
north         NO    Margot Weber        4.5    .89    5      9
central       CT    Ann Stephens        5.7    .94    5     13
```

4.7.1 Printing: The *p* Command (and the *--quiet* option)

EXAMPLE 4.5

```
% sed '/north/p' datafile
northwest         NW       Charles Main        3.0   .98   3    34
northwest         NW       Charles Main        3.0   .98   3    34
western           WE       Sharon Gray         5.3   .97   5    23
southwest         SW       Lewis Dalsass       2.7   .8    2    18
southern          SO       Suan Chin           5.1   .95   4    15
southeast         SE       Patricia Hemenway   4.0   .7    4    17
eastern           EA       TB Savage           4.4   .84   5    20
northeast         NE       AM Main Jr.         5.1   .94   3    13
northeast         NE       AM Main Jr.         5.1   .94   3    13
north             NO       Margot Weber        4.5   .89   5     9
north             NO       Margot Weber        4.5   .89   5     9
central           CT       Ann Stephens        5.7   .94   5    13
```

EXPLANATION

Prints all lines to standard output by default. If the pattern *north* is found, *sed* will print that line in addition to all the other lines.

EXAMPLE 4.6

```
1 % sed -n '/north/p' datafile
  northwest     NW      Charles Main       3.0   .98   3   34
  northeast     NE      AM Main Jr.        5.1   .94   3   13
  north         NO      Margot Weber       4.5   .89   5    9

2 % sed --quiet '/north/p' datafile
  northwest     NW      Charles Main       3.0   .98   3   34
  northeast     NE      AM Main Jr.        5.1   .94   3   13
  north         NO      Margot Weber       4.5   .89   5    9
```

EXPLANATION

1 The *-n* option suppresses the default behavior of *sed* when used with the *p* command. Without the *-n* option, *sed* will print duplicate lines of output as shown in the preceding example. Only the lines containing the pattern *north* are printed when *-n* is used.

2 The *--quiet* option does the same the as *-n*.

```
% cat datafile
northwest    NW    Charles Main        3.0    .98    3    34
western      WE    Sharon Gray         5.3    .97    5    23
southwest    SW    Lewis Dalsass       2.7    .8     2    18
southern     SO    Suan Chin           5.1    .95    4    15
southeast    SE    Patricia Hemenway   4.0    .7     4    17
eastern      EA    TB Savage           4.4    .84    5    20
northeast    NE    AM Main Jr.         5.1    .94    3    13
north        NO    Margot Weber        4.5    .89    5     9
central      CT    Ann Stephens        5.7    .94    5    13
```

4.7.2 Deleting: The *d* Command

EXAMPLE 4.7

```
% sed '3d' datafile
northwest       NW      Charles Main          3.0    .98    3    34
western         WE      Sharon Gray           5.3    .97    5    23
southern        SO      Suan Chin             5.1    .95    4    15
southeast       SE      Patricia Hemenway     4.0    .7     4    17
eastern         EA      TB Savage             4.4    .84    5    20
northeast       NE      AM Main Jr.           5.1    .94    3    13
north           NO      Margot Weber          4.5    .89    5     9
central         CT      Ann Stephens          5.7    .94    5    13
```

EXPLANATION

Deletes the third line. All other lines are printed to the screen by default.

EXAMPLE 4.8

```
% sed '3,$d' datafile
northwest       NW      Charles Main          3.0    .98    3    34
western         WE      Sharon Gray           5.3    .97    5    23
```

EXPLANATION

The third line through the last line are deleted. The remaining lines are printed. The dollar sign ($) represents the last line of the file. The comma is called the *range operator*. In this example, the range of addresses starts at line *3* and ends at the last line, which is represented by the dollar sign ($).

EXAMPLE 4.9

```
% sed '$d' datafile
northwest       NW      Charles Main          3.0    .98    3    34
western         WE      Sharon Gray           5.3    .97    5    23
southwest       SW      Lewis Dalsass         2.7    .8     2    18
southern        SO      Suan Chin             5.1    .95    4    15
southeast       SE      Patricia Hemenway     4.0    .7     4    17
eastern         EA      TB Savage             4.4    .84    5    20
northeast       NE      AM Main Jr.           5.1    .94    3    13
north           NO      Margot Weber          4.5    .89    5     9
```

EXPLANATION

Deletes the last line. The dollar sign ($) represents the last line. The default is to print all of the lines except those affected by the *d* command.

EXAMPLE 4.10

```
% sed '/north/d' datafile
western        WE    Sharon Gray         5.3   .97   5   23
southwest      SW    Lewis Dalsass       2.7   .8    2   18
southern       SO    Suan Chin           5.1   .95   4   15
southeast      SE    Patricia Hemenway   4.0   .7    4   17
eastern        EA    TB Savage           4.4   .84   5   20
central        CT    Ann Stevens         5.7   .94   5   13
```

EXPLANATION

All lines containing the pattern *north* are deleted. The remaining lines are printed.

4.7.3 Substitution: The *s* Command

EXAMPLE 4.11

```
% sed 's/west/north/g' datafile
northnorth     NW    Charles Main        3.0   .98   3   34
northern       WE    Sharon Gray         5.3   .97   5   23
southnorth     SW    Lewis Dalsass       2.7   .8    2   18
southern       SO    Suan Chin           5.1   .95   4   15
southeast      SE    Patricia Hemenway   4.0   .7    4   17
eastern        EA    TB Savage           4.4   .84   5   20
northeast      NE    AM Main Jr.         5.1   .94   3   13
north          NO    Margot Weber        4.5    89   5    9
central        CT    Ann Stephens        5.7   .94   5   13
```

EXPLANATION

The *s* command is for substitution. The *g* flag at the end of the command indicates that the substitution is global across the line; that is, if multiple occurrences of *west* are found, all of them will be replaced with *north*. Without the *g* command, only the first occurrence of *west* on each line would be replaced with *north*.

```
% cat datafile
northwest      NW    Charles Main        3.0   .98   3   34
western        WE    Sharon Gray         5.3   .97   5   23
southwest      SW    Lewis Dalsass       2.7   .8    2   18
southern       SO    Suan Chin           5.1   .95   4   15
southeast      SE    Patricia Hemenway   4.0   .7    4   17
eastern        EA    TB Savage           4.4   .84   5   20
northeast      NE    AM Main Jr.         5.1   .94   3   13
north          NO    Margot Weber        4.5   .89   5    9
central        CT    Ann Stephens        5.7   .94   5   13
```

EXAMPLE 4.12

```
% sed -n 's/^west/north/p' datafile
northern          WE        Sharon Gray           5.3    .97    5    23
```

EXPLANATION

The *s* command is for substitution. The *-n* option with the *p* flag at the end of the command tells *sed* to print only those lines where the substitution occurred; that is, if *west* is found at the beginning of the line and is replaced with *north,* just those lines are printed.

EXAMPLE 4.13

```
% sed 's/[0-9][0-9]$/&.5/' datafile
northwest         NW        Charles Main          3.0    .98    3    34.5
western           WE        Sharon Gray           5.3    .97    5    23.5
southwest         SW        Lewis Dalsass         2.7    .8     2    18.5
southern          SO        Suan Chin             5.1    .95    4    15.5
southeast         SE        Patricia Hemenway     4.0    .7     4    17.5
eastern           EA        TB Savage             4.4    .84    5    20.5
northeast         NE        AM Main Jr.           5.1    .94    3    13.5
north             NO        Margot Weber          4.5    .89    5     9
central           CT        Ann Stephens          5.7    .94    5    13.5
```

EXPLANATION

The ampersand[a] (*&*) in the replacement string represents exactly what was found in the search string. Each line that ends in two digits will be replaced by itself, and *.5* will be appended to it.

a. To represent a literal ampersand in the replacement string, it must be escaped, \&

EXAMPLE 4.14

```
% sed -n 's/Hemenway/Jones/gp' datafile
southeast         SE        Patricia Jones        4.0    .7     4    17
```

EXPLANATION

All occurrences of *Hemenway* are replaced with *Jones*, and only the lines that changed are printed. The *-n* option combined with the *p* command suppresses the default output. The *g* stands for global substitution across the line.

EXAMPLE 4.15

```
% sed -n 's/\(Mar\)got/\1ianne/p' datafile
north           NO      Marianne Weber      4.5   .89   5    9
```

EXPLANATION

The pattern *Mar* is enclosed in parentheses and saved as tag 1 in a special register. It will be referenced in the replacement string as \1. *Margot* is then replaced with *Marianne*.

EXAMPLE 4.16

```
% sed 's#3#88#g' datafile
northwest       NW      Charles Main        88.0  .98   88 884
western         WE      Sharon Gray         5.88  .97    5 288
southwest       SW      Lewis Dalsass       2.7   .8     2  18
southern        SO      Suan Chin           5.1   .95    4  15
southeast       SE      Patricia Hemenway   4.0   .7     4  17
eastern         EA      TB Savage           4.4   .84    5  20
northeast       NE      AM Main Jr.         5.1   .94   88 188
north           NO      Margot Weber        4.5   .89    5   9
central         CT      Ann Stephens        5.7   .94    5 188
```

EXPLANATION

The character after the *s* command is the delimiter between the search string and the replacement string. The delimiter character is a forward slash by default, but can be changed (only when the *s* command is used). Whatever character follows the *s* command is the new string delimiter. This technique can be useful when searching for patterns containing a forward slash, such as pathnames or birthdays.

```
% cat datafile
northwest     NW    Charles Main        3.0    .98    3     34
western       WE    Sharon Gray         5.3    .97    5     23
southwest     SW    Lewis Dalsass       2.7    .8     2     18
southern      SO    Suan Chin           5.1    .95    4     15
southeast     SE    Patricia Hemenway   4.0    .7     4     17
eastern       EA    TB Savage           4.4    .84    5     20
northeast     NE    AM Main Jr.         5.1    .94    3     13
north         NO    Margot Weber        4.5    .89    5      9
central       CT    Ann Stephens        5.7    .94    5     13
```

4.7.4 Range of Selected Lines: The Comma

EXAMPLE 4.17

```
% sed -n '/west/,/east/p' datafile
northwest       NW      Charles Main        3.0   .98   3   34
western         WE      Sharon Gray         5.3   .97   5   23
southwest       SW      Lewis Dalsass       2.7   .8    2   18
southern        SO      Suan Chin           5.1   .95   4   15
southeast       SE      Patricia Hemenway   4.0   .7    4   17
```

EXPLANATION

All lines in the range of patterns between *west* and *east* are printed. If *west* were to appear on a line after *east,* the lines from *west* to the next *east* or to the end of file, whichever comes first, would be printed. The arrows mark the range.

EXAMPLE 4.18

```
% sed -n '5,/^northeast/p' datafile
southeast       SE      Patricia Hemenway   4.0   .7    4   17
eastern         EA      TB Savage           4.4   .84   5   20
northeast       NE      AM Main Jr.         5.1   .94   3   13
```

EXPLANATION

Prints the lines from line *5* through the first line that begins with *northeast.*

EXAMPLE 4.19

```
% sed '/west/,/east/s/$/**VACA**/' datafile
northwest    NW   Charles Main        3.0  .98   3   34**VACA**
western      WE   Sharon Gray         5.3  .97   5   23**VACA**
southwest    SW   Lewis Dalsass       2.7  .8    2   18**VACA**
southern     SO   Suan Chin           5.1  .95   4   15**VACA**
southeast    SE   Patricia Hemenway   4.0  .7    4   17**VACA**
eastern      EA   TB Savage           4.4  .84   5   20
northeast    NE   AM Main Jr.         5.1  .94   3   13
north        NO   Margot Weber        4.5  .89   5   9
central      CT   Ann Stephens        5.7  .94   5   13
```

EXPLANATION

For lines in the range between the patterns *east* and *west*, the end of line (*$*) is replaced with the string ***VACA***. The newline is moved over to the end of the new string. The arrows mark the range.

4.7.5 Multiple Edits: The *e* Command

EXAMPLE 4.20

```
% sed -e '1,3d' -e 's/Hemenway/Jones/' datafile
southern       SO      Suan Chin          5.1   .95   4   15
southeast      SE      Patricia Jones     4.0   .7    4   17
eastern        EA      TB Savage          4.4   .84   5   20
northeast      NE      AM Main            5.1   .94   3   13
north          NO      Margot Weber       4.5   .89   5    9
central        CT      Ann Stephens       5.7   .94   5   13
```

EXPLANATION

The *-e* option allows multiple edits. The first edit removes lines *1* through *3*. The second edit substitutes *Hemenway* with *Jones*. Because both edits are done on a per-line basis (i.e., both commands are executed on the current line in the pattern space), the order of the edits may affect the outcome differently. For example, if both commands had performed substitutions on the line, the first substitution could affect the second substitution.

EXAMPLE 4.21

```
% sed --expression='s/TB/Tobias/' --expression='/north/d' datafile
western     WE   Sharon Gray         5.3    .97    5    23
southwest   SW   Lewis Dalsass       2.7    .8     2    18
southern    SO   Suan Chin           5.1    .95    4    15
southeast   SE   Patricia Hemenway   4.0    .7     4    15
eastern     EA   Tobias Savage       4.4    .84    5    20
central     CT   Ann Stephens        5.7    .94    5    13
```

EXPLANATION

The *-e* option allows multiple edits. A more descriptive option for *-e* is *--expression* assigned the value of the *sed* expression. The first edit tells *sed* to substitute the regular expression, *TB*, with *Tobias*, and the second expression removes all lines containing the pattern *north*.

```
% cat datafile
northwest    NW    Charles Main          3.0    .98    3    34
western      WE    Sharon Gray           5.3    .97    5    23
southwest    SW    Lewis Dalsass         2.7    .8     2    18
southern     SO    Suan Chin             5.1    .95    4    15
southeast    SE    Patricia Hemenway     4.0    .7     4    17
eastern      EA    TB Savage             4.4    .84    5    20
northeast    NE    AM Main Jr.           5.1    .94    3    13
north        NO    Margot Weber          4.5    .89    5     9
central      CT    Ann Stephens          5.7    .94    5    13
```

4.7.6 Reading from Files: The *r* Command

EXAMPLE 4.22

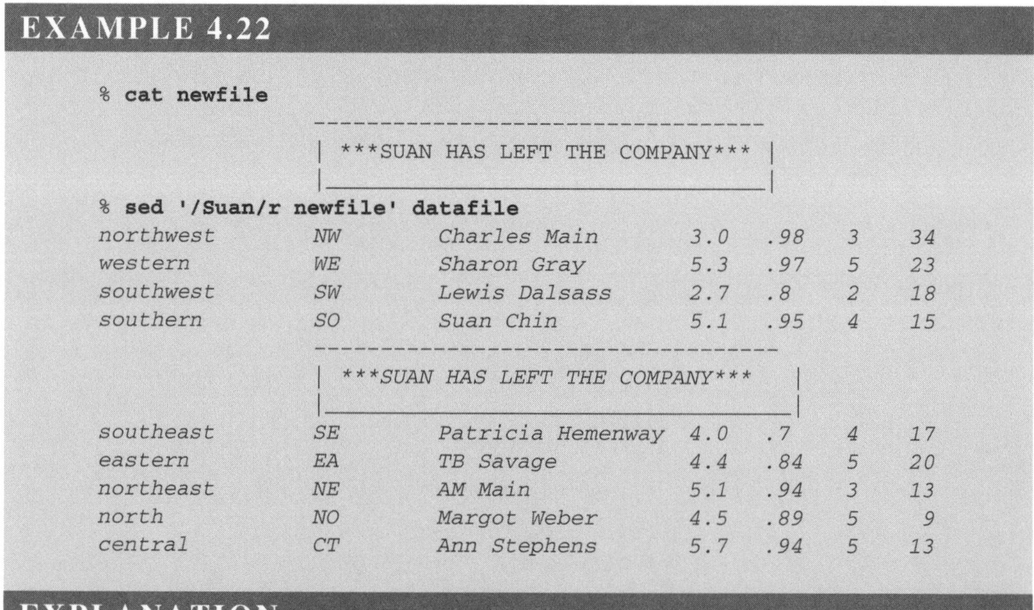

```
% cat newfile
              ---------------------------------
              | ***SUAN HAS LEFT THE COMPANY*** |
              |_________________________________|
% sed '/Suan/r newfile' datafile
northwest     NW      Charles Main         3.0   .98   3   34
western       WE      Sharon Gray          5.3   .97   5   23
southwest     SW      Lewis Dalsass        2.7   .8    2   18
southern      SO      Suan Chin            5.1   .95   4   15
              ---------------------------------
              | ***SUAN HAS LEFT THE COMPANY***   |
              |___________________________________|
southeast     SE      Patricia Hemenway    4.0   .7    4   17
eastern       EA      TB Savage            4.4   .84   5   20
northeast     NE      AM Main              5.1   .94   3   13
north         NO      Margot Weber         4.5   .89   5    9
central       CT      Ann Stephens         5.7   .94   5   13
```

EXPLANATION

The *r* command reads specified lines from a file.The contents of *newfile* are read into the input file *datafile*, after the line where the pattern *Suan* is matched. If *Suan* had appeared on more than one line, the contents of *newfile* would have been read in under each occurrence.

4.7.7 Writing to Files: The *w* Command

EXAMPLE 4.23

```
% sed -n '/north/w newfile2' datafile
cat newfile2
northwest       NW      Charles Main        3.0   .98   3   34
northeast       NE      AM Main Jr.         5.1   .94   3   13
north           NO      Margot Weber        4.5   .89   5    9
```

EXPLANATION

The *w* command writes specified lines to a file. All lines containing the pattern *north* are written to a file called *newfile2*.

4.7.8 Appending: The *a* Command

EXAMPLE 4.24

```
% sed '/^north  /a\\
--->THE NORTH SALES DISTRICT HAS MOVED<---' datafile
northwest       NW      Charles Main        3.0   .98   3   34
western         WE      Sharon Gray         5.3   .97   5   23
southwest       SW      Lewis Dalsass       2.7   .8    2   18
southern        SO      Suan Chin           5.1   .95   4   15
southeast       SE      Patricia Hemenway   4.0   .7    4   17
eastern         EA      TB Savage           4.4   .84   5   20
northeast       NE      AM Main Jr.         5.1   .94   3   13
north           NO      Margot Weber        4.5   .89   5    9
--->THE NORTH SALES DISTRICT HAS MOVED<---
central         CT      Ann Stephens        5.7   .94   5   13
```

EXPLANATION

The *a* command is the append command. The string --->*The NORTH SALES DISTRICT HAS MOVED*<--- is appended after lines beginning with the pattern *north,* when *north* is followed by a space. The text that will be appended must be on the line following the append command.

Sed requires a backslash after the *a* command. The second backslash is used by the TC shell to escape the newline so that its closing quote can be on the next line.[a] If more than one line is appended, each line, except the last one, must also end in a backslash.

a. The Bash, Bourne, and Korn shells do not require the second backslash to escape the newline, because they do not require quotes to be matched on the same line, only that they match.

```
% cat datafile
northwest    NW    Charles Main        3.0   .98   3   34
western      WE    Sharon Gray         5.3   .97   5   23
southwest    SW    Lewis Dalsass       2.7   .8    2   18
southern     SO    Suan Chin           5.1   .95   4   15
southeast    SE    Patricia Hemenway   4.0   .7    4   17
eastern      EA    TB Savage           4.4   .84   5   20
northeast    NE    AM Main Jr.         5.1   .94   3   13
north        NO    Margot Weber        4.5   .89   5    9
central      CT    Ann Stephens        5.7   .94   5   13
```

4.7.9 Inserting: The *i* Command

EXAMPLE 4.25

```
% sed '/eastern/i\\
NEW ENGLAND REGION\\
-------------------------------------' datafile
northwest       NW      Charles Main        3.0   .98   3   34
western         WE      Sharon Gray         5.3   .97   5   23
southwest       SW      Lewis Dalsass       2.7   .8    2   18
southern        SO      Suan Chin           5.1   .95   4   15
southeast       SE      Patricia Hemenway   4.0   .7    4   17
NEW ENGLAND REGION
------------------------------------
eastern         EA      TB Savage           4.4   .84   5   20
northeast       NE      AM Main Jr.         5.1   .94   3   13
north           NO      Margot Weber        4.5   .89   5    9
central         CT      Ann Stephens        5.7   .94   5   13
```

EXPLANATION

The *i* command is the insert command. If the pattern *eastern* is matched, the *i* command causes the text following the backslash to be inserted above the line containing *eastern*. A backslash is required after each line to be inserted, except the last one. (The extra backslash is for the TC shell.)

4.7.10 Next: The *n* Command

EXAMPLE 4.26

```
% sed '/eastern/{ n; s/AM/Archie/; }' datafile
northwest    NW    Charles Main        3.0   .98   3   34
western      WE    Sharon Gray         5.3   .97   5   23
southwest    SW    Lewis Dalsass       2.7   .8    2   18
southern     SO    Suan Chin           5.1   .95   4   15
southeast    SE    Patricia Hemenway   4.0   .7    4   17
eastern      EA    TB Savage           4.4   .84   5   20
northeast    NE    Archie Main Jr.     5.1   .94   3   13
north        NO    Margot Weber        4.5   .89   5    9
central      CT    Ann Stephens        5.7   .94   5   13
```

EXPLANATION

If the pattern *eastern* is matched on a line, the *n* command causes *sed* to get the next line of input (the line with *AM Main Jr.*), replace the pattern space with this line, substitute (*s*) *AM* with *Archie*, print the line, and continue.

4.7.11 Transform: The *y* Command

EXAMPLE 4.27

```
% sed '1,3y/abcdefghijklmnopqrstuvwxyz/ABCDEFGHIJKL
MNOPQRSTUVWXYZ/'  datafile
NORTHWEST    NW    CHARLES MAIN        3.0   .98   3   34
WESTERN      WE    SHARON GRAY         5.3   .97   5   23
SOUTHWEST    SW    LEWIS DALSASS       2.7   .8    2   18
southern     SO    Suan Chin           5.1   .95   4   15
southeast    SE    Patricia Hemenway   4.0   .7    4   17
eastern      EA    TB Savage           4.4   .84   5   20
northeast    NE    AM Main Jr.         5.1   .94   3   13
north        NO    Margot Weber        4.5   .89   5    9
central      CT    Ann Stephens        5.7   .94   5   13
```

EXPLANATION

For lines *1* through *3*, the *y* command translates all lowercase letters to uppercase letters. Regular expression metacharacters do not work with this command.

```
% cat datafile
northwest     NW     Charles Main        3.0    .98    3     34
western       WE     Sharon Gray         5.3    .97    5     23
southwest     SW     Lewis Dalsass       2.7    .8     2     18
southern      SO     Suan Chin           5.1    .95    4     15
southeast     SE     Patricia Hemenway   4.0    .7     4     17
eastern       EA     TB Savage           4.4    .84    5     20
northeast     NE     AM Main Jr.         5.1    .94    3     13
north         NO     Margot Weber        4.5    .89    5      9
central       CT     Ann Stephens        5.7    .94    5     13
```

4.7.12 Quit: The *q* Command

EXAMPLE 4.28

```
% sed '5q' datafile
northwest       NW      Charles Main        3.0   .98   3   34
western         WE      Sharon Gray         5.3   .97   5   23
southwest       SW      Lewis Dalsass       2.7   .8    2   18
southern        SO      Suan Chin           5.1   .95   4   15
southeast       SE      Patricia Hemenway   .0    .7    4   17
```

EXPLANATION

After the line *5* is printed, the *q* command causes the *sed* program to *quit*.

EXAMPLE 4.29

```
% sed  '/Lewis/{ s/Lewis/Joseph/;q; }' datafile
northwest       NW      Charles Main        3.0   .98   3   34
western         WE      Sharon Gray         5.3   .97   5   23
southwest       SW      Joseph Dalsass      2.7   .8    2   18
```

EXPLANATION

When the pattern *Lewis* is matched on a line, the substitution command (*s*) first replaces *Lewis* with *Joseph*, and then the *q* command causes the *sed* program to quit.

4.7.13 Holding and Getting: The *h* and *g* Commands

EXAMPLE 4.30

```
% sed -e '/northeast/h'  -e  '$G'  datafile
northwest      NW     Charles Main        3.0   .98   3    34
western        WE     Sharon Gray         5.3   .97   5    23
southwest      SW     Lewis Dalsass       2.7   .8    2    18
southern       SO     Suan Chin           5.1   .95   4    15
southeast      SE     Patricia Hemenway   4.0   .7    4    17
eastern        EA     TB Savage           4.4   .84   5    20
-->northeast   NE     AM Main Jr.         5.1   .94   3    13
north          NO     Margot Weber        4.5   .89   5    9
central        CT     Ann Stephens        5.7   .94   5    13
-->northeast   NE     AM Main Jr.         5.1   .94   3    13
```

EXPLANATION

As *sed* processes the file, each line is stored in a temporary buffer called the *pattern space.* Unless the line is deleted or suppressed from printing, the line will be printed to the screen after it is processed. The pattern space is then cleared and the next line of input is stored there for processing. In this example, after the line containing the pattern *northeast* is found, it is placed in the pattern space and the *h* command copies it and places it in another special buffer called the *holding buffer.* In the second *sed* instruction, when the last line is reached (*$*) the *G* command tells *sed* to get the line from the holding buffer and put it back in the pattern space buffer, appending it to the line that is currently stored there—in this case, the last line. Simply stated: Any line containing the pattern *northeast* will be copied and appended to the end of the file. (See Figure 4.1.)

```
% cat datafile
northwest      NW     Charles Main        3.0    .98    3    34
western        WE     Sharon Gray         5.3    .97    5    23
southwest      SW     Lewis Dalsass       2.7    .8     2    18
southern       SO     Suan Chin           5.1    .95    4    15
southeast      SE     Patricia Hemenway   4.0    .7     4    17
eastern        EA     TB Savage           4.4    .84    5    20
northeast      NE     AM Main Jr.         5.1    .94    3    13
north          NO     Margot Weber        4.5    .89    5     9
central        CT     Ann Stephens        5.7    .94    5    13
```

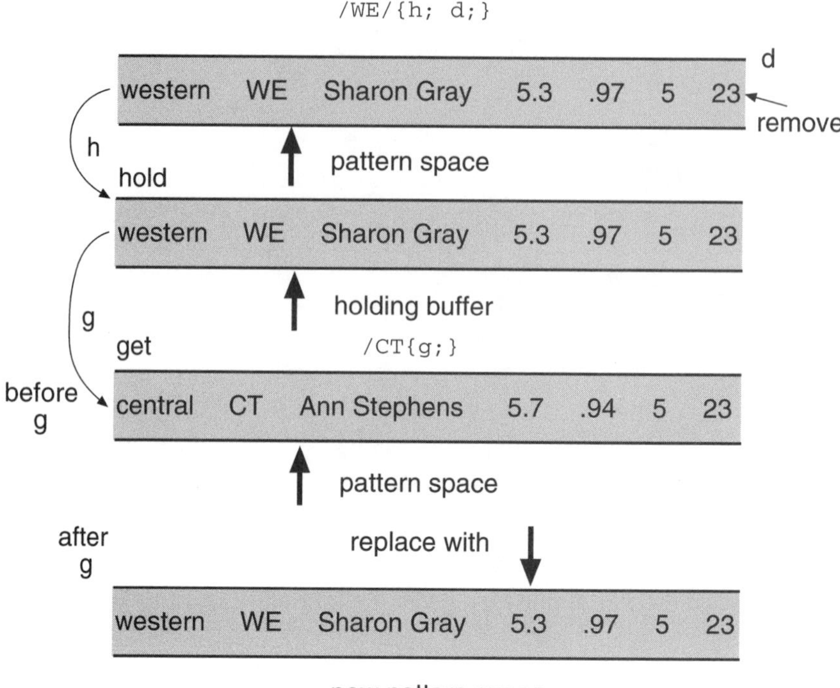

Figure 4.1 The pattern space and holding buffer. See Example 4.33.

EXAMPLE 4.31

```
% sed -e '/WE/{h; d; }' -e '/CT/{G; }' datafile
northwest       NW      Charles Main        3.0   .98   3   34
southwest       SW      Lewis Dalsass       2.7   .8    2   18
southern        SO      Suan Chin           5.1   .95   4   15
southeast       SE      Patricia Hemenway   4.0   .7    4   17
eastern         EA      TB Savage           4.4   .84   5   20
northeast       NE      AM Main Jr.         5.1   .94   3   13
north           NO      Margot Weber        4.5   .89   5    9
central         CT      Ann Stephens        5.7   .94   5   13
--> western     WE      Sharon Gray         5.3   .97   5   23
```

EXPLANATION

If the pattern *WE* is found on a line, the *h* command causes the line to be copied from the pattern space into a holding buffer. When stored in the holding buffer, the line can be retrieved (*G* or *g* command) at a later time. In this example, when the pattern *WE* is found, the line where it was found is stored in the pattern buffer first. The *h* command then puts a copy of the line in the holding buffer. The *d* command deletes the copy in the pattern buffer. The second command searches for *CT* in a line, and when it is found, *sed* gets (*G*) the line that was stored in the holding buffer and appends it to the line currently in the pattern space. Simply stated: The line containing *WE* is moved and appended after the line containing *CT*. (See "Holding and Exchanging: The h and x Commands" on page 117.)

EXAMPLE 4.32

```
% sed -e '/northeast/h'  -e  '$g'  datafile
northwest      NW      Charles Main          3.0   .98   3   34
western        WE      Sharon Gray           5.3   .97   5   23
southwest      SW      Lewis Dalsass         2.7   .8    2   18
southern       SO      Suan Chin             5.1   .95   4   15
southeast      SE      Patricia Hemenway     4.0   .7    4   17
eastern        EA      TB Savage             4.4   .84   5   20
--> northeast  NE      AM Main Jr.           5.1   .94   3   13
north          NO      Margot Weber          4.5   .89   5    9
--> northeast  NE      AM Main Jr.           5.1   .94   3   13
```

EXPLANATION

As *sed* processes the file, each line is stored in a temporary buffer called the *pattern space*. Unless the line is deleted or suppressed from printing, the line will be printed to the screen after it is processed. The pattern space is then cleared and the next line of input is stored there for processing. In this example, after the line containing the pattern *northeast* is found, it is placed in the pattern space. The *h* command takes a copy of it and places it in another special buffer called the *holding buffer*. In the second *sed* instruction, when the last line is reached (*$*), the *g* command tells *sed* to get the line from the holding buffer and put it back in the pattern space buffer, replacing the line that is currently stored there—in this case, the last line. Simply stated: The line containing the pattern *northeast* is copied. The copy overwrites the last line in the file.

```
% cat datafile
northwest     NW    Charles Main         3.0   .98   3   34
western       WE    Sharon Gray          5.3   .97   5   23
southwest     SW    Lewis Dalsass        2.7   .8    2   18
southern      SO    Suan Chin            5.1   .95   4   15
southeast     SE    Patricia Hemenway    4.0   .7    4   17
eastern       EA    TB Savage            4.4   .84   5   20
northeast     NE    AM Main Jr.          5.1   .94   3   13
north         NO    Margot Weber         4.5   .89   5    9
central       CT    Ann Stephens         5.7   .94   5   13
```

EXAMPLE 4.33

```
% sed -e '/WE/{h; d; }' -e '/CT/{g; }' datafile
northwest     NW    Charles Main         3.0   .98   3   34
southwest     SW    Lewis Dalsass        2.7   .8    2   18
southern      SO    Suan Chin            5.1   .95   4   15
southeast     SE    Patricia Hemenway    4.0   .7    4   17
eastern       EA    TB Savage            4.4   .84   5   20
northeast     NE    AM Main Jr.          5.1   .94   3   13
north         NO    Margot Weber         4.5   .89   5    9
western       WE    Sharon Gray          5.3   .97   5   23
```

EXPLANATION

If the pattern *WE* is found, the *h* command copies the line into the *holding buffer*; the *d* command deletes the line in the pattern space. When the pattern *CT* is found, the *g* command gets the copy in the holding buffer and overwrites the line currently in the pattern space. Simply stated: Any line containing the pattern *WE* will be moved to overwrite lines containing *CT*. (See Figure 4.1 on page 114.)

4.7.14 Holding and Exchanging: The *h* and *x* Commands

EXAMPLE 4.34

```
% sed -e '/Patricia/h'  -e '/Margot/x' datafile
northwest       NW      Charles Main        3.0   .98   3    34
western         WE      Sharon Gray         5.3   .97   5    23
southwest       SW      Lewis Dalsass       2.7   .8    2    18
southern        SO      Suan Chin           5.1   .95   4    15
southeast       SE      Patricia Hemenway   4.0   .7    4    17
eastern         EA      TB Savage           4.4   .84   5    20
northeast       NE      AM Main Jr.         5.1   .94   3    13
southeast       SE      Patricia Hemenway   4.0   .7    4    17
central         CT      Ann Stephens        5.7   .94   5    13
```

EXPLANATION

The *x* command exchanges (swaps) the contents of the holding buffer with the current pattern space. When the line containing the pattern *Patricia* is found, it will be stored in the holding buffer. When the line containing *Margot* is found, the pattern space will be exchanged for the line in the holding buffer. Simply stated: The line containing *Margot* will be replaced with the line containing *Patricia.*

4.8 *sed* Scripting

A *sed script* is a list of *sed* commands in a file. To let *sed* know your commands are in a file, when invoking *sed* at the command line, use the *-f* option followed by the name of the *sed* script. *Sed* is very particular about the way you type lines into the script. There cannot be any trailing white space or text at the end of the command. If commands are not placed on a line by themselves, they must be terminated with a semicolon. A line from the input file is copied into the pattern buffer, and all commands in the *sed* script are executed on that line. After the line has been processed, the next line from the input file is placed in the pattern buffer, and all commands in the script are executed on that line. *Sed* gets "garbled" if your syntax is incorrect.

The nice thing about *sed* scripts is that you don't have to worry about the shell's interaction as you do when at the command line. Quotes are not needed to protect *sed* commands from interpretation by the shell. In fact, you cannot use quotes in a *sed* script at all, unless they are part of a search pattern.

```
% cat datafile
northwest    NW   Charles Main       3.0   .98   3   34
western      WE   Sharon Gray        5.3   .97   5   23
southwest    SW   Lewis Dalsass      2.7   .8    2   18
southern     SO   Suan Chin          5.1   .95   4   15
southeast    SE   Patricia Hemenway  4.0   .7    4   17
eastern      EA   TB Savage          4.4   .84   5   20
northeast    NE   AM Main Jr.        5.1   .94   3   13
north        NO   Margot Weber       4.5   .89   5    9
central      CT   Ann Stephens       5.7   .94   5   13
```

4.8.1 *sed* Script Examples

EXAMPLE 4.35

```
% cat sedding1   (Look at the contents of the sed script.)
1  # My first sed script by Jack Sprat
2  /Lewis/a\
3     Lewis is the TOP Salesperson for April!!\
      Lewis is moving to the southern district next month.\
4     CONGRATULATIONS!
5  /Margot/c\
      *******************\
      MARGOT HAS RETIRED\
      ********************
6  1i\
   EMPLOYEE DATABASE\
   ---------------------
7  $d

% sed -f sedding1 datafile   (Execute the sed script commands; the
                              input file is datafile.)
EMPLOYEE DATABASE
---------------------
northwest     NW     Charles Main       3.0   .98   3   34
western       WE     Sharon Gray        5.3   .97   5   23
southwest     SW     Lewis Dalsass      2.7   .8    2   18
Lewis is the TOP Salesperson for April!!
Lewis is moving to the southern district next month
CONGRATULATIONS!
southern      SO     Suan Chin          5.1   .95   4   15
southeast     SE     Patricia Hemenway  4.0   .7    4   17
eastern       EA     TB Savage          4.4   .84   5   20
northeast     NE     AM Main Jr.        5.1   .94   3   13

********************
MARGOT HAS RETIRED
**********************
```

EXPLANATION

1. This line is a comment. Comments must be on lines by themselves and start with a pound sign (*#*).
2. If a line contains the pattern *Lewis*, the next three lines are appended to that line.
3. Each line being appended, except the last one, is terminated with a backslash. The backslash must be followed immediately with a newline. If there is any trailing text, even one space after the newline, *sed* will complain.
4. The last line to be appended does not have the terminating backslash. This indicates to *sed* that this is the last line to be appended and that the next line is another command.
5. Any lines containing the pattern *Margot* will be replaced (*c* command) with the next three lines of text.
6. The next two lines will be inserted (*i* command) above line *1*.
7. The last line (*$*) will be deleted.

EXAMPLE 4.36

```
% cat sedding2 (Look at the contents of the sed script.)
# This script demonstrates the use of curly braces to nest addresses
# and commands. Comments are preceded by a pound sign (#) and must
# be on a line by themselves. Commands are terminated with a newline
# or semicolon. If, using the Unix version of sed, there is any
# text after a command, even one space, you receive an error message:
#       sed: Extra text at end of command:

1  /western/, /southeast/{
      /^ *$/d
      /Suan/{ h; d; }
   }
2   /Ann/g
3   s/TB \(Savage\)/Thomas \1/

% sed -f sedding2 datafile
northwest       NW        Charles Main        3.0    .98    3     34
western         WE        Sharon Gray         5.3    .97    5     23
southwest       SW        Lewis Dalsass       2.7    .8     2     18
southeast       SE        Patricia Hemenway   4.0    .7     4     17
eastern         EA        Thomas Savage       4.4    .84    5     20
northeast       NE        AM Main Jr.         5.1    .94    3     13
north           NO        Margot Weber        4.5    .89    5      9
southern        SO        Suan Chin           5.1    .95    4     15
```

EXPLANATION

1 In the range of lines starting at *western* and ending at *southeast*, blank lines are deleted, and lines matching *Suan* are copied from the pattern buffer into the holding buffer, then deleted from the pattern buffer.

2 When the pattern *Ann* is matched, the *g* command copies the line in the holding buffer to the pattern buffer, overwriting what is in the pattern buffer.

3 All lines containing the pattern *TB Savage* are replaced with *Thomas* and the pattern that was tagged, *Savage*. In the search string, *Savage* is enclosed in escaped parentheses, tagging the enclosed string so that it can be used again. It is tag number `1`, referenced by `\1`.

EXAMPLE 4.37

```
1 % cat bye4now (Display the contents of the sed script.)
   # The sed script
   $a\
       Thankyou for coming
               bye

2 % sed -e 's/Charles/Jimmy/' -f bye4now datafile
northwest     NW     Jimmy Main          3.0       .98      3        34
western       WE     Sharon Gray         5.3       .97      5        23
southwest     SW     Lewis Dalsass       2.7       .8       2        18
southern      SO     Suan Chin           5.1       .95      4        15
southeast     SE     Patricia Hemenway   4.0       .7       4        15
eastern       EA     TB Savage           4.4       .84      5        20
northeast     NE     AM Main Jr.         5.1       .94      3        13
north         NO     Margot Weber        4.5       .89      5        9
central       CT     Ann Stephens        5.7       .94      5        13

       Thankyou for coming
               bye

3 % sed --file=bye4now --expression='s/Charles/Jimmy/' datafile
northwest     NW     Jimmy Main          3.0       .98      3        34
western       WE     Sharon Gray         5.3       .97      5        23
southwest     SW     Lewis Dalsass       2.7       .8       2        18
southern      SO     Suan Chin           5.1       .95      4        15
southeast     SE     Patricia Hemenway   4.0       .7       4        15
eastern       EA     TB Savage           4.4       .84      5        20
northeast     NE     AM Main Jr.         5.1       .94      3        13
north         NO     Margot Weber        4.5       .89      5        9
central       CT     Ann Stephens        5.7       .94      5        13

       Thankyou for coming
               bye
```

EXPLANATION

1 The contents of a *sed* script called *bye4now* are displayed. *$a* means: Append the following text after the last line of the input file.

2 The *-e* option is used to evaluate the *sed* substitution command, i.e., substitute *Charles* with *Jimmy*. The *-f* option is used to read commands from the *sed* script *bye4now*.

3 The long format of the *-f* option, *--file*, is assigned the name of the *sed* script, followed by the long form of the *-e* option, *--expression*, and the *sed* substitution command.

4.8.2 *sed* Review

Table 4.4 lists *sed* commands and what they do.

Table 4.4 *sed* Review

Command	*What It Does*
sed -n '/sentimental/p' filex	Prints to the screen all lines containing *sentimental*. The file *filex* does not change. Without the *-n* option, all lines with *sentimental* will be printed twice.
sed '1,3d' filex > newfilex	Deletes lines *1*, *2*, and *3* from *filex* and saves changes in *newfilex*.
sed '/[Dd]aniel/d' filex	Deletes lines containing *Daniel* or *daniel*.
sed -n '15,20p' filex	Prints only lines *15* through *20*.
sed '1,10s/Montana/MT/g' filex	Substitutes *Montana* with *MT* globally in lines *1* through *10*.
sed '/March/\!d' filex (tcsh) *sed '/March/!d' filex (sh)*	Deletes all lines not containing *March*. (The backslash is used in *tcsh* to escape the history character.)
sed '/report/s/5/8/' filex	Changes the first occurrence of *5* to *8* on all lines containing *report*.
sed 's/....//' filex	Deletes the first four characters of each line; i.e., substitutes the first four characters with nothing.
sed 's/...$//' filex	Deletes the last three characters of each line; i.e., substitutes the last three characters with nothing.
sed '/east/,/west/s/North/South/' filex	For any lines falling in the range from *east* to *west*, substitutes *North* with *South*.
sed -n '/Time off/w timefile' filex	Writes all lines containing *Time off* to the file *timefile*.
sed 's/\([Oo]ccur\)ence/\1rence/' file	Substitutes either *Occurence* or *occurence* with *Occurrence* or *occurrence*.
sed -n 'l' filex	Prints all lines showing nonprinting characters as *\nn* where *nn* is the octal value of the character, and showing tabs as >.

LINUX TOOLS LAB 2

sed Exercise

Steve Blenheim:238-923-7366:95 Latham Lane, Easton, PA 83755:11/12/56:20300
Betty Boop:245-836-8357:635 Cutesy Lane, Hollywood, CA 91464:6/23/23:14500
Igor Chevsky:385-375-8395:3567 Populus Place, Caldwell, NJ 23875:6/18/68:23400
Norma Corder:397-857-2735:74 Pine Street, Dearborn, MI 23874:3/28/45:245700
Jennifer Cowan:548-834-2348:583 Laurel Ave., Kingsville, TX 83745:10/1/35:58900
Jon DeLoach:408-253-3122:123 Park St., San Jose, CA 04086:7/25/53:85100
Karen Evich:284-758-2857:23 Edgecliff Place, Lincoln, NB 92743:7/25/53:85100
Karen Evich:284-758-2867:23 Edgecliff Place, Lincoln, NB 92743:11/3/35:58200
Karen Evich:284-758-2867:23 Edgecliff Place, Lincoln, NB 92743:11/3/35:58200
Fred Fardbarkle:674-843-1385:20 Parak Lane, DeLuth, MN 23850:4/12/23:780900
Fred Fardbarkle:674-843-1385:20 Parak Lane, DeLuth, MN 23850:4/12/23:780900
Lori Gortz:327-832-5728:3465 Mirlo Street, Peabody, MA 34756:10/2/65:35200
Paco Gutierrez:835-365-1284:454 Easy Street, Decatur, IL 75732:2/28/53:123500
Ephram Hardy:293-259-5395:235 CarltonLane, Joliet, IL 73858:8/12/20:56700
James Ikeda:834-938-8376:23445 Aster Ave., Allentown, NJ 83745:12/1/38:45000
Barbara Kertz:385-573-8326:832 Ponce Drive, Gary, IN 83756:12/1/46:268500
Lesley Kirstin:408-456-1234:4 Harvard Square, Boston, MA 02133:4/22/62:52600
William Kopf:846-836-2837:6937 Ware Road, Milton, PA 93756:9/21/46:43500
Sir Lancelot:837-835-8257:474 Camelot Boulevard, Bath, WY 28356:5/13/69:24500
Jesse Neal:408-233-8971:45 Rose Terrace, San Francisco, CA 92303:2/3/36:25000
Zippy Pinhead:834-823-8319:2356 Bizarro Ave., Farmount, IL 84357:1/1/67:89500
Arthur Putie:923-835-8745:23 Wimp Lane, Kensington, DL 38758:8/31/69:126000
Popeye Sailor:156-454-3322:945 Bluto Street, Anywhere, USA 29358:3/19/35:22350
Jose Santiago:385-898-8357:38 Fife Way, Abilene, TX 39673:1/5/58:95600
Tommy Savage:408-724-0140:1222 Oxbow Court, Sunnyvale, CA 94087:5/19/66:34200
Yukio Takeshida:387-827-1095:13 Uno Lane, Ashville, NC 23556:7/1/29:57000
Vinh Tranh:438-910-7449:8235 Maple Street, Wilmington, VM 29085:9/23/63:68900

(Refer to the database called "*datebook*" on the CD.)

1. Print the version and copyright information of the version of *sed* you are using.
2. What are three ways to suppress *sed*'s default output?
3. What option displays a list of *sed*'s command line options and what they do?
4. If you find bugs in this version of *sed*, where do you send your report?
5. Change *Fred*'s name to *Frederick.*
6. Delete the first three lines.
7. Print lines *6* through *12.*
8. Delete lines containing *Lane.*

9. Print all lines where the birthdays are in *November* or *December.*
10. Append three stars to the end of lines starting with *Karen*.
11. Replace the line containing *Jose* with *JOSE HAS RETIRED*.
12. Change *Popeye*'s birthday to *11/14/46*.
13. Delete all blank lines.
14. Exchange the line containing *Paco* with the line containing *Vinh*.
15. Move the line beginning with *Tommy* to overwrite the last line of the file.
16. Write a *sed* script that will:
    a. Insert above the first line the title *PERSONNEL FILE*
    b. Remove the salaries ending in *500*.
    c. Print the contents of the file with the last names and first names reversed.
    d. Append at the end of the file *THE END*.

CHAPTER

5

GAWK UTILITY: GAWK AS A LINUX TOOL

5.1 What's *awk*? What's *nawk*? What's *gawk*?

Awk is a UNIX/Linux programming language used for manipulating data and generating reports. *Nawk* is a newer version, and *Gawk* is the Gnu version. The data may come from standard input, one or more files, or as output from a process. *Awk* can be used at the command line for simple operations, or it can be written into programs for larger applications. Because *awk* can manipulate data, it is an indispensable tool used in shell scripts and for managing small databases.

Awk scans a file (or input) line by line, from the first to the last line, searching for lines that match a specified pattern and performing selected actions (enclosed in curly braces) on those lines. If there is a pattern with no specific action, all lines that match the pattern are displayed; if there is an action with no pattern, all input lines specified by the action are executed upon.

Gawk is the Gnu Project's implementation of the *awk* programming language. It conforms to the definition of the language in the POSIX 1003.2 Command Language And Utilities Standard and to the same *awk* (*nawk*) authored by Aho, Kernighan, and Weinberger. *Gawk* also provides more recent Bell Labs *awk* extensions and some Gnu-specific extensions.

5.1.1 What Does *awk* Stand for?

Awk stands for the first initials in the last names of each of the authors of the language, Alfred Aho, Brian Kernighan, and Peter Weinberger. They could have called it *wak* or *kaw*, but for whatever reason, *awk* won out. *Gawk* stands for the same thing; it's just the Gnu version.

5.1.2 Which *awk*?

There are a number of versions of *awk*: old *awk*, new *awk*, Gnu *awk (gawk)*, POSIX *awk*, and so on. *Awk* was originally written in 1977, and in 1985, the original implementation was improved so that *awk* could handle larger programs. Additional features include user-defined functions, dynamic regular expressions, processing multiple input files, and more. On most systems, the command is *awk* if using the old version, *nawk* if using the new version, and *gawk* if using the Gnu version.[1] This chapter is based on *gawk,* the version of *awk* that is part of the Linux distribution. Version information can be displayed with the *--version* option to *awk.*

EXAMPLE 5.1

```
% awk --version
GNU Awk 3.0.3
Copyright (C) 1989, 1991-1997 Free Software Foundation.

This program is free software; you can redistribute it and/or modify
it under the terms of the GNU General Public License as published by
the Free Software Foundation; either version 2 of the License, or
(at your option) any later version.

This program is distributed in the hope that it will be useful,
but WITHOUT ANY WARRANTY; without even the implied warranty of
MERCHANTABILITY or FITNESS FOR A PARTICULAR PURPOSE.  See the
GNU General Public License for more details.

You should have received a copy of the GNU General Public License
along with this program; if not, write to the Free Software
Foundation, Inc., 59 Temple Place - Suite 330, Boston, MA  02111-
1307, USA.
```

On many systems the command, *awk*, is linked to the version being used. When describing *awk* and its many features, we will use the command *awk*, assuming that it is linked to *gawk* as shown in the following example.

EXAMPLE 5.2

```
% ls -l /bin/awk
lrwxrwxrwx   1 root     root          4 May 12 04:47 /bin/awk -> gawk
```

1. With Red Hat Linux, the Gnu version, *gawk*, is linked to *awk*. This text pertains primarily to the new *awk*, *nawk*, with Gnu extensions. The Gnu implementation, *gawk*, is fully upward-compatible with *nawk*.

5.2 *awk*'s Format

An *awk* program consists of the *awk* command, the program instructions enclosed in quotes (or in a file), and the name of the input file. If an input file is not specified, input comes from standard input (*stdin*), the keyboard.

Awk instructions consist of patterns, actions, or a combination of patterns and actions. A pattern is a statement consisting of an expression of some type. If you do not see the keyword *if*, but you *think* the word *if* when evaluating the expression, it is a pattern. Actions consist of one or more statements separated by semicolons or newlines and enclosed in curly braces. Patterns cannot be enclosed in curly braces, and consist of regular expressions enclosed in forward slashes or expressions consisting of one or more of the many operators provided by *awk*.

Awk commands can be typed at the command line or in *awk* script files. The input lines can come from files, pipes, or standard input.

5.2.1 Input from Files

In the following examples, the percent sign (%) is the C shell prompt.

FORMAT

```
% awk 'pattern' filename
% awk '{action}' filename
% awk 'pattern {action}' filename
```

Here is a sample file called *employees*:

EXAMPLE 5.3

```
% cat employees
Tom Jones       4424    5/12/66     543354
Mary Adams      5346    11/4/63     28765
Sally Chang     1654    7/22/54     650000
Billy Black     1683    9/23/44     336500

% awk '/Mary/'  employees
Mary Adams      5346    11/4/63     28765
```

EXPLANATION

Awk prints all lines that contain the pattern *Mary*.

EXAMPLE 5.4

```
% cat employees
Tom Jones        4424     5/12/66     543354
Mary Adams       5346     11/4/63     28765
Sally Chang      1654     7/22/54     650000
Billy Black      1683     9/23/44     336500

% awk '{print $1}' employees
Tom
Mary
Sally
Billy
```

EXPLANATION

Awk prints the first field of file *employees*, where the field starts at the left margin of the line and is delimited by white space.

EXAMPLE 5.5

```
% cat employees
Tom Jones        4424     5/12/66     543354
Mary Adams       5346     11/4/63     28765
Sally Chang      1654     7/22/54     650000
Billy Black      1683     9/23/44     336500

% awk '/Sally/{print $1, $2}' employees
Sally Chang
```

EXPLANATION

Awk prints the first and second fields of file *employees*, only if the line contains the pattern *Sally*. Remember, the field separator is white space.

5.2.2 Input from Commands

The output from a Linux command or commands can be piped to *awk* for processing. Shell programs commonly use *awk* for manipulating commands.

FORMAT

```
% command | awk 'pattern'
% command | awk '{action}'
% command | awk 'pattern {action}'
```

EXAMPLE 5.6

```
1  % df | awk '$4 > 75000'
   /oracle    (/dev/dsk/c0t0d057 ):390780 blocks     105756 files
   /opt       (/dev/dsk/c0t0d058 ):1943994 blocks     49187 files

2  % rusers  | awk '/root$/{print  $1}'
   owl
   crow
   bluebird
```

EXPLANATION

1 The *df* command reports the free disk space on file systems. The output of the *df* command is piped to *awk*. If the fourth field is greater than 75,000 blocks, the line is printed.

2 The *rusers* command prints those logged on remote machines on the network. The output of the *rusers* command is piped to *awk* as input. The first field is printed if the regular expression *root* is matched at the end of the line (*$*); that is, all machine names are printed where *root* is logged on.

5.2.3 *awk* Command Line Options

Awk has a number of comand line options. *Gawk* has two formats for command line options: the Gnu long format starting with a double dash (--) and a word, and the traditional short POSIX format, consisting of a dash and one letter. *Gawk* specific options are used with the *-W* option or its corresponding long option. Any arguments provided to long options are either joined by an = sign (with no intervening spaces), or may be provided in the next command line argument. The *--help* option to *gawk* lists all the *gawk* options. See Table 5.1.

EXAMPLE 5.7

```
% awk --help
Usage: awk [POSIX or GNU style options] -f progfile [--] file ...
       awk [POSIX or GNU style options] [--] 'program' file ...
POSIX options:          GNU long options:
       -f progfile             --file=progfile
       -F fs                   --field-separator=fs
       -v var=val              --assign=var=val
       -m[fr] val
       -W compat               --compat
       -W copyleft             --copyleft
       -W copyright            --copyright
       -W help                 --help
       -W lint                 --lint
       -W lint-old             --lint-old
       -W posix                --posix
       -W re-interval          --re-interval
       -W source=program-text  --source=program-text
       -W traditional          --traditional
       -W usage                --usage
       -W version              --version

Report bugs to bug-gnu-utils@prep.ai.mit.edu,
with a Cc: to arnold@gnu.ai.mit.edu
```

Table 5.1 *gawk* Command Line Options

Options	***Meaning***
-F fs, *--field-separator fs*	Specifies the input field separator,where *fs* is either a string or regular expression; e.g., FS=":" or FS="[\t:]"
-v var=value, *--assign var=value*	Assigns a *value* to a user-defined variable, *var* before the *awk* script starts execution. Available to the BEGIN block.
-f scriptfile, *--file scriptfile*	Reads *awk* commands from the scriptfile.
-mf nnn, *-mr nnn*	Sets memory limits to the value of *nnn*. With *-mf* as the option, limits the maximum number of fields to *nnn*; with *-mr* as the option sets the maximum number of records. Not applicable for *gawk*.
-W traditional, *-W compat,* *--traditional* *--compat*	Runs in compatibility mode so that *gawk* behaves exactly as UNIX versions of *awk*. All *gawk* extensions are ignored. Both modes do the same thing; *--traditional* is preferred.

Table 5.1 *gawk* Command Line Options (Continued)

Options	*Meaning*
-W copyleft *-W copyright* *--copyleft*	Prints abbreviated version of copyright information.
-W help *-W usage* *--help* *--usage*	Prints the available *awk* options and a short summary of what they do.
-W lint *--lint*	Prints warnings about the use of constructs that may not be portable to traditional versions of UNIX *awk*.
-W lint-old, *--lint-old*	Provides warnings about constructs that are not portable to the original version of UNIX implementations.
-W posix *--posix*	Turns on the compatibility mode. Does not recognize: \x escape sequences, newlines as a field separator character if *FS* is assigned a single space, the function keyword, *func*, operators ** and **= to replace ^ and ^=, and *fflush.*
-W re-interval, *--re-interval*	Allows the use of interval regular expressions (see "The POSIX Character Class" on page 147); i.e., the bracketed expressions such as [[:alpha:]]
-W source program-text *--source program-text*	Uses *program-text* as *awk*'s source code allowing *awk* commands at the command line to be intermixed with *-f* files; e.g., *awk -W source '{print $1} -f cmdfile inputfile*
-W version *--version*	Prints version and bug reporting information.
--	Signals the end of option processing.

5.3 Formatting Output

5.3.1 The *print* Function

The action part of the *awk* command is enclosed in curly braces. If no action is specified and a pattern is matched, *awk* takes the default action, which is to print the lines that are matched to the screen. The *print* function is used to print easy and simple output that does not require fancy formatting. For more sophisticated formatting, the *printf* or *sprintf* functions are used. If you are familiar with C, then you already know how *printf* and *sprintf* work.

The *print* function can also be explicitly used in the action part of *awk* as *{print}*. The *print* function accepts arguments as variables, computed values, or string constants. Strings must be enclosed in double quotes. Commas are used to separate the arguments; if commas are not provided, the arguments are concatenated together. The comma evaluates to the value of the output field separator (*OFS*), which is by default a space.

The output of the *print* function can be redirected or piped to another program, and the output of another program can piped to *awk* for printing. (See "Redirection" on page 22 and "Pipes" on page 25.)

EXAMPLE 5.8

```
% date
Wed Jan 12 22:23:16 PST 2000

% date | awk '{ print "Month: " $2 "\nYear: " , $6 }'
Month: Jan
Year: 2000
```

EXPLANATION

The output of the Linux *date* command will be piped to *awk*. The string *Month:* is printed, followed by the second field, the string containing the newline character, *\n*, and *Year:*, followed by the sixth field (*$6*).

Escape Sequences. Escape sequences are represented by a backslash and a letter or number. They can be used in strings to represent tabs, newlines, form feeds, and so forth (see Table 5.2).

Table 5.2 Escape Sequences

Escape Sequence	***Meaning***
\b	Backspace
\f	Form feed
\n	Newline
\r	Carriage return
\t	Tab
\047	Octal value 47, a single quote
\c	*c* represents any other character, e.g., \

EXAMPLE 5.9

```
Tom Jones       4424    5/12/66     543354
Mary Adams      5346    11/4/63     28765
Sally Chang     1654    7/22/54     650000
Billy Black     1683    9/23/44     336500

% awk '/Sally/{print "\t\tHave a nice day, " $1, $2 "\!"}' employees
        Have a nice day, Sally Chang!
```

EXPLANATION

If the line contains the pattern *Sally*, the *print* function prints two tabs, the string *Have a nice day*, the first (where *$1* is *Sally*) and second fields (where *$2* is *Chang*), followed by a string containing two exclamation marks.

5.3.2 The *OFMT* Variable

When printing numbers, you may want to control the format of the number. Normally this would be done with the *printf* function, but the special *awk* variable, *OFMT*, can be set to control the printing of numbers when using the *print* function. It is set by default to "*%.6g*"—six significant digits to the right of the decimal are printed. (The following section describes how this value can be changed.)

EXAMPLE 5.10

```
% awk  'BEGIN{OFMT="%.2f"; print 1.2456789, 12E-2}'
1.25  0.12
```

EXPLANATION

The *OFMT* variable is set so that floating point numbers (*f*) will be printed with two numbers following the decimal point. The percent sign (%) indicates a format is being specified.

5.3.3 The *printf* Function

When printing output, you may want to specify the amount of space between fields so that columns line up neatly. Because the *print* function with tabs does not always guarantee the desired output, the *printf* function can be used for formatting fancy output.

The *printf* function returns a formatted string to standard output, like the *printf* statement in C. The *printf* statement consists of a quoted control string that may be imbedded with format specifications and modifiers. The control string is followed by a comma and a list of comma-separated expressions that will be formatted according to the specifications stated in the control string. Unlike the *print* function, *printf* does not provide a newline. The escape sequence, *\n*, must be provided if a newline is desired.

For each percent sign and format specifier, there must be a corresponding argument. To print a literal percentage, two percent signs must be used. See Table 5.3 for a list of conversion characters and Table 5.4 for *printf* modifiers. The format specifiers are preceded by a percent sign. See Table 5.5 for a list of format specifiers.

When an argument is printed, the place where the output is printed is called the *field*, and the *width* of the field is the number of characters contained in that field.

The pipe symbol (vertical bar) in the following examples, when part of the *printf* string, is part of the text and is used to indicate where the formatting begins and ends.

EXAMPLE 5.11

```
1   % echo "Linux" | awk '{printf "|%-15s|\n", $1}'
    (Output)
    |Linux          |

2   % echo "Linux" | awk '{ printf "|%15s|\n", $1}'
    (Output)
    |          Linux|
```

EXPLANATION

1 The output of the *echo* command, *Linux*, is piped to *awk*. The *printf* function contains a control string. The percent sign alerts *printf* that it will be printing a *15*-space, left-justified string enclosed in vertical bars and terminated with a newline. The dash after the percent sign indicates left justification. The control string is followed by a comma and *$1*. The string *Linux* will be formatted according to the format specification in the control string.

2 The string *Linux* is printed in a right-justified, 15-space string, enclosed in vertical bars, and terminated with a newline.

EXAMPLE 5.12

```
% cat employees
Tom Jones      4424   5/12/66   543354
Mary Adams     5346   11/4/63   28765
Sally Chang    1654   7/22/54   650000
Billy Black    1683   9/23/44   336500

% awk '{printf "The name is: %-15s ID  is %8d\n", $1, $3}' employees
The name is Tom                ID is    4424
The name is Mary               ID is    5346
The name is Sally              ID is    1654
The name is Billy              ID is    1683
```

EXPLANATION

The string to be printed is enclosed in double quotes. The first format specifier is *%-15s*. It has a corresponding argument, *$1*, positioned directly to the right of the comma after the closing quote in the control string. The percent sign indicates a format specification: The dash means left justify, the *15s* means 15-space string. At this spot, print a left-justified, 15-space string followed by the string *ID is* and a number.

The *%8d* format specifies that the decimal (integer) value of *$2* will be printed in its place within the string. The number will be right-justified and take up eight spaces. Placing the quoted string and expressions within parentheses is optional.

Table 5.3 Conversion Characters

Conversion Character	*Definition*
c	Character
s	String
d	Decimal number
ld	Long decimal number
u	Unsigned decimal number
lu	Long unsigned decimal number
x	Hexadecimal number
lx	Long hexidecimal number
o	Octal number
lo	Long octal number
e	Floating point number in scientific notation (*e*-notation)
f	Floating point number
g	Floating point number using either *e* or *f* conversion, whichever takes the least space

Table 5.4 *printf* Modifiers

Character	***Definition***
-	Left-justification modifier.
#	Integers in octal format are displayed with a leading 0; integers in hexadecimal form are displayed with a leading 0*x*.
+	For conversions using *d*, *e*, *f*, and *g*, integers are displayed with a numeric sign + or –.
0	The displayed value is padded with zeros instead of white space.

Table 5.5 Format Specifiers

printf *Format Specifier*	***What It Does***
Given *x = A, y = 15, z = 2.3,* and *$1 = Bob Smith*	
%c	Prints a single ASCII character. *printf("The character is %c\n", x)* prints: *The character is A*
%d	Prints a decimal number. *printf("The boy is %d years old\n", y)* prints: *The boy is 15 years old*
%e	Prints the *e* notation of a number. *printf("z is %e\n", z)* prints: *z is 2.3e+01*
%f	Prints a floating point number. *printf("z is %f\n", 2.3 *2)* prints: *z is 4.600000*
%o	Prints the octal value of a number. *printf("y is %o\n", y)* prints: *z is 17*
%s	Prints a string of characters. *printf("The name of the culprit is %s\n", $1)* prints: *The name of the culprit is Bob Smith*
%x	Prints the hex value of a number. *printf ("y is %x\n", y)* prints: *x is f*

5.4 *awk* Commands from within a File

If *awk* commands are placed in a file, the *-f* option is used with the name of the *awk* file, followed by the name of the input file to be processed. A record is read into *awk*'s buffer and each of the commands in the *awk* file are tested and executed for that record. After *awk* has finished with the first record, it is discarded and the next record is read into the buffer, and so on. If an action is not controlled by a pattern, the default behavior is to print the entire record. If a pattern does not have an action associated with it, the default is to print the record where the pattern matches an input line.

EXAMPLE 5.13

```
(The Database)
   $1     $2     $3    $4      $5
   Tom    Jones  4424  5/12/66  543354
   Mary   Adams  5346  11/4/63  28765
   Sally  Chang  1654  7/22/54  650000
   Billy  Black  1683  9/23/44  336500

   % cat awkfile
1  /^Mary/{print "Hello Mary!"}
2  {print $1, $2, $3}

3  % awk -f awkfile employees
   Tom Jones 4424
   Hello Mary!
   Mary Adams 5346
   Sally Chang 1654
   Billy Black 1683

4  % awk -W source '/^Sally/' -f awkfile employees
   Tom Jones 4424
   Hello Mary!
   Mary Adams 5346
   Sally Chang 1654 7/22/54 650000
   Sally Chang 1654
   Billy Black 1683
```

EXPLANATION

1. If the record begins with the regular expression *Mary*, the string "*Hello Mary*!" is printed. The action is controlled by the pattern preceding it. Fields are separated by white space.
2. The first, second, and third field of *each* record are printed. The action occurs for each line because there is not a pattern controlling the action.
3. *Awk* reads commands from the script, *awkfile*.
4. When the *-W* option (specific to *gawk*) is followed by the argument, *source*, *awk* can intermix *awk* commands provided at the command line as well as those coming from a script file when the script file is preceded by the *-f* option. In this example, *awk* will search for *Sally* at the beginning of the line, and then get the rest of its commands from *awkfile*. The *-W* option is provided with Gnu *awk*, not UNIX versions of *awk*.

5.5 Records and Fields

5.5.1 Records

Awk does not see input data as an endless string of characters, but as having a format or structure. By default, each line is called a *record* and is terminated with a newline.

The Record Separator. By default, the output and input record separator (line separator) is a carriage return, stored in the built-in *awk* variables *ORS* and *RS*, respectively. The *ORS* and *RS* values can be changed, but only in a limited fashion.

The *$0* Variable. An entire record is referenced as *$0* by *awk*. (When *$0* is changed by substitution or assignment, the value of *NF*, the number of fields, may be changed.) The newline value is stored in *awk*'s built-in variable *RS*, a carriage return by default.

EXAMPLE 5.14

```
% cat employees
Tom Jones      4424      5/12/66      543354
Mary Adams     5346      11/4/63      28765
Sally Chang    1654      7/22/54      650000
Billy Black    1683      9/23/44      336500

% awk '{print $0}' employees
Tom Jones      4424      5/12/66      543354
Mary Adams     5346      11/4/63      28765
Sally Chang    1654      7/22/54      650000
Billy Black    1683      9/23/44      336500
```

EXPLANATION

The *awk* variable *$0* holds the current record. It is printed to the screen. By default, *awk* would also print the record if the command were:

```
% awk '{print}' employees
```

The *NR* Variable. The number of each record is stored in *awk*'s built-in variable, *NR*. After a record has been processed, the value of *NR* is incremented by one.

EXAMPLE 5.15

```
% cat employees
Tom Jones       4424      5/12/66      543354
Mary Adams      5346      11/4/63      28765
Sally Chang     1654      7/22/54      650000
Billy Black     1683      9/23/44      336500

% awk '{print NR, $0}'  employees
1 Tom Jones     4424      5/12/66      543354
2 Mary Adams    5346      11/4/63      28765
3 Sally Chang   1654      7/22/54      650000
4 Billy Black   1683      9/23/44      336500
```

EXPLANATION

Each record, *$0*, is printed as it is stored in the file and is preceded with the number of the record, *NR*.

5.5.2 Fields

Each record consists of words called *fields* which, by default, are separated by white space, that is, blank spaces or tabs. Each of these words is called a *field*, and *awk* keeps track of the number of fields in its built-in variable, *NF*. The value of *NF* can vary from line to line, and the limit is implementation-dependent, typically 100 fields per line. New fields can be created. The following example has four records (lines) and five fields (columns). Each record starts at the first field, represented as *$1*, then moves to the second field, *$2*, and so forth.

EXAMPLE 5.16

```
(Fields are represented by a dollar sign ($) and the field number.)
(The Database)

        $1        $2        $3        $4         $5
        Tom       Jones     4424      5/12/66    543354
        Mary      Adams     5346      11/4/63    28765
        Sally     Chang     1654      7/22/54    650000
        Billy     Black     1683      9/23/44    336500
```

EXAMPLE 5.16 (CONTINUED)

```
% awk '{print NR, $1, $2, $5}'  employees
1 Tom Jones 543354
2 Mary Adams 28765
3 Sally Chang 650000
4 Billy Black 336500
```

EXPLANATION

Awk will print the number of the record (*NR*), and the first, second, and fifth fields (columns) of each line in the file.

EXAMPLE 5.17

```
% awk  '{print $0, NF}'  employees
Tom Jones     44234  5/12/66  543354  5
Mary Adams    5346   11/4/63  28765   5
Sally Chang   1654   7/22/54  650000  5
Billy Black   1683   9/23/44  336500  5
```

EXPLANATION

Awk will print each record (*$0*) in the file, followed by the number of fields.

5.5.3 Field Separators

The Input Field Separator. *Awk*'s built-in variable, *FS*, holds the value of the input field separator. When the default value of *FS* is used, *awk* separates fields by spaces and/or tabs, stripping leading blanks and tabs. The *FS* can be changed by assigning a new value to it, either in a *BEGIN* statement or at the command line. For now, we will assign the new value at the command line. To change the value of *FS* at the command line, the *-F* option is used, followed by the character representing the new separator.

Changing the Field Separator at the Command Line. When the *-F* option follows the *awk* command, it is used to change the input field separator. The string immediately following *-F* determines the new field separator. The string can contain metacharacters to represent multiple field separators. See the following examples.

EXAMPLE 5.18

```
% cat employees2
Tom Jones:4424:5/12/66:543354
Mary Adams:5346:11/4/63:28765
Sally Chang:1654:7/22/54:650000
Billy Black:1683:9/23/44:336500

% awk -F: '/Tom Jones/{print $1, $2}'  employees2
Tom Jones  4424
```

EXPLANATION

The *-F* option is used to reassign the value of the input field separator at the command line. When a colon is placed directly after the *-F* option, *awk* will look for colons to separate the fields in the *employees2* file.

Using More Than One Field Separator. You may specify more than one input separator. If more than one character is used for the field separator, *FS*, then the string is a regular expression and is enclosed in square brackets. In the following example, the field separator is a space, colon, or tab. (The old version of *awk* did not support this feature.)

EXAMPLE 5.19

```
% awk -F'[ :\t]'  '{print $1, $2, $3}' employees2
Tom Jones 4424
Mary Adams 5346
Sally Chang 1654
Billy Black 1683
```

EXPLANATION

The *-F* option is followed by a regular expression enclosed in brackets. If a space, colon, or tab is encountered, *awk* will use that character as a field separator. The expression is surrounded by quotes so that the shell will not pounce on the metacharacters for its own use. (Remember that the shell uses brackets for filename expansion.)

The Output Field Separator. The default output field separator is a single space and is stored in *awk*'s internal variable, *OFS*. In all of the examples thus far, we have used the *print* statement to send output to the screen. The comma that is used to separate fields in *print* statements evaluates to whatever the *OFS* has been set. If the default is used, the comma inserted between *$1* and *$2* will evaluate to a single space and the *print* function will print the fields with a space between them. The *OFS* can be changed.

EXAMPLE 5.20

```
% cat employees2
Tom Jones:4424:5/12/66:543354
Mary Adams:5346:11/4/63:28765
Sally Chang:1654:7/22/54:650000
Billy Black:1683:9/23/44:336500

(The Command Line)
% awk -F: '/Tom Jones/{print $1, $2, $3, $4}' employees2
Tom Jones  4424 5/12/66  543354
```

EXPLANATION

The output field separator, a space, is stored in *awk*'s *OFS* variable. The comma between the fields evaluates to whatever is stored in *OFS*. The fields are printed to standard output separated by a space.

EXAMPLE 5.21

```
% awk -F: '/Tom Jones/{print $1 $2 $3 $4}' employees2
Tom Jones44245/12/66543354
```

EXPLANATION

The fields are jammed together because the comma was not used to separate the fields. The *OFS* will not be evaluated unless the comma separates the fields.

EXAMPLE 5.22

```
% awk -F: '/Tom Jones/{print $0}' employees2
Tom Jones:4424:5/12/66:543354
```

EXPLANATION

The *$0* variable holds the current record exactly as it is found in the input file. The record will be printed as-is.

5.6 Patterns and Actions

5.6.1 Patterns

Awk patterns control what actions *awk* will take on a line of input. A pattern consists of a regular expression, an expression resulting in a true or false condition, or a combination of these. The default action is to print each line where the expression results in a true condition. When reading a pattern expression, there is an implied *if* statement. When an *if* is implied, there can be no curly braces surrounding it. When the *if* is explicit, it becomes an action statement and the syntax is different. (See "Conditional Statements" on page 207.)

EXAMPLE 5.23

```
% cat employees
    Tom Jones     4424   5/12/66   543354
    Mary Adams    5346   11/4/63   28765
    Sally Chang   1654   7/22/54   650000
    Billy Black   1683   9/23/44   336500

(The Command Line)
1   awk '/Tom/' employees
    Tom Jones     4424   5/12/66   543354

2   awk '$3 < 4000' employees
    Sally Chang   1654   7/22/54   650000
    Billy Black   1683   9/23/44   336500
```

EXPLANATION

1 If the pattern *Tom* is matched in the input file, the record is printed. The default action is to print the line if no explicit action is specified. This is equivalent to:

```
awk '$0 ~ /Tom/{print $0}' employees
```

2 If the third field is less than *4000*, the record is printed.

5.6.2 Actions

Actions are statements enclosed within curly braces and separated by semicolons.[2] If a pattern precedes an action, the pattern dictates when the action will be performed. Actions can be simple statements or complex groups of statements. Statements are separated by semicolons, or by a newline if placed on their own line.

2. On some versions of *awk*, actions must be separated by semicolons or newlines, and the statements within the curly braces also must be separated by semicolons or newlines. *Nawk* and *gawk* require the use of semicolons or newlines to separate statements within an action, but do not require the use of semicolons to separate actions; for example, the two actions that follow do not need a semicolon:

```
gawk '/Tom/{print "hi Tom"};{x=5}'  file
```

FORMAT

```
{ action }
```

EXAMPLE 5.24

```
{ print $1, $2 }
```

EXPLANATION

The action is to print fields *1* and *2*.

Patterns can be associated with actions. Remember, actions are statements enclosed in curly braces. A pattern controls the action from the first open curly brace to the first closing curly brace. If an action follows a pattern, the first opening curly brace must be on the same line as the pattern. Patterns are *never* enclosed in curly braces.

FORMAT

```
pattern{ action statement; action statement; etc. }
        or
pattern{
        action statement
        action statement
}
```

EXAMPLE 5.25

```
% awk '/Tom/{print "Hello there, "  $1}' employees
Hello there, Tom
```

EXPLANATION

If the record contains the pattern *Tom,* the string *"Hello there, Tom"* will print.

A pattern with no action displays all lines matching the pattern. String-matching patterns contain regular expressions enclosed in forward slashes.

5.7 Regular Expressions

A *regular expression* to *awk* is a pattern that consists of characters enclosed in forward slashes. *Awk* supports the use of regular expression metacharacters (same as *egrep*) to modify the regular expression in some way. If a string in the input line is matched by the regular expression, the resulting condition is true, and any actions associated with the expression are executed. If no action is specified and an input line is matched by the regular expression, the record is printed. See Table 5.6.

EXAMPLE 5.26

```
% awk  '/Mary/'  employees
Mary Adams  5346  11/4/63  28765
```

EXPLANATION

Awk will display all lines in the *employees* file containing the regular expression pattern *Mary.*

EXAMPLE 5.27

```
% awk  '/Mary/{print $1, $2}'  employees
Mary Adams
```

EXPLANATION

Awk will display the first and second fields of all lines in the *employees* file containing the regular expression pattern *Mary.*

Table 5.6 Regular Expression Metacharacters

^	Matches at the beginning of string
$	Matches at the end of string
.	Matches for a single character
*	Matches for zero or more of preceding character
+	Matches for one or more of preceding character
?	Matches for zero or one of preceding character
[ABC]	Matches for any one character in the set of characters, i.e., *A, B,* or *C*
[^ABC]	Matches character not in the set of characters, i.e., *A, B,* or *C*
[A-Z]	Matches for any character in the range from *A* to *Z*
A|B	Matches either *A* or *B*
(AB)+	Matches one or more sets of *AB*

Table 5.6 Regular Expression Metacharacters (Continued)

*	Matches for a literal asterisk
&	Used in the replacement string, to represent what was found in the search string (e.g., can be used with *sub, gsub*, etc.)
A{m} *A{m,}* *A{m,n}*	Repetition of character *A*, *m* times, at least *m* times, or between *m* and *n* times
\y[a]	Matches an empty string either at the beginning or end of a word
\B	Matches an empty string within a word
\<	Matches an empty string at the beginning of a word—also called beginning of word anchor
\>	Matches an empty string at the end of a word—also called end of word anchor
\w	Matches an alphanumeric word character
\W	Matches a nonalphanumeric word character
\‘	Matches an empty string at the beginning of a string
\’	Matches an empty string at the end of a string

a. *All metacharacters from here to the end of the table are specific to gawk, not UNIX versions of awk.*

EXAMPLE 5.28

```
% awk '/^Mary/' employees
    Mary Adams  5346  11/4/63  28765
```

EXPLANATION

Awk will display all lines in the *employees* file that start with the regular expression *Mary.*

EXAMPLE 5.29

```
% awk '/^[A-Z][a-z]+ /' employees
  Tom Jones     4424    5/12/66    543354
  Mary Adams    5346    11/4/63    28765
  Sally Chang   1654    7/22/54    650000
  Billy Black   1683    9/23/44    336500
```

EXPLANATION

Awk will display all lines in the *employees* file where the line begins with an uppercase letter at the beginning of the line, followed by one or more lowercase letters, followed by a space.

The POSIX Character Class. POSIX (the Portable Operating System Interface) is an industry standard to ensure that programs are portable across operating systems. In order to be portable, POSIX recognizes that different countries or locales may differ in the way characters are encoded, different alphabets, the symbols used to represent currency, and how times and dates are represented. To handle different types of characters, POSIX added to the basic and extended regular expressions, the bracketed character class of characters shown in Table 5.7. *Gawk* supports this new character class of metacharacters, whereas *awk* and *nawk* do not.

The class, *[:alnum:]* is another way of saying *A-Za-z0-9*. To use this class, it must be enclosed in another set of brackets for it to be recognized as a regular expression. For example, *A-Za-z0-9,* by itself, is not a regular expression, but *[A-Za-z0-9]* is. Likewise, *[:alnum:]* should be written *[[:alnum:]]*. The difference between using the first form, *[A-Za-z0-9]* and the bracketed form, *[[:alnum:]]* is that the first form is dependent on ASCII character encoding, whereas the second form allows characters from other languages to be represented in the class, such as Swedish rings and German umlauts.

Table 5.7 Bracketed Character Class Added by POSIX

Bracket Class	*Meaning*
[:alnum:]	alphanumeric characters
[:alpha:]	alphabetic characters
[:cntrl:]	control characters
[:digit:]	numeric characters
[:graph:]	nonblank characters (not spaces, control characters, etc.)
[:lower:]	lowercase letters
[:print:]	like *[:graph:]*, but includes the space character
[:punct:]	punctuation characters
[:space:]	all white-space characters (newlines, spaces, tabs)
[:upper:]	uppercase letters
[:xdigit:]	allows digits in a hexadecimal number (*0-9a-fA-F*)

EXAMPLE 5.30

```
% awk '/[[:lower:]]+g[[:space:]]+[[:digit:]]/' employees
Sally Chang 1654 7/22/54 650000
```

EXPLANATION

Awk searches for one or more lowercase letters, followed by a *g*, followed by one or more spaces, followed by a digit.

5.7.1 The Match Operator

The match operator, the tilde (~), is used to match an expression within a record or field.

EXAMPLE 5.31

```
% cat employees
   Tom Jones      44234     5/12/66     543354
   Mary Adams     5346      11/4/63     28765
   Sally Chang    1654      7/22/54     650000
   Billy Black    1683      9/23/44     336500

% awk '$1 ~ /[Bb]ill/' employees
   Billy Black      1683      9/23/44      336500
```

EXPLANATION

Awk will display any lines matching *Bill* or *bill* in the first field.

EXAMPLE 5.32

```
% awk '$1 !~ /ly$/' employees
   Tom Jones      4424      5/12/66     543354
   Mary Adams     5346      11/4/63     28765
```

EXPLANATION

Awk will display any lines not matching *ly,* when *ly* is at the end of the first field.

5.8 *awk* Commands in a Script File

When you have multiple *awk* pattern/action statements, it is often much easier to put the statements in a script. The script is a file containing *awk* comments and statements. If statements and actions are on the same line, they are separated by semicolons. If statements are on separate lines, semicolons are not necessary. If an action follows a pattern, the opening curly brace must be on the same line as the pattern. Comments are preceded by a pound (#) sign.

EXAMPLE 5.33

```
% cat employees
   Tom Jones:4424:5/12/66:54335
   Mary Adams:5346:11/4/63:28765
   Billy Black:1683:9/23/44:336500
   Sally Chang:1654:7/22/54:65000
   Jose Tomas:1683:9/23/44:33650

(The Awk Script)
% cat info
1   # My first awk script by Jack Sprat
    # Script name: info; Date: February 28, 2000
2   /Tom/{print  "Tom's birthday is "$3}
3   /Mary/{print NR, $0}
4   /^Sally/{print "Hi Sally. "  $1 " has a salary of  $" $4 "."}
    # End of info script

(The Command Line)
5   % awk -F: -f info employees2
    Tom's birthday is 5/12/66
    2 Mary Adams:5346:11/4/63:28765
    Hi Sally. Sally Chang has a salary of $65000.
    Tom's birthday is 9/23/44     <-- Finds Jose Thomas
```

EXPLANATION

1. These are comment lines.
2. If the regular expression *Tom* is matched against an input line, the string "*Tom's birthday is*" and the value of the third field (*$3*) is printed.
3. If the regular expression *Mary* is matched against an input line, the action block prints *NR*, the number of the current record, and the record.
4. If the regular expression *Sally* is found at the beginning of the input line, the string "*Hi Sally*" is printed, followed by the value of the first field (*$1*), the string "*has a salary of $*", and the value of the fourth field (*$4*).
5. The *awk* command is followed by the *-F:* option, specifying the colon to be the field separator. The *-f* option is followed by the name of the *awk* script. *Awk* will read instructions from the *info* file. The input file, *employees2,* is next.

5.9 Review

The examples in this section use a sample database, called *datafile*. In the database, the **input field separator**, *FS*, is white space, the default. The **number of fields**, *NF*, is *8*. The number may vary from line to line, but in this file, the number of fields is fixed. The **record separator**, *RS*, is the newline, which separates each line of the file. *Awk* keeps track of the number of each record in the *NR* variable. The **output field separator**, *OFS*, is a space. If a comma is used to separate fields, when the line is printed, each field printed will be separated by a space.

5.9.1 Simple Pattern Matching

```
% cat datafile
northwest     NW     Joel Craig        3.0     .98    3     4
western       WE     Sharon Kelly      5.3     .97    5    23
southwest     SW     Chris Foster      2.7     .8     2    18
southern      SO     May Chin          5.1     .95    4    15
southeast     SE     Derek Johnson     4.0     .7     4    17
eastern       EA     Susan Beal        4.4     .84    5    20
northeast     NE     TJ Nichols        5.1     .94    3    13
north         NO     Val Shultz        4.5     .89    5     9
central       CT     Sheri Watson      5.7     .94    5    13
```

EXAMPLE 5.34

```
% awk '/west/'  datafile
northwest     NW     Joel Craig        3.0   .98   3    4
western       WE     Sharon Kelly      5.3   .97   5   23
southwest     SW     Chris Foster      2.7   .8    2   18
```

EXPLANATION

All lines containing the pattern *west* are printed.

EXAMPLE 5.35

```
% awk '/^north/' datafile
northwest     NW     Joel Craig        3.0   .98   3    4
northeast     NE     TJ Nichols        5.1   .94   3   13
north         NO     Val Shultz        4.5   .89   5    9
```

EXPLANATION

All lines beginning with the pattern *north* are printed.

EXAMPLE 5.36

```
% awk '/^(no|so)/' datafile
northwest       NW      Joel Craig        3.0   .98   3    4
southwest       SW      Chris Foster      2.7   .8    2   18
southern        SO      May Chin          5.1   .95   4   15
southeast       SE      Derek Johnson     4.0   .7    4   17
northeast       NE      TJ Nichols        5.1   .94   3   13
north           NO      Val Shultz        4.5   .89   5    9
```

EXPLANATION

All lines beginning with the pattern *no* or *so* are printed.

5.9.2 Simple Actions

EXAMPLE 5.37

```
% awk '{print $3, $2}' datafile
Joel NW
Sharon WE
Chris SW
May SO
Derek SE
Susan EA
TJ NE
Val NO
Sheri CT
```

EXPLANATION

The output field separator, *OFS*, is a space by default. The comma between *$3* and *$2* is translated to the value of the *OFS*. The third field is printed, followed by a space and the second field.

```
% cat datafile
northwest       NW      Joel Craig        3.0   .98   3    4
western         WE      Sharon Kelly      5.3   .97   5   23
southwest       SW      Chris Foster      2.7   .8    2   18
southern        SO      May Chin          5.1   .95   4   15
southeast       SE      Derek Johnson     4.0   .7    4   17
eastern         EA      Susan Beal        4.4   .84   5   20
northeast       NE      TJ Nichols        5.1   .94   3   13
north           NO      Val Shultz        4.5   .89   5    9
central         CT      Sheri Watson      5.7   .94   5   13
```

EXAMPLE 5.38

```
% awk '{print $3 $2}' datafile
JoelNW
SharonWE
ChrisSW
MaySO
DerekSE
SusanEA
TJNE
ValNO
SheriCT
```

EXPLANATION

The third field is followed by the second field. Because the comma does not separate fields *$3* and *$2*, the output is displayed without spaces between the fields.

EXAMPLE 5.39

```
1   % awk 'print $1' datafile
    awk: syntax error near line 1
    awk: bailing out near line 1

2   % nawk 'print $1' datafile
    nawk: syntax error at source line 1
    context is
         >>> print <<<  $1
    nawk: bailing out at source line 1

3   % gawk 'print $1' datafile
    awk: cmd. line:1: print $1
    awk: cmd. line:1: ^parse error
```

EXPLANATION

1 This is the *awk* (old *awk*) error message. Old *awk* programs were difficult to debug because almost all errors produced this same message. The curly braces are missing in the action statement.

2 This is the *nawk* (new *awk*) error message. *Nawk* error messages are much more verbose than those of the old *awk*. In this program, the curly braces are missing in the action statement.

3 Gnu *awk*, *gawk*, displays its diagnostics in a style a little different from traditional versions of *awk*.

EXAMPLE 5.40

```
% awk '{print $0}' datafile
northwest     NW    Joel Craig        3.0   .98   3    4
western       WE    Sharon Kelly      5.3   .97   5   23
southwest     SW    Chris Foster      2.7   .8    2   18
southern      SO    May Chin          5.1   .95   4   15
southeast     SE    Derek Johnson     4.0   .7    4   17
eastern       EA    Susan Beal        4.4   .84   5   20
northeast     NE    TJ Nichols        5.1   .94   3    3
north         NO    Val Shultz        4.5   .89   5    9
central       CT    Sheri Watson      5.7   .94   5   13
```

EXPLANATION

Each record is printed. *$0* holds the current record.

EXAMPLE 5.41

```
% awk '{print "Number of fields: "NF}' datafile
Number of fields: 8
Number of fields: 8
Number of fields: 8
Number of fields: 8
Number of fields: 8
Number of fields: 8
Number of fields: 8
Number of fields: 8
Number of fields: 8
```

EXPLANATION

There are eight fields in each record. The built-in *awk* variable *NF* holds the number of fields and is reset for each record.

```
% cat datafile
northwest     NW    Joel Craig        3.0   .98   3    4
western       WE    Sharon Kelly      5.3   .97   5   23
southwest     SW    Chris Foster      2.7   .8    2   18
southern      SO    May Chin          5.1   .95   4   15
southeast     SE    Derek Johnson     4.0   .7    4   17
eastern       EA    Susan Beal        4.4   .84   5   20
northeast     NE    TJ Nichols        5.1   .94   3   13
north         NO    Val Shultz        4.5   .89   5    9
central       CT    Sheri Watson      5.7   .94   5   13
```

5.9.3 Regular Expressions in Pattern and Action Combinations

EXAMPLE 5.42

```
% awk '/northeast/{print $3, $2}' datafile
TJ NE
```

EXPLANATION

If the record contains (or matches) the pattern *northeast*, the third field, followed by the second field, is printed.

EXAMPLE 5.43

```
% awk '/E/' datafile
western         WE      Sharon Kelly      5.3   .97   5   23
southeast       SE      Derek Johnson     4.0   .7    4   17
eastern         EA      Susan Beal        4.4   .84   5   20
northeast       NE      TJ Nichols        5.1   .94   3   13
```

EXPLANATION

If the record contains an *E*, the entire record is printed.

EXAMPLE 5.44

```
% awk '/^[ns]/{print $1}' datafile
northwest
southwest
southern
southeast
northeast
north
```

EXPLANATION

If the record begins with an *n* or *s*, the first field is printed.

EXAMPLE 5.45

```
% awk '$5 ~ /\.[7-9]+/' datafile
southwest       SW      Chris Foster    2.7   .8    2    18
central         CT      Sheri Watson    5.7   .94   5    13
```

EXPLANATION

If the fifth field (*$5*) contains a literal period, followed by one or more numbers between *7* and *9*, the record is printed.

EXAMPLE 5.46

```
% awk '$2 !~ /E/{print $1, $2}' datafile
northwest NW
southwest SW
southern SO
north NO
central CT
```

EXPLANATION

If the second field does not contain the pattern *E*, the first field followed by the second field (*$1, $2*) is printed.

```
% cat datafile
northwest     NW    Joel Craig       3.0    .98   3    4
western       WE    Sharon Kelly     5.3    .97   5   23
southwest     SW    Chris Foster     2.7    .8    2   18
southern      SO    May Chin         5.1    .95   4   15
southeast     SE    Derek Johnson    4.0    .7    4   17
eastern       EA    Susan Beal       4.4    .84   5   20
northeast     NE    TJ Nichols       5.1    .94   3   13
north         NO    Val Shultz       4.5    .89   5    9
central       CT    Sheri Watson     5.7    .94   5   13
```

EXAMPLE 5.47

```
% awk '$3 ~ /^Joel/{print $3 " is a nice guy."}' datafile
Joel is a nice guy.
```

EXPLANATION

If the third field (*$3*) begins with the pattern *Joel*, the third field followed by the string "*is a nice guy.*" is printed. Note that a space is included in the string if it is to be printed.

EXAMPLE 5.48

```
% awk '$8 ~ /[0-9][0-9]$/{print $8}' datafile
23
18
15
17
20
13
13
```

EXPLANATION

If the eighth field (*$8*) ends in two digits, it is printed.

EXAMPLE 5.49

```
% awk '$4 ~ /Chin$/{print "The price is $" $8 "."}' datafile
The price is $15.
```

EXPLANATION

If the fourth field (*$4*) ends with *Chin*, the string enclosed in double quotes (*"The price is"*), the eighth field (*$8*), and the string containing a period are printed.

EXAMPLE 5.50

```
% awk '/TJ/{print $0}' datafile
northeast       NE      TJ Nichols      5.1   .94   3   13
```

EXPLANATION

If the record contains the pattern *TJ*, *$0* (the record) is printed.

5.9.4 Input Field Separators

```
% cat datafile2
Joel Craig:northwest:NW:3.0:.98:3:4
Sharon Kelly:western:WE:5.3:.97:5:23
Chris Foster:southwest:SW:2.7:.8:2:18
May Chin:southern:SO:5.1:.95:4:15
Derek Johnson:southeast:SE:4.0:.7:4:17
Susan Beal:eastern:EA:4.4:.84:5:20
TJ Nichols:northeast:NE:5.1:.94:3:13
Val Shultz:north:NO:4.5:.89:5:9
Sheri Watson:central:CT:5.7:.94:5:13
```

EXAMPLE 5.51

```
% awk '{print $1}' datafile2
Joel
Sharon
Chris
May
Derek
Susan
TJ
Val
Sheri
```

EXPLANATION

The default input field separator is white space. The first field (*$1*) is printed.

```
% cat datafile2
Joel Craig:northwest:NW:3.0:.98:3:4
Sharon Kelly:western:WE:5.3:.97:5:23
Chris Foster:southwest:SW:2.7:.8:2:18
May Chin:southern:SO:5.1:.95:4:15
Derek Johnson:southeast:SE:4.0:.7:4:17
Susan Beal:eastern:EA:4.4:.84:5:20
TJ Nichols:northeast:NE:5.1:.94:3:13
Val Shultz:north:NO:4.5:.89:5:9
Sheri Watson:central:CT:5.7:.94:5:13
```

EXAMPLE 5.52

```
% awk -F: '{print $1}' datafile2
Joel Craig
Sharon Kelly
Chris Foster
    <more output here>
Val Shultz
Sheri Watson
```

EXPLANATION

The *-F* option specifies the colon as the input field separator. The first field (*$1*) is printed.

EXAMPLE 5.53

```
% awk '{print "Number of fields: "NF}' datafile2
Number of fields: 2
Number of fields: 2
Number of fields: 2
    <more of the same output here>
Number of fields: 2
Number of fields: 2
```

EXPLANATION

Because the field separator is the default, white space, the number of fields for each record is 2. The only space is between the first and last name.

EXAMPLE 5.54

```
% awk -F: '{print "Number of fields: "NF}' datafile2
Number of fields: 7
Number of fields: 7
Number of fields: 7
    <more of the same output here>
Number of fields: 7
Number of fields: 7
```

EXPLANATION

Because the field separator is a colon, the number of fields in each record is *7*.

EXAMPLE 5.55

```
% awk -F"[ :]" '{print $1, $2}' datafile2
Joel Craig
Sharon Kelly
Chris Foster
May Chin
Derek Johnson
Susan Beal
TJ Nichols
Val Shultz
Sheri Watson
```

EXPLANATION

Multiple field separators can be specified with *awk* as a regular expression. Either a space or a colon will be designated as a field separator. The first and second fields (*$1, $2*) are printed.

```
% cat datafile
northwest    NW    Joel Craig       3.0    .98    3     4
western      WE    Sharon Kelly     5.3    .97    5    23
southwest    SW    Chris Foster     2.7    .8     2    18
southern     SO    May Chin         5.1    .95    4    15
southeast    SE    Derek Johnson    4.0    .7     4    17
eastern      EA    Susan Beal       4.4    .84    5    20
northeast    NE    TJ Nichols       5.1    .94    3    13
north        NO    Val Shultz       4.5    .89    5     9
central      CT    Sheri Watson     5.7    .94    5    13
```

5.9.5 *awk* Scripting

EXAMPLE 5.56

```
  % cat awk.sc1
  #This is a comment
  # This is my first awk script
1 /^north/{print $1, $2, $3}
2 /^south/{print "The " $1 " district."}

  % awk -f awk.sc1 datafile
3 northwest NW Joel
  The southwest district.
  The southern district.
  The southeast district.
  northeast NE TJ
  north NO Val
```

EXPLANATION

1. If the record begins with the pattern *north*, the first, second, and third fields (*$1, $2, $3*) are printed.
2. If the record begins with the pattern *south*, the string *The*, followed by the value of the first field (*$1*), and the string *district* are printed.
3. The *-f* option precedes the name of the *awk* script file, followed by the input file that is to be processed.

LINUX TOOLS LAB 3

(File: lab3.data)

Mike Harrington:(510) 548-1278:250:100:175
Christian Dobbins:(408) 538-2358:155:90:201
Susan Dalsass:(206) 654-6279:250:60:50
Archie McNichol:(206) 548-1348:250:100:175
Jody Savage:(206) 548-1278:15:188:150
Guy Quigley:(916) 343-6410:250:100:175
Dan Savage:(406) 298-7744:450:300:275
Nancy McNeil:(206) 548-1278:250:80:75
John Goldenrod:(916) 348-4278:250:100:175
Chet Main:(510) 548-5258:50:95:135
Tom Savage:(408) 926-3456:250:168:200
Elizabeth Stachelin:(916) 440-1763:175:75:300

The database above contains the names, phone numbers, and money contributions to the party campaign for the past three months.

1. Print all the phone numbers.
2. Print *Dan*'s phone number.
3. Print *Susan*'s name and phone number.
4. Print all last names beginning with *D*.
5. Print all first names beginning with either a *C* or *E*.
6. Print all first names containing only four characters.
7. Print the first names of all those in the *916* area code.
8. Print *Mike*'s campaign contributions. Each value should be printed with a leading dollar sign; e.g., $250 $100 $175.
9. Print last names followed by a comma and the first name.
10. Print all lines that end in a space, followed by three digits, using the POSIX character class.
11. Write an *awk* script called *facts* that:
    a. Prints full names and phone numbers for the *Savages*.
    b. Prints *Chet*'s contributions.
    c. Prints all those who contributed *$250* the first month.

CHAPTER

THE GAWK UTILITY: EVALUATING EXPRESSIONS

6.1 Comparison Expressions

Comparison expressions match lines where the action is performed if the condition is true. These expressions use relational operators and are used to compare numbers or strings. Table 6.1 provides a list of the relational operators. The value of the expression is 1 if the expression evaluates true, and 0 if false.

6.1.1 Relational Operators

Table 6.1 Relational Operators

Operator	*Meaning*	*Example*
<	Less than	x < y
<=	Less than or equal to	x <= y
==	Equal to	x == y
!=	Not equal to	x != y
>=	Greater than or equal to	x >= y
>	Greater than	x > y
~	Matched by regular expression	x ~ /y/
!~	Not matched by regular expression	x !~ /y/

EXAMPLE 6.1

```
(The Database)
% cat employees
   Tom Jones      4423       5/12/66      543354
   Mary Adams     5346       11/4/63      28765
   Sally Chang    1654       7/22/54      650000
   Billy Black    1683       9/23/44      336500

(The Command Line)
1  % awk '$3 == 5346' employees
   Mary Adams     5346       11/4/63      28765

2  % awk '$3 > 5000{print $1} ' employees
   Mary

3  % awk '$2 ~ /Adam/ ' employees
   Mary Adams     5346       11/4/63      28765

4  % awk '$2 !~ /Adam/ ' employees
   Tom Jones      4423       5/12/66      543354
   Sally Chang    1654       7/22/54      650000
   Billy Black    1683       9/23/44      336500
```

EXPLANATION

1. If the third field is equal to *5346*, the condition is true and *awk* will perform the default action—print the line. When an *if* condition is implied, it is a conditional pattern test.
2. If the third field is greater than *5000*, *awk* prints the first field.
3. If the second field matches the regular expression *Adam*, the record is printed.
4. If the second field does not match the regular expression *Adam*, the record is printed. If an expression is a numeric value and is being compared to a string value with an operator that requires a numeric comparison, the string value will be converted to a numeric value. If the operator requires a string value, the numeric value will be converted to a string value.

6.1.2 Conditional Expressions

A conditional expression uses two symbols, the question mark and the colon, to evaluate expressions. It is really just a short way to achieve the same result as doing an *if/else* statement. The general format is:

FORMAT

```
conditional expression1 ? expression2 : expression3
```

This produces the same result as the *if/else* shown here. (A complete discussion of the *if/else* construct is given later.)

```
{
if (expression1)
        expression2
else
        expression3
}
```

EXAMPLE 6.2

```
% awk '{max=($1 > $2) ? $1 : $2; print max}' filename
```

EXPLANATION

If the first field is greater than the second field, the value of the expression after the question mark is assigned to *max*; otherwise the value of the expression after the colon is assigned to *max*.

This is comparable to:

```
if ($1 > $2 )
        max=$1
else
        max=$2
```

6.1.3 Computation

Computation can be performed within patterns. *Awk* performs all arithmetic in floating point. The arithmetic operators are provided in Table 6.2.

EXAMPLE 6.3

```
% awk '$3 * $4 > 500' filename
```

EXPLANATION

Awk will multiply the third field (*$3*) by the fourth field (*$4*), and if the result is greater than *500*, it will display those lines. (*Filename* is assumed to be a file containing the input.)

Table 6.2 Arithmetic Operators

Operator	*Meaning*	*Example*
+	Add	x + y
–	Subtract	x - y
*	Multiply	x * y
/	Divide	x / y
%	Modulus	x % y
^	Exponentiation	x ^ y

6.1.4 Compound Patterns

Compound patterns are expressions that combine patterns with logical operators (see Table 6.3). An expression is evaluated from left to right.

Table 6.3 Logical Operators

Operator	*Meaning*	*Example*
&&	Logical AND	a && b
||	Logical OR	a || b
!	NOT	! a

EXAMPLE 6.4

```
% awk '$2 > 5 && $2 <= 15' filename
```

EXPLANATION

Awk will display those lines that match both conditions; that is, where the second field (*$2*) is greater than *5* AND the second field (*$2*) is also less than or equal to *15*. With the *&&* operator, BOTH conditions must be true. (*Filename* is assumed to be a file containing the input.)

EXAMPLE 6.5

```
% awk '$3 == 100 || $4 > 50' filename
```

EXPLANATION

Awk will display those lines that match one of the conditions; that is, where the third field is equal to *100* OR the fourth field is greater than *50*. With the || operator, only one of the conditions must be true. (*Filename* is assumed to be a file containing the input.)

EXAMPLE 6.6

```
% awk '!($2 < 100 && $3 < 20)' filename
```

EXPLANATION

If both conditions are true, *awk* will negate the expression and display those lines—so the lines displayed will have one or both conditions false. The unary *!* operator negates the result of the condition so that if the expression yields a true condition, the *not* will make it false, and vice versa. (*Filename* is assumed to be a file containing the input.)

6.1.5 Range Patterns

Range patterns match from the first occurrence of one pattern to the first occurrence of the second pattern, then match for the next occurrence of the first pattern to the next occurrence of the second pattern, etc. If the first pattern is matched and the second pattern is not found, *awk* will display all lines to the end of the file.

EXAMPLE 6.7

```
% awk '/Tom/,/Suzanne/' filename
```

EXPLANATION

Awk will display all lines, inclusive, that range between the first occurrence of *Tom* and the first occurrence of *Suzanne*. If *Suzanne* is not found, *awk* will continue processing lines until the end of file. If, after the range between *Tom* and *Suzanne* is printed, *Tom* appears again, *awk* will start displaying lines until another *Suzanne* is found or the file ends.

6.1.6 A Data Validation Program

Using the *awk* commands discussed so far, the password-checking program from the book *The AWK Programming Language*[1] illustrates how the data in a file can be validated.

EXAMPLE 6.8

```
(The Password Database)
1 % cat /etc/passwd
tooth:pwHfudo.eC9sM:476:40:Contract Admin.:/home/rickenbacker/tooth:/bin/csh
lisam:9JY7OuS2f31HY:4467:40:Lisa M. Spencer:/home/fortune1/lisam:/bin/csh
goode:v7Ww.nWJCeSIQ:32555:60:Goodwill Guest User:/usr/goodwill:/bin/csh
bonzo:eTZbu6M2jM7VA:5101:911: SSTOOL Log account :/home/sun4/bonzo:/bin/csh
info:mKZsrioPtW9hA:611:41:Terri Stern:/home/chewie/info:/bin/csh
cnc:IN1IVqVj1bVv2:10209:41:Charles Carnell:/home/christine/cnc:/bin/csh
bee:*:347:40:Contract Temp.:/home/chanel5/bee:/bin/csh
friedman:oyuIiKoFTV0TE:3561:50:Jay Friedman:/home/ibanez/friedman:/bin/csh
chambers:Rw7R1k77yUY4.:592:40:Carol Chambers:/usr/callisto2/chambers:/bin/csh
gregc:nkLul0g:7777:30:Greg Champlin FE Chicago
ramona:gbDQLdDBeRc46:16660:68:RamonaLeininge MWA CustomerService Rep:/home/forsh:

(The Awk Commands)
2   % cat /etc/passwd | awk -F: '\
3   NF != 7{\
4   printf("line %d, does not have 7 fields: %s\n",NR,$0)} \
5   $1 !~ /[A-Za-z0-9]/{printf("line %d, nonalphanumeric user id: %s\n",NR,$0)} \
6   $2 == "*" {printf("line %d, no password: %s\n",NR,$0)} '

(The Output)
    line 7, no password: bee:*:347:40:Contract Temp.:/home/chanel5/bee:/bin/csh
    line 10, does not have 7 fields: gregc:nk2EYi7kLul0g:7777:30:Greg Champlin
    FE Chicago
    line 11, does not have 7 fields: ramona:gbDQLdDBeRc46:16660:68:Ramona
    Leininger MWA Customer Service Rep:/home/forsh:
```

EXPLANATION

1. The contents of the */etc/passwd* file are displayed.
2. The *cat* program sends its output to *awk*. *Awk*'s field separator is a colon.
3. If the number of fields (*NF*) is not equal to *7*, the following action block is executed.
4. The *printf* function prints the string "*line <number>, does not have 7 fields*" followed by the number of the current record (*NR*) and the record itself (*$0*).
5. If the first field (*$1*) does not contain any alphanumeric characters, the *printf* function prints the string "*nonalphanumeric user id,*" followed by the number of the record and the record.
6. If the second field (*$2*) equals an asterisk, the string "*no passwd*" is printed, followed by the number of the record and the record itself.

---

1. Aho, Weinberger, and Kernighan, *The Awk Programming Language*. Addison Wesley, 1988.

6.2 Review

6.2.1 Equality Testing

```
% cat datafile
northwest    NW    Joel Craig       3.0   .98   3   4
western      WE    Sharon Kelly     5.3   .97   5   23
southwest    SW    Chris Foster     2.7   .8    2   18
southern     SO    May Chin         5.1   .95   4   15
southeast    SE    Derek Johnson    4.0   .7    4   17
eastern      EA    Susan Beal       4.4   .84   5   20
northeast    NE    TJ Nichols       5.1   .94   3   13
north        NO    Val Shultz       4.5   .89   5   9
central      CT    Sheri Watson     5.7   .94   5   13
```

EXAMPLE 6.9

```
% awk '$7 == 5' datafile
western      WE     Sharon Kelly     5.3   .97   5   23
eastern      EA     Susan Beal       4.4   .84   5   20
north        NO     Val Shultz       4.5   .89   5    9
central      CT     Sheri Watson     5.7   .94   5   13
```

EXPLANATION

If the seventh field (*$7*) is equal to the number *5*, the record is printed.

EXAMPLE 6.10

```
% awk '$2 == "CT"{print $1, $2}' datafile
central        CT
```

EXPLANATION

If the second field is equal to the string *CT*, fields one and two (*$1*, *$2*) are printed. Strings must be quoted.

```
% cat datafile
northwest     NW    Joel Craig       3.0   .98   3    4
western       WE    Sharon Kelly     5.3   .97   5   23
southwest     SW    Chris Foster     2.7   .8    2   18
southern      SO    May Chin         5.1   .95   4   15
southeast     SE    Derek Johnson    4.0   .7    4   17
eastern       EA    Susan Beal       4.4   .84   5   20
northeast     NE    TJ Nichols       5.1   .94   3   13
north         NO    Val Shultz       4.5   .89   5    9
central       CT    Sheri Watson     5.7   .94   5   13
```

6.2.2 Relational Operators

EXAMPLE 6.11

```
% awk '$7 != 5' datafile
northwest        NW      Joel Craig        3.0   .98   3    4
southwest        SW      Chris Foster      2.7   .8    2   18
southern         SO      May Chin          5.1   .95   4   15
southeast        SE      Derek Johnson     4.0   .7    4   17
northeast        NE      TJ Nichols        5.1   .94   3   13
```

EXPLANATION

If the seventh field (*$7*) is not equal to the number *5*, the record is printed.

EXAMPLE 6.12

```
% awk '$7 < 5 {print $4, $7}' datafile
Craig 3
Foster 2
Chin 4
Johnson 4
Nichols 3
```

EXPLANATION

If the seventh field (*$7*) is less than *5*, fields *4* and *7* are printed.

EXAMPLE 6.13

```
% awk '$6 > .9 {print $1, $6}' datafile
northwest .98
western .97
southern .95
northeast .94
central .94
```

EXPLANATION

If the sixth field (*$6*) is greater than *.9*, fields *1* and *6* are printed.

EXAMPLE 6.14

```
% awk '$8 <= 17 { print $8}' datafile
4
15
17
13
9
13
```

EXPLANATION

If the eighth field (*$8*) is less than or equal to *17*, it is printed.

EXAMPLE 6.15

```
% awk '$8 >= 17 {print $8}' datafile
23
18
17
20
```

EXPLANATION

If the eighth field is greater than or equal to *17*, the eighth field is printed.

```
% cat datafile
northwest     NW     Joel Craig       3.0    .98    3    4
western       WE     Sharon Kelly     5.3    .97    5    23
southwest     SW     Chris Foster     2.7    .8     2    18
southern      SO     May Chin         5.1    .95    4    15
southeast     SE     Derek Johnson    4.0    .7     4    17
eastern       EA     Susan Beal       4.4    .84    5    20
northeast     NE     TJ Nichols       5.1    .94    3    13
north         NO     Val Shultz       4.5    .89    5    9
central       CT     Sheri Watson     5.7    .94    5    13
```

6.2.3 Logical Operators

EXAMPLE 6.16

```
% awk '$8 > 10 && $8 < 17' datafile
southern        SO        May Chin         5.1   .95   4    15
northeast       NE        TJ Nichols       5.1   .94   3    13
central         CT        Sheri Watson     5.7   .94   5    13
```

EXPLANATION

If the eighth field (*$8*) is greater than *10* AND less than *17*, the record is printed. The record will be printed only if both expressions are true.

EXAMPLE 6.17

```
% awk '$2 == "NW" || $1 ~ /south/{print $1, $2}' datafile
northwest NW
southwest SW
southern SO
southeast SE
```

EXPLANATION

If the second field (*$2*) is equal to the string *"NW"* OR the first field (*$1*) contains the pattern *south*, the first and second fields (*$1*, *$2*) are printed. The record will be printed if only one of the expressions is true.

6.2.4 Logical Not Operator

EXAMPLE 6.18

```
% awk '!($8 == 13){print $8}' datafile
4
23
18
15
17
20
9
```

EXPLANATION

If the eighth field (*$8*) is equal to *13*, the *!* (not operator) NOTs the expression and prints the eighth field (*$8*). The *!* is a unary negation operator.

6.2.5 Arithmetic Operators

EXAMPLE 6.19

```
% awk '/southern/{print $5 + 10}' datafile
15.1
```

EXPLANATION

If the record contains the regular expression *southern*, *10* is added to the value of the fifth field (*$5*) and printed. Note that the number prints in floating point.

EXAMPLE 6.20

```
% awk '/southern/{print $8 + 10}' datafile
25
```

EXPLANATION

If the record contains the regular expression *southern*, *10* is added to the value of the eighth field (*$8*) and printed. Note that the number prints in decimal.

```
% cat datafile
northwest     NW     Joel Craig       3.0     .98    3     4
western       WE     Sharon Kelly     5.3     .97    5    23
southwest     SW     Chris Foster     2.7     .8     2    18
southern      SO     May Chin         5.1     .95    4    15
southeast     SE     Derek Johnson    4.0     .7     4    17
eastern       EA     Susan Beal       4.4     .84    5    20
northeast     NE     TJ Nichols       5.1     .94    3    13
north         NO     Val Shultz       4.5     .89    5     9
central       CT     Sheri Watson     5.7     .94    5    13
```

EXAMPLE 6.21

```
% awk '/southern/{print $5 + 10.56}' datafile
15.66
```

EXPLANATION

If the record contains the regular expression *southern*, *10.56* is added to the value of the fifth field (*$5*) and printed.

EXAMPLE 6.22

```
% awk '/southern/{print $8 - 10}' datafile
5
```

EXPLANATION

If the record contains the regular expression *southern*, *10* is subtracted from the value of the eighth field (*$8*) and printed.

EXAMPLE 6.23

```
% awk '/southern/{print $8 / 2}' datafile
7.5
```

EXPLANATION

If the record contains the regular expression *southern*, the value of the eighth field (*$8*) is divided by *2* and printed.

EXAMPLE 6.24

```
% awk '/northeast/{print $8 / 3}' datafile
4.33333
```

EXPLANATION

If the record contains the regular expression *northeast*, the value of the eighth field (*$8*) is divided by *3* and printed. The precision is six places to the right of the decimal point.

EXAMPLE 6.25

```
% awk '/southern/{print $8 * 2}' datafile
30
```

EXPLANATION

If the record contains the regular expression *southern*, the eighth field (*$8*) is multiplied by *2* and printed.

EXAMPLE 6.26

```
% awk '/northeast/ {print $8 % 3}' datafile
1
```

EXPLANATION

If the record contains the regular expression *northeast*, the eighth field (*$8*) is divided by *3* and the remainder (modulus) is printed.

EXAMPLE 6.27

```
% awk '$3 ~ /^Susan/\
{print "Percentage: "$6 + .2 " Volume: " $8}' datafile
Percentage: 1.04 Volume: 20
```

EXPLANATION

If the third field (*$3*) begins with the regular expression *Susan*, the *print* function prints the result of the calculations and the strings in double quotes.

```
% cat datafile
northwest    NW   Joel Craig       3.0   .98   3    4
western      WE   Sharon Kelly     5.3   .97   5   23
southwest    SW   Chris Foster     2.7   .8    2   18
southern     SO   May Chin         5.1   .95   4   15
southeast    SE   Derek Johnson    4.0   .7    4   17
eastern      EA   Susan Beal       4.4   .84   5   20
northeast    NE   TJ Nichols       5.1   .94   3   13
north        NO   Val Shultz       4.5   .89   5    9
central      CT   Sheri Watson     5.7   .94   5   13
```

6.2.6 Range Operator

EXAMPLE 6.28

```
% awk '/^western/,/^eastern/' datafile
western      WE     Sharon Kelly     5.3   .97   5   23
southwest    SW     Chris Foster     2.7   .8    2   18
southern     SO     May Chin         5.1   .95   4   15
southeast    SE     Derek Johnson    4.0   .7    4   17
eastern      EA     Susan Beal       4.4   .84   5   20
```

EXPLANATION

All records within the range beginning with the regular expression *western* are printed until a record beginning with the expression *eastern* is found. Records will start being printed again if the pattern *western* is found and will continue to print until *eastern* or end of file is reached.

6.2.7 Conditional Operator

EXAMPLE 6.29

```
% awk '{print ($7 > 4 ? "high "$7 : "low "$7)}' datafile
low 3
high 5
low 2
low 4
low 4
high 5
low 3
high 5
high 5
```

EXPLANATION

If the seventh field (*$7*) is greater than *4*, the *print* function gets the value of the expression after the question mark (the string *high* and the seventh field); else the *print* function gets the value of the expression after the colon (the string *low* and the value of the seventh field).

6.2.8 Assignment Operators

EXAMPLE 6.30

```
% awk '$3 == "Chris"{ $3 = "Christian"; print}' datafile
southwest SW Christian Foster 2.7 .8 2 18
```

EXPLANATION

If the third field (*$3*) is equal to the string *Chris*, the action is to assign *Christian* to the third field (*$3*) and print the record. The double equal tests its operands for equality, whereas the single equal is used for assignment.

EXAMPLE 6.31

```
% awk '/Derek/{$8 += 12; print $8}' datafile
29
```

EXPLANATION

If the regular expression *Derek* is found, *12* is added and assigned to *(+=)*, the eighth field (*$8*), and that value is printed. Another way to write this is: `$8 = $8 + 12.`

EXAMPLE 6.32

```
% awk '{$7 %= 3; print $7}' datafile
0
2
2
1
1
2
0
2
2
```

EXPLANATION

For each record, the seventh field (*$7*) is divided by *3*, and the remainder of that division (modulus) is assigned to the seventh field and printed.

LINUX TOOLS LAB 4

(File lab4.data)

Mike Harrington:(510) 548-1278:250:100:175
Christian Dobbins:(408) 538-2358:155:90:201
Susan Dalsass:(206) 654-6279:250:60:50
Archie McNichol:(206) 548-1348:250:100:175
Jody Savage:(206) 548-1278:15:188:150
Guy Quigley:(916) 343-6410:250:100:175
Dan Savage:(406) 298-7744:450:300:275
Nancy McNeil:(206) 548-1278:250:80:75
John Goldenrod:(916) 348-4278:250:100:175
Chet Main:(510) 548-5258:50:95:135
Tom Savage:(408) 926-3456:250:168:200
Elizabeth Stachelin:(916) 440-1763:175:75:300

The database above contains the names, phone numbers, and money contributions to the party campaign for the past three months.

1. Print the first and last names of those who contributed more than *$100* in the second month.
2. Print the names and phone numbers of those who contributed less than *$85* in the last month.
3. Print the names of those who contributed between *$75* and *$150* in the first month.
4. Print the names of those who contributed less than *$800* over the three-month period.
5. Print the names and addresses of those with an average monthly contribution greater than *$200*.

6. Print the first name of those not in the *916* area code.
7. Print each record preceded by the number of the record.
8. Print the name and total contribution of each person.
9. Add *$10* to *Chet*'s second contribution.
10. Change *Tom Savage*'s name to *Steve Hanson*.

CHAPTER

7

THE GAWK UTILITY: GAWK PROGRAMMING

7.1 Variables

7.1.1 Numeric and String Constants

Numeric constants can be represented as integers like 243, floating point numbers like 3.14, or numbers using scientific notation like .723E–1 or 3.4e7. Strings, such as *"Hello world"*, are enclosed in double quotes.

Initialization and Type Coercion. Just mentioning a variable in your *awk* program causes it to exist. A variable can be a string, a number, or both. When it is set, it becomes the type of the expression on the right-hand side of the equal sign.

Uninitialized variables have the value zero or the value " ", depending on the context in which they are used.

`name = "Nancy"`	*name is a string*
`x++`	***x*** *is a number;* ***x*** *is initialized to zero and incremented by 1*
`number = 35`	*number is a number*

To coerce a string to be a number:

```
name + 0
```

To coerce a number to be a string:

```
number " "
```

All fields and array elements created by the *split* function are considered strings, unless they contain only a numeric value. If a field or array element is null, it has the string value of null. An empty line is also considered to be a null string.

7.1.2 User-Defined Variables

User-defined variables consist of letters, digits, and underscores, and cannot begin with a digit. Variables in *awk* are not declared. *Awk* infers data type by the context of the variable in the expression. If the variable is not initialized, *awk* initializes string variables to null and numeric variables to zero. If necessary, *awk* will convert a string variable to a numeric variable, and vice versa. Variables are assigned values with *awk*'s assignment operators. See Table 7.1.

Table 7.1 Assignment Operators

Operator	*Meaning*	*Equivalence*
=	a = 5	a = 5
+=	a = a + 5	a += 5
-=	a = a - 5	a -= 5
*=	a = a * 5	a *= 5
/=	a = a / 5	a /= 5
%=	a = a % 5	a %= 5
^=	a = a ^ 5	a ^= 5

The simplest assignment takes the result of an expression and assigns it to a variable.

FORMAT

```
variable = expression
```

EXAMPLE 7.1

```
% awk '$1 ~  /Tom/ {wage = $2 * $3; print wage}'  filename
```

EXPLANATION

Awk will scan the first field for *Tom* and when there is a match, it will multiply the value of the second field by the value of the third field and assign the result to the user-defined variable *wage.* Because the multiplication operation is arithmetic, *awk* assigns *wage* an initial value of zero. (The % is the UNIX prompt and *filename* is an input file.)

Increment and Decrement Operators. To add one to an operand, the *increment operator* is used. The expression *x++* is equivalent to *x = x + 1*. Similarly, the *decrement operator* subtracts one from its operand. The expression *x –* is equivalent to *x = x – 1*. This notation is useful in looping operations when you simply want to increment or decrement a counter. You can use the increment and decrement operators either preceding the operator, as in ++x, or after the operator, as in *x++*. If these expressions are used in assignment statements, their placement will make a difference in the result of the operation.

```
{x = 1;  y = x++ ; print x, y}
```

The ++ here is called a *postincrement operator*; *y* is assigned the value of one, and then *x* is increased by one, so that when all is said and done, **y *will equal one, and* x *will equal two.***

```
{ x = 1; y = ++x;  print x, y}
```

The ++ here is called a *preincrement operator*; *x* is incremented first, and the value of two is assigned to *y*, so that when this statement is finished, **y *will equal two, and* x *will equal two*.**

User-Defined Variables at the Command Line. A variable can be assigned a value at the command line and passed into an *awk* script. See "Processing Command Arguments in awk" on page 220 for more on processing arguments and *ARGV*, the array of command line arguments.

EXAMPLE 7.2

```
% awk -F: -f awkscript   month=4  year=2000 filename
```

EXPLANATION

Month and *year* are user-defined variables assigned the values *4* and *2000*, respectively. In the *awk* script, these variables may be used as though they were created in the script. Note: If *filename* precedes the arguments, the variables will not be available in the *BEGIN* statements. (See "BEGIN Patterns" on page 186.)

The *-v* Option (*awk*). The *-v* option provided by *awk* allows command line arguments to be processed within a *BEGIN* statement. For each argument passed at the command line, there must be a *-v* option preceding it.

Field Variables. Field variables can be used like user-defined variables, except they reference fields. New fields can be created by assignment. A field value that is referenced and has no value will be assigned the null string. If a field value is changed, the *$0* variable is recomputed using the current value of *OFS* as a field separator. The number of fields allowed is usually limited to 100.

EXAMPLE 7.3

```
% awk ' { $5 = 1000 * $3 / $2;  print } '  filename
```

EXPLANATION

If *$5* does not exist, *awk* will create it and assign the result of the expression *1000 * $3 / $2* to the fifth field (*$5*). If the fifth field exists, the result will be assigned to it, overwriting what is there.

EXAMPLE 7.4

```
% awk ' $4 == "CA" { $4  = "California"; print}'  filename
```

EXPLANATION

If the fourth field (*$4*) is equal to the string *CA*, *awk* will reassign the fourth field to *California.* The double quotes are essential. Without them, the strings become user-defined variables with an initial value of null.

Built-In Variables. Built-in variables have uppercase names. They can be used in expressions and can be reset. See Table 7.2 for a list of built-in variables.

Table 7.2 Built-In Variables

Variable Name	*Variable Contents*
ARGC	Number of command line argument.
ARGIND	Index in *ARGV* of the current file being processed from the command line (*gawk* only).
ARGV	Array of command line arguments.
CONVFMT	Conversion format for numbers, *%.6g*, by default (*gawk* only).
ENVIRON	An array containing the values of the current environment variables passed in from the shell.
ERRNO	Contains a string describing a system error occurring from redirection when reading from the *getline* function or when using the *close* function (*gawk* only).
FIELDWIDTHS	A white-space separated list of fieldwidths used instead of FS when splitting records of fixedfield width (*gawk* only).
FILENAME	Name of current input file.

Table 7.2 Built-In Variables (Continued)

Variable Name	*Variable Contents*
FNR	Record number in current file.
FS	The input field separator, by default a space.
IGNORECASE	Turns off case-sensitivity in regular expressions and string operations (*gawk* only).
NF	Number of fields in current record.
NR	Number of records so far.
OFMT	Output format for numbers.
OFS	Output field separator.
ORS	Output record separator.
RLENGTH	Length of string matched by *match* function.
RS	Input record separator.
RSTART	Offset of string matched by *match* function.
RT	The record terminator. *Gawk* sets it to the input text that matched the character or regex specified by *RS*.
SUBSEP	Subscript separator.

EXAMPLE 7.5

```
(The Employees Database)

% cat employees2
   Tom Jones:4423:5/12/66:543354
   Mary Adams:5346:11/4/63:28765
   Sally Chang:1654:7/22/54:650000
   Mary Black:1683:9/23/44:336500

(The Command Line)

% awk  -F:  '{IGNORECASE=1}; \
  $1 == "mary adams"{print NR, $1, $2,$NF}' employees2


(The Output)
   2  Mary Adams 5346  28765
```

EXPLANATION

The *-F* option sets the field separator to a colon. The gawk built-in variable, *IGNORECASE* variable, when set to a nonzero value, turns off *awk*'s case-sensitivity when doing case-sensitive string and regular expression operations. The string *"mary adams"* will be matched, even though in the input file, her name is spelled *"Mary Adams."* The *print* function prints the record number, the first field, the second field, and the last field (*$NF*).

7.1.3 *BEGIN* Patterns

The *BEGIN* pattern is followed by an action block that is executed *before awk* processes any lines from the input file. In fact, a *BEGIN* block can be tested without any input file, because *awk* does not start reading input until the *BEGIN* action block has completed. The *BEGIN* action is often used to change the value of the built-in variables, *OFS, RS, FS,* and so forth, to assign initial values to user-defined variables, and to print headers or titles as part of the output.

EXAMPLE 7.6

```
% awk 'BEGIN{FS=":"; OFS="\t"; ORS="\n\n"}{print $1,$2,$3}' file
```

EXPLANATION

Before the input file is processed, the field separator (*FS*) is set to a colon, the output field separator (*OFS*) to a tab, and the output record separator (*ORS*) to two newlines. If there are two or more statements in the action block, they should be separated with semicolons or placed on separate lines (use a backslash to escape the newline character if at the shell prompt).

EXAMPLE 7.7

```
% awk 'BEGIN{print "MAKE      YEAR"}'
make year
```

EXPLANATION

Awk will display *MAKE YEAR*. The *print* function is executed before *awk* opens the input file, and even though the input file has not been assigned, *awk* will still print *MAKE* and *YEAR*. When debugging *awk* scripts, you can test the *BEGIN* block actions before writing the rest of the program.

7.1.4 *END* Patterns

END patterns do not match any input lines, but execute any actions that are associated with the *END* pattern. *END* patterns are handled *after* all lines of input have been processed.

EXAMPLE 7.8

```
% awk 'END{print "The number of records is " NR }'  filename
The number of records is 4
```

EXPLANATION

The *END* block is executed after *awk* has finished processing the file. The value of *NR* is the number of the last record read.

EXAMPLE 7.9

```
% awk '/Mary/{count++}END{print "Mary was found " count " times."}'
employees2
Mary was found 2 times.
```

EXPLANATION

For every line that contains the pattern *Mary*, the value of the *count* variable is incremented by one. After *awk* has processed the entire file, the *END* block prints the string "*Mary was found,*" the value of *count*, and the string "*times.*"

7.2 Redirection and Pipes

7.2.1 Output Redirection

When redirecting output from within *awk* to a UNIX file, the shell redirection operators are used. The filename must be enclosed in double quotes. When the > symbol is used, the file is opened and truncated. Once the file is opened, it remains opened until explicitly closed or the *awk* program terminates. Output from subsequent *print* statements to that file will be appended to the file.

The >> symbol is used to open the file, but does not clear it out; instead it simply appends to it.

EXAMPLE 7.10

```
% awk '$4 >= 70 {print $1, $2  > "passing_file" }' filename
```

EXPLANATION

If the value of the fourth field is greater than or equal to *70*, the first and second fields will be printed to the file *passing_file*.

7.2.2 Input Redirection (*getline*)

The *getline* Function. The *getline* function is used to read input from the standard input, a pipe, or a file other than from the current file being processed. It gets the next line of input and sets the *NF, NR,* and the *FNR* built-in variables. The *getline* function returns one if a record is found and zero if EOF (end of file) is reached. If there is an error, such as failure to open a file, the *getline* function returns a value of -1.

EXAMPLE 7.11

```
% awk 'BEGIN{ "date" | getline d; print d}' filename
Thu Jan 14 11:24:24 PST 2000
```

EXPLANATION

Will execute the UNIX *date* command, pipe the output to *getline*, assign it to the user-defined variable *d*, and then print *d*.

EXAMPLE 7.12

```
% awk 'BEGIN{ "date " | getline d; split( d, mon) ; print mon[2]}'
filename
Oct
```

EXPLANATION

Will execute the *date* command and pipe the output to *getline.* The *getline* function will read from the pipe and store the input in a user-defined variable, *d*. The *split* function will create an array called *mon* out of variable *d*, and then the second element of the array *mon* will be printed.

EXAMPLE 7.13

```
% awk 'BEGIN{while("ls" | getline) print}'
a.out
db
dbook
getdir
file
sortedf
```

EXPLANATION

Will send the output of the *ls* command to *getline*; for each iteration of the loop, *getline* will read one more line of the output from *ls* and then print it to the screen. An input file is not necessary, because the *BEGIN* block is processed before *awk* attempts to open input.

EXAMPLE 7.14

```
(The Command Line)
1   % awk 'BEGIN{ printf "What is your name?" ;\
        getline name < "/dev/tty"}\
2   $1 ~ name {print "Found " name " on line ", NR "."}\
3   END{print "See ya,  " name "."}' filename

(The Output)
    What is your name?  Ellie < Waits for input from user >
    Found Ellie on line 5.
    See ya, Ellie.
```

EXPLANATION

1. Will print to the screen "*What is your name?*" and wait for user response; the *getline* function will accept input from the terminal (*/dev/tty*) until a newline is entered, and then store the input in the user-defined variable *name*.
2. If the first field matches the value assigned to *name*, the *print* function is executed.
3. The *END* statement prints out "*See ya,*" and then the value *Ellie*, stored in variable *name,* is displayed.

EXAMPLE 7.15

```
(The Command Line)

% awk 'BEGIN{while (getline < "/etc/passwd"  > 0 )lc++; print lc}'
file

(The Output)
16
```

EXPLANATION

Awk will read each line from the */etc/passwd* file, increment *lc* until EOF is reached, and then print the value of *lc,* which is the number of lines in the *passwd* file.

Note: The value returned by *getline* is minus one if the file does not exist. If the end of file is reached, the return value is zero, and if a line was read, the return value is one. Therefore, the command

```
while ( getline < "/etc/junk")
```

would start an infinite loop if the file */etc/junk* did not exist, because the return value of minus one yields a true condition.

7.3 Pipes

If you open a pipe in an *awk* program, you must close it before opening another one. The command on the right-hand side of the pipe symbol is enclosed in double quotes. Only one pipe can be opened at a time.

EXAMPLE 7.16

```
(The Database)
% cat names
john smith
alice cheba
george goldberg
susan goldberg
tony tram
barbara nguyen
elizabeth lone
dan savage
eliza goldberg
john goldenrod
```

EXAMPLE 7.16 (CONTINUED)

```
(The Command Line)
% awk '{print $1, $2 | "sort -r +1 -2 +0 -1 "}' names

(The Output)
tony tram
john smith
dan savage
barbara nguyen
elizabeth lone
john goldenrod
susan goldberg
george goldberg
eliza goldberg
alice cheba
```

EXPLANATION

Awk will pipe the output of the *print* statement as input to the UNIX *sort* command, which does a reversed sort using the second field as the primary key and the first field as the secondary key. The UNIX command must be enclosed in double quotes. (See "*sort*" on page 718 in Appendix A.)

7.4 Closing Files and Pipes

If you plan to use a file or pipe in an *awk* program again for reading or writing, you may want to close it first, because it remains open until the script ends. Once opened, the pipe remains opened until *awk* exits. Therefore, statements in the *END* block will also be affected by the pipe. The first line in the *END* block closes the pipe.

EXAMPLE 7.17

```
(In Script)
1   { print $1, $2, $3 | " sort -r +1 -2 +0 -1"}
    END{
2   close("sort -r +1 -2 +0 -1")
     <rest of statements>  }
```

EXPLANATION

1. *Awk* pipes each line from the input file to the UNIX *sort* utility.
2. When the *END* block is reached, the pipe is closed. The string enclosed in double quotes must be identical to the pipe string where the pipe was initially opened.

The *system* Function. The built-in *system* function takes a Linux (operating system command) command as its argument, executes the command, and returns the exit status to the *awk* program. It is similar to the C standard library function, also called *system()*. The Linux command must be enclosed in double quotes. If the *system* function (*gawk* only) is given an empty string as its argument, the output buffers will be flushed.

FORMAT

```
system( "Linux Command")
```

EXAMPLE 7.18

```
(In Script)
   {
1  system ( "cat  " $1 )
2  system ( "clear" )
   }
```

EXPLANATION

1. The *system* function takes the UNIX *cat* command and the value of the first field in the input file as its arguments. The *cat* command takes the value of the first field, a filename, as its argument. The UNIX shell causes the *cat* command to be executed.
2. The *system* function takes the UNIX *clear* command as its argument. The shell executes the command, causing the screen to be cleared.

The *fflush* Function. The *fflush* function was added to *awk* in 1994 (Bell Labs) and is not included in the POSIX standard. *Gawk* uses it to flush output buffers. If *fflush* is not given an argument, it flushes the buffer for standard output. If the null string is given as an argument, e.g., *fflush(" ")*, the buffers for all open files and pipes are flushed.

7.5 Review

7.5.1 Increment and Decrement Operators

```
% cat datafile
northwest    NW   Joel Craig      3.0   .98   3    4
western      WE   Sharon Kelly    5.3   .97   5   23
southwest    SW   Chris Foster    2.7   .8    2   18
southern     SO   May Chin        5.1   .95   4   15
southeast    SE   Derek Johnson   4.0   .7    4   17
```

```
eastern      EA   Susan Beal      4.4  .84  5  20
northeast    NE   TJ Nichols      5.1  .94  3  13
north        NO   Val Shultz      4.5  .89  5   9
central      CT   Sheri Watson    5.7  .94  5  13
```

EXAMPLE 7.19

```
% awk '/^north/{count += 1; print count}' datafile
1
2
3
```

```
% cat datafile
northwest    NW   Joel Craig      3.0  .98  3   4
western      WE   Sharon Kelly    5.3  .97  5  23
southwest    SW   Chris Foster    2.7  .8   2  18
southern     SO   May Chin        5.1  .95  4  15
southeast    SE   Derek Johnson   4.0  .7   4  17
eastern      EA   Susan Beal      4.4  .84  5  20
northeast    NE   TJ Nichols      5.1  .94  3  13
north        NO   Val Shultz      4.5  .89  5   9
central      CT   Sheri Watson    5.7  .94  5  13
```

EXPLANATION

If the record begins with the regular expression *north*, a user-defined variable, *count*, is created; *count* is incremented by 1 and its value is printed.

EXAMPLE 7.20

```
% awk '/^north/{count++; print count}' datafile
1
2
3
```

EXPLANATION

The auto-increment operator increments the user-defined variable *count* by 1. The value of *count* is printed.

EXAMPLE 7.21

```
% awk '{x = $7--; print "x = "x ", $7 = "$7}' datafile
x = 3, $7 = 2
x = 5, $7 = 4
x = 2, $7 = 1
x = 4, $7 = 3
x = 4, $7 = 3
x = 5, $7 = 4
x = 3, $7 = 2
x = 5, $7 = 4
x = 5, $7 = 4
```

EXPLANATION

After the value of the seventh field (*$7*) is assigned to the user-defined variable *x*, the auto-decrement operator decrements the seventh field by one. The value of *x* and the seventh field are printed.

7.5.2 Built-In Variables

EXAMPLE 7.22

```
% awk '/^north/{print "The record number is " NR}' datafile
The record number is 1
The record number is 7
The record number is 8
```

EXPLANATION

If the record begins with the regular expression *north*, the string "*The record is*" and the value of *NR* (record number) are printed.

EXAMPLE 7.23

```
% awk '{print NR, $0}' datafile
1 northwest     NW     Joel Craig       3.0   .98   3    4
2 western       WE     Sharon Kelly     5.3   .97   5   23
3 southwest     SW     Chris Foster     2.7   .8    2   18
4 southern      SO     May Chin         5.1   .95   4   15
5 southeast     SE     Derek Johnson    4.0   .7    4   17
6 eastern       EA     Susan Beal       4.4   .84   5   20
7 northeast     NE     TJ Nichols       5.1   .94   3   13
8 north         NO     Val Shultz       4.5   .89   5    9
9 central       CT     Sheri Watson     5.7   .94   5   13
```

EXPLANATION

The value of *NR*, the number of the current record, and the value of *$0*, the entire record, are printed.

EXAMPLE 7.24

```
% awk 'NR==2,NR==5{print NR, $0}' datafile
2 western       WE      Sharon Kelly      5.3   97    5    23
3 southwest     SW      Chris Foster      2.7    8    2    18
4 southern      SO      May Chin          5.1   95    4    15
5 southeast     SE      Derek Johnson     4.0    7    4    17
```

EXPLANATION

If the value of *NR* is in the *range* between 2 and 5 (record numbers 2–5), the number of the record (*NR*) and the record (*$0*) are printed.

```
% cat datafile
northwest    NW    Joel Craig       3.0    .98    3     4
western      WE    Sharon Kelly     5.3    .97    5    23
southwest    SW    Chris Foster     2.7    .8     2    18
southern     SO    May Chin         5.1    .95    4    15
southeast    SE    Derek Johnson    4.0    .7     4    17
eastern      EA    Susan Beal       4.4    .84    5    20
northeast    NE    TJ Nichols       5.1    .94    3    13
north        NO    Val Shultz       4.5    .89    5     9
central      CT    Sheri Watson     5.7    .94    5    13
```

EXAMPLE 7.25

```
% awk '/^north/{print NR, $1, $2, $NF, RS}' datafile
1 northwest NW 4

7 northeast NE 13

8 north NO 9
```

EXPLANATION

If the record begins with the regular expression *north*, the number of the record (*NR*), followed by the first field, the second field, the value of the last record (*NF* preceded by a dollar sign), and the value of *RS* (a newline) are printed. Because the *print* function generates a newline by default, *RS* will generate another newline, resulting in double spacing between records.

```
% cat datafile2
Joel Craig:northwest:NW:3.0:.98:3:4
Sharon Kelly:western:WE:5.3:.97:5:23
Chris Foster:southwest:SW:2.7:.8:2:18
May Chin:southern:SO:5.1:.95:4:15
Derek Johnson:southeast:SE:4.0:.7:4:17
Susan Beal:eastern:EA:4.4:.84:5:20
TJ Nichols:northeast:NE:5.1:.94:3:13
Val Shultz:north:NO:4.5:.89:5:9
Sheri Watson:central:CT:5.7:.94:5:131.
```

EXAMPLE 7.26

```
% awk -F: 'NR == 5{print NF}' datafile2
7
```

EXPLANATION

The field separator is set to a colon at the command line with the *-F* option. If the number of the record (*NR*) is *5*, the number of fields (*NF*) is printed.

EXAMPLE 7.27

```
% awk 'BEGIN{OFMT="%.2f";print 1.2456789,12E-2}' datafile2
1.25 0.12
```

EXPLANATION

The *OFMT*, output format variable for the *print* function, is set so that floating point numbers will be printed with a decimal-point precision of two digits. The numbers *1.23456789* and *12E-2* are printed in the new format.

```
% cat datafile
northwest     NW    Joel Craig        3.0    .98    3    4
western       WE    Sharon Kelly      5.3    .97    5    23
southwest     SW    Chris Foster      2.7    .8     2    18
southern      SO    May Chin          5.1    .95    4    15
southeast     SE    Derek Johnson     4.0    .7     4    17
eastern       EA    Susan Beal        4.4    .84    5    20
northeast     NE    TJ Nichols        5.1    .94    3    13
north         NO    Val Shultz        4.5    .89    5    9
central       CT    Sheri Watson      5.7    .94    5    13
```

EXAMPLE 7.28

```
% awk '{$9 = $6 * $7; print $9}' datafile
2.94
4.85
1.6
3.8
2.8
4.2
2.82
4.45
4.7
```

EXPLANATION

The result of multiplying the sixth field (*$6*) and the seventh field (*$7*) is stored in a new field, *$9*, and printed. There were eight fields; now there are nine.

EXAMPLE 7.29

```
% awk '{$10 = 100; print NF, $9, $0}' datafile
10  northwest NW    Joel Craig    3.0    .98    3    4     100
10  western   WE    Sharon Kelly  5.3    .97    5    23    100
10  southwest SW    Chris Foster  2.7    .8     2    18    100
10  southern  SO    May Chin      5.1    .95    4    15    100
10  southeast SE    Derek Johnson 4.0    .7     4    17    100
10  eastern   EA    Susan Beal    4.4    .84    5    20    100
10  northeast NE    TJ Nichols    5.1    .94    3    13    100
10  north     NO    Val Shultz    4.5    .89    5    9     100
10  central   CT    Sheri Watson  5.7    .94    5    13    100
```

EXPLANATION

The tenth field (*$10*) is assigned *100* for each record. This is a new field. The ninth field (*$9*) does not exist, so it will be considered a null field. The number of fields is printed (*NF*), followed by the value of *$9*, the null field, and the entire record (*$0*). The value of the tenth field is *100*.

EXAMPLE 7.30

```
% awk 'NR==1{print ENVIRON["USER"], ENVIRON["HOME"]}' datafile
ellie  /home/ellie
```

EXPLANATION

If *NR* is 1, i.e. the first record, *awk* prints the values of two of its environment variables, *USER* and *HOME*. The environment variables are passed into *awk* from the parent process, normally a shell, and are stored in a special associative array called *ENVIRON*.

7.5.3 *BEGIN* Patterns

EXAMPLE 7.31

```
% awk 'BEGIN{print "---------EMPLOYEES---------"}'
---------EMPLOYEES---------
```

EXPLANATION

The *BEGIN* pattern is followed by an action block. The action is to print out the string "---------*EMPLOYEES*---------" before opening the input file. Note that an input file has not been provided and *awk* does not complain.

EXAMPLE 7.32

```
% awk 'BEGIN{print "\t\t---------EMPLOYEES-------\n"}\
 {print $0}' datafile
                ---------EMPLOYEES-------
northwest       NW       Joel Craig       3.0   .98   3    4
western         WE       Sharon Kelly     5.3   .97   5   23
southwest       SW       Chris Foster     2.7   .8    2   18
southern        SO       May Chin         5.1   .95   4   15
southeast       SE       Derek Johnson    4.0   .7    4   17
eastern         EA       Susan Beal       4.4   .84   5   20
northeast       NE       TJ Nichols       5.1   .94   3   13
north           NO       Val Shultz       4.5   .89   5    9
central         CT       Sheri Watson     5.7   .94   5   13
```

EXPLANATION

The *BEGIN* action block is executed first. The title "---------*EMPLOYEES*-------" is printed. The second action block prints each record in the input file. When breaking lines, the backslash is used to suppress the carriage return. Lines can be broken at a semicolon or a curly brace.

```
% cat datafile2
Joel Craig:northwest:NW:3.0:.98:3:4
Sharon Kelly:western:WE:5.3:.97:5:23
Chris Foster:southwest:SW:2.7:.8:2:18
May Chin:southern:SO:5.1:.95:4:15
Derek Johnson:southeast:SE:4.0:.7:4:17
Susan Beal:eastern:EA:4.4:.84:5:20
TJ Nichols:northeast:NE:5.1:.94:3:13
Val Shultz:north:NO:4.5:.89:5:9
Sheri Watson:central:CT:5.7:.94:5:131.
```

EXAMPLE 7.33

```
% awk 'BEGIN{ FS=":";OFS="\t"};/^Sharon/{print $1, $2, $7 }'
datafile2
Sharon Kelly       western      23
```

EXPLANATION

The *BEGIN* action block is used to initialize variables. The *FS* variable (field separator) is assigned a colon. The *OFS* variable (output field separator) is assigned a tab (*\t*). If a record begins with the regular expression *Sharon*, the first, second, and eighth fields (*$1*, *$2*, *$8*) are printed. Each field in the output is separated by a tab.

7.5.4 *END* Patterns

```
% cat datafile
northwest    NW    Joel Craig       3.0    .98    3     4
western      WE    Sharon Kelly     5.3    .97    5    23
southwest    SW    Chris Foster     2.7    .8     2    18
southern     SO    May Chin         5.1    .95    4    15
southeast    SE    Derek Johnson    4.0    .7     4    17
eastern      EA    Susan Beal       4.4    .84    5    20
northeast    NE    TJ Nichols       5.1    .94    3    13
north        NO    Val Shultz       4.5    .89    5     9
central      CT    Sheri Watson     5.7    .94    5    13
```

EXAMPLE 7.34

```
% awk 'END{print "The total number of records is " NR}' datafile
The total number of records is 9
```

EXPLANATION

After *awk* has finished processing the input file, the statements in the *END* block are executed. The string "*The total number of records is*" is printed, followed by the value of *NR*, the number of the last record.

EXAMPLE 7.35

```
% awk '/^north/{count++}END{print count}' datafile
3
```

EXPLANATION

If the record begins with the regular expression *north*, the user-defined variable *count* is incremented by one. When *awk* has finished processing the input file, the value stored in the variable *count* is printed.

7.5.5 *awk* Script with *BEGIN* and *END*

EXAMPLE 7.36

```
% cat awk.sc2
    # Second awk script-- awk.sc2
1   BEGIN{ FS=":"; OFS="\t"
        print "  NAME\t\tDISTRICT\tQUANTITY"
        print "___________________________________________________\n"
    }

2       {print $1"\t  " $3"\t\t" $7}
        {total+=$7}
        /north/{count++}

3   END{
        print "---------------------------------------------"
        print "The total quantity is " total
        print "The number of northern salespersons is " count "."
    }
```

```
% cat datafile2
Joel Craig:northwest:NW:3.0:.98:3:4
Sharon Kelly:western:WE:5.3:.97:5:23
Chris Foster:southwest:SW:2.7:.8:2:18
May Chin:southern:SO:5.1:.95:4:15
Derek Johnson:southeast:SE:4.0:.7:4:17
Susan Beal:eastern:EA:4.4:.84:5:20
TJ Nichols:northeast:NE:5.1:.94:3:13
Val Shultz:north:NO:4.5:.89:5:9
Sheri Watson:central:CT:5.7:.94:5:131.
```

EXAMPLE 7.36 (CONTINUED)

```
(The Output)
% awk -f awk.sc2 datafile2
    NAME         DISTRICT QUANTITY
  ____________________________________________
  Joel Craig     NW        4
  Sharon Kelly   WE        23
  Chris Foster   SW        18
  May Chin       SO        15
  Derek Johnson  SE        17
  Susan Beal     EA        20
  TJ Nichols     NE        13
  Val Shultz     NO        9
  Sheri Watson   CT        13
  ----------------------------------------------
  The total quantity is 132
  The number of northern salespersons is 3.
```

EXPLANATION

1 The *BEGIN* block is executed first. The field separator (*FS*) and the output field separator (*OFS*) are set. Header output is printed.

2 The body of the *awk* script contains statements that are executed for each line of input coming from *data.file2*.

3 Statements in the *END* block are executed after the input file has been closed, i.e., before *awk* exits.

4 At the command line, the *awk* program is executed. The *-f* option is followed by the script name, *awk.sc2*, and then by the input file, data.file2.

7.5.6 The *printf* Function

EXAMPLE 7.37

```
% awk '{printf "$%6.2f\n",$6 * 100}' datafile
$ 98.00
$ 97.00
$ 80.00
$ 95.00
$ 70.00
$ 84.00
$ 94.00
$ 89.00
$ 94.00
```

EXPLANATION

The *printf* function formats a floating point number to be right-justified (the default) with a total of *6* digits, one for the decimal point, and two for the decimal numbers to the right of the period. The number will be rounded up and printed.

EXAMPLE 7.38

```
% awk '{printf "|%-15s|\n",$4}' datafile
|Craig          |
|Kelly          |
|Foster         |
|Chin           |
|Johnson        |
|Beal           |
|Nichols        |
|Shultz         |
|Watson         |
```

EXPLANATION

A left-justified, *15*-space string is printed. The fourth field (*$4*) is printed enclosed in vertical bars to illustrate the spacing.

```
% cat datafile
northwest     NW    Joel Craig        3.0    .98    3     4
western       WE    Sharon Kelly      5.3    .97    5    23
southwest     SW    Chris Foster      2.7    .8     2    18
southern      SO    May Chin          5.1    .95    4    15
southeast     SE    Derek Johnson     4.0    .7     4    17
eastern       EA    Susan Beal        4.4    .84    5    20
northeast     NE    TJ Nichols        5.1    .94    3    13
north         NO    Val Shultz        4.5    .89    5     9
central       CT    Sheri Watson      5.7    .94    5    13
```

7.5.7 Redirection and Pipes

EXAMPLE 7.39

```
% awk '/north/{print $1, $3, $4 > "districts"}' datafile
% cat districts
northwest Joel Craig
northeast TJ Nichols
north Val Shultz
```

EXPLANATION

If the record contains the regular expression *north*, the first, third, and fourth fields (*$1*, *$3*, *$4*) are printed to an output file called "*districts*". Once the file is opened, it remains opened until closed or the program terminates. The filename "*districts*" must be enclosed in double quotes.

EXAMPLE 7.40

```
% awk '/south/{print $1, $2, $3 >> "districts"}' datafile
% cat districts
northwest Joel Craig
northeast TJ Nichols
north Val Shultz
southwest SW Chris
southern SO May
southeast SE Derek
```

EXPLANATION

If the record contains the pattern *south*, the first, second, and third fields (*$1*, *$2*, *$3*) are appended to the output file "*districts*".

7.5.8 Opening and Closing a Pipe

EXAMPLE 7.41

```
% cat awk.sc3
# awk script using pipes -- awk.sc3
1   BEGIN{
2       printf "  %-22s%s\n", "NAME", "DISTRICT"
        print "--------------------------------------"

3   }
```

EXAMPLE 7.41 (CONTINUED)

```
4   /west/{count++}
5   {printf "%s %s\t\t%-15s\n", $3, $4, $1| "sort +1" }

6   END{
7       close "sort +1"
        printf "The number of sales persons in the western "
                printf "region is " count ".\n"}
```

```
(The Output)
   %awk -f awk.sc3 datafile
1   NAME          DISTRICT
2   -------------------------------------------------------
3   Susan Beal    eastern
    May Chin      southern
    Joel Craig    northwest
    Chris Foster southwest
    Derek Johnsonsoutheast
    Sharon Kelly western
    TJ Nichols    northeast
    Val Shultz    north
    Sheri Watson central
    The number of sales persons in the western region is 3.
```

EXPLANATION

1. The special *BEGIN* pattern is followed by an action block. The statements in this block are executed first, before *awk* processes the input file.
2. The *printf* function displays the string *NAME* as a 22-character, left-justified string, followed by the string *DISTRICT*, which is right-justified.
3. The *BEGIN* block ends.
4. Now *awk* will process the input file, one line at a time. If the pattern *west* is found, the action block is executed, i.e., the user-defined variable *count* is incremented by one. The first time *awk* encounters the *count* variable, it will be created and given an initial value of zero.
5. The *print* function formats and sends its output to a pipe. After all of the output has been collected, it will be sent to the *sort* command
6. The *END* block is started.
7. The pipe (*sort +1*) must be closed with exactly the same command that opened it; in this example "*sort +1*". Otherwise, the *END* statements will be sorted with the rest of the output.

LINUX TOOLS LAB 5

(File lab5.data)

```
Mike Harrington:(510) 548-1278:250:100:175
Christian Dobbins:(408) 538-2358:155:90:201
Susan Dalsass:(206) 654-6279:250:60:50
Archie McNichol:(206) 548-1348:250:100:175
Jody Savage:(206) 548-1278:15:188:150
Guy Quigley:(916) 343-6410:250:100:175
Dan Savage:(406) 298-7744:450:300:275
Nancy McNeil:(206) 548-1278:250:80:75
John Goldenrod:(916) 348-4278:250:100:175
Chet Main:(510) 548-5258:50:95:135
Tom Savage:(408) 926-3456:250:168:200
Elizabeth Stachelin:(916) 440-1763:175:75:300
```

The database above contains the names, phone numbers, and money contributions to the party campaign for the past three months.

Write an *awk* script to produce the following output:

```
% awk -f gawk.sc db
                    ***CAMPAIGN 2000 CONTRIBUTIONS***
-----------------------------------------------------------------------------
NAME                  PHONE            Jan    |   Feb   |    Mar   | Total Donated
-----------------------------------------------------------------------------
Mike Harrington      (510) 548-1278   250.00    100.00    175.00        525.00
Christian Dobbins    (408) 538-2358   155.00     90.00    201.00        446.00
Susan Dalsass        (206) 654-6279   250.00     60.00     50.00        360.00
Archie McNichol      (206) 548-1348   250.00    100.00    175.00        525.00
Jody Savage          (206) 548-1278    15.00    188.00    150.00        353.00
Guy Quigley          (916) 343-6410   250.00    100.00    175.00        525.00
Dan Savage           (406) 298-7744   450.00    300.00    275.00       1025.00
Nancy McNeil         (206) 548-1278   250.00     80.00     75.00        405.00
John Goldenrod       (916) 348-4278   250.00    100.00    175.00        525.00
Chet Main            (510) 548-5258    50.00     95.00    135.00        280.00
Tom Savage           (408) 926-3456   250.00    168.00    200.00        618.00
Elizabeth Stachelin  (916) 440-1763   175.00     75.00    300.00        550.00
-----------------------------------------------------------------------------
                                    SUMMARY
-----------------------------------------------------------------------------
The campaign received a total of $6137.00 for this quarter.
The average donation for the 12 contributors was $511.42.
The highest contribution was $300.00.
The lowest contribution was $15.00.
```

7.6 Conditional Statements

The conditional statements in *awk* were borrowed from the C language. They are used to control the flow of the program in making decisions.

7.6.1 *if* Statements

Statements beginning with the *if* construct are action statements. With *conditional patterns*, the *if* is implied; with a conditional *action* statement, the *if* is explicitly stated, and followed by an expression enclosed in parentheses. If the expression evaluates true (nonzero or non-null), the statement or block of statements following the expression is executed. If there is more than one statement following the conditional expression, the statements are separated either by semicolons or a newline, and the group of statements must be enclosed in curly braces so that the statements are executed as a block.

FORMAT

```
if (expression) {
    statement; statement; ...
}
```

EXAMPLE 7.42

```
1   % awk '{if ( $6 > 50 ) print $1 "Too high"}' filename

2   % awk '{if ($6 > 20 && $6  <= 50){safe++; print "OK"}}' filename
```

EXPLANATION

1. In the *if* action block, the expression is tested. If the value of the sixth field is greater than *50*, the *print* statement is executed. Because the statement following the expression is a single statement, curly braces are not required. (*filename* represents the input file.)
2. In the *if* action block, the expression is tested. If the sixth field is greater than *20* AND the sixth field is less than or equal to *50*, the statements following the expression are executed as a block and must be enclosed in curly braces.

7.6.2 *if/else* Statements

The *if/else* statement allows a two-way decision. If the expression after the *if* keyword is true, the block of statements associated with that expression are executed. If the first expression evaluates to false or zero, the block of statements after the *else* keyword is executed. If multiple statements are to be included with the *if* or *else*, they must be blocked with curly braces.

FORMAT

```
{if (expression) {
    statement; statement; ...
        }
else{
    statement; statement; ...
    }
}
```

EXAMPLE 7.43

```
1   % awk '{if( $6 > 50) print  $1 " Too high" ;\
       else print "Range  is OK"}' filename
2   % awk '{if ( $6 > 50 ) { count++; print $3 } \
       else { x+5; print $
    }' filename
```

EXPLANATION

1 If the first expression is true, that is, the sixth field (*$6*) is greater than *50*, the *print* function prints the first field and "*Too high*"; otherwise, the statement after the *else*, "*Range is OK*," is printed.

2 If the first expression is true, that is, the sixth field (*$6*) is greater than *50*, the block of statements is executed; otherwise, the block of statements after the *else* is executed. Note that the blocks are enclosed in curly braces.

7.6.3 *if/else else if* Statements

The *if/else else if* allows a multiway decision. If the expression following the keyword *if* is true, the block of statements associated with that expression is executed and control starts again after the last closing curly brace associated with the final *else*. Otherwise, control goes to the *else if* and that expression is tested. When the first *else if* condition is true, the statements following the expression are executed. If none of the conditional expressions test true, control goes to the *else* statements. The *else* is called the default action because if none of the other statements are true, the *else* block is executed.

FORMAT

```
{if ( expression ) {
    statement; statement; ...
{
else if (expression){
    statement; statement; ...
}
else if (expression){
    statement; statement; ...
}
else{
    statement
}
}
```

EXAMPLE 7.44

```
(In the Script)
1    {if ( $3 > 89 && $3 < 101 ) Agrade++
2    else if ( $3 > 79 ) Bgrade++
3    else if ( $3 > 69 ) Cgrade++
4    else if ( $3 > 59 ) Dgrade++
5    else Fgrade++
     }
     END{print "The number of failures is" Fgrade }
```

EXPLANATION

1 The *if* statement is an action and must be enclosed in curly braces. The expression is evaluated from left to right. If the first expression is false, the whole expression is false; if the first expression is true, the expression after the logical AND (*&&*) is evaluated. If it is true, the variable *Agrade* is incremented by one.

2 If the first expression following the *if* keyword evaluates to false (0), the *else if* expression is tested. If it evaluates to true, the statement following the expression is executed; that is, if the third field (*$3*) is greater than *79*, *Bgrade* is incremented by one.

3 If the first two statements are false, the *else if* expression is tested, and if the third field (*$3*) is greater than *69*, *Cgrade* is incremented.

4 If the first three statements are false, the *else if* expression is tested, and if the third field is greater than *59*, *Dgrade* is incremented.

5 If none of the expressions tested above is true, the *else* block is executed. The curly brace ends the action block. *Fgrade* is incremented.

7.7 Loops

Loops are used to repeatedly execute the statements following the test expression if a condition is true. Loops are often used to iterate through the fields within a record and to loop through the elements of an array in the *END* block. *Awk* has three types of loops: the *while* loop, the *for* loop, and the *special for* loop, which will be discussed later when working with *awk* arrays.

7.7.1 *while* Loop

The first step in using a *while* loop is to set a variable to an initial value. The value is then tested in the *while* expression. If the expression evaluates to true (nonzero), the body of the loop is entered and the statements within that body are executed. If there is more than one statement within the body of the loop, those statements must be enclosed in curly braces. Before ending the loop block, the variable controlling the loop expression must be updated or the loop will continue forever. In the following example, the variable is reinitialized each time a new record is processed.

The *do/while* loop is similar to the *while* loop, except that the expression is not tested until the body of the loop is executed at least once.

EXAMPLE 7.45

```
% awk '{ i=1; while ( i <= NF ) { print NF, $i ; i++ } }'  filename
```

EXPLANATION

The variable *i* is initialized to one; while *i* is less than or equal to the number of fields (*NF*) in the record, the *print* statement will be executed, then *i* will be incremented by one. The expression will then be tested again, until the variable *i* is greater than the value of *NF*. The variable *i* is not reinitialized until *awk* starts processing the next record.

7.7.2 *for* Loop

The *for* loop and *while* loop are essentially the same, except the *for* loop requires three expressions within the parentheses: the initialization expression, the test expression, and the expression to update the variables within the test expression. In *awk*, the first statement within the parentheses of the *for* loop can perform only one initialization. (In C, you can have multiple initializations separated by commas.)

EXAMPLE 7.46

```
% awk '{ for( i = 1; i <= NF; i++) print NF,$i }' filex
```

EXPLANATION

The variable *i* is initialized to one and tested to see whether it is less than or equal to the number of fields (*NF*) in the record. If so, the *print* function prints the value of *NF* and the value of *$i* (the *$* preceding the *i* is the number of the *i*th field), then *i* is incremented by one. (Frequently the *for* loop is used with arrays in an *END* action to loop through the elements of an array.) See "Arrays" on page 213.

7.7.3 Loop Control

***break* and *continue* Statements.** The *break* statement lets you break out of a loop if a certain condition is true. The *continue* statement causes the loop to skip any statements that follow if a certain condition is true, and returns control to the top of the loop, starting at the next iteration.

EXAMPLE 7.47

```
  (In the Script)
      {for ( x = 3; x <= NF; x++ )
1          if ( $x < 0 ){ print "Bottomed out!"; break}
           # breaks out of for loop
      }

      {for ( x = 3; x <= NF; x++ )
2         if ( $x == 0 ) { print "Get next item"; continue}
          # starts next iteration of  the for loop
      }
```

EXPLANATION

1. If the value of the field *$x* is less than zero, the *break* statement causes control to go to the statement after the closing curly brace of the loop body; i.e., breaks out of the loop.
2. If the value of the field *$x* is equal to zero, the *continue* statement causes control to start at the top of the loop and start execution, in the third expression at the *for* loop at *x++*.

7.8 Program Control Statements

7.8.1 *next* Statement

The *next* statement gets the next line of input from the input file, restarting execution at the top of the *awk* script.

EXAMPLE 7.48

```
(In Script)
{ if ($1 ~ /Peter/){next}
   else {print}
}
```

EXPLANATION

If the first field contains *Peter*, *awk* skips over this line and gets the next line from the input file. The script resumes execution at the beginning.

7.8.2 *exit* Statement

The *exit* statement is used to terminate the *awk* program. It stops processing records, but does not skip over an *END* statement. If the *exit* statement is given a value between 0 and 255 as an argument (exit 1), this value can be printed at the command line to indicate success or failure by typing:

EXAMPLE 7.49

```
(In Script)
   {exit(1) }

(The Command Line)
% echo $status  (csh, tcsh)
   1

$ echo $? (bash, sh, ksh, tcsh)
   1
```

EXPLANATION

An exit status of zero indicates success, and an exit value of nonzero indicates failure (a convention in UNIX/Linux). It is up to the programmer to provide the exit status in a program. The exit value returned in this example is 1.

7.9 Arrays

Arrays in *awk* are called *associative arrays* because the subscripts can be either numbers or strings. The subscript is often called the key and is associated with the value assigned to the corresponding array element. The keys and values are stored internally in a table where a hashing algorithm is applied to the value of the key in question. Due to the techniques used for hashing, the array elements are not stored in a sequential order, and when the contents of the array are displayed, they may not be in the order you expected.

An array, like a variable, is created by using it, and *awk* can infer whether or not it is used to store numbers or strings. Array elements are initialized with numeric value zero and string value null, depending on the context. You do not have to declare the size of an *awk* array. *Awk* arrays are used to collect information from records and may be used for accumulating totals, counting words, tracking the number of times a pattern occurred, and so forth.

7.9.1 Subscripts for Associative Arrays

Using Variables as Array Indexes. A variable can be used as an index value in an array subscript. The value of the variable can be a number or a string.

EXAMPLE 7.50

```
(The Input File)
% cat employees
   Tom Jones      4424      5/12/66             543354
   Mary Adams     5346      11/4/63             28765
   Sally Chang    1654      7/22/54             650000
   Billy Black    1683      9/23/44             336500

(The Command Line)
1   % awk '{name[x++]=$2};END{for(i=0; i<NR; i++)\
    print i, name[i]}' employees
    0 Jones
    1 Adams
    2 Chang
    3 Black

2   % awk '{id[NR]=$3};END{for(x = 1; x <= NR; x++)\
    print id[x]}'  employees
    4424
    5346
    1654
    1683
```

EXPLANATION

1 The subscript in array *name* is a user-defined variable, *x*. The ++ indicates a numeric context. *Awk* initializes *x* to zero and increments *x* by one *after* (post-increment operator) it is used. The value of the second field is assigned to each element of the *name* array. In the *END* block, the *for* loop is used to loop through the array, printing the value that was stored there, starting at subscript zero. Because the subscript is just a key, it does not have to start at zero. It can start at any value, either a number or a string.

2 The *awk* variable *NR* contains the number of the current record. By using *NR* as a subscript, the value of the third field is assigned to each element of the array for each record. At the end, the *for* loop will loop through the array, printing out the values that were stored there.

The *special for* Loop. The *special for* loop is used to read through an associative array in cases where the *for* loop is not practical; that is, when strings are used as subscripts or the subscripts are not consecutive numbers. The *special for* loop uses the subscript as a key into the value associated with it.

FORMAT

```
{for(item in arrayname){
        print arrayname[item]
    }
}
```

EXAMPLE 7.51

```
(The Input File)
% cat db
    Tom Jones
    Mary Adams
    Sally Chang
    Billy Black
    Tom Savage
    Tom Chung
    Reggie Steel
    Tommy Tucker

(The Command Line, For Loop)
1   % awk '/^Tom/{name[NR]=$1};\
    END{for( i = 1; i <= NR; i++ )print name[i]}' db
    Tom



    Tom
```

EXAMPLE 7.51 (CONTINUED)

```
     Tom

     Tommy

(The Command Line, Special For Loop)
2    % awk '/^Tom/{name[NR]=$1};\
     END{for(i in name){print name[i]}}' db
     Tom
     Tommy
     Tom
     Tom
```

EXPLANATION

1 If the regular expression *Tom* is matched against an input line, the *name* array is assigned a value. Because the subscript used is *NR*, the number of the current record, the subscripts in the array will not be in numeric order. Therefore, when printing the array with the traditional *for* loop, there will be null values printed where an array element has no value.

2 The *special for* loop iterates through the array, printing only values where there was a subscript associated with that value. The order of the printout is random due to the way the associative arrays are stored (hashed).

Using Strings as Array Subscripts. A subscript may consist of a variable containing a string or literal string. If the string is a literal, it must be enclosed in double quotes.

EXAMPLE 7.52

```
(The Input File)
% cat datafile3
tom
mary
sean
tom
mary
mary
bob
mary
alex
```

EXAMPLE 7.52 (CONTINUED)

```
(The Script)
    # awk.sc script
1   /tom/ { count["tom"]++ }
2   /mary/ { count["mary"]++ }
3   END{print "There are " count["tom"] "Toms in the file and "\
     count["mary"]" Marys in the file."}

(The Command Line)
  % awk -f awk.sc datafile3
    There are 2 Toms in the file and 4 Marys in the file.
```

EXPLANATION

1 An array called *count* consists of two elements, *count["tom"]* and *count["mary"]*. The initial value of each of the array elements is zero. Every time *tom* is matched, the value of the array is incremented by one.

2 The same procedure applies to *count["mary"]*. Note: Only one *tom* is recorded for each line, even if there are multiple occurrences on the line.

3 The *END* pattern prints the value stored in each of the array elements.

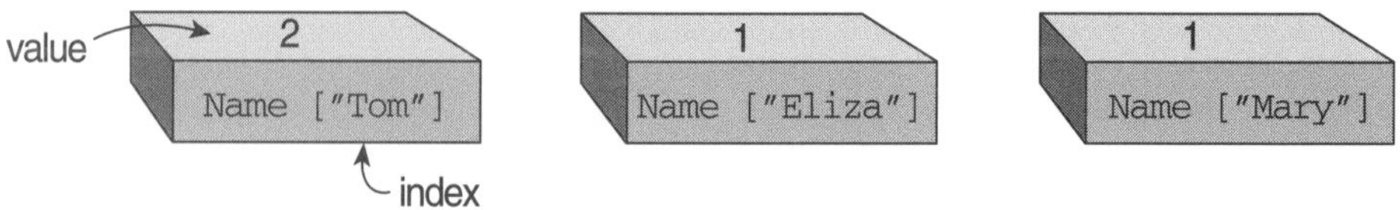

Figure 7.1 Using strings as subscripts in an array. (See Example 7.52.)

Using Field Values as Array Subscripts. Any expression can be used as a subscript in an array. Therefore, fields can be used. The program in Example 7.52 counts the frequency of all names appearing in the second field and introduces a new form of the *for* loop.

```
for( index_value in array ) statement
```

The *for* loop found in the *END* block of the previous example works as follows: the variable *name* is set to the index value of the *count* array. After each iteration of the *for* loop, the *print* action is performed, first printing the *value of the index*, and then the *value stored* in that element. (The order of the printout is not guaranteed.)

EXAMPLE 7.53

```
(The Input File)
% cat datafile4
    4234  Tom     43
    4567  Arch    45
    2008  Eliza   65
    4571  Tom     22
    3298  Eliza   21
    4622  Tom     53
    2345  Mary    24

(The Command Line)
% awk '{count[$2]++}END{for(name in count)print name,count[name] }'
datafile4
Tom 3
Arch 1
Eliza 2
Mary 1
```

EXPLANATION

The *awk* statement first will use the second field as an index in the *count* array. The index varies as the second field varies, thus the first index in the *count* array is *Tom* and the value stored in *count["Tom"]* is one.

Next, *count ["Arch"]* is set to one, *count["Eliza"]* to one, and *count["Mary"]* to one. When *awk* finds the next occurrence of *Tom* in the second field, *count["Tom"]* is incremented, now containing the value 2. The same thing happens for each occurrence of *Arch, Eliza,* and *Mary.*

EXAMPLE 7.54

```
(The Input File)
% cat datafile4
    4234  Tom     43
    4567  Arch    45
    2008  Eliza   65
    4571  Tom     22
    3298  Eliza   21
    4622  Tom     53
    2345  Mary    24
```

EXAMPLE 7.54 (CONTINUED)

```
(The Command Line)
    % awk  '{dup[$2]++; if (dup[$2] > 1){name[$2]++ }}\
    END{print "The duplicates were";\
    for (i in name){print i, name[i]}}' datafile4

(The Output)
    Tom 2
    Eliza 2
```

EXPLANATION

The subscript for the *dup* array is the value in the second field, that is, the name of a person. The value stored there is initially zero, and it is incremented by one each time a new record is processed. If the name is a duplicate, the value stored for that subscript will go up to two, and so forth. If the value in the *dup* array is greater than one, a new array called *name* also uses the second field as a subscript and keeps track of the number of names greater than one.

Arrays and the *split* Function. *Awk*'s built-in *split* function allows you to split up a string into words and store them in an array. You can define the field separator or use the value currently stored in *FS*.

FORMAT

```
split(string, array, field separator)
split (string, array)
```

EXAMPLE 7.55

```
(The Command Line)
    % awk 'BEGIN{ split( "3/15/2000", date, "/");\
    print "The month is " date[1] \
     "and the year is " date[3] }'  filename

(The Output)
The month is 3 and the year is 2000.
```

EXPLANATION

The string "*3/15/2000*" is stored in the array *date,* using the forward slash as the field separator. Now *date[1]* contains *3*, *date[2]* contains *15*, and *date[3]* contains *2000*. The field separator is specified in the third argument; if not specified, the value of *FS* is used as the separator.

The *delete* Function. The *delete* function removes an array element.

EXAMPLE 7.56

```
% awk '{line[x++]=$2}END{for(x in line) delete(line[x])}' filename
```

EXPLANATION

The value assigned to the array *line* is the value of the second field. After all the records have been processed, the *special for* loop will go through each element of the array, and the *delete* function will in turn remove each element.

Multidimensional Arrays in *awk*. Although *awk* does not officially support multidimensional arrays, a syntax is provided that gives the appearance of a multidimensional array. This is done by concatenating the indices into a string separated by the value of a special built-in variable, *SUBSEP*. The *SUBSEP* variable contains the value *"\034,"* an unprintable character that is so unusual that it is unlikely to be found as an index character. The expression *matrix[2,8]* is really the array *matrix[2 SUBSEP 8],* which evaluates to *matrix["2\0348"].* The index becomes a unique string for an associative array.

EXAMPLE 7.57

```
% cat numbers          (The Input File)
1 2 3 4 5
2 3 4 5 6
6 7 8 9 10

% awk.scnum                (The Script)
1   {nf=NF
2   for(x = 1; x <= NF; x++ ){
3       matrix[NR, x] = $x
        }
    }
4   END { for (x=1; x <= NR; x++ ){
        for (y = 1; y <= nf; y++ )
              printf "%d ", matrix[x,y]
    printf"\n"
        }
    }

% awk -f awk.scnum numbers            (The Output)
    1 2 3 4 5
    2 3 4 5 6
    6 7 8 9 10
```

EXPLANATION

1 The variable *nf* is assigned the value of *NF*, the number of fields. (This program assumes a fixed number of five fields per record.)

2 The *for* loop is entered, storing the number of each field on the line in the variable *x*.

3 The *matrix* array is a two-dimensional array. The two indices, *NR* (number of the current record) and *x*, are assigned the value of each field.

4 In the *END* block, the two *for* loops are used to iterate through the *matrix* array, printing out the values stored there. This example does nothing more than demonstrate that multidimensional arrays can be simulated.

7.9.2 Processing Command Arguments in *awk*

ARGV. Command line arguments are available to *awk* and *gawk* with the built-in array called *ARGV*. These arguments include the command *awk*, but not any of the options passed to *awk*. The index of the *ARGV* array starts at zero.

ARGC. *ARGC* is a built-in variable that contains the number of command line arguments.

EXAMPLE 7.58

```
% cat argvs          (The Script)
# This script is called argvs
BEGIN{
    for ( i=0; i < ARGC; i++ ){
        printf("argv[%d] is %s\n", i, ARGV[i])
        }
    printf("The number of arguments, ARGC=%d\n", ARGC)
}

(The Output)
% awk -f argvs datafile
argv[0] is awk
argv[1] is datafile
The number of arguments, ARGC=2
```

EXPLANATION

In the *for* loop, *i* is set to zero, *i* is tested to see if it is less than the number of command line arguments (*ARGC*), and the *printf* function displays each argument encountered, in turn. When all of the arguments have been processed, the last *printf* statement outputs the number of arguments, *ARGC*. The example demonstrates that *awk* does not count command line options as arguments.

EXAMPLE 7.59

```
(The Command Line)
    % awk -f argvs datafile "Peter Pan" 12
    argv[0] is awk
    argv[1] is datafile
    argv[2] is Peter Pan
    argv[3] is 12
    The number of arguments, ARGC=4
```

EXPLANATION

As in the last example, each of the arguments is printed. The *awk* command is considered the first argument, whereas the *-f* option and script name, *argvs*, are excluded.

EXAMPLE 7.60

```
(The Datafile)
% cat datafile5
    Tom Jones:123:03/14/56
    Peter Pan:456:06/22/58
    Joe Blow:145:12/12/78
    Santa Ana:234:02/03/66
    Ariel Jones:987:11/12/66

(The Script)
% cat arging.sc
    # This script is called arging.sc
1   BEGIN{FS=":"; name=ARGV[2]
2           print "ARGV[2] is " ARGV[2]
    }
    $1  ~ name { print $0 }

(The Command Line)
    % awk -f arging.sc datafile5 "Peter Pan"
    ARGV[2] is Peter Pan
    Peter Pan:456:06/22/58
    awk: arging.sc:5: (FILENAME=datafile5 FNR=6 fatal; cannot
   open file 'Peter Pan' for reading (No such file or directory)
```

EXPLANATION

1. In the *BEGIN* block, the variable *name* is assigned the value of *ARGV[2]*, *Peter Pan*.
2. *Peter Pan* is printed, but then *awk* tries to open *Peter Pan* as an input file after it has processed and closed the *datafile5*. *Awk* treats arguments as input files.

EXAMPLE 7.61

```
(The Script)
% cat arging2.sc
    BEGIN{FS=":"; name=ARGV[2]
        print "ARGV[2] is " ARGV[2]
        delete ARGV[2]
    }
    $1  ~ name { print $0 }

(The Command Line)
    % awk -f arging2.sc datafile5 "Peter Pan"
    ARGV[2] is Peter Pan
    Peter Pan:456:06/22/58
```

EXPLANATION

Awk treats the elements of the *ARGV* array as input files; after an argument is used, it is shifted to the left and the next one is processed, until the *ARGV* array is empty. If the argument is deleted immediately after it is used, it will not be processed as the next input file.

7.10 *awk* Built-In Functions

7.10.1 String Functions

The *sub* and *gsub* Functions. The *sub* function matches the regular expression for the largest and leftmost substring in the record, and then replaces that substring with the substitution string. If a target string is specified, the regular expression is matched for the largest and leftmost substring in the target string, and the substring is replaced with the substitution string. If a target string is not specified, the entire record is used.

FORMAT

```
sub (regular expression, substitution string);
sub (regular expression, substitution string, target string)
```

EXAMPLE 7.62

```
1  % awk '{sub(/Mac/, "MacIntosh");print}' filename
2  % awk '{sub(/Mac/, "MacIntosh", $1); print}' filename
```

EXPLANATION

1 The first time the regular expression *Mac* is matched in the record ($0), it will be replaced with the string "*MacIntosh.*" The replacement is made only on the first occurrence of a match on the line. (See *gsub* for multiple occurrences.)

2 The first time the regular expression *Mac* is matched in the first field of the record, it will be replaced with the string "*MacIntosh.*" The replacement is made only on the first occurrence of a match on the line for the target string. The *gsub* function substitutes a regular expression with a string globally, that is, for every occurrence where the regular expression is matched in each record ($0).

FORMAT

```
gsub(regular expression, substitution string)
gsub(regular expression, substitution string, target string)
```

EXAMPLE 7.63

```
1   % awk '{ gsub(/CA/, "California"); print }' datafile
2   % awk '{ gsub(/[Tt]om/, "Thomas", $1 ); print  }'  filename
```

EXPLANATION

1 Everywhere the regular expression *CA* is found in the record (*$0*), it will be replaced with the string "*California*".

2 Everywhere the regular expression *Tom* or *tom* is found in the first field, it will be replaced with the string "*Thomas*".

The *index* Function. The *index* function returns the first position where a substring is found in a string. Offset starts at position 1.

FORMAT

```
index(string, substring)
```

EXAMPLE 7.64

```
% awk '{ print index("hollow", "low") }' filename
4
```

EXPLANATION

The number returned is the *position* where the substring *low* is found in *hollow,* with the offset starting at one.

The *length* Function. The *length* function returns the number of characters in a string. Without an argument, the *length* function returns the number of characters in a record.

FORMAT

```
length ( string )
length
```

EXAMPLE 7.65

```
% awk '{ print length("hello") }' filename
5
```

EXPLANATION

The *length* function returns the number of characters in the string *hello.*

The *substr* Function. The *substr* function returns the substring of a string starting at a position where the first position is one. If the length of the substring is given, that part of the string is returned. If the specified length exceeds the actual string, the string is returned.

FORMAT

```
substr(string, starting position)
substr(string, starting position, length of string)
```

EXAMPLE 7.66

```
% awk  ' { print substr("Santa Claus", 7, 6 )} '  filename
Claus
```

EXPLANATION

In the string "*Santa Claus*", print the substring starting at position *7* with a length of *6* characters.

The *match* Function. The *match* function returns the index where the regular expression is found in the string, or zero if not found. The *match* function sets the built-in variable *RSTART* to the starting position of the substring within the string, and *RLENGTH* to the number of characters to the end of the substring. These variables can be used with the *substr* function to extract the pattern. (Works only with *awk* and *gawk*.)

FORMAT

```
match(string, regular expression)
```

EXAMPLE 7.67

```
% awk 'END{start=match("Good ole USA", /[A-Z]+$/); print start}'
filename
10
```

EXPLANATION

The regular expression, /[A–Z]+$/, says search for consecutive uppercase letters at the end of the string. The substring "*USA*" is found starting at the tenth character of the string "*Good ole USA.*" If the string cannot be matched, *0* is returned.

EXAMPLE 7.68

```
1 % awk 'END{start=match("Good ole USA", /[A-Z]+$/);\
  print RSTART, RLENGTH}' filename
  10 3
2 % awk 'BEGIN{ line="Good ole USA"}; \
  END{ match( line, /[A-Z]+$/);\
  print substr(line, RSTART,RLENGTH)}' filename
  USA
```

EXPLANATION

1. The *RSTART* variable is set by the *match* function to the starting position of the regular expression matched. The *RLENGTH* variable is set to the length of the substring.
2. The *substr* function is used to find a substring in the variable *line*, and uses the *RSTART* and *RLENGTH* values (set by the *match* function) as the beginning position and length of the substring.

The *toupper* and *tolower* Functions (*gawk* only). The *toupper* function returns a string with all the lowercase characters translated to uppercase, and leaves nonalphabetic characters unchanged. Likewise, the *tolower* function tranlates all uppercase letters to lowercase. Strings must be quoted.

FORMAT

```
toupper (string)
tolower (string)
```

EXAMPLE 7.69

```
% awk 'BEGIN{print toupper("linux"), tolower("BASH 2.0")}'
LINUX bash 2.0
```

The *split* Function. The *split* function splits a string into an array using whatever field separator is designated as the third parameter. If the third parameter is not provided, *awk* will use the current value of *FS*.

FORMAT

```
split (string, array, field separator)
split (string, array)
```

EXAMPLE 7.70

```
% awk 'BEGIN{split("12/25/99",date,"/");print date[2]}' filename
25
```

EXPLANATION

The *split* function splits the string "*12/25/99*" into an array, called *date*, using the forward slash as the separator. The array subscript starts at *1*. The second element of the *date* array is printed.

The *sprintf* Function. The *sprintf* function returns an expression in a specified format. It allows you to apply the format specifications of the *printf* function.

FORMAT

```
variable=sprintf("string with format specifiers ", expr1, expr2, ...
, expr2)
```

EXAMPLE 7.71

```
% awk '{line = sprintf ( "%-15s %6.2f ", $1 , $3 );\
        print line}'  filename
```

EXPLANATION

The first and third fields are formatted according to the *printf* specifications (a left-justified, *15*-space string and a right-justified, *6*-character floating point number). The result is assigned to the user-defined variable *line*. See "The printf Function" on page 202.

7.10.2 Time Functions

Gawk provides two functions for getting the time and formatting time stamps. They are the *systime* and *strftime* functions.

The *systime* function. The *systime* function returns the time of day in non-leap year seconds since January 1, 1970 (called the Epoch).

FORMAT

```
systime()
```

EXAMPLE 7.72

```
% awk 'BEGIN{now=systime(); print now}'
939515282
```

EXPLANATION

The return value of the *systime* function is returned to a user-defined variable, now. The value is the time of day in non-leap year seconds since January 1, 1970.

The *strftime* function. The *strftime* function formats the time using the C library *strftime* function. The format specifications are in the form *%T %D*, etc. (See Table 7.3). The timestamp is in the same form as the return value from *systime*. If the timestamp is omitted, then the current time of day is used as the default.

Table 7.3 Date and Time Format Specifications

Date Format	*Definition*
	Assume the current date and time as:
	Date: Sunday, October 17, 1999 ***Time: 15:26:26 PDT***
%a	Abbreviated weekday name (*Sun*)
%A	Full weekday name (*Sunday*)
%b	Abbreviated month name *(Oct)*
%B	Full month name *(October)*
%c	Date and time for locale *(Sun Oct 17 15:26:46 1999)*
%d	Day of month in decimal (*17*)
%D	Date as *10/17/99*[a]
%e	Day of the month, padded with space if only one digit.
%H	Hour for a 24 hour clock in decimal (*15*)
%I	Hour for a 12 hour clock in decimal (*03*)
%j	Day of the year since January 1 in decimal (*290*)
%m	Month in decimal (*10*)
%M	Minute in decimal (*26*)
%p	AM/PM notation assuming a 12 hour clock (*PM*)
%S	Second as a decimal number *(26*)
%U	Week number of the year (with the first Sunday as the first day of week one) as a decimal number (*42*)
%w	Weekday (Sunday is 0) as a decimal number (0)
%W	The week number of the year (the first Monday as the first day of week one) as a decimal number (*41*)
%x	Date representation for locale (*10/17/99*)
%X	Time representation for locale (*15:26:26*)
%y	Year as two digits in decimal (99)
%Y	Year with century (*1999*)
%Z	Time zone (*PDT*)
%%	A literal percent sign (%)

a. *%D* and *%e* are available only on some versions of *gawk*.

FORMAT

```
systime([format specification][,timestamp])
```

EXAMPLE 7.73

```
% awk 'BEGIN{now=strftime("%D", systime()); print now}'
10/09/99

% awk 'BEGIN{now=strftime("%T"); print now}'
17:58:03

% awk 'BEGIN{now=strftime("%m/%d/%y"); print now}'
10/09/99
```

EXPLANATION

The *strftime* function formats the time and date according to the format instruction provided as an argument. (See Table 7.3.) If *systime* is given as a second argument or no argument is given at all, the current time for this locale is assumed. If a second argument is given, it must be in the same format as the return value from the *systime* function.

7.10.3 Built-In Arithmetic Functions

Table 7.4 lists the built-in arithmetic functions where *x* and *y* are arbitrary expressions.

Table 7.4 Arithmetic Functions

Name	*Value Returned*
atan2(x,y)	Arctangent of *y/x* in the range
cos(x)	Cosine of *x*, with *x* in radians
exp(x)	Exponential function of *x, e*
int(x)	Integer part of *x*; truncated toward 0 when $x > 0$
log(x)	Natural (base *e*) logarithm of *x*
rand( )	Random number *r*, where $0 < r < 1$
sin(x)	Sine of *x*, with *x* in radians
sqrt(x)	Square root of *x*
srand(x)	*x* is a new seed for rand( )[a]

a. From Aho, Wienburger, Kernighan. *The AWK Programming Language*. Addison Wesley, 1988, p. 19.

7.10.4 Integer Function

The *int* function truncates any digits to the right of the decimal point to create a whole number. There is no rounding off.

EXAMPLE 7.74

```
1   % awk  'END{print 31/3}' filename
    10.3333
2   % awk 'END{print int(31/3)}' filename
    10
```

EXPLANATION

1. In the *END* block, the result of the division is to print a floating point number.
2. In the *END* block, the *int* function causes the result of the division to be truncated at the decimal point. A whole number is displayed.

7.10.5 Random Number Generator

The *rand* Function. The *rand* function generates a pseudorandom floating point number greater than or equal to zero and less than one.

EXAMPLE 7.75

```
% awk '{print rand()}'  filename
0.513871
0.175726
0.308634

% awk '{print rand()}'  filename
0.513871
0.175726
0.308634
```

EXPLANATION

Each time the program runs, the same set of numbers is printed. The *srand* function can be used to seed the *rand* function with a new starting value. Otherwise, the same sequence is repeated each time *rand* is called.

The *srand* Function. The *srand* function without an argument uses the time of day to generate the seed for the *rand* function. *Srand(x)* uses *x* as the seed. Normally, *x* should vary during the run of the program.

EXAMPLE 7.76

```
% awk 'BEGIN{srand()};{print rand()}' filename
0.508744
0.639485
0.657277

% awk 'BEGIN{srand()};{print rand()}' filename
0.133518
0.324747
0.691794
```

EXPLANATION

The *srand* function sets a new seed for *rand*. The starting point is the time of day. Each time *rand* is called, a new sequence of numbers is printed.

EXAMPLE 7.77

```
% awk 'BEGIN{srand()};{print 1 + int(rand() * 25)}' filename
6
24
14
```

EXPLANATION

The *srand* function sets a new seed for *rand*. The starting point is the time of day. The *rand* function selects a random number between 0 and 25 and casts it to an integer value.

7.11 User-Defined Functions

A user-defined function can be placed anywhere in the script that a pattern action rule can.

FORMAT

```
function name ( parameter, parameter, parameter, ... ) {
    statements
    return expression
(The return statement and expression are optional )
}
```

Variables are passed by value and are local to the function where they are used. Only copies of the variables are used. Arrays are passed by address or by reference, so array elements can be directly changed within the function. Any variable used within the function that has *not* been passed in the parameter list is considered a global variable; that is, it is visible to the entire *awk* program, and if changed in the function, is changed throughout the program. The only way to provide local variables within a function is to include them in the parameter list. Such parameters are usually placed at the end of the list. If there is not a formal parameter provided in the function call, the parameter is initially set to null. The return statement returns control and possibly a value to the caller.

EXAMPLE 7.78

```
(The Command Line Display of grades File before Sort)
   % cat  grades
   44 55 66 22 77 99
   100 22 77 99 33 66
   55 66 100 99 88 45

(The Script)
% cat sorter.sc
   # Script is called sorter
   # It sorts numbers in ascending order
   function sort ( scores, num_elements, temp, i, j ) {
      # temp,i,and j will be local and private,
      # with an initial value of null.
      for( i = 2; i <= num_elements ; ++i ) {
          for ( j = i; scores [j-1] > scores[j]; --j ){
             temp = scores[j]
             scores[j] = scores[j-1]
             scores[j-1] = temp
          }
      }
   }
   {for ( i = 1; i <= NF; i++)
      grades[i]=$i
   sort(grades, NF)     # Two arguments are passed
   for( j = 1; j <= NF; ++j )
      printf( "%d ", grades[j] )
   printf("\n")
   }

(After the Sort)

   %  awk -f sorter.sc grades
   22 44 55 66 77 99
   22 33 66 77 99 100
   45 55 66 88 99 100
```

EXPLANATION

1 The function called *sort* is defined. The function can be defined anywhere in the script. All variables, except those passed as parameters, are global in scope. If changed in the function, they will be changed throughout the *awk* script. Arrays are passed by reference. Five formal arguments are enclosed within the parentheses. The array *scores* will be passed by reference, so that if any of the elements of the array are modified within the function, the original array will be modified. The variable *num_elements* is a local variable, a copy of the original. The variables *temp, i,* and *j* are local variables in the function.

2 The outer *for* loop will iterate through an array of numbers, as long as there are at least two numbers to compare.

3 The inner *for* loop will compare the current number with the previous number, *scores[j –1]*). If the previous array element is larger than the current one, *temp* will be assigned the value of the current array element, and the current array element will be assigned the value of the previous element.

4 The outer loop block ends.

5 This is the end of the function definition.

6 The first action block of the script starts here. The *for* loop iterates through each field of the current record, creating an array of numbers.

7 The *sort* function is called, passing the array of numbers from the current record and the number of fields in the current record.

8 When the *sort* function has completed, program control starts here. The *for* loop prints the elements in the sorted array.

7.12 Review

```
% cat datafile
northwest    NW   Joel Craig        3.0   .98   3    4
western      WE   Sharon Kelly      5.3   .97   5   23
southwest    SW   Chris Foster      2.7   .8    2   18
southern     SO   May Chin          5.1   .95   4   15
southeast    SE   Derek Johnson     4.0   .7    4   17
eastern      EA   Susan Beal        4.4   .84   5   20
northeast    NE   TJ Nichols        5.1   .94   3   13
north        NO   Val Shultz        4.5   .89   5    9
central      CT   Sheri Watson      5.7   .94   5   13
```

EXAMPLE 7.79

```
% awk '{if ( $8 > 15 ){ print $3 " has a high rating"}\
else print $3 "---NOT A COMPETITOR---"}' datafile

Joel---NOT A COMPETITOR---
Sharon has a high rating
Chris has a high rating
May---NOT A COMPETITOR---
Derek has a high rating
Susan has a high rating
TJ---NOT A COMPETITOR---
Val---NOT A COMPETITOR---
Sheri---NOT A COMPETITOR---
```

EXPLANATION

The *if* statement is an action statement. If there is more than one statement following the expression, it must be enclosed in curly braces. (Curly braces are not required in this example, because there is only one statement following the expression.) The expression reads—*if* the eighth field is greater than *15*, print the third field and the string "*has a high rating*"; *else* print the third field and "*---NOT A COMPETITOR---*".

EXAMPLE 7.80

```
% awk '{i=1; while(i<=NF && NR < 2){print $i; i++}}' datafile
northwest
NW
Joel
Craig
3.0
.98
3
4
```

EXPLANATION

The user-defined variable *i* is assigned *1*. The *while* loop is entered and the expression tested. If the expression evaluates true, the *print* statement is executed; the value of the *i*th field is printed. The value of *i* is printed, next the value is incremented by *1*, and the loop is reentered. The loop expression will become false when the value of *i* is greater than *NF* and the value of *NR* is two or more. The variable *i* will not be reinitialized until the next record is entered.

```
% cat datafile
northwest    NW    Joel Craig        3.0    .98    3    4
western      WE    Sharon Kelly      5.3    .97    5    23
southwest    SW    Chris Foster      2.7    .8     2    18
southern     SO    May Chin          5.1    .95    4    15
southeast    SE    Derek Johnson     4.0    .7     4    17
eastern      EA    Susan Beal        4.4    .84    5    20
northeast    NE    TJ Nichols        5.1    .94    3    13
north        NO    Val Shultz        4.5    .89    5    9
central      CT    Sheri Watson      5.7    .94    5    13
```

EXAMPLE 7.81

```
% awk '{ for( i=3 ; i <= NF && NR == 3 ; i++ ){ print $i }}' datafile
Chris
Foster
2.7
.8
2
18
```

EXPLANATION

This is similar to the *while* loop in functionality. The initialization, test, and loop control statements are all in one expression. The value of *i (i = 3)* is initialized once for the current record. The expression is then tested. If *i* is less than or equal to *NF*, and *NR* is equal to *3*, the *print* block is executed. After the value of the *i*th field is printed, control is returned to the loop expression. The value of *i* is incremented and the test is repeated.

EXAMPLE 7.82

```
(The Command Line)
% cat awk.sc4
# Awk script illustrating arrays
BEGIN{OFS="\t"}
{ list[NR] = $1 }     # The array is called list. The index is the
                      # number of the current record. The value of the
                      # first field is assigned to the array element.
END{ for( n = 1; n <= NR; n++){
            print list[n]} # for loop is used to loop
                           # through the array.
}
```

EXAMPLE 7.82 (CONTINUED)

```
(The Command Line)
% awk -f awk.sc4 datafile
northwest
western
southwest
southern
southeast
eastern
northeast
north
central
```

EXPLANATION

The array, *list*, uses NR as an index value. Each time a line of input is processed, the first field is assigned to the *list* array. In the *END* block, the *for* loop iterates through each element of the array.

EXAMPLE 7.83

```
(The Command Line)
% cat awk.sc5
# Awk script with special for loop
/north/{name[count++]=$3}
END{ print "The number living in a northern district: " count
     print "Their names are: "
     for ( i in name )        # special awk for loop is used to
           print name[i]      # iterate through the array.
}

% awk -f awk.sc5 datafile
The number living in a northern district: 3
Their names are:
Joel
TJ
Val
```

EXPLANATION

Each time the regular expression *north* appears on the line, the *name* array is assigned the value of the third field. The index *count* is incremented each time a new record is processed, thus producing another element in the array. In the *END* block, the *special for* loop is used to iterate through the array.

```
% cat datafile
northwest    NW    Joel Craig        3.0    .98    3    4
western      WE    Sharon Kelly      5.3    .97    5    23
southwest    SW    Chris Foster      2.7    .8     2    18
southern     SO    May Chin          5.1    .95    4    15
southeast    SE    Derek Johnson     4.0    .7     4    17
eastern      EA    Susan Beal        4.4    .84    5    20
northeast    NE    TJ Nichols        5.1    .94    3    13
north        NO    Val Shultz        4.5    .89    5    9
central      CT    Sheri Watson      5.7    .94    5    13
```

EXAMPLE 7.84

```
(The Command Line)
% cat awk.sc6
# Awk and the special for loop
{region[$1]++}  # The index is the first field of each record

END{for(item in region){
        print region[item], item
    }
}

% awk -f awk.sc6 datafile

1 central
1 northwest
1 western
1 southeast
1 north
1 southern
1 northeast
1 southwest
1 eastern

% awk -f awk.sc6 datafile3
4 Mary
2 Tom
1 Alax
1 Bob
1 Sean
```

EXPLANATION

The *region* array uses the first field as an index. The value stored is the number of times each region was found. The *END* block uses the special *awk for* loop to iterate through the array called *region*.

LINUX TOOLS LAB 6

(File lab6.data)

```
Mike Harrington:(510) 548-1278:250:100:175
Christian Dobbins:(408) 538-2358:155:90:201
Susan Dalsass:(206) 654-6279:250:60:50
Archie McNichol:(206) 548-1348:250:100:175
Jody Savage:(206) 548-1278:15:188:150
Guy Quigley:(916) 343-6410:250:100:175
Dan Savage:(406) 298-7744:450:300:275
Nancy McNeil:(206) 548-1278:250:80:75
John Goldenrod:(916) 348-4278:250:100:175
Chet Main:(510) 548-5258:50:95:135
Tom Savage:(408) 926-3456:250:168:200
Elizabeth Stachelin:(916) 440-1763:175:75:300
```

The database above contains the names, phone numbers, and money contributions to the party campaign for the past three months.

Write a *awk* script that will produce the following report:

```
                    ***FIRST QUARTERLY REPORT****
                    ***CAMPAIGN 2000 CONTRIBUTIONS***
-----------------------------------------------------------------------------
  NAME                  PHONE             Jan  |    Feb   |    Mar   | Total Donated
-----------------------------------------------------------------------------
Mike Harrington       (510) 548-1278   250.00    100.00    175.00      525.00
Christian Dobbins     (408) 538-2358   155.00     90.00    201.00      446.00
Susan Dalsass         (206) 654-6279   250.00     60.00     50.00      360.00
Archie McNichol       (206) 548-1348   250.00    100.00    175.00      525.00
Jody Savage           (206) 548-1278    15.00    188.00    150.00      353.00
Guy Quigley           (916) 343-6410   250.00    100.00    175.00      525.00
Dan Savage            (406) 298-7744   450.00    300.00    275.00     1025.00
Nancy McNeil          (206) 548-1278   250.00     80.00     75.00      405.00
John Goldenrod        (916) 348-4278   250.00    100.00    175.00      525.00
Chet Main             (510) 548-5258    50.00     95.00    135.00      280.00
Tom Savage            (408) 926-3456   250.00    168.00    200.00      618.00
Elizabeth Stachelin   (916) 440-1763   175.00     75.00    300.00      550.00
-----------------------------------------------------------------------------
                                   SUMMARY
-----------------------------------------------------------------------------
The campaign received a total of $6137.00 for this quarter.
The average donation for the 12 contributors was $511.42.
The highest total contribution was $1025.00 made by Dan Savage.
                    ***THANKS Dan***
The following people donated over $500 to the campaign.
They are eligible for the quarterly drawing!!
Listed are their names (sorted by last names) and phone numbers:
   John Goldenrod--(916) 348-4278
   Mike Harrington--(510) 548-1278
   Archie McNichol--(206) 548-1348
   Guy Quigley--(916) 343-6410
   Dan Savage--(406) 298-7744
   Tom Savage--(408) 926-3456
   Elizabeth Stachelin--(916) 440-1763
      Thanks to all of you for your continued support!!
```

7.13 Odds and Ends

Some data, read in from tape or from a spreadsheet, may not have obvious field separators, but the data does have fixed-width columns. To preprocess this type of data, the *substr* function is useful. (The files in this section are found on the CD in directory *chap07/OddsAndEnds*.)

7.13.1 Fixed Fields

In the following example, the fields are of a fixed width, but are not separated by a field separator. The *substr* function is used to create fields. For *gawk,* see the "The FIELDWIDTHS Variable" on page 241.

EXAMPLE 7.85

```
% cat fixed
031291ax5633(408)987-0124
021589bg2435(415)866-1345
122490de1237(916)933-1234
010187ax3458(408)264-2546
092491bd9923(415)134-8900
112990bg4567(803)234-1456
070489qr3455(415)899-1426

% awk '{printf substr($0,1,6)" ";printf substr($0,7,6)" ";\
     print substr($0,13,length)}' fixed
031291  ax5633  (408)987-0124
021589  bg2435  (415)866-1345
122490  de1237  (916)933-1234
010187  ax3458  (408)264-2546
092491  bd9923  (415)134-8900
112990  bg4567  (803)234-1456
070489  qr3455  (415)899-1426
```

EXPLANATION

The first field is obtained by getting the substring of the entire record, starting at the first character, offset by *6* places. Next, a space is printed. The second field is obtained by getting the substring of the record, starting at position *7*, offset by *6* places, followed by a space. The last field is obtained by getting the substring of the entire record, starting at position *13* to the position represented by the length of the line. (The length function returns the length of the current line (*$0*) if it does not have an argument.)

Empty Fields. If the data is stored in fixed-width fields, it is possible that some of the fields are empty. In the following example, the *substr* function is used to preserve the fields, whether or not they contain data.

EXAMPLE 7.86

```
1   % cat db
    xxx xxx
    xxx abc xxx
    xxx a   bbb
    xxx     xx

    % cat awkfix
    # Preserving empty fields. Field width is fixed.
    {
2   f[1]=substr($0,1,3)
3   f[2]=substr($0,5,3)
4   f[3]=substr($0,9,3)
5   line=sprintf("%-4s%-4s%-4s\n", f[1],f[2], f[3])
6   print line
    }
    % awk -f awkfix db
    xxx xxx
    xxx abc xxx
    xxx a   bbb
    xxx     xx
```

EXPLANATION

1 The contents of the file *db* are printed. There are empty fields in the file.

2 The first element of the *f* array is assigned the substring of the record, starting at position *1* and offset by *3*.

3 The second element of the *f* array is assigned the substring of the record, starting at position *5* and offset by *3*.

4 The second element of the *f* array is assigned the substring of the record, starting at position *9* and offset by *3*.

5 The elements of the array are assigned to the user-defined variable *line* after being formatted by the *sprintf* function.

6 The value of *line* is printed and the empty fields are preserved.

The *FIELDWIDTHS* Variable. The *FIELDWIDTHS* variable (*gawk* only) can be used if the file has fields of a fixed width. The value assigned to this variable is a space separated list of numbers, in which each number in the list represents the number of characters in a field. The value of *FS* will be ignored if *FIELDWIDTHS* is set.

EXAMPLE 7.87

```
% cat fixedfile
abc1245556
xxxyyyzzzz

% awk 'BEGIN{FIELDWIDTHS="3 3 4"}{print $2}' fixedfile
124
yyy
```

EXPLANATION

Gawk includes a variable called *FIELDWIDTHS* to govern the way it splits up a line into fields. The variable is assigned a space separated list, 3 3 4, meaning that each record consists of three fixed width fields: The first is 3 characters in length, the second 3 characters and the last is 4 characters. Even though there are no separators in *fixedfile*, the records will be split into fields according to the value assigned to *FIELDWIDTHS*.

Numbers with $, Commas, or Other Characters. In the following example, the price field contains a dollar sign and comma. The script must eliminate these characters to add up the prices to get the total cost. This is done using the *gsub* function.

EXAMPLE 7.88

```
% cat vendor
access tech:gp237221:220:vax789:20/20:11/01/90:$1,043.00
alisa systems:bp262292:280:macintosh:new updates:06/30/91:$456.00
alisa systems:gp262345:260:vax8700:alisa talk:02/03/91:$1,598.50
apple computer:zx342567:240:macs:e-mail:06/25/90:$575.75
caci:gp262313:280:sparc station:network11.5:05/12/91:$1,250.75
datalogics:bp132455:260:microvax2:pagestation
maint:07/01/90:$1,200.00
dec:zx354612:220:microvax2:vms sms:07/20/90:$1,350.00

% awk -F: '{gsub(/\$/,"");gsub(/,/,""); cost +=$7};\
END{print "The total cost is $" cost}' vendor
The total cost is $7474
```

EXPLANATION

The first *gsub* function globally substitutes the literal dollar sign (\$) with the null string, and the second *gsub* function substitutes commas with a null string. The user-defined *cost* variable is then totalled by adding the seventh field to *cost* and assigning the result back to *cost*. In the *END* block, the string *"The total cost is $"* is printed, followed by the value of *cost*.[a]

a. For details on how commas are added back into the program, see *The Awk Programming Language* by Alfred Aho, Brian Kernighan, and Peter Wienberger, Addison Wesley, 1988, p. 72.

7.13.2 Bundling and Unbundling Files

The Bundle Program. In *The AWK Programming Language* by Alfred Aho, Brian Kernighan, and Peter Wienberger, the program to bundle files together is very short and to the point. We are trying to combine several files into one file to save disk space, to send files through electronic mail, and so forth. The following *awk* command will print every line of each file, preceded with the filename.

EXAMPLE 7.89

```
% awk '{ print FILENAME, $0 }' file1 file2 file3 > bundled
```

EXPLANATION

The name of the current input file, *FILENAME,* is printed, followed by the record (*$0*) for each line of input in *file1*. After *file1* has reached the end of file, *awk* will open the next file, *file2*, and do the same thing, and so on. The output is redirected to a file called *bundled.*

Unbundle. The following example displays how to unbundle files, or put them back into separate files.

EXAMPLE 7.90

```
%  awk '$1 != previous { close(previous); previous=$1};\
    {print substr($0, index($0, " ") + 1) > $1}' bundled
```

EXPLANATION

The first field is the name of the file. If the name of the file is not equal to the value of the user-defined variable *previous* (initially null), the action block is executed. The file assigned to *previous* is closed, and *previous* is assigned the value of the first field. Then the *substr* of the record, the starting position returned from the index function (the position of the first space + 1), is redirected to the filename contained in the first field.

To bundle the files so that the filename appears on a line by itself, above the contents of the file use, the following command:

```
% awk '{if(FNR==1){print FILENAME;print $0}\
else print $0}'  file1 file2 file3 > bundled
```

The following command will unbundle the files:

```
% awk 'NF==1{filename=$NF} ;\
NF != 1{print $0 > filename}' bundled
```

7.13.3 Multiline Records

In the sample data files used so far, each record is on a line by itself. In the following sample datafile, called *checkbook,* the records are separated by blank lines and the fields are separated by newlines. To process this file, the record separator (*RS*) is assigned a value of null, and the field separator (*FS*) is assigned the newline.

EXAMPLE 7.91

```
(The Input File)
    % cat checkbook
    1/1/99
    #125
    -695.00
    Mortgage

    1/1/99
    #126
    -56.89
    PG&E

    1/2/99
    #127
    -89.99
    Safeway
```

EXAMPLE 7.91 (CONTINUED)

```
    1/3/99
    +750.00
    Pay Check

    1/4/99
    #128
    -60.00
    Visa

(The Script)
    % cat awkchecker
1   BEGIN{RS=""; FS="\n";ORS="\n\n"}
2   {print  NR, $1,$2,$3,$4}

(The Output)
    % awk -f awkchecker checkbook
    1 1/1/99   #125   -695.00   Mortgage

    2 1/1/99   #126   -56.89   PG&E

    3 1/2/99   #127   -89.99   Safeway

    4 1/3/99   +750.00   Pay Check

    5 1/4/99   #128   -60.00   Visa
```

EXPLANATION

1. In the *BEGIN* block, the record separator (*RS*) is assigned null, the field separator (*FS*) is assigned a newline, and the output record separator (*ORS*) is assigned two newlines. Now each line is a field and each output record is separated by two newlines.
2. The number of the record is printed, followed by each of the fields.

7.13.4 Generating Form Letters

The following example is modified from a program in *The Awk Programming Language*. The tricky part of this is keeping track of what is actually being processed. The input file is called *data.file*. It contains just the data. Each field in the input file is separated by colons. The other file is called *form.letter*. It is the actual form that will be used to create the letter. This file is loaded into *awk*'s memory with the *getline* function. Each line of the form letter is stored in an array. The program gets its data from *data.file,* and the letter is created by substituting real data for the special strings preceded by # and @ found in *form.letter*. A temporary variable, *temp*, holds the actual line that will be displayed after the data has been substituted. This program allows you to create personalized form letters for each person listed in *data.file*.

EXAMPLE 7.92

```
(The Awk Script)
% cat form.awk
# form.awk is an awk script that requires access to 2 files: The
# first file is called "form.letter". This file contains the
# format for a form letter. The awk script uses another file,
# "data.form", as its input file. This file contains the
# information that will be substituted into the form letters in
# place of the numbers preceded by pound signs. Today's date
# is substituted in the place of "@date" in "form.letter".
BEGIN{ FS=":"; n=1
while(getline < "form.letter" >  0)
    form[n++] = $0   #Store lines from form.letter in an array
"date" | getline d; split(d, today, " ")
    # Output of date is Sun Mar 2 14:35:50   PST 1999
thisday=today[2]". "today[3]", "today[6]
}
{ for( i = 1; i < n; i++ ){
    temp=form[i]
    for ( j = 1; j <=NF; j++ ){
         gsub("@date", thisday, temp)
         gsub("#" j, $j , temp )
    }
print temp
}
}

% cat form.letter
The form letter, form.letter, looks like this:
*******************************************************
Subject: Status Report for Project "#1"
To: #2
From: #3
Date: @date
This letter is to tell you, #2, that project "#1" is up to
date.
We expect that everything will be completed and ready for
shipment as scheduled on #4.

Sincerely,

#3
*******************************************************
```

The file, *data.form*, is awk's **input file** containing the data that will replace the #1–4 and the @date in *form.letter*.

EXAMPLE 7.92 (CONTINUED)

```
% cat data.form
    Dynamo:John Stevens:Dana Smith, Mgr:4/12/1999
    Gallactius:Guy Sterling:Dana Smith, Mgr:5/18/99

(The Command Line)

    % awk  -f form.awk  data.form
    *******************************************************
    Subject: Status Report for Project "Dynamo"
    To: John Stevens
    From: Dana Smith, Mgr
    Date: Mar. 2, 1999
    This letter is to tell you, John Stevens, that project
    "Dynamo" is up to date.
    We expect that everything will be completed and ready for
    shipment as scheduled on 4/12/1999.

    Sincerely,

    Dana Smith, Mgr
    Subject: Status Report for Project "Gallactius"
    To: Guy Sterling
    From: Dana Smith, Mgr
    Date: Mar. 2, 1999
    This letter is to you, Guy Sterling, that project "Gallactius"
    is up to date.
    We expect that everything will be completed and ready for
    shipment as scheduled on 5/18/99.

    Sincerely,

    Dana Smith, Mgr
```

EXPLANATION

1 In the *BEGIN* block, the field separator (*FS*) is assigned a colon; a user-defined variable *n* is assigned 1.

2 In the *while* loop, the *getline* function reads a line at a time from the file called *form.letter.* If *getline* fails to find the file, it returns a –1. When it reaches the end of file, it returns zero. Therefore, by testing for a return value of greater than one, we know that the function has read in a line from the input file.

3 Each line from *form.letter* is assigned to an array called *form.*

4 The output from the UNIX *date* command is piped to the *getline* function and assigned to the user-defined variable *d*. The *split* function then splits up the variable *d* with white space, creating an array called *today.*

EXPLANATION (CONTINUED)

5 The user-defined variable *thisday* is assigned the month, day, and year.

6 The *BEGIN* block ends.

7 The *for* loop will loop *n* times.

8 The user-defined variable *temp* is assigned a line from the *form* array.

9 The nested *for* loop is looping through a line from the input file, *data.form*, *NF* number of times. Each line stored in the *temp* variable is checked for the string *@date*. If *@date* is matched, the *gsub* function replaces it with today's date (the value stored in *this day*).

10 If a *#* and a number are found in the line stored in *temp*, the *gsub* function will replace the *#* and number with the value of the corresponding field in the input file, *data.form*. For example, if the first line stored is being tested, *#1* would be replaced with *Dynamo*, *#2* with *John Stevens*, *#3* with *Dana Smith, #4* with *4/12/1999,* and so forth.

11 The line stored in *temp* is printed after the substitutions.

7.13.5 Interaction with the Shell

Now that you have seen how *awk* works, you will find that *awk* is a very powerful utility when writing shell scripts. You can embed one-line *awk* commands or *awk* scripts within your shell scripts. The following is a sample of a Bash shell program embedded with *awk* commands.

EXAMPLE 7.93

```
#!/bin/bash
# Scriptname: bash.sc
# This bash shell script will collect data for awk to use in
# generating form letter(s). See above.
echo "Hello $LOGNAME. "
echo "This report is for the month and year:"
1   cal | awk 'NR==1{print $0}'

    if [[ -f data.form   || -f formletter? ]]
    then
       rm data.form formletter?  2> /dev/null
    fi
    let num=1
    while true
    do
```

EXAMPLE 7.93 (CONTINUED)

```
        echo "Form letter #$num:"
        echo -n "What is the name of the project? "
        read project
        echo -n "Who is the status report from? "
        read sender
        echo -n "Who is the status report to? "
        read recipient
        echo -n "When is the completion date scheduled? "
        read due_date
        echo $project:$recipient:$sender:$due_date > data.form
        echo -n "Do you wish to generate another form letter? "
        read answer
        if [[ "$answer" != [Yy]* ]]
        then
            break
        else
2           awk -f form.awk  data.form  > formletter$num
        fi
        (( num+=1 ))
    done
    awk -f form.awk data.form > formletter$num
```

EXPLANATION

1 The Linux *cal* command is piped to *awk*. The first line which contains the current month and year is printed.

2 The *awk* script *form.awk* generates form letters, which are redirected to a UNIX file.

7.14 Review

7.14.1 String Functions

```
% cat datafile
northwest    NW    Joel Craig        3.0    .98    3     4
western      WE    Sharon Kelly      5.3    .97    5    23
southwest    SW    Chris Foster      2.7    .8     2    18
southern     SO    May Chin          5.1    .95    4    15
southeast    SE    Derek Johnson     4.0    .7     4    17
eastern      EA    Susan Beal        4.4    .84    5    20
northeast    NE    TJ Nichols        5.1    .94    3    13
north        NO    Val Shultz        4.5    .89    5     9
central      CT    Sheri Watson      5.7    .94    5    13
```

EXAMPLE 7.94

```
% awk 'NR==1{gsub(/northwest/,"southeast", $1) ;print}' datafile
southeast          NW          Joel Craig          3.0    .98    3     4
```

EXPLANATION

If this is the first record *(NR == 1)*, **globally substitute** the regular expression *northwest* with *southeast,* if *northwest* is found in the first field.

EXAMPLE 7.95

```
% awk 'NR==1{print substr($3, 1, 3)}' datafile
Joe
```

EXPLANATION

If this is the first record, display the **substring** of the third field, starting at the first character, and extracting a length of *3* characters. The substring *Joe* is printed.

EXAMPLE 7.96

```
% awk 'NR==1{print length($1)}' datafile
9
```

EXPLANATION

If this is the first record, the **length** (number of characters) in the first field is printed.

EXAMPLE 7.97

```
% awk 'NR==1{print index($1,"west")}' datafile
6
```

EXPLANATION

If this is the first record, print the first position where the substring *west* is found in the first field. The string *west* starts at the sixth position (**index**) in the string *northwest.*

EXAMPLE 7.98

```
% awk '{if(match($1,/^no/)){print substr($1,RSTART,RLENGTH)}}'
datafile
no
no
no
```

```
% cat datafile
northwest    NW    Joel Craig       3.0    .98    3    4
western      WE    Sharon Kelly     5.3    .97    5    23
southwest    SW    Chris Foster     2.7    .8     2    18
southern     SO    May Chin         5.1    .95    4    15
southeast    SE    Derek Johnson    4.0    .7     4    17
eastern      EA    Susan Beal       4.4    .84    5    20
northeast    NE    TJ Nichols       5.1    .94    3    13
north        NO    Val Shultz       4.5    .89    5     9
central      CT    Sheri Watson     5.7    .94    5    13
```

EXPLANATION

If the *match* function finds the regular expression */^no/* in the first field, the index position of the leftmost character is returned. The built-in variable *RSTART* is set to the index position and the *RLENGTH* variable is set to the length of the matched substring. The *substr* function returns the string in the first field starting at position *RSTART, RLENGTH* number of characters.

EXAMPLE 7.99

```
% awk 'BEGIN{split("10/14/98",now,"/");print now[1],now[2],now[3]}'
10 14 98
```

EXPLANATION

The string *10/14/98* is **split** into an array called *now*. The delimiter is the forward slash. The elements of the array are printed, starting at the first element of the array.

```
% cat datafile2
Joel Craig:northwest:NW:3.0:.98:3:4
Sharon Kelly:western:WE:5.3:.97:5:23
Chris Foster:southwest:SW:2.7:.8:2:18
May Chin:southern:SO:5.1:.95:4:15
Derek Johnson:southeast:SE:4.0:.7:4:17
Susan Beal:eastern:EA:4.4:.84:5:20
TJ Nichols:northeast:NE:5.1:.94:3:13
Val Shultz:north:NO:4.5:.89:5:9
Sheri Watson:central:CT:5.7:.94:5:13
```

EXAMPLE 7.100

```
% awk -F: '/north/{split($1, name, " ");\
print "First name: "name[1];\
print "Last name: " name[2]; \
print "\n--------------------"}' datafile2

First name: Joel
Last name: Craig
--------------------
First name: TJ
Last name: Nichols
--------------------
First name: Val
last name: Shultz
--------------------
```

EXPLANATION

The input field separator is set to a colon (*-F:*). If the record contains the regular expression *north*, the first field is **split** into an array called *name*, where a space is the delimiter. The elements of the array are printed.

```
% cat datafile
northwest    NW   Joel Craig       3.0   .98   3    4
western      WE   Sharon Kelly     5.3   .97   5   23
southwest    SW   Chris Foster     2.7   .8    2   18
southern     SO   May Chin         5.1   .95   4   15
southeast    SE   Derek Johnson    4.0   .7    4   17
eastern      EA   Susan Beal       4.4   .84   5   20
northeast    NE   TJ Nichols       5.1   .94   3   13
north        NO   Val Shultz       4.5   .89   5    9
central      CT   Sheri Watson     5.7   .94   5   13
```

EXAMPLE 7.101

```
% awk '{line=sprintf("%10.2f%5s",$7,$2); print line}' datafile
      3.00   NW
      5.00   WE
      2.00   SW
      4.00   SO
      4.00   SE
      5.00   EA
      3.00   NE
      5.00   NO
      5.00   CT
```

EXPLANATION

The *sprintf* function formats the seventh and the second fields (*$7, $2*) using the formatting conventions of the *printf* function. The formatted string is returned and assigned to the user-defined variable *line* and printed.

7.14.2 Command Line Arguments

EXAMPLE 7.102

```
% cat argvs.sc
# Testing command line arguments with ARGV and ARGC using a for loop.

BEGIN{
      for(i=0;i < ARGC;i++)
       printf("argv[%d] is %s\n", i, ARGV[i])
      printf("The number of arguments, ARGC=%d\n", ARGC)
}

% awk -f argvs.sc datafile
argv[0] is awk
argv[1] is datafile
The number of arguments, ARGC=2
```

EXPLANATION

The *BEGIN* block contains a *for* loop to process the **command line arguments**. *ARGC* is the number of arguments and *ARGV* is an array that contains the actual arguments. *awk* does not count options as arguments. The only valid arguments in this example are the *awk* command and the input file, *datafile*.

EXAMPLE 7.103

```
% awk 'BEGIN{name=ARGV[1]};\
 $0 ~ name {print $3 , $4}'  "Derek" datafile
awk: can't open Derek
 source line number 1


% awk 'BEGIN{name=ARGV[1]; delete ARGV[1]};\
 $0 ~ name {print $3, $4}'   "Derek" datafile
Derek Johnson
```

EXPLANATION

1 The name *"Derek"* was set to the variable *name* in the *BEGIN* block. In the pattern-action block, *awk* attempted to open *"Derek"* as an input file and failed.

2 After assigning *"Derek"* to the variable *name, ARGV[1]* is deleted. When starting the pattern-action block, *awk* does not try to open *"Derek"* as the input file, but opens *datafile* instead.

```
% cat datafile
northwest    NW    Joel Craig       3.0    .98    3     4
western      WE    Sharon Kelly     5.3    .97    5    23
southwest    SW    Chris Foster     2.7    .8     2    18
southern     SO    May Chin         5.1    .95    4    15
southeast    SE    Derek Johnson    4.0    .7     4    17
eastern      EA    Susan Beal       4.4    .84    5    20
northeast    NE    TJ Nichols       5.1    .94    3    13
north        NO    Val Shultz       4.5    .89    5     9
central      CT    Sheri Watson     5.7    .94    5    13
```

7.14.3 Reading Input (*getline*)

EXAMPLE 7.104

```
% awk 'BEGIN{ "date" | getline d; print d}' datafile
Thu Jan 15 11:24:24 PST 2000
```

EXPLANATION

The UNIX *"date"* command is piped to the *getline* function. The results are stored in the variable *d* and printed.

EXAMPLE 7.105

```
% awk 'BEGIN{ "date " | getline d; split( d, mon) ;print mon[2]}' datafile
Jan
```

EXPLANATION

The UNIX/Linux *date* command is piped to the *getline* function and the results are stored in *d*. The *split* function splits the string *d* into an array called *mon*. The second element of the array is printed.

EXAMPLE 7.106

```
% awk 'BEGIN{ printf "Who are you looking for?" ; getline name <
"/dev/tty"};'
```

EXPLANATION

Input is read from the terminal, */dev/tty*, and stored in the array called *name*.

EXAMPLE 7.107

```
% awk 'BEGIN{while(getline < "/etc/passwd"  > 0 ){lc++}; print lc}'
datafile
16
```

EXPLANATION

The *while* loop is used to loop through the */etc/passwd* file one line at a time. Each time the loop is entered, a line is read by *getline* and the value of the variable *lc* is incremented. When the loop exits, the value of *lc* is printed, i.e., the number of lines in the */etc/passwd* file. As long as the return value from *getline* is not *0*, i.e., a line has been read, the looping continues.

7.14.4 Control Functions

EXAMPLE 7.108

```
% awk '{if ( $5 > 4.5) next; print $1}' datafile
northwest
southwest
southeast
eastern
north
```

EXPLANATION

If the fifth field is greater than *4.5*, the next line is read from the input file (*datafile*) and processing starts at the beginning of the *awk* script (after the *BEGIN* block). Otherwise, the first field is printed.

EXAMPLE 7.109

```
% awk '{if ($2 ~ /S/){print ; exit 0}}' datafile
southwest        SW       Chris    Foster  2.7      .8       2        18

% echo $status ( csh, tcsh ) or echo $? (bash, sh, ksh)
0
```

EXPLANATION

If the second field contains an *S*, the record is printed and the *awk* program exits. The TC shell and C shell status variable contains the exit value. If using the Bash, Bourne, or Korn shells, the *$?* variable contains the exit status.

```
% cat datafile
northwest     NW    Joel Craig         3.0    .98    3     4
western       WE    Sharon Kelly       5.3    .97    5    23
southwest     SW    Chris Foster       2.7    .8     2    18
southern      SO    May Chin           5.1    .95    4    15
southeast     SE    Derek Johnson      4.0    .7     4    17
eastern       EA    Susan Beal         4.4    .84    5    20
northeast     NE    TJ Nichols         5.1    .94    3    13
north         NO    Val Shultz         4.5    .89    5     9
central       CT    Sheri Watson       5.7    .94    5    13
```

7.14.5 User-Defined Functions

EXAMPLE 7.110

```
(The Command Line)
% cat awk.sc7
1   BEGIN{largest=0}
2   {maximum=max($5)}

3   function max ( num ) {
4       if ( num > largest){ largest=num }
        return largest
5   }
6   END{ print "The maximum is " maximum "."}
% awk -f awk.sc7 datafile
The maximum is 5.7.
```

EXPLANATION

1 In the *BEGIN* block, the user-defined variable *largest* is initialized to zero.

2 For each line in the file, the variable *maximum* is assigned the value returned from the function *max*. The function *max* is given *$5* as its argument.

3 The user-defined function *max* is defined. The function statements are enclosed in curly braces. Each time a new record is read from the input file, *datafile*, the function *max* will be called.

4 It will compare the values in *num* and *largest* and return the larger of the two numbers.

5 The function definition block ends.

6 The *END* block prints the final value in *maximum*.

LINUX TOOLS LAB 7

(File lab7.data)

```
Mike Harrington:(510) 548-1278:250:100:175
Christian Dobbins:(408) 538-2358:155:90:201
Susan Dalsass:(206) 654-6279:250:60:50
Archie McNichol:(206) 548-1348:250:100:175
Jody Savage:(206) 548-1278:15:188:150
Guy Quigley:(916) 343-6410:250:100:175
Dan Savage:(406) 298-7744:450:300:275
Nancy McNeil:(206) 548-1278:250:80:75
John Goldenrod:(916) 348-4278:250:100:175
Chet Main:(510) 548-5258:50:95:135
Tom Savage:(408) 926-3456:250:168:200
Elizabeth Stachelin:(916) 440-1763:175:75:300
```

The database above contains the names, phone numbers, and money contributions to the party campaign for the past three months.

1. Write a user-defined function to return the average of all the contributions for a given month. The month will be passed in at the command line.
2. Write another user-defined function that will print the date this report was generated.

CHAPTER

8

THE INTERACTIVE BASH SHELL

8.1 Introduction

With an interactive shell, the standard input, output, and error are tied to a terminal. When using the Bourne Again shell interactively, you will type Linux/UNIX commands at the *bash* prompt and wait for a response. *Bash* provides you with a large assortment of built-in commands and command line shortcuts, such as history, aliases, file and command completion, command line editing, and many more. Some of the features were present in the standard UNIX Bourne shell but the Gnu project has expanded the shell to include a number of new features as well adding POSIX compliancy. With the release of *bash* 2.x, so many features of the UNIX Korn shell and C shell have been included that the *bash* shell is a fully functional shell at both the interactive and programming level, while upwardly compatible with the standard Bourne shell. For Linux and UNIX users, *bash* offers an alternative to the standard UNIX shells, *sh*, *csh*, and *ksh*.

This chapter focuses on how you interact with *bash* at the command line and how to customize your working environment. You will learn how to take advantage of all shortcuts and built-in features in order to create an efficient and fun working environment. The next chapter takes you a step further. Then you will be ready to write *bash* shell scripts to further tailor the working environment for yourself by automating everyday tasks and developing sophisticated scripts, and if you are an administrator, doing the same not only for yourself but also for whole groups of users.

8.1.1 Versions of Bash

The Bourne Again shell is a Capricorn, born on January 10, 1988, fathered by Brian Fox and later adopted by Chet Ramey, who now officially maintains *bash*, enhances it, and fixes bugs. The first version of *bash* was 0.99. The latest version (as of this writing) is version 2.03. Major enhancements were completed in version 2.0. There are a number of operating systems that are still using version 1.14.7 and all versions are freely available under the Gnu public license. To see what version you are using, use the *-version* option to *bash* or print the value of the *BASH_VERSION* environment variable.

EXAMPLE 8.1

```
$ bash -version
GNU bash, version 2.03.0(1)-release (i686-pc-linux-gnu)
Copyright 1998 Free Software Foundation, Inc.

$ echo $BASH_VERSION
2.03.0(1)-release
```

8.1.2 Startup

If the *bash* shell is your login shell, it follows a chain of processes before you see a shell prompt.[1]

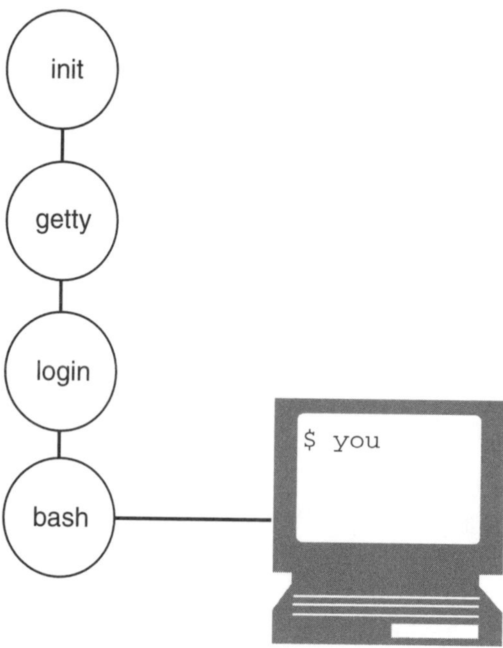

Figure 8.1 Starting the *bash* shell.

When the system boots, the first process to run is called *init*, PID #1. It spawns a getty process. This process opens up the terminal ports, providing a place where standard input comes from and a place where standard output and errors go, and puts a login prompt on your screen. The */bin/login* program is then executed. The *login* program prompts for a password, encrypts and verifies the password, sets up an initial environment, and starts up

1. To get the latest version of *bash,* go to Web site: http://www.delorie.com/gnu/.

the login shell, */bin/bash*, the last entry in the *passwd* file. The *bash* process looks for the system file, */etc/profile,* and executes its commands. It then looks in the user's home directory for an initialization file called *.bash_profile*. After executing commands from *.bash_profile*[2], it will execute a command from the user's ENV file, usually called *.bashrc*, and finally the default dollar sign ($) prompt appears on your screen and the shell waits for commands. (For more on initialization files, see "The Environment" on page 262.)

Changing the Login Shell with *chsh*. The *chsh* command allows you to change your login shell. For example, if you are currently using the standard Bourne shell and would rather have *bash* as your login shell, you can use *chsh* to change your login shell. If a shell is not given on the command line, *chsh* prompts for one. All valid shells are listed in the */etc/shells* file. (See Table 8.1.)

Table 8.1 The *chsh* Command

Option	*What It Does*
-l,--list-shells	Prints the list of available shells listed in */etc/shells* and exits
-s, --shell	Specifies the login shell
-u, --help	Prints a usage message and exits
-v, --version	Prints version information and exits

EXAMPLE 8.2

```
1 $ chsh -l
/bin/bash
/bin/sh
/bin/ash
/bin/bsh
/bin/tcsh
/bin/csh
/bin/ksh
/bin/zsh

2 $ chsh
Changing shell for ellie.
New shell [/bin/sh] tcsh
chsh: shell must be a full pathname.
```

2. There are a number of different initialization files used by *bash*; they are discussed on the next pages.

EXPLANATION

1 Lists all available shells on this Linux system.
2 Asks the user to type the full pathname for a new login shell. Fails unless a full pathname such as, */bin/tcsh*, is given.

8.1.3 The Environment

The environment of a process consists of variables, open files, the current working directory, functions, resource limits, signals, and so forth. It defines those features that are inherited from one shell to the next and the configuration for the working environment. The configuration for the user's shell is defined in the shell initialization files.

The Initialization Files. The *bash* shell has a number of startup files that are sourced. Sourcing a file causes all settings in the file to become part of the current shell; i.e., a subshell is not created. (The source command is discussed in "The source or dot Command" on page 281.) The initialization files are sourced depending on the whether the shell is a login shell, an interactive shell (but not the login shell), or a noninteractive shell (a shell script).

When you log on, before the shell prompt appears, the system-wide initialization file, *etc/profile*, is sourced. Next, if it exists, the *.bash_profile* in the user's home directory is sourced. It sets the user's aliases and functions and then sets user-specific environment variables and startup scripts.

If the user doesn't have a *.bash_profile*, but does have a file called *.bash_login*, that file will be sourced, and if he doesn't have a *.bash_login*, but does have a *.profile*, it will be sourced. (The *.bash_login* file is similar to the C shell's *.login* file and the *.profile* is normally sourced by the Bourne shell when it starts up.)

Here is a summary of the order that *bash* processes its initialization files (see Figure 8.2):[3]

```
if /etc/profile exists, source it,
   if ~/.bash_profile exists, source it,
      if  ~/.bashrc exists, source it,
   else if ~/.bash_login exists, source it,
   else if ~/.profile exists, source it.
```

The */etc/profile* File. The */etc/profile* file is a system-wide initialization file set up by the system administrator to perform tasks when the user logs on. It is executed when the *bash* shell starts up. It is also available to all Bourne and Korn shell users on the system and normally performs such tasks as checking the mail spooler for new mail and displaying the message of the day from the */etc/motd* file. (The following examples will make more sense after you have completed this chapter.)

3. If the shell is invoked with the *-noprofile* option, none of the initialization files are read.

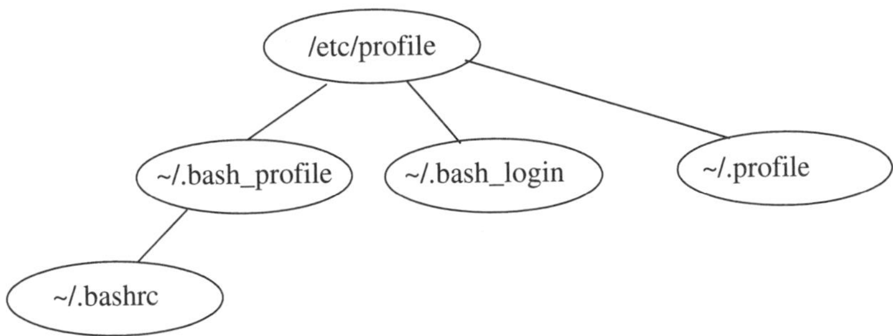

Figure 8.2 Order of processing initialization files.

EXAMPLE 8.3

```
(Sample /etc/profile)
# /etc/profile

# System wide environment and startup programs
# Functions and aliases go in /etc/bashrc

PATH="$PATH:/usr/X11R6/bin"
PS1="[\u@\h \W]\\$ "

ulimit -c 1000000
if [ 'id -gn' = 'id -un' -a 'id -u' -gt 14 ]; then
    umask 002
else
    umask 022
fi

USER='id -un'
LOGNAME=$USER
MAIL="/var/spool/mail/$USER"

HOSTNAME='/bin/hostname'
HISTSIZE=1000
HISTFILESIZE=1000
export PATH PS1 HOSTNAME HISTSIZE HISTFILESIZE USER LOGNAME MAIL

for i in /etc/profile.d/*.sh ; do
     if [ -x $i ]; then
          . $i
     fi
done

unset i #
```

EXPLANATION

1 The PATH variable is assigned locations where the shell should search for commands.
2 The primary prompt is assigned. It will be displayed in the shell window as the user's name (\u),the @ symbol, the host machine (\W),and a dollar sign.
3 The *ulimit* command (a shell built-in command) is set to limit the maximum size of core files created to 1000000 bytes. Core files are memory dumps of programs that have crashed, and they take up a lot of disk space.
4 This line reads: if the user's group name is equal to the user's name and the user's id number is greater than 14... (see 5)
5 Then set the umask to 002. When directories are created they will get 775 permissions and files will get 664 permissions. Otherwise, the umask is set to 022, giving 755 to directories and 644 to files.
6 The USER variable is assigned the username (*id -un*).
7 The LOGNAME variable is set to the value in $USER.
8 The MAIL variable is assigned the path to the mail spooler where the user's mail is saved.
9 The HOSTNAME variable is assigned the name of the user's host machine.
10 The HISTSIZE variable is set to 1000. HISTSIZE controls the number of history items that are remembered (from the history list stored in the shell's memory) and saved in the history file after the shell exits.
11 The HISTFILESIZE is set to limit the number of commands stored in the history file to 1000, i.e., the history file is truncated after it reaches 1000 lines. (See "History" on page 292.)
12 These variables are exported so that they will be available in subshells and child processes.
13 For each file (ending in *.sh*) in the *etc/profile.d* directory... (see 14)
14 Check to see if the file is executable, and if it is... (see 15)
15 Execute (source) the file with the dot command. The files in the */etc/profile.d* directory: *lang.sh* and *mc.sh*, respectively, set the Linux character and font sets and create a function called *mc* that starts up a visual/browser file manager program, called *Midnight Commander*. To see how the file manager works, type *mc* at the *bash* prompt.
16 The *done* keyword marks the end of the *for* loop.
17 The variable *i* is unset, i.e., removed from shell's name space. The value of *i* is whatever was assigned to it while in the *for* loop, if anything was assigned at all.

The *~/.bash_profile* File. If the *~/.bash_profile* is found in the user's home directory, it is sourced after the */etc/profile*. If *~/.bash_profile* doesn't exist, *bash* will look for another user-defined file, *~./bash_login*, and source it, and if *~./bash_login* doesn't exist, it will source the *~/.profile*, if it exists. Only one of the three files (*~/.bash_profile*, *~/.bash_login*, or *~/.profile*) will be sourced. *Bash* will also check to see if the user has a *.bashrc* file and then source it.

EXAMPLE 8.4

```
(Sample .bash_profile)

    # .bash_profile
    # The file is sourced by bash only when the user logs on.

    # Get the aliases and functions
1   if [ -f ~/.bashrc ]; then
2           . ~/.bashrc
    fi

    # User specific environment and startup programs

3   PATH=$PATH:$HOME/bin
4   ENV=$HOME/.bashrc      #  or BASH_ENV=$HOME/.bashrc
5   USERNAME="root"

6   export USERNAME ENV PATH
7   mesg n
8   if [ $TERM = linux ]
    then
            startx    # Start the X Window system
    fi
```

EXPLANATION

1. If there is a file called *.bashrc* in the user's home directory... (see 2)
2. Execute (source) the *.bashrc* file for the login shell.
3. The *PATH* variable is appended with a path to the user's *bin* directory, normally the place where shell scripts are stored.
4. The *BASH_ENV*[a] *(ENV)* file is set to the pathname for the *.bashrc* file, an initialization file that will be sourced for interactive *bash* shells and and scripts only if the *BASH_ENV (ENV)* variable is set. The *.bashrc* file contains user-defined aliases and functions.
5. The variable *USERNAME* is set to *root.*
6. The variables are exported so that they are available to subshells and other processes will know about them.
7. The *mesg* command is executed with the *n* option, disallowing others to write to the terminal.
8. If the value of the *TERM* variable is "linux," then *startx* will start the X window system (the graphical user interface allowing multiple virtual consoles), rather than starting an interactive session in the Linux console window. Because the *~/.bash_profile* is only sourced when you log in, the login shell would be the best place to start up your X windows session.

a. *BASH_ENV* is used by versions of Bash starting at 2.0.

The *BASH_ENV* (*ENV*) Variable. Before *bash* version 2.0, the *BASH_ENV* file was simply called the *ENV* file (same as in Korn shell). The *BASH_ENV (ENV)* variable is set in the *~/.bash_profile*. It is assigned the name of a file that will be executed every time an interactive *bash* shell or *bash* script is started. The *BASH_ENV (ENV)* file will contain special *bash* variables and aliases. The name is conventionally *.bashrc*, but you can call it anything you want. The *BASH_ENV* (*ENV*) file is not processed when the privileged option is on (*bash -p* or *set -o privileged*) or the *--norc* command line option is used *(bash -norc* or *bash --norc* (*bash 2.x* +)).

The *.bashrc* File. The *BASH_ENV* (*ENV*) variable is assigned (by convention) the name *.bashrc*. This file is automatically sourced every time a new or interactive *bash* shell or *bash* script starts. It contains settings that pertain only to the Bash shell.

EXAMPLE 8.5

```
 (Sample .bashrc)
#If the .bashrc file exists, it is in the user's home directory.
#It contains aliases (nicknames for commands) and user-defined
#functions.

    # .bashrc

    # User specific aliases and functions


1   set -o vi
2   set -o noclobber
3   set -o ignoreeof
4   alias rm='rm -i'
    alias cp='cp -i'
    alias mv='mv -i'
5   stty erase ^h
   # Source global definitions
6  if [ -f /etc/bashrc ]; then
      . /etc/bashrc
   fi
7   case "$-" in
8    *i*) echo This is an interactive bash shell
               ;;
9    *)    echo This shell is noninteractive
               ;;
    esac
10  history_control=ignoredups

11  function cd { builtin cd $1; echo $PWD; }
```

EXPLANATION

1 The *set* command with the *-o* switch turns on or off special built-in options. (See "The set -o Options" on page 270.) If the switch is *-o*, a minus sign, the option is turned on, and if a plus sign, the option is turned off. The *vi* option allows interactive command line editing. For example, *set -o vi* turns on interactive command-line editing, whereas *set vi +o* turns it off. (See Table 8.2 on page 270.)

2 The *noclobber* option is turned on, which prevents the user from overwriting files when using redirection; e.g., *sort filex > filex.* (See "Standard I/O and Redirection" on page 363.)

3 When exiting a shell, normally you can type ^d (Control-D). With *ignoreeof* set, you must type *exit*.

4 The alias for *rm*, *rm -i*, causes *rm* to be interactive (*-i*), i.e., it will ask the user if it's OK to remove files before actually removing them.The alias for the *cp*, *cp -i*, command causes the copy to be interactive.

5 The *stty* command is used to set the terminal backspace key to erase. ^h represents the Backspace key.

6 If a file called */etc/bashrc* exists, source it.

7 If the shell is interactive, the special variable, *$-*, will contain an "i." If not, you are probably running a script. The *case* command evaluates *$-*.

8 If the value returned from *$-* matches **i**, i.e., any string containing an "i," then the shell prints *"This is an interactive shell."*

9 Otherwise, the shell prints *"This shell is noninteractive."* If you start up a script, or a new shell at the prompt, you will be able to tell whether or not your shell is interactive. It is only here to let you test your understanding of the terms "interactive" and "noninteractive" shell.

10 The *history_control* setting is used to control how commands are saved in the history file. This line says *"Don't save commands in the history file, if they're already there."*; i.e., ignore duplicates.

11 This is a user-defined function. When the user changes directories, the present working directory, *PWD*, is printed. The function is named *cd* and contains within its definition, the command *cd.* The special built-in command, called *builtin*, precedes the *cd* command within the function definition to prevent the function from going into an infinite recursion; i.e., from calling itself indefinitely.

The */etc/bashrc* File. System-wide functions and aliases can be set in the */etc/bashrc* file. The primary prompt is often set here.

EXAMPLE 8.6

```
(Sample /etc/bashrc)

   # System wide functions and aliases
   # Environment stuff goes in /etc/profile

   # For some unknown reason bash refuses to inherit
   # PS1 in some circumstances that I can't figure out.
   # Putting PS1 here ensures that it gets loaded every time.
1  PS1="[\u@\h \W]\\$ "

2  alias which="type -path"
```

EXPLANATION

1 System-wide functions and aliases are set here. The primary *bash* prompt is set to the name of the user (\u), and @ symbol, the host machine (\h), the basename of the current working directory, and a dollar sign. (See Table 8.3 on page 276.) This prompt will appear for all interactive shells.

2 Aliases, nicknames for commands, are usually set in the user's *.bashrc* file. The alias was preset and is available when *bash* starts up. You use it when you want to find out where a program resides on disk; i.e., what directory it is found in; e.g., *which ls* will print */bin/ls.*

The *~/.profile* File. The *.profile* file is a user-defined initialization file, found in the user's home directory, and sourced once at login if running *sh* (Bourne shell) or if running *bash,* and *bash* cannot find any other of the initialization files listed above. It allows a user to customize and modify his shell environment. Environment and terminal settings are normally put here, and if a window application or database application is to be initiated, it is started here.

EXAMPLE 8.7

```
(Sample .profile)
# A login initialization file sourced when running as sh or the
#.bash_profile or .bash_login are not found.

1   TERM=xterm
2   HOSTNAME=`uname -n`
3   EDITOR=/bin/vi
4   PATH=/bin:/usr/ucb:/usr/bin:/usr/local:/etc:/bin:/usr/bin:.
5   PS1="$HOSTNAME $ > "
6   export TERM HOSTNAME EDITOR PATH PS1
7   stty erase ^h
8   go () { cd $1; PS1=`pwd`; PS1=`basename $PS1`; }
9   trap '$HOME/.logout' EXIT
10  clear
```

EXPLANATION

1 The *TERM* variable is assigned the value of the terminal type, *xterm*.

2 Because the *uname -n* command is enclosed in back quotes, the shell will perform command substitution, i.e., the output of the command (the name of the host machine) will be assigned to the variable *HOSTNAME*.

3 The *EDITOR* variable is assigned */bin/vi*. Programs such as *mail* and *history* will now have this variable available when defining an editor.

4 The *PATH* variable is assigned the directory entries that the shell searches in order to find a Linux program. If, for example, you type *ls*, the shell will search the *PATH* until it finds that program in one of the listed directories. If it never finds the program, the shell will tell you so.

5 The primary prompt is assigned the value of *HOSTNAME*, the machine name, and the *$* and > symbols.

6 All of the variables listed are exported. They will be known by child processes started from this shell.

7 The *stty* command sets terminal options. The Erase key is set to *^h*, so that when you press the Backspace key, the letter typed preceding the cursor is erased.

8 A function called *go* is defined. The purpose of this function is to take one argument, a directory name, *cd* to that directory, and set the primary prompt to the present working directory. The *basename* command removes all but the last entry of the path. The prompt will show you the current directory.

9 The *trap* command is a signal handling command. When you exit the shell, that is, log out, the *.logout* file will be executed. The *.logout* file is a user-defined file containing commands that will be executed just before logging out, commands that will clean up temp files or log the time of log out, etc.

10 The *clear* command clears the screen.

The *~/.bash-logout* File. When the user logs out (exits the login shell), if a file called *~/.bash_logout* exists, it is sourced. This file normally contains commands to clean up temporary files, truncate the history file, record the time of logout, etc.

Options to Prevent Startup Files from Being Executed. If *bash* is invoked with the *--noprofile* option (e.g., *bash --noprofile*), then the */etc/profile*, *~/.bash_profile*, *~/.bash_login*, or *~/.profile* startup files will not be sourced.

If invoked with the *-p* option (e.g., *bash -p*), *bash* will not read the user's *~/.profile* file.

If *bash* is invoked as *sh* (Bourne shell), it tries to mimic the behavior of the Bourne shell as closely as possible. For a login shell, it attempts to source only */etc/profile* and *~/.profile*, in that order. The *-noprofile* option may still be used to disable this behavior. If the shell is invoked as *sh,* it does not attempt to source any other startup files.

The *.inputrc* File. Another default initalization file, *.inputrc*, is also read when *bash* starts up. This file, if it exists in the user's home directory, contains variables to customize key stroke behavior and settings that bind strings, macros, and control functions to keys. The names for the key bindings and what they do are found in the Readline Library, a library that is used by applications that manipulate text. The bindings are used particularly by the built-in *emacs* and *vi* editors, when performing command line editing. (See "Command Line Editing" on page 301 for more on *readline*.)

8.1.4 Setting Bash Options with the Built-In *set* and *shopt* Commands

The *set -o* Options. The *set* command can take options when the *-o* switch is used. Options allow you to customize the shell environment. They are either on or off, and are normally set in the *BASH_ENV (ENV)* file. Many of the options for the *set* command are set with an abbreviated form. For example, *set -o noclobber* can also be written, *set -C*. (See Table 8.2.)

Table 8.2 The Built-In *set* Command Options

Name of Option	*Shortcut Switch*	*What It Does*
allexport	*-a*	Automatically marks new or modified variables for export from the time the option is set, until unset.
braceexpand	*-B*	Enables brace expansion, and is a default setting.
emacs		For command line editing, uses the *emacs* built-in editor, and is a default setting
errexit	*-e*	If a command returns a nonzero exit status (fails), exits. Not set when reading initialization files.

Table 8.2 The Built-In *set* Command Options (Continued)

Name of Option	***Shortcut Switch***	***What It Does***
histexpand	*-H*	Enables ! and !! when performing history substitution, and is a default setting.
history		Enables command line history; on by default.
ignoreeof		Disables EOF (Control-D) from exiting a shell; must type exit. Same as setting shell variable, IGNOREEOF=10.
keyword	*-k*	Places keyword arguments in the environment for a command.
interactive-comments		For interactive shells, a leading # is used to comment out any text remaining on the line.
monitor	*-m*	Allows job control.
noclobber	*-C*	Protects files from being overwritten when redirection is used.
noexec	*-n*	Reads commands, but does not execute them. Used to check the syntax of scripts. Not on when running interactively.
noglob	*-d*	Disables pathname expansion; i.e., turns off wildcards.
notify	*-b*	Notifies user when background job finishes
nounset	*-u*	Displays an error when expanding a variable that has not been set.
onecmd	*-t*	Exit after reading and executing one command.
physical	*-P*	If set, does not follow symbolic links when typing *cd* or *pwd*. The physical directory is used instead.
posix		Shell behavior is changed if the default operation doesn't match the POSIX standard.
privileged	*-p*	When set, the shell does not read the *.profile* or *ENV* file and shell functions are not inherited from the environment; automatically set for *setuid* scripts.
posix		Change the default behavior to POSIX 1003.2.
verbose	*-v*	Turns on the *verbose* mode for debugging.
vi		For command line editing, uses the *vi* built-in editor.
xtrace	*-x*	Turns on the echo mode for debugging.

FORMAT

```
set -o option   Turns on the option.
set +o option   Turns off the option.
set -[a-z]   Abbreviation for an option; the minus turns it on.
set +[a-z]   Abbreviation for an option; the plus turns it off.
```

EXAMPLE 8.8

```
1   set -o allexport
2   set +o allexport
3   set -a
4   set +a
```

EXPLANATION

1 Sets the *allexport* option. This option causes all variables to be automatically exported to subshells.

2 Unsets the *allexport* option. All variables will now be local in the current shell.

3 Sets the *allexport* option. Same as 1. Not every option has an abbreviation. (See Table 8.2.)

4 Unsets the *allexport* option. Same as 2.

EXAMPLE 8.9

```
1  $ set -o
   braceexpand     on
   errexit         off
   hashall         on
   histexpand      on
   keyword         off
   monitor         on
   noclobber       off
   noexec          off
   noglob          off
   notify          off
   nounset         off
   onecmd          off
   physical        off
   privileged      off
   verbose         off
   xtrace          off
```

EXAMPLE 8.9 (CONTINUED)

```
     history          on
     ignoreeof        off
     interactive-comments on
     posix            off
     emacs            off
     vi               on

  2  $ set -o noclobber
  3  $ date > outfile
  4  $ ls > outfile
     bash: outfile: Cannot clobber existing file.
  5  $ set +o noclobber
  6  $ ls > outfile
  7  $ set -C
```

EXPLANATION

1. With the *-o* option, the set command lists all the options currently set or not set.
2. To set an option, the *-o* option is used. The *noclobber* option is set. It protects you from overwriting files when using redirection. Without *noclobber,* the file to the right of the > symbol is truncated if it exists, and created if it doesn't exist.
3. The output of the Linux *date* command is redirected to a file called *outfile*.
4. This time, the *outfile* exists. By attempting to redirect the output of *ls* to *outfile*, the shell complains that the file already exists. Without *noclobber* set, it would be clobbered.
5. With the *+o* option to the set command, *noclobber* is turned off.
6. This time, trying to overwrite *outfile* is fine because *noclobber* is no longer set.
7. Using the *-C* switch to the *set* command is an alternate way of turning on *noclobber.* *+C* would turn it off.

The *shopt* Built-In (Version 2.x+). The *shopt (shell options)* built-in command is used in newer versions of *bash* as an alternative to the *set* command. In many ways *shopt* duplicates the *set* built-in command, but it adds more options for configuring the shell. See Table 8.31 on page 375 for a list of all the *shopt* options. In the following example, *shopt* with the *-p* option prints all the available options settings. The *-u* switch indicates an unset option and *-s* indicates one that is currently set.

EXAMPLE 8.10

```
1   $ shopt -p
    shopt -u cdable_vars
    shopt -u cdspell
    shopt -u checkhash
    shopt -u checkwinsize
    shopt -s cmdhist
    shopt -u dotglob
    shopt -u execfail
    shopt -s expand_aliases
    shopt -u extglob
    shopt -u histreedit
    shopt -u histappend
    shopt -u histverify
    shopt -s hostcomplete
    shopt -u huponexit
    shopt -s interactive_comments
    shopt -u lithist
    shopt -u mailwarn
    shopt -u nocaseglob
    shopt -u nullglob
    shopt -s promptvars
    shopt -u restricted_shell
    shopt -u shift_verbose
    shopt -s sourcepath

2   $ shopt -s cdspell
3   $ shopt -p cdspell
    shopt -s cdspell
4   $ cd /hame
    /home
5   $ pwd
    /home
6   $ cd /ur/lcal/ban
    /usr/local/man
7   $ shopt -u cdspell
8   $ shopt -p cdspell
    shopt -u cdspell
```

EXPLANATION

1. With the *-p* (for print) option, the *shopt* command lists all settable shell options and their current values, either set (*-s*) or unset (*-u*).
2. With the *-s* option, *shopt* sets (or turns on) an option. The *cdspell* option causes the shell to correct minor spelling errors on directory names given as arguments to the *cd* command. It will correct simple typos, insert missing letters, and even transpose letters if it can.

EXPLANATION (CONTINUED)

3 With the *-p* option and the name of the option, *shopt* indicates whether or not the option is set. The option has been set (*-s*).

4 In this example, the user tries to *cd* to his home directory, but misspells *home*. The shell fixes the spelling; i.e., *hame* becomes *home*. The directory is changed to */home*.

5 The output of the *pwd* command displays the current working directory, showing that the directory was really changed even though the user spelled it wrong.

6 This time the directory name is missing letters and has a misspelling for the last entry, *ban*. The shell makes a pretty good attempt to spell out the correct pathname by inserting the missing letters, and correcting *ban* to *man*. Because the "b" in *ban* is the first misspelled character, the shell searches in the directory for an entry that might end with "a" and "n." It finds *man*.

7 With the *-u* switch[a], *shopt* unsets (or turns off) the option.

8 With the *-p* switch and the name of the option, *shopt* indicates whether or not the option is set. The *cdspell* option has been unset (*-u*).

a. The words switch or option are interchangeable. They are arguments to a command that contain a leading dash.

8.1.5 The Prompts

When used interactively, the shell prompts you for input. When you see the prompt, you know that you can start typing commands. The *bash* shell provides four prompts: the primary prompt is a dollar sign (*$*), and the secondary prompt, a right angle bracket symbol (>). The third and fourth prompts, *PS3* and *PS4* respectively, will be discussed later. The prompts are displayed when the shell is running interactively. You can change these prompts.

The variable, *PS1*, is set to a string containing the primary prompt. Its value, the dollar sign, appears when you log on and waits for user input, normally a *Linux* command. The variable *PS2* is the secondary prompt, initially set to the right angle bracket character. It appears if you have partially typed a command and then pressed the carriage return. You can change the primary and secondary prompts.

The Primary Prompt. The dollar sign (or *bash $*) is the default primary prompt. You can change your prompt. Normally prompts are defined in */etc/bashrc* or the user initialization file, *.bash_profile*, or *.profile* (Bourne shell).

EXAMPLE 8.11

```
1   $ PS1="$(uname -n) > "
2   chargers >
```

EXPLANATION

1 The default primary prompt is a dollar sign (*bash $*). The *PS1* prompt is being reset to the name of the machine[a] (*uname -n*) and a > symbol.

2 The new prompt is displayed.

a. The command, *uname -n*, is executed because it is enclosed in a set of parentheses preceded by a dollar sign. An alternative would be to enclose the command in back quotes. See "Command Substitution" on page 353.)

Setting the Prompt with Special Escape Sequences. By inserting special backslash-escape sequences into the prompt string, you can customize the prompts. Table 8.3 lists the special sequences.

Table 8.3 Prompt String Settings

Backslash Sequence	*What It Evaluates To*
\t	the current time in HH:MM:SS format
\d	the date in "Weekday Month Date" format (e.g., "Tue May 26")
\n	newline
\s	the name of the shell, the basename of $0 (the portion following the final slash)
\w	the current working directory
\W	the basename of the current working directory
\u	the username of the current user
\h	the hostname
\#	the command number of this command
\!	the history number of this command
\$	if the effective UID is 0, a #, otherwise a $
\nnn	the character corresponding to the octal number *nnn*
\\	a backslash
\[	begin a sequence of nonprinting characters, which could be used to embed a terminal control sequence into the prompt
\]	end a sequence of nonprinting characters

Table 8.3 Prompt String Settings (Continued)

Backslash Sequence	*What It Evaluates To*
New in Bash Version 2.x+	
\a	the ASCII bell character
\@	the current time in 12 hours AM/PM format
\H	the hostname
\T	the current time in 12-hour format: HH:MM:SS
\e	the ASCII escape character (033)
\v	the version of *bash*, e.g., 2.03
\V	the release and pathlevel of *bash*; e.g., 2.03.0

EXAMPLE 8.12

```
1    $ PS1="[\u@\h \W]\\$ "
     [ellie@homebound ellie]$

2    $ PS1="\W:\d> "
     ellie:Tue May 18>
```

EXPLANATION

1. You customize the primary *bash* prompt using special backslash-escape sequences. *\u* evaluates to the user's login name, *\h* to the host machine, and *\W* is the basename for the current working directory. There are two backslashes. The first backslash escapes the second backslash, resulting in *\$*. The dollar sign is protected from shell interpretation and thus printed literally.
2. The primary prompt is assigned *\W*, the escape sequence evaluating to the basename of the current working directory, and *\d*, the escape sequence evaluating to today's date.

The Secondary Prompt. The *PS2* variable is assigned a string called the secondary prompt. Its value is displayed to standard error, which is the screen by default. This prompt appears when you have not completed a command or more input is expected. The default secondary prompt is >.

EXAMPLE 8.13

```
1   $ echo "Hello
2   > there"
3   Hello
    there
4   $

5   $ PS2="----> "
6   $ echo 'Hi
7   ------>
    ------>
    ------> there'
     Hi


    there
    $

8 $ PS2="\s:PS2 > "
  $ echo 'Hello
   bash:PS2 > what are
   bash:PS2 > you
   bash:PS2 > trying to do?
   bash:PS2 > '
   Hello
   what are
   you
   trying to do?
$
```

EXPLANATION

1 The double quotes must be matched after the string "*Hello.*

2 When a newline is entered, the secondary prompt appears. Until the closing double quotes are entered, the secondary prompt will be displayed.

3 The output of the *echo* command is displayed.

4 The primary prompt is displayed.

5 The secondary prompt is reset.

6 The single quote must be matched after the string *'Hi.*

7 When a newline is entered, the new secondary prompt appears. Until the closing single quote is entered, the secondary prompt will be displayed.

8 The *PS2* prompt is set to the name of the shell (*\s*) followed by a string consisting of a colon, *PS2* and >, followed by a space.

The Search Path. *Bash* uses the *PATH* variable to locate commands typed at the command line. The path is a colon-separated list of directories used by the shell when searching for commands. The default path is system-dependent, and is set by the administrator who installs *bash*. The path is searched from left to right. The dot at the end of the path represents the current working directory. If the command is not found in any of the directories listed in the path, the shell sends to standard error the message "*filename: not found.*" The path is normally set in the *.bash_profile* if running the *bash shell* or *.profile* file if using *sh,* the Bourne shell.

If the dot is not included in the path and you are executing a command or script from the current working directory, the name of the script must be preceded with a ./, such as *./program_name*, so that shell can find the program.

EXAMPLE 8.14

```
(Printing the PATH)
1   $ echo $PATH
    /usr/gnu/bin:/usr/local/bin:/usr/ucb:/bin:/usr/bin:.

(Setting the PATH)
2
    $ PATH=$HOME:/usr/ucb:/usr:/usr/bin:/usr/local/bin:
3   $ export PATH
4   $ runit
    bash: runit: command not found
5   $ ./runit
    < program starts running here >
```

EXPLANATION

1 By echoing *$PATH*, the value of the *PATH* variable is displayed. The path consists of a list of colon-separated elements and is searched from left to right. The dot at the end of the path represents the user's current working directory.

2 To set the path, a list of colon-separated directories are assigned to the *PATH* variable. Note that in this path, the dot is not at the end of the path, perhaps as a security measure.

3 By exporting the path, child processes will have access to it. It is not necessary to export the PATH on a separate line: It could be written: ***export PATH=$HOME:/usr/ucb:/bin:.***, etc., on the same line.

4 Because the dot is not in the search path, when the program, *runit*, is executed in the present working directory, *bash* can't find it.

5 Because the program name is preceded with a dot and a slash (./), the shell will be able to find it, and execute it, if it is the current working directory.

The *hash* Command. The *hash* command controls the internal hash table used by the shell to improve efficiency in searching for commands. Instead of searching the path each time a command is entered, the first time you type a command, the shell uses the search path to find the command, and then stores it in a table in the shell's memory. The next time you use the same command, the shell uses the *hash* table to find it. This makes it much faster to access a command than having to search the complete path. If you know that you will be using a command often, you can add the command to the *hash* table. You can also remove commands from the table. The output of the *hash* command displays the number of times the shell has used the table to find a command (*hits*) and the full pathname of the command. The *hash* command with the *-r* option clears the hash table. An argument of -- disables option checking for the rest of the arguments. Hashing is automatically implemented by *bash*. Although you can turn it off, if there isn't any compelling reason to do so, don't.

EXAMPLE 8.15

```
(Printing the PATH)

(Command line)
1   hash
    hits     command
    1        /usr/bin/mesg
    4        /usr/bin/man
    2        /bin/ls

2   hash -r
3   hash
    No commands in hash table

4   hash find
    hits     command
    0        /usr/bin/find
```

EXPLANATION

1. The *hash* command displays the full pathname of commands that have been executed in this login session.(Built-in commands are not listed) The number of hits is the number of times the *hash* table has been used to find the command.
2. The *-r* option to the *hash* command erases all remembered locations in the *hash* table.
3. After the *-r* option was used in the last command, the *hash* command reports that there are no commands currently in the table.
4. If you know you are going to use a command often, you can add it to the *hash* table by giving it as an argument to the *hash* command. The *find* command has been added. The table has zero hits, because the command hasn't been used yet.

The *source* or *dot* Command. The *source* command (from the C shell) is a built-in *bash* shell command. The *dot* command, simply a period, (from the Bourne shell) is another name for *source*. Both commands take a script name as an argument. The script will be executed in the environment of the current shell; that is, a child process will not be started. All variables set in the script will become part of the current shell's environment. Likewise, all variables set in the current shell will become part of the script's environment. The *source* (or *dot*) command is normally used to reexecute any of the initialization files, e.g., *.bash_profile*, *.profile*, etc, if they have been modified. For example, if one of the settings, such as the *EDITOR* or *TERM* variable, has been changed in the *.bash_profile* since you logged on, you can use the *source* command to reexecute commands in the *.bash_profile* without logging out and then logging back on. A file, such as *.bash_profile*, or for that matter any shell script, does not need execute permissions to be sourced with either the *dot* or the *source* commands.

EXAMPLE 8.16

```
$ source .bash_profile
$ . .bash_profile
```

EXPLANATION

The *source or dot* command executes the initialization file, *.bash_profile,* within the context of the current shell. Local and global variables are redefined within this shell. The *dot* command makes it unnecessary to log out and then log back in again after the file has been modified.[a]

a. If the *.bash_profile* were executed directly as a script, a child shell would be started. Then the variables would be set in the child shell, and when the child shell exited, the parent shell would not have any of the settings available to it.

8.1.6 The Command Line

After you log on, the *bash* shell displays its primary prompt, a dollar sign, by default. The shell is your command interpreter. When the shell is running interactively, it reads commands from the terminal and breaks the command line into words. A command line consists of one or more words (or tokens), separated by white space (blanks and/or tabs), and terminated with a newline, generated by pressing the Enter key. The first word is the command, and subsequent words are the command's arguments. The command may be a *Linux/UNIX* executable program such as *ls* or *date*, a user-defined function, a built-in command such as *cd* or *pwd*, or a shell script. The command may contain special characters, called metacharacters, which the shell must interpret while parsing the command line. If a command line is too long, the backslash character, followed by a newline, will allow you to continue typing on the next line. The secondary prompt will appear until the command line is terminated.

The Order of Processing Commands. The first word on the command line is the command to be executed. The command may be a keyword, an alias, a function, a special built-in command or utility, an executable program, or a shell script. The command is executed according to its type in the following order:

1. Aliases
2. Keywords (such as *if, function, while, until*)
3. Functions
4. Built-in commands
5. Executables and scripts

Special built-in commands and functions are defined within the shell, and therefore, are executed from within the context of the current shell, making them much faster in execution. Scripts and executable programs such as *ls* and *date* are stored on disk, and the shell, in order to execute them, must first locate them within the directory hierarchy by searching the *PATH* environment variable; the shell then forks a new shell which executes the script. To find out the type of command you are using—i.e., a built-in command, an alias, a function, or an executable, etc.—use the built-in *type* command. (See Example 8.17.)

EXAMPLE 8.17

```
$ type pwd
pwd is a shell builtin
$ type test
test is a shell builtin
$ type clear
clear is /usr/bin/clear
$ type m
m is aliased to 'more'
$ type bc
bc is /usr/bin/bc
$ type if
if is a shell keyword
$ type -path cal
/usr/bin/cal
$ type which
which is aliased to 'type -path'
$ type greetings
greetings is a function
greetings ()
{
        echo "Welcome to my world!";
}
```

Built-In Commands and the *help* Command. Built-in commands are commands that are part of the internal source code for the shell. They are built-in and readily available to the shell, whereas commands such as *date, cal,* and *finger*, are compiled binary programs that reside on the disk. There is less overhead in executing a built-in because it involves no disk operations. Built-in commands are executed by the shell before the programs on disk. *Bash* has added a new online help system so that you can see all the built-ins, or a description for a particular built-in; *help*, itself, is a built-in command. See Table 8.32 on page 377 for a complete list of built-in commands.

EXAMPLE 8.18

```
1  $ help help
   help: help [pattern ...]
   Display helpful information about built-in commands. if PATTERN
   is specified, gives detailed help on all commands matching
   PATTERN, otherwise a list of the built-ins is printed.

2  $ help pw
   pwd: pwd
       Print the current working directory.
```

Changing the Order of Command Line Processing. *Bash* provides three built-in commands that can override the order of command line processing: ***command***, ***builtin***, and ***enable***.

The *command* built-in eliminates aliases and functions from being looked up in the order of processing. Only built-ins and executables, found in the search path, will be processed.

The *builtin* command looks up only built-ins, ignoring functions and executables found in the path.

The *enable* built-in command turns built-ins on and off. By default, built-ins are enabled. Disabling a built-in allows an executable command found on the disk to be to be executed without specifying a full pathname, even if it has the same name as a built-in. (In normal processing, *bash* searches for built-ins before disk executable commands.) Built-ins become disabled by using the *-n* switch. A classic example causing confusion for new shell programmers, is naming a script, *test.* Because *test* is a built-in command, the shell will try to execute it rather than the user's script, (a built-in is normally executed before any executable program). By typing: *enable -n test*, the *test* built-in is disabled, and the user's script will take precedence.

Without options, the *enable* built-in prints a list of all the built-ins. Each of the following built-ins are described in "Shell Built-In Commands" on page 377.

EXAMPLE 8.19

```
1 $ enable
enable .
enable :
enable [
enable alias
enable bg
enable bind
enable break
enable builtin
enable cd
enable command
enable continue
enable declare
enable dirs
    .....
enable read
enable readonly
enable return
enable set
enable shift
enable shopt
    .....
enable type
enable typeset
enable ulimit
enable umask
enable unalias
enable unset
enable wait

2 enable -n test

3 function cd { builtin cd; echo $PWD; }
```

EXPLANATION

1. The *enable* built-in, without any options, displays a complete list of all *bash* shell built-in commands. This example shows just part of that list.
2. With the *-n* switch, the *test* built-in command is disabled. Now, you execute your script named "test" without worrying about the built-in *test* being executed instead. It's not good practice to name a script by the same name as an operating system command, because if you try to run the same script in another shell, the disabling of built-ins doesn't exist.
3. The function is called *cd*. The *builtin* command causes the *cd* within the function definition to be called instead of the function *cd*, which would cause an endless recursive loop.

The Exit Status. After a command or program terminates, it returns an exit status to the parent process. The exit status is a number between 0 and 255. By convention, when a program exits, if the status returned is zero, the command was successful in its execution. When the exit status is nonzero, the command failed in some way. If a command is not found by the shell, the exit status returned is 127. If a fatal signal causes the command to terminate, the exit status is 128 plus the value of the signal that caused it to die.

The shell status variable, *?*, is set to the value of the exit status of the last command that was executed. Success or failure of a program is determined by the programmer who wrote the program.

EXAMPLE 8.20

```
1   $ grep ellie /etc/passwd
    ellie:MrHJEFd2YpkJY:501:501::/home/ellie:/bin/bash
2   $ echo $?
    0

3   $ grep nicky /etc/passwd
4   $ echo $?
    1

5   $ grep ellie /junk
    grep: /junk: No such file or directory
6   $ echo $?
    2

7   $ grip ellie /etc/passwd
    bash: grip: command not found
8   $ echo $?
    127

9   $ find / -name core ^C     User presses Control-C
10   $ echo $?
     130
```

EXPLANATION

1. The *grep* program searches for the pattern *"ellie"* in the */etc/passwd* file and is successful. The line from */etc/passwd* is displayed.
2. The *?* variable is set to the exit value of the *grep* command. Zero indicates successful status.
3. The *grep* program cannot find user *nicky* in the */etc/passwd* file.
4. The *grep* program cannot find the pattern; the *?* variable return value is nonzero. An exit status of *1* indicates failure.

EXPLANATION (CONTINUED)

5 The *grep* fails because the */junk* file cannot be opened.The *grep* error message is sent to standard error, the screen.

6 If *grep* cannot find the file, it returns an exit status of *2*.

7 The command, *grip*, is not found by the shell.

8 Because the command is not found, the exit status, *127*, is returned.

9 The find command is interrupted when the SIGINT signal is sent by pressing Control-C. The signal number for Ctrl-C is 2.

10 The status returned from a process that has been killed is 128 + the number of the signal; i.e., 128 + 2.

Multiple Commands at the Command Line. A command line can consist of multiple commands. Each command is separated by a semicolon, and the command line is terminated with a newline. The exit status is that of the last command in the chain of commands.

EXAMPLE 8.21

```
$ ls; pwd; date
```

EXPLANATION

The commands are executed from left to right, one after the other, until the newline is reached.

Grouping Commands. Commands may also be grouped so that all of the output is either piped to another command or redirected to a file.

EXAMPLE 8.22

```
$  ( ls; pwd; date ) > outputfile
```

EXPLANATION

The output of each of the commands is sent to the file called *outputfile*. The spaces inside the parentheses are necessary.

Conditional Execution of Commands. With conditional execution, two command strings are separated by the special metacharacters, double ampersands (*&&*) and double vertical bars (||). The command on the right of either of these metacharacters will or will not be executed based on the exit condition of the command on the left.

EXAMPLE 8.23

```
$ cc prgm1.c -o prgm1 && prgm1
```

EXPLANATION

If the first command is successful (has a zero exit status), the second command after the *&&* is executed; i.e., if the *cc* program can successfully compile *prgm1.c*, the resulting executable program, *prgm1*, will be executed.

EXAMPLE 8.24

```
$ cc prog.c >& err || mail bob < err
```

EXPLANATION

If the first command fails (has a nonzero exit status), the second command after the || is executed; i.e., if the *cc* program cannot compile *prog.c*, the errors are sent to a file called *err*, and user *bob* will be mailed the *err* file.

Commands in the Background. Normally, when you execute a command, it runs in the foreground, and the prompt does not reappear until the command has completed execution. It is not always convenient to wait for the command to complete. When you place an ampersand (&) at the end of the command line, the shell will return the shell prompt immediately and execute the command in the background concurrently. You do not have to wait to start up another command. The output from a background job will be sent to the screen as it processes. Therefore, if you intend to run a command in the background, the output of that command might be redirected to a file or piped to another device, such as a printer, so that the output does not interfere with what you are doing.

The *!* variable contains the PID number of the last job put in the background. (See "Job Control" on page 288 for more on background processing.)

EXAMPLE 8.25

```
1   $ man sh | lp&
2   [1] 1557
3   $ kill -9 $!
```

EXPLANATION

1 The output of the *man* command (the manual pages for the *Linux* command) is piped to the printer. The ampersand at the end of the command line puts the job in the background.

2 There are two numbers that appear on the screen: the number in square brackets indicates that this is the first job to be placed in the background; the second number is the PID, or the process identification number of this job.

3 The shell prompt appears immediately. While your program is running in the background, the shell is waiting for another command in the foreground. The *!* variable evaluates to the PID of the job most recently put in the background. If you get it in time, you will kill this job before it goes to the print queue.

8.1.7 Job Control

Job control is a powerful feature of the *bash* shell that allows you to selectivly run programs, called *jobs*, in the background or foreground. A running program is called a process or a job and each process has a process id number, called the PID. Normally, a command typed at the command line is running in the foreground and will continue until it has finished unless you send a signal by pressing Ctrl-C or Ctrl-\ to terminate it. With job control you can send a job to the background and let it keep running; you can stop a job by pressing Ctrl-Z, which sends the job to the background and suspends it; you can cause a stopped job to run in the background; you can bring a background job back to the foreground; and you can even kill the jobs you have running in the background or foreground. For a list of job commands, see Table 8.4 on page 290.

By default, job control is already set (some older versions of UNIX do not support this feature). If disabled, it can be reset by any one of the following commands:

FORMAT

```
set -m              (set job control in the .bashrc file)
set -o monitor      (set job control in the .bashrc file)
bash -m -i          (set job control when invoking interactive bash)
```

EXAMPLE 8.26

```
1   $ vi
    [1]+  Stopped       vi

2   $ sleep 25&
    [2] 4538

3   $ jobs
    [2]+  Running       sleep 25&
    [1]-  Stopped         vi
```

EXAMPLE 8.26 (CONTINUED)

```
4   $ jobs -l
    [2]+ 4538    Running         sleep 25&
    [1]- 4537      Stopped          vi

5   $ jobs %%
    [2]+ 4538    Running          sleep 25&

6   $ fg %1

7   $ jobs -x echo %1
    4537

8   $ kill %1    or   kill 4537

    [1]+    Stopped        vi
    Vim: Caught deadly signal TERM
    Vim: Finished.
    [1]+    Exit 1        vi
```

EXPLANATION

1 After the *vi* editor is invoked, you can press ^Z (Control-Z) to suspend the *vi* session. The editor will be suspended in the background, and after the message *Stopped* appears, the shell prompt will appear immediately.

2 The ampersand at the end of the command causes the *sleep* command, with an argument of *25*, to execute in the background. The notation [2] means that this is the second job to be run in the background and the PID of this job is *4538*.

3 The *jobs* command displays the jobs currently in the background.

4 The *jobs* command with the *-l* option displays the processes (jobs) running in the background and the PID numbers of those jobs.

5 The *%%* argument causes *jobs* to display the most recent command put in the job table.

6 The *fg* command followed by a percent sign and the job number will bring that numbered job into the foreground. Without a number, *fg* brings the most recently backgrounded job back into the foreground.

7 The *-x* option can be used to print just the PID number of the job. *%1* refers to the *vi* session that was stopped in the first example.

8 The *kill* command sends a TERM signal to the process and kills it. The *vi* program is killed. You can specify either the job number or the PID number as arguments to the *kill* command.

Table 8.4 Job Control Commands

Command	*Meaning*
jobs	Lists all the jobs running.
^Z (Ctrl-Z)	Stops (suspends) the job; the prompt appears on the screen.
bg	Starts running the stopped job in the background.
fg	Brings a background job to the foreground.
stop	Suspends a background job.
stty tostop	Suspends a background job if it sends output to the terminal.
kill	Sends the *kill* signal to a specified job.
wait [n]	Waits for a specified job and returns its exit status, where *n* is a PID or job number.

Argument to jobs command	*Represents*
%n	Job number *n*.
%sting	Job name starting with string.
%?string	Job name containing string.
%%	Current job.
%+	Current job.
%-	Previous job, before current job.
-r	Lists all running jobs.
-s	Lists all suspended jobs.

New Jobs Options. Two new options were added to the *jobs* command in *bash* versions 2.x. They are the *-r* and *-s* options. The *-r* option lists all running jobs, and the *-s* option lists all stopped jobs.

The *disown* Built-In. The *disown* built-in command (*bash* 2.x) removes a specified job from the job table. After the job has been removed, the shell will no longer recognize it as a viable job process and it can only be referenced by its process id number.

8.2 Command Line Shortcuts

8.2.1 Command and Filename Completion

To save typing, *bash* implements command and filename completion, a mechanism that allows you to type part of a command or filename, press the Tab key, and the rest of the word will be completed for you.

If you type the first letters in a command, and press the Tab key, *bash* will attempt to complete the command and execute it. If *bash* cannot complete the filename or command, because neither exists, the terminal may beep and the cursor will stay at the end of the command. If there is more than one command starting with those characters and you press the Tab key a second time, all commands that start with those characters will be listed.

If there are several files starting with the same letters, *bash* will complete the shortest name that matches, expand out the filename until the characters differ, and then flash the cursor for you to complete the rest.

EXAMPLE 8.27

```
1   $ ls
    file1 file2 foo foobarckle fumble

2   $ ls fu[tab]          expands to filename to fumble

3   $ ls fx[tab]          terminal beeps, nothing happens

4   $ ls fi[tab]          expands to file_   (_ is a cursor)

5   $ ls fi[tab][tab]     lists all possibilities
    file1 file2

6   $ ls foob[tab]        expands to foobarckle

7   $ da[tab]             completes the date command
    date
    Tue Feb 29 18:53:40 PST 2000

8   $ ca[tab][tab]          lists all commands starting with ca
    cal     captoinfo   case    cat
```

EXPLANATION

1 All files are listed for the current working directory.

2 After *fu* is typed, the Tab key is pressed, causing the spelling of the filename to be completed to *fumble*, and listed.

EXPLANATION (CONTINUED)

3 Because none of the files start with *fx*, the terminal beeps and the cursor remains but does nothing. (The terminal may not beep it that feature has been disabled.)

4 There are a number of files starting with *fi*; the filenames are completed until the letters are no longer the same. If another Tab key is pressed, all files with that spelling are listed.

5 By pressing two Tab keys, a list of all files beginning with *file* is printed.

6 When the Tab key is pressed, the filename is expanded to *foobarckle*.

7 When the Tab key is pressed after *da*, the only command that begins with *da* is the *date* command. The command name is expanded and executed.

8 When the Tab key is pressed after *ca*, nothing happens because more than one command starts with *ca*. Pressing the Tab key twice lists all commands starting with *ca*.

8.2.2 History

The history mechanism keeps a numbered record of the commands that you have typed at the command line in a history list. During a login session, the commands you type are stored in the the shell's memory in a history *list* and then appended to the history *file* when you exit. You can recall a command from the history list and reexecute it without retyping the command. The *history* built-in command displays the history list. The default name for the history file is *.bash_history,* and it is located in your home directory.

When *bash* starts accessing the history file, the *HISTSIZE* variable specifies how many commands can be accessed from the history file. The default size is 500. The *HISTFILE* variable specifies the name of the command history file (*~/.bash_history* is the default) where commands are stored. If unset, the command history is not saved when an interactive shell exits.

The history file grows from one login session to the next. The *HISTFILESIZE* variable controls the maximum number of lines contained in the history file. When this variable is assigned a value, the history file is truncated when it surpasses that number of lines. The default size is 500.

The *fc -l* command can be used to display or edit commands in the history list.

Table 8.5 History Variables

FCEDIT	The pathname of the Linux editor that uses the *fc* command.
HISTCMD	The history number, or index in the history list, of the current command. If HISTCMD is unset, it loses its special properties, even if it is subsequently reset.
HISTCONTROL	If set to a value of *ignorespace*, lines which begin with a space character are not entered on the history list. If set to a value of *ignoredups*, lines matching the last history line are not entered. A value of *ignoreboth* combines the two options. If unset, or if set to any other value than those above, all lines read by the parser are saved on the history list.
HISTFILE	Specifies file in which to store command history. The default value is *~/.bash_history.* If unset, the command history is not saved when an interactive shell exits.
HISTFILESIZE	The maximum number of lines contained in the history file. When this variable is assigned a value, the history file is truncated, if necessary, to contain no more than that number of lines. The default value is 500.
HISTIGNORE	A colon-separated list of patterns used to decide which command lines should be saved on the history list. Each pattern is anchored to the beginning of the line and consists of normal shell pattern matching characters. An & can be used in the pattern causing the *history* command to ignore duplicates; e.g., *ty??:&* would match for any command line starting with "ty" followed by two characters, and any duplicates of that command. Those commands would not be placed in the history list.
HISTSIZE	The number of commands to remember in the command history. The default value is 500.

8.2.3 Accessing Commands from the History File

The Arrow Keys. To access commands from the history file, you can use the arrow keys on the keyboard to move up and down through the history file, and from left to right. You can edit any of the lines from the history file by using the standard keys for deleting, updating, backspacing, etc. As soon as you have edited the line, pressing the carriage return (Enter key) will cause the command line to be reexecuted.

Table 8.6 The Arrow Keys

↑	Up arrow moves up the history list.
↓	Down arrow moves down the history list.
→	Right arrow moves cursor to right of history command.
←	Left arrow moves left on history command.

The *history* Built-In Command. The *history* built-in command displays the history of commands typed preceded by an event number.

EXAMPLE 8.28

```
1 $ history
   982  ls
   983  for i in 1 2 3
   984  do
   985  echo $i
   986  done
   987  echo $i
   988  man xterm
   989  adfasdfasdfadfasdfasdfadfasdfasdf
   990  id -gn
   991  id -un
   992  id -u
   993  man id
   994  more /etc/passwd
   995  man ulimit
   996  man bash
   997  man baswh
   998  man bash
   999  history
  1000  history
```

EXPLANATION

1 The built-in *history* command displays a list of numbered commands from the history list. Any lines listed with an * have been modified.

The *fc* Command. The *fc* command, also called the *fix* command, can be used in two ways: (1) to select commands from the history list, and (2) to edit the commands in either the *vi* or *emacs* editor, or for that matter, any editor on your system.

In the first form, *fc* with the *-l* option can select specific lines or ranges of lines from the history list. When the *-l* switch is on, the output goes to the screen. For example, *fc -l*, the default, prints the last 16 lines from the history list, *fc -l 10* selects lines numbered 10 through the end of the list, and *fc -l -3* selects the last three lines. The *-n* switch turns off the numbering of commands in the history list. With this option on, you could select a range of commands and redirect them to a file, which in turn could be executed as a shell script. The *-r* switch reverses the order of the commands.

The second form of *fc* is described in "Command Line Editing" on page 301.

Table 8.7 The *fc* Command

fc arguments	*Meaning*
-e editor	Puts history list into editor
-l n-m	Lists commands in range from *n* to *m*
-n	Turns off numbering of history list
-r	Reverses the order of the history list
-s string	Accesses command starting with string

EXAMPLE 8.29

```
1  $ fc -l
    4        ls
    5        history
    6        exit
    7        history
    8        ls
    9        pwd
   10        clear
   11        cal 2000
   12        history
   13        vi file
   14        history
   15        ls -l
   16        date
   17        more file
   18        echo a b c d
   19        cd
   20        history
2  $ fc -l -3
   19        cd
   20        history
   21        fc -l
3 $  fc -ln
       exit
       history
       ls
       pwd
       clear
       cal 2000
       history
       vi file
       history
       ls -l
```

EXAMPLE 8.29 (CONTINUED)

```
            date
            more file
            echo a b c d
            cd
            history
            fc -l
            fc -l -3

4 $ fc -ln -3 > saved

5 $ more saved
            fc -l
            fc -l -3
            fc -ln
6 $ fc -l 15
  15         ls -l
  16         date
  17         more file
  18         echo a b c d
  19         cd
  20         history
  21         fc -l
  22         fc -l -3
  23         fc -ln
  24         fc -ln -3 > saved
  25         more saved
  26         history
7 $ fc -l 15 20
  15         ls -l
  16         date
  17         more file
  18         echo a b c d
  19         cd
  20         history
```

EXPLANATION

1. *fc -l* selects the last 16 commands from the history list.
2. *fc -l -3* selects the last three commands from the history list.
3. *fc* with the *-ln* options prints the history list without line numbers.
4. The last three commands, without line numbers, from the history list are redirected to a file called *saved.*
5. The contents of the file, *saved*, are displayed.
6. Commands from the history list, starting at number 15, are listed.
7. Commands numbered 15 through 20 are displayed.

If *fc* is given the *-s* option, a string pattern can be used to reexecute a previous command; e.g., *fc -s rm* will cause the most previous line containing the pattern *rm* to be reexecuted. To emulate the Korn shell's *redo* command, you can create a *bash* alias called *r*, e.g., *alias r='fc -s'* so that if you type *r vi* at the command line, the last history item containing that pattern will be reexecuted; in this case, the *vi* editor will be started just as it was the last time it started, including any arguments passed.

EXAMPLE 8.30

```
1   $ history
     1     ls
     2     pwd
     3     clear
     4     cal 2000
     5     history
     6     ls -l
     7     date
     8     more file
     9     echo a b c d

2   $ fc -s da
    date
    Thu Jul  15 12:33:25 PST 1999

3   $ alias r="fc -s"
4   $ date +%T
    18:12:32

5   $ r d
    date +%T
    18:13:19
```

EXPLANATION

1 The built-in *history* command displays the history list.

2 *fc* with the *-s* option searches for the last command that began with string *da.* The *date* command is found in the history list and is reexecuted.

3 An alias, a user-defined nickname, called *r* is assigned the command *fc -s.* This means that any time *r* is typed at the command line, it will be substituted with *fc -s.*

4 The *date* command is executed. It will print the current time.

5 The alias is used as a shortcut to the *fs -s* command. The last command beginning with a *d* is reexecuted.

Reexecuting History Commands (bang! bang!). To reexecute a command from the history list, the exclamation point (called bang) is used. If you type two exclamation points (!!) *bang, bang,* the last command in the history list is reexecuted. If you type an exclamation point, followed by a number, the command listed by that number is reexecuted. If you type an exclamation point and a letter or string, the last command that started with that letter or string is reexecuted. The caret (^) is also used as a shortcut method for editing the previous command. See Table 8.8 for a complete list of history substitution characters.

Table 8.8 Substitution and History

Event Designators	*Meaning*
!	Indicates the start of history substitution.
!!	Reexecutes the previous command.
!*N*	Reexecutes the Nth command from the history list.
!-*N*	Reexecutes the Nth command back from present command.
!*string*	Reexecutes the last command starting with *string.*
!?*string*?	Reexecutes the last command containing *string.*
!?*string*?%	Reexecutes the most recent command line argument from the history list containing *string.*
!$	Uses the last argument from the last history command in the current command line.
!! *string*	Appends string to the previous command and executes.
!N *string*	Appends string to *N*th command in history list and executes.
!N:*s/old/new/*	In previous *N*th command, substitutes the first occurrence of old string with new string.
!N:*gs/old/new/*	In previous *N*th command, globally substitutes old string with new string.
^*old*^*new*^	In last *history* command, substitutes old string with new string.
command !N:wn	Executes current command appending an argument *(wn)* from the *N*th previous command. *Wn* is a number starting at 0, 1, 2, ... designating the number of the word from the previous command; word 0 is the command itself, and 1 is its first argument, etc. (See Example 8.32.)

EXAMPLE 8.31

```
1   $ date
    Mon Jul  12 12:27:35 PST 1999

2   $ !!
    date
    Mon Jul  12 12:28:25 PST 1999

3   $ !106
    date
    Mon Jul  12 12:29:26 PST 1999

4   $ !d
    date
    Mon Jul  12 12:30:09 PST 1999

5   $ dare
    dare: Command not found.

6   $ ^r^t
    date
    Mon Jul  12 12:33:25 PST 1999
```

EXPLANATION

1 The Linux *date* command is executed at the command line. The history list is updated. This is the last command on the list.

2 The *!!* (bang bang) gets the last command from the history list; the command is reexecuted.

3 Command number 106 from the history list is reexecuted.

4 The last command on the history list that started with the letter *d* is reexecuted.

5 The command is mistyped. It should be *date*, not *dare*.

6 The carets are used to substitute letters from the last command on the history list. The first occurrence of an *r* is replaced with a *t*; i.e., *dare* becomes *date*.

EXAMPLE 8.32

```
1  $ ls  file1 file2 file3
   file1 file2 file3

   $ vi !:1
   vi file1

2  $ ls file1 file2 file
   file1 file2 file3

   $ ls !:2
   ls file2
   file2

3  $ ls file1 file2 file3
   $ ls  !:3
   ls file3
   file3

4  $ echo a b c
   a b c
   $ echo !$
   echo c
   c

5  $ echo a b c
   a b c
   $ echo !^
   echo a
   a

6  % echo a b c
   a b c
   % echo !*
   echo a b c
   a b c

7  % !!:p
   echo a b c
```

EXPLANATION

1 The *ls* command lists *file1, file2,* and *file3.* The history list is updated. The command line is broken into words, starting with word number zero. If the word number is preceded by a colon, that word can be extracted from the history list. The *!:1* notation means "*get the first argument from the last command on the history list and replace it in the command string.*" The first argument from the last command is *file1.* (Word *0* is the command itself.)

EXPLANATION (CONTINUED)

2 The *!:2* is replaced with the second argument of the last command, *file2*, and given as an argument to *ls*. *File2* is printed. (*file2* is the third word.)

3 *ls !:3* reads "*go to the last command on the history list and get the fourth word (words start at zero) and pass it to the* ls *command as an argument.*" (*file3* is the fourth word.)

4 The bang (*!*) with the dollar sign (*$*) refers to the last argument of the last command on the history list. The last argument is *c*.

5 The caret (^) represents the first argument after the command. The bang (*!*) with the ^ refers to the first argument of the last command on the history list. The first argument of the last command is *a*.

6 The asterisk (*) represents all arguments after the command. The bang (*!*) with the * refers to all of the arguments of the last command on the history list.

7 The last command from the history list is printed but not executed. The history list is updated. You could now perform caret substitutions on that line.

Command Line Editing. The *bash* shell provides two built-in editors, *emacs* and *vi*, so that you can interactively edit your history list. This feature has been implemented through a package called the Readline Library (See "The Readline Library and Binding Keys" on page 306 for a list of *readline* functions). When you use the editing features at the command line, whether in *vi* or *emacs* mode, the *readline* functions determine which keys will perform certain functions. For example, if using *emacs*, Ctrl-P allows you to scroll upward in the command line history, whereas if using *vi*, the K key moves upward through the history list. *Readline* also controls the arrow keys, cursor movement, changing, deleting, inserting text, and redoing or undoing corrections. Another feature of *readline* is the completion feature previously discussed in "Command and Filename Completion" on page 291. This allows you to type part of a command, filename, or variable, and then, by pressing the Tab key, the rest of the word is completed. There are many more features provided by the Readline library designed to help manipulate text at the command line.

The *emacs* built-in editor is the default built-in editor and is modeless, whereas the *vi* built-in editor works in two modes, one to execute commands on lines and the other to enter text. If you use either UNIX or Linux, you are probably familiar with one of these editors. To enable the *vi* editor, add the *set* command listed below[4] and put this line in your *~/.bashrc* file. To set *vi*, type what's shown in the following example, at either the prompt or in the *~/.bashrc* file.

---

4. If the set *-o* (editor) has not been set, but the EDITOR variable has been set to either *emacs* or *vi*, then bash will use that definition.

EXAMPLE 8.33

```
set -o vi
```

EXPLANATION

Sets the built-in editor, *vi*, for command line editing of the history list.

To switch to the *emacs* editor, type:

EXAMPLE 8.34

```
set -o emacs
```

EXPLANATION

Sets the built-in editor, *emacs*, for command line editing of the history list.

The *vi* Built-In Editor. To edit the history list, go to the command line and press the ESC key. Then press the *K* key if you want to scroll upward in the history list, and the *J* key[5] to move downward, just like standard *vi* motion keys. When you find the command that you want to edit, use the standard keys that you would use in *vi* for moving left and right, deleting, inserting, and changing text. (See Table 8.9.) After making the edit, press the Enter key. The command will be executed and added to the bottom of the history list.

Table 8.9 *vi* Commands

Command	*Function*
Moving Through the History File	
ESC k *or* +	Move up the history list.
ESC j *or* -	Move down the history list.
G	Move to first line in history file.
5G	Move to fifth command in history file for *string*.
/string	Search upward through history file.
?	String search downward through history file.

5. *vi* is case-sensitive; an uppercase *J* and a lowercase *j* are different commands.

Table 8.9 *vi* Commands (Continued)

Command	*Function*
Moving Around on a Line	
h	Move left on a line.
l	Move right on a line.
b	Move backward a word.
e *or* w	Move forward a word.
^ *or* 0	Move to beginning of first character on the line.
$	Move to end of line.
Editing with vi	
a A	Append text.
i I	Insert text.
Editing with vi (continued)	
dd dw x	Delete text into a buffer (line, word, or character).
cc C	Change text.
u U	Undo.
yy Y	Yank (copy a line into buffer).
p P	Put yanked or deleted line down below or above the line.
r R	Replace a letter or any amount of text on a line.

The *emacs* Built-In Editor. If using the emacs built-in editor, like *vi*, start at the command line. To start moving upward through the history file, press ^P. To move down, press ^N. Use *emacs* editing commands to change or correct text, then press Enter, and the command will be reexecuted. See Table 8.10.

Table 8.10 *emacs* Commands

Command	*Function*
Ctrl-P	Move up history file.
Ctrl-N	Move down history file.
ESC <	Move to first line of history file.
ESC >	Move to last line of history file.
Ctrl-B	Move backward one character.

Table 8.10 *emacs* Commands (Continued)

Command	***Function***
Ctrl-R	Search backward for string.
ESC B	Move backward one word.
Ctrl-F	Move forward one character.
ESC F	Move forward one word.
Ctrl-A	Move to the beginning of the line.
Ctrl-E	Move to the end of the line.
ESC <	Move to the first line of the history file.
ESC >	Move to the last line of the history file.
Editing with emacs	
Ctrl-U	Delete the line.
Ctrl-Y	Put the line back.
Ctrl-K	Delete from cursor to the end line.
Ctrl-D	Delete a letter.
ESC D	Delete one word forward.
ESC H	Delete one word backward.
ESC space	Set a mark at cursor position.
Ctrl-X Ctrl-X	Exchange cursor and mark.
Ctrl-P Ctrl-Y	Push region from cursor to mark into a buffer (Ctrl-P) and put it down (Ctrl-Y).

***FCEDIT* and Editing Commands.** If the *fc* command is given the *-e* option followed by the name of a *Linux* editor, that editor is invoked containing history commands selected from the history list; e.g., *fc -e vi -1 -3* will invoke the *vi* editor, create a temporary file in */tmp*, with the last three commands from the history list in the *vi* buffer. The commands can be edited or commented out. (Preceding the command with a # will comment it.) If the user quits the editor, the commands will all be echoed and executed.[6]

If the editor name is not given, the value of the *FCEDIT* variable is used (typically set in the initialization files, either *bash_profile* or *.profile*), and the value of the *EDITOR* variable is used if *FCEDIT* is not set. When editing is complete, and you exit the editor, all of the edited commands are echoed and executed.

6. Whether the user save and quits the editor, or simply quits the editor, the commands will all be executed, unless they are commented or deleted.

EXAMPLE 8.35

```
1   $ FCEDIT=/bin/vi
2   $ pwd
3   $ fc
< Starts up the full screen vi editor with the pwd command on line 1>
```

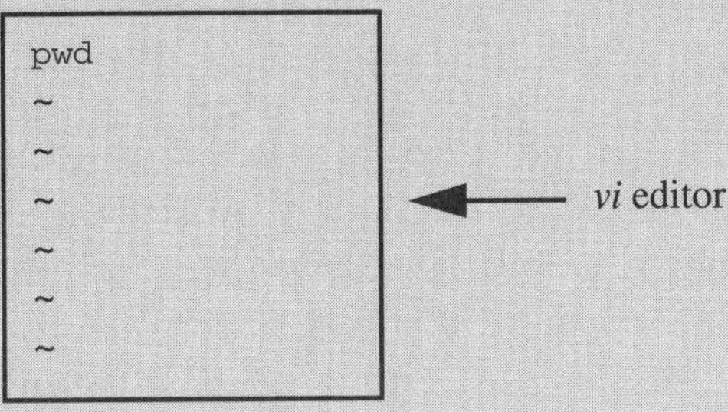


```
4   $ history
    1 date
    2 ls -l
    3 echo "hello"
    4 pwd

5   $ fc -3 -1        start vi, edit, write/quit, and execute
                       last 3 commands:
```

EXPLANATION

1 The *FCEDIT* variable can be assigned the pathname for any of the *Linux* text editors you have on your system, such as *vi, emacs,* etc. If not set, the *vi* editor is the default.

2 The *pwd* command is typed at the command line. It will be placed in the *history* file.

3 The *fc* command caused the editor (set in *FCEDIT*) to be invoked with the last command typed in the editor window. After the user writes and quits the editor, any commands typed there will be executed.

4 The *history* command lists recently typed commands.

5 The *fc* command is used to start up the editor with the last three commands from the *history* file in the editor's buffer.

8.2.4 The Readline Library and Binding Keys

The *Readline* Library. The Readline library (type: *man readline*) is a set of library routines, copyright of the Free Software Foundation, Inc. that controls the way keys function when typing text at the command line. When any program which uses the Readline library starts up, such as the shell, an init file (normally called *~./inputrc*) is read, and readline prompts the user for input. It then reads a line from the terminal and returns it. You can also type different key strokes to edit what you have previously typed. Readline uses an *emacs* style notation for denoting key strokes; e.g., *C-h* means *Control-H*, *M-x* means *Meta-X*. (If the Meta key is not on your keyboard, either the Escape or the Alt key can be used instead.) To use *vi* key bindings, instead of the default *emacs* bindings, just turn on the *vi* command line editor with *set -o vi* as shown in "Command Line Editing" on page 301 or by adding the following line to the initialization file *~/.inputrc* for *readline*:

```
set editing-mode vi
```

To customize *readline*, put commands that control keys and how they function in a file called *~/.inputrc*. (The filename can be different if assigned to the *INPUTRC* environment variable.) When a shell or any other program that uses the Readline library starts, the *.inputrc* file is read, and the key settings and variables defined in that file are set.

You can see how the keys are bound by looking at the output of the built-in *bind* command. To see a complete list of key bindings and definitions, see the *readline* manual page. It lists all the key bindings and what they control.

Binding Keys. There are several ways to bind keys in the *.inputrc* file. You can use an English name for the key, such as *Ctrl-T* to represent the *Control* and *T* characters, or you can use the escape sequence, *\C-t*. To assign a value to the key, use either a built-in *readline* command such as *backward-kill-line*, a macro, or a *readline* variable. The functions for both *emacs* and *vi* can be viewed by looking at the output of the built-in *bind*[7] command. Type at the *bash* prompt:

find -v[8] *or* **bind -p**

- **The English Format**
  To bind keys with the English format, the key sequence is spelled out, followed by a colon, followed by the command or macro that defines the behavior of the key sequence. In the following example, *C-u* is bound to the function *universal-argument*, and *C-o* is bound to run the macro "*>& output*". [9]

---

7. For a complete list of options to *bind*, type: *help bind*.
8. On bash 2.x.
9. Some of these examples for binding keys are from the *bash man* page, where *readline* is defined.

EXAMPLE 8.36

(English format for binding keys)
(from ~/.inputrc file)

1. Control-U: universal-argument
2. Meta-Rubout: backward-kill-word
3. Control-O: ">& output"[a]

a. To try these key bindings, put them in *~/.inputrc*. To test a binding, do one of the following: (1) log out and back on, (2) start a new bash shell, or (3) type Cotnrol-X, Control-R.

EXPLANATION

1 *Control-U* is set to the universal argument. By pressing the Control key and U together, the *universal argument* is set for the next command typed at the command line. For example, if you press *Control-U,* you will see on a line by itself: **(arg: 4)**. Then if you use an *emacs* command that can take an argument, such as *Control-P,* instead of moving up one line in the history list, you will be moved 4 lines up. If you type a number after you see the string: **(arg: 4)**, the number you type will replace the 4 to a new argument count. Typing 6, for example, would change the universal argument count to: **(arg: 6)**. Thereafter, each time you press *Control-U*, while at the (arg: #) prompt the number will be multiplied by 4, making it (**arg:24**). Always multiplies arg by 4.

To test the new setting, type a line of text. Then press *Control-U.* Next press a left or right arrow key. You will be moved to the left or right by the number of characters shown after the universal argument prompt, by default a multiple of 4.

2 The *Meta* and *Rubout* key (Alt and Del keys) are assigned the *readline* command, *backward-kill-word.* Using this combination of keys will erase a word from the point of the cursor backward.

3 The *Control-O* sequence is assigned a macro, a string of text. When the *Control-O* keys are pressed, the string *">&output"* will appear on the screen. This can be used to redirect the output and errors from a command to a file called *output.* For example, if you typed at the command line prompt: *find / -type d -print* and then pressed *Control-O*, you would see *find / -type d -print >& output.*

- **The Escape Format**
  If you are using the Escape key sequence, the key sequence is surrounded by double quotes. In the following example, *\C-u* represents *Control-U*, *\C-x\C-r* represents *Control-X* to be followed immediately by *Control-R*, and the last example demonstrates an escape sequence that binds the F1 function key if that key is entered at the *Linux* console window.

EXAMPLE 8.37

(The escape sequences)
(from ~/.inputrc file)

1. \C-u: universal-argument
2. \C-x\C-r: re-read-init-file
3. \e[11~: Function Key 1

EXPLANATION

1 The escape sequence is in double quotes. This syntax produces the same binding and result as in the previous example where the English notation was used: *Control-U: universal-argument.*

2 The escape sequence *\C-x\C-r* can be used to reread the *~/.inputrc* file if you have edited it, similar to sourcing the *.bashrc* file. Otherwise, the changes made will not be reflected unless you start another shell.

3 This escape sequence is generated by the Function key 1 on terminals where the terminal type is *linux*. In this example the function key is bound to a string. No doubt you would want to do something more interesting. However, be careful when binding function keys. They may already have a specific function of their own, such as turning off the display or locking the screen.

- **Macros and Escape Sequences**
  Macros are strings of quoted text that can be assigned to key sequences to define what the keys do. For example, if the sequence *\C-o* is assigned the macro string "| *more*", every time the user presses *Control-O*, the macro will be expanded to "| *more*". Within the key sequences and macro definitions, you can also embed escape sequences to represent special characters as listed in Table 8.11. The backslash can also be used for other characters in a string so that they will be treated as literals.

Table 8.11 Escape Sequences

\C-	Control prefix
\M-	Meta prefix
\e	An escape character
\\	A backslash
\"	A double quote

Table 8.11 Escape Sequences (Continued)

\'	A single quote
a	Alert (bell)
b	Backspace
d	Delete
f	Form feed
n	Newline
r	Carriage return
t	Horizontal tab
v	Vertical tab
nnn	A three digit octal number representing the corresponding ASCII code for that character.
xnnn	A three digit hex number representing the corresponding ASCII code for that character.

***Readline* Variables.** There are also a number of *readline* variables that can be set in the *~/.inputrc* file to modify the way *readline* behaves. To set a *readline* variable, the format is:

```
set variable value
```

For some of the variables, either *On* or *Off* can be given as a value. A list of the variables and their values is given in Table 8.12.

FORMAT

```
set variable value
```

EXAMPLE 8.38

1. set editing-mode vi
2. set expand-tilde On

Table 8.12 Readline Variables

bell-style (audible)	Controls the terminal bell. If set to none, bell never rings. If set to visible, readline uses a visible bell if one is available. If set to audible, readline attempts to ring the terminal's bell.
comment-begin	Used by readline's *insert-comment* command; by default a #.
completion-query-items	Controls the number of completions the user can ask to see. The default is 100.
convert-meta (On)	Converts characters with the eighth bit set to an ASCII key sequence by stripping the eighth bit and prepending an escape character (in effect, using escape as the metaprefix).
disable-completion (Off)	If set to *On*, inhibits word completion.
editing-mode (emacs)	Sets the key bindings for command line editing to either *emacs* or *vi*. *Emacs* is the default.
enable-keypad (Off)	When set to *On*, readline will try to enable the application keypad when it is called. Some systems need this to enable the arrow keys.
expand-tilde (Off)	If set to *On*, tilde expansion is performed when readline attempts word completion.
horizontal-scroll-mode (Off)	When set to *On*, makes readline use a single line for display (even if you type past the right margin of the screen), scrolling the input horizontally on a single screen line when it becomes longer than the screen width rather than wrapping to a new line.
input-meta (Off)	If set to *On*, readline will enable eight-bit input(that is, it will not strip the high bit from the characters it reads), regardless of what the terminal claims it can support. The name meta-flag is a synonym for this variable.
isearch-terminators (''-[C-J'')	The string of characters that should terminate an incremental search without subsequently executing the character as a command. If this variable has not been given a value, the characters ESC and C-J will terminate an incremental search.
keymap (emacs)	Sets the current readline keymap. The set of valid keymap names is *emacs, emacs-standard, emacs-meta, emacs-ctlx,vi, vi-command*, and *vi-insert*. *Vi* is equialent to *vi-command* and *emacs* to *emacs-standard*. The default is *emacs*; the value of *editing-mode* also effects the default keymap.
mark-directories (On)	If set to *On*, appends completed directory names with a slash.

Table 8.12 Readline Variables (Continued)

mark-modified-lines (Off)	If set to *On*, modified history lines that have been modified are preceded by an asterisk (*).
meta-flag (Off)	If set to *On*, eight-bit input is accepted.
output-meta (Off)	If set to *On*, displays characters with the eighth bit set directly rather than as a metaprefixed escape sequence.
print-completions-horizontally (Off)	If set to *On*, readline will display completions with matches sorted horizontally in alphabetical order, rather than down the screen.
show-all-if-ambiguous (Off)	If set to *On*, words which have more than one possible completion cause the matches to be listed immediately instead of ringing the bell.
visible-stats (Off)	If set to *On*, appends a character to a filename, denoting the file's type (reported by the *stat* system call) when listing completions.

To see the readline variables, use the *bind* built-in command as shown in Example 8.39.

EXAMPLE 8.39

```
1  $ bind -V
completion-ignore-case is set to 'off'
convert-meta is set to 'on'
disable-completion is set to 'off'
enable-keypad is set to 'off'
expand-tilde is set to 'off'
horizontal-scroll-mode is set to 'off'
input-meta is set to 'off'
mark-directories is set to 'on'
mark-modified-lines is set to 'on'
meta-flag is set to 'off'
output-meta is set to 'off'
print-completions-horizontally is set to 'off'
show-all-if-ambiguous is set to 'off'
visible-stats is set to 'off'
bell-style is set to 'none'
comment-begin is set to ''
completion-query-items is set to '100'
editing-mode is set to 'vi'
keymap is set to 'vi-insert'
```

Simple Conditionals. There are several *readline* conditional constructs you can put in the *.inputrc* file to test for specific conditions before setting key bindings. For example, there may be a key binding that will work only if you are using the *emacs* built-in editor, or the terminal type is *linux*, or is specific to a certain type of application such as the shell or *xterm*.

The conditional *readline* constructs for testing are: *$if*, *$else*, and *$endif*, and *$include*.

The *$if* construct allows you to bind keys to *readline* commands based on the editing mode, the terminal being used, or the application using *readline*. The *$endif* terminates the *$if* construct and the *$else* is used for branching if the test fails.

The *$include* construct takes a single filename as its argument and reads commands and bindings from that file.

Table 8.13 Tests for *$if*

Test	*Example*	*What It Does*
mode=editor	*$if mode=emacs*	Tests whether *readline* is in *emacs* mode; can also test for *vi* mode.
term=terminal	*$if term=sun*	Tests if terminal is *sun* or *sun-cmd*.
application	*$if bash*	Tests if the appliction using readline is a *bash* shell.
filename	*$include /etc/inputrc*	Reads key bindings from */etc/inputrc*.

Setting Up the *.inputrc* File. The following example demonstrates how to set up an *.inputrc* file with *readline* commands and variables described in this section. This file belongs in your home directory. To reexecute the file after you have created it, or made changes to it, type the *Ctrl-x, Ctrl-r* sequence. Otherwise, to test, you can start a new shell by typing "bash" at the prompt. Every time you start a new shell, the *.inputrc* file is reread by the Readline library.

EXAMPLE 8.40

```
(Sample .inputrc file)

1  # set editing-mode vi   value of  editing-mode variable also
      # affects the default keymap.
2  set bell-style none
3  set mark-directories On
4  set mark-modified-lines On
5  Control o: "| more"
```

EXAMPLE 8.40 (CONTINUED)

```
6 "C-x\C-r": re-read-init-file
7 $if mode=emacs
8        Control-t: universal-argument

9 $endif
10 $if term=linux
         "\e[12~": "Welcome to the Linux World!\n"
   $endif
```

EXPLANATION

1 When you set the editing mode to *vi,* the key bindings for the *vi* editor are in effect when performing command line editing. It has been commented here.

2 The terminal bell is turned off. Now it won't beep at you when you reach the end of a line, or cannot perform filename completion, etc.

3 If the variable, *mark-directories*, is turned *On*, directory names will be appended with a slash when filename completion is performed.

4 The lines in the history list are commands that have been previously entered. If any of these commands have been altered, a star will be prepended to the line containing the command, if the *mark-modified-lines* variable is *On*.

5 In this example, the key sequence is in the English format and the keys are bound to a macro. If the Control and O keys are pressed at the same time, the macro will be expanded. For example, if you type: *ls Ctrl-O* , you will get: *ls | more*

6 This example uses the *emacs* style escape sequence key format to represent the key sequence. If *Control-x* is typed, followed by *Control-r*, the *~/.inputrc* file is reread by *readline*.

7 The *$if* directive is used to test if the editor being used by *readline* is *emacs*.

8 If the editor is *emacs*, *Control-T* is bound to the universal argument, a *readline* command. If the *Control-T* key sequence is entered, the universal argument can be used to modify the command most recently typed. (See explanation of universal argument in Example 8.36.)

9 The *$endif* construct ends the conditional *$if* and its statements.

10 If the terminal is the virtual console, *linux*, when the F1 function key is pressed, *Welcome to the Linux world!* is displayed.

8.2.5 Aliases

An *alias* is a *bash* user-defined abbreviation for a command. Aliases are useful if a command has a number of options and arguments or the syntax is difficult to remember. Aliases set at the command line are not inherited by subshells. Aliases are normally set in the *.bashrc* file. Because the *.bashrc* is executed when a new shell is started, any aliases set there will be reset for the new shell. Aliases may also be passed into shell scripts but will cause potential portability problems unless they are set directly within the script.

Listing Aliases. The *alias* built-in command lists all set aliases. The alias is printed first, followed by the real command or commands it represents.

EXAMPLE 8.41

```
$ alias
alias co='compress'
alias cp='cp -i'
alias mroe='more'
alias mv='mv -i'
alias ls='ls --colorztty'
alias uc='uncompress'
```

EXPLANATION

The *alias* command lists the alias (nickname) for the command and the real command the alias represents after the = sign.

Creating Aliases. The *alias* command is used to create an alias. The first argument is the name of the alias, the nickname for the command. The rest of the line consists of the command or commands that will be executed when the alias is executed. *Bash* aliases cannot take arguments (see "Defining Functions" on page 360). Multiple commands are separated by a semicolon, and commands containing spaces and metacharacters are surrounded by single quotes.

EXAMPLE 8.42

```
$ alias m=more
$ alias mroe=more
$ alias lF='ls -alF'
$ alias r='fc -s'
```

EXPLANATION

1 The nickname for the *more* command is set to *m*.

2 The alias for the *more* command is set to *mroe*. This is handy if you can't spell.

3 The alias definition is enclosed in quotes because of the white space. The alias *lF* is a nickname for the command *ls -alF.*

4 The alias *r* will be used instead of *fc -s* to recall commands from the history list by a specified pattern; e.g., *r vi* will reexecute the last command in the history list containing the pattern *vi.*

Deleting Aliases. The *unalias* command is used to delete an alias. To temporarily turn off an alias, precedethe alias name by a backslash.

EXAMPLE 8.43

```
1   % unalias mroe
2   % \ls
```

EXPLANATION

1 The *unalias* command deletes the alias *mroe* from the list of defined aliases.

2 The alias *ls* is temporarily turned off for this execution of the command only.

8.2.6 Manipulating the Directory Stack

If you find that as you work, you *cd* up and down the directory tree into many of the same directories, you can make it easy to access those directories by pushing them onto a directory stack and manipulating the stack. The *pushd* built-in command pushes directories onto a stack and the *popd* command removes them. (See Example 8.44.) The stack is a list of directories with the directory at the left being the most recent directory pushed onto the stack. The directories can be listed with the built-in *dirs* command.

The *dirs* Built-In Command. The built-in command, *dirs*, with a *-l* option, displays the directory stack with each of its directories in full pathname format; without an option, *dirs* uses a tilde to denote the home directory. With a *+n* option, *dirs* displays the *nth* directory entry counting from the left in the directory list, starting a 0. With *-n* option, it does the same thing, but starts at the right-hand side of the directory list with 0.

The *pushd* and *popd* Commands. The *pushd* command, with a directory as an argument, causes the new directory to be added to the directory stack and, at the same time, changes to that directory. If the argument is a *+n* where *n* is a number, *pushd* rotates the stack so that the *n*th directory from the stack, starting at the left-hand side, is pushed onto the top of the stack. With a *-n* option, it does the same thing but starts at the right-hand side. Without arguments, *pushd* exchanges the top two elements of the directory stack, making it easy to switch back and forth between directories.

The *popd* command removes a directory from the top of the stack, and changes to that directory. With *+n,* where *n* is a number, *popd* removes the *n*th entry, starting at the left of the list shown by *dirs*.

EXAMPLE 8.44

```
1   > pwd
    /home/ellie

    > pushd ..
    /home ~

    > pwd
    /home

2   > pushd        # swap the two top directories on the stack
    ~ /home

    > pwd
    /home/ellie

3   > pushd perlclass
    ~/perlclass  ~  /home

4   > dirs
    ~/perlclass ~ /home

5   > dirs -l
    /home/ellie/perlclass /home/ellie  /home

6   > popd
    ~/home

    > pwd
    /home/ellie

7   > popd
    /home

    > pwd
    /home

8   > popd
    bash: popd: Directory stack empty.
```

EXPLANATION

1 First the *pwd* command displays the present working directory, */home/ellie*. Next the *pushd* command with **..** as its argument, pushes the parent directory (**..**) onto the directory stack. The output of *pushd* indicates that */home* is at the top of the directory stack (starting at the left-hand side of the displayed list) and the user's home directory, represented by the tilde character (~) is at the bottom of the stack. *pushd* also changes the directory to the one that was pushed onto the stack; i.e., **..** which translates to */home*. The new directory is displayed with the second *pwd* command.

2 *Pushd*, without arguments, exchanges the two top directory entries on the stack and changes to the swapped directory; in this example, the directory is switched back to the user's home directory, */home/ellie*.

3 The *pushd* command will push its argument, *~/perlclass,* onto the stack, and change to that directory.

4 The built-in *dirs* command displays the directory stack, with the top level starting at left-hand side of the listing. The tilde expands to the user's home directory.

5 With the *-l* option, *dirs* list displays the directory stack with full pathnames instead of using tilde expansion.

6 The *popd* command removes a directory from the top of the stack, and changes to that directory.

7 The *popd* command removes another directory from the top of the stack, and changes to that directory.

8 The *popd* command cannot remove any more directory entries because the stack is empty, and issues an error message saying so.

8.2.7 Metacharacters (Wildcards)

Metacharacters are special characters used to represent something other than themselves. Shell metacharacters are called *wildcards*. Table 8.14 lists metacharacters and what they do.

Table 8.14 Metacharacters

Metacharacter	*Meaning*
\	Literally interprets the following character.
&	Processes in the background.
;	Separates commands.
$	Substitutes variables.

Table 8.14 Metacharacters (Continued)

Metacharacter	*Meaning*
?	Matches for a single character.
[abc]	Matches for one character from a set of characters; e.g., *a*, *b*, or *c*.
[!abc]	Matches for one character *not* from the set of characters; e.g., not *a*, *b*, or *c*.
*	Matches for zero or more characters.
(cmds)	Executes commands in a subshell.
{cmds}	Executes commands in current shell.

8.2.8 Filename Substitution (Globbing)

When evaluating the command line, the shell uses metacharacters to abbreviate filenames or pathnames that match a certain set of characters. The filename substitution metacharacters listed in Table 8.15 are expanded into an alphabetically listed set of filenames. The process of expanding the metacharacter into filenames is also called *filename substitution,* or *globbing*. If a metacharacter is used and there is no filename that matches it, the shell treats the metacharacter as a literal character.

Table 8.15 Shell Metacharacters and Filename Substitution

Metacharacter	*Meaning*
*	Matches zero or more characters.
?	Matches exactly one character.
[abc]	Matches one character in the set *a, b*, or *c*.
[!abc]	Matches one character not in the set, not *a*, *b*, or *c*.
{a,ile,ax}	Matches for a character or set of characters.
[! a–z]	Matches one character *not* in the range from *a* to *z*.
\	Escapes or disables the metacharacter.

The Asterisk. The asterisk is a wildcard that matches for zero or more of any characters in a filename.

EXAMPLE 8.45

```
1   $ ls *
    abc abc1 abc122 abc123 abc2 file1 file1.bak file2 file2.bak none
    nonsense nobody nothing nowhere one
2   $ ls *.bak
    file1.bak file2.bak
3   $ echo a*
    ab abc1 abc122 abc123 abc2
```

EXPLANATION

1 The asterisk expands to all of the files in the present working directory. All of the files are passed as arguments to *ls* and displayed.

2 All files starting with zero or more characters and ending with *.bak* are matched and listed.

3 All files starting with *a*, followed by zero or more characters, are matched and passed as arguments to the *echo* command.

The Question Mark. The question mark represents a single character in a filename. When a filename contains one or more question marks, the shell performs filename substitution by replacing the question mark with the character it matches in the filename.

EXAMPLE 8.46

```
1   $ ls
    abc   abc122   abc2   file1.bak   file2.bak   nonsense   nothing   one
    abc1   abc123   file1   file2   none   noone   nowhere

2   $ ls a?c?
    abc1 abc2

3   $ ls ??
    ls: ??: No such file or directory

4   $ echo  abc???
    abc122 abc123

5   $ echo ??
    ??
```

EXPLANATION

1 The files in the current directory are listed.

2 Filenames starting with *a*, followed by a single character, followed by *c* and a single character, are matched and listed.

3 Filenames containing exactly two characters are listed, if found. Because there are not any two-character files, the question marks are treated as a literal filename. Such a file is not found, and the error message is printed.

4 Filenames starting with *abc* and followed by exactly three characters are expanded and displayed by the *echo* command.

5 There are no files in the directory that contain exactly two characters. The shell treats the question mark as a literal question mark if it cannot find a match.

The Square Brackets. The brackets are used to match filenames containing *one* character in a set or range of characters.

EXAMPLE 8.47

```
1   $ ls
    abc abc122 abc2 file1.bak file2.bak nonsense nothing
    one abc1 abc123 file1 file2 none noone nowhere

2   $ ls abc[123]
    abc1  abc2

3   $ ls abc[1-3]
    abc1  abc2

4   $ ls [a-z][a-z][a-z]
    abc one

5   $ ls [!f-z]???
    abc1  abc2

6   $ ls abc12[23]
    abc122 abc123
```

EXPLANATION

1 All of the files in the present working directory are listed.

2 All filenames containing four characters are matched and listed if the filename starts with *abc*, followed by *1*, *2*, or *3*. Only one character from the set in the brackets is matched.

EXPLANATION (CONTINUED)

3 All filenames containing four characters are matched and listed, if the filename starts with *abc* and is followed by a number in the range from *1* to *3*.

4 All filenames containing three characters are matched and listed, if the filename contains exactly three lowercase alphabetic characters.

5 All filenames containing four characters are listed if the first character is *not* a letter between *f* and *z* (*[!f-z]*, followed by three of any characters, where *?* represents a single character.

6 Files are listed if the filenames contain *abc12* followed by *2* or *3*.

Brace Expansion. The curly braces match for any of a list of comma-separated strings. Normally the strings are filenames. Any characters prepended to the opening curly brace are called the *preamble*, and any characters appended to the closing curly brace are called the *postamble*. Both the *preamble* and *postamble* are optional. There can be no unquoted white space within the braces.

EXAMPLE 8.48

```
1   $ ls
    a.c b.c abc ab3 ab4 ab5 file1 file2 file3 file4 file5 foo
    faa fumble

2   $ ls f{oo,aa,umble}
    foo faa fumble

3   $ ls a{.c,c,b[3-5]}
    a.c ab3 ab4 ab5

4   $ mkdir /usr/local/src/bash/{old,new,dist,bugs}

5   $ chown root /usr/{ucb/{ex,edit},lib/{ex?.?*,how_ex}}

6   $ echo fo{o, um}*
    fo{o, um}*

7   $ echo {mam,pap,ba}a
    mama papa baa

8   $ echo post{script,office,ure}
    postscript postoffice posture
```

EXPLANATION

1 All the files in the current directory are listed.

2 Files starting with *f* and followed by the strings *oo*, *aa*, or *umble* are listed. Spaces inside the curly braces will cause the error message *Missing }*.

3 Files starting with *a* followed by *.c, c*, or *b3, b4*, or *b5* are listed. (The square brackets can be used inside the curly braces.)

4 Four new directories will be made in */usr/local/src/bash: old, new, dist, and bugs.*

5 Root ownership will be given to files, *ex* and *edit,* in directory */usr /ucb* and to files named *ex* followed by one character, a period, and at least one more character, and a file called *how_ex* in directory */usr/lib* .

6 Brace expansion will not occur if there are any unquoted spaces within the braces.

7 Brace expansion does not necessarily always cause expansion of filenames. In this example the postamble, *a*, is added to each of the strings within the curly braces and echoed back after the expansion.

8 The preamble is the string *post*, followed by a comma-separated list enclosed within braces. Brace expansion is performed and the resulting strings are displayed.

Escaping Metacharacters. To use a metacharacter as a literal character, use the backslash to prevent the metacharacter from being interpreted.

EXAMPLE 8.49

```
1   $ ls
    abc file1 youx

2   $ echo How are you?
    How are youx

3   $ echo How are you\?
    How are you?

4   $ echo  When does this line \
    > ever end\?
    When does this line ever end?
```

EXPLANATION

1 The files in the present working directory are listed. (Note the file *youx*.)

EXPLANATION (CONTINUED)

2 The shell will perform filename expansion on the *?*. Any files in the current directory starting with *y-o-u* and followed by exactly one character are matched and substituted in the string. The filename *youx* will be substituted in the string to read *How are youx* (probably not what you want to happen).

3 By preceding the question mark with a backslash, it is escaped, meaning that the shell will not try to interpret it as a wildcard.

4 The newline is escaped by preceding it with a backslash. The secondary prompt is displayed until the string is terminated with a newline. The question mark (*?*) is escaped to protect it from filename expansion.

Tilde and Hyphen Expansion. The tilde character was adopted by the *bash* shell (from the C shell) for pathname expansion. The tilde by itself evaluates to the full pathname of the user's home directory.[10] When the tilde is appended with a username, it expands to the full pathname of that user.

When the plus sign follows the tilde, the value of the *PWD* (present working directory), replaces the tilde. The tilde followed by the hyphen character is replaced with the previous working directory; *OLDPWD* also refers to the previous working directory.

EXAMPLE 8.50

```
1  $ echo ~
   /home/jody/ellie

2  $ echo ~joe
   /home/joe

3  $ echo ~+
   /home/jody/ellie/perl

4  $ echo ~-
   /home/jody/ellie/prac

5  $ echo $OLDPWD
   /home/jody/ellie/prac

6  $ cd -
   /home/jody/ellie/prac
```

10. The tilde character will not be expanded if enclosed in either double or single quotes.

EXPLANATION

1 The tilde evaluates to the full pathname of the user's home directory.

2 The tilde preceding the username evaluates to the full pathname of *joe's* home directory.

3 The ~+ notation evaluates to the full pathname of the working directory.

4 The ~– notation evaluates to the previous working directory.

5 The *OLDPWD* variable contains the previous working directory.

6 The hyphen refers to the previous working directory; *cd* to go to the previous working directory and display the directory.

Controlling Wildcards (Globbing). If the *bash noglob* variable is set or if the *set* command is given a *-f* option, filename substitution, called globbing, is turned off, meaning that all metacharacters represent themselves; they are not used as wildcards. This can be useful when searching for patterns containing metacharacters in programs like *grep, sed*, or *awk*. If globbing is not set, all metacharacters must be escaped with a backslash to turn off wildcard interpretation.

The built-in *shopt* command (*bash* versions 2.x) also supports options for controlling globbing.

EXAMPLE 8.51

```
1   $ set noglob or set -f

2   $ print * ?? [] ~ $LOGNAME
    * ?? [] /home/jody/ellie ellie

3   $ unset noglob or set +f

4   $ shopt -s dotglob    # Only available in bash versions 2.x

5   $ echo *bash*
    .bash_history .bash_logout .bash_profile .bashrc bashnote
    bashtest
```

EXPLANATION

1 The *-f* option is given as an argument to the *set* command. It turns off the special meaning of wildcards used for filename expansion.

2 The filename expansion metacharacters are displayed as themselves without any interpretation. Note that the tilde and the dollar sign are still expanded, because they are not used for filename expansion.

EXPLANATION (CONTINUED)

3 If either *noglob* is unset or the *+f* option is set, filename metacharacters will be expanded.

4 The *shopt* built-in allows you to set options for the shell. The *dotglob* option allows filenames to be matched with globbing metacharacters, even in they start with a dot. Normally the files starting with a dot are invisible and not recognized when performing filename expansion.

5 Because the *dotglob* option was set in line 4, when the wildcard, *, is used for filename expansion, the filenames starting with a dot are also expanded if the filename contains the pattern, *bash.*

Extended Filename Globbing (*bash 2.x*). Derived from Korn shell pattern matching, *bash 2.x* has included this extended functionality, allowing regular expression type syntax. The regular expression operators are not recognized unless the *extglob* option to the *shopt* command is turned on:

```
shopt -s extglob
```

Table 8.16 Extended Pattern Matching

Regular Expression	*Its Meaning*
abc?(2|9)1	*?* matches zero or one occurrences of any pattern in the parentheses. The vertical bar represents an OR condition; e.g., either *2* or *9*. Matches *abc21*, *abc91*, or *abc1*.
abc([0–9])*	* matches zero or more occurrences of any pattern in the parentheses. Matches *abc* followed by zero or more digits; e.g., *abc*, *abc1234*, *abc3*, *abc2*, etc.
abc+([0–9])	+ matches one or more occurrences of any pattern in the parentheses. Matches *abc* followed by one or more digits; e.g., *abc3*, *abc123*, etc.
no@(one|ne)	@ matches exactly one occurrence of any pattern in the parentheses. Matches *noone* or *none.*
no!(thing|where)	*!* matches all strings *except* those matched by any of the patterns in the parentheses. Matches *no*, *nobody*, or *noone*, but not *nothing* or *nowhere.*

EXAMPLE 8.52

```
1   $ shopt -s extglob

2   $ ls
    abc      abc122   f1    f3     nonsense   nothing   one
    abc1     abc2     f2    none   noone      nowhere

3   $ ls abc?(1|2)
    abc      abc1     abc2

4   $ ls abc*([1-5])
    abc      abc1     abc122    abc2

5   $ ls abc+([0-5])
    abc1     abc122   abc2

6   $ ls no@(thing|ne)
    none     nothing

7   $ ls no!(thing)
    none     nonsense   noone     nowhere
```

EXPLANATION

1. The *shopt* built-in is used to set the *extglob* (extended globbing) option, allowing *bash* to recognize extended pattern matching characters.
2. All the files in the present working directory are listed.
3. Matches filenames starting with *abc* and followed by *zero characters or one* of either of the patterns in parentheses. Matches *abc*, *abc1*, or *abc2*.
4. Matches filenames starting with *abc* and followed by *zero or more* numbers between *1* and *5*. Matches *abc, abc1, abc122, abc123*, and *abc2*.
5. Matches filenames starting with *abc* and followed by *one or more* numbers between *0* and *5*. Matches *abc1, abc122, abc123,* and *abc2*.
6. Matches filenames starting with *no* and followed by *exactly thing* or *ne*. Matches *nothing* or *none*.
7. Matches filenames starting with *no* and followed by anything except *one* or *nsense*. Matches *none, nothing,* and *nowhere*. The *!* means *not*.

8.3 Variables

Types of Variables. There are two types of variables: local and environment. Local variables are known only to the shell in which they were created. Environment variables are available to any child processes spawned from the shell from which they were created. Some variables are created by the user and others are special shell variables.

Naming Conventions. Variable names must begin with an alpha or underscore character. The remaining characters can be alphas, decimal digits (0 to 9), or an underscore character. Any other characters mark the termination of the variable name. Names are case-sensitive. When assigning a value to a variable, do not include any white space surrounding the equal sign. To set the variable to null, follow the equal sign with a newline. The simplest format for creating a local variable is simply to assign a value to a variable in the format:

FORMAT

```
variable=value
```

EXAMPLE 8.53

```
name=Tommy
```

The *declare* Built-In. There are two built-in commands, *declare* and *typeset*, used to create variables, with options to control the way the variable is set. The *typeset* command (from Korn shell) is exactly the same as the *declare* command (*bash*). The *bash* documentation says, "The *typeset* command is supplied for compatibility with the Korn shell; however, it has been deprecated in favor of the *declare* built-in command."[11] So from this point on we'll use the *declare* built-in (even though we could just as easily have chosen to use *typeset*).

Without arguments, *declare* lists all set variables. Normally read-only variables cannot be reassigned or unset. If read-only variables are created with *declare*, they <u>cannot</u> be unset, but they <u>can</u> be reassigned. Integer-type variables can also be assigned with *declare*.

FORMAT

```
declare variable=value
```

EXAMPLE 8.54

```
declare name=Tommy
```

---

11. Bash Reference Manual: http://www.delorie.com/gnu/docs/bash/bashref_56.html.

Table 8.17 Declare options

Option	*Meaning*
-f	Lists functions names and definitions
-r	Makes variables read-only
-x	Exports variable names to subshells
-i	Makes variables integer types
-a[a]	Treats variable as an array; i.e., assigns elements
-F	Lists just function names

a. *-a* and *-F* are implemented only on versions of *bash* 2.x.

8.3.1 Local Variables and Scope

The scope of a variable refers to where the variable is visible within a program. For the shell, the scope of local variables is confined to the shell in which the variable is created.

When assigning a value, there can be no white space surrounding the equal sign. To set the variable to null, the equal sign is followed by a newline.[12]

A dollar sign is used in front of a variable to extract the value stored there.

The *local* function can be used to create local variables, but this is only used within functions. (See "Defining Functions" on page 360.)

Setting Local Variables. Local variables can be set by simply assigning a value to a variable name, or by using the *declare* built-in function as shown in Example 8.55.

EXAMPLE 8.55

```
1  $ round=world or declare round=world
   $ echo $round
   world

2  $ name="Peter Piper"
   $ echo $name
   Peter Piper

3  $ x=
   $ echo $x

4  $ file.bak="$HOME/junk"
   bash: file.bak=/home/jody/ellie/junk: not found
```

12. A variable set to a value or to null will be displayed by using the *set* command, but an unset variable will not.

EXPLANATION

1 The local variable *round* is assigned the value *world.* When the shell encounters the dollar sign preceding a variable name, it performs variable substitution. The value of the variable is displayed. (Don't confuse the prompt (*$*) with the *$* used to perform variable substitution.)

2 The local variable *name* is assigned the value "*Peter Piper.*" The quotes are needed to hide the white space so that the shell will not split the string into separate words when it parses the command line. The value of the variable is displayed.

3 The local variable *x* is not assigned a value. It will be assigned null. The null value, an empty string, is displayed.

4 The period in the variable name is illegal. The only characters allowed in a variable name are numbers, letters, and the underscore. The shell tries to execute the string as a command.

EXAMPLE 8.56

```
1   $ echo $$
     1313
2   $ round=world
    $ echo $round
     world
3   $ bash   Start a subshell

4   $ echo $$
     1326
5   $ echo $round
6   $ exit   Exits this shell, returns to parent shell

7   $ echo $$
     1313
8   $ echo $round
     world
```

EXPLANATION

1 The value of the double dollar sign variable evaluates to the PID of the current shell. The PID of this shell is *1313.*

2 The local variable *round* is assigned the string value *world*, and the value of the variable is displayed.

3 A new *bash* shell is started. This is called a *subshell*, or *child shell.*

4 The PID of this shell is *1326*. The parent shell's PID is *1313.*

EXPLANATION

5. The local variable *round* is not defined in this shell. A blank line is printed.
6. The *exit* command terminates this shell and returns to the parent shell. (Control-D will also exit this shell.)
7. The parent shell returns. Its PID is displayed.
8. The value of the variable *round* is displayed. It is local to this shell.

Setting Read-Only Variables. A read-only variable is a special variable that cannot be redefined or unset. If, however, the *declare* function is used, a read-only variable can be redefined, but not unset.

EXAMPLE 8.57

```
1  $ name=Tom
2  $ readonly name
   $ echo $name
   Tom

3  $ unset name
   bash: unset: name: cannot unset: readonly variable
4  $ name=Joe
   bash: name: readonly variable

5  $ declare -r city='Santa Clara'
6  $ unset city
   bash: unset: city: cannot unset: readonly variable

7  $ declare city='San Francisco'     # What happened here?
   $ echo $city
   San Francisco
```

EXPLANATION

1. The local variable *name* is assigned the value *Tom.*
2. The variable is made read-only.
3. A read-only variable cannot be unset.
4. A read-only variable cannot be redefined.
5. The *declare* built-in command assigns a read-only variable, *city*, the value *Santa Clara.* Quotes are necessary when assigning a string containing white space.
6. Since it is read-only, the variable cannot be unset.
7. When a read-only variable is created with the *declare* command, it cannot be unset, but it can be reassigned.

8.3.2 Environment Variables

Environment variables are available to the shell in which they are created and any subshells or processes spawned from that shell. They are often called global variables to differentiate them from local variables. By convention, environment variables are capitalized. Environment variables are variables that have been exported with the *export* built-in command.

The shell in which a variable is created is called the *parent shell.* If a new shell is started from the parent shell, it is called the *child shell.* Environment variables are passed to any child process started from the shell where the environment variables were created. They are passed from parent to child to grandchild, etc., but not the other direction; i.e., a child process can create an environment variable, but cannot pass it back to its parent, only to its children.[13] Some of the environment variables, such as *HOME, LOGNAME, PATH,* and *SHELL,* are set before you log on by the */bin/login* program. Normally, environment variables are defined and stored in the *.bash_profile* file in the user's home directory. See Table 8.19 for a list of environment variables.

Setting Environment Variables. To set environment variables, the *export* command is used either after assigning a value or when the variable is set. The *declare* built-in, given the *-x* option, will do the same. (Do not use the dollar sign on a variable when exporting it.)

FORMAT

```
export variable=value
variable=value; export variable
declare -x variable=value
```

EXAMPLE 8.58

```
export NAME=john
PS1= '\d:\W:$USER> ' ; export PS1
declare -x TERM=linux
```

Table 8.18 The Export Command and Its Options

Option	*Value*
--	Marks the end of option processing; the remaining parameters are arguments.
-f	Name-value pairs are treated as functions, not variables.
-n	Converts a global (exported) variable to a local variable. The variable will not be exported to child processes.
-p	Displays all the global variables.

13. Like DNA, inheritance goes one direction only, from parent to child.

EXAMPLE 8.59

```
1  $ export TERM=linux    or declare -x TERM=linux

2  $ NAME="John Smith"
   $ export NAME
   $ echo $NAME
   John Smith

3  $ echo $$
   319               pid number for parent shell

4  $ bash             Start a subshell

5  $ echo $$
   340               pid number for new shell

6  $ echo $NAME
   John Smith

7  $ declare -x NAME="April Jenner"
   $ echo $NAME
   April Jenner

8  $ exit
                     Exit the subshell and go back to parent shell
9  $ echo $$
   319               pid number for parent shell
10 $ echo $NAME
   John Smith
```

EXPLANATION

1 The *TERM* variable is assigned *linux*. The variable is exported at the same time. Now, processes started from this shell will inherit the variable. You can use *declare -x* to do the same thing.

2 The variable *NAME* is defined and exported to make it available to subshells started from the shell.

3 The value of this shell's PID is printed.

4 A new *bash* shell is started. The new shell is called the *child*. The original shell is its *parent*.

5 The PID of the new *bash* shell is stored in the *$$* variable and its value is echoed.

6 The variable, set in the parent shell, was exported to this new shell and is displayed.

EXPLANATION (CONTINUED)

7 The built-in *declare* function is another way to set a variable. With the *-x* switch, *declare* marks the variable for export. The variable is reset to *April Jenner.* It is exported to all subshells, but will not affect the parent shell. Exported values are not propagated upward to the parent shell.

8 This *bash* child shell is exited.

9 The PID of the parent is displayed again.

10 The variable NAME contains its original value. Variables retain their values when exported from parent to child shell. The child cannot change the value of a variable for its parent.

Table 8.19 *Bash* Environment Variables
** only on version of bash 2.x*

Variable Name	*Meaning*
_ (underscore)	The last argument to the previous command.
BASH	Expands to the full pathname used to invoke this instance of bash.
*BASH_ENV**	Same as ENV but set only in *bash* versions 2.0 or above.
BASH_VERSION	Expands to the version number of this instance of *bash.*
*BASH_VERSINFO**	Version information about this version of *bash* if the version is 2.0 or above.
CDPATH	The search path for the *cd* command. This is a colon-separated list of directories in which the shell looks for destination directories specified by the *cd* command. A sample value is *.:~:/usr.*
COLUMNS	If set, defines the width of the edit window for shell edit modes and the select command.
*DIRSTACK**	The current contents of the directory stack if the *bash* version is 2.0 or above.
EDITOR	Pathname for a built-in editor: *emacs*, *gmacs*, or *vi*.
EUID	Expands to the effective user ID of the current user, initialized at shell startup.
ENV	The environment file that is executed every time a new *bash* shell is started, including a script. Normally the filename assigned to this variable is *.bashrc*. The value of *ENV* is subjected to parameter expansion, command substitution, and arithmetic expansion before being interpreted as a pathname.
FCEDIT	Default editor name for the *fc* command.

Table 8.19 *Bash* Environment Variables (Continued)
** only on version of bash 2.x*

Variable Name	*Meaning*
FIGNORE	A colon-separated list of suffixes to ignore when performing filename completion. A filename whose suffix matches one of the entries in *FIGNORE* is excluded from the list of matched filenames. A sample value is *.o:~*.
*GLOBIGNORE**	A list of files that will be ignored during filename expansion (called globbing).
*GROUPS**	An array of groups to which the current user belongs.
HISTCMD	The history number, or index in the history list, of the current command. If *HISTCMD* is unset, it loses its special properties, even if it is subsequently reset.
HISTCONTROL	If set to a value of *ignorespace*, lines which begin with a space character are not entered on the history list. If set to a value of *ignoredups*, lines matching the last history line are not entered. A value of *ignoreboth* combines the two options. If unset, or if set to any other value than those above, all lines read by the parser are saved on the history list.
HISTFILE	Specifies file in which to store command history. The default value is *~/.bash_history.* If unset, the command history is not saved when an interactive shell exits.
HISTFILESIZE	The maximum number of lines contained in the history file. When this variable is assigned a value, the history file is truncated, if necessary, to contain no more than that number of lines. The default value is 500.
HISTSIZE	The number of commands to remember in the command history. The default value is 500.
HOME	Home directory; used by *cd* when no directory is specified.
HOSTFILE	Contains the name of a file in the same format as in */etc/hosts* that should be read when the shell needs to complete a hostname. The file may be changed interactively; the next time hostname completion is attempted *bash* adds the contents of the new file to the already existing database.
HOSTTYPE	Automatically set to the type of machine on which *bash* is executing. The default is system-dependent.
IFS	Internal field separators, normally SPACE, TAB, and NEWLINE, used for field splitting of words resulting from command substitution, lists in loop constructs, and reading input.
IGNOREEOF	Controls the action of the shell on receipt of an *EOF* character as the sole input. If set, the value is the number of consecutive *EOF* characters typed as the first characters on an input line before *bash* exits. If the variable exists but does not have a numeric value, or has no value, the default value is 10. If it does not exist, *EOF* signifies the end of input to the shell. This is only in effect for interactive shells.

Table 8.19 *Bash* Environment Variables (Continued)
** only on version of bash 2.x*

Variable Name	*Meaning*
INPUTRC	The filename for the *readline* startup file, overriding the default of *~./inputrc*.
*LANG**	Used to determine the locale category for any category not specifically selected with a variable starting with *LC_*.
*LC_ALL**	Overrides the value of *LANG* and any other *LC_* variable.
*LC_COLLATE**	Determines the collation order used when sorting the results of pathname expansion and the behavior of range expressions, equivalence classes, and collating sequences when matching pathnames and patterns.
*LC_MESSSAGES**	Determines the locale used to translate double-quoted strings preceded by a *$*.
LINENO	Each time this parameter is referenced, the shell substitutes a decimal number representing the current sequential line number (starting with 1) within a script or function.
*MACHTYPE**	Contains a string describing the system on which *bash* is executing.
MAIL	If this parameter is set to the name of a mail file and the *MAILPATH* parameter is not set, the shell informs the user of the arrival of mail in the specified file.
MAILCHECK	This parameter specifies how often (in seconds) the shell will check for the arrival of mail in the files specified by the *MAILPATH* or *MAIL* parameters. The default value is 600 seconds (10 minutes). If set to zero, the shell will check before issuing each primary prompt.
MAILPATH	A colon-separated list of filenames. If this parameter is set, the shell informs the user of the arrival of mail in any of the specified files. Each filename can be followed by a % and a message that will be printed when the modification time changes. The default message is "*you have mail.*"
MAIL__WARNING	If set, and a file that *bash* is checking for mail has been accessed since the last time it was checked, the message *"The mail in [filename where mail is stored] has been read"* is printed.
OLDPWD	Last working directory.
OPTARG	The value of the last option argument processed by the *getopts* built-in command.
OPTERR	If set to 1, displays error messages from the *getopts* built-in.
OPTIND	The index of the next argument to be processed by the *getopts* built-in command.
OSTYPE	Automatically set to a string that describes the operating system on which *bash* is executing. The default is system-dependent.

Table 8.19 *Bash* Environment Variables (Continued)
** only on version of bash 2.x*

Variable Name	*Meaning*
PATH	The search path for commands. It is a colon-separated list of directories in which the shell looks for commands. The default path is system-dependent, and is set by the administrator who installs *bash*. A common value is: */usr/gnu/bin:/usr/local/bin:/usr/ucb:/bin:/usr/bin:.*
PIPESTATUS	An array containing a list of exit status values from processes in the most recently executed foreground jobs in a pipeline.
PROMPT_COMMAND	The command assigned to this variable is executed before the primary prompt is displayed.
PPID	Process *id* of the parent process.
PS1	Primary prompt string, by default *$*.
PS2	Secondary prompt string, by default >.
PS3	Selection prompt string used with the *select* command, by default *#?*.
PS4	Debug prompt string used when tracing is turned on, by default +. Tracing can be turned on with *set -x*.
PWD	Present working directory; set by *cd*.
RANDOM	Each time this parameter is referenced, a random integer is generated. The sequence of random numbers may be initialized by assigning a value to *RANDOM*. If *RANDOM* is unset, it loses its special properties, even if it is subsequently reset.
REPLY	Set when *read* is not supplied arguments.
SECONDS	Each time *SECONDS* is referenced, the number of seconds since shell invocation is returned. If a value is assigned to *SECONDS*, the value returned upon subsequent references is the number of seconds since the assignment plus the value assigned. If *SECONDS* is unset, it loses its special properties, even if it is subsequently reset.
SHELL	When the shell is invoked, it scans the environment for this name. The shell gives default values to *PATH*, *PS1*, *PS2*, *MAILCHECK*, and *IFS*. *HOME* and *MAIL* are set by *login(1)*.
SHELLOPTS	Contains a list of enabled shell options, such as *braceexpand*, *hashall*, *monitor*, etc.
SHLVL	Incremented by one each time an instance of *bash* is started.
TMOUT	Specifies number of seconds to wait for input before exiting.
FORMAT	Used to format the output of the *time* reserved word on a command pipeline.
UID	Expands to the user ID of the current user, initialized at shell startup.

Unsetting Variables. Both local and environment variables can be unset by using the *unset* command, unless the variables are set as read-only.

EXAMPLE 8.60

```
unset name; unset TERM
```

EXPLANATION

The *unset* command removes the variable from the shell's memory.

Printing the Values of Variables: The *echo* Command. The built-in *echo* command prints its arguments to standard output. *Echo*, with the *-e* option, allows the use of numerous escape sequences that control the appearance of the output. Table 8.20 lists the *echo* options and escape sequences.

Table 8.20 *echo* Options and Escape Sequences

Option	*Meaning*
-e	Allows interpretation of the escape sequences shown below
-n	Suppresses newline at the end of a line of output
-E[a]	Disables the interpretation of these escape characters, even on systems where they are interpreted by default (*bash* 2.x)
Escape Sequence	
\a[a]	Alert (bell)
\b	Backspace
\c	Prints the line without a newline
\f	Form feed
\n	Newline
\r	Return
\t	Tab
\v	Vertical tab
\\	Backslash
\nnn	The character whose ASCII code is *nnn* (octal)

a. Not available in *bash* versions prior to 2.x.

When using the escape sequences, don't forget to use the *-e* switch!

EXAMPLE 8.61

```
1   $ echo The username is $LOGNAME.
    The username is ellie.

2   $ echo -e "\t\tHello there\c"
                Hello there$

3   $ echo -n "Hello there"
    Hello there$
```

EXPLANATION

1. The *echo* command prints its arguments to the screen. Variable substitution is performed by the shell before the *echo* command is executed.
2. The *echo* command, with the *-e* option, supports escape sequences similar to those of the C programming language. The *$* is the shell prompt.
3. When the *-n* option is on, the line is printed without the newline. The escape sequences are not supported by this version of *echo*.

The *printf* Command. The Gnu version of *printf*[14] can be used to format printed output. It prints the formatted string, in the same way as the C *printf* function. The format consists of a string that may contain formatting instructions to describe how the printed output will look. The formatting instructions are designated with a % followed by specifiers (*diouxXfeEgGcs*) where *%f* would represent a floating point number and *%d* would represent a whole (decimal) number.

To see a complete listing of *printf* specifiers and how to use them, type at the command line prompt: *printf --help*. To see what version of *printf* you are using, type: *printf --version*. If you are using *bash 2.x*, the built-in *printf* command uses the same format as the executable version in */usr/bin*.

FORMAT

```
printf format [argument...]
```

EXAMPLE 8.62

```
printf "%10.2f%5d\n" 10.5  25
```

14. On *bash* versions 2.x, *printf* is a built-in command.

Table 8.21 Format Specifiers for the *printf* Command

Format specifier	*Value*
\”	Double quote
\0*NNN*	An octal character where *NNN* represents 0 to 3 digits
\\	Backslash
\a	Alert or beep
\b	Backspace
\c	Produce no further output
\f	Form feed
\n	New line
\r	Carriage return
\t	Horizontal tab
\v	Vertical tab
\x*NNN*	Hexadecimal character, where *NNN* is 1 to 3 digits
%%	A single %
%b	ARGUMENT as a string with ‘\’ escapes interpreted

EXAMPLE 8.63

```
1   $ printf --version
    printf (GNU sh-utils) 1.16

2   $ type printf
    printf is a shell builtin

3   $ printf "The number is %.2f\n" 100
    The number is 100.00

4   $ printf "%-20s%-15s%10.2f\n" "Jody" "Savage" 28
    Jody                Savage              28.00

5   $ printf "|%-20s|%-15s|%10.2f|\n" "Jody" "Savage" 28
    Jody                |Savage         |     28.00|

6   $ printf "%s's average was %.1f%%.\n" "Jody" $(( (80+70+90)/3 ))
    Jody's average was 80.0%.
```

EXPLANATION

1. The Gnu version of the *printf* command is printed. This is not a built-in command, but a Linux executable found in */usr/bin.*
2. If using *bash2.x*, *printf* is a built-in command.
3. The argument *100* is printed as a floating point number with only 2 places to the right of the decimal point printing, designated by the format specification *%.2f* in the format string. Note that unlike C, there are no commas separating the arguments.
4. This time the format string specifies that three conversions will take place: the first one is *%-20s* (a left-justified, 20-character string), next is *%-15s* (a left-justified, 15-character string, and last *%10.2f* (a right-justified, 10-character floating point number, one of those characters is the period and the last two characters are the two numbers to the right of the decimal point). Each argument is formatted in the order of the corresponding % signs, so that string *"Jody"* corresponds to first %, string *"Savage"* corresponds to the second %, and the number *28* to the last % sign.
5. This line is the same as line 4 except vertical bars have been added to demonstrate left- and right-justification of the strings.
6. The *printf* command formats the string *Jody* and formats the result of the arithmetic expansion. (See "Arithmetic Expansion" on page 356.) Two percents (%%) signs are needed to print one percent sign (%).

Variable Expansion Modifiers (Parameter Expansion). Variables can be tested and modified by using special modifiers. The modifier provides a shortcut conditional test to check if a variable has been set, and then assigns a value to the variable based on the outcome of the test. See Table 8.22 for a list of variable modifiers.

Table 8.22 Variable Modifiers

Modifier	***Value***
${variable:–word}	If *variable* is set and is non-null, substitute its value; otherwise, substitute *word.*
${variable:=word}	If *variable* is set or is non-null, substitute its value; otherwise, set it to *word.* The value of *variable* is substituted permanently. Positional parameters may not be assigned in this way.
${variable:+word}	If variable is set and is non-null, substitute *word*; otherwise, substitute nothing.
${variable:?word}	If *variable* is set and is non-null, substitute its value; otherwise, print *word* and exit from the shell. If *word* is omitted, the message "*parameter null or not set*" is printed.
${variable:offset}[a]	Gets the substring of the value in *variable*, starting at offset, where offset starts at 0 to the end of the string.
${variable:offset:length}	Gets the substring of the value in *variable,* starting at offset, length characters over.

a. Not available on bash versions prior to 2.0.

Using the colon with any of the modifiers (-, =, +, ?) checks whether the variable is not set or is *null;* without the colon, a variable set to null is considered to be set.

EXAMPLE 8.64

```
(Substitute Temporary Default Values)
1   $ fruit=peach
2   $ echo ${fruit:-plum}
    peach

3   $ echo ${newfruit:-apple}
    apple
4   $ echo $newfruit

5   $ echo $EDITOR          # More realistic example

6   $ echo ${EDITOR:-/bin/vi}
    /bin/vi
7   $ echo $EDITOR

8   $ name=
    $ echo ${name-Joe}
9   $ echo ${name:-Joe}
    Joe
```

EXPLANATION

1 The variable *fruit* is assigned the value *peach.*

2 The special modifier will check to see if the variable *fruit* has been set. If it has, the value is printed; if not, *plum* is substituted for *fruit* and its value is printed.

3 The variable *newfruit* has not been set. The value *apple* will be temporarily substituted for *newfruit.*

4 The setting was only temporary. The variable *newfruit* is not set.

5 The environment variable *EDITOR* has not been set.

6 The *:-* modifier substitutes *EDITOR* with */bin/vi.*

7 The *EDITOR* was never set. Nothing prints.

8 The variable *name* is set to null. By not prefixing the modifier with a colon, the variable is considered to be set, even if to null, and the new value *Joe* is not assigned to *name.*

9 The colon causes the modifier to check that a variable is either *not* set or is set to null. In either case, the value *Joe* will be substituted for *name.*

EXAMPLE 8.65

```
(Substitute Permanent Default Values)
1   $ name=

2   $ echo  ${name:=Peter}
    Peter

3   $ echo $name
    Patty

4   $ echo ${EDITOR:=/bin/vi}
    /bin/vi

5   $ echo $EDITOR
    /bin/vi
```

EXPLANATION

1 The variable *name* is assigned the value *null.*

2 The special modifier *:=* will check to see if the variable name has been set. If it has been set, it will not be changed; if it is either null or not set, it will be assigned the value to the right of the equal sign. *Peter* is assigned to *name* since the variable is set to null. The setting is permanent.

3 The variable *name* still contains the value *Peter.*

4 The value of the variable *EDITOR* is set to */bin/vi.*

5 The value of the variable *EDITOR* is displayed.

EXAMPLE 8.66

```
(Substitute Temporary Alternate Value)
1   $ foo=grapes

2   $ echo ${foo:+pears}
    pears

3   $ echo $foo
    grapes
    $
```

EXPLANATION

1 The variable *foo* has been assigned the value *grapes*.

2 The special modifier *:+* will check to see if the variable has been set. If it has been set, *pears* will temporarily be substituted for *foo*; if not, null is returned.

3 The variable *foo* now has its original value.

EXAMPLE 8.67

```
(Creating Error Messages Based On Default Values)

1   $ echo ${namex:?"namex is undefined"}
    namex: namex is undefined

2   $ echo ${y?}
    y: parameter null or not set
```

EXPLANATION

1 The *:?* modifier will check to see if the variable has been set. If not, the string to the right of the *?* is printed to standard error, after the name of the variable. If in a script, the script exits.

2 If a message is not provided after the *?*, the shell sends a default message to standard error.

EXAMPLE 8.68

```
(Creating Substring[a])

1   $ var=notebook

2   $ echo ${var:0:4}
    note

3   $ echo ${var:4:4}
    book

4   $ echo ${var:0:2}
    no
```

a. Not available in versions of *bash* prior to 2.x.

EXPLANATION

1 The variable is assigned the value, *notebook*.

2 The substring of *var,* starts at offset 0; the *n* in *notebook*, and has a length of 4 characters, ending at the *e*.

3 The substring of *var,* starts at offset 4; the *b* in *notebook*, and has a length of 4 characters, ending at the *k*.

4 The substring of *var*, starts at offset 0; the *n* in *notebook*, and has a length of 2 characters, ending at the *o*.

Variable Expansion of Substrings. Pattern-matching arguments are used to strip off certain portions of a string from either the front or end of the string. The most common use for these operators is stripping off pathname elements from the head or tail of the path. See Table 8.23.

Table 8.23 Variable Expansion Substrings[a]

Expression	*Function*
${variable%pattern}	Matches the *smallest trailing portion* of the value of *variable* to *pattern* and removes it.
${variable%%pattern}	Matches the *largest trailing portion* of the value of *variable* to *pattern* and removes it.
${variable#pattern}	Matches the *smallest leading portion* of the value of *variable* to *pattern* and removes it.

Table 8.23 Variable Expansion Substrings[a] (Continued)

Expression	*Function*
${variable##pattern}	Matches the *largest leading portion* of the value of *variable* to *pattern* and removes it.
${#variable}	Substitutes the number of characters in the variable. If * or @, the length is the number of positional parameters.

a. Not available on versions of *bash* prior to 2.x.

EXAMPLE 8.69

```
1   $ pathname="/usr/bin/local/bin"
2   $ echo ${pathname%/bin*}
    /usr/bin/local
```

EXPLANATION

1 The local variable *pathname* is assigned */usr/bin/local/bin.*

2 The % removes the *smallest trailing portion* of *pathname* containing the pattern */bin,* followed by zero or more characters; that is, it strips off */bin.*

EXAMPLE 8.70

```
1   $ pathname="usr/bin/local/bin"
2   $ echo ${pathname%%/bin*}
    /usr
```

EXPLANATION

1 The local variable *pathname* is assigned */usr/bin/local/bin.*

2 The %% removes the *largest trailing portion* of *pathname* containing the pattern */bin,* followed by zero or more characters; that is, it strips off */bin/local/bin*

EXAMPLE 8.71

```
1   $ pathname=/home/lilliput/jake/.bashrc
2   $ echo ${pathname#/home}
    /lilliput/jake/.bashrc
```

EXPLANATION

1 The local variable *pathname* is assigned */home/liliput/jake/.bashrc.*

2 The # removes the *smallest leading portion* of *pathname* containing the pattern */home*; that is, */home* is stripped from the beginning of the path variable.

EXAMPLE 8.72

```
1   $ pathname=/home/liliput/jake/.bashrc
2   $ echo ${pathname##*/}
    .bashrc
```

EXPLANATION

1 The local variable *pathname* is assigned */home/liliput/jake/.bashrc.*

2 The ## removes the *largest leading portion* of *pathname* containing zero or more characters up to and including the last slash; that is, it strips off */home/lilliput/jake* from the path variable.

EXAMPLE 8.73

```
1   $ name="Ebenezer Scrooge"
2   $ echo  ${#name}
    16
```

EXPLANATION

1 The variable, *name*, is assigned the string *Ebenezer Scrooge.*

2 The ${#variable} syntax, displays the number of characters in the string assigned to the variable, *name.* There are 16 characters in *Ebenezer Scrooge.*

Positional Parameters. Normally, the special built-in variables, often called positional parameters, are used in shell scripts when passing arguments from the command line, or used in functions to hold the value of arguments passed to the function. The variables are called positional parameters because they are referenced by numbers 1, 2, 3, and so on, representing their respective positions in the parameter list. See Table 8.24.

The name of the shell script is stored in the *$0* variable. The positional parameters can be set, reset, and unset with the *set* command.

Table 8.24 Positional Parameters

Expression	*Function*
$0	References the name of the current shell script.
$1–$9	Positional parameters *1–9*.
${10}	Positional parameter *10*.
$#	Evaluates to the number of positional parameters.
*$**	Evaluates to all the positional parameters.
$@	Same as *$**, except when double quoted.
"$"*	Evaluates to "*$1 $2 $3*," etc.
"$@"	Evaluates to "*$1*" "*$2*" "*$3*," etc.

EXAMPLE 8.74

```
1   $ set punky tommy bert jody
    $ echo $*                 Prints all the positional parameters
    punky tommy bert jody

2   $ echo $1                 Prints the first position
    punky

3   $ echo $2 $3              Prints the second and third position
    tommy bert

4   $ echo $#                 Prints the total number of positional
    4                         parameters

5   $ set a b c d e f g h i j k l m
    $ print $10               Prints the first positional parameter
    a0                        followed by a 0.

    $ echo ${10} ${11}        Prints the 10th and 11th positions
    j k

6   $ echo $#
    13

7   $ echo $*
    a b c d e f g h i j k l m
```

EXAMPLE 8.74 (CONTINUED)

```
8   $ set file1 file2 file3
    $ echo \$$#
    $3

9   $ eval echo \$$#
    file3

10  $ set --              Unsets all positional parameters
```

EXPLANATION

1 The *set* command assigns values to positional parameters. The *$** special variable contains all of the parameters set.

2 The value of the first positional parameter, *punky,* is displayed.

3 The value of the second and third parameters, *tommy* and *bert,* are displayed.

4 The *$#* special variable contains the number of positional parameters currently set.

5 The *set* command resets all of the positional parameters. The original parameter list is cleared. To print any positional parameters beyond 9, use the curly braces to keep the two digits together. Otherwise, the value of the first positional parameter is printed, followed by the number appended to it.

6 The number of positional parameters is now *13.*

7 The values of all the positional parameters are printed.

8 The dollar sign is escaped; $# is the number of arguments. The *echo* command displays *$3*, a literal dollar sign followed by the number of positional parameters.

9 The *eval* command parses the command line a second time before executing the command. The first time parsed by the shell, the print would display *$3*; the second time, after *eval*, the *print* displays the value of *$3*, *file3.*

10 The *set* command with the option, --, clears or unsets all positional parameters.

Other Special Variables. The shell has special variables consisting of a single character. The dollar sign preceding the character allows you to access the value stored in the variable. See Table 8.25.

Table 8.25 Special Variables

Variable	*Meaning*
$	The PID of the shell
–	The *sh* options currently set
?	The exit value of last executed command
!	The PID of the last job put in the background

EXAMPLE 8.75

```
1   $ echo The pid of this shell is $$
    The pid of this shell is 4725

2   $ echo The options for this shell are $-
    The options for this shell are imh

3   $ grep dodo /etc/passwd
    $ echo $?
    1

4   $ sleep 25&
    4736
    $ echo $!
    4736
```

EXPLANATION

1 The *$* variable holds the value of the PID for this process.

2 The - variable lists all options for this interactive *bash* shell.

3 The *grep* command searches for the string *dodo* in the */etc/passwd* file. The *?* variable holds the exit status of the last command executed. Since the value returned from *grep* is *1*, *grep* is assumed to have failed in its search. An exit status of zero indicates a successful exit.

4 The *!* variable holds the PID number of the last command placed in the background. The *&* appended to the *sleep* command sends the command to the background.

8.3.3 Quoting

Quoting is used to protect special metacharacters from interpretation and prevent parameter expansion. There are three methods of quoting: the backslash, single quotes, and double quotes. The characters listed in Table 8.26 are special to the shell and must be quoted.

Table 8.26 Special Metacharacters Requiring Quotes

Metacharacter	*Meaning*
;	Command separator
&	Background processing
( )	Command grouping; creates a subshell
{ }	Command grouping; does not create a subshell
|	Pipe
<	Input redirection
>	Output redirection
newline	Command termination
space/tab	Word delimiter
$	Variable substitution character
* [ ] ?	Shell metacharacters for filename expansion

Single and double quotes must be matched. Single quotes protect special metacharacters, such as $, *, ?, |, >, and <, from interpretation. Double quotes also protect special metacharacters from being interpreted, but allow variable and command substitution characters (the dollar sign and back quotes) to be processed. Single quotes will protect double quotes and double quotes will protect single quotes.

Unlike the Bourne shell, *bash* tries to let you know if you have mismatched quotes. If running interactively, a secondary prompt appears when quotes are not matched; if in a shell script, the file is scanned and if the quote is not matched, the shell will attempt to match it with the next available quote. If the shell cannot match it with the next available quote, the program aborts and the message *bash:unexpected EOF while looking for* ` " ' appears on the terminal. Quoting can be a real hassle for even the best of shell programmers! See Appendix C for shell quoting rules.

The Backslash. The backslash is used to quote (or escape) a single character from interpretation. The backslash is not interpreted if placed in single quotes. The backslash will protect the dollar sign ($), back quotes (` `), and the backslash from interpretation if enclosed in double quotes.

EXAMPLE 8.76

```
1   $ echo Where are you going\?
    Where are you going?

2   $ echo Start on this line and \
    >  go to the next line.
    Start on this line and go to the next line.

3   $ echo \\
    \

4   $ echo '\\'
    \\

5   $ echo '\$5.00'
    \$5.00

6   $ echo  "\$5.00"
    $5.00

7   $ echo 'Don\'t you need $5.00?'
    >
    >'

    Don\t you need .00?
```

EXPLANATION

1 The backslash prevents the shell from performing filename substitution on the question mark.

2 The backslash escapes the newline, allowing the next line to become part of this line.

3 Because the backslash itself is a special character, it prevents the backslash following it from interpretation.

4 The backslash is not interpreted when enclosed in single quotes.

5 All characters in single quotes are treated literally. The backslash does not serve any purpose here.

6 When enclosed in double quotes, the backslash prevents the dollar sign from being interpreted for variable substitution.

EXPLANATION (CONTINUED)

7 The backslash is not interpreted when inside single quotes; therefore, the shell sees three single quotes (the one at the end of the string is not matched). A secondary prompt appears, waiting for a closing single quote. When the shell finally gets the closing quote, it strips out all of the quotes and passes the string on to the *echo* command. Because the first two quotes were matched, the rest of the string *t you need $5.00?* was not enclosed within any quotes. The shell tried to evaluate $5; it was empty and *.00* printed.

Single Quotes. Single quotes must be matched. They protect all metacharacters from interpretation. To print a single quote, it must be enclosed in double quotes or escaped with a backslash.

EXAMPLE 8.77

```
1   $ echo 'hi there
    > how are you?
    > When will this end?
    > When the quote is matched
    > oh'
    hi there
    how are you?
    When will this end?
    When the quote is matched
    oh

2   $ echo Don\'t you need '$5.00?'
    Don't you need $5.00?

3   $ echo 'Mother yelled, "Time to eat!"'
    Mother yelled, "Time to eat!"
```

EXPLANATION

1 The single quote is not matched on the line. The Bourne shell produces a secondary prompt. It is waiting for the quote to be matched.

2 The single quotes protect all metacharacters from interpretation. The apostrophe in *"Don't"* is escaped with a backslash (the backslash protects a single character, rather than a string). Otherwise, it would match the single quote before the $. Then the single quote at the end of the string would not have a mate. The *$* and the *?* are enclosed in a pair of single quotes, protecting them from shell interpretation; i.e., treating them as literals.

3 The single quotes protect the double quotes in this string.

Double Quotes. Double quotes must be matched, will allow variable and command substitution, and protect any other special metacharacters from being interpreted by the shell.

EXAMPLE 8.78

```
1   $ name=Jody

2   $ echo "Hi $name, I'm glad to meet you!"
    Hi Jody, I'm glad to meet you!

3   $ echo "Hey $name, the time is $(date)"
    Hey Jody, the time is Wed Jul 14 14:04:11 PST 2000
```

EXPLANATION

1 The variable *name* is assigned the string *Jody*.

2 The double quotes surrounding the string will protect all special metacharacters from interpretation, with the exception of *$* in *$name*. Variable substitution is performed within double quotes.

3 Variable substitution and command substitution are both performed when enclosed within double quotes. The variable *name* is expanded, and the command in parentheses, *date*, is executed. (See "Command Substitution" below.)

8.3.4 Command Substitution

Command substitution is used when assigning the output of a command to a variable or when substituting the output of a command within a string. All shells use back quotes to perform command substitution.[15] *Bash* allows two forms: the older form, where the command(s) is placed within back quotes, and the new Korn style form, where the command(s) is placed within a set of parentheses preceded by a dollar sign.

Bash performs the expansion by executing the command and returning the standard output of the command, with any trailing newlines deleted. When the old-style backquote form of substitution is used, the backslash retains its literal meaning except when followed by $, ‘, or \. When using the $(command) form, all characters between the parentheses make up the command; none are treated specially.

Command substitutions may be nested. To nest when using the old form, the inner backquotes must be escaped with backslashes.

15. The *bash* shell allows back quotes for command substitution for upward-compatibility, but provides an alternate method as well.

FORMAT

```
`Linux command`    Old method with back quotes

$(Linux command)   New method
```

EXAMPLE 8.79

```
   (Old Way)
1  $ echo "The hour is `date +%H`"
   The hour is 09

2  $ name=`awk -F: '{print $1}' database`
   $ echo $name
   Ebenezer Scrooge

3  $ ls `ls /etc`
   shutdown

4  $ set `date`
5  $ echo $*
   Wed Jul 14 09:35:21 PDT 1999
6  $ echo $2 $6
   Jul 1999

7  $ echo `basename \`pwd\``
   ellie
```

EXPLANATION

1 The output of the *date* command is substituted into the string.

2 The output of the *awk* command is assigned to the variable *name*, and displayed.

3 The output of the *ls* command, enclosed in back quotes, is a list of files from the */etc* directory. The filenames will be arguments to the first *ls* command. All files with the same name in */etc* in the current directory are listed. (The files that are not matches in this directory will cause an error message, such as ls: *termcap: No such file or directory.*)

4 The *set* command assigns the output of the *date* command to positional parameters. White space separates the list of words into its respective parameters.

5 The *$** variable holds all of the parameters. The output of the *date* command was stored in the *$** variable. Each parameter is separated by white space.

6 The second and sixth parameters are printed.

7 To set the variable *dirname* to the name (only) of the present working directory, command substitution is nested. The *pwd* command is executed first, passing the full pathname of the present working directory as an argument to the Linux command *basename*. The *basename* command strips off all but the last element of a pathname. When nesting commands within backquotes, the backquotes for the inner command must be escaped with a backslash.

The *bash alternate* for using back quotes in command substitution is presented below in Example 8.80.

EXAMPLE 8.80

```
(The New Way)
1   $ d=$(date)
    $ echo $d
     Wed Jul 14 09:35:21 PDT 1999

2   $ lines = $(cat filex)

3   $ echo The time is $(date +%H)
    The time is 09

4   $ machine=$(uname -n)
    $ echo $machine
    jody

5   $ pwd
    /usr/local/bin
    $ dirname="$(basename $(pwd)) "         Nesting commands
    $ echo $dirname
    bin

6   $ echo $(cal)            Newlines are lost
    July 1999 S M Tu W Th F S 1 2 3 4 5 6 7 8 9 10 11 12 13 14 15
    16 17 18 19 20 21 22 23 24 25 26 27 28 29 30 31

7   $ echo "$(cal)"
         July 1999
     S  M  Tu  W   Th F  S
                    1  2  3
     4  5  6  7     8  9 10
    11 12 13 14    15 16 17
    18 19 20 21    22 23 24
    25 26 27 28    29 30 31
```

EXPLANATION

1. The *date* command is enclosed within parentheses. The output of the command is substituted into the expression, then assigned to the variable *d,* and displayed.
2. The output from the *cat* command is assigned to the variable *lines.*
3. Again the *date* command is enclosed in parentheses. The output of *date +%H,* the current hour, is substituted for the expression and echoed to the screen.

EXPLANATION (CONTINUED)

4 The variable, *machine*, is assigned the output of *uname -n*, the name of the host machine. The value of the *machine* variable is echoed to the screen.

5 The output of the *pwd* command (present working directory) is */usr/local/bin.*The variable *dirname* is assigned the output resulting from command substitution where the command substitutions are nested. *$(pwd)* is the first command substitution to be be performed. The output of the *pwd* command is substituted in the expression, then the *basename* program will use the results of that substitution, */usr/local/bin*, as its argument, resulting in: *basename /usr/local/bin.*

6 The output of the *cal* (the current month) command is echoed. The trailing newlines are deleted when command substitution is performed.

7 When you put the whole command substitution expression in double quotes, the trailing newlines are preserved, and calendar looks like it should.

8.3.5 Arithmetic Expansion

The shell performs arithmetic expansion by evaluating an arithmetic expression and substituting the result. The expression is treated as if it were in double quotes and the expressions may be nested. For a complete discussion of arithmetic operations, and arithmetic evaluations, see "The let Command" on page 394.

There are two formats for evaluating arithmetic expressions:

FORMAT

```
$[ expression ]
$(( expression ))
```

EXAMPLE 8.81

```
echo $[ 5 + 4 - 2 ]
7
echo $[ 5 + 3 * 2]
11
echo $[(5 + 3) * 2]
16
echo $(( 5 + 4 ))
9
echo $(( 5 / 0 ))
bash: 5/0: division by 0 ( error token is "0")
```

8.3.6 Order of Expansion

When you are performing the expansion of variables, commands, arithmetic expressions, and pathnames, the shell is programmed to follow a specific order when scanning the command line. Assuming that the variables are not quoted, the processing is performed in the following order:

1. Brace expansion
2. Tilde expansion
3. Parameter expansion
4. Variable substitution
5. Command substitution
6. Arithmetic expansion
7. Word splitting
8. Pathname expansion

8.3.7 Arrays (Versions 2.x)

Versions of *bash 2.x*, provide for creation of one-dimensional arrays. Arrays allow you to collect a list of words into one variable name, such as a list of numbers, a list of names, or a list of files. Arrays are created with the built-in function, *declare -a*, or can be created on the fly by giving a subscript to a variable name, such as, *x[0]=5*. The index value is an integer starting at 0. There is no maximum size limit on the array, and indices do not have to be ordered numbers, i.e., *x[0], x[1], x[2]*.... To extract an element of an array, the syntax is *${arrayname[index]}*. If *declare* is given the *-a* and *-r* options, a read-only array is created.

FORMAT

```
declare -a variable_name
variable = ( item1 item2 item3 ... )
```

EXAMPLE 8.82

```
declare -a nums=(45 33 100 65)
declare -ar names    (array is readonly)
names=( Tom  Dick  Harry)
states=( ME  [3]=CA  CT )
x[0]=55
n[4]=100
```

When assigning values to an array, they are automatically started at index 0 and incremented by 1 for each additional element added. You do not have to provide indices in an assignment, and if you do, they do not have to be in order. To unset an array, use the *unset* command followed by the array name, and to unset one element of the array, use *unset* and the arrayname[subscript] syntax.

The *declare*, *local*, and *read-only* built-ins also can take the *-a* option to declare an array. The *read* command with the *-a* option is used to read in a list of words from standard input into array elements.

EXAMPLE 8.83

```
1   $ declare -a friends

2   $ friends=(Sheryl Peter Louise)

3   $ echo ${friends[0]}
    Sheryl

4   $ echo ${friends[1]}
    Peter

5   $ echo ${friends[2]}
    Louise

6   $ echo "All the friends are ${friends[*]}"
    All the friends are Sheryl Peter Louise

7   $ echo "The number of elements in the array is ${#friends[*]}"
    The number of elements in the array is 3

8   $ unset friends  or unset ${friends[*]}
```

EXPLANATION

1 The *declare* built-in command is used to explicitly declare an array, but it is not necessary. Any variable that uses a subscript, such as *variable[0]*, when being assigned a value, will automatically be treated as an array.

2 The array, *friends*, is assigned a list of values: *Sheryl*, *Peter*, and *Louise*.

3 The first element of the *friends* array is accessed by enclosing the array name and its subscript in curly braces, with an index of 0 used as the value of the subscript. *Sheryl* is printed.

4 The second element of the *friends* array is accessed by using the index value of 1.

5 The third element of the *friends* array is accessed by using the index value of 2.

6 When you place the asterisk within the subscript, all of the elements of the array can be accessed. This line displays all the elements in the *friends* array.

7 The syntax, *${#friends[*]}*, produces the size of the array; i.e., the number of elements in the array. On the other hand, *${#friends[0]}*, produces the number of characters in the value of the first element of the array. There are six characters in *Sheryl*.

8 The *unset* built-in command deletes the whole array. Just one element of the array can be removed by typing: *unset friends[1]*; this would remove *Sheryl*.

EXAMPLE 8.84

```
1  $ x[3]=100
   $ echo ${x[*]}
   100

2  $ echo ${x[0]}

3  $ echo ${x[3]}
   100

4  $ states=(ME  [3]=CA  [2]=CT)
   $ echo ${states[*]}
   ME CA CT

5  $ echo ${states[0]}
   ME

6  $ echo ${states[1]}

7  $ echo ${states[2]}
   CT

8  $ echo ${states[3]}
   CA
```

EXPLANATION

1. The third element of the array, *x*, is being assigned 100. It doesn't matter if the index number is 3, but because the first two elements do not exist yet, the size of the array is only 1. *${x[*]}* displays the one element of the array, *x*.
2. *x[1]* has no value, and neither do *x[1]* and *x[2]*.
3. *x[3]* has a value of *100*.
4. The *states* array is being assigned *ME* at index *0*, *CA* at index *3*, and *CT* at index *2*. In this example, you can see that *bash* doesn't care at what index you store values, and that the index numbers do not have to be contiguous.
5. The first element of the *states* array is printed.
6. There is nothing stored in *states[1]*.
7. The third element of the *states* array, *states[2]*, was assigned *CT*.
8. The fourth element of the *states* array, *states[3]*, was assigned *CA*.

8.3.8 Functions (Introduction)

Bash functions are used to execute a group of commands with a name within the context of the current shell (a child process is not forked). They are like scripts, only more efficient. Once defined, functions become part of the shell's memory so that when the function is called, the shell does not have to read it in from the disk as it does with a file. Often functions are used to improve the modularity of a script. Once defined, functions can be used again and again. Although functions can be defined at the prompt when running interactively, they are often defined in the user's initialization file, *.bash_profile*. They must be defined before they are invoked.

Defining Functions. There are two ways to declare a *bash* function. One way, the old Bourne shell way, is to give the function name followed by a set of empty parentheses, followed by the function definition. The new way (Korn shell way) is to use the *function* keyword followed by the function name and then the function definition. If using the new way, the parentheses are optional. The function definition is enclosed in curly braces. It consists of commands separated by semicolons. The last command is terminated with a semicolon. Spaces around the curly braces are required. Any arguments passed to the function are treated as positional parameters within the function. The positional parameters in a function are local to the function. The *local* built-in function allows local variables to be created within the function definition. Functions may also be recursive, i.e., call themselves an unlimited number of times.

FORMAT

```
function_name () { commands ; commands; }
function function_name { commands ; commands; }
function function_name () { commands ; commands; }
```

EXAMPLE 8.85

```
1  $ function greet { echo "Hello $LOGNAME, today is $(date)"; }
2  $ greet
   Hello ellie, today is Wed Jul 14 14:56:31 PDT  1999

3  $ greet () { echo "Hello $LOGNAME, today is $(date)"; }
4  $ greet
   Hello ellie, today is Wed Jul 14 15:16:22 PDT  1999

5  $ declare -f
   declare -f greet()
   {
      echo "Hello $LOGNAME, today is $(date)"
   }
```

EXAMPLE 8.85 (CONTINUED)

```
6   $ declare -F[a]
    declare -f greet

7   $ export -f greet

8   $ bash                    Start subshell
9   $ greet
    Hello ellie, today is Wed Jul 14 17:59:24 PDT  1999
```

a. Only on *bash* version 2.x.

EXPLANATION

1 The keyword, *function,* is followed by the name of the function, *greet.* The function definition is surrounded by curly braces. There must be a space after the opening curly brace. Statements on the same line are terminated with a semicolon.

2 When the *greet* function is invoked, the command(s) enclosed within the curly braces are executed in the context of the current shell.

3 The *greet* function is defined again using the Bourne shell syntax, the name of the function, followed by an empty set of parentheses, and the function definition.

4 The *greet* function is invoked again.

5 The *declare* command with the *-f* switch, lists all functions defined in this shell and their definitions.

6 The *declare* command with the *-F* switch lists only function names.

7 The *export* command with the *-f* switch makes the function global, i.e., available to subshells.

8 A new *bash* shell is started.

9 The function is defined for this child shell because it was exported.

EXAMPLE 8.86

```
1   $ function fun {
          echo "The current working directory is $PWD."
          echo "Here is a list of your files: "
          ls
          echo "Today is $(date +%A).";
    }
2   $ fun
    The current working directory is /home.
    Here is a list of your files:
    abc       abc123    file1.bak  none       nothing   tmp
    abc1      abc2      file2      nonsense   nowhere   touch
    abc122    file1     file2.bak  noone      one
    Today is Wednesday.

3   $ function welcome { echo "Hi $1 and $2"; }
4   $ welcome tom joe
    Hi tom and joe

5   $ set jane anna lizzy
6   $ echo $*
    jane anna lizzy

7   $ welcome johan joe
    hi johan and joe

8   $ echo  $1 $2
    johan joe

9   $ unset -f welcome      # unsets the function
```

EXPLANATION

1. The function *fun* is named and defined. The keyword, *function*, is followed by the function's name and a list of commands enclosed in curly braces. Commands are listed on separate line; if they are listed on the same line, they must be separated by semicolons. A space is required after the first curly brace or you will get a syntax error. A function must be defined before it can be used.
2. The function behaves just like a script when invoked. Each of the commands in the function definition are executed in turn.
3. There are two positional parameters used in the function *welcome*. When arguments are given to the function, the positional parameters are assigned those values.
4. The arguments to the function, *tom* and *joe*, are assigned to *$1* and *$2*, respectively. The positional parameters in a function are private to the function and will not interfere with any used outside the function.

EXPLANATION (CONTINUED)

5 The positional parameters are set at the command line. These variables have nothing to do with the ones set in the function.

6 *$** displays the values of the currently set positional parameters.

7 The function *welcome* is called. *Johan* and *joe* are the values assigned to the positional parameters.

8 The positional variables assigned at the command line are unaffected by those set in the function.

9 The *unset* built-in command with the *-f* switch unsets the function. It is no longer defined.

Listing and Unsetting Functions. To list functions and their definitions, use the *declare* command. In *bash* versions 2.x and above, *declare -F* lists just function names. The function and its definition will appear in the output, along with the exported and local variables. Functions and their definitions are unset with the *unset -f* command.

8.3.9 Standard I/O and Redirection

When the shell starts up, it inherits three files: *stdin, stdout*, and *stderr.* Standard input normally comes from the keyboard. Standard output and standard error normally go to the screen. There are times when you want to read input from a file or send output or errors to a file. This can be accomplished by using I/O redirection. See Table 8.27 for a list of redirection operators.

Table 8.27 Redirection

Redirection Operator	*What It Does*
<	Redirects input
>	Redirects output
>>	Appends output
2>	Redirects error
&>	Redirects output and error
>&	Redirects output and error (preferred way)
2>&1	Redirects error to where output is going
1>&2	Redirects output to where error is going
>|	Overrides *noclobber* when redirecting output
<> *filename*	Uses file as both standard input and output if a device file (from */dev*)

EXAMPLE 8.87

```
1  $ tr '[A-Z]'  '[a-z]' < myfile
                                  Redirect  input

2  $ ls > lsfile                  Redirect output
   $ cat lsfile
   dir1
   dir2
   file1
   file2
   file3

3  $ date >> lsfile               Redirect and append otuput
   $ cat lsfile
   dir1
   dir2
   file1
   file2
   file3
   Sun Sept 17 12:57:22 PDT 1999

4  $ cc prog.c 2> errfile    Redirect error

5  $ find . -name \*.c -print > foundit 2> /dev/null
    Redirect output to foundit and errors to /dev/null,
    respectively.

6  $ find . -name \*.c -print >& foundit
    Redirect both output and errors to foundit.

7  $ find . -name \*.c -print > foundit 2>&1
    Redirect output to foundit and send errors to where output
    is going; i.e. foundit

8  $ echo "File needs an argument" 1>&2
      Send standard output to error
```

EXPLANATION

1. Instead of getting input from the keyboard, standard input is redirected from the file *myfile* to the *Linux tr* command. All uppercase letters are converted to lowercase.
2. Instead of sending output to the screen, the *ls* command redirects its output to the file *lsfile*.
3. The output of the *date* command is redirected and appended to *lsfile*.

EXPLANATION (CONTINUED)

4 The C program source file *prog.c* is compiled. If the compile fails, the standard error is redirected to the file *errfile*. Now you can take your error file to the local guru for an explanation (of sorts)!

5 The *find* command starts searching in the current working directory for filenames ending in *.c,* and prints the filenames to a file named *foundit.* Errors from the *find* command are sent to */dev/null.*

6 The *find* command starts searching in the current working directory for filenames ending in *.c,* and prints the filenames to a file named *foundit.* The errors are also sent to *foundit.*

7 Same as 6.

8 The *echo* command sends its message to standard error. Its standard output is merged with standard error.

The *exec* Command and Redirection. The *exec* command can be used to replace the current program with a new one without starting a new process. Standard output or input can be changed with the *exec* command without creating a subshell. (See Table 8.28 below.) If a file is opened with *exec*, subsequent *read* commands will move the file pointer down the file a line at a time until the end of the file. The file must be closed to start reading from the beginning again. However, if using *Linux* utilities such as *cat* and *sort*, the operating system closes the file after each command has completed.

Table 8.28 The *exec* Command

exec Command	*What It Does*
exec ls	*ls* executes in place of the shell. When *ls* is finished, the shell in which it was started does not return.
exec < filea	Opens *filea* for reading standard input.
exec > filex	Opens *filex* for writing standard output.
exec 3< datfile	Opens *datfile* as file descriptor *3* for reading input.
sort <&3	*Datfile* is sorted.
exec 4>newfile	Opens *newfile* as file descriptor (fd) *4* for writing.
ls >&4	Output of *ls* is redirected to *newfile.*
exec 5<&4	Makes fd *5* a copy of fd *4.*
exec 3<&–	Closes fd *3.*

EXAMPLE 8.88

```
1   $ exec date
    Thu Oct 14 10:07:34  PDT 1999
     <Login prompt appears if you are in your login shell >

2   $ exec > temp
    $ ls
    $ pwd
    $ echo Hello
3   $ exec > /dev/tty
4   $ echo Hello
    Hello
```

EXPLANATION

1 The *exec* command executes the *date* command in the current shell (does not fork a child shell). Because the *date* command is executed in place of the current shell, when the *date* command exits, the shell terminates. If a *bash* shell had been started from the *tcshell*, the *bash* shell would exit and the *tcshell* prompt would appear. If you are in your login shell when you try this, you will be logged out. If you are working interactively in a shell window, the window exits.

2 The *exec* command opens standard output for the current shell to the *temp* file. Output from *ls, pwd,* and *echo* will no longer go to the screen, but to *temp*. (See Figure 8.3.)

3 The *exec* command reopens standard output to the terminal. Now, output will go to the screen as shown in line 4.

4 Standard output has been directed back to the terminal (*/dev/tty*).

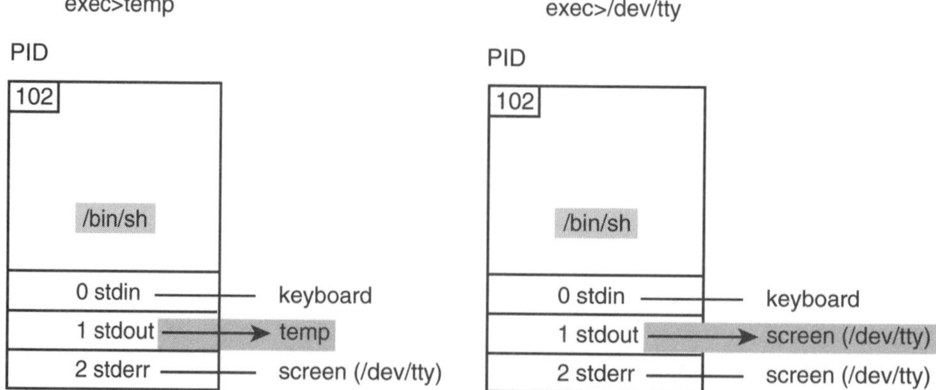

Figure 8.3 The *exec* command and file descriptors.

EXAMPLE 8.89

```
1   > bash
2   $ cat doit
    pwd
    echo hello
    date
3   $ exec < doit
    /home/homebound/ellie/shell
    hello
    Thu Oct 14 10:07:34  PDT 1999
4   >
```

EXPLANATION

1. From a *tcshell* prompt, *bash* is started up. (This is done so that when the *exec* command exits, the user will not be logged out.)
2. The contents of a file called *doit* are displayed.
3. The *exec* command opens standard input to the file called *doit.* Input is read from the file instead of from the keyboard. The commands from the file *doit* are executed in place of the current shell. When the last command exits, so does the shell.
4. The *bash* shell exited when the *exec* command completed. The *tcshell* prompt appeared. It was the parent shell. If you had been in your login shell when the *exec* finished, you would be logged out; if in a window, the window would have disappeared.

EXAMPLE 8.90

```
1   $ exec 3> filex
2   $ who >& 3
3   $ date >& 3
4   $ exec 3>&-
5   $ exec 3<filex
6   $ cat <&3
    ellie   tty1   Jul 21 09:50
    ellie   ttyp1  Jul 21 11:16  (:0.0)
    ellie   ttyp0  Jul 21 16:49  (:0.0)
    Wed Jul 21 17:15:18 PDT 1999
7   $ exec 3<&-
8   $ date >& 3
    date: write error: Bad file descriptor
```

EXPLANATION

1 File descriptor *3* (fd *3*) is assigned to *filex* and opened for redirection of output. See Figure 8.4(a).

2 The output of the *who* command is sent to fd *3*, *filex*.

3 The output of the *date* command is sent to fd *3*; *filex* is already opened, so the output is appended to *filex*.

4 Fd *3* is closed.

5 The *exec* command opens fd *3* for reading input. Input will be redirected from *filex*. See Figure 8.4(b).

6 The *cat* program reads from fd *3*, assigned to *filex*.

7 The *exec* command closes fd *3*. (Actually, the operating system will close the file once end of file is reached.)

8 When attempting to send the output of the *date* command to fd *3*, *bash* reports an error condition, because *fd 3* was previously closed.

exec 3>filex

101 /bin/sh

0	stdin
1	stdout
2	stderr
3	filex

a. opened for writing

exec 3<filex

102 /bin/sh

0	stdin
1	stdout
2	stderr
3	filex

b. opened for reading

Figure 8.4 *Exec* and file descriptors.

8.3.10 Pipes

A *pipe* takes the output from the command on the left-hand side of the pipe symbol and sends it to the input of the command on the right-hand side of the pipe symbol. A pipeline can consist of more than one pipe.

The purpose of the next commands in Example 8.91 is to count the number of people logged on (*who*), save the output of the command in a file (*tmp*), use the *wc -l* to count the number of lines in the *tmp* file (*wc -l*), and then remove the *tmp* file (i.e., find the number of people logged on).

EXAMPLE 8.91

```
1   $ who > tmp
2   $ wc -l tmp
    4 tmp
3   $ rm tmp

Using a pipe saves disk space and time.

4   $ who | wc -l
            4

5   $ du .. | sort -n | sed -n '$p'
    1980    ..

6   $ ( du / | sort -n | sed -n '$p' ) 2> /dev/null
    1057747  /
```

EXPLANATION

1. The output of the *who* command is redirected to the *tmp* file.
2. The *wc -l* command displays the number of lines in *tmp*.
3. The *tmp* file is removed.
4. With the pipe facility, you can perform all three of the preceding steps in one step. The output of the *who* command is sent to an anonymous kernel buffer; the *wc -l* command reads from the buffer and sends its output to the screen. See Figure 8.5.
5. The output of the *du* command, the number of disk blocks used per directory, starting in the parent directory (..), is piped to the *sort* command and sorted numerically. It is then piped to the *sed* command, which prints the last line of the output it receives. See Figure 8.6.
6. The *du* command (starting in the root directory) will send error messages to *stderr* (the screen) if it is unable to get into a directory because the permissions have been turned off. When you put the whole command line in a set of parentheses, all the output is sent to the screen, and all the errors are directed to the *Linux* bit bucket, */dev/null*.

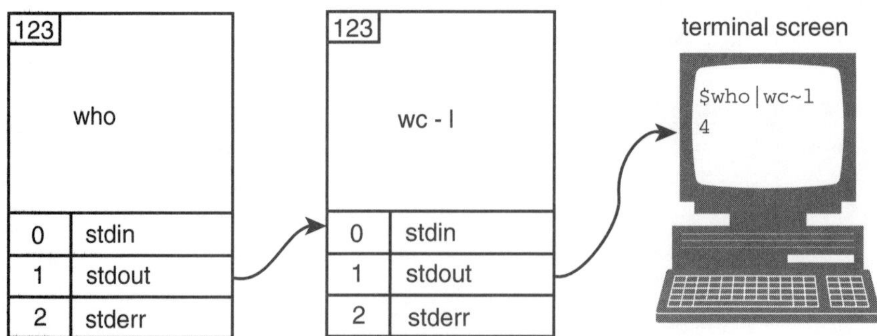

Figure 8.5 The pipe.

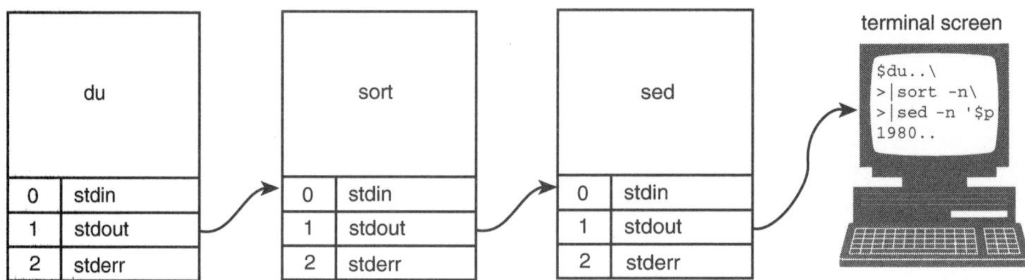

Figure 8.6 Multiple pipes (filter).

8.3.11 The *Here* Document and Redirecting Input

The *here* document is a special form of quoting. It accepts inline text for a program expecting input, such as *mail, sort*, or *cat*, until a user-defined terminator is reached. It is often used in shell scripts for creating menus. The command receiving the input is appended with a << symbol, followed by a user-defined word or symbol, and a newline. The next lines of text will be the lines of input to be sent to the command. The input is terminated when the user-defined word or symbol is then placed on a line by itself in the leftmost column (it cannot have spaces surrounding it). The word is used in place of Control-D to stop the program from reading input.

If the terminator is preceded by the <<- operator, leading tabs, and only tabs, may precede the final terminator. The user-defined terminating word or symbol must match exactly from "here" to "here." The following examples illustrate the use of the *here* document at the command line to demonstrate the syntax. It is much more practical to use them in scripts.

EXAMPLE 8.92

```
1   $ cat << FINISH               # FINISH is a user-defined
2   > Hello there $LOGNAME            terminator
3   > The time is $(date +%T).
    > I can't wait to see you!!!
4   > FINISH                      # terminator matches first

5   Hello there ellie             # FINISH on line 1.
    The time is 19:42:12.
    I can't wait to see you!!!
6   $
```

EXPLANATION

1 The *Linux cat* program will accept input until the word *FINISH* appears on a line by itself.

2 A secondary prompt appears. The following text is input for the *cat* command. Variable substitution is performed within the "here" document.

3 Command substitution, *$(date +%T)*, is performed within the *here* document. Could have also used the older form of command substitution: *'date +T'*.

4 The user-defined terminator *FINISH* marks the end of input for the *cat* program. It cannot have any spaces before or after it and is on a line by itself.

5 The output from the *cat* program is displayed.

6 The shell prompt reappears.

EXAMPLE 8.93

```
1   $ cat <<- DONE
    >  Hello there
    >       What's up?
    >Bye now The time is `date`.
2   >    DONE
      Hello there
           What's up?
    Bye now The time is Sun Feb 819:48:23 PST 1999.
    $
```

EXPLANATION

1 The *cat* program accepts input until *DONE* appears on a line by itself. The <<- operator allows the input and final terminator to be preceded by one or more tabs. Typing this example at the command line may cause problems with the Tab key; the example will work fine, if run from a script.

2 The final matching terminator, *DONE*, is preceded by a tab. The output of the *cat* program is displayed on the screen.

8.3.12 Shell Invocation Options

When the shell is started using the *bash* command, it can take options to modify its behavior. There are two types of options: single-character options and multicharacter options. The single-character options consist of a single leading dash followed by a single character. The multicharacter options consist of two leading dashes and any number of characters. Multicharacter options must appear before single-character options. An interactive login shell normally starts up with *-i* (starts an interactive shell) , *-s* (reads from standard input), and *-m* (enables job control). See Table 8.29.

Table 8.29 *Bash* 2.x Shell Invocation Options

Option	*Meaning*
-c string	Commands are read from *string*. Any arguments after *string* are assigned to positional parameters, starting at $0.
-D	A list of double quoted strings, preceded by a *$*, are printed to standard output. These strings are subject to language translation when the current locale is not C or POSIX. The *-n* option is implied; no commands will be executed.
-i	Shell is in the interactive mode. TERM, QUIT, and INTERRUPT are ignored.
-s	Commands are read from standard input and allows the setting of positional parameters.
-r	Starts a restricted shell.
--	Signals the end of options and disables further option processing. Any arguments after -- or - are treated as filenames and arguments.
--dump-strings	Same as *-D*.
--help	Displays a usage message for a built-in command and exits.
--login	Causes *bash* to be invoked as a login shell.
--noediting	When *bash* is running interactively, does not use the Readline library.

Table 8.29 *Bash* 2.x Shell Invocation Options (Continued)

Option	*Meaning*
--noprofile	When starting up, *bash* does not read the initialization files: */etc/profile*, *~/.bash_profile*, *~/.bash_login*, or *~/.profile*.
--norc	For interactive shells, *bash* will not read the *~/.bashrc* file. Turned on by default, if running shell as *sh*.
--posix	Changes the behavior of *bash* to match the POSIX 1003.2 standard, if otherwise it wouldn't.
--quiet	Displays no information at shell startup, the default.
--rcfile file	If *bash* is interactive, uses this intialization file instead of *~/.bashrc*.
--restricted	Starts a restricted shell.
--verbose	Turns on verbose; same as *-v*.
--version	Displays version information about this *bash* shell and exits.

8.3.13 The *set* Command and Options

The *set* command can be used to turn shell options on and off, as well as for handling command line arguments. To turn an option on, the dash (-) is prepended to the option; to turn an option off, the plus sign (+) is prepended to the option. See Table 8.30 for a list of *set* options.

EXAMPLE 8.94

```
1   $ set -f

2   $ echo *
    *

3   $ echo ??
    ??

4   $ set +f
```

EXPLANATION

1. The *f* option is turned on, disabling filename expansion.
2. The asterisk is not expanded.
3. The question marks are not expanded.
4. The *f* is turned off; filename expansion is enabled.

Table 8.30 The Built-In *set* Command Options

Name of Option	*Shortcut Switch*	*What It Does*
allexport	*-a*	Automatically marks new or modified variables for export from the time the option is set, until unset.
braceexpand	*-B*	Enables brace expansion, and is a default setting.
emacs		For command line editing, uses the *emacs* built-in editor, and is a default setting.
errexit	*-e*	If a command returns a nonzero exit status (fails), exits. Not set when reading initialization files.
histexpand	*-H*	Enables *!* and *!!* when performing history substitution, and is a default setting.
history		Enables command line history; on by default.
ignoreeof		Disables EOF (*Control-D*) from exiting a shell; must type *exit*. Same as setting shell variable, IGNOREEOF=10.
keyword	*-k*	Places keyword arguments in the environment for a command.
interactive_comments		For interactive shells, a leading # is used to comment out any text remaining on the line.
monitor	*-m*	Allows job control.
noclobber	*-C*	Protects files from being overwritten when redirection is used.
noexec	*-n*	Reads commands, but does not execute them. Used to check the syntax of scripts. Not on when running interactively.
noglob	*-d*	Disables pathname expansion; i.e., turns off wildcards.
notify	*-b*	Notifies user when background job finishes.
nounset	*-u*	Displays an error when expanding a variable that has not been set.
onecmd	*-t*	Exits after reading and executing one command.
physical	*-P*	If set, does not follow symbolic links when typing *cd* or *pwd*. The physical directory is used instead.

Table 8.30 The Built-In *set* Command Options (Continued)

Name of Option	*Shortcut Switch*	*What It Does*
posix		Shell behavior is changed if the default operation doesn't match the POSIX standard.
privileged	*-p*	When set, the shell does not read the *.profile* or *ENV* file and shell functions are not inherited from the environment; automatically set for *setuid* scripts.
posix		Change the default behavior to POSIX 1003.2.
verbose	*-v*	Turns on the *verbose* mode for debugging.
vi		For command line editing, uses the *vi* built-in editor.
xtrace	*-x*	Turns on the echo mode for debugging.

8.3.14 The *shopt* Command and Options

The *shopt* (*bash* 2.x) command can also be used to turn shell options on and off.

Table 8.31 The *shopt* Command Options

Option	*Meaning*
cdable_vars	If an argument to the *cd* built-in command is not a directory, it is assumed to be the name of a variable whose value is the directory to change to.
cdspell	Corrects minor errors in the spelling of a directory name in a *cd* command. The errors checked for are transposed characters, a missing character, and a character too many. If a correction is found, the corrected path is printed, and the command proceeds. Only used by interactive shells.
checkhash	*Bash* checks that a command found in the hash table exists before trying to execute it. If a hashed command no longer exists, a normal path search is performed.
checkwinsize	*Bash* checks the window size after each command and, if necessary, updates the values of LINES and COLUMNS.
cmdhist	*Bash* attempts to save all lines of a multiple-line command in the same history entry. This allows easy re-editing of multiline commands.
dotglob	*Bash* includes filenames beginning with a ". " in the results of filename expansion.

Table 8.31 The *shopt* Command Options (Continued)

Option	***Meaning***
execfail	A noninteractive shell will not exit if it cannot execute the file specified as an argument to the *exec* built-in command. An interactive shell does not exit if *exec* fails.
expand_aliases	Aliases are expanded. Enabled by default.
extglob	The extended pattern matching features (regular expression metacharacters derived from Korn shell for filename expansion) are enabled.
histappend	The history list is appended to the file named by the value of the HISTFILE variable when the shell exits, rather than overwriting the file.
histreedit	If Readline is being used, a user is given the opportunity to re-edit a failed history substitution.
histverify	If set, and Readline is being used, the results of history substitution are not immediately passed to the shell parser. Instead, the resulting line is loaded into the Readline editing buffer, allowing further modification.
hostcomplete	If set, and Readline is being used, *bash* will attempt to perform hostname completion when a word containing "@" is being completed. Enabled by default.
huponexit	If set, *bash* will send SIGHUP (hangup signal) to all jobs when an interactive login shell exits.
interactive_comments	Allows a word beginning with "#" to cause that word and all remaining characters on that line to be ignored in an interactive shell. Enabled by default.
lithist	If enabled, and the *cmdhist* option is enabled, multiline commands are saved to the history with embedded newlines rather than using semicolon separators where possible.
mailwarn	If set, and a file that *bash* is checking for mail has been accessed since the last time it was checked, the message "The mail in mailfile has been read" is displayed.
nocaseglob	If set, *bash* matches filenames in a case-insensitive fashion when performing filename expansion.
nullglob	If set, *bash* allows filename patterns which match no files to expand to a null string, rather than themselves.
promptvars	If set, prompt strings undergo variable and parameter expansion after being expanded. Enabled by default.

Table 8.31 The *shopt* Command Options (Continued)

Option	***Meaning***
restricted_shell	The shell sets this option if it is started in restricted mode. The value may not be changed. This is not reset when the startup files are executed, allowing the startup files to discover whether or not a shell is restricted.
shift_verbose	If this is set, the shift built-in prints an error message when the shift count exceeds the number of positional parameters.
sourcepath	If set, the *source* built-in uses the value of PATH to find the directory containing the file supplied as an argument. Enabled by default.
source	A synonym for **.** (a dot)

8.3.15 Shell Built-In Commands

The shell has a number of commands that are built-in to its source code. Because the commands are built-in, the shell doesn't have to locate them on disk, making execution much faster. The *help* feature provided with *bash* give you online help for any built-in command. The built-in commands are listed in Table 8.32.

Table 8.32 Built-In Commands

Command	***What It Does***
:	Do-nothing command; returns exit status zero.
. file	The *dot* command reads and executes command from file.
break [n]	See "Looping Commands" on page 440.
.	Executes program in context of current process; same as source.
alias	Lists and creates "nicknames" for existing commands.
bg	Puts a job in the background.
bind	Display current key and function bindings, or binds keys to a *readline* function or macro.
break	Breaks out of the innermost loop.
builtin [sh-builtin [args]]	Runs a shell built-in, passing it args, and returning 0 exit status. Useful if a function and built-in have the same name.
cd [arg]	Changes the directory to home if no arg or to arg.

Table 8.32 Built-In Commands (Continued)

Command	***What It Does***
command command [arg]	Runs a command even if a function has the same name; i.e., bypasses function lookup.
continue [n]	See "Looping Commands" on page 440.
declare [var]	Displays all variables or declares variables with optional attributes.
dirs	Displays a list of currently remembered directories resulting from *pushd.*
disown	Removes an active job from the job table.
echo [args]	Displays args terminated with a newline
enable	Enables and disables shell built-in commands.
eval [args]	Reads args as input to the shell and executes the resulting command(s).
exec command	Runs command in place of this shell.
exit [n]	Exits the shell with status *n.*
export [var]	Makes *var* known to subshells.
fc	History's fix command for editing history commands.
fg	Puts background job into foreground.
getopts	Parses and processes command line options.
hash	Controls the internal hash table for quicker searches for commands.
help [command]	Displays helpful info about built-in commands and, if command is specified, detailed help about that built-in command.
history	Displays the history list with line numbers.
jobs	Lists jobs put in the background.
kill [-signal process]	Sends the signal to the PID number or job number of the process. Type at the prompt: *kill -l*
getopts	Used in shell scripts to parse command line and check for legal options.
let	Used for evaluating arithmetic expressions and assigning results of arithmetic calculations to variables.
local	Used in functions to restrict the scope of variables to the function.
logout	Exits the login shell.
popd	Removes entries from the directory stack.

Table 8.32 Built-In Commands (Continued)

Command	*What It Does*
pushd	Adds entries to the directory stack.
pwd	Prints present working directory.
read [var]	Reads line from standard input into variable *var*.
readonly [var]	Makes variable *var* read-only. Cannot be reset.
return [n]	Returns from a function where *n* is the exit value given to the return.
set	Sets options and positional parameters. See "The set Command and Positional Parameters" on page 397.
shift [n]	Shifts positional parameters to the left *n* times.
stop pid	Halts execution of the process number PID.
suspend	Stops execution of the current shell (but not if a login shell).
test	Checks file types and evaluates conditional expressions.
times	Prints accumulated user and system *times* for processes run from this shell.
trap [arg] [n]	When shell receives signal *n* (0, 1, 2, or 15), executes *arg*.
type [command]	Prints the type of command; e.g., *pwd* is a built-in shell command.
typeset	Same as declare. Sets variables and gives them attributes.
ulimit	Diplays and sets process resource limits.
umask [octal digits]	Sets user file creation mode mask for owner, group, and others.
unalias	Unsets aliases.
unset [name]	*Unset* value of variable or function.
wait [pid#n]	Waits for background process with PID number *n* and reports termination status.

THE BOURNE SHELL LAB EXERCISES

Lab 1—Getting Started

1. What process puts the login prompt on your screen?
2. What process assigns values to HOME, LOGNAME, and PATH?
3. How do you know what shell you are using?
4. What command will allow you to change your login shell?
5. Where is your login shell assigned? (What file?)
6. Explain the difference between the */etc/profile* and *~/.bash_profile* file. Which one is executed first?
7. Edit your *.bash_profile* file as follows.
   a. Welcome the user.
   b. Add your home directory to the path if it is not there.
   c. Set erase to the backspace key using *stty*.
   d. Type: *source.bash_profile*
   What is the function of the source command?
8. What is the *BASH_ENV* file? When is it executed?
9. What is the default primary prompt?
   a. Change the prompt to include the time of day and your home directory.
   b. What is the default secondary prompt? What is its function?
10. Explain the function of each of the following settings:
    a. set *-o ignoreeof*
    b. set *-o noclobber*
    c. set *-o emacs*
    d. set *-o vi*
11. In what file are the settings in the previous example stored? Why are they stored there?
12. What does *shopt -p* do? Why use *shopt* instead of *set*?
13. What is a built-in command? How can you tell if a command is a built-in or an executable? What is the purpose of the *builtin* command? The *enable* command?
14. What would cause the shell to return an exit status of 127?

Lab 2—Job Control

1. What is the difference between a program and a process? What is a job?
2. What is the PID of your shell?
3. How do you stop a job?
4. What command brings a background job into the foreground?
5. How do you list all running jobs? All stopped jobs?
6. What is the purpose of the *kill* command?
7. What does *jobs -l* display? What does *kill -l* display?

Lab 3—Command Completion, History, and Aliases

1. What is filename completion?
2. What is the name of the file that stores a history of commands entered at the command line?
3. What does the HISTSIZE variable control? What does HISTFILESIZE control?
4. What does bang, bang mean?
5. How would you reexecute the last command that started with a "v"?
6. How would you reexecute the 125th command? How would you print the history list in reverse?
7. How do you set interactive editing to use the *vi* editor? In what initialization file would you put this setting?
8. What is the *fc* command?
9. What is the purpose of the Readline library? From what initialization file does it read instructions?
10. What is key binding? How do you find out what keys are bound?
11. What is the universal argument?
12. Create an alias for the following commands:

    a. clear

    b. fc -s

    c. ls --color=tty

    d. kill -l

Lab 4—Shell Metacharacters

1. Make a directory called *wildcards*. *Cd* to that directory and type at the prompt:

    ```
    touch ab abc a1 a2 a3 all a12 ba ba.1 ba.2 filex filey AbC ABC
    ABc2 abc
    ```

2. Write and test the command that will:

    a. List all files starting with *a*.

    b. List all files ending in at least one digit.

    c. List all files starting with *a* or *A*.

    d. List all files ending in a period, followed by a digit.

    e. List all files containing just two alphas.

    f. List three character files where all letters are uppercase.

    g. List files ending in *10*, *11*, or *12*.

    h. List files ending in *x* or *y*.

    i. List all files ending in a digit, an uppercase letter, or a lowercase letter.

    j. List all files *not* starting with a *b* or *B*.

    k. Remove two character files starting with *a* or *A*.

Lab 5—Redirection

1. What are the names of the three file streams associated with your terminal?

2. What is a file descriptor?

3. What command would you use to:

    a. Redirect the output of the *ls* command to a file called *lsfile*?

    b. Redirect and append the output of the *date* command to *lsfile*?

    c. Redirect the output of the *who* command to *lsfile*? What happened?

4. What happens when you type *cp* all by itself?

5. How do you save the error message from the above example to a file?

6. Use the *find* command to find all files, starting from the parent directory, of type *directory*. Save the standard output in a file called *found* and any errors in a file called *found.errs*.

7. Take the output of three commands and redirect the output to a file called *gottem_all*?

8. Use a pipe(s) with the *ps* and *wc* commands to find out how many processes you are currently running.

Lab 6—Variables

1. What is a positional parameter? Type at the command line:
   set dogs cats birds fish
   a. How do you list all of the positional parameters?
   b. Which positional parameter is assigned *birds*?
   c. How do you print the number of positional parameters?
   d. How do you remove all the positional parameters from the shell's memory?
2. What is an environment variable? What is the command used to list them? Create an environment variable called CITY and assign it the value of your home town. How do you export it?
3. What is a local variable? Set a local variable to your name. Print its value. Unset it.
4. What is the function of *declare -i*?
5. What does the *$$* variable display? What does the *$!* display?

CHAPTER

9

PROGRAMMING WITH THE BASH SHELL

9.1 Introduction

When commands are executed from within a file, instead of from the command line, the file is called a shell script and the shell is running noninteractively. When the *bash* shell starts running noninteractively, it looks for the environment variable, *BASH_ENV* (*ENV*) and starts up the file (normally *.bashrc*) assigned as its value. After the *BASH_ENV* file has been read, the shell will start executing commands in the script.[1]

9.1.1 The Steps in Creating a Shell Script

A shell script is normally written in an editor and consists of commands interspersed with comments. Comments are preceded by a pound sign and consist of text used to document what is going on.

The First Line. The first line at the top left corner of the script will indicate the program that will be executing the lines in the script. This line, commonly called the *shbang* line, is written as:

```
#!/bin/bash
```

The *#!* is called a magic number and is used by the kernel to identify the program that should be interpreting the lines in the script. This line must be the top line of your script. The *bash* program can also accept arguments to modify its behavior. See "Bash Options" on page 474 for a list of *bash* options.

1. When *bash* starts interactively, if the *-norc* or *--norc* option is given, the *BASH_ENV* or *ENV* file will not be read.

Comments. *Comments* are lines preceded by a pound sign (#) and can be on a line by themselves or on a line following a script command. They are used to document your script. It is sometimes difficult to understand what the script is supposed to do if it is not commented. Although comments are important, they are often too sparse or not used at all. Try to get used to commenting what you are doing not only for someone else, but also for yourself. Two days from now you may not recall exactly what you were trying to do.

Executable Statements and *bash* Shell Constructs. A *bash* shell program consists of a combination of Linux commands, *bash* shell commands, programming constructs, and comments.

Making the Script Executable. When you create a file, it is not given the execute permission. You need this permission to run your script. Use the *chmod* command to turn on the execute permission.

EXAMPLE 9.1

```
1   $ chmod +x myscript
2   $ ls -lF  myscript
    -rwxr-xr-x    1  ellie    0 Jul   13:00 myscript*
```

EXPLANATION

1 The *chmod* command is used to turn on the execute permission for the user, group, and others.

2 The output of the *ls* command indicates that all users have execute permission on the *joker* file. The asterisk at the end of the filename also indicates that this is an executable program.

A Scripting Session. In the following example, the user will create a script in the editor. After the user saves the file, the execute permissions are turned on, and the script is executed. If there are errors in the program, the shell will respond immediately.

EXAMPLE 9.2

```
(The Script)
1   #!/bin/bash
2   # This is the first Bash shell program of the day.
    # Scriptname: greetings
    # Written by:  Barbara Bashful
3   echo "Hello $LOGNAME, it's nice talking to you."
4   echo "Your present working directory is `pwd`."
    echo "You are working on a machine called `uname -n`."
    echo "Here is a list of your files."
5   ls  # list files in the present working directory
6   echo  "Bye for now $LOGNAME. The time is `date +%T`!"

(The Command Line)
    $ greetings      # Don't forget to turn turn on x permission!
    bash: ./greetings: Permission denied.

    $ chmod +x greetings
    $ greetings  or  ./greetings
3   Hello barbara, it's nice talking to you.
4   Your present working directory is /home/lion/barbara/prog
    You are working on a machine called lion.
    Here is a list of your files.

5   Afile        cplus    letter     prac
    Answerbook   cprog    library    prac1
    bourne       joke     notes      perl5
6   Bye for now barbara. The time is 18:05:07!
```

EXPLANATION

1. The first line of the script, *#!/bin/bash*, lets the kernel know what interpreter will execute the lines in this program, in this case the *bash* (Bourne Again shell) interpreter.
2. The comments are nonexecutable lines preceded by a pound sign. They can be on a line by themselves or appended to a line after a command.
3. After variable substitution is performed by the shell, the *echo* command displays the line on the screen.
4. After command substitution is performed by the shell, the *echo* command displays the line on the screen.
5. The *ls* command is executed. The comment will be ignored by the shell.
6. The *echo* command displays the string enclosed within double quotes. Variables and command substitution (back quotes) are expanded when placed within double quotes. In this case, the quotes were really not necessary.

9.2 Reading User Input

9.2.1 Variables (Review)

In the last chapter we talked about declaring and unsetting variables. Variables are set local to the current shell or as environment variables. Unless your shell script will invoke another script, variables are normally set as local variables within a script. (See in Chapter 8, "Variables" on page 327.)

To extract the value from a variable, preceed the variable with a dollar sign. You can enclose the variable within double quotes and the dollar sign will be interpreted by the shell for variable expansion. Variable expansion is not performed if the variable is enclosed in single quotes.

EXAMPLE 9.3

```
1   name="John Doe" or declare name="John Doe"    (local variable)
2   export NAME="John Doe"      (global variable)
3   echo "$name" "$NAME"        (extract the value)
```

9.2.2 The *read* Command

The *read* command is a built-in command used to read input from the terminal or from a file (see Table 9.1). The *read* command takes a line of input until a newline is reached. The newline at the end of a line will be translated into a null byte when read. If no names are supplied, the line read is assigned to the special built-in variable, *REPLY*. You can also use the *read* command to cause a program to stop until the user enters a carriage return. To see how the *read* command is most effectively used for reading lines of input from a file, see "Looping Commands" on page 425. The *-r* option to read causes the backslash-newline pair to be ignored; the backslash is treated as part of the line. The *read* command has four options to control its behavior:-*a*, -*e*, -*p*, and -*r*.[2]

Table 9.1 The *read* Command

Format	*Meaning*
read answer	Reads a line from standard input and assigns it to the variable *answer*.
read first last	Reads a line from standard input to the first white space or newline, putting the first word typed into the variable *first* and the rest of the line into the variable *last*.
read	Reads a line from standard input and assigns it to the built-in variable, *REPLY*.

2. Options -*a*, -*e*, and -*p* are available only in *bash* versions 2.x.

Table 9.1 The *read* Command (Continued)

Format	*Meaning*
read -a arrayname	Reads a list of words into an array called *arrayname.*[a]
read -e	Used in interactive shells with command line editing in effect; e.g., if editor is *vi*, *vi* commands can be used on the input line.[a]
read -p prompt	Prints a prompt, waits for input, and stores input in *REPLY* variable.[a]
read -r line	Allows the input to contain a backslash.[a]

a. Not implemented on versions of *bash* prior to 2.0.

EXAMPLE 9.4

```
(The Script)
    #!/bin/bash
    # Scriptname: nosy
    echo -e "Are you happy? \c"
1   read answer
    echo "$answer is the right response."
    echo -e "What is your full name? \c"
2   read first middle last
    echo "Hello  $first"

    echo -n "Where do you work? "
3   read
4   echo I guess $REPLY keeps you busy!
------------------------------------------------a
5    read -p "Enter your job title: "
6    echo "I thought you might be an $REPLY."

7    echo -n "Who are your best friends? "
8    read -a friends
9    echo "Say hi to ${friends[2]}."

------------------------------------------------------------

(The Output)
    $ nosy
    Are you happy? Yes
1   Yes is the right response.
2   What is your full name? Jon Jake Jones
    Hello Jon
3   Where do you work? the Chico Nut Factory
4   I guess the Chico Nut Factory keeps you busy!
5   Enter your job title: Accountant
6   I thought you might be an Accountant.
7,8 Who are your best friends?  Melvin Tim Ernesto
9   Say hi to Ernesto.
```

a. The commands listed below this line are not implemented on versions of *bash* prior to 2.x.

EXPLANATION

1 The *read* command accepts a line of user input and assigns the input to the variable *answer.*

2 The *read* command accepts input from the user and assigns the first word of input to the variable *first*, the second word of input to the variable *middle*, and all the rest of the words up to the end of the line to the variable *last*.

3 A line is read from standard input and stored in the built-in *REPLY* variable.

4 The value of the *REPLY* variable is printed.

5 With the *-p* option, the *read* command produces a prompt, *Enter your job title:* and stores the line of input in the special built-in *REPLY* variable.

6 The value of the *REPLY* variable is displayed in the string.

7 The user is asked to enter input.

8 With the *-a* option, the *read* command takes input as an array of words. The array is called *friends*. The elements read into the array are *Melvin, Tim,* and *Ernesto.*

9 The third element of the *friends* array, *Ernesto*, is printed. Array indices start at 0.

EXAMPLE 9.5

```
   (The Script)
     #!/bin/bash
     # Scriptname: printer_check
     # Script to clear a hung up printer
1    if [ $LOGNAME != root ]
     then
         echo "Must have root privileges to run this program"
         exit 1
     fi
2    cat << EOF
     Warning: All jobs in the printer queue will be removed.
     Please turn off the printer now. Press return when you
     are ready to continue. Otherwise press Control C.
     EOF
3    read JUNK       # Wait until the user turns off the printer
     echo
4    /etc/rc.d/init.d/lpd stop       # Stop the printer
5    echo -e "\nPlease turn the printer on now."
6    echo "Press return to continue"
```

EXAMPLE 9.5 (CONTINUED)

```
7   read JUNK                   # Stall until the user turns the printer
                                # back on
    echo                        # A blank line is printed
8   /etc/rc.d/init.d/lpd start     # Start the printer
```

EXPLANATION

1. Checks to see if user is *root*. If not, sends an error and exits.
2. Creates a "here" document. Warning message is displayed on the screen.
3. The *read* command waits for user input. When the user presses Enter, the variable *JUNK* accepts whatever is typed. The variable is not used for anything. The *read* in this case is used to wait until the user turns off the printer, comes back, and presses Enter.
4. The *lpd* program stops the printer daemon.
5. Now it's time to turn the printer back on!
6. The user is asked to press the carriage return when ready.
7. Whatever the user types is read into the variable *JUNK*, and when Enter is pressed, the program will resume execution.
8. The *lpd* program starts the print daemons.

9.3 Arithmetic

9.3.1 Integers (*declare* and *let* Commands)

The *declare* Command. Variables can be declared as integers with the *declare -i* command. If you attempt to assign any string value, *bash* assigns 0 to the variable. Arithmetic can be performed on variables that have been declared as integers. (If the variable has not been declared as an integer, the built-in *let* command allows arithmetic operations. See "The let Command" on page 394.) If you attempt to assign a floating point number, *bash* reports a syntax error. Numbers can also be represented in different bases such as *binary, octal, and hex*.

EXAMPLE 9.6

```
1   $ declare -i num

2   $ num=hello
    $ echo $num
    0

3   $ num=5 + 5
    bash: +: command not found

4   $ num=5+5
    $ echo $num
    10

5   $ num=4*6
    $ echo $num
    24

6   $ num="4 * 6"
    $ echo $num
    24

7   $ num=6.5
    bash: num: 6.5: sytax error in expression (remainder of
     expression is ".5")
```

EXPLANATION

1 The *declare* command with the *-i* option creates an integer variable *num.*

2 Trying to assign the string *hello* to the integer variable *num* causes the string to be stored as zero.

3 The white space must be quoted or removed unless the *let* command is used.

4 The white space is removed and arithmetic is performed.

5 Multiplication is performed and the result assigned to *num.*

6 The white space is quoted so that the multiplication can be performed and to keep the shell from expanding the wildcard (*).

7 Because the variable is set to integer, adding a fractional part causes a *bash* syntax error.

Listing Integers. The *declare* command with only the *-i* argument will list all preset integers and their values, as shown in the following display.

```
$ declare -i
declare -ir EUID="15"          # effective user id
declare -ir PPID="235"         # parent process id
declare -ir UID="15"           # user id
```

Representing and Using Different Bases. Numbers can be represented in decimal (base 10 and the default), octal (base 8), hexadecimal (base 16), ranging from base 2 to 36.

FORMAT

```
variable=base#number-in-that-base
```

EXAMPLE 9.7

```
n=2#101    Base is 2; number 101 is in base 2
```

EXAMPLE 9.8

```
(The Command Line)
1  $ declare -i x=017
   $ echo $x
   15
2  $ x=2#101
   $ echo $x
   5
3  $ x=8#17
   $ echo $x
   15
4  $ x=16#b
   $ echo $x
   11
```

EXPLANATION

1 The *declare* function is used to assign an integer variable *x* the octal value 017. Octal numbers must start with a leading zero. *15*, the decimal value of *017*, is printed.

2 The variable, *x*, is assigned the value of *101* (binary). *2* represents the base, separated by a #, and the number in that base, *101*. The value of *x* is printed as decimal, *5*.

EXPLANATION (CONTINUED)

3 The variable, *x*, is assigned the value of 17 (octal). *x*. The value of *x* is printed as decimal, *15*.

4 The variable, *x*, is assigned the value of b (hexadecimal). The value of *x* is decimal *11*.

The *let* Command. The *let* command is a *bash* shell built-in command that is used to perform integer arithmetic and numeric expression testing. To see what *let* operators your version of *bash* supports, type at the prompt:

```
help let
```

A list of the operators is also found in Table 9.4 on page 407.

EXAMPLE 9.9

```
1   $ i=5   or let i=5

2   $ let i=i+1
    $ echo $i
    6

3   $ let "i = i + 2"
    $ echo $i
    8

4   $ let "i+=1"
    $ echo $i
    9

5   $ i=3

6   $ (( i+=4))
    $ echo $i
    7

7   $ (( i=i-2 ))
    $ echo $i
    5
```

EXPLANATION

1 The variable *i* is assigned the value *5*.

2 The *let* command will add *1* to the value of *i*. The *$* (dollar sign) is not required for variable substitution when performing arithmetic.

EXPLANATION (CONTINUED)

3 The quotes are needed if the arguments contain white space.

4 The shortcut operator, +=, is used to add *1* to the value of *i*.

5 The variable *i* is assigned the value 5.

6 The double parentheses can be used to replace *let*.[a]
4 is added and assigned to *i*.

7 2 is subtracted from *i*. We could have also written: *i–=2*

a. Double parentheses (( )) are used to replace *let* on versions of Bash 2.x.

9.3.2 Floating Point Arithmetic

Bash supports only integer arithmetic, but the *bc*, *awk*, and *nawk* utilities are useful if you need to perform more complex calculations.

EXAMPLE 9.10

```
(The Command Line)
1   $ n=`echo "scale=3; 13 / 2" | bc`
    $ echo $n
    6.500

2   product=`gawk -v x=2.45 -v y=3.123 'BEGIN{printf "%.2f\n",x*y}'`
    $ echo $product
    7.65
```

EXPLANATION

1 The output of the *echo* command is piped to the *bc* program. The scale is set to *3*, which is the number of significant digits to the right of the decimal point that will be printed. The calculation is to divide *13* by *2*. The entire pipeline is enclosed in back quotes. Command substitution will be performed and the output assigned to the variable *n*.

2 The *gawk* program gets its values from the argument list passed in at the command line, *x=2.45 y=3.123*. After the numbers are multiplied, the *printf* function formats and prints the result with a precision of two places to the right of the decimal point. The output is assigned to the variable *product*.

9.4 Positional Parameters and Command Line Arguments

9.4.1 Positional Parameters

Information can be passed into a script via the command line. Each word (separated by white space) following the script name is called an argument.

Command line arguments can be referenced in scripts with positional parameters; for example, *$1* for the first argument, *$2* for the second argument, *$3* for the third argument, and so on. After *$9*, curly braces are used to keep the number as one number. For example, positional parameter *10* is referenced as *${10}*. The *$#* variable is used to test for the number of parameters, and *$** is used to display all of them. Positional parameters can be set or reset with the *set* command. When the *set* command is used, any positional parameters previously set are cleared out. See Table 9.2.

Table 9.2 Positional Parameters

Positional Parameter	*What It References*
$0	References the name of the script.
$#	Holds the value of the number of positional parameters.
*$**	Lists all of the positional parameters.
$@	Means the same as *$**, except when enclosed in double quotes.
"$"*	Expands to a single argument (e.g., "*$1 $2 $3*").
"$@"	Expands to separate arguments (e.g., "*$1*" "*$2*" "*$3*").
$1 ... ${10}	References individual positional parameters.

EXAMPLE 9.11

```
(The Script)
    #!/bin/bash
    # Scriptname: greetings2
    echo "This script is called $0."
1   echo "$0 $1 and $2"
    echo "The number of positional parameters is $#"
    ----------------------------------------------------------
```

EXAMPLE 9.11 (CONTINUED)

```
(The Command Line)
   $ chmod +x greetings2
2  $ greetings2
   This script is called  greetings2.
   greetings  and
   The number of positional paramters is

3  $ greetings2 Tommy
   This script is called greetings2.
   greetings Tommy and
   The number of positional parameters is 1

4  $ greetings2 Tommy Kimberly
   This script is called greetings2.
   greetings Tommy and Kimberly
   The number of positional parameters is 2
```

EXPLANATION

1 In the script *greetings2*, positional parameter *$0* references the script name, *$1* the first command line agreement, and *$2* the second command line agreement.

2 The *greetings2* script is executed without any arguments passed. The output illustrates that the script is called *greetings2* (*$0* in the script) and that *$1* and *$2* were never assigned anything; therefore, their values are null and nothing is printed.

3 This time, one argument is passed, *Tommy*. *Tommy* is assigned to positional parameter *1*.

4 Two arguments are entered, *Tommy* and *Kimberly*. *Tommy* is assigned to *$1* and *Kimberly* is assigned to *$2*.

9.4.2 The *set* Command and Positional Parameters

The *set* command with arguments resets the positional parameters.[3] Once reset, the old parameter list is lost. To unset all of the positional parameters, use *set --*. *$0* is always the name of the script.

---

3. Remember, without arguments, the *set* command displays all the variables that have been set for this shell, local and exported. With options, the *set* command turns on and off shell control options such as *-x* and *-v*.

EXAMPLE 9.12

```
(The Script)
   #!/bin/bash
   # Scriptname: args
   # Script to test command line arguments
1  echo The name of this script is $0.
2  echo The arguments are $*.
3  echo The first argument is $1.
4  echo The second argument is $2.
5  echo The number of arguments is $#.
6  oldargs=$*
7  set Jake Nicky Scott     # reset the positional parameters
8  echo All the positional parameters are $*.
9  echo The number of postional parameters is $#.
10 echo "Good-bye for now, $1."
11 set $(date)              # reset the positional parameters
12 echo The date is $2 $3, $6.
13 echo "The value of \$oldargs is $oldargs."
14 set $oldargs
15 echo $1 $2 $3

(The Output)
   $ args a b c d
1  The name of this script is args.
2  The arguments are a b c d.
3  The first argument is a.
4  The second argument is b.
5  The number of arguments is 4.
8  All the positional parameters are Jake Nicky Scott.
9  The number of positional parameters is 3.
10 Good-bye for now, Jake.
12 The date is Mar 25, 2000.
13 The value of $oldargs is a b c d.
```

EXPLANATION

1 The name of the script is stored in the *$0* variable.

2 *$** represents all of the positional parameters.

3 *$1* represents the first positional parameter (command line argument).

4 *$2* represents the second positional parameter.

5 *$#* is the total number of positional parameters (command line arguments).

6 All positional parameters are saved in a variable called *oldargs*.

EXPLANATION (CONTINUED)

7 The *set* command allows you to reset the positional parameters, clearing out the old list. Now, *$1* is *Jake, $2* is *Nicky,* and *$3* is *Scott.*

8 *$** represents all of the parameters, *Jake, Nicky,* and *Scott.*

9 *$#* represents the number of parameters, *3.*

10 *$1* is *Jake.*

11 After command substitution is performed, i.e., *date* is executed, the positional parameters are reset to the output of the *date* command.

12 The new values of *$2, $3,* and *$6* are displayed.

13 The values saved in *oldargs* are printed.

14 The *set* command creates positional parameters from the values stored in *oldargs.*

15 The first three positional parameters are displayed.

EXAMPLE 9.13

```
(The Script)
    #!/bin/bash
    # Scriptname: checker
    # Script to demonstrate the use of special variable
    # modifiers and arguments
1   name=${1:?"requires an argument" }
    echo Hello $name

(The Command Line)
2   $ checker
    checker: 1: requires an argument
3   $ checker Sue
    Hello Sue
```

EXPLANATION

1 The special variable modifier *:?* will check whether *$1* has a value. If not, the script exits and the message is printed.

2 The program is executed without an argument. *$1* is not assigned a value; an error is displayed.

3 The *checker* program is given a command line argument, *Sue*. In the script, *$1* is assigned *Sue*. The program continues.

How $* and $@ Differ. The $* and $@ differ only when enclosed in double quotes. When $* is enclosed within double quotes, the parameter list becomes a single string. When $@ is enclosed within double quotes, each of the parameters is quoted; that is, each word is treated as a separate string.

EXAMPLE 9.14

```
1   $ set 'apple pie' pears peaches
2   $ for i in $*
    > do
    > echo $i
    > done
    apple
    pie
    pears
    peaches

3   $ set 'apple pie' pears peaches
4   $ for i in "$*"
    > do
    > echo $i
    > done
    apple pie pears peaches

5   $ set 'apple pie' pears peaches
6   $ for i in $@
    > do
    > echo $i
    > done
    apple
    pie
    pears
    peaches

7   $ set 'apple pie' pears peaches
8   $ for i in "$@"          # At last!!
    > do
    > echo $i
    > done
    apple pie
    pears
    peaches
```

EXPLANATION

1 The positional parameters are set.

2 When *$** is expanded, the quotes surrounding *apple pie* are stripped; *apple* and *pie* become two separate words. The *for* loop assigns each of the words, in turn, to the variable *i*, and then prints the value of *i*. Each time through the loop, the word on the left is shifted off, and the next word is assigned to the variable *i*.

3 The positional parameters are set.

4 By enclosing *$** in double quotes, the entire parameter list becomes one string, *apple pie pears peaches*. The entire list is assigned to *i* as a single word. The loop makes one iteration.

5 The positional parameters are set.

6 Unquoted, *$@* and *$** behave the same way (see entry 2 of this explanation).

7 The positional parameters are set.

8 By surrounding *$@* with double quotes, each of the positional parameters is treated as a quoted string. The list would be *apple pie*, *pears*, and *peaches*. The desired result is finally achieved.

9.5 Conditional Constructs and Flow Control

9.5.1 Exit Status

Conditional commands allow you to perform some task(s) based on whether or not a condition succeeds or fails. The *if* command is the simplest form of decision-making; the *if/else* commands allow a two-way decision; and the *if/elif/else* commands allow a multiway decision.

Bash allows you to test two types of conditions: the success or failure of commands or whether or not an expression is true or false. In either case, the exit status is always used. An exit status of zero indicates success or true, and an exit status that is nonzero indicates failure or false. The *?* status variable contains a numeric value representing the exit status. To refresh your memory on how exit status works, look at the following Example 9.15.

EXAMPLE 9.15

```
   (At the Command Line)

1  $ name=Tom
2  $ grep "$name"  /etc/passwd
   Tom:8ZKX2F:5102:40:Tom Savage:/home/tom:/bin/sh
```

EXAMPLE 9.15

```
3   $ echo $?
    0                  Success!
4   $ name=Fred
5   $ grep "$name" /etc/passwd
    $ echo $?
     1                 Failure
```

EXPLANATION

1. The variable *name* is assigned the string *Tom*.
2. The *grep* command will search for string *Tom* in the *passwd* file.
3. The *?* variable contains the exit status of the last command executed; in this case, the exit status of *grep*. If *grep* is successful in finding the string *Tom*, it will return an exit status of zero. The *grep* command was successful.
4. The variable *name* is assigned *Fred*.
5. The *grep* command searches for Fred in the *passwd* file and is unable to find him. The *?* variable has a value of 1, indicating that *grep* failed.

9.5.2 The Built-In *test* Command

To evaluate an expression, the built-in *test* command is commonly used. This command is also linked to the bracket symbol. Either the *test* command itself can be used, or the expression can be enclosed in set of single brackets. Shell metacharacter expansion is not performed on expressions evaluated with the simple *test* command or when square brackets are used. Since word splitting is performed on variables, strings containing white space must be quoted. (See Example 9.16.)

On versions of *bash 2.x*, double brackets [[ ]] (the built-in compound *test* command) can be used to evaluate expressions. Word splitting is not performed on variables and pattern matching is done, allowing the expansion of metacharacters. A literal string containing white space must be quoted and if a string (with or without white space) is to be evaluated as an exact string, rather than part of a pattern, it too must be enclosed in quotes. The logical operators && (and) and || (or) replace the *-a* and *-o* operators used with the simple *test* command. (See Example 9.17.)

Although the *test* command can evaluate arithmetic expressions, you may prefer to use the *let* command with its rich set of C-like operators (*bash 2.x*). The *let* command can be represented alternatively by enclosing its expression in a set of double parentheses. (See Example 9.18.)

Whether you are using the *test* command, compound command, or *let* command, the result of an expression is tested, with zero status indicating success and nonzero status indicating failure. (See Table 8.14 on page 317.)

The following examples illustrate how the exit status is tested with the built-in *test* command and the alternate form of *test*, a set of single brackets [ ]; the compound command, a set of double brackets [[ ]]; and the *let* command, a set of double parentheses (( )).

EXAMPLE 9.16

```
    The test Command
    (At the Command Line)

1   $ name=Tom

4   $ test $name != Tom
5   $ echo $?
    1             Failure
6   $ [ $name = Tom ]
        # Brackets replace the test command
7   $ echo $?
    0
8   $ [ $name = [Tt]?? ]
    $ echo $?
    1
9   $ x=5
    $ y=20
10  $ [ $x -gt $y ]
    $ echo $?
    1
11  $ [ $x -le $y ]
    $ echo $?
    0
```

EXPLANATION

1 The variable *name* is assigned the string *Tom.*

2 The *grep* command will search for string *Tom* in the *passwd* file.

3 The *?* variable contains the exit status of the last command executed, in this case, the exit status of *grep*. If *grep* is successful in finding the string *Tom*, it will return an exit status of zero. The *grep* command was successful.

4 The *test* command is used to evaluate strings, numbers, and perform file testing. Like all commands, it returns an exit status. If the exit status is zero, the expression is true; if the exit status is one, the expression evaluates to false. There *must* be spaces surrounding the equal sign. The value of *name* is tested to see if it is not equal to *Tom.*

5 The test fails and returns an exit status of one.

6 The brackets are an alternate notation for the *test* command. There must be spaces after the first bracket. The expression is tested to see if *name* evaluates to the string *Tom. Bash* allows either a single or double equal sign to be used to test for equality of strings.

7 The exit status of the test is 0. The test was successful because *$name* is equal to *Tom.*

EXPLANATION (CONTINUED)

8 The *test* command does not allow wildcard expansion. Because the question mark is treated as a literal character, the test fails. *Tom* and *[Tt]??* are not equal.The exit status is one indicating that the text in line 8 failed.

9 *x* and *y* are given numeric values.

10 The *test* command uses numeric relational operators to test its operands; in this example it tests if *$x* is greater than (*-gt*) *$y*, and returns 0 exit status if true, 1 if false. (See Table 9.3 on page 406.)

11 Tests if *$x* less than or equal to (*-le*) *$y*, returning 0 exit status if true,1 if false.

EXAMPLE 9.17

```
The compound test command (bash 2.x)
    $ name=Tom; friend=Joseph
1   $ [[ $name == [Tt]om ]]          Wildcards allowed
    $ echo $?
    0
2   $ [[ $name == [Tt]om && $friend == "Jose" ]]
    $ echo $?
    1
3   $ shopt -s extglob               Turns on extended pattern matching
4   $ name=Tommy
5   $ [[ $name == [Tt]o+(m)y ]]
    $ echo $?
    0
```

EXPLANATION

1 If using the compound *test* command, shell metacharacters can be used in string tests. In this example, the expression is tested for string equality where *name* can match either *Tom* or *tom* or *tommy*, etc. If the expression is true, the exit status (?) is 0.

2 The logical operators && (and) and || (or) can be used with the compound test. If && is used, both expressions must be true, and if the first expression evaluates as false, no further checking is done. With the || logical operator, only one of the expressions must be true. If the first expression evaluates true, no further checking is done. Note that *"Jose"* is quoted. If not quoted, the *friend* variable would be checked to see if it contained the pattern *Jose*. *Jose* would match, and so would *Joseph*. The expression evaluates to false because the second condition is not true. The exit status is 1.

3 Extended pattern matching is turned on with the built-in *shopt* command.

4 The variable is assigned the value *Tommy*.

5 In this test, the expression is tested for string equality using the new pattern-matching metacharacters. It tests if *name* matches a string starting with *T* or *t*, followed by an *o*, one or more *m* characters, and a *y*.

EXAMPLE 9.18

```
    The let Command (bash 2.x)
    (At the Command Line)
1   $ x=2
    $ y=3

2   (( x > 2 ))
    echo $?
    1

3   (( x < 2 ))
    echo $?
    0

4   (( x == 2 && y == 3 ))
    echo $?
    0

5   (( x > 2 || y < 3 ))
    echo $?
    1
```

EXPLANATION

1. *x* and *y* are assigned numeric values.
2. The double parens replace the *let* command to evaluate the numeric expression. If x is greater than y, the exit status is *0*. Because the condition is not true, the exit status is *1*. The *?* variable holds the exit status of the last command executed; i.e., the (( )) command. Note: To evaluate a variable, the dollar sign is not necessary when the variable is enclosed in (( )).
3. The double parens evaluate the expression. If *x* is less than 2, and exit status of 0 is returned; otherwise, 1 is returned.
4. The compound expression is evaluated. The expression is tested as follows: if *x* is equal to *2* and *y* is equal to *3* (i.e., both expressions are true), then an exit status of 0 is returned; otherwise, 1 is returned.
5. The compound expression is evaluated. The expression is tested as follows: if *x* is greater than *2* or *y* is less than *3* (i.e. one of the expressions is true), then an exit status of 0 is returned; otherwise, 1 is returned.

Table 9.3 The *test* Command Operators

Test Operator	*Test for True If*
String Test	
[string1 = string2] *[string1==string2]*	*String1* is equal to *String2 (space surrounding = required).* (Can be used instead of the single = sign on *bash* versions 2.x.)
[string1 != string2]	*String1* is not equal to *String2 (space surrounding != required).*
[string]	*String* is not null.
[-z string]	Length of *string* is zero.
[-n string]	Length of *string* is nonzero.
[-l string]	Length of *string* (number of characters).
Examples:	*test -n $word* or *[-n $word]* *test tom = sue* or *[tom = sue]*
Logical Test	
[string1 -a string1]	Both *string1* and *string2* are true.
[string1 -o string2]	Either *string1* or *string2* is true.
[! string1]	Not a *string1* match.
Logical Test (Compound Test)[a]	
[[pattern1 && pattern2]]	Both *pattern1* and *pattern2* are true.
[[pattern1 || pattern2]]	Either *pattern1* or *pattern2* is true.
[[! pattern]]	Not a *pattern* match.
Integer Test	
[int1 -eq int2]	*Int1* is equal to *int2*.
[int1 -ne int2]	*Int1* is not equal to *int2*.
[int1 -gt int2]	*Int1* is greater than *int2*.
[int1 -ge int2]	*Int1* is greater than or equal to *int2*.
[int1 -lt int2]	*Int1* is less than *int2*.
[int1 -le int2]	*Int1* is less than or equal to *int2*.
Binary Operators for File Testing	
[file1 -nt file2]	True if *file1* is newer than (according to modification date) *file2*.
[file1 -ot file2]	True if *file1* is older than *file2*.
[file1 -ef file2]	True if *file1* and *file2* have the same device or inode numbers.

a. With the compound test, *pattern* can contain pattern matching metacharacters; for exact string testing, *pattern2* must be enclosed in quotes.

Table 9.4 The *let* Command Operators

<table>
<tr><th>Operator</th><th>Meaning</th></tr>
<tr><td>- +</td><td>Unary minus and plus</td></tr>
<tr><td>! ~</td><td>Logical and bitwise not (negation)</td></tr>
<tr><td>* / %</td><td>Multiply, divide, remainder</td></tr>
<tr><td>+ -</td><td>Add, subtract</td></tr>
<tr><td colspan="2">let operators not implemented prior to bash 2.x:</td></tr>
<tr><td><< >></td><td>Bitwise left shift, right shift</td></tr>
<tr><td><= >= < ></td><td>Comparison operators</td></tr>
<tr><td>== !=</td><td>Equal to and not equal to</td></tr>
<tr><td>&</td><td>Bitwise and</td></tr>
<tr><td>^</td><td>Bitwise exclusive or</td></tr>
<tr><td>|</td><td>Bitwise or</td></tr>
<tr><td>&&</td><td>Logical and</td></tr>
<tr><td>||</td><td>Logical or</td></tr>
<tr><td>= *= /= %= += -= <<= >>= &= ^= |=</td><td>Assignment and shortcut assignment</td></tr>
</table>

9.5.3 The *if* Command

The simplest form of conditional is the *if* command. The command (a *bash* built-in or executable) following the *if* construct is executed and its exit status is returned. The exit status is usually determined by the programmer who wrote the utility. If the exit status is zero, the command succeeded and the statement(s) after the *then* keyword are executed. In the C shell, the expression following the *if* command is a Boolean-type expression as in C. But in the Bash, Bourne, and Korn shells, the statement following the *if* is a command or group of commands. If the exit status of the command being evaluated is zero, the block of statements after the *then* is executed until *fi* is reached. The *fi* terminates the *if* block. If the exit status is nonzero, meaning that the command failed in some way, the statement(s) after the *then* keyword are ignored and control goes to the line directly after the *fi* statement.

It is important that you know the exit status of the commands being tested. For example, the exit status of *grep* is reliable in letting you know whether *grep* found the pattern it was searching for in a file. If *grep* is successful in its search, it returns a zero exit status; if not, it returns one. The *sed* and *gawk* programs also search for patterns, but they will report a successful exit status whether they find the pattern. The criteria for success with *sed* and *gawk* is correct syntax, not functionality.

FORMAT

```
    if command
    then
       command
       command
    fi
------------------------------------

(Using test for numbers and strings -- old format)

    if test expression
    then
       command
    fi
            or

    if [ string/numeric expression ] then
           command
    fi
-------------------------------------

(Using test for strings -- new formst)

    if [[ string expression ]] then
           command
    fi

(Using let for numbers -- new format)

   if (( numeric expression ))

--------------------------------------
```

EXAMPLE 9.19

```
if grep "$name" /etc/passwd > /dev/null 2>&1
then
     echo Found $name!
fi
```

EXPLANATION

1. The *grep* command searches for its argument, *name*, in the */etc/passwd* database. Standard output and standard error are redirected to */dev/null*, the Linux bit bucket.

2. If the exit status of the *grep* command is zero, the program goes to the *then* statement and executes commands until *fi* is reached. Indentation of commands between the *then* and *fi* keywords is a convention used to make the program more readable, and hence, easier to debug.

3. The *fi* terminates the list of commands following the *then* statement.

EXAMPLE 9.20

```
1   echo  "Are you o.k. (y/n) ?"
    read answer
2   if [ "$answer" = Y -o "$answer" = y ]
    then
         echo  "Glad to hear it."
3   fi

4   if [ $answer = Y -o "$answer" = y ]
    [: too many arguments

    ------------------------------------------
5   if [[ $answer == [Yy]* || $answer == Maybe ]]a
    then
         echo  "Glad to hear it."
    fi

6   shopt -s extglob

7   answer="not really"

8   if [[ $answer = [Nn]o?( way|t really) ]]
    then
         echo "So sorry. "
    fi
```

a. Lines 5 through 8 are only implemented on versions of *bash 2.x*.

EXPLANATION

1. The user is asked the question and told to respond. The *read* command waits for a response.

2. The *test* command, represented by square brackets, is used to test expressions. It returns an exit status of zero if the expression is true and nonzero if the expression is false. If the variable *answer* evaluates to *Y* or *y*, the commands after the *then* statement are executed. (The *test* command does not allow the use of wildcards when testing expressions, and spaces must surround the square brackets, as well as the = operators. See Table 9.3.) *$answer* is double quoted to hold it together as a single string. Otherwise the test command will fail.

3. The *fi* terminates the *if* on line 2.

4. The *test* command fails if more than one word appears before the = operator. For example, if the user entered "*yes, you betcha,*" the *answer* variable would evaluate to three words, causing the *test* to fail, *unless $answer* is enclosed in double quotes. The resulting error message is shown here.

5. The compound command operators [[ ]] allow the expansion of shell metacharacters in a string expression. The variable does not need quotes surrounding it, even if it contains more than one word, as it did with the old *test* command.

6. The *shopt* built-in, if set to *extglob*, allows expanded parameter expansion. See Table 8.16 on page 325.

7. The *answer* variable is set to the string *"not really"*.

8. Extended pattern matching is used here. The expression reads: if the value of the *answer* variable matches a string starting with *no* or *No* and if followed by zero or one occurrences of the expression in the parentheses, the expression is true. The expression could be evaluated to *no, No, no way, No way, not really,* or *Not really.*

The *exit* Command and the *?* Variable. The *exit* command is used to terminate the script and return to the command line. You may want the script to exit if some condition occurs. The argument given to the *exit* command is a number ranging from 0 to 255. If the program exits with zero as an argument, the program exited with success. A nonzero argument indicates some kind of failure. The argument given to the *exit* command is stored in the shell's *?* variable.

EXAMPLE 9.21

```
(The Script)
$ cat bigfiles
    # Name: bigfiles
    # Purpose: Use the find command to find any files in the root
    # partition that have not been modified within the past n (any
    # number within 30 days) days and are larger than 20 blocks
    # (512 byte blocks)

1   if (( $# != 2 ))[a]            # [ $# -ne 2 ]
    then
        echo  "Usage:   $0 mdays size " 1>&2
        exit 1
2   fi
3   if (( $1 <  0 || $1 > 30 ))[b]      # [ $1 -lt 0 -o $1 -gt 30 ]
    then

        echo "mdays is out of range"
        exit 2
4   fi
5   if (( $2 <= 20 ))         # [ $2 -le 20 ]
    then
        echo "size is out of range"
        exit 3
6   fi

7   find / -xdev -mtime $1 -size +$2

(The Command Line)
    $ bigfiles
    Usage: bigfiles mdays size

    $ echo $?
    1

    $ bigfiles 400 80
    mdays is out of range

    $ echo $?
    2

    $ bigfiles 25 2
    size is out of range

    $ echo $?
    3

    $ bigfiles 2 25
     (Output of find prints here)
```

a. Not implemented on versions prior to *bash 2.x*. On older versions could also be written: `if let $(( $# != 2 ))`

b. Same as above. On older versions could also be written: `if let  $(( $1 <  0 || $1 > 30 )`

EXPLANATION

1 The statement reads: *If the number of arguments is not equal to 2, print the error message and send it to standard error, then exit the script with an exit status of 1.* Either the built-in *test* command or the *let* command can be used to test numeric expressions.

2 The *fi* marks the end of the block of statements after *then.*

3 The statement reads: *If the value of the first positional parameter passed in from the command line is less than 0 or greater than 30, then print the message and exit with a status of 2.* See Table 9.4 on page 407 for numeric operators.

4 The *fi* ends the *if* block.

5 The statement reads: *If the value of the second positional parameter passed in at the command line is less than or equal to 20 (512-byte blocks), then print the message and exit with a status of 3.*

6 The *fi* ends the *if* block.

7 The *find* command starts its search in the root directory. The *-xdev* option prevents *find* from searching other partitions. The *-mtime* option takes a number argument, which is the number of days since the file was modified, and the *-size* option takes a number argument, which is the size of the file in 512-byte blocks.

Checking for Null Values. When checking for null values in a variable, use double quotes to hold the null value or the *test* command will fail.

EXAMPLE 9.22

```
(The Script)

1   if [ "$name" = "" ]
        # Alternative to    [ ! "$name" ]  or   [ -z "$name" ]
    then
        echo The name variable is null
    fi

(From System showmount program, which displays all remotely mounted
systems)
    remotes=$(/usr/sbin/showmount)
2   if [ "X${remotes}" != "X" ]
    then
        /usr/sbin/wall ${remotes}
                    ...
3   fi
```

EXPLANATION

1 If the *name* variable evaluates to null, the test is true. The double quotes are used to represent null.

2 The *showmount* command lists all clients remotely mounted from a host machine. The command will list either one or more clients, or nothing. The variable *remotes* will either have a value assigned or will be null. The letter ***X*** precedes the variable *remotes* when being tested. If *remotes* evaluates to null, no clients are remotely logged on and ***X*** will be equal to ***X***, causing the program to start execution again on line 3. If the variable has a value, for example, the hostname *pluto*, the expression would read *if* ***Xpluto != X***, and the *wall* command would be executed. (All users on remote machines will be sent a message.) The purpose of using *X* in the expression is to guarantee that even if the value of *remotes* is null, there will always be a placeholder on either side of the *!=* operator in the expression.

3 The *fi* terminates the *if*.

Nested *if* Commands. When *if* statements are nested, the *fi* statement always goes with the nearest *if* statement. Indenting the nested *ifs* makes it easier to see which *if* statement goes with which *fi* statement.

9.5.4 The *if/else* Command

The *if/else* commands allow a two-way decision-making process. If the command after the *if* fails, the commands after the *else* are executed.

FORMAT

```
if  command
then
   command(s)
else
   command(s)
fi
```

EXAMPLE 9.23

```
(The Script)
   #!/bin/bash
   #Scriptname: grepit
1  if grep "$name" /etc/passwd >& /dev/null; then
      echo Found $name!
3  else
4        echo  "Can't find $name."
         exit 1
5  fi
```

EXPLANATION

1 The *grep* command searches for its argument, *name*, in the NIS *passwd* database. Because the user does not need to see the output, standard output and standard error are redirected to */dev/null*, the Linux bit bucket.

2 If the exit status of the *ypmatch* command is zero, program control goes to the *then* statement and executes commands until *else* is reached.

3 The commands under the *else* statement are executed if the *ypmatch* command fails to find *$name* in the *passwd* database; that is, the exit status of *ypmatch* must be nonzero for the commands in the *else* block to be executed.

4 If the value in *$name* is not found in the *passwd* database, this *echo* statement is executed and the program exits with a value of 1, indicating failure.

5 The *fi* terminates the *if*.

EXAMPLE 9.24

```
   (The Script)
   #!/bin/bash
   # Scriptname: idcheck
   # purpose:check user id to see if user is root.
   # Only root has a uid of 0.
   # Format for id output:uid=9496(ellie) gid=40 groups=40
   # root's uid=0

1     id=`id | gawk -F'[=(]'  '{print $2}'`     # get user id
      echo your user id is:  $id
2     if  (( id == 0 ))[a]    #    [ $id -eq 0 ] (See cd file: idcheck2)
      then
3        echo "you are superuser."
4     else
         echo "you are not superuser."
5     fi

      (The Command Line)
6     $ idcheck
      Your user id is: 9496
      You are not  superuser.
7     $ su
      Password:
8     # idcheck
      your user id is: 0
      you are superuser
```

a. Not implemented on versions of *bash* prior to 2.x.

EXPLANATION

1 The *id* command is piped to the *gawk* command. *Nawk* uses an equal sign and open parenthesis as field separators, extracts the user id from the output, and assigns the output to the variable *id*.

2,3,4 If the value of *id* is equal to zero, then line 3 is executed. If *id* is not equal to zero, the *else* statements are executed.

5 The *fi* marks the end of the *if* command.

6 The *idcheck* script is executed by the current user, whose uid is 9496.

7 The *su* command switches the user to *root*.

8 The # prompt indicates that the superuser (root) is the new user. The uid for root is *0*.

9.5.5 The *if/elif/else* Command

The *if/elif/else* commands allow a multiway decision-making process. If the command following the *if* fails, the command following the *elif* is tested. If that command succeeds, the commands under its *then* statement are executed. If the command after the *elif* fails, the next *elif* command is checked. If none of the commands succeeds, the *else* commands are executed. The *else* block is called the default.

FORMAT

```
if  command
then
    command(s)
elif  command
then
    commands(s)
elif  command
then
    command(s)
else
    command(s)
fi
```

EXAMPLE 9.25

```
(The Script)
    #!/bin/bash
    # Scriptname: tellme
    # Using the old-style test command
1   echo -n "How old are you? "
    read age
2   if [ $age -lt 0 -o $age -gt 120 ]
    then
        echo  "Welcome to our planet! "
        exit 1
    fi
3   if  [ $age -ge 0 -a $age -le 12 ]
    then
        echo  "A child is a garden of verses"
    elif  [ $age -ge 12 -a $age -le 19 ]
    then
        echo  "Rebel without a cause"
    elif  [ $age -ge 20 -a  $age -le 29 ]
    then
        echo  "You got the world by the tail!!"
    elif  [ $age -ge  30 -a  $age -le 39 ]
    then
        echo  "Thirty something..."
4   else
        echo  "Sorry I asked"
5   fi


(The Output)
    $ tellme
    How old are you? 200
    Welcome to our planet!

    $ tellme
    How old are you? 13
    Rebel without a cause

    $ tellme
    How old are you? 55
    Sorry I asked
```

EXAMPLE 9.25 (CONTINUED)

```
------------------------------------------------------------
    # Using the new (( )) compound let command
    #!/bin/bash
    # Scriptname: tellme2

1   echo -n "How old are you? "
    read age
2   if (( age < 0 || age > 120 ))
    then
        echo  "Welcome to our planet! "
        exit 1
    fi
3   if ((age >= 0 && age <= 12))
    then
        echo  "A child is a garden of verses"
    elif ((age >= 13 && age <= 19 ))
    then
         echo  "Rebel without a cause"
    elif  (( age >= 19 &&  age <=  29 ))
    then
        echo  "You got the world by the tail!!"
    elif  (( age >=  30 &&  age <= 39 ))
    then
        echo  "Thirty something..."
4   else
        echo  "Sorry I asked"
5   fi
```

EXPLANATION

1. The user is asked for input. The input is assigned to the variable *age*.
2. A numeric test is performed by the *test* command. If *age* is less than *0* or greater than *120*, the *echo* command is executed and the program terminates with an exit status of one. The interactive shell prompt will appear.
3. A numeric test is performed by the *test* command. If *age* is greater than or equal to *0* and less than or equal to *12*, the *test* command returns exit status zero, true, and the statement after the *then* is executed. Otherwise, program control goes to the *elif*. If that test is false, the next *elif* is tested.
4. The *else* construct is the default. If none of the above statements are true, the *else* commands will be executed.
5. The *fi* terminates the initial *if* statement.

9.5.6 File Testing

Often when you are writing scripts, your script will require that there are certain files available and that those files have specific permissions, are of a certain type, or have other attributes. You will find file testing a necessary part of writing dependable scripts.

Table 9.5 File Test Operators

Test Operator	*Test for True If*
File Test	
-b filename	Block special file.
-c filename	Character special file.
-d filename	Directory existence.
-e filename	File existence.
-f filename	Regular file existence and not a directory.
-G filename	True if file exists and is owned by the effective group id.
-g filename	Set–group–ID is set.
-k filename	Sticky bit is set.
-L filename	File is a symbolic link.
-p filename	File is a named pipe.
-O filename	File exists and is owned by the effective user id.
-r filename	File is readable.
-S filename	File is a socket.
-s filename	File is nonzero size.
-t fd	True if *fd* (file descriptor) is opened on a terminal.
-u filename	Set–user–ID bit is set.
-w filename	File is writeable.
-x filename	File is executable.

EXAMPLE 9.26

```
(The Script)
    #!/bin/bash
    # Using the old style test command
    # filename: perm_check
    file=./testing

1   if [ -d $file ]
    then
        echo "$file is a directory"
2   elif [ -f $file ]
    then
3       if [  -r $file -a -w $file -a -x $file ]
        then  # nested if command
                echo "You have read,write,and execute \
                permission on $file."
4       fi
5   else
        echo  "$file is neither a file nor a directory. "
6   fi

-------------------------------------------------------a
Using the new compound operator for test (( ))

#!/bin/bash
# filename: perm_check2
file=./testing

1   if [[ -d $file ]]
    then
        echo "$file is a directory"
2   elif [[ -f $file ]]
    then
3       if [[ -r $file && -w $file && -x $file ]]
        then  # nested if command
                echo "You have read,write,and execute \
                permission on $file."
4       fi
5   else
        echo  "$file is neither a file nor a directory. "
6   fi
```

a. New style test with compound operators not implemented before *bash 2.x*.

EXPLANATION

1. If the file *testing* is a directory, print "*testing is a directory.*"
2. If the file *testing* is not a directory, *else if* the file is a plain file, then...
3. f the file *testing* is readable and writeable, and executable, then...
4. The *fi* terminates the innermost *if* command.
5. The *else* commands are executed *if* lines 1 and 2 are not true.
6. This *fi* goes with the first *if*.

9.5.7 The *null* Command

The *null* command, represented by a colon, is a built-in, do-nothing command that returns an exit status of zero. It is used as a placeholder after an *if* command when you have nothing to say, but need a command or the program will produce an error message because it requires something after the *then* statement. Often the null command is used as an argument to the *loop* command to make the loop a forever loop.

EXAMPLE 9.27

```
(The Script)
     #!/bin/bash
     # filename: name_grep
1    name=Tom
2    if grep "$name" databasefile >& /dev/null
     then
3                            :
4    else
         echo  "$1 not found in databasefile"
         exit 1
     fi
```

EXPLANATION

1. The variable *name* is assigned the string *Tom.*
2. The *if* command tests the exit status of the *grep* command. If *Tom* is found in the database file, the *null* command, a colon, is executed and does nothing. Both output and errors are redirected to */dev/null.*
3. The colon is the *null* command. It does nothing other than returning a *0* exit status.
4. What we really want to do is print an error message and exit if *Tom* is *not found.* The commands after the *else* will be executed if the *grep* command fails.

EXAMPLE 9.28

```
(The Command Line)
1   $ DATAFILE=
2   $ : ${DATAFILE:=$HOME/db/datafile}
    $ echo $DATAFILE
    /home/jody/ellie/db/datafile
3   $ : ${DATAFILE:=$HOME/junk}
    $ echo $DATAFILE
    /home/jody/ellie/db/datafile
```

EXPLANATION

1 The variable *DATAFILE* is assigned null.

2 The colon command is a "do-nothing" command. The modifier (:=) returns a value that can be assigned to a variable or used in a test. In this example, the expression is passed as an argument to the do-nothing command. The shell will perform variable substitution; that is, assign the pathname to *DATAFILE* if *DATAFILE* does not already have a value. The variable *DATAFILE* is permanently set.

3 Because the variable has already been set, it will not be reset with the default value provided on the right of the modifier.

EXAMPLE 9.29

```
(The Script)
    #!/bin/bash
1   # Script name: wholenum
    # Purpose:The expr command tests that the user enters an
    # integer
    #
    echo "Enter a number."
    read number
2   if expr "$number" + 0 >& /dev/null
    then
3       :
    else
4       echo "You did not enter an integer value."
        exit 1
5   fi
```

EXPLANATION

1 The user is asked to enter an integer. The number is assigned to the variable *number.*

2 The *expr* command evaluates the expression. If addition can be performed, the number is a whole number and *expr* returns a successful exit status. All output is redirected to the bit bucket */dev/null.*

3 If *expr* is successful, it returns a zero exit status, and the colon command does nothing.

4 If the *expr* command fails, it returns a nonzero exit status, the *echo* command displays the message, and the program exits.

5 The *fi* ends the *if* block.

9.5.8 The *case* Command

The *case* command is a multiway branching command used as an alternative to *if/elif* commands. The value of the *case* variable is matched against *value1, value2*, and so forth, until a match is found. When a value matches the *case* variable, the commands following the value are executed until the double semicolons are reached. Then execution starts after the word *esac* (*case* spelled backward).

If the *case* variable is not matched, the program executes the commands after the *), the default value, until ;; or *esac* is reached. The *) value functions the same as the *else* statement in *if/else* conditionals. The *case* values allow the use of shell *wildcards* and the vertical bar (pipe symbol) for OR-ing two values.

FORMAT

```
case variable in
value1)
    command(s)
    ;;
value2)
    command(s)
    ;;
*)
command(s)
     ;;
esac
```

EXAMPLE 9.30

```
(The Script)
    #!/bin/bash
    # Scriptname: xcolors
1   echo -n "Choose a foreground color for your xterm window: "
2   read color
2   case "$color" in
3   [Bb]l??)
4       xterm -fg blue -fn terminal &
5       ;;
6   [Gg]ree*)
        xterm -fg darkgreen -fn terminal &
        ;;
7   red | orange)        # The vertical bar means "or"
        xterm -fg "$color"  -fn terminal &
        ;;
8   *)
        xterm -fn terminal
        ;;
9   esac
10  echo  "Out of case command"
```

EXPLANATION

1 The user is asked for input. The input is assigned to the variable *color.*

2 The *case* command evaluates the expression *$color.*

3 If the color begins with a *B* or *b*, followed by the letter *l* and any two characters, the *case* expression matches the first value. The value is terminated with a single closed parenthesis. The wildcards are shell metacharacters used for filename expansion.The *xterm* command sets the foreground color to blue.

4 The statement is executed if the value in line number 3 matches the *case* expression.

5 The double semicolons are required after the last command in this block of commands. Control branches to line 10 when the semicolons are reached. The script is easier to debug if the semicolons are on their own line.

6 If the *case* expression matches a *G* or *g*, followed by the letters *ree* and ending in zero or more of any other characters, the *xterm* command is executed. The double semicolons terminate the block of statements and control branches to line 10.

7 The vertical bar is used as an OR conditional operator. If the *case* expression matches either *red* or *orange*, the *xterm* command is executed.

8 This is the default value. If none of the above values match the *case* expression, the commands after the **)* are executed.

9 The *esac* statement terminates the *case* command.

10 After one of the *case* values are matched, execution continues here.

Creating Menus with the *here* Document and *case* Command. The *here* document and *case* command are often used together. The *here* document is used to create a menu of choices that will be displayed to the screen. The user will be asked to select one of the menu items, and the *case* command will test against the set of choices to execute the appropriate command.

EXAMPLE 9.31

```
(From the .bash_profile File)
   echo  "Select a terminal type:  "
1  cat <<- ENDIT
      1) linux
      2) xterm
      3) sun
2  ENDIT
3  read choice
4  case "$choice" in
5  1)  TERM=linux
       export TERM
       ;;
   2)  TERM=xterm
       export TERM
       ;;
6  3)  TERM=sun
       export TERM
       ;;
7  esac
8  echo "TERM is $TERM."

(The Output)
$ . .bash_profile
   Select a terminal type:
   1) linux
   2) xterm
   3) sun
   2           <-- User input
   TERM is xterm.
```

EXPLANATION

1. If this segment of script is put in the *.bash_profile*, when you log on, you will be given a chance to select the proper terminal type. The *here* document is used to display a menu of choices.
2. The user-defined *ENDIT* terminator marks the end of the *here* document.
3. The *read* command stores the user input in the variable *TERM*.

EXPLANATION (CONTINUED)

4 The *case* command evaluates the variable *TERM* and compares that value with one of the values preceding the closing parenthesis: *1, 2*, or *.

5 The first value tested is 1. If there is a match, the terminal is set to a *linux*. The *TERM* variable is exported so that subshells will inherit it.

6 A default value is not required. The *TERM* variable is normally assigned in */etc/profile* at login time. If the choice is 3, the terminal is set to a *sun*.

7 The *esac* terminates the *case* command.

8 After the *case* command has finished, this line is executed.

9.6 Looping Commands

Looping commands are used to execute a command or group of commands a set number of times or until a certain condition is met. The Bourne shell has three types of loops: the *for* loop, the *while* loop, and the *until* loop.

9.6.1 The *for* Command

The *for* looping command is used to execute commands a finite number of times on a list of items. For example, you might use this loop to execute the same commands on a list of files or usernames. The *for* command is followed by a user-defined variable, the keyword *in*, and a list of words. The first time in the loop, the first word from the wordlist is assigned to the variable, and then shifted off the list. Once the word is assigned to the variable, the body of the loop is entered, and commands between the *do* and *done* keywords are executed. The next time around the loop, the second word is assigned to the variable, and so on. The body of the loop starts at the *do* keyword and ends at the *done* keyword. When all of the words in the list have been shifted off, the loop ends and program control continues after the *done* keyword.

FORMAT

```
for variable in word_list
do
    command(s)
done
```

EXAMPLE 9.32

```
(The Script)
    #!/bin/bash
    # Scriptname: forloop
1   for pal in Tom Dick Harry Joe
2   do
3       echo  "Hi $pal"
4   done
5   echo  "Out of loop"

(The Output)
$ forloop
    Hi Tom
    Hi Dick
    Hi Harry
    Hi Joe
    Out of loop
```

EXPLANATION

1 This *for* loop will iterate through the list of names, *Tom, Dick, Harry,* and *Joe*, shifting each one off (to the left and assigning its value to the user-defined variable, *pal*) after it is used. As soon as all of the words are shifted and the wordlist is empty, the loop ends and execution starts after the *done* keyword. The first time in the loop, the variable *pal* will be assigned the word *Tom*. The second time through the loop, *pal* will be assigned *Dick*, the next time *pal* will be assigned *Harry*, and the last time *pal* will be assigned *Joe*.

2 The *do* keyword is required after the wordlist. If it is used on the same line, the list must be terminated with a semicolon. Example:

```
for pal in Tom Dick Harry Joe; do
```

3 This is the body of the loop. After *Tom* is assigned to the variable *pal,* the commands in the body of the loop (i.e., all commands between the *do* and *done* keywords) are executed.

4 The *done* keyword ends the loop. Once the last word in the list (*Joe*) has been assigned and shifted off, the loop exits, and execution starts at line 2.

5 Control resumes here when the loop exits.

EXAMPLE 9.33

```
(The Command Line)
1  $ cat mylist
   tom
   patty
   ann
   jake

(The Script)
   #!/bin/bash
   # Scriptname: mailer
2  for person in $(cat mylist)
   do
3      mail $person < letter
       echo $person was sent a letter.
4  done
5  echo "The letter has been sent."
```

EXPLANATION

1. The contents of a file, called *mylist*, are displayed.
2. Command substitution is performed and the contents of *mylist* becomes the wordlist. The first time in the loop, *tom* is assigned to the variable *person*, then it is shifted off to be replaced with *patty*, and so forth.
3. In the body of the loop, each user is mailed a copy of a file called *letter*.
4. The *done* keyword marks the end of this loop iteration.
5. When all of the users in the list have been sent mail and the loop has exited, this line is executed.

EXAMPLE 9.34

```
(The Script)
   #!/bin/bash
   # Scriptname: backup
   # Purpose:
   # Create backup files and store them in a backup directory
   #
1  dir=/home/jody/ellie/backupscripts
```

EXAMPLE 9.34 (CONTINUED)

```
2   for file in memo[1-5]
    do
3       if [ -f $file ]
        then
             cp $file $dir/$file.bak
             echo "$file is backed up in $dir"
        fi
4   done

(The Output)
    memo1 is backed up in /home/jody/ellie/backupscripts
    memo2 is backed up in /home/jody/ellie/backupscripts
    memo3 is backed up in /home/jody/ellie/backupscripts
    memo4 is backed up in /home/jody/ellie/backupscripts
    memo5 is backed up in /home/jody/ellie/backupscripts
```

EXPLANATION

1. The variable *dir* is assigned the directory where the backup scripts are to be stored.
2. The wordlist will consist of all files in the current working directory with names starting with *memo* and ending with numbers between *1* and *5*. Each filename will be assigned, one at time, to the variable *file* for each iteration of the loop.
3. When the body of the loop is entered, the file will be tested to make sure it exists and is a real file. If so, it will be copied into the directory */home/jody/ellie/backupscripts* with the *.bak* extension appended to its name.
4. The *done* marks the end of the loop.

The $* and $@ Variables in Wordlists. When expanded, the $* and $@ are the same unless enclosed in double quotes. $* evaluates to one string, whereas $@ evaluates to a list of separate words.

EXAMPLE 9.35

```
(The Script)
    #!/bin/bash
    # Scriptname: greet
1   for name in $*          # same as for name in $@
2   do
       echo Hi $name
3   done
```

EXAMPLE 9.35 (CONTINUED)

```
(The Command Line)
    $ greet Dee Bert Lizzy Tommy
    Hi Dee
    Hi Bert
    Hi Lizzy
    Hi Tommy
```

EXPLANATION

1 *$** and *$@* expand to a list of all the positional parameters, in this case, the arguments passed in from the command line: *Dee*, *Bert*, *Lizzy*, and *Tommy*. Each name in the list will be assigned, in turn, to the variable *name* in the *for* loop.

2 The commands in the body of the loop are executed until the list is empty.

3 The *done* keyword marks the end of the loop body.

EXAMPLE 9.36

```
(The Script)
    #!/bin/bash
    # Scriptname: permx
1   for file          # Empty wordlist
    do

2     if [ -f $file -a ! -x $file ] or if [[ -f $file && ! -x $file ]][a]
      then

3              chmod +x $file
               echo $file now has execute permission
      fi
    done

(The Command Line)
4   $ permx *
    addon now has execute permission
    checkon now has execute permission
    doit now has execute permission
```

a. *Bash* 2.x only.

EXPLANATION

1 If the *for* loop is not provided with a wordlist, it iterates through the positional parameters. This is the same as *for file* in *$**.

2 The filenames are coming in from the command line. The shell expands the asterisk (*) to all filenames in the current working directory. If the file is a plain file and does not have execute permission, line 3 is executed.

3 Execute permission is added for each file being processed.

4 At the command line, the asterisk will be evaluated by the shell as a wildcard and all files in the current directory will be replaced for the *. The files will be passed as arguments to the *permx* script.

9.6.2 The *while* Command

The *while* command evaluates the command following it and, if its exit status is zero, the commands in the body of the loop (commands between *do* and *done*) are executed. When the *done* keyword is reached, control is returned to the top of the loop and the *while* command checks the exit status of the command again. Until the exit status of the command being evaluated by the *while* becomes nonzero, the loop continues. When the exit status reaches nonzero, program execution starts after the *done* keyword.

FORMAT

```
while command
do
    command(s)
done
```

EXAMPLE 9.37

```
(The Script)
    #!/bin/bash
    # Scriptname: num
1   num=0     # Initialize num
2   while (( $num < 10 ))[a]    # or  while [ num -lt 10 ]
    do
        echo  -n "$num "
3       let num+=1              # Increment num
    done
4   echo -e "\nAfter loop exits, continue running here"

(The Output)
    0 1 2 3 4 5 6 7 8 9
4   After loop exits, continue running here
```

a. Versions of *bash* 2.x use this form.

EXPLANATION

1 This is the initialization step. The variable *num* is assigned *0*.

2 The *while* command is followed by the *let* command. The *let* command evaluates the arithmetic expression, returning an exit status of 0 (true) if the condition is true; i.e., if the value of *num* is less than *10*, the body of the loop is entered.

3 In the body of the loop, the value of *num* is incremented by one. If the value of *num* never changes, the loop would iterate infinitely or until the process is killed.

4 After the loop exits, the *echo* command (with the *-e* option) prints a newline and the string.

EXAMPLE 9.38

```
(The Script)
    #!/bin/bash
    # Scriptname: quiz
1   echo "Who was the 2nd U.S. president to be impeached?"
    read answer
2   while [[ "$answer" != "Bill Clinton" ]]
3   do
        echo  "Wrong try again!"
4       read answer
5   done
6   echo You got it!

(The Output)
    $ quiz
    Who was the 2nd U.S. president to be impeached? Ronald Reagon
    Wrong try again!
    Who was the 2nd U.S. president to be impeached?  I give up
    Wrong try again!
    Who was the 2nd U.S. president to be impeached?  Bill Clinton
    You got it!
```

EXPLANATION

1 The *echo* command prompts the user *Who was the 2nd U.S. president to be impeached?* The *read* command waits for input from the user. The input will be stored in the variable *answer*.

2 The *while* loop is entered and the *test* command, the bracket, tests the expression. If the variable *answer* does not exactly equal the string *Bill Clinton*, the body of the loop is entered and commands between the *do* and *done* are executed.

EXPLANATION (CONTINUED)

3 The *do* keyword is the start of the loop body.

4 The user is asked to re-enter input.

5 The *done* keyword marks the end of the loop body. Control is returned to the top of the *while* loop, and the expression is tested again. As long as *answer* does not evaluate to *Bill Clinton*, the loop will continue to iterate. When the user enters *Bill Clinton*, the loop ends. Program control goes to line 6.

6 When the body of the loop ends, control starts here.

EXAMPLE 9.39

```
  (The Script)
  $ cat sayit
     #!/bin/bash
     # Scriptname: sayit
     echo  Type q to quit.
     go=start
1    while [ -n "$go" ]    # Make sure to double quote the variable
     do
2        echo -n I love you.
3        read word
4        if [[ $word == [Qq] ]]
         then          # [ "$word" = q -o "$word" = Q ]  Old style
                   echo "I'll always love you!"
                   go=
         fi
     done

  (The Output)
     $ sayit
     Type q to quit.
     I love you.          When user presses the enter key, the program
                           continues
     I love you.
     I love you.
     I love you.
     I love you.q
     I'll always love you!
     $
```

EXPLANATION

1 The command after the *while* is executed and its exit status tested. The *-n* option to the *test* command tests for a nonnull string. Because *go* initially has a value, the test is successful, producing a zero exit status. If the variable *go* is not enclosed in double quotes and the variable is null, the *test* command would complain:

```
go: test: argument expected
```

2 The loop is entered. The string *I love you* is echoed to the screen.

3 The *read* command waits for user input.

4 The expresson is tested. If the user enters a *q* or *Q*, the string "*I'll always love you!*" is displayed, and the variable *go* is set to null. When the *while* loop is re-entered, the test is unsuccessful because the variable is null. The loop terminates. Control goes to the line after the *done* statement. In this example, the script will terminate because there are no more lines to execute.

9.6.3 The *until* Command

The *until* command is used like the *while* command, but executes the loop statements only if the command after *until* fails, i.e., if the command returns an exit status of nonzero. When the *done* keyword is reached, control is returned to the top of the loop and the *until* command checks the exit status of the command again. Until the exit status of the command being evaluated by *until* becomes zero, the loop continues. When the exit status reaches zero, the loop exits, and program execution starts after the *done* keyword.

FORMAT

```
until command
do
    command(s)
done
```

EXAMPLE 9.40

```
    #!/bin/bash
1   until who | grep linda
2   do
        sleep 5
3   done
    talk linda@dragonwings
```

EXPLANATION

1 The *until* loop tests the exit status of the last command in the pipeline, *grep*. The *who* command lists who is logged on this machine and pipes its output to *grep*. The *grep* command will return a zero exit status (success) only when it finds user *linda*.

2 If user *linda* has not logged on, the body of the loop is entered and the program sleeps for five seconds.

3 When *linda* logs on, the exit status of the *grep* command will be zero and control will go to the statements following the *done* keyword.

EXAMPLE 9.41

```
(The Script)
$ cat hour
    #!/bin/bash
    # Scriptname: hour
1   let hour=0
2   until (( hour > 24 ))[a] # or [ $hour -gt 24 ]
    do
3       case "$hour" in
        [0-9]|1[0-1])echo  "Good morning!"
             ;;
        12)  echo  "Lunch time."

             ;;
        1[3-7])echo  "Siesta time."
             ;;
        *)   echo  "Good night."
             ;;
        esac
4       let hour+=1     # Don't forget to increment the hour
5   done

(The Output)
$ hour
    Good morning!
    Good morning!
        ...
    Lunch time.
    Siesta time.
        ...
    Good night.
        ...
```

a. Versions of *bash* 2.x use this form.

EXPLANATION

1 The variable *hour* is initialized to *0*.

2 The *let* command tests the arithmetic expression to test for an hour greater than or equal to *24*. If the hour is not greater than or equal to *24*, the body of the loop is entered. The *until* loop is entered if the command following it returns a nonzero exit status. Until the condition is true, the loop continues to iterate.

3 The *case* command evaluates the *hour* variable and tests each of the *case* statements for a match.

4 The *hour* variable is incremented with the *let* command before control returns to the top of the loop.

5 The *done* command marks the end of the loop body.

9.6.4 The *select* Command and Menus

The *here* document is an easy method for creating menus, but *bash* introduces another looping mechanism, called the *select* loop, used primarily for creating menus. A menu of numerically listed items is displayed to standard error. The PS3 prompt is used to prompt the user for input; by default, *PS3* is #?. After the *PS3* prompt is displayed, the shell waits for user input. The input should be one of the numbers in the menu list. The input is stored in the special shell *REPLY* variable. The number in the *REPLY* variable is associated with the string to the right of the parentheses in the list of selections.

The *case* command is used with the *select* command to allow the user to make a selection from the menu and, based on that selection, execute commands. The *LINES* and *COLUMNS* variables can be used to determine the layout of the menu items displayed on the terminal. (These variables are built in to versions of *bash 2.x,* but are not built in to earlier versions; if they have not been defined, you can define and export them in the *.bash_profile.*) The output is displayed to standard error, each item preceded by a number and closing parenthesis, and the PS3 prompt is displayed at the bottom of the menu. Because the *select* command is a looping command, it is important to remember to use either the *break* command to get out of the loop, or the *exit* command to exit the script.

FORMAT

```
select var in wordlist
do
    command(s)
done
```

EXAMPLE 9.42

```
(The Script)
    #!/bin/bash
    # Script name: runit
1   PS3="Select a program to execute: "
2   select program  in 'ls -F' pwd date
3   do
4         $program
5   done

(The Command Line)
    Select a program to execute: 2
    1) ls -F
    2) pwd
    3) date
    /home/ellie
    Select a program to execute: 1
    1) ls -F
    2) pwd
    3) date
    12abcrty abc12  doit* progs/  xyz
    Select a program to execute: 3
    1) ls -F
    2) pwd
    3) date
    Sun Mar 12 13:28:25 PST 2000
```

EXPLANATION

1. The *PS3* prompt is assigned the string that will appear below the menu that the *select* loop displays. This prompt is *$#* by default and is sent to standard error, the screen.
2. The *select* loop consists of a variable, called program, and the 3 word list that will be displayed in the menu: *ls -F*, *pwd*, and *date*. The words in this list are Linux commands, but they could be any words, e.g., *red, green, yellow*, or *cheese, bread, milk, crackers*. If the word has space, it must be quoted; e.g., *'ls-F'*
3. The *do* keyword starts the body of the *select* loop.
4. When the user selects numbers in the menu, that number will be equated with the word value to the right of the number after the parentheses. For example, if he selects number 2, that is associated with *pwd* and *pwd* is stored in the *program* variable. *$program* evaluates to the executable command, *pwd*; the command is executed.
5. The *done* keyword marks the end of the body of statements in the *select* loop. Control will return to the top of the loop. This loop will continue to execute, until the user presses ^C.

EXAMPLE 9.43

```
(The Script)
    #!/bin/bash
    # Scriptname name: goodboys
1   PS3="Please choose one of the three boys : "
2   select choice in tom dan guy
3   do
4       case $choice in
         tom)
             echo Tom is a cool dude!
5            break;;         # break out of the select loop
6        dan | guy )
             echo Dan and Guy are both wonderful.
             break;;
         *)
7            echo "$REPLY is not one of your choices" 1>&2
             echo "Try again."
             ;;
8       esac
9   done

(The Command Line)

    $ goodboys
    1) tom
    2) dan
    3) guy
    Please choose one of the three boys : 2
    Dan and Guy are both wonderful.

    $ goodboys
    1) tom
    2) dan
    3) guy
    Please choose one of the three boys : 4
    4 is not one of your choices
    Try again.
    Please choose one of the three boys : 1
    Tom is a cool dude!
    $
```

EXPLANATION

1 The PS3 prompt will be printed above the menu created by the *select* loop on line 2.

2 The *select* loop is entered. It causes the words in its list to be displayed as a numbered menu.

3 The loop body starts here.

EXPLANATION (CONTINUED)

4 The variable choice is assigned the first value on the list, after which the value is shifted off the list and the next item will be first.

5 The *break* statement sends loop control after line 9.

6 If either *dan* or *guy* are selected, the following *echo* command is executed, followed by the *break* command, sending control after line 9.

7 The built-in REPLY variable contains the number of the current list item; i.e., 1, 2, or 3.

8 This marks the end of the *case* command.

9 The *done* marks the end of the *select* loop.

EXAMPLE 9.44

```
(The Script)
    #!/bin/bash
    # Script name: ttype
    # Purpose: set the terminal type
    # Author: Andy Admin
1   COLUMNS=60
2   LINES=1
3   PS3="Please enter the terminal type: "
4   select choice in wyse50 vt200 xterm sun
    do
5      case $REPLY in
       1)
6            export TERM=$choice
             echo "TERM=$choice"
             break;;               # break out of the select loop
       2 | 3 )
             export TERM=$choice

             echo "TERM=$choice"
             break;;
       4)
             export TERM=$choice
             echo "TERM=$choice"
             break;;
       *)
7            echo -e "$REPLY is not a valid choice. Try again\n" 1>&2
8            REPLY=   # Causes the menu to be redisplayed
              ;;
       esac
9   done
```

EXAMPLE 9.44 (CONTINUED)

```
(The Command Line)
    $ ttype
    1) wyse50    2) vt200    3) xterm    4) sun
    Please enter the terminal type : 4
    TERM=sun

    $ ttype
    1) wyse50    2) vt200    3) xterm    4) sun
    Please enter the terminal type : 3
    TERM=xterm

    $ ttype
    1) wyse50    2) vt200    3) xterm    4) sun
    Please enter the terminal type : 7
    7 is not a valid choice. Try again.

    1) wyse50    2) vt200    3) xterm    4) sun
     Please enter the terminal type: 2
    TERM=vt200
```

EXPLANATION

1 The *COLUMNS* variable is set to the width of the terminal display in columns for menus created with the *select* loop. The default is 80.

2 The *LINES* variable controls the vertical display of the *select* menu on the terminal. The default is 24 lines. When you change the *LINES* value to *1*, the menu items will be printed on one line, instead of vertically as in the last example.

3 The *PS3* prompt is set and will appear under the menu choices.

4 The *select* loop will print a menu with four selections: *wyse50*, *vt200*, *vt100*, and *sun*. The variable *choice* will be assigned one of these values based on the user's response held in the *REPLY* variable. If *REPLY* is 1, *wyse50* is assigned to *choice*; if *REPLY* is 2, *vt200* is assigned to *choice*; if *REPLY* is 3, *xterm* is assigned to *choice*; and if *REPLY* is 4, *sun* is assigned to *choice*.

5 The *REPLY* variable evaluates to the user's input selection.

6 The terminal type is assigned, exported, and printed.

7 If the user does not enter a number between 1 and 4, he or she will be prompted again. Note that the menu does not appear, just the *PS3* prompt.

8 If the *REPLY* variable is set to null, *e.g., REPLY=*, the menu will be redisplayed.

9 The end of the *select* loop.

9.6.5 Looping Commands

If some condition occurs, you may want to break out of a loop, return to the top of the loop, or provide a way to stop an infinite loop. The Bourne shell provides loop control commands to handle these kinds of situations.

The *shift* Command. The *shift* command shifts the parameter list to the left a specified number of times. The *shift* command without an argument shifts the parameter list once to the left. Once the list is shifted, the parameter is removed permanently. Often, the *shift* command is used in a *while* loop when iterating through a list of positional parameters.

FORMAT

```
shift [n]
```

EXAMPLE 9.45

```
(Without a Loop)
(The Script)
    #!/bin/bash
    # Scriptname: shifter
1   set joe mary tom sam
2   shift
3   echo $*
4   set $(date)
5   echo  $*
6   shift 5
7   echo  $*
8   shift 2

(The Output)
3   mary tom sam
5   Thu Mar 16 10:00:12 PST 2000
7   2000
8   shift: shift count must be <= $#
```

EXPLANATION

1. The *set* command sets the positional parameters. *$1* is assigned *joe*, *$2* is assigned *mary, $3* is assigned *tom*, and *$4* is assigned *sam*. *$** represents all of the parameters.
2. The *shift* command shifts the positional parameters to the left; *joe* is shifted off.
3. The parameter list is printed after the shift.
4. The *set* command resets the positional parameters to the output of the Linux *date* command.
5. The new parameter list is printed.

EXPLANATION (CONTINUED)

6 This time the list is shifted *5* times to the left.

7 The new parameter list is printed.

8 By attempting to shift more times than there are parameters, the shell sends a message to standard error stating that the *shift* command cannot shift more off more parameters that it has. *$#* is the total number of positional parameters. On versions of *bash* 2.x no error message occurs.

EXAMPLE 9.46

```
(With a Loop)
(The Script)
    #!/bin/bash
    # Name: doit
    # Purpose: shift through command line arguments
    # Usage: doit [args]
1    while (( $# > 0 ))[a]   # or [ $# -gt 0 ]
     do
2       echo  $*
3       shift
4    done

(The Command Line)
    $ doit a b c d e
    a b c d e
    b c d e
    c d e
    d e
    e
```

a. Not implemented of versions of *bash* prior to 2.x.

EXPLANATION

1 The *let* command tests the numeric expression. If the number of positional parameters (*$#*) is greater than *0*, the body of the loop is entered. The positional parameters are coming from the command line as arguments. There are five.

2 All positional parameters are printed.

3 The parameter list is shifted once to the left.

4 The body of the loop ends here; control returns to the top of the loop. Each time the loop is entered, the *shift* command causes the parameter list to be decreased by one. After the first shift, *$#* (number of positional parameters) is four. When *$#* has been decreased to zero, the loop ends.

EXAMPLE 9.47

```
(The Script)
    #!/bin/bash
    # Scriptname: dater
    # Purpose: set positional parameters with the set command
    # and shift through the parameters.

1   set $(date)
2   while (( $# > 0 )) # or  [ $# -gt 0 ]  Old style
    do
3       echo $1
4       shift
    done

(The Output)
$ dater
    Wed
    Mar
    15
    19:25:00
    PST
    2000
```

EXPLANATION

1. The *set* command takes the output of the *date* command and assigns the output to positional parameters *$1* through *$6.*
2. The *while* command tests whether the number of positional parameters (*$#*) is greater than *0.* If true, the body of the loop is entered.
3. The *echo* command displays the value of *$1*, the first positional parameter.
4. The *shift* command shifts the parameter list once to the left. Each time through the loop, the list is shifted until the list is empty. At that time, *$#* will be zero and the loop terminates.

The *break* Command. The built-in *break* command is used to force immediate exit from a loop, but not from a program. (To leave a program, the *exit* command is used.) After the *break* command is executed, control starts after the *done* keyword. The *break* command causes an exit from the innermost loop, so if you have nested loops, the *break* command takes a number as an argument, allowing you to break out of a specific outer loop. If you are nested in three loops, the outermost loop is loop number 3, the next nested loop is loop number 2, and the innermost nested loop is loop number 1. The *break* is useful for exiting from an infinite loop.

FORMAT

```
break [n]
```

EXAMPLE 9.48

```
    #!/bin/bash
    # Scriptname: loopbreak
1   while true; do
2       echo Are you ready to move on\?
        read answer
3       if [[  "$answer"  ==  [Yy] ]]
        then
4           break
5       else
            ....commands...
        fi
6   done
7   print "Here we are"
```

EXPLANATION

1 The *true* command is a Linux command that always exits with zero status. It is often used to start an infinite loop. It is okay to put the *do* statement on the same line as the *while* command, as long as a semicolon separates them. The body of the loop is entered.

2 The user is asked for input. The user's input is assigned to the variable *answer.*

3 If *$answer* evaluates to *Y* or *y*, control goes to line 4.

4 The *break* command is executed, the loop is exited, and control goes to line 7. The line *Here we are* is printed. Until the user answers with a *Y* or *y*, the program will continue to ask for input. This could go on forever!

5 If the test fails in line 3, the *else* commands are executed. When the body of the loop ends at the *done* keyword, control starts again at the top of the *while* at line 1.

6 This is the end of the loop body.

7 Control starts here after the *break* command is executed.

The *continue* Command. The *continue* command returns control to the top of the loop if some condition becomes true. All commands below the *continue* will be ignored. If nested within a number of loops, the *continue* command returns control to the innermost loop. If a number is given as its argument, control can then be started at the top of any loop.

If you are nested in three loops, the outermost loop is loop number 3, the next nested loop is loop number 2, and the innermost nested loop is loop number 1.[4]

FORMAT

```
continue [n]
```

EXAMPLE 9.49

```
(The mailing List)
    $ cat mail_list
    ernie
    john
    richard
    melanie
    greg
    robin

(The Script)
    #!/bin/bash
    # Scriptname: mailem
    # Purpose: To send a list
1   for name in $(cat  mail_list)
    do
2       if [[ $name == richard ]] ; then
3           continue
        else
4           mail $name < memo
        fi
5   done
```

EXPLANATION

1. After command substitution, *$(cat mail_list)* or *`cat mail_list`*, the *for* loop will iterate through the list of names from the file called *mail_list.*
2. If the name matches *richard*, the *continue* command is executed and control goes back to top of the loop where the loop expression is evaluated. Because *richard* has already been shifted off the list, the next user, *melanie*, will be assigned to the variable *name*. Old style: *if ["$name" = richard] ; then*
3. The *continue* command returns control to the top of the loop, skipping any commands in the rest of the loop body.
4. All users in the list, except *richard*, will be mailed a copy of the file *memo.*
5. This is the end of the loop body.

---

4. If the *continue* command is given a number higher than the number of loops, the loop exits.

Nested Loops and Loop Control. When you are using nested loops, the *break* and *continue* commands can be given a numeric, integer argument so that control can go from the inner loop to an outer loop.

EXAMPLE 9.50

```
(The Script)
    #!/bin/bash
    # Scriptname: months
1   for month in Jan Feb Mar Apr May Jun Jul Aug Sep Oct Nov Dec
    do
2       for week in  1 2 3 4
        do
            echo -n "Processing the month of $month. O.K.? "
            read ans
3           if [ "$ans" = n  -o -z "$ans" ]
            then
4               continue 2
            else
                echo -n "Process  week $week of $month? "
                read ans
                if [ "$ans" = n -o -z "$ans"  ]
                then
5                   continue
                else
                   echo "Now processing week $week of $month."
                   sleep 1
                       # Commands go here
                   echo  "Done processing..."
                fi
            fi
6       done
7   done

(The Output)
$ months
  Processing the month of Jan. O.K.?
  Processing the month of Feb. O.K.? y
  Process  week 1 of Feb? y
  Now processing  week 1 of Feb.
  Done processing...
  Processing the month of Feb. O.K.? y
  Process week 2 of Feb? y
  Now processing week 2 of Feb.
  Done processing...
  Processing the month of Feb. O.K.? n
  Processing the month of Mar. O.K.? n
  Processing the month of Apr. O.K.? n
  Processing the month of May. O.K.? n
```

EXPLANATION

1 The outer *for* loop is started. The first time in the loop, *Jan* is assigned to *month.*

2 The inner *for* loop starts. The first time in this loop, *1* is assigned to *week.* The inner loop iterates completely before going back to the outer loop.

3 If the user enters either an *n* or presses Enter, line 4 is executed.

4 The *continue* command with an argument of 2 starts control at the top of the second outermost loop. The *continue* without an argument returns control to the top of the innermost loop.

5 Control is returned to the innermost *for* loop.

6 This *done* terminates the innermost loop.

7 This *done* terminates the outermost loop.

9.6.6 I/O Redirection and Subshells

Input can be piped or redirected to a loop from a file. Output can also be piped or redirected to a file from a loop. The shell starts a subshell to handle I/O redirection and pipes. Any variables defined within the loop will not be known to the rest of the script when the loop terminates.

Redirecting the Output of the Loop to a File. Output from a *bash* loop can be sent to a file rather than to the screen. See Example 9.51.

EXAMPLE 9.51

```
(The Command Line)
1   $ cat memo
    abc
    def
    ghi

(The Script)
    #!/bin/bash
    # Program name: numberit
    # Put line numbers on all lines of memo
2   if let $(( $# <  1 ))
    then
3       echo  "Usage: $0 filename " >&2
        exit 1
    fi
4   count=1                          # Initialize count
```

EXAMPLE 9.51 (CONTINUED)

```
5   cat $1 | while read line
    # Input is coming from file provided at command line
    do
6      let $((count == 1)) && echo "Processing file $1..." > /dev/tty
7      echo -e "$count\t$line"
8      let count+=1
9   done > tmp$$                     # Output is going to a temporary file
10  mv tmp$$ $1

(The Command Line)
11  $ numberit memo
    Processing file memo...

12  $ cat memo
    1   abc
    2   def
    3   ghi
```

EXPLANATION

1 The contents of file *memo* are displayed.

2 If the user did not provide a command line argument when running this script, the number of arguments (*$#*) will be less than one and the error message appears.

3 The usage message is sent to *stderr* (*>&2*) if the number of arguments is less than *1*.

4 The *count* variable is assigned the value *1*.

5 The Linux *cat* command displays the contents of the filename stored in *$1*, and the output is piped to the *while* loop. The *read* command is assigned the first line of the file the first time in the loop, the second line of the file the next time through the loop, and so forth. The *read* command returns a zero exit status if it is successful in reading input and one if it fails.

6 If the value of *count* is *1*, the *echo* command is executed and its output is sent to */dev/tty*, the screen.

7 The *echo* command prints the value of *count*, followed by the line in the file.

8 The *count* is incremented by one.

9 The output of this entire loop, each line of the file in *$1*, is redirected to the file *tmp$$*, with the exception of the first line of the file, which is redirected to the terminal, */dev/tty*.[a]

10 The *tmp* file is renamed to the filename assigned to *$1*.

11 The program is executed. The file to be processed is called *memo*.

12 The file *memo* is displayed after the script has finished, demonstrating that line numbers have been prepended to each line.

a. *$$* expands to the PID number of the current shell. By appending this number to the filename, the filename is made unique.

Piping the Output of a Loop to a Linux Command. Output can be either piped to another command(s) or redirected to a file.

EXAMPLE 9.52

```
(The Script)
    #!/bin/bash
1   for i in 7 9 2 3 4  5
2   do
        echo  $i
3   done | sort -n


(The Output)
    2
    3
    4
    5
    7
    9
```

EXPLANATION

1 The *for* loop iterates through a list of unsorted numbers.

2 In the body of the loop, the numbers are printed. This output will be piped into the *Linux sort* command, a numerical sort.

3 The pipe is created after the *done* keyword. The loop is run in a subshell.

Running Loops in the Background. Loops can be executed to run in the background. The program can continue without waiting for the loop to finish processing.

EXAMPLE 9.53

```
(The Script)
    #!/bin/bash
1   for person in bob jim joe sam
    do
2       mail $person < memo
3   done &
```

EXPLANATION

1 The *for* loop shifts through each of the names in the wordlist: *bob, jim, joe,* and *sam.* Each of the names is assigned to the variable *person*, in turn.

2 In the body of the loop, each person is sent the contents of the *memo* file.

3 The ampersand at the end of the *done* keyword causes the loop to be executed in the background. The program will continue to run while the loop is executing.

9.6.7 IFS and Loops

The shell's internal field separator (IFS) evaluates to spaces, tabs, and the newline character. It is used as a word (token) separator for commands that parse lists of words, such as *read, set,* and *for*. It can be reset by the user if a different separator will be used in a list. Before changing its value, it is a good idea to save the original value of the IFS in another variable. Then it is easy to return to its default value, if needed.

EXAMPLE 9.54

```
(The Script )
$ cat runit2
    #/bin/bash
    # Script is called runit.
    # IFS is the internal field separator and defaults to
    # spaces, tabs, and newlines.
    # In this script it is changed to a colon.
1   names=Tom:Dick:Harry:John
2   oldifs="$IFS"  # save the original value of IFS
3   IFS=":"
4   for persons in $names
    do
5       echo  Hi $persons
    done
6   IFS="$oldifs"              # reset the IFS to old value
7   set Jill Jane Jolene       # set positional parameters
8   for girl in $*
    do
9       echo Howdy $girl
    done

(The Output)
$ runit2
5   Hi Tom
    Hi Dick
    Hi Harry
    Hi John
9   Howdy Jill
    Howdy Jane
    Howdy Jolene
```

EXPLANATION

1 The *names* variable is set to the string *Tom:Dick:Harry:John*. Each of the words is separated by a colon.

2 The value of *IFS*, white space, is assigned to another variable, *oldifs*. Since the value of the *IFS* is white space, it must be quoted to preserve it.

EXPLANATION (CONTINUED)

3 The *IFS* is assigned a colon. Now the colon is used to separate words.

4 After variable substitution, the *for* loop will iterate through each of the names, using the colon as the internal field separator between the words.

5 Each of the names in the wordlist are displayed.

6 The *IFS* is reassigned its original value stored in *oldifs*.

7 The positional parameters are set. *$1* is assigned *Jill*, *$2* is assigned *Jane*, and *$3* is assigned *Jolene*.

8 *$** evaluates to all the positional parameters, *Jill, Jane,* and *Jolene*. The *for* loop assigns each of the names to the *girl* variable, in turn, through each iteration of the loop.

9 Each of the names in the parameter list is displayed.

9.7 Functions

Functions were introduced to the Bourne shell in ATT's UNIX SystemVR2 and have been enhanced in the Bourne Again shell. A function is a name for a command or group of commands. Functions are used to modularize your program and make it more efficient. They are executed in context of the current shell. In other words, a child process is not spawned as it is when running an executable program such as *ls*. You may even store functions in another file and load them into your script when you are ready to use them.

Here is a review of some of the important rules about using functions.

1. The shell determines whether you are using an alias, a function, a built-in command, or an executable program (or script) found on the disk. It looks for aliases first, then functions, built-in commands, and last, executables.
2. A function must be defined before it is used.
3. The function runs in the current environment; it shares variables with the script that invoked it, and lets you pass arguments by assigning them as positional parameters. Local variables can be created within a function by using the *local* function.
4. If you use the *exit* command in a function, you exit the entire script. If you exit the function, you return to where the script left off when the function was invoked.
5. The *return* statement in a function returns the exit status of the last command executed within the function or the value of the argument given.
6. Functions can be exported to subshells with the *export -f* built-in command.
7. To list functions and definitions, use the *declare -f* command. To list just function names, use *declare -F*.[5]

5. Only on *bash* versions 2.x.

8. Traps, like variables, are global within functions. They are shared by both the script and the functions invoked in the script. If a trap is defined in a function, it is also shared by the script. This could have unwanted side effects.
9. If functions are stored in another file, they can be loaded into the current script with the *source* or *dot* command.
10. Functions can be recursive; i.e., they can call themselves. There is no limit imposed for the number of recursive calls.

FORMAT

```
function function_name { commands ; commands; }
```

EXAMPLE 9.55

```
function dir { echo "Directories: ";ls -l|awk '/^d/ {print $NF}'; }
```

EXPLANATION

The keyword, *function*, is followed by the name of the function is *dir*. (Sometimes empty parentheses follow the function name, but they are not necessary.) The commands within the curly braces will be executed when *dir* is typed. The purpose of the function is to list only the subdirectories below the present working directory. The spaces surrounding the first curly brace are required.

To Unset a Function. To remove a function from memory, use the *unset* command.

FORMAT

```
unset -f function_name
```

Exporting Functions. Functions may be exported so that subshells know about them.

FORMAT

```
export -f function_name
```

9.7.1 Function Arguments and the Return Value

Because the function is executed within the current shell, the variables will be known to both the function and the shell. Any changes made to your environment in the function will also be made to the shell.

The Built-In *local* Function. To create local variables that are private to the function and will disappear after the function exits, use the built-in *local* function. See Example 9.57.

Arguments. Arguments can be passed to functions by using positional parameters. The positional parameters are private to the function; that is, arguments to the function will not affect any positional parameters used outside the function. See Example 9.56.

The Built-In *return* Function. The *return* command can be used to exit the function and return control to the program at the place where the function was invoked. (Remember, if you use *exit* anywhere in your script, including within a function, the script terminates.) The return value of a function is really just the value of the exit status of the last command in the script, unless you give a specific argument to the *return* command. If a value is assigned to the *return* command, that value is stored in the *?* variable and can hold an integer value between zero and 256. Because the *return* command is limited to returning only an integer between zero and 256, you can use command substitution to capture the output of a function. Place the entire function in parentheses preceded by a *$*, e.g., *$(function_name)*, or traditional back quotes to capture and assign the output to a variable just as you would if getting the output of a Linux command.

EXAMPLE 9.56

```
(Passing Arguments)
(The Script)
   #!/bin/bash
   # Scriptname: checker
   # Purpose: Demonstrate function and arguments

1  function Usage { echo "error: $*" 2>&1; exit 1; }

2  if (( $# != 2 ))
   then
3          Usage "$0: requires two arguments"
   fi
4  if [[ ! ( -r $1 && -w $1 ) ]]
   then
5          Usage "$1: not readable and writeable"
   fi
```

EXAMPLE 9.56 (CONTINUED)

```
6    echo The arguments are: $*
 <   Program continues here >

(Output)
$ checker
error: checker: requires two arguments

$ checker file1 file2
error: file1: not readable and writeable

$ checker filex file2
The arguments are filex file2
```

EXPLANATION

1 The function called *Usage* is defined. It will be used to send an error message to standard error (the screen). Its arguments consist of any string of characters sent when the function is called. The arguments are stored in *$**, the special variable that contains all positional parameters. Within a function, positional parameters are local and have no effect on those positional parameters used outside the function.

2 If the number of arguments begin passed into the script from the command line does not equal 2, the program branches to line 3.

3 When the *Usage* function is called, the string *"$0: requires two arguments"* is passed to the function and stored in the *$** varable. The *echo* statement will then send the message to standard error and the script will exit with an exit status of 1 to indicate that something went wrong.[a]

4, 5 If the first argument coming into the program from the command line is not the name of a readable and writeable file, the *Usage* function will be called with *"$1: not readable and writeable"* as its argument.

6 The arguments coming into the script from the command line are stored in *$**. This has no effect on the *$** in the function.

a. With the old test form, the expression is written: `if [ ! \( -r $1 -a -w $1 \) ]`

EXAMPLE 9.57

```
(Using the return Command)
(The Script)
$ cat do_increment
    #!/bin/bash
    # Scriptname: do_increment
1    increment ()  {
2       local sum;      # sum is known only in this function
3       let "sum=$1 + 1"
4       return $sum     # Return the value of sum to the script.
    }
5   echo  -n "The sum is "
6   increment 5      # Call function increment; pass 5 as a
                     # parameter. 5 becomes $1 for the increment
                     # function.
7   echo $?          # The return value is stored in $?
8   echo  $sum       # The variable "sum" is not known here

(The Output)
$ do_increment
4,6   The sum is 6
7
```

EXPLANATION

1 The function called *increment* is defined.

2 The built-in *local* function makes variable, *sum*, local (private) to this function. It will not exist outside the function. When the function exits, it will be removed.

3 When the function is called, the value of the first argument, *$1*, will be incremented by one and the result assigned to *sum*.

4 The *return* built-in command, when given an argument, returns to the main script after the line where the function was invoked. It stores its argument in the *?* variable.

5 The string is echoed to the screen.

6 The *increment* function is called with an argument of *5*.

7 When the function returns, its exit status is stored in the *?* variable. The exit status is the exit value of the last command executed in the function unless an explicit argument is used in the *return* statement. The argument for *return* must be an integer between 0 and 255.

8 Although the *sum* was defined in the function *increment*, it is local in scope, and therefore also not known outside the function. Nothing is printed.

EXAMPLE 9.58

```
(Using Command Substitution)
(The Script)
$ cat do_square
    #!/bin/bash
    # Scriptname: do_square
1   function square {
      local sq    # sq is local to the function
      let "sq=$1 * $1"
      echo  "Number to be squared is $1."
2     echo  "The result is $sq "
    }
3   echo "Give me a number to square. "
    read number
4   value_returned=$(square $number) # Command substitution
5   echo   "$value_returned"

(The Output)
$ do_square
3   Give me a number to square.
    10
5   Number to be squared is 10.
     The result is 100
```

EXPLANATION

1. The function called *square* is defined. Its purpose, when called, is to multiply its argument, *$1*, times itself.
2. The result of squaring the number is printed.
3. The user is asked for input. This is the line where the program starts executing.
4. The function *square* is called with a number (input from the user) as its argument. Command substitution is performed because the function is enclosed in parentheses preceded by a *$*. The output of the function, both of its *echo* statements, is assigned to the variable *value_returned.*
5. The value returned from the command substitution is printed.

9.7.2 Functions and the *source* (or *dot*) Command

Storing Functions. Functions are often defined in the *.profile* file, so that when you log in, they will be defined. Functions can be exported, and they can be stored in a file. Then when you need the function, the *source* or *dot* command is used with the name of the file to activate the definitions of the functions within it.

EXAMPLE 9.59

```
1   $ cat myfunctions
2   function go() {
        cd $HOME/bin/prog
        PS1=''pwd' > '
        ls
    }
3   function greetings() { echo "Hi $1! Welcome to my world." ; }

4   $ source myfunctions
5   $ greetings george
    Hi george! Welcome to my world.
```

EXPLANATION

1. The file *myfunctions* is displayed. It contains two function definitions.
2. The first function defined is called *go*. It sets the primary prompt to the present working directory.
3. The second function defined is called *greetings*. It will greet the name of the user passed in as an argument.
4. The *source or dot* command loads the contents of the file *myfunctions* into the shell's memory. Now both functions are defined for this shell.
5. The *greetings* function is invoked and executed.

EXAMPLE 9.60

```
(The .dbfunctions file  shown below contains functions to be used by
the main program.  See cd for complete script.)
1   $ cat dbfunctions
2   function addon () {# Function defined in file .dbfunctions
3       while true
        do
             echo "Adding information "
             echo "Type the full name of employee "
             read name
             echo "Type address for employee "
             read address
             echo "Type start date for employee (4/10/88 ) :"
             read startdate
```

EXAMPLE 9.60 (CONTINUED)

```
                echo $name:$address:$startdate
                echo -n "Is this correct? "
                read ans
                case "$ans"  in
                [Yy]*)
                            echo "Adding info..."
                            echo $name:$address:$startdate>>datafile
                            sort -u datafile -o datafile
                            echo -n "Do you want to go back to the main \
                               menu? "
                     read ans
                     if [[ $ans == [Yy] ]]
                     then

4                         return     # return to calling program
                     else

5                         continue   # go to the top of the loop
                     fi
                     ;;
                *)
                echo "Do you want to try again? "
                read answer
                case "$answer" in
                [Yy]*) continue;;
                *) exit;;
                esac
                     ;;
        esac
    done
6   }   # End of function definition

------------------------------------------------------------
(The Command Line)
7   $ more mainprog
    #!/bin/bash
    # Scriptname: mainprog
    # This is the main script that will call the function, addon

    datafile=$HOME/bourne/datafile
8   source dbfunctions    # The file is loaded into memory
       if [ ! -e $datafile ]
    then
       echo "$(basename $datafile) does not exist" >&2
       exit 1
    fi
```

EXAMPLE 9.60 (CONTINUED)

```
9    echo "Select one: "
     cat <<EOF
         [1] Add info
         [2] Delete info
         [3] Update info
         [4] Exit
     EOF
     read choice
     case $choice in
10       1)   addon        # Calling the addon function
               ;;
         2)   delete       # Calling the delete function
               ;;
         3)   update
               ;;
         4)
              echo Bye
              exit 0
               ;;
          *)  echo Bad choice
                  exit 2
               ;;
     esac
     echo Returned from function call
     echo The name is $name
     # Variable set in the function are known in this shell.
done
```

EXPLANATION

1 The *.dbfunctions* file is displayed.

2 The *addon* function is defined. Its function is to add new information to the *datafile.*

3 A *while* loop is entered. It will loop forever unless a loop control statement such as *break* or *continue* is included in the body of the loop.

4 The *return* command sends control back to the calling program where the function was called.

5 Control is returned to the top of the *while* loop.

6 The closing curly brace ends the function definition.

7 This is the main script. The function *addon* will be used in this script.

8 The *source* command loads the file *.dbfunctions* into the program's memory. Now the function *addon* is defined for this script and available for use. It is as though you had just defined the function right here in the script.

9 A menu is displayed with the *here* document. The user is asked to select a menu item.

10 The *addon* function is invoked.

9.8 Trapping Signals

While your program is running, if you press Control-C or Control-\, your program terminates as soon as the signal arrives. There are times when you would rather not have the program terminate immediately after the signal arrives. You could arrange to ignore the signal and keep running or perform some sort of cleanup operation before actually exiting the script. The *trap* command allows you to control the way a program behaves when it receives a signal.

A *signal* is defined as an asynchronous message that consists of a number that can be sent from one process to another, or by the operating system to a process if certain keys are pressed or if something exceptional happens.[6] The *trap* command tells the shell to terminate the command currently in execution upon the receipt of a signal. If the *trap* command is followed by commands within quotes, the command string will be executed upon receipt of a specified signal. The shell reads the command string twice, once when the trap is set, and again when the signal arrives. If the command string is surrounded by double quotes, all variable and command substitution will be performed when the trap is set the first time. If single quotes enclose the command string, variable and command substitution do not take place until the signal is detected and the trap is executed.

Use the command *kill -l* or *trap -l* to get a list of all signals. Table 9.6 on page 460 provides a list of signal numbers and their corresponding names.

FORMAT

```
trap 'command; command' signal-number
trap 'command; command' signal-name
```

EXAMPLE 9.61

```
trap 'rm tmp*; exit 1'  0 1 2 15
trap 'rm tmp*; exit 1'  EXIT HUP INT TERM
```

EXPLANATION

When any of the signals *1* (hangup), *2* (interrupt), or *15* (software termination) arrives, remove all the *tmp* files and exit.

If an interrupt comes in while the script is running, the *trap* command lets you handle the interrupt signal in several ways. You can let the signal behave normally (default), ignore the signal, or create a handler function to be called when the signal arrives.

Signal names such as *HUP* and *INT* are normally prefixed with *SIG*, for example, *SIGHUP, SIGINT,* and so forth.[7] The *bash* shell allows you to use symbolic names for the

6. Bolsky, Morris I. and Korn, David G. *The New KornShell Command And Programming, 2nd ed.* Prentice Hall. 1995. p. 327.
7. SIGKILL, number 9, often called a "sure kill," is not trapable.

signals, which are the signal names without the *SIG* prefix, or you can use the numeric value for the signal. See Table 9.6. A pseudo signal name *EXIT,* or the number 0, will cause the trap to be executed when the shell exits.

Table 9.6 Signal Numbers and Signals (*kill -l*)

1) SIGHUP	9) SIGKILL	18) SIGCONT	26) SIGVTALRM
2) SIGINT	10) SIGUSR1	19) SIGSTOP	27) SIGPROF
3) SIGQUIT	11) SIGSEGV	20) SIGTSTP	28) SIGWINCH
4) SIGILL	12) SIGUSR2	21) SIGTTIN	29) SIGIO
5) SIGTRAP	13) SIGPIPE	22) SIGTTOU	30) SIGPWR
6) SIGABRT	14) SIGALRM	23) SIGURG	
7) SIGBUS	15) SIGTERM	24) SIGXCPU	
8) SIGFPE	17) SIGCHLD	25) SIGXFSZ	

Resetting Signals. To reset a signal to its default behavior, the *trap* command is followed by the signal name or number. *Traps* set in functions are recognized by the shell that invoked the function, once the function has been called. Any traps set outside the function are also recognized with the function.

EXAMPLE 9.62

```
trap 2   or   trap INT
```

EXPLANATION

Resets the default action for signal 2, *SIGINT.* The default action is to kill the process when the interrupt key (Control-C) is pressed.

Ignoring Signals. If the *trap* command is followed by a pair of empty quotes, the signals listed will be ignored by the process.

EXAMPLE 9.63

```
trap " " 1 2   or    trap "" HUP INT
```

EXPLANATION

Signals *1* (*SIGHUP*) and *2* (*SIGINT*) will be ignored by the shell process.

Listing Traps. To list all traps and the commands assigned to them, type *trap*.

EXAMPLE 9.64

```
(At the command line)
1  $ trap 'echo "Caught ya!; exit"' 2
2  $ trap
   trap -- 'echo "Caught ya!; exit 1"' SIGINT
3  $ trap -
```

EXPLANATION

1. The *trap* command is set to exit on signal 2 (Control-C).
2. The *trap* command without an argument lists all set traps.
3. If the argument is a dash, all signals are reset to their original values, whatever they were when the shell started up.

EXAMPLE 9.65

```
(The Script)
    #!/bin/bash
    # Scriptname: trapping
    # Script to illustrate the trap command and signals
    # Can use the signal numbers or bash abbreviations seen
    # below. Cannot use SIGINT, SIGQUIT, etc.
1   trap 'echo "Control-C will not terminate $0."'  INT
2   trap 'echo "Control-\ will not terminate $0."'  QUIT
3   trap 'echo "Control-Z will no stop $0."'        TSTP
4   echo  "Enter any string after the prompt.
    When you are ready to exit, type \"stop\"."
5   while true
    do
6       echo -n "Go ahead...> "
7       read
8       if [[ $REPLY == [Ss]top ]]
        then
9            break
        fi
10  done
```

EXAMPLE 9.65 (CONTINUED)

```
(The Output)
    $ trapping
4   Enter any string after the prompt.
    When you are ready to exit, type "stop".
6   Go ahead...> this is it^C
1   Control-C will not terminate trapping.
6   Go ahead...> this is it again^Z
3   Control-Z will not terminate trapping.
6   Go ahead...> this is never it|^\
2   Control-\ will not terminate trapping.
6   Go ahead...> stop
    $
```

EXPLANATION

1. The first *trap* catches the *INT* signal, Control-C. If Control-C is pressed while the program is running, the command enclosed in quotes will be executed. Instead of aborting, the program will print *Control-C will not terminate trapping* and continue to prompt the user for input.
2. The second *trap* command will be executed when the user presses Control-\, the *QUIT* signal. The string *Control-\ will not terminate trapping* will be displayed and the program will continue to run. This signal, *SIGQUIT* by default, kills the process and produces a core file.
3. The third *trap* command will be executed when the user presses Control-Z, the *TSTP* signal. The string *Control-Z will not terminate trapping* will be displayed, and the program will continue to run. This signal normally causes the program to be suspended in the background if job control is implemented.
4. The user is prompted for input.
5. The *while* loop is entered.
6. The string *Go ahead...>* is printed and the program waits for input (see *read* on the next line).
7. The *read* command assigns user input to the built-in *REPLY* variable.
8. If the value of *REPLY* matches *Stop* or *stop*, the *break* command causes the loop to exit and the program will terminate. Entering *Stop* or *stop* is the only way we will get out of this program unless it is killed with the *kill* command.
9. The *break* command causes the body of the loop to be exited.
10. The *done* keyword marks the end of the loop.

Resetting Signals. To reset a signal to its default behavior, the *trap* command is followed by the signal name or number.

EXAMPLE 9.66

```
trap 2
```

EXPLANATION

Resets the default action for signal 2, *SIGINT*, which is used to kill a process, i.e., Control-C.

EXAMPLE 9.67

```
trap 'trap 2' 2
```

EXPLANATION

Sets the default action for signal 2 (*SIGINT*) to execute the command string within quotes when the signal arrives. The user must press Control-C twice to terminate the program. The first *trap* catches the signal, the second *trap* resets the trap back to its default action, which is to kill the process.

Traps in Functions. If you use a trap to handle a signal in a function, it will affect the entire script, once the function is called. The trap is global to the script. In the following example, the trap is set to ignore the interrupt key, ^C. This script had to be killed with the *kill* command to stop the looping. It demonstrates potential undesirable side effects when using traps in functions.

EXAMPLE 9.68

```
(The Script)
   #!/bin/bash
1  function trapper () {
       echo "In trapper"
2      trap 'echo "Caught in a trap!"' INT
       # Once set, this trap affects the entire script. Anytime
       # ^C is entered, the script will ignore it.
   }
3  while :
   do
       echo "In the main script"
```

EXAMPLE 9.68 (CONTINUED)

```
4        trapper
5        echo "Still in main"
         sleep 5
     done

(The Output)
$ trapper
     In the main script
     In trapper
     Still in main
     ^CCaught in a trap!
     In the main script
     In trapper
     Still in main
     ^CCaught in a trap!
     In the main script
```

EXPLANATION

1 The *trapper* function is defined. All variables and traps set in the function are global to the script.

2 The *trap* command will ignore INT, signal 2, the interrupt key (^C). If ^C is pressed, the message *Caught in a trap* is printed, and the script continues forever. The script can be killed with the *kill* command or Ctrl-\.

3 The main script starts a forever loop.

4 The function *trapper* is called.

5 When the function returns, execution starts here.

9.9 Debugging

By using the *-n* option to the *bash* command, you can check the sytnax of your scripts without really executing any of the commands. If there is a syntax error in the script, the shell will report the error. If there are no errors, nothing is displayed.

The most commonly used method for debugging scripts is the *set* command with the *-x* option, or *bash*, invoked with the *-x* option, and the scriptname. See Table 9.7 on page 465 for a list of debugging options. These options allow an execution trace of your script. Each command from your script is displayed after substitution has been performed, and then the command is executed. When a line from your script is displayed, it is preceded with a plus (+) sign.

With the verbose option turned on, or by invoking the shell with the *-v* option (*bash -v* scriptname), each line of the script will be displayed just as it was typed in the script, and then executed.

Table 9.7 Debugging Options

Command	*Option*	*What It Does*
bash -x scriptname	Echo option	Displays each line of script after variable substitutions and before execution
bash -v scriptname	Verbose option	Displays each line of script before execution, just as you typed it
bash -n scriptname	Noexec option	Interprets but does not execute commands
set -x	Turns on echo	Traces execution in a script
set +x	Turns off echo	Turns off tracing

EXAMPLE 9.69

```
(The Script)
$ cat todebug
    #!/bin/bash
    # Scriptname: todebug

1   name="Joe Shmoe"
    if [[ $name == "Joe Blow" ]]
    then
         printf "Hello $name\n"
    fi

    declare -i num=1
    while (( num < 5 ))
    do
         let num+=1
    done
    printf "The total is %d\n", $num

(The Output)
2 bash -x todebug
+ name=Joe Shmoe
+ [[ Joe Shmoe == \J\o\e\ \B\l\o\w ]]
+ declare -i num=1
+ ((  num < 5  ))
+ let num+=1
+ ((  num < 5  ))
+ let num+=1
+ ((  num < 5  ))
+ let num+=1
+ ((  num < 5  ))
+ let num+=1
+ ((  num < 5  ))
+ printf 'The total is %d\n,' 5
The total is 5
```

EXPLANATION

1 The script is called *todebug*. You can watch the script run with the *-x* switch turned on. Each iteration of the loop is displayed and the values of variables are printed as they are set and when they change.

2 *Bash* is invoked with the *-x* option. Echoing is turned on. Each line of the script will be displayed to the screen prepended with a plus sign (+). Variable substitution is performed before the line is displayed. The result of the execution of the command appears after the line has been displayed.

9.10 Processing Command Line Options with *getopts*

If you are writing scripts that require a number of command line options, positional parameters are not always the most efficient. For example, the Linux *ls* command takes a number of command line options and arguments. (An option requires a leading dash; an argument does not.) Options can be passed to the program in several ways: *ls -laFi, ls -i -a -l -F, ls -ia -F*, and so forth. If you have a script that requires arguments, positional parameters might be used to process the arguments individually, such as *ls -l -i -F* . Each dash option would be stored in *$1, $2*, and *$3*, respectively. But, what if the user listed all of the options as one dash option, as in *ls -liF*? Now the *-liF* would all be assigned to *$1* in the script. The *getopts* function makes it possible to process command line options and arguments in the same way they are processed by the *ls* program.[8] The *getopts* function will allow the *runit* program to process its arguments using any variety of combinations.

EXAMPLE 9.70

```
(The Command Line )
1   $ runit -x -n  200 filex

2   $ runit -xn200 filex

3   $ runit -xy

4   $ runit -yx -n 30

5   $ runit -n250 -xy filey

( any other combination of these arguments )
```

8. See the UNIX manual pages (Section 3) for the C library function *getopt*.

EXPLANATION

1 The program *runit* takes four arguments: *x* is an option, *n* is an option requiring a number argument after it, and *filex* is an argument that stands alone.

2 The program *runit* combines the options *x* and *n* and the number argument *200*; *filex* is also an argument.

3 The program *runit* is invoked with the *x* and *y* options combined.

4 The program *runit* is invoked with the *y* and *x* options combined; the *n* option is passed separately, as is the number argument, *30*.

5 The program *runit* is invoked with the *n* option combined with the number argument, the *x* and *y* options are combined, and the *filey* is separate.

Before getting into all the details of the *runit* program, we examine the line from the program where *getopts* is used to see how it processes the arguments.

EXAMPLE 9.71

```
(A Line from the Script Called "runit")

    while getopts :xyn: name
```

EXPLANATION

1 *x*, *y*, and *n* are the options. In this example the first option is preceded by a colon. This tells *getopts* to use silent error reporting. If there is a colon after one of the options, the option expects an argument separated from it by white space. An argument is a word that does not begin with a dash. *-n* requires an argument.

2 Any options typed at the command line must begin with a dash.

3 Any options that do not contain a dash tell *getopts* that the option list has ended.

4 Each time *getopts* is called, it places the next option value it finds in the variable *name*. (You can use any variable name here.) If an illegal argument is given, *name* is assigned a question mark.

***getopts* Scripts.** The following examples illustrate how *getopts* processes arguments.

EXAMPLE 9.72

```
    (The Script)
    $ cat opts1
       #!/bin/bash
       # Program opts1
       # Using getopts -- First try --
    1  while getopts xy options
       do
    2      case $options in
    3      x) echo "you entered -x as an option";;
           y) echo "you entered -y as an option";;
           esac
       done
    (The Command Line)
    4  $ opts1 -x
       you entered -x as an option
    5  $ opts1 -xy
       you entered -x as an option
       you entered -y as an option
    6  $ opts1 -y
       you entered -y as an option
    7  $ opts1 -b
       opts1:   illegal option --  b
    8  $ opts1 b
```

EXPLANATION

1 The *getopts* command is used as a condition for the *while* command. The valid options for this program are listed after the *getopts* command; they are *x* and *y*. Each option is tested in the body of the loop, one after the other. Each option will be assigned to the variable *options*, without the leading dash. When there are no longer any arguments to process, *getopts* will exit with a nonzero status, causing the *while* loop to terminate.

2 The *case* command is used to test each of the possible options found in the *options* variable, either *x* or *y*.

3 If *x* was an option, the string *You entered x as an option* is displayed.

4 At the command line, the *opts1* script is given an *x* option, a legal option to be processed by *getopts*.

5 At the command line, the *opts1* script is given an *xy* option; *x* and *y* are legal options to be processed by *getopts*.

6 At the command line, the *opts1* script is given a *y* option, a legal option to be processed by *getopts*.

7 The *opts1* script is given a *b* option, an illegal option. *Getopts* sends an error message to *stderr*.

8 An option without a dash prepended to it is not an option and causes *getopts* to stop processing arguments.

EXAMPLE 9.73

```
   (The Script)
   $ cat opts2
      #!/bin/bash
      # Program opts2
      # Using getopts -- Second try --
1     while getopts xy options 2> /dev/null
      do
2         case $options in
          x) echo "you entered -x as an option";;
          y) echo "you entered -y as an option";;
3         \?) echo "Only -x and -y are valid options"  1>&2;;
          esac
      done
   (The Command Line)
      $ opts2 -x
      you entered -x as an option

      $ opts2 -y
      you entered -y as an option

      $ opts2 xy

      $ opts2 -xy
      you entered -x as an option
      you entered -y as an option

4     $ opts2 -g
      Only -x and -y are valid options

5     $ opts2 -c
      Only -x and -y are valid options
```

EXPLANATION

1. If there is an error message from *getopts*, it is redirected to */dev/null.*
2. If the option is a bad option, a question mark will be assigned to the *options* variable. The *case* command can be used to test for the question mark, allowing you to print your own error message to standard error.
3. If the *options* variable is assigned the question mark, the *case* statement is executed. The question mark is protected with the backslash so that the shell does not see it as a wildcard and try to perform filename substitution.
4. *g* is not a legal option. A question mark is assigned to the variable *options,* and the error message is displayed.
5. *c* is not a legal option. A question mark is assigned to the variable *options,* and the error message is displayed.

Special *getopts* Variables. The *getopts* function provides two variables to help keep track of arguments: *OPTIND* and *OPTARG*. *OPTIND* is a special variable that is initialized to one and is incremented each time *getopts* completes processing a command line argument to the number of the next argument *getopts* will process. The *OPTARG* variable contains the value of a legal argument. See Examples 9.74 and 9.75.

EXAMPLE 9.74

```
(The Script)
$ cat opts3
    #!/bin/bash
    # Program opts3
    # Using getopts -- Third try --
1   while getopts dq: options
    do
        case $options in
2             d) echo "-d is a valid switch ";;
3             q) echo "The argument for -q is $OPTARG";;
              \?) echo "Usage:opts3 -dq filename ... " 1>&2;;
        esac
    done

(The Command Line)
4   $ opts3 -d
    -d is a valid switch

5   $ opts3 -q  foo
    The argument for -q is foo

6   $ opts3 -q
    Usage:opts3 -dq filename ...

7   $ opts3 -e
    Usage:opts3 -dq filename ...

8   $ opts3 e
```

EXPLANATION

1 The *while* command tests the exit status of *getopts*; if *getopts* can successfully process an argument, it returns zero exit status, and the body of the *while* loop is entered. The colon appended to the argument list means that the *q* option requires an argument. The argument will be stored in the special variable, OPTARG.

2 One of the legal options is *d*. If *d* is entered as an option, the *d* (without the dash) is stored in the *options* variable.

EXPLANATION (CONTINUED)

3 One of the legal options is *q*. The *q* option requires an argument. There must be a space between the *q* option and its argument. If *q* is entered as an option followed by an argument, the *q*, without the dash, is stored in the *options* variable and the argument is stored in the OPTARG variable. If an argument does not follow the *q* option, the question mark is stored in the variable *options*.

4 The *d* option is a legal option to *opts3*.

5 The *q* option with an argument is also a legal option to *opts3*.

6 The *q* option without an argument is an error.

7 The *e* option is invalid. A question mark is stored in the *options* variable if the option is illegal.

8 The option is prepended with neither a dash nor a plus sign. The *getopts* command will not process it as an option and returns a nonzero exit status. The *while* loop is terminated.

EXAMPLE 9.75

```
$ cat opts4
    #!/bin/bash
    # Program opts4
    # Using getopts -- Fourth try --
1   while getopts xyz: arguments 2>/dev/null
    do
        case $arguments  in
2       x) echo "you entered -x as an option .";;
        y) echo "you entered -y as an option." ;;
3       z) echo "you entered -z as an option."
             echo "\$OPTARG is $OPTARG.";;
4       \?) echo "Usage opts4 [-xy] [-z  argument]"
              exit 1;;
        esac
    done
5   echo "The number of arguments passed was $(( $OPTIND - 1 ))"

(The Command Line)
    $ opts4 -xyz foo
    You entered -x as an option.
    You entered -y as an option.
    You entered -z as an option.
    $OPTARG is foo.
    The number of arguments passed was 2.
```

EXAMPLE 9.75 (CONTINUED)

```
$ opts4 -x -y -z  boo
You entered -x as an option.
You entered -y as an option.
You entered -z as an option.
$OPTARG is boo.
The number of arguments passed was 4.

$ opts4 -d
Usage: opts4  [-xy] [-z argument]
```

EXPLANATION

1 The *while* command tests the exit status of *getopts*; if *getopts* can successfully process an argument, it returns zero exit status, and the body of the *while* loop is entered. The colon appended to the *z* option tells *getopts* that an argument must follow the *-z* option. If the option takes an argument, the argument is stored in the *getopts* built-in variable *OPTARG*.

2 If *x* is given as an option, it is stored in the variable *arguments*.

3 If *z* is given as an option with an argument, the argument is stored in the built-in variable *OPTARG*.

4 If an invalid option is entered, the question mark is stored in the variable *arguments*, and an error message is displayed.

5 The special *getopts* variable, *OPTIND*, holds the number of the next option to be processed. Its value is always one more than the actual number of command line arguments.

9.11 The *eval* Command and Parsing the Command Line

The *eval* command evaluates a command line, performs all shell substitutions, and then executes the command line. It is used when normal parsing of the command line is not enough.

EXAMPLE 9.76

```
1   $ set a b c d
2   $ echo The last argument is \$$#
3   The last argument is $4

4   $ eval echo The last argument is \$$#
    The last argument is d

5   $ set -x
    $ eval echo The last argument is \$$#
    + eval echo the last argument is '$4'
    ++ echo the last argument is d
    The last argument is d
```

EXPLANATION

1 Four positional parameters are set.

2 The desired result is to print the value of the last positional parameter. The \$ will print a literal dollar sign. The *$#* evaluates to 4, the number of positional parameters. After the shell evaluates the *$#*, it does not parse the line again to get the value of *$4*.

3 *$4* is printed instead of the last argument.

4 After the shell performs variable substitution, the *eval* command performs the variable substitution and then executes the *echo* command.

5 Turn on the echoing to watch the order of parsing.

EXAMPLE 9.77

```
  (From Shutdown Program)
1  eval `/usr/bin/id | /usr/bin/sed 's/[^a-z0-9=].*//'`
2  if [ "${uid:=0}" -ne 0 ]
   then
3     echo $0: Only root can run $0
      exit 2
   fi
```

EXPLANATION

1 This is a tricky one. The *id* program's output is sent to *sed* to extract the *uid* part of the string. The output for *id* is:

uid=9496(ellie) gid=40 groups=40
uid=0(root) gid=1(daemon) groups=1(daemon)

The *sed* regular expression reads: *Starting at the beginning of the string, find any character that is not a letter, number, or an equal sign and remove that character and all characters following it.* The result is to substitute everything from the first opening parenthesis to the end of the line with nothing. What is left is either: *uid=9496* or *uid=0.*

After *eval* evaluates the command line, it then executes the resulting command:

uid=9496
or
uid=0

For example, if the user's id is *root*, the command executed would be *uid=0.* This creates a local variable in the shell called *uid* and assigns zero to it.

2 The value of the *uid* variable is tested for zero, using command modifiers.

3 If the *uid* is not zero, the *echo* command displays the script name (*$0*) and the message.

9.12 Bash Options

9.12.1 Shell Invocation Options

When the shell is started using the *bash* command, it can take options to modify its behavior. There are two types of options: single-character options and multicharacter options. The single-character options consist of a single leading dash followed by a single character. The multicharacter options consist of two leading dashes and any number of characters. Multicharacter options must appear before single-character options. An interactive login shell normally starts up with *-i* (start an interactive shell), *-s* (read from standard input), and *-m* (enable job control). See Table 9.8 on page 475.

Table 9.8 *Bash* 2.x Shell Invocation Options

Option	***Meaning***
-c string	Commands are read from *string*. Any arguments after *string* are assigned to positional parameters, starting at *$0*.
-D	A list of double quoted strings, preceded by a *$*, are printed to standard output. These strings are subject to language translation when the current locale is not C or POSIX. The *-n* option is implied; no commands will be executed.
-i	Shell is in the interactive mode. *TERM*, *QUIT*, and *INTERRUPT* are ignored.
-s	Commands are read from standard input and allow the setting of positional parameters.
-r	Starts a restricted shell.
--	Signals the end of options and disables further option processing. Any arguments after -- or - are treated as filenames and arguments.
--dump-strings	Same as *-D*.
--help	Displays a usage message for a built-in command and exits.
--login	Causes *bash* to be invoked as a login shell.
--noediting	When *bash* is running interactively, does not use the Readline library.
--noprofile	When starting up, *bash* does not read the initialization files: */etc/profile*, *~/.bash_profile*, *~/.bash_login*, or *~/.profile*.
--norc	For interactive shells, *bash* will not read the *~/.bashrc* file. Turned on by default, if running shell as *sh*.
--posix	Changes the behavior of *bash* to match the POSIX 1003.2 standard, if otherwise it wouldn't.
--quiet	Displays no information at shell startup, the default.
--rcfile file	If *bash* is interactive, uses this intialization file instead of *~/.bashrc*.
--restricted	Starts a restricted shell.
--verbose	Turns on verbose; same as *-v*.
--version	Displays version information about this *bash* shell and exit.

Table 9.9 *Bash* (Versions Prior to 2.x) Shell Invocation Options

-c string	Commands are read from *string*. Any arguments after *string* are assigned to positional parameters, starting at *$0*.
-D	A list of double quoted strings, preceded by a *$*, are printed to standard output. These strings are subject to language translation when the current locale is not C or POSIX. The *-n* option is implied; no commands will be executed.
-i	Shell is in the interactive mode. *TERM*, *QUIT*, and *INTERRUPT* are ignored.
-s	Commands are read from standard input and allows the setting of positional parameters.
-r	Starts a restricted shell.
-	Signals the end of options and disables further option processing. Any arguments after -- or - are treated as filenames and arguments.
-login	Causes *bash* to be invoked as a login shell.
-nobraceexpansion	Curly brace expansion is turned off.
-nolineediting	When *bash* is running interactively, does not use the Readline library.
-noprofile	When starting up, *bash* does not read the initialization files: */etc/profile*, *~/.bash_profile*, *~/.bash_login*, or *~/.profile*.
-posix	Changes the behavior of *bash* to match the POSIX standard, if otherwise, it wouldn't.
-quiet	Displays no information at shell startup, the default.
-rcfile file	If *bash* is interactive, uses this intialization file instead of *~/.bashrc*.
-verbose	Turns on verbose; same as *-v*.
-version	Displays version information about this *bash* shell and exit.

9.12.2 The *set* Command and Options

The *set* command can be used to turn shell options on and off, as well as for handling command line arguments. To turn an option on, the dash (-) is prepended to the option; to turn an option off, the plus sign (+) is prepended to the option. See Table 9.10 on page 477 for a list of *set* options.

EXAMPLE 9.78

```
1    $ set -f

2    $ echo *
     *

3    $ echo ??
     ??

4    $ set +f
```

EXPLANATION

1. The *f* option is turned on, disabling filename expansion.
2. The asterisk is not expanded.
3. The question marks are not expanded.
4. The *f* is turned off; filename expansion is enabled.

Table 9.10 The Built-In *set* Command Options

Name of Option	*Shortcut Switch*	*What It Does*
allexport	*-a*	Automatically marks new or modified variables for export from the time the option is set, until unset.
**braceexpand*	*-B*	Enables brace expansion, and is a default setting.
emacs		For command line editing, uses the *emacs* built-in editor, and is a default setting
errexit	*-e*	If a command returns a nonzero exit status (fails), exits. Not set when reading initialization files.
**histexpand*	*-H*	Enables *!* and *!!* when performing history substitution, and is a default setting.
**history*		Enables command line history; on by default.
ignoreeof		Disables EOF (Control-D) from exiting a shell; must type exit. Same as setting shell variable, *IGNOREEOF=10.*

Table 9.10 The Built-In *set* Command Options (Continued)

Name of Option	*Shortcut Switch*	*What It Does*
**keyword*	*-k*	Places keyword arguments in the environment for a command.
interactive-comments		For interactive shells, a leading # is used to comment out any text remaining on the line.
monitor	*-m*	Allows job control.
noclobber	*-C*	Protects files from being overwritten when redirection is used.
noexec	*-n*	Reads commands, but does not execute them. Used to check the syntax of scripts. Not on when running interactively.
noglob	*-d*	Disables pathname expansion; i.e., turns off wildcards.
notify	*-b*	Notifies user when background job finishes
nounset	*-u*	Displays an error when expanding a variable that has not been set.
**onecmd*	*-t*	Exits after reading and executing one command.
physical	*-P*	If set, does not follow symbolic links when typing *cd* or *pwd*. The physical directory is used instead.
posix		Shell behavior is changed if the default operation doesn't match the POSIX standard.
privileged	*-p*	When set, the shell does not read the *.profile* or *ENV* file and shell functions are not inherited from the environment; automatically set for *setuid* scripts.
posix		Changes the default behavior to POSIX 1003.2
verbose	*-v*	Turns on the *verbose* mode for debugging.
vi		For command line editing, uses the *vi* built-in editor.
xtrace	*-x*	Turns on the echo mode for debugging.

* Asterisk indicates option applies only to versions of *bash 2.x*.

9.12.3 The *shopt* Command and Options

The *shopt* (*bash 2.x*) command can also be used to turn shell options on and off.

Table 9.11 The *shopt* Command Options

Option	*Meaning*
cdable_vars	If an argument to the *cd* built-in command is not a directory, it is assumed to be the name of a variable whose value is the directory to change to.
cdspell	Corrects minor errors in the spelling of a directory name in a *cd* command. The errors checked for are transposed characters, a missing character, and a character too many. If a correction is found, the corrected path is printed, and the command proceeds. Only used by interactive shells.
checkhash	*Bash* checks that a command found in the hash table exists before trying to execute it. If a hashed command no longer exists, a normal path search is performed.
checkwinsize	*Bash* checks the window size after each command and, if necessary, updates the values of *LINES* and *COLUMNS*.
cmdhist	*Bash* attempts to save all lines of a multiple-line command in the same history entry. This allows easy re-editing of multiline commands.
dotglob	*Bash* includes filenames beginning with a "." in the results of filename expansion.
execfail	A noninteractive shell will not exit if it cannot execute the file specified as an argument to the *exec* built-in command. An interactive shell does not exit if *exec* fails.
expand_aliases	Aliases are expanded. Enabled by default.
extglob	The extended pattern matching features (regular expression metacharacters derived from Korn shell for filename expansion) are enabled.
histappend	The history list is appended to the file named by the value of the *HISTFILE* variable when the shell exits, rather than overwriting the file.
histreedit	If Readline is being used, a user is given the opportunity to re-edit a failed history substitution.
histverify	If set, and Readline is being used, the results of history substitution are not immediately passed to the shell parser. Instead, the resulting line is loaded into the Readline editing buffer, allowing further modification.
hostcomplete	If set, and Readline is being used, *bash* will attempt to perform hostname completion when a word containing an "@" is being completed Enabled by default.

Table 9.11 The *shopt* Command Options (Continued)

Option	***Meaning***
huponexit	If set, *bash* will send *SIGHUP* (hangup signal) to all jobs when an interactive login shell exits.
interactive_comments	Allows a word beginning with "#" to cause that word and all remaining characters on that line to be ignored in an interactive shell. Enabled by default.
lithist	If enabled, and the *cmdhist* option is enabled, multiline commands are saved to the history with embedded newlines rather than using semicolon separators where possible.
mailwarn	If set, and a file that *bash* is checking for mail has been accessed since the last time it was checked, the message *The mail in mailfile has been read* is displayed.
nocaseglob	If set, *bash* matches filenames in a case-insensitive fashion when performing filename expansion.
nullglob	If set, *bash* allows filename patterns which match no files to expand to a null string, rather than themselves.
promptvars	If set, prompt strings undergo variable and parameter expansion after being expanded. Enabled by default.
restricted_shell	The shell sets this option if it is started in restricted mode. The value may not be changed. This is not reset when the startup files are executed, allowing the startup files to discover whether or not a shell is restricted.
shift_verbose	If this is set, the shift built-in prints an error message when the shift count exceeds the number of positional parameters.
sourcepath	If set, the *source* built-in uses the value of *PATH* to find the directory containing the file supplied as an argument. Enabled by default.
source	A synonym for **.** (a dot)

9.13 Shell Built-In Commands

The shell has a number of commands that are built-in to its source code. Because the commands are built-in, the shell doesn't have to locate them on disk, making execution much faster. The *help* feature provided with bash give you online help for any built-in command. The built-in commands are listed in Table 9.12 on page 481.

Table 9.12 Built-In Commands

Command	*What It Does*
:	Do-nothing command; returns exit status zero.
. file	The *dot* command reads and executes command from file.
break [n]	See the looping commands on page 443.
:	Do-nothing command; returns 0 exit status.
.	Executes program in context of current process; same as source.
alias	Lists and creates "nicknames" for existing commands.
bg	Puts a job in the background.
*bind**	Displays current key and function bindings, or binds keys to a *readline* function or macro.
break	Breaks out of the innermost loop.
*builtin [sh-builtin [args]]**	Runs a shell built-in, passing it args, and returning 0 exit status. Useful if a function and built-in have the same name.
cd [arg]	Changes the directory to home if no arg or to arg.
command command [arg]*	Runs a command even if a function has the same name; i.e., bypasses function lookup.
continue [n]	See the looping commands on page 444.
*declare [var]**	Displays all variables or declares variables with optional attributes.
dirs	Displays a list of currently remembered directories resulting from *pushd.*
disown	Removes an active job from the job table.
echo [args]	Displays *args* terminated with a newline.
*enable**	Enables and disables shell built-in commands.
eval [args]	Reads *args* as input to the shell and executes the resulting command(s).
exec command	Runs command in place of this shell.
exit [n]	Exits the shell with status *n*.
export [var]	Makes *var* known to subshells.
fc	History's fix command for editing history commands.

Table 9.12 Built-In Commands (Continued)

Command	*What It Does*
fg	Puts background job into foreground.
getopts	Parses and processes command line options.
hash	Controls the internal hash table for quicker searches for commands.
*help [command]**	Displays helpful info about built-in commands and, if command is specified, detailed help about that built-in command.
history	Displays the history list with line numbers.
jobs	Lists jobs put in the background.
kill [-signal process]	Sends the signal to the pid number or job number of the process. Type *kill -l* for a list of signals.
getopts	Used in shell scripts to parse command line and check for legal options.
let	Used for evaluating arithmetic expressions and assigning results of arithmetic calculations to variables.
local	Used in functions to restrict the scope of variables to the function.
logout	Exits the login shell.
popd	Removes entries from the directory stack.
pushd	Adds entries to the directory stack.
pwd	Prints present working directory.
read [var]	Reads line from standard input into variable *var.*
readonly [var]	Makes variable *var* read-only. Cannot be reset.
return [n]	Returns from a function where *n* is the exit value given to the return.
set	Sets options and positional parameters. See Table 9.2 on page 396.
shift [n]	Shifts positional parameters to the left *n* times.
stop pid	Halts execution of the process number pid.
suspend	Stops execution of the current shell (but not if a login shell).
test	Checks file types and evaluates conditional expressions.
times	Prints accumulated user and system *times* for processes run from this shell.

Table 9.12 Built-In Commands (Continued)

Command	***What It Does***
trap [arg] [n]	When shell receives signal *n* (0, 1, 2, or 15), executes *arg.*
type [command]	Prints the type of command; e.g., *pwd* is a built-in shell command.
typeset	Same as declare. Sets variables and gives them attributes.
ulimit	Diplays and sets process resource limits.
umask [octal digits]	Sets user file creation mode mask for owner, group, and others.
unalias	Unsets aliases.
unset [name]	*Unset* value of variable or function.
wait [pid#n]	Waits for background process with pid number *n* and reports termination status.

THE BASH SHELL LAB EXERCISES

Lab 1—First Script

1. Write a script called *greetme* that will:

   a. Contain a comment section with your name, the name of this script, and the purpose of this script.

   b. Greet the user.

   c. Print the date and the time.

   d. Print a calendar for this month.

   e. Print the name of your machine.

   f. Print the name and release of this operating system, (*cat /etc/motd*).

   g. Print a list of all files in your parent directory.

   h. Print all the processes *root* is running.

   i. Print the value of the *TERM*, *PATH*, and *HOME* variables.

   j. Print your disk usage (*du*).

   k. Use the *id* command to print your group ID.

l. Print "*Please couldn't you loan me $50.00?*"

m. Tell the user "*Good bye*" and the current hour (see *man* pages for the *date* command).

2. Make sure your script is executable.

```
chmod +x greetme
```

3. What was the first line of your script? Why do you need this line?

Lab 2—Command Line Arguments

1. Write a script called *rename* that will take two arguments: the first argument is the name of the original file and the second argument is the new name for the file.

   If the user does not provide two arguments, a usage message will appear on the screen and the script will exit. Here is an example of how the script works:

```
$ rename
Usage: rename oldfilename newfilename
$

$ rename file1 file2
file1 has been renamed file2
Here is a listing of the directory:
a file2
b file.bak
```

2. The following *find* command (SunOS) will list all files in the *root* partition that are larger than 100K and that have been modified in the last week. (Check your *man* pages for the correct *find* syntax on this system.)

```
find / -xdev -mtime -7 -size +200 -print
```

3. Write a script called *bigfiles* that will take two arguments: one will be the *mtime* and one the *size* value. An appropriate error message will be sent to *stderr* if the user does not provide two arguments.

4. If you have time, write a script called *vib* that creates backup files for *vi*. The backup files will have the extension *.bak* appended to the original name.

Lab 3—Getting User Input

1. Write a script called *nosy* that will:

   a. Ask the user's full name—first, last, and middle name.

   b. Greet the user by his or her first name.

   c. Ask the user's year of birth and calculate his or her age (use *expr*).

d. Ask the user's login name and print his or her user ID (*from /etc/passwd*).

e. Tell the user his or her home directory.

f. Show the user the processes he or she is running.

g. Tell the user the day of the week, and the current time in nonmilitary time. The output should resemble:

"The day of the week is Tuesday and the current time is 04:07:38 PM."

2. Create a text file called *datafile* (unless this file has already been provided for you). Each entry consists of fields separated by colons. The fields are:

   a. First and last name

   b. Phone number

   c. Address

   d. Birthdate

   e. Salary

3. Create a script called *lookup* that will:

   a. Contain a comment section with the script name, your name, the date, and the reason for writing this script. The reason for writing this script is to display the datafile in sorted order.

   b. Sort the *datafile* by last names.

   c. Show the user the contents of the *datafile*.

   d. Tell the user the number of entries in the file.

4. Try the *-x* and *-v* options for debugging your script. How did you use these commands? How do they differ?

Lab 4—Conditional Statements

1. Write a script called *checking* that will:

   a. Take a command line argument, a user's login name.

   b. Will test to see if a command line argument was provided.

   c. Will check to see if the user is in the */etc/passwd* file. If so, will print:

   "Found <user> in the /etc/passwd file."

   Otherwise will print:

   "No such user on our system."

2. In the *lookup* script, ask the user if he or she would like to add an entry to the *datafile*. If the answer is *yes* or *y*:

    a. Prompt the user for a new name, phone, address, birthday, and salary. Each item will be stored in a separate variable. You will provide the colons between the fields and append the information to the *datafile*.

    b. Sort the file by last names. Tell the user you added the entry, and show him or her the line preceded by the line number.

Lab 5—Conditionals and File Testing

1. Rewrite *checking*. After checking whether the named user is in the */etc/passwd* file, the program will check to see if the user is logged on. If so, the program will print all the processes that are running; otherwise it will tell the user:

    "<user> is not logged on."

2. Use the *let* command to evaluate a set of grades. The script will ask the user for his or her numeric grade on an examination. (Use *declare -i*). The script will test that the grade is within a legal range between 0 and 100. If not, the program will exit. If the grade is within the legal range, the user's letter grade will be displayed, e.g., *You received an A. Excellent!* The range is:

    A (90-100) B (80-89) C (70-79) D (60-69) F (Below 60)

3. The *lookup* script depends on the *datafile* in order to run. In the *lookup* script, check to see if the *datafile* exists and if it is readable and writeable. Add a menu to the *lookup* script to resemble the following:

    [1] Add entry.
    [2] Delete entry.
    [3] View entry.
    [4] Exit.

    You already have the *Add entry* part of the script written. The *Add entry* routine should now include code that will check to see if the name is already in the *datafile* and if it is, tell the user so. If the name is not there, add the new entry.

    Now write the code for the *Delete entry*, *View entry*, and *Exit* functions.

    The *Delete* part of the script should first check to see if the entry exists before trying to remove it. If it does, notify the user; otherwise, remove the entry and tell the user you removed it. On exit, make sure that you use a digit to represent the appropriate exit status.

    How do you check the exit status from the command line?

Lab 6—The Case Statement

1. The *ps* command is different on BSD (Berkeley UNIX) and System 5 (ATT UNIX). Linux uses the BSD options to *ps*. On System 5, the command to list all processes is:

   ```
   ps -ef
   ```

   On Linux, the command is:

   ```
   ps aux
   ```

   Write a program called *systype* that will check for a number of different system types. The cases to test for will be:

   AIX
   LINUX
   HP–UX
   SCO
   OSF1
   ULTRIX
   SunOS (Solaris / SunOs)
   OS

   Solaris, HP–UX, SCO, and IRIX are ATT-type systems. The rest are BSDish.

   The version of UNIX you are using will be printed to *stdout*. The system name can be found with the *uname -s* command or from the */etc/motd* file.

2. Write a script called *timegreet* that will:

   a. Provide a comment section at the top of the script, with your name, the date, and the purpose of the program.

   b. Convert the following program to use the *case* command rather than *if/elif*.

   ```
   #!/bin/bash
   # Comment section
   you=$LOGNAME
   hour=$( date +%H )
   echo "The time is: $( date +%T )"
   if (( hour > 0 && hour < 12 ))
   then
      echo "Good morning, $you!"
   elif (( hour == 12 ))
   then
      echo "Lunch time!"
   elif (( hour > 12 && hour < 16 ))
   then
      echo "Good afternoon, $you!"
   else
      echo "Good night, $you. Sweet dreams."
   fi
   ```

Lab 7—Loops

Select one of the following:

1. Write a program called *mchecker* to check for new mail and write a message to the screen if new mail has arrived.

   a. The program will get the size of the mail spool file for the user. (The spool files are found in */usr/mail/$LOGNAME* on ATT systems and */usr/spool/mail/$USER* on Linux and UCB systems. Use the *find* command if you cannot locate the file.) The script will execute in a continuous loop, once every 30 seconds. Each time the loop executes, it will compare the size of the mail spool file with its size from the previous loop. If the new size is greater than the old size, a message will be printed on your screen, saying *Username, You have new mail.*

The size of a file can be found by looking at the output from *ls -l, wc -c or* from the *find* command.

2. Write a script that will:

   a. Provide a comment section at the top of the script, with your name, the date, and the purpose of the program.

   b. Use the *select* loop to produce a menu of foods.

   c. Produce output to resemble the following:

1) steak and potatoes
2) fish and chips
3) soup and salad
Please make a selection. 1
Stick to your ribs.
Watch your cholesterol.
Enjoy your meal.

1) steak and potatoes
2) fish and chips
3) soup and salad
Please make a selection. 2
British are coming!
Enjoy your meal.

1) steak and potatoes
2) fish and chips
3) soup and salad
Please make a selection. 3
Health foods...
Dieting is so boring.
Enjoy your meal.

3. Write a program called *dusage* that will mail a list of users, one at a time, a listing of the number of blocks they are currently using. The list of users will be in a file called *potential_hogs*. One of the users listed in the *potential_hogs* file will be *admin*.

    a. Use file testing to check that *potential_hogs* file exists and is readable.

    b. A loop will be used to iterate through the list of users. Only those users who are using over 500 blocks will be sent mail. The user *admin* will be skipped over (i.e., he or she does not get a mail message). The mail message will be stored in a *here document* in your *dusage* script.

    c. Keep a list of the names of each person who received mail. Do this by creating a log file. After everyone on the list has been sent mail, print the number of people who received mail and a list of their names.

Lab 8—Functions

1. Rewrite the last program, *systype,* as a function that returns the name of the system. Use this function to determine what options you will use with the *ps* command in the *checking* program.

2. The *ps* command to list all processes on ATT UNIX is:

```
ps -ef
```

3. On Linux/BSD UNIX, the command is:

```
ps -aux   or ps aux
```
[9]

4. Write a function called *cleanup* that will remove all temporary files and exit the script. If the interrupt or hangup signal is sent while the program is running, the *trap* command will call the *cleanup* function.

5. Use a *here document* to add a new menu item to the *lookup* script to resemble the following:

    [1] Add entry
    [2] Delete entry
    [3] Change entry
    [4] View entry
    [5] Exit

    Write a function to handle each of the items in the menu. After the user has selected a valid entry, and the function has completed, ask if the user would like to see the menu again. If an invalid entry is entered, the program should print:

    "Invalid entry, try again."

    and the menu will be redisplayed.

9. Using the leading dash with Linux will produce a warning. See the man page.

6. Create a submenu under *View entry* in the *lookup* script. The user will be asked if he or she would like to view specific information for a selected individual:

   a) Phone
   b) Address
   c) Birthday
   d) Salary

7. Use the *trap* command in a script to perform a cleanup operation if the interrupt signal is sent while the program is running.

CHAPTER 10

THE INTERACTIVE TC SHELL

10.1 Introduction

An interactive shell is one in which the standard input, output, and errors are connected to a terminal. When using the TC shell (*tcsh*) interactively, you will be typing commands at the *tcsh* prompt and waiting for a response. The TC[1] shell is a program that starts up at login time and interprets commands. It is a public domain enhanced version of its predecessor, the Berkeley UNIX C shell. Additional features include command line editing, fancy prompts, programmable completions (filenames, commands, and variables), spelling correction, etc.

The primary *tcsh* source distribution is at *ftp.astron.com,* also *ftp.gw.com*, and *ftp.primate.wisc.edu.*[2] Although *tcsh* is included in most Linux distributions, it can be ported to a number of operating systems, including Solaris, Windows NT, HP-UX, QNX, etc.

This chapter focuses on how to use the TC shell interactively and how to set up your initial working environment. The next chapter will guide you through the programming constructs provided with the TC shell for writing script files. Then, instead of typing commands at the prompt, you will be storing them in a file and executing the file.

10.1.1 Versions of *tcsh*

To find out what version of *tcsh* you are using, type at the shell prompt:

```
which tcsh
```

To tell you in what directory *tcsh* is installed (normally */bin*), and to print the version information, type:

```
/directory_path/tcsh -c 'echo $version'
```

---

1. The T in *tcsh* has historical origins dating back to the TENEX and TOP-10s operating systems used by DEC for its PDP-10 computer. These systems had a form of command completion for the monitor. The creator of the *tcsh* admired features of these systems, and hence, added the T to the C shell.
2. See tutorial at *www.tac.nyc.ny.us/mirrors/tcsh-book.*

EXAMPLE 10.1

```
1  which tcsh
   /bin/tcsh

2 /bin/tcsh -c 'echo $version'
  tcsh 6.07.09 (Astron) 1998-07-07 (i386-intel-linux) options
  8b,nls,dl,al,rh,color
```

10.1.2 Startup

Before the TC shell displays a prompt, it is preceded by a number of processes. See Figure 10.1.

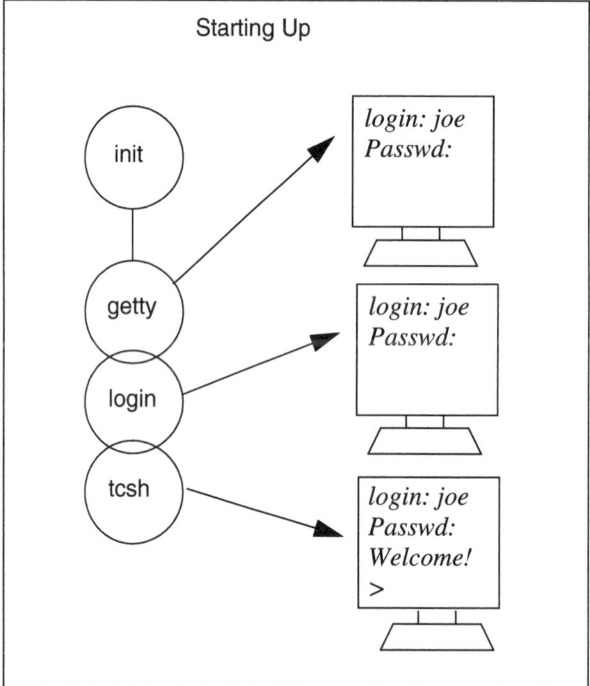

Figure 10.1 System startup and the TC shell.

After the system boots, the first process to run is called *init*, process identification number (PID) 1. It spawns a *getty* process. These processes are responsible for opening up the terminal ports, for providing a place where input comes from (*stdin)* and where standard output (*stdout*) and error (*stderr*) go, and for putting a login prompt on your screen. After the user types his user name, the */bin/login* program is executed. The login program prompts for a password, encrypts and verifies your password, sets up an initial working environment, and then initiates the shell, */bin/tcsh*. The TC shell looks in the */etc* directory for a system startup file called */etc/csh.cshrc* and */etc/csh.login* (if it exists). It then looks in the user's home directory for a file called *~/.tcshrc*, another initialization file used to customize the *tcsh* environment. If that file is not found, it will look for another file that does the same job, called *~/.cshrc* (normally invoked when running *csh*). After executing commands in the *.tcshrc* file (or *.cshrc*), it will execute the history file, commonly called *.history*. Then commands in the *~/.login* file are executed, and finally the *.cshdirs* file is executed. Each of these files will be explained in "The Environment" below.[3]

The */etc/csh.cshrc* and *~/.tcshrc* files will be executed every time a new TC shell is started. The *.login* file is executed only once when the user logs on, and also contains commands and variables to initialize the user's environment. After executing commands from all the startup files, the prompt (> is the default) appears on your screen and the *tcsh* awaits commands. See Figure 10.2.

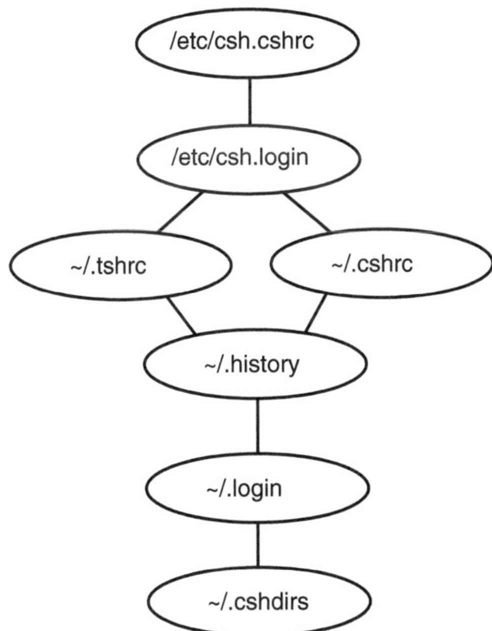

Figure 10.2 If any of these initialization files exist, they are sourced in this sequence.

When logging out, the user presses Control-D or will be automatically logged out if the *autologout* shell variable has been set. Before logging off, the shell looks for a file called */etc/csh.logout* or *~/.logout* in the home directory and if either is located, its commands will be executed. The *.logout* file normally contains commands to clean up temporary files, append data to logfiles, wish the user a good day, etc.

3. The order in which these files are read can be changed when *tcsh* is compiled.

10.2 The TC Shell Environment

10.2.1 Initialization Files

After the *tcsh* program starts, it is programmed to execute a systemwide startup file, */etc/csh.cshrc*, and then two shell initialization files in the user's home directory: the *.tcshrc* file and then the *.login* file. These files allow users to initialize their own environment.

EXAMPLE 10.2

```
# /etc/csh.cshrc

# System wide environment and startup programs for csh users

1  if ($?PATH) then
2      setenv PATH "${PATH}:/usr/X11R6/bin"
   else
3      setenv PATH "/bin:/usr/bin:/usr/local/bin:/usr/X11R6/bin"
   endif

4  if ($?prompt) then
5       [ "$SHELL" = /bin/tcsh ]
6       if ($status == 0) then
7            set prompt='[%n@%m %c]$ '
8       else
9            set prompt=\[`id -nu`@`hostname -s`\]\$\
10      endif
   endif
11 limit coredumpsize 1000000

12  [ `id -gn` = `id -un` -a `id -u` -gt 14 ]
13  if $status then
14       umask 022
    else
15       umask 002
    endif

16  setenv HOSTNAME `/bin/hostname`
17  set history=1000

18  test -d /etc/profile.d
19    if ($status == 0) then
20       set nomatch
21          foreach i ( /etc/profile.d/*.csh )
22             test -f $i
               if ($status == 0) then
23                        source $i
               endif
         end
24      unset nonomatch
      endif
```

EXPLANATION

1 *$?PATH* is a test to see if the *PATH* variable has been set; it returns 1 if true.

2 If the *PATH* variable has been set, */usr/X11R6/bin* is appended to it. This is a directory that contains the *X* windows files.

3 If the *PATH* variable has not been previously set, this line sets it to: */bin:/usr/bin:/usr/local/bin:/usr/X11R6/bin*

4 This line checks to see if the prompt has been set.

5 When you place the expression in square brackets, the expression will be tested and if the result of the expression is true, a zero exit status is returned; otherwise a nonzero exit status is returned. If the value of the *SHELL* environment variable is */bin/tcsh*, the exit status will be 0.

6 The *status* variable contains the exit status of the last command executed, which in this example, is the previous test on line 5.

7 If the status from the last command was zero, the prompt for the */bin/tcsh* is set. The prompt will be set to the user's name followed by an @ symbol, the hostname, and the current working directory (all enclosed in *[ ]*), followed by a dollar sign; e.g., *[ellie@homebound ~]$*

8 If the status was nonzero, the *else* branches program control to line 9.

9 This line sets the prompt for the standard *csh* program. It will print the user's name (*id -un*), an @ symbol, and the short name for his host machine, i.e., the hostname cut at the first dot, and a *$*.

10 The *endif* terminates the inner *if* block.

11 The size of core files (usually created when a program crashes for some illegal system operation) is limited to 1000000 bytes. Core files are created if you abort a running program with Control-\.

12 If the group id number and the user id number are the same, and the user id number is greater than 14, then the next line will be executed; otherwise, the line under the *else* will be executed. Typically, user ids below 14 are for special users, such as *root, daemon, adm, lp,* etc. (See */etc/passwd*. The user id is in field number 3.)

13 If the test in the previous line returned a nonzero exit status, line 14 is executed, else line 15 is executed.

14 The *umask* sets the file creation mask; i.e., the initial permissions for files and directories when created. Directories will get 755 (rwxr-xr-x) and files will get 644 (*rw-r--r--*) when they are created.

15 *Umask* is set so that when a directory is created, its permissions will be 775 (*rwxrwxr-x*) and files will get 664 (*rw-rw-r--*).

EXPLANATION (CONTINUED)

16 The environment variable *HOSTNAME* is assigned the output of the */bin/hostname* command.

17 The *history* variable is set to 1000. When commands are typed at the command line, they are saved in a history list. When you set the history variable to 1000, no more than 1000 commands will be displayed when the *history* command is typed.

18 The *test* command returns zero exit status if the */etc/profile.d* directory exists, and nonzero if it doesn't.

19 If the status is 0, the directory exists, and the program branches to line 20.

20 The *nonomatch* variable is set to prevent the shell from sending an error message if any of its special metacharacters (*, ?, []) cannot be matched.

21 The *foreach* loop assigns each file, with a *.csh* extension (**.csh*) in the */etc/profile.d* directory, to the variable *i*, in turn, looping until each file has been tested (lines 22–24).

22 If the filename assigned to variable *i* is a regular file (*-f*), then go to the next line.

23 If the test returned a 0 status (true), then source the file; i.e., execute it in the context of the current environment.

24 The *end* keyword marks the end of the loop body.

The ~/.tcshrc File. The *.tcshrc* file contains *tcsh* variable settings and is executed every time a *tcsh* subshell is started. Aliases and history are normally set here.

EXAMPLE 10.3

```
# (The .tcshrc File)
1  if ( $?prompt ) then
2     set prompt = "\! stardust > "
3     set history = 100
4     set savehist = 5
5     set noclobber
6     set rmstar

7     set cdpath = ( /home/jody/ellie/bin /usr/local/bin /usr/bin )
8     set ignoreeof
9     alias m more
      alias status 'date;du -s'
      alias cd 'cd \!*;set prompt = "\! <$cwd> "'
10 endif
```

EXPLANATION

1 If the prompt has been set (*$?prompt*), the shell is running interactively; i.e., it is not running in a script. Prompts are set only for interactive shells.

2 The primary prompt is set to the number of the current history event, the name *stardust*, and a > character. This will change the > prompt, the default.

3 The *history* variable is set to *100*. This controls the number of history events that will appear on the screen. The last 100 commands you entered will be displayed when you type *history.* (See "History" on page 508.)

4 Normally, when you log out, the history list is cleared. The *savehist* variable allows you to save a specified number of commands from the end of the history list. In this example, the last five commands will be saved in a file in your home directory, the *.history* file, so that when you log in again, the shell can check to see if that file exists and put the history lines saved at the top of the new history list.

5 The *noclobber* variable is set to protect the user from inadvertently removing files when using redirection. For example, *sort myfile > myfile* will destroy *myfile*. With *noclobber* set, the message *"file exists"* will appear on the screen if you attempt to redirect output to an existing file.

6 If the *tcsh* variable, *rmstar*, is set, the user will be asked if he really wants to remove all his files after entering *rm* *; i.e., he is given a chance to save himself from removing all files in his current working directory.

7 The *cdpath* variable is assigned a list of path elements. When changing directories, if you specify just the directory name, and that directory is not a subdirectory directly below the current working directory, the shell will search the *cdpath* directory entries to see if it can find the directory in any of those locations and then will change the directory.

8 The *ignoreeof* variable prevents you from logging out with ^D (Control-D). Linux utilities that accept input from the keyboard, such as the *mail* program, are terminated by pressing ^D. Often, on a slow system, the user will be tempted to press ^D more than once. The first time, the *mail* program would be terminated; the second time, the user is logged out. By setting *ignoreeof*, you are required to type *logout* to log out.

9 The *aliases* are set to give a shorthand notation for a single command or group of commands. Now when you type the alias, the command(s) assigned to it will be executed. The alias for the *more* command is *m*. Every time you type *m*, the *more* command is executed. The *status* alias prints the date and a summary of the user's disk usage. The *cd* alias creates a new prompt every time the user changes directories. The new prompt will contain the number of the current history event (\!*) and the current working directory (*$cwd*) surrounded by < >. (See "Aliases" on page 537.)

10 The *endif* marks the end of the block of statements following the *if* construct on line 1.

The ~/.login File. The *.login* file is executed one time when you first log in. It normally contains environment variables and terminal settings. It is the file where window applications are usually started. Because environment variables are inherited by processes spawned from this shell and only need to be set once, and terminal settings do not have to be reset for every process, those settings belong in the *.login* file.

EXAMPLE 10.4

```
# (The .login File)
1   stty -istrip
2   stty erase ^h
3   stty kill ^u
    #
    # If possible start the windows system.
    # Give a user a chance to bail out
    #
4   if ( $TERM == "linux" ) then
5             echo "Starting X windows.  Press control C \
                   to exit within the next 5 seconds "
              sleep 5
6             startx
7   endif
8   set autologout=60
```

EXPLANATION

1. The *stty* command sets options for the terminal. Input characters will not be stripped to seven bits if *-istrip* is used.
2. The *stty* command sets Control-H, the Backspace key, to erase.
3. Any line beginning with # is a comment. It is not an executable statement.
4. If the current terminal window (*tty*) is the console (*linux*), the next line is executed; otherwise, program control goes to the last *endif.*
5. This line is echoed to the screen, and if the user does not press Control-C to kill the process, the program will sleep (pause) for five seconds, and then the *X* windows program will start.
6. The *startx* program launches *X* windows.
7. The *endif* marks the end of the innermost *if* construct.
8. The *autologout* variable is set to 60 so that after 60 minutes of inactivity, the user will automatically be logged out (from the login shell).

10.2.2 The Search Path

The *path* variable is used by the shell to locate commands typed at the command line. The search is from left to right. The dot represents the current working directory. If the command is not found in any of the directories listed in the path, or in the present working directory, the shell sends the message "*Command not found.*" to standard error. It is recommended that the path be set in the *.login* file.[4] The search path is set differently in the *tcshell* than it is in the *bash* and *Korn* shells. Each element is separated by white space in the *tcshell*, but separated by colons in the other shells.

The *tcshell* internally updates the environment variable for *PATH* to maintain compatibility with other programs, such as the Bash, Bourne, or Korn shells that may be started from this shell and will need to use the *path* variable.

EXAMPLE 10.5

```
# Path is set in the ~/.tcshrc file.

1   set path = (/usr/bin /bin /usr/bsd /usr/local/bin  .)

2   echo $path
    /usr/bin /bin /usr/bsd /usr/local/bin .

# The environment variable PATH will display as a colon-separated list

3   echo $PATH
    /usr/bin:/bin:/usr/bsd:/usr/local/bin:.
```

EXPLANATION

1 The search path is set for *tcsh*. It consists of a space separated list of directories searched from left to right by *tcsh* when a command is entered at the command line. The search path is local to the current shell. (See "Setting Local Variables" on page 567.)

2 The value of the *path* variable is displayed

3 The value of the environment variable, *PATH*, is displayed. It is a colon-separated list of the same directories as listed in the *path* variable, and is passed to other programs or applications invoked from the current shell. (*Bash*, *sh*, and *ksh* set the path as a colon-separated list.)

The *rehash* Command. The shell builds an internal hash table consisting of the contents of the directories listed in the search path. (If the dot is in the search path, the files in the dot directory, the current working directory, are not put in the hash table.) For efficiency,

4. Do not confuse the search path variable with the *cdpath* variable set in the *.cshrc* file.

the shell uses the hash table to find commands that are typed at the command line, rather than searching the path each time. If a new command is added to one of the directories already listed in the search path, the internal hash table must be recomputed. You do this by typing:

```
rehash
```

The hash table is also automatically recomputed when you change your path or start another shell.

The *hashstat* Command. The *hashstat* command displays performance statistics to show the effectiveness of its search for commands from the hash table. The statistics are in terms of "hits" and "misses." If the shell finds most of its commands you used at the end of your path, it has to work harder than if they were at the front of the path, resulting in a higher number of misses than hits. In such cases, you can put the most heavily hit directory toward the front of the path to improve performance.[5] The *unhash* built-in command disables the use of the internal hash table.

```
> hashstat
1024 hash buckets of 16 bits each
```

The *source* Command. The *source* command is a built-in shell command, that is, part of the shell's internal code. It is used to execute a command or set of commands from a file. Normally, when a command is executed, the shell forks a child process to execute the command, so that any changes made will not affect the original shell, called the parent shell. The *source* command causes the program to be executed in the current shell, so that any variables set within the file will become part of the environment of the current shell. The *source* command is normally used to reexecute the *.tcshrc*, *.cshrc* or *.login* if either has been modified. For example, if the *path* is changed after logging in, type

```
> source .login or source .tcshrc
```

10.2.3 The Shell Prompts

The TC shell has three prompts: the *primary* prompt (a > symbol), the *secondary* prompt (a question mark (*?*) followed by a *tcsh* command such as *while*, *foreach*, or *if*), and a third prompt used for the spelling correction feature. The primary prompt is the prompt that is displayed on the terminal after you have logged in. It can be reset. If you are writing scripts at the prompt that require *tcsh* programming constructs, for example, decision-making or looping, the secondary prompt will appear so that you can continue on to the next line. It will continue to appear after each newline, until the construct has been properly terminated. The third prompt appears to confirm automatic spelling correction if spelling correction is turned on. (See "Spelling Correction" on page 536.) It contains the string *CORRECT > corrected command (y|n|e|a)?*. The prompts can be customized by adding special formatting sequences to the prompt string. See Table 10.1.

---

5. On machines without vfork(2), prints the number and size of hash buckets.

Table 10.1 Prompt Strings

%/	The current working directory.
%~	The current working directory, where ~ represents the user's home directory and other users' home directories are represented by *~user.*
%c[[0]n], *%.[[0]n]*	The trailing component of the current working directory, or if *n* (a digit) is given, *n* trailing components.
%C	Like *%c*, but without ~ substitution.
%h, %!, !	The current history event number.
%M	The full hostname.
%m	The hostname up to the first ".".
%S (%s)	Start (stop) standout mode.
%B (%b)	Start (stop) boldfacing mode.
%U (%u)	Start (stop) underline mode.
%t, %@	The time of day in 12-hour AM/PM format.
%T	Like *%t*, but in 24-hour format.
%p	The "precise" time of day in 12-hour AM/PM format, with seconds.
%P	Like *%p*, but in 24-hour format.
^c	*c* is parsed as in bindkey.
\c	*c* is parsed as in bindkey.
%%	A single %.
%n	The user name.
%d	The weekday in "Day" format.
%D	The day in "dd" format.
%w	The month in "Mon" format.
%W	The month in "mm" format.
%y	The year in "yy" format.
%Y	The year in "yyyy" format.
%l	The shell's *tty.*

Table 10.1 Prompt Strings (Continued)

%L	Clears from the end of the prompt to the end of the display or the end of the line.
%$	Expands the shell or environment variable name immediately after the $.
%#	> (or the first character of the *promptchars* shell variable) for normal users, # (or the second character of *promptchars*) for the superuser.
%{string%}	Includes string as a literal escape sequence. It should be used only to change terminal attributes and should not move the cursor location. This cannot be the last sequence in *prompt*.
%?	The return code of the command executed just before the prompt.
%R	In *prompt2*, the status of the parser. In *prompt3*, the corrected string. In *history*, the history string.

The Primary Prompt. When running interactively, the prompt waits for you to type a command and press the Enter key. If you do not want to use the default prompt, reset it in the *.tcshrc* file and it will be set for this and all TC shells subsequently started. If you only want it set for this login session, set it at the shell prompt.

EXAMPLE 10.6

```
1   > set prompt = '[ %n@%m %c]# '
2   [ ellie@homebound ~]#  cd ..
3   [ ellie@homebound /home]#  cd ..
```

EXPLANATION

1 The primary prompt is assigned the user's login name (*%n*), followed by the host-name (*%m*), a space, and the current working directory. The string is enclosed in square brackets, followed by a #.

2 The new prompt is displayed. The ~ appearing in the prompt represents the user's home directory. The *cd* command changes directory to the parent directory.

3 The new prompt indicates the current working directory, */home*. In this way the user always know what directory he is in.

The Secondary Prompt. The secondary prompt appears when you are writing online scripts at the prompt. The secondary prompt can be changed. Whenever shell programming constructs are entered, followed by a newline, the secondary prompt appears and continues to appear until the construct is properly terminated. Writing scripts correctly at the prompt takes practice. Once the command is entered and you press Enter, you cannot back up, and the *tcsh* history mechanism does not save commands typed at the secondary prompt.

EXAMPLE 10.7

```
1    > foreach pal (joe tom ann)
2    foreach? echo Hi $pal
3    foreach? end
     Hi joe
     Hi tom
     Hi ann
4    >
```

EXPLANATION

1 This is an example of online scripting. Because the TC shell is expecting further input after the *foreach* loop is entered, the secondary prompt appears. The *foreach* loop processes each word in the parenthesized list.

2 The first time in the loop, *joe* is assigned to the variable *pal*. The user *joe* is sent the contents of *memo* in the mail. Then next time through the loop, *tom* is assigned to the variable *pal*, and so on.

3 The *end* statement marks the end of the loop. When all of the items in the parenthesized list have been processed, the loop ends and the primary prompt is displayed.

4 The primary prompt is displayed.

EXAMPLE 10.8

```
> set prompt2='%R %% '
> foreach name ( joe tom ann )
foreach % echo Hi $name
foreach % end
Hi joe
Hi tom
Hi ann
>
```

EXPLANATION

1 The secondary prompt, *prompt2*, is reset to the formatted string where *%R* is the name of the conditional or looping construct entered in line 2 at the primary prompt. The two percent signs will evaluate to one percent sign.

2 The *foreach* command has been started. This is a looping construct that must end with the keyword *end*. The secondary prompt will continue to appear until the loop is properly terminated.

3 The secondary prompt is *foreach %*.

4 After the *end* keyword is typed, the loop executes.

5 The primary prompt reappears awaiting user input.

10.2.4 The Command Line

After logging in, the TC shell displays its primary prompt, by default a > symbol. The shell is your command interpreter. When the shell is running interactively, it reads commands from the terminal and breaks the command line into words. A command line consists of one or more words (or tokens) separated by white space (blanks and/or tabs) and terminated by a newline, generated by pressing the Enter key. The first word is the command, and subsequent words are the command's options and/or arguments. The command may be a Linux executable program such as *ls* or *pwd*, an alias, a built-in command such as *cd* or *jobs*, or a shell script. The command may contain special characters, called *metacharacters,* that the shell must interpret while parsing the command line. If the last character in the command line is a backslash, followed by a newline, the line can be continued to the next line.[6]

Exit Status and the *printexitvalue* Variable. After a command or program terminates, it returns an *exit status* to the parent process. The exit status is a number between 0 and 255. By convention, when a program exits, if the status returned is zero, the program was successful in its execution. When the exit status is nonzero, then it failed in some way. If the program terminated abnormally, then 0200 is added to the status. Built-in commands that fail, return an exit status of 1; otherwise, they return a status of 0.

The *tcsh status* variable or *?* variable is set to the value of the exit status of the last command that was executed. Success or failure of a program is determined by the programmer who wrote the program. By setting the *tcsh* variable, *printexitvalue*, any time a program exits with a value other than zero, its status will automatically be printed.

6. The length of the command line can be at least 256 characters.

EXAMPLE 10.9

```
1 > grep "ellie" /etc/passwd
    ellie:GgMyBsSJavd16s:501:40:E Quigley:/home/jody/ellie:/bin/tcsh
2 > echo $status   or echo $?
    0
3 > grep "nicky" /etc/passwd
4 > echo $status
    1
5 > grep "scott" /etc/passsswd
    grep: /etc/passsswd: No such file or directory
6 > echo $status
    2
7 > set printexitvalue
  > grep "XXX" /etc/passwd
  Exit 1
  >
```

EXPLANATION

1. The *grep* program searches for the pattern "*ellie*" in the */etc/passwd* file and is successful. The line from */etc/passwd* is displayed.
2. The *status* variable is set to the exit value of the *grep* command; *0* indicates success. The *?* variable also holds the exit status. This is the variable used by the *bash* and *ksh* shells for checking exit status. (It is not used by *csh.*)
3. The *grep* program cannot find user *nicky* in the */etc/passwd* file.
4. The *grep* program cannot find the pattern, so it returns an exit status of *1.*
5. The *grep* fails because the file */etc/passsswd* cannot be opened.
6. *Grep* cannot find the file, so it returns an exit status of *2.*
7. The special *tcsh* variable *printexitvalue* is set. It will automatically print the exit value of any command that exits with a nonzero value.

Command Grouping. A command line can consist of multiple commands. Each command is separated by a semicolon and the command line is terminated with a newline.

EXAMPLE 10.10

```
> ls; pwd; cal 2000
```

EXPLANATION

The commands are executed from left to right until the newline is reached.

Commands may also be grouped so that all of the output is either piped to another command or redirected to a file. The shell executes commands in a subshell.

EXAMPLE 10.11

```
1   > ( ls ; pwd; cal 2000 ) > outputfile
2   > pwd; ( cd / ; pwd ) ; pwd
    /home/jody/ellie
    /
    /home/jody/ellie
```

EXPLANATION

1. The output of each of the commands is sent to the file called *outputfile*. Without the parentheses, the output of the first two commands would go to the screen, and only the output of the *cal* command would be redirected to the output file.
2. The *pwd* command displays the present working directory. The parentheses cause the commands enclosed within them to be processed by a subshell. The *cd* command is built-in to the shell. While in the subshell, the directory is changed to *root* and the present working directory is displayed. When out of the subshell, the present working directory of the original shell is displayed.

Conditional Execution of Commands. With conditional execution, two command strings are separated by two special metacharacters, two ampersands, or double vertical lines. The command on the right of either of these metacharacters will or will not be executed based on the exit condition of the command on the left.

EXAMPLE 10.12

```
> grep '^tom:' /etc/passwd && mail tom < letter
```

EXPLANATION

If the first command is successful (has a zero exit status), the second command after the *&&* is executed. If the *grep* command successfully finds *tom* in the *passwd* file, the command on the right will be executed: The *mail* program will send *tom* the contents of the *letter* file.

EXAMPLE 10.13

```
> grep '^tom:' /etc/passwd || echo "tom is not a user here."
```

EXPLANATION

If the first command fails (has a nonzero exit status), the second command after the || is executed. If the *grep* command does not find *tom* in the *passwd* file, the command on the right will be executed: The *echo* program will print *"tom is not a user here"* to the screen.

Commands in the Background. Normally, when you execute a command, it runs in the foreground, and the prompt does not reappear until the command has completed execution. It is not always convenient to wait for the command to complete. When you place an ampersand at the end of the command line, the shell prompt will return immediately so that you do not have to wait for the last command to complete before starting another one. The command running in the background is called a *background job* and its output will be sent to the screen as it processes. It can be confusing if two commands are sending output to the screen concurrently. To avoid confusion, you can send the output of the job running in the background to a file or pipe it to another device such as a printer. It is often handy to start a new shell window in the background. Then you will have access to both the window from which you started and the new shell window.

EXAMPLE 10.14

```
1   > man tcsh | lpr &
2   [1] 4664
3   >
```

EXPLANATION

1 The output from the *man* pages for the *tcsh* program is piped to the printer. The ampersand at the end of the command line puts the job in the background.

2 There are two numbers that appear on the screen: the number in square brackets indicates that this is the first job to be placed in the background; the second number is the PID of this job.

3 The shell prompt appears immediately. While your program is running in the background, the shell is prompting you for another command in the foreground.

10.3 Command Line Shortcuts

10.3.1 History

The history mechanism is built into the TC shell. It keeps in memory a sequentially numbered list of the commands, called *events*, that you have typed at the command line. As well as the number of the history event, it also keeps track of the time the event was entered at the terminal. When the shell reads a command from the terminal, it breaks the command line into words (using white space to designate a word break), saves the line to the history list, parses it, and then executes it. The previous command typed is always saved. You can recall a command at any time from the history list and reexecute it without retyping the command. During a login session, the commands you type are appended to the history list until you exit, at which time they can be saved in a file in your home directory, called *.history*[7]. The terms history list and history file can be somewhat confusing. The history list consists of the command lines currently held in the shell's memory. The history file, normally called *.history*, is the text file where those commands are saved for future use. The built-in variable, *savehist*, saves the history list to the *.history* file when you log out, and loads its contents into memory when you start up. (See *-S* and *-L* options to the *history* command in Table 10.2.) The *history* built-in command displays the history list. It supports a number of arguments to control how the history is displayed.

Table 10.2 The *history* Command and Options

Option	*Meaning*
-h	Prints history list without numbers.
-T	Prints timestamps in comment form.
-r	Prints history list in reverse.
-S [filename]	Saves history list to *.history or filename* if given.
-L [filename]	Appends history file (*.history* or *filename*) to the history list.
-M [filename]	Like *-L*, except merges contents of history file with current history list.
-c	Clears the history list in memory, not the history file.
n	*n* is a number, e.g., *history 5*, controlling the number of lines displayed.

7. The name of the *.history* file can be changed by assigning the new name to the *histfile* shell variable.

Although the default name for the history file is *.history,* its name can be changed by assigning an alternative name to the built-in shell variable, *histfile*. The *history* shell variable is set to a number specifying how many commands to display and the *histdup* variable can be set so that duplicate entries are not added to the history file.

EXAMPLE 10.15

```
(The Command Line)
> history
1 17:12    cd
2 17:13    ls
3 17:13    more /etc/fstab
4 17:24    /etc/mount
5 17:54    sort index
6 17:56    vi index
```

EXPLANATION

The history list displays the last commands that were typed at the command line. Each event in the list is preceded with a number (called an event number) and the time that it was entered at the command line.

The *history* Variable. The TC shell *history* variable can be set to the number of events from the history list that will be displayed on the terminal. Normally, this is set in the */etc/.cshrc* or *~/.tcshrc* file, the user's initialization file. It is set to 100 by default. You can also provide an optional second value for the history variable to control the way the history is formatted. This value uses the same formatting sequences as the prompt variable. (See Table 10.1.) The default format string for history is: *%h\t%T\t%R\n*.

EXAMPLE 10.16

```
1   set history=1000

2   set history= ( 1000 '%B%h %R\n' )

3   history
    136 history
    137 set history = ( 1000 '%B%h %R\n' )
    138 history
    139 ls
    140 pwd
    141 cal
    141 pwd
    142 cd
```

EXPLANATION

1 The last 1000 commands typed at the terminal can be displayed on the screen by typing the *history* command.

2 The last 1000 commands typed at the terminal are displayed. The format string causes the history list to be displayed in bold text (*%B*) first with the event number (*%h*), then a space, and finally the command that was typed (*%R*) at the command line followed by a newline (*\n*).

3 When you type *history*, the new format is shown. This is only a selected section of the real history list.

Saving History and the *savehist* Variable. To save history events across logins, set the *savehist* variable. This variable is normally set in the *.tcshrc* file, the user's initialization file. If the first value assigned to *savehist* is a number, it cannot exceed the number set in the *history* variable, if the *history* variable is set. If the second value is set to *merge*, the history list is merged with the existing history file instead of replacing it. It is sorted by timestamp, and the most recent events saved.

EXAMPLE 10.17

```
1   set savehist
2   set savehist = 1000
3   set savehist = 1000 merge
```

EXPLANATION

1 The commands from the history list are saved in the history file and will be at the top of the history list the next time you log in.

2 The history file is replaced with the last 1000 commands from the history list, and saved. It will be displayed when you next log in.

3 Rather than replacing the existing history file, the current history list will be merged with the existing history file when you log out, and loaded into memory after you log in.

Displaying History. The *history* command displays the events in the history list. The history command also has options that control the number of events and the format of the events that will be displayed. The numbering of events does not necessarily start at one. If you have 100 commands on the history list, and you have set the history variable to 25, you will only see the last 25 commands saved.

EXAMPLE 10.18

```
1    > set history = 10
2    > history
     1 ls
     2 vi file1
     3 df
     4 ps -eaf
     5 history
     6 more /etc/passwd
     7 cd
     8 echo $USER
     9 set
     10 ls
```

EXPLANATION

1. The history variable is set to 10. Only the last 10 lines of the history list will be displayed, even if there may be many more.
2. The last 10 events from the history are displayed. Each command is numbered.

EXAMPLE 10.19

```
1    > history -h          print without line numbers
     ls
     vi file1
     df
     ps -eaf
     history
     more /etc/passwd
     cd
     echo $USER
     set
     history -n

2    > history -c
```

EXPLANATION

1. With the *h* option, the history list is displayed without line numbers.
2. With the *c* option, the history list is cleared.

EXAMPLE 10.20

```
> history -r        # print the history list in reverse
11 history -r
10 history -h
 9 set
 8 echo $USER
 7 cd
 6 more /etc/passwd
 5 history
 4 ps -eaf
 3 df
 2 vi file1
 1 ls
```

EXPLANATION

The history list is displayed in reverse order.

EXAMPLE 10.21

```
> history 5         # prints the last 5 events on the history list
7   echo $USER
8   cd
9   set
10  history -n
11  history 5
```

EXPLANATION

The last five commands on the history list are executed.

Accessing Commands from the History File. There are several ways to access and repeat commands from the history list. You can use the arrow keys to scroll up and down the history list, and to move left and right across lines, editing as you go; you can use a mechanism called history substitution to reexecute and fix spelling mistakes; or you can use the built-in *emacs* or *vi* editors to retrieve, edit, and execute previous commands. We'll step through each of these procedures and then you can choose whatever way works best for you.

1. **The Arrow Keys**
   To access commands from the history list, you can use the arrow keys on the keyboard to move up and down through the history list, and from left to right You can edit any of the lines in the history list by using the standard keys for deleting, backspacing, etc. As soon as you have edited the line, pressing the carriage return (Enter key) will cause the command line to be reexecute. You can also use stan-

dard *emacs* or *vi* commands to edit the history list. (See Table 10.5 on page 518 and Table 10.6 on page 519). The arrow keys behave the same way for both the *vi* and *emacs* keybindings. (See Table 10.3.)

Table 10.3 The Arrow Keys

↑	Up arrow moves up the history list.
↓	Down arrow moves down the history list.
→	Right arrow moves cursor to right of history command.
←	Left arrow moves cursor to left of history command.

2. **Reexecuting and Bang! Bang!**
To reexecute a command from the history list, use the exclamation point (bang) to start history substitution. The exclamation point can begin anywhere on the line and can be escaped with a backslash. If the *!* is followed by a space, tab, or newline, it will not be interpreted. There are a number of ways to use history substitution to designate what part of the history list you want to redo. (See Table 10.4 on page 516.) If you type two exclamation points (*!!*), the last command is reexecuted. If you type the exclamation point followed by a number, the number is associated with the command from the history list and the command is executed. If you type an exclamation point and a letter, the last command that started with that letter is executed. The caret (^) is also used as a shortcut method for editing the previous command.

    After history substitution is performed, the history list is updated with the results of the substitution shown in the command. For example, if you type *!!* the last command will be reexecuted and saved in the history list in its expanded form. If you want the last command to be added to the history list in its literal form; i.e., *!!*, then set the *histlit* shell variable.

EXAMPLE 10.22

```
1   > date
    Mon Feb  8 12:27:35 PST 2000

2   > !!
    date
    Mon Aug  10 12:28:25 PST 2000

3   > !3
    date
    Mon Aug  10 12:29:26 PST 2000

4   > !d
    date
    Mon Aug  10 12:30:09 PST 2000
```

EXAMPLE 10.22 (CONTINUED)

```
5   > dare
    dare: Command not found.

6   > ^r^t
    date
    Mon Apr  10 16:15:25 PDT 2000

7   > history
    1 16:16  ls
    2 16:16  date
    3 16:17  date
    4 16:18  date
    5 16:18  dare
    6 16:18  date

8   > set histlit

9   > history
    1 16:18  ls
    2 16:19  date
    3 16:19  !!
    4 16:20  !3
    5 16:21  dare
    6 16:21  ^r^t
```

EXPLANATION

1 The Linux *date* command is executed at the command line. The history list is updated. This is the last command on the list.

2 The *!!* (bang bang) gets the last command from the history list; the command is reexecuted.

3 The third command on the history list is reexecuted.

4 The last command on the history list that started with the letter *d* is reexecuted.

5 The command is mistyped.

6 The carets are used to substitute letters from the last command on the history list. The first occurrence of an *r* is replaced with a *t*.

7 The *history* command displays the history list, after history substitution has been performed.

8 By setting *histlit,* the shell will perform history substitution, but will put the literal command typed, on the history list; i.e., just as it was typed.

9 When *histlit* is set, the output of the *history* command shows what commands were literally typed before history substitution took place. (This is just a demo; the history numbers are not accurate.)

EXAMPLE 10.23

```
1   % cat file1 file2 file3

       <Contents of files displayed here>

    > vi !:1
     vi file1

2   > cat file1 file2 file3

    <Contents of file, file2, and file3 are displayed here>

    > ls !:2
     ls file2
     file2

3   > cat file1 file2 file3
    > ls  !:3
     ls file3
     file3

4   > echo a b c
     a b c
    > echo !$
     echo c
     c

5   > echo a b c
     a b c
    > echo !^
     echo a
     a

6   > echo a b c
     a b c
    > echo !*
     echo a b c
     a b c

7   > !!:p
    echo a b c
```

EXPLANATION

1 The *cat* command displays the contents of *file1* to the screen. The history list is updated. The command line is broken into words, starting with word number zero. If the word number is preceded by a colon, that word can be extracted from the history list. The *!:1* notation means "*get the first argument from the last command on the history list and replace it in the command string.*" The first argument from the last command is *file1*. (Word *0* is the command itself.)

2 The *!:2* is replaced with the second argument of the last command, *file2*, and given as an argument to *ls*. *File2* is printed. (*File2* is the third word.)

3 *ls !:3* reads "*go to the last command on the history list and get the fourth word (words start at zero) and pass it to the* ls *command as an argument.*" (*File3* is the fourth word.)

4 The bang (*!*) with the dollar sign (*$*) refers to the last argument of the last command on the history list. The last argument is *c*.

5 The caret (^) represents the first argument after the command. The bang (*!*) with the ^ refers to the first argument of the last command on the history list. The first argument of the last command is *a*.

6 The asterisk (*) represents all arguments after the command. The bang (*!*) with the * refers to all of the arguments of the last command on the history list.

7 The last command from the history list is printed but not executed. The history list is updated. You could now perform caret substitutions on that line.

Table 10.4 Substitution and History

Event Designators	*Meaning*
!	Indicates the start of history substitution.
!!	Reexecutes the previous command.
!N	Reexecutes the *N*th command from the history list.
!-N	Reexecutes the *N*th command back from present command.
!string	Reexecutes the last command starting with *string*.
!?string?	Reexecutes the last command containing *string*.
!?string?%	Reexecutes the most recent command line argument from the history list containing *string*.
*!^*	Uses the first argument of the last history command in the current command line.
*!**	Uses all of the arguments from the last history command in the current command line.

Table 10.4 Substitution and History (Continued)

Event Designators	*Meaning*
!$	Uses the last argument from the last history command in the current command line.
!! string	Appends string to the previous command and executes.
!N string	Appends string to *N*th command in history list and executes.
!N:s/old/new/	In previous *N*th command, substitutes the first occurrence of old string with new string.
!N:gs/old/new/	In previous *N*th command, globally substitutes old string with new string.
*^old^new^*	In last history command, substitutes old string with new string.
command !N:wn	Executes current command appending an argument (*wn*) from the *N*th previous command. *wn* is a number starting at 0, 1, 2, ... designating the number of the word from the previous command; word 0 is the command itself, and 1 is its first argument, etc.
!N:p	Puts the command at the bottom of the history list and prints it, but doesn't execute it.

10.3.2 The Built-In Command Line Editors

The command line can be edited by using the same type of key sequences that you use in either the *emacs* or *vi* editors. You can use editor commands to scroll up and down the history list. Once the command is found, it can be edited, and by pressing the Enter key, reexecuted. When the shell was compiled, it was given a default set of keybindings for the *emacs* editor.

The *bindkey* Built-In Command. The built-in *bindkey* command is used to select either *vi* or *emacs* for command line editing and to list and set key bindings for the respective editors. To use *vi* as your command line editor, use *bindkey* with the *-v* option:

```
bindkey -v
```

and to go back to *emacs:*

```
bindkey -e
```

To see a list of editor commands and a short description of what each does, type:

```
bindkey -l
```

And to see the actual keys and how they are bound, type:

```
bindkey
```

To actually bind keys to commands, see "Binding Keys" on page 520.

The *vi* Built-In Editor. To edit the history list, go to the command line and press the ESC key. Then press the K key if you want to scroll upward in the history list, and the J key to move downward, just like standard *vi* motion keys. When you find the command that you want to edit, use the standard keys that you would use in *vi* for moving left and right, deleting, inserting, and changing text. See Table 10.5. After making the edit, press the Enter key. The command will be executed and added to the bottom of the history list. If you want to add or insert text, then use any of the insertion commands (*i, e, o, O*, etc.). Remember, *vi* has two modes: the command mode and the insert mode. You are always in the insert mode when you are actually typing text. To get back to the command mode, press the Escape key (ESC).

Table 10.5 *vi* Commands

Command	***Function***
Moving Through the History File	
ESC k *or* +	Move up the history list.
ESC j *or* -	Move down the history list.
G	Move to first line in history file.
5G	Move to fifth command in history file.
/string	Search upward through history file.
?	String search downward through history file.
Moving Around on a Line	
h	Move left on a line.
l	Move right on a line.
b	Move backward a word.
e *or* w	Move forward a word.
^ *or* 0	Move to beginning of first character on the line.
$	Move to end of line.
Editing with vi	
a A	Append text.
i I	Insert text.
dd dw x	Delete text into a buffer (line, word, or character).
cc C	Change text.
u U	Undo.
yy Y	Yank (copy a line into buffer).
p P	Put yanked or deleted line down below or above the line.
r R	Replace a letter or any amount of text on a line.

The *emacs* Built-In Editor. If you are using the *emacs* built-in editor, like *vi*, start at the command line. To start moving upward through the history file, press ^P. To move down, press ^N . Use *emacs* editing commands to change or correct text, then press Enter, and the command will be reexecuted. See Table 10.6.

Table 10.6 *emacs* Commands

Command	***Function***
Ctrl-P	Move up history file.
Ctrl-N	Move down history file.
ESC <	Move to first line of history file.
ESC >	Move to last line of history file.
Ctrl-B	Move backward one character.
Ctrl-R	Search backward for string.
ESC B	Move back one word.
Ctrl-F	Move forward one character.
ESC F	Move forward one word.
Ctrl-A	Move to the beginning of the line.
Ctrl-E	Move to the end of the line.
ESC <	Move to the first line of the history file.
ESC >	Move to the last line of the history file.
Editing with emacs	
Ctrl-U	Delete the line.
Ctrl-Y	Put the line back.
Ctrl-K	Delete from cursor to the end line.
Ctrl-D	Delete a letter.
ESC D	Delete one word forward.
ESC H	Delete one word backward.
ESC space	Set a mark at cursor position.
Ctrl-X Ctrl-X	Exchange cursor and mark.
Ctrl-P Ctrl-Y	Push region from cursor to mark into a buffer (Ctrl-P) and put it down (Ctrl-Y).

Binding Keys. The *bindkey* built-in command lists all the standard keybindings including keybindings for *emacs* and *vi.* The keybindings are divided up into four groups: the standard key bindings, alternative key bindings, multicharacter key bindings, and the arrow key bindings. The *bindkey* command also allows you to change the current bindings of keys.

EXAMPLE 10.24

```
1   > bindkey
    Standard key bindings
    "^@"             ->  is undefined
    "^A"             ->  beginning-of-line
    "^B"             ->  backward-char
    "^C"             ->  tty-sigintr
    "^D"             ->  list-or-eof
    "^E"             ->  end-of-line
    "^F"             ->  forward-char
    "^L"             ->  clear-screen
    "^M"             ->  newline
              ...     ....
    Alternative key bindings
    "^@"             ->  is undefined
    "^A"             ->  beginning-of-line
    "^B"             ->  is undefined
    "^C"             ->  tty-sigintr
    "^D"             ->  list-choices
    "^E"             ->  end-of-line
    "^F"             ->  is undefined
         ......  .....
    Multi-character bindings
    "^[[A"           -> up-history
    "^[[B"           -> down-history
    "^[[C"           -> forward-char
    "^[[D"           -> backward-char
    "^[OA"           -> up-history
    "^[OB"           -> down-history
         ...   ....
    Arrow key bindings
    down             -> down-history
    up               -> up-history
    left             -> backward-char
    right            -> forward-char
```

The *-l* option to *bindkey* lists the editor commands and what they do. See Example 10.25.

EXAMPLE 10.25

```
> bindkey -l

backward-char
          Move back a character
backward-delete-char
          Delete the character behind cursor
backward-delete-word
          Cut from beginning of current word to cursor - saved in cut
          buffer
backward-kill-line
          Cut from beginning of line to cursor - save in cut buffer
backward-word
          Move to beginning of current word
beginning-of-line
          Move to beginning of line
capitalize-word
          Capitalize the characters from cursor to end of current
          word
change-case
          Vi change case of character under cursor and advance one
          character
change-till-end-of-line
          Vi change to end of line
clear-screen
Standard key bindings
          .....    ...
```

The *bindkey* command can also display the values for individual key bindings as shown in Example 10.26. The *emacs* mappings are shown by default, but with the *-a* option to *bindkey*, the alternate mappings for *vi* keys are displayed. The arguments to *bindkey* are specified as a sequence of special characters to represent the key sequences followed by the editing command key to which the key will be bound. You can bind keys not only to *emacs* or *vi* editor commands, but also to Linux commands and strings.

Table 10.7 Keybinding Characters

Characters	*Meaning*
^C	Control-C
^[	ESC
^?	DEL
\a	Control-G (bell)
\b	Control-H (backspace)

Table 10.7 Keybinding Characters (Continued)

Characters	*Meaning*
\e	ESC (escape)
\f	Formfeed
\n	Newline
\r	Return
\t	Tab
\v	Control-K (vertical tab)
\nnn	ASCII octal number

EXAMPLE 10.26

```
1   > bindkey ^L
    "^L"      ->     clear-screen

2   > bindkey ^C
    "^C"      ->     tty-sigintr

3   > bindkey "j"
    "j"       ->     self-insert-command

4   > bindkey -v

5   > bindkey -a "j"
    "j"       ->     down-history
```

EXPLANATION

1 The *bindkey* command with a Control key (^L) displays to what command the control key is bound. ^L causes the screen to be cleared.

2 Control-C (^C) is bound to the interrupt signal, which normally terminates a process.

3 Lowercase "j" is an *emacs* self-insert-command which does nothing but insert that letter into the buffer.

4 In order to see the alternate *vi* key bindings, be sure you have set the *vi* command line editor with: *bindkey -v* as shown here.

5 With the *-a* option, *bindkey* displays the alternate key mapping for "j"; i.e., the *vi* key for moving down the history list.

EXAMPLE 10.27

```
1   > bindkey "^T" clear-screen

2   > bindkey "^T"
    "^T"       ->     clear-screen

3   > bindkey -a "^T"
    "^T"       ->     undefined-key

4   > bindkey -a  [Control-v Control t] clear-screen
         Press keys one after the other

5   > bindkey -a [Control-v Control t]
    "^T"        ->     clear-screen

6   > bindkey -s '\ehi'  'Hello to you!\n'
    > echo [Esc]hi    Press escape followed by 'h' and 'i'
      Hello to you!
    >
7   > bindkey '^[hi'
    "^[hi"     ->   "Hello to you!"

8   > bindkey -r '\[hi'

9   > bindkey '\ehi'
    Unbound extended key "^[hi"

10  > bindkey -c '\ex' 'ls | more'
```

EXPLANATION

1 Control-T is bound to the command to clear the screen, a default *emacs* key mapping. This key sequence was not originally bound to anything. Now when the Control and T keys are pressed together, the screen will be cleared.

2 The *bindkey* command, with the key sequence as an argument, will display the mapping for that sequence, if there is one.

3 With the *-a* option and a key sequence, *bindkey* displays the value of the alternate key map, *vi*. In this example, *bindkey* with the *-a* option and the key sequence shows that the alternate mapping (*vi*) does not have this sequence bound to anything.

4 With the *-a* option, *bindkey* can bind keys to the alternate key map, *vi*. By pressing Control-V followed by Control-T, the key sequence is created and assigned the value *clear-screen*. Control-V/Control-T can also be represented as *"^T"* as shown in the previous example.

5 The *bindkey* function displays the alternate mapping for ^T and its command.

EXPLANATION (CONTINUED)

6 With the *-s* command, *bindkey* will bind a literal string to a key sequence. Here the string *"Hello to you!\n"* is bound to the escape sequence *hi*. By pressing the ESC key and then an *h* and an *i*, the string will be sent to standard output.

7 The *bindkey* command displays the binding for the escape sequence *hi*. The *^[* is another way to represent ESC (escape).

8 With the *-r* option, *bindkey* removes a key binding.

9 Because the key binding was removed, the output says that this extended key sequence is not bound.

10 With the *-c* option, *bindkey* can bind a key sequence to a Linux command. In this example, pressing the Escape key, followed by the "x" key will cause the command *ls* to be piped to *more*.

Table 10.8 *bindkey* Options

bindkey	***Lists All Key Bindings***
bindkey -a	Allow alternate key mapping.
bindkey -d	Restore default bindings.
bindkey -e	Use *emacs* bindings.
bindkey -l	Display all editing commands and what they mean.
bindkey -u	Display usage message.
bindkey -v	Use *vi* key bindings.
bindkey *key*	Display binding for *key*.
bindkey *key* command	Bind *key* to *emacs* or *vi* command.
bindkey -c *key command*	Bind *key* to UNIX/Linux *command*.
bindkey -s *key* string	Bind *key* to string.
bindkey -r *key*	Remove *key* binding.

10.3.3 Command, Filename, and Variable Completion

To save typing, *tcsh* has a mechanism called *completion* that allows you to type part of a command, filename, or variable, and then by pressing the Tab key, have the rest of the word completed for you.

If you type the first few letters of a command, and press the Tab key, *tcsh* will attempt to complete the command name. If *tcsh* cannot complete the command, because it doesn't exist, the terminal will beep and the cursor will stay at the end of the command. If there is more than one command starting with those characters, by pressing Control-D, all commands that start with those characters will be listed.

Filename and variable completion work the same as command completion. With filename completion, if there are several files starting with the same letters, *tcsh* will complete the shortest name that matches, expand out the filename until the characters differ, and then flash the cursor for you to complete the rest. See Example 10.28.

The *autolist* Variable. If the *autolist* variable is set, and there are a number of possible completions, all of the possible commands, variables, or filenames will be listed depending on what type of completion is being performed when the tab key is entered.

EXAMPLE 10.28

```
1   > ls
    file1 file2 foo foobarckle fumble

2   > ls fu[tab]          expands to filename to fumble

3   > ls fx[tab]          terminal beeps, nothing happens

4   > ls fi[tab]          expands to file_  (_ is a cursor)

5   > set autolist

6   > ls f[tab]           lists all possibilities
    file1 file2 foo foobarckle fumble

7   > ls foob[tab]        expands to foobarckle

8   > da[tab]             completes the date command
    date
    Fri Aug 9 21:15:38 PDT 2000

9   > ca[tab]             lists all commands starting with ca
    cal    captoinfo  case   cat

10  > echo $ho[tab]me     expands shell variables
    /home/ellie/

11  > echo $h[tab]
    history home
```

EXPLANATION

1. All files are listed for the current working directory.
2. After *fu* is typed, the Tab key is pressed, causing the filename to be completed to *fumble*, and listed.

EXPLANATION (CONTINUED)

3 Because none of the files start with *fx*, the terminal beeps and the cursor remains but does nothing.

4 There are a number of files starting with *fi*; the filenames are completed until the letters are no longer the same. When you press Control-D, all files with that spelling are listed.

5 The *autolist* variable is set. If there are a number of choices, when you press the Tab key, *autolist* displays all the possibilities.

6 After you press the Tab key, a list of all files beginning with *f* are printed.

7 When the Tab key is pressed, the filename is expanded to *foobarckle*.

8 When the Tab key is pressed after *da*, the only command that begins with *da* is the *date* command. The command name is expanded and executed.

9 Because *autolist* is set, when the Tab key is pressed after *ca*, all commands starting with *ca* are listed. If *autolist* is not set, type Control-D to get a list.

10 The leading *$* on a word indicates that the shell should perform variable expansion when the Tab key is pressed to complete the word. The variable *home* is completed.

11 Variable completion is ambiguous in this example. When completion is attempted by pressing the Tab key, all possible shell variables are listed.

The *fignore* Variable. The shell variable, *fignore*, can be set to ignore certain filename extensions when filename completion is in use. For example, you may not want to expand files that end in *.o* because they are unreadable object files. Or maybe you don't want the *.gif* files to be accidently removed when filenames are expanded. For whatever reason, the *fignore* variable can be assigned a list of extensions for files that will be excluded from filename expansion.

EXAMPLE 10.29

```
1   > ls
    baby         box.gif    file2     prog.c
    baby.gif     file1      file3     prog.o

2   > set fignore = (.o .gif )

3   > echo ba[tab]     Completes baby but ignores baby.gif
    baby

4   > echo box[tab].gif     fignore is ignored if only one completion
    box.gif                             is possible

5   > vi prog[tab]            expands to prog.c
    Starts vi with prog.c as its argument
```

EXPLANATION

1 The files in the current working directory are listed. Note that some of the files have extensions on their names.

2 The *fignore* variable allows you to list those filename extensions that should be ignored when filename completion is performed. All filenames ending in either *.o* or *.gif* will be ignored.

3 By pressing the Tab key, only the file, *baby*, is listed, not *baby.gif*. The *.gif* files are ignored.

4 Even though *.gif* is listed as a suffix to be ignored, *fignore* will not take effect when there are no other possible completions, such as the same filename without the *.gif* extension as in line 3.

5 When the *vi* editor is invoked, *prog* is expanded to *prog.c*.

The *complete* Shell Variable. This is a variable that does a lot! It is a little tricky trying to decipher all it can do from the *tcsh* man page, but you may find some of these examples helpful for a start. You can control what kind of completion you are doing. For example maybe you only want completion to expand directory names, or a filename depending on its position in the command line, or maybe you would like certain commands to be expanded and others excluded, or even create a list of possible words that can be expanded. Whatever it is you want to do with completion, no doubt, the *complete* shell variable will accommodate you.

Filename completion can be even more sophisticated if the *complete* shell variable is set to *enchance*. This causes tab completion to ignore case; to treat hyphens, periods, and underscores as word separators; and to consider hyphens and underscores as equivalent.

EXAMPLE 10.30

```
1   > set complete=enchance

2   > ls g..[tab]    expands to gawk-3.0.3
    gawk-3.0.3

3   > ls GAW[tab]    expands to gawk-3.0.3
    gawk-3.0.3
```

EXPLANATION

1 By setting the *complete* shell variable to *enchance*, tab completion will ignore case; will treat hyphens, periods, and underscores as word separators; and will consider hyphens and underscores as equivalent.

EXPLANATION (CONTINUED)

2 With *enhance* set, filename completion expands *g..* to any files starting with a *g*, followed by any two characters (..), and any characters to complete the filename, including hyphens, periods, etc.

3 With *enhance* set, filename completion expands *GAW* to any files starting with *GAW*, where *GAW* can be any combination of upper and lowercase letters, and the remaining characters can be any characters even if they contain hyphens, periods, and underscores.

Programming Completions. To customize completions to a more specific functionality, you can program the completions, and then store them in the *~/.tcshrc* file, making them part of your *tcsh* environment each time you start a new TC shell. The purpose of programming completions is to improve efficiency and select types of commands and arguments that will be affected. (The Tab key for word completion, and Control-D to list possible completions still work the same way as they did for simple completions.)

Types of Completions. There three types of completions: *p, n,* and *c*. A *p*-type completion is position-dependent. It rules the way a completion is performed based on the *position* of a word in the command line, where position 0 is the command, position 1 is the first argument, position 2, the second argument, etc. Suppose, for example, you wanted to guarantee that any time a completion is performed for the built-in *cd* command, the first (and only) argument to *cd* is completed only if it is a directory name, nothing else; then you can program the completion as shown in the following example:

```
complete  cd   'p/1/d/'
```

The *complete* command is followed by the *cd* command and what is called the completion *rule*. The *p* stands for the word position in the command line. The command, *cd*, is position 0 and its first argument is position 1. The pattern part of the rule is enclosed in slashes (*p/1/* means position 1, the first argument to *cd*), and will be affected by the completion rule. The *d* part of the pattern is called a *word type*. See Table 10.9 on page 530 for a complete list of word types. The *d* word type means that only directories are to be affected by the completion. A filename or alias, for example, would not be completed if given as the first argument to *cd*. The rule states that whenever tab completion is performed on the *cd* command, it will only take place if the first argument is a directory, and Control-D will only list directories if the match is ambiguous; i.e., there is more than one possible completion. See Example 10.31 for *p*-type completions.

EXAMPLE 10.31

```
   # p-type completions (positional completion)

1  > complete
   alias     'p/1/a/'
   cd        'p/1/d/'
   ftp       'p/1/( owl ftp.funet.fi prep.ai.mit.edu )'
   man       'p/*/c/'

2  > complete  vi  'p/*/t/'

3  > complete vi
   vi  'p/*/t/'

4  > set autolist

5  > man fin[tab]     Completes command names
   find     find2perl   findaffix  findsmb  finger

6  > vi b[tab]        Completes only  filenames, not directories
   bashtest binded bindings bindit

7  > vi na[tab]mes

8  > cd sh[tab]ellsolutions/

9  > set hosts = ( netcom.com 192.100.1.10 192.0.0.200 )

10 > complete telnet 'p/1/$hosts/'

11 > telnet net[tab]com.com
   telnet netcom.com

12 > alias m[tab]   Completes alias names
   mc mroe mv

13 > ftp prep[tab]
```

EXPLANATION

1 The *complete* built-in command, without arguments, lists all programmed completions. The following examples (lines 2 through 11) use these completion rules.

2 This rule states that if tab completion is used when typing arguments to the *vi* command, that all arguments (*), must be of type "t" (i.e., plain text files) for completion to performed.

3 The *complete* command, with the name of a command as its argument, displays the completion rule for that command. The completion rule for *vi* is displayed.

EXPLANATION (CONTINUED)

4 By setting the built-in command, *autolist,* all possible tab completions will automatically be printed. (You don't have to press Control-D.)

5 The *man* command has a programmed completion: *complete man 'p/1/c/'*. This rule states that the first argument given to the *man* command must be a command, because *c* is defined as a command word type. In this example, completion is attempted with the letters *fin* as the argument to *man.* All manual commands starting with *fin* will be displayed.

6 Only filenames will be completed, because the *vi* editor completion was programmed to complete only text files, not directories.

7 According to the *vi* completion rule, only text filenames will be completed, no matter how many arguments are passed.

8 When filename completion is performed on the first argument to the built-in *cd* command, the only word that will be completed must be the name of a directory as stated in the completion rule. The argument in this example will expand to a directory called *shellsolutions.*

9 The variable *hosts* is set to a list of IP addresses or hostnames.

10 The completion rule for *telnet* states that completion will be performed if position 1 contains one of the hostnames set in the *hosts* variable. This is a list word type completion.

11 The *telnet* command is executed and the word beginning with *net,* followed by pressing the Tab key, is completed to *netcom.com*, which is one of the hostnames in the *hosts* variable, previously set.

12 The *alias* completion is performed if the user types the word *alias* followed by a word that will be expanded to all aliases that contain that word. Word type *a* means only aliases are expanded for *p*, postition 1.

Table 10.9 Completion Word Types

Word	*Type*
a	alias
b	editor key-binding commands
c	commands (built-in or external commands)
C	external commands which begin with the supplied path prefix
d	directory
D	directories which begin with the supplied path prefix

Table 10.9 Completion Word Types (Continued)

Word	***Type***
e	environment variables
f	filenames (not directory)
F	filenames which begin with the supplied path prefix
g	groupnames
j	jobs
l	limits
n	nothing
s	shell variables
S	signals
t	plain ("text") files
T	plain ("text") files beginning with the supplied path prefix
v	any variables
u	usernames
X	command names for which completions have been defined
x	like *n*, but prints a message if ^D is typed
C, D, F, T	like *c, d, f, t*, but selects completions from a given directory
(list)	selects completions from words in a list

A *c*-type completion is used to complete a pattern in the current word. The current word refers to the pattern enclosed in forward slashes. It rules that if the pattern is matched, any completion performed will finish the pattern.

EXAMPLE 10.32

```
# c-type completions

1   > complete
    stty      'c/-/(raw xcase noflsh)/'
    bash      'c/-no/(profile rc braceexpansion)/'
    find      'c/-/(user name type exec)/'
    man       'c/perl/(delta faq toc data modlib locale)/'

2   > stty -r[tab]aw
    stty -raw
```

EXAMPLE 10.32 (CONTINUED)

```
3   > bash -nop[tab]rofile
    bash -noprofile

4   > find / -n[tab]ame .tcshrc -p[tab]rint
    find / -name .tcshrc -print

5   > man perlde[tab]lta
    man perldelta

6   > uncomplete stty
    > complete
    bash      'c/-no/(profile rc braceexpansion)/'
    find      'c/-/(user name type exec)/'
    man       'c/perl/(delta faq toc data modlib locale)/'

7   > uncomplete *
```

EXPLANATION

1 These examples demonstrate a *c*-type completion. If the pattern in the first set of forward slashes is typed, that pattern will be completed by one of the words listed in the parentheses when a character(s) from that list is typed, followed by the Tab key.

2 When the *stty* command is typed, followed by a dash (-) character, the word will be completed to *-raw*, if a dash, an *r*, and the Tab key are entered. One of the words from the rule list in parentheses (*raw xcase noflsh*) can be completed.

3 When the *bash* command is typed, followed by the pattern, *-no*, that pattern will be completed to *-noprofile*, if the pattern *-no* is followed by a *p* and the Tab key. Completion is performed from one of the words in the rule list (*profile rc braceexpansion*); in this example, resulting in *-noprofile*.

4 Arguments to the *find* command are completed if the dash (-) character is completed by typing significant characters from any of the words in the *find* rule list (*user name type exec*).

5 When the *man* command is typed, the pattern *perl* is completed to *perldelta* since the pattern is followed by one of the words from the list (*delta faq toc data modlib locale*).

6 The *uncomplete* built-in command removes the completion rule for *stty*. The other completion rules remain.

7 The *uncomplete* built-in command, with the asterisk as its argument, removes all completion rules.

N-type completions match the first word and complete the second one.

EXAMPLE 10.33

```
# n-type completions (next word completion)

1   > complete
    rm   'n/-r/d/'
    find 'n/-exec/c/'

2   > ls -ld testing
    drwxr-sr-x  2  ellie  root   1024 Aug 29 11:02 testing

3   > rm -r te[tab]sting
```

EXPLANATION

1. These examples demonstrate an *n*-type completion. If the word in the first set of forward slashes is typed (the current word) and matched, the next word (in the second set of forward slashes) will be completed according to the word type. The *complete* command lists two *n*-type completions, one for the *rm* command and one for the *find* command. When the *rm* command is executed with the *-r* switch, the word following *-r* must be of type directory if completion is to be performed. The rule for the *find* command is: if the *-exec* option is given, any words following it must be commands if completion is to be performed.
2. The output of the *ls* command shows that *testing* is a directory.
3. Filename completion is successful for the *rm* command because word completion is attempted for a directory named *testing*. If *testing* were a plain file, the completion would not have been performed.

10.3.4 Manipulating the Directory Stack

If you find that as you work, you *cd* up and down the directory tree into many of the same directories, you can make it easy to access those directories by pushing them onto a directory stack and manipulating the stack. The directory stack is often compared to stacking trays in a cafeteria where the trays are stacked on top of each other, the first one being at the bottom of the stack. The *pushd* built-in command pushes directories onto a stack and the *popd* command removes them. (See following Examples.) The stack is a numbered list of directories with the top directory being the most recent directory pushed onto the stack. The directories are numbered starting with the top directory at 0, the next one numbered 1, etc. The built-in command, *dirs*, with a *-v* option, displays the numbered directory stack.

The *pushd* and *popd* Commands. The *pushd* command with a directory as an argument causes the new directory to be added to the directory stack and, at the same time, changes to that directory. If the argument is a dash (-), the dash refers to the previous working directory. If the argument is a + and a number (*n*), *pushd* extracts the *n*th directory from the stack and pushes it onto the top, then changes to that directory. Without arguments, *pushd* exchanges the top two elements of the directory stack, making it easy to switch back and forth between directories. There are a number of shell variables that control the way *pushd* works. (See "Setting Local Variables" on page 567.)

To save a directory stack across login sessions, you must set the *savedirs* variable in one of the *tcsh* initialization files (e.g., *~/.tcshrc*). The directory stack will be stored in a file called *~/.cshdirs* and will be automatically sourced when the shell starts up.

The *popd* command removes a directory from the top of the stack, and changes to that directory.

Table 10.10 Directory Stack Variables

pushdtohome	If set, *pushd* without arguments, is same as *pushd ~* or *cd*.
dunique	Before pushing a directory onto the stack, removes any directories with the same name.
pushdsilent	Doesn't print the directory stack when *pushd* is executed.
deextract	If set, *pushd +n* extracts the *n*th directory from the directory stack before pushing it onto the stack.
pushtohome	Without arguments, pushes to ~, the user's home directory.
dirsfile	Can be assigned a filename where the directory stack can be saved across logins.
savedirs	Saves the directory stack across logins.
dirstack	Used to display the stack or assign directories to it.

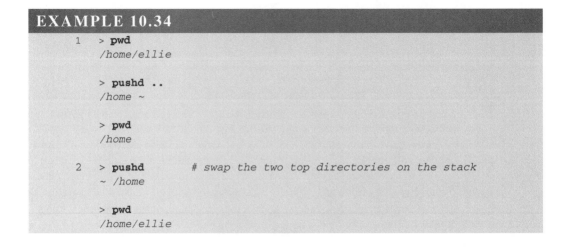

EXAMPLE 10.34

```
1   > pwd
    /home/ellie

    > pushd ..
    /home ~

    > pwd
    /home

2   > pushd         # swap the two top directories on the stack
    ~ /home

    > pwd
    /home/ellie
```

EXAMPLE 10.34 (CONTINUED)

```
3   > pushd perlclass
    ~/perlclass  ~  /home

4   > dirs -v
    0       ~/perlclass
    1       ~
    2       /home

5   > popd
    ~       /home
    > pwd
    /home/ellie

6   > popd
    /home

    > pwd
    /home

7   > popd
    popd: Directory stack empty.
```

Directory stack

0	~/perlclass
1	~
2	/home

EXPLANATION

1 First the *pwd* command displays the present working directory, */home/ellie*. Next the *pushd* command with **..** as its argument, pushes the parent directory (**..**) onto the directory stack. The output of *pushd* indicates that */home* is at the top of the directory stack and the user's home directory (~), */home/ellie*, is at the bottom of the stack. *pushd* also changes the directory to the one that was pushed onto the stack; i.e., **..** which translates to */home*. The new directory is displayed with the second *pwd* command.

2 *pushd*, without arguments, exchanges the two top directory entries on the stack and changes to the swapped directory; in this example, the directory is switched back to the user's home directory, */home/ellie*.

3 The *pushd* command will push its argument, *~/perlclass,* onto the stack, and change to that directory.

4 The built-in *dirs* command displays the numbered directory stack, with 0 being the top level. See the directory stack chart on the right side of Example 10.34.

5 The *popd* command removes a directory from the top of the stack, and changes to that directory.

6 The *popd* command removes another directory from the top of the stack, and changes to that directory.

7 The *popd* command cannot remove any more directory entries because the stack is empty, and issues an error message saying so.

10.3.5 Spelling Correction

Spelling correction, a feature added to the TC shell, is the ability to correct spelling errors in filenames, commands, and variables. If using the *emacs* built-in editor, the spelling error can be corrected by using the spelling correction keys, bound to the *Meta-s* or *Meta-S* keys (use the ALT or ESC key if you don't have Meta) and *Meta-$* to correct an entire line. The value of the prompt, *prompt3,* displays the spelling correction prompt.[8]

If you are using the *vi* built-in editor, set the built-in variable *correct*, and the shell will prompt you to fix the spelling.

EXAMPLE 10.35

```
1   > fimger[Alt-s]     Replaces fimger with finger

2   > set correct=all

3   > dite

    CORRECT>date (y|n|e|a)? yes
    Wed Aug 11 19:26:27 PDT 2000

4   > dite

    CORRECT>date (y|n|e|a)? no
    dite: Command not found.
    >

5   > dite

    CORRECT>date (y|n|e|a)? edit
    > dite█        Waits for user to edit and then executes command

6   > dite

    CORRECT>date (y|n|e|a)? abort
    >
```

EXPLANATION

1 By pressing the *Meta* (or ALT or ESC) key together with an *s*, the spelling of a command, filename, or variable can be corrected. This does not work if you are using the built-in *vi* editor.

8. From the *tcsh* man page: "Beware: Spelling correction is not guaranteed to work the way one intends, and is provided as an experimental feature. Suggestions and improvements are welcome."

EXPLANATION (CONTINUED)

2 By setting *correct* to *all, tcsh* will attempt to correct all spelling errors in the command line. This feature is available for both *emacs* and *vi* keybindings.

3 Because the command was incorrectly spelled, the third prompt, *prompt3*, "*CORRECT>date (y|n|e|a)?*" appears on the screen, and the user is supposed to type the letter *y* if he wants the spelling corrected, an *n* if he doesn't, an *e* if he wants to edit the line himself, or an *a* if he wants to abort the whole operation.

4 If the user wants the command to be unchanged, he types an *n* for no.

5 If the user wants to edit the correction, he types an *e*, and he will be prompted to fix or enhance the command himself.

6 If the correction is incorrect or not wanted, the user types an *a*, and the spelling correction is aborted.

Table 10.11 The *correct* Variable Arguments

Argument	***What It Does***
cmd	spell-corrects commands
complete	completes commands
all	spell-corrects entire command line

10.3.6 Aliases

An *alias* is a TC shell user-defined abbreviation for a command. Aliases are useful if a command has a number of options and arguments or the syntax is difficult to remember. Aliases set at the command line are not inherited by subshells. Aliases are normally set in the *.tcshrc* file. Because the *.tcshrc* is executed when a new shell is started, any aliases set there will get reset for the new shell. Aliases may also be passed into shell scripts but will cause potential portability problems, unless they are directly set within the script.

The TC shell has some additional preset aliases, which remain undefined until you define them. They are: *beepcmd*, *cwdcmd*, *periodic*, and *precomd*. These aliases are listed and defined in "Special Aliases (tcsh Only)" on page 602.

Listing Aliases. The *alias* built-in command lists all set aliases. The alias is printed first, followed by the real command or commands it represents.

EXAMPLE 10.36

```
> alias
apache   $HOME/apache/httpd -f $HOME/apache/conf/httpd.conf
co       compress
cp       cp -i
ls1      enscript -B -r -Porange -f Courier8 !* &
mailq    /usr/lib/sendmail -bp
mc       setenv MC '/usr/bin/mc -P !*'; cd $MC; unsetenv MC
mroe     more
mv       mv -i
uc       uncompress
uu       uudecode
vg       vgrind -t -s11 !:1 | lpr -t
weekly   (cd /home/jody/ellie/activity; ./weekly_report; echo
Done)
```

EXPLANATION

The *alias* command lists the alias (nickname) for the command in the first column and the real command the alias represents in the second column.

Creating Aliases. The *alias* command is used to create an alias. The first argument is the name of the alias, the nickname for the command. The rest of the line consists of the command or commands that will be executed when the alias is executed. Multiple commands are separated by a semicolon, and commands containing spaces and metacharacters are surrounded by single quotes.

FORMAT

```
alias
alias aliasname command
alias aliasname 'command command(s)'
unalias aliasname
```

EXAMPLE 10.37

```
1   > alias m more
2   > alias mroe more
3   > alias lf ls-F
4   > alias cd 'cd \!*; set prompt = "%/ > "'
```

EXAMPLE 10.37 (CONTINUED)

```
5   > cd ..
6   /home/jody >   cd /          # new prompt displayed
    / >

7   > set tperiod = 60
    > alias periodic 'echo You have worked an hour, nonstop'
8   > alias Usage 'echo "Error: \!* " ; exit 1'
```

EXPLANATION

1 The nickname for the *more* command is set to *m*.

2 The alias for the *more* command is set to *mroe*. This is handy if you can't spell.

3 The alias *lf* is a nickname for the *tcsh* built-in command *ls-F*. It lists files like *ls -F*, but is faster.

4 When *cd* is executed, the alias for *cd* will cause *cd* to go to the directory named as an argument and will then reset the prompt to the current working directory (*%/*) followed by the string " > ". The *!** is used by the alias in the same way it is used by the history mechanism. The backslash prevents the history mechanism from evaluating the *!** first before the alias has a chance to use it. The *\!** represents the arguments from the most recent command on the history list. The alias definition is enclosed in quotes because of the white space.

5 After the *cd* command changes to the parent directory, the prompt is expanded to the current working directory (*%/*) and a > symbol.[a]

6 The new directory is */home/jody* which is reflected in the prompt; after changing directory to root (*/*), the prompt again reflects the change.

7 The *tperiod* variable is set to 60 minutes.The alias, *periodic*, is a preset alias. Every 60 minutes, the echo statement will be displayed.

8 This alias is useful in scripts to produce a diagnostic message and to then exit the script. For an example of this alias in use, see Example 11.29 on page 644.

a. If using */bin/csh* as your shell, replace *%/* with *$cwd* when setting the prompt.

Deleting Aliases. The *unalias* command is used to delete an alias. To temporarily turn off an alias, precede the alias name by a backslash.

EXAMPLE 10.38

```
1   > unalias mroe
2   > \cd ..
```

EXPLANATION

1 The *unalias* command deletes the alias *mroe* from the list of defined aliases.

2 The alias *cd* is temporarily turned off for this execution of the command only.

Alias Loop. An alias loop occurs when an alias definition references another alias that references back to the original alias.

EXAMPLE 10.39

```
1   > alias m more
2   > alias mroe m
3   > alias m mroe          # Causes a loop
4   > m datafile
    Alias loop.
```

EXPLANATION

1 The alias is *m*. The alias definition is *more*. Every time *m* is used, the *more* command is executed.

2 The alias is *mroe*. The alias definition is *m*. If *mroe* is typed, the alias *m* is invoked and the *more* command is executed.

3 This is the culprit. If alias *m* is used, it invokes alias *mroe*, and alias *mroe* references back to *m*, causing an alias loop. Nothing bad happens. You just get an error message.

4 Alias *m* is used. It is circular. *M* calls *mroe* and *mroe* calls *m*, then *m* calls *mroe*, etc. Rather than looping forever, the TC shell catches the problem and displays an error message.

10.4 Job Control

Job control is a powerful feature of the TC shell that allows you to run programs, called *jobs*, in the background or foreground. Normally, a command typed at the command line is running in the foreground and will continue until it has finished. If you have a windowing program, job control may not be necessary, because you can simply open another window to start a new task. On the other hand, with a single terminal, job control is a very useful feature. For a list of job commands, see Table 10.12.

Table 10.12 Job Control Commands

Command	*Meaning*
jobs	Lists all the jobs running.
^Z (Ctrl-Z)	Stops (suspends) the job; the prompt appears on the screen.
bg	Starts running the stopped job in the background.
fg	Brings a background job to the foreground.
kill	Sends the *kill* signal to a specified job.

Argument to Jobs Command	*Represents*
%n	Job number *n*.
%string	Job name starting with string.
%?string	Job name containing string.
%%	Current job.
%+	Current job.
%-	Previous job, before current job.

10.4.1 Background Jobs

The Ampersand. If a command takes a long time to complete, you can append the command with an ampersand and the job will execute in the background. The *tcsh* prompt returns immediately and now you can type another command. Now the two commands are running concurrently, one in the background and one in the foreground. They both send their standard output to the screen. If you place a job in the background, it is a good idea to redirect its output either to a file or pipe it to a device such as a printer.

EXAMPLE 10.40

```
> find . -name core -exec rm {} \; &
[1]  543
>
```

EXPLANATION

1. The *find* command runs in the background. (Without the *-print* option, the *find* command does not send any output to the screen).[a]
2. The number in square brackets indicates this is the first job to be run in the background and the PID for this process is *543*.
3. The prompt returns immediately. The shell waits for user input.

a. The *find* syntax requires a semicolon at the end of an *exec* statement. The semicolon is preceded by a backslash to prevent the shell from interpreting it.

The Suspend Key Sequence. To suspend a program, the suspend key sequence, ^Z, is issued. The job is now suspended (stopped), the shell prompt is displayed, and the program will not resume until the *fg* or *bg* commands are issued. (When using the *vi* editor, the ZZ command writes and saves a file. Do not confuse this with ^Z, which would suspend the *vi* session.) If you try to log out when a job is suspended, the message "*There are suspended jobs*" appears on the screen.

The *jobs* Command and the *listjobs* Variable. The *tcsh* built-in command, *jobs*, displays the programs that are currently active and either running or suspended in the background. *Running* means the job is executing in the background. When a job is *suspended*, it is stopped; it is not in execution. In both cases, the terminal is free to accept other commands. If you attempt to exit the shell while jobs are stopped, the warning, *"There are suspended jobs"* will appear on the screen. When you attempt to exit immediately a second time, the shell will go ahead and terminate the suspended jobs. You set the *tcsh* built-in *listjobs* variable if you want to automatically print a message when you suspend a job.

EXAMPLE 10.41

```
(The Command Line)

1   > jobs
2   [1]  +             Suspended     vi filex
    [2]  -             Running       sleep 25

3   > jobs -l
    [1]  +    355      Suspended     vi filex
    [2]  -    356      Running       sleep 25

4   [2] Done                         sleep 25
```

EXAMPLE 10.41 (CONTINUED)

```
5   > set listjobs = long
    > sleep 1000
    Press Control-Z to suspend job

    [1]  +  3337 Suspended             sleep 1000
    >

6   > set notify
```

EXPLANATION

1 The *jobs* command lists the currently active jobs.

2 The notation *[1]* is the number of the first job; the plus sign indicates that the job is not the most recent job to be placed in the background; the dash indicates that this is the most recent job put in the background; *Suspended* means that this job was stopped with ^Z and is not currently active.

3 The *-l* option (long listing) displays the number of the job as well as the PID of the job. The notation *[2]* is the number of the second job, in this case, the last job placed in the background. The dash indicates that this is the most recent job. The *sleep* command is running in the background.

4 After *sleep* has been running for *25* seconds, the job will complete and a message saying that it has finished appears on the screen.

5 The *tcsh listjobs* variable, when set to *long*, will print the number of a job as well as its process id number when it is suspended. (See Table 10.25 on page 603 for a list of built-in *tcsh* variables.).

6 Normally the shell notifies you if a job is stopped just before it prints a prompt, but if the shell variable *notify* is set, the shell will notify you immediately if there is any change in the status of a background job. For example, if you are working in the *vi* editor, and a background job is terminated, a message will appear immediately in your *vi* window like this:
[1]   Terminated   sleep 20

10.4.2 Foreground and Background Commands

The *fg* command brings a background job into the foreground. The *bg* command starts a suspended job running in the background. A percent sign and the number of a job can be used as arguments to *fg* and *bg* if you want to select a particular job for job control.

EXAMPLE 10.42

```
1   > jobs
2   [1] + Suspended                     vi filex
    [2] - Running                       cc prog.c -o prog

3   > fg %1
    vi filex
    (vi session starts)

4   > kill %2
    [2] Terminated                      c prog.c -o prog

5   > sleep 15
    (Press ^z)

     Suspended
6   > bg
    [1] sleep 15 &
    [1] Done    sleep 15
```

EXPLANATION

1. The *jobs* command lists currently running processes, called jobs.
2. The first job stopped is the *vi* session, the second job is the *cc* command.
3. The job numbered *[1]* is brought to the foreground. The number is preceded with a percent sign.
4. The *kill* command is built-in. It sends the *TERM* (terminate) signal, by default, to a process. The argument is either the number or the PID of the process.
5. The *sleep* command is stopped by pressing ^Z. The *sleep* command is not using the CPU and is suspended in the background.
6. The *bg* command causes the last background job to start executing in the background. The *sleep* program will start the countdown in seconds before execution resumes.[a]

a. Programs such as *grep*, *sed*, and *awk* have a set of metacharacters, called regular expression metacharacters, for pattern matching. These should not be confused with shell metacharacters.

10.4.3 Scheduling Jobs

The *sched* built-in command allows you to create a list of jobs that will be scheduled to run at some specific time. The *sched* command, without arguments, displays a numbered list of all the scheduled events. It sets times in the form *hh:mm* (hour:minute) where hour can be in military or 12 hour AM/PM format. Time can also be specified as a relative time with a + sign; i.e., relative to the current time, and with a - sign, the event is removed from the list.[9]

FORMAT

```
sched
sched [+]hh:mm  command
sched -n
```

EXAMPLE 10.43

```
1   > sched 14:30  echo '^G Time to start your lecture!'

2   > sched 5PM  echo Time to go home.

3   > sched +1:30 /home/ellie/scripts/logfile.sc

4   > sched
    1     17:47 /home/scripts/logfile.sc
    2     5PM  echo Time to go home.
    3     14:30  echo '^G Time to start your lecture!'

5   > sched -2
    > sched
    1     17:47 /home/scripts/logfile.sc
    2     14:30  echo '^G Time to start your lecture!'
```

EXPLANATION

1 The *sched* command schedules the echo command to be executed at 14:30. At that time a beep will sound (Control-G)[a] and the message will be displayed.

2 The *sched* command will schedule the echo command to be executed at 5 PM.

3 The script, *logfile.sc*, is scheduled to be executed 1 hour and 30 minutes from now.

4 The *sched* command displays the scheduled events, in numeric order, the last one first.

5 With a numeric argument, *sched* will remove the numbered job from the scheduled list. Job number 2 was removed, as shown in the output of *sched*.

a. To get the ^G into the echo statement, type Ctrl-M followed by Ctrl-V, followed by Ctrl-G.

---

9. From the *tcsh* man page: "A command in the scheduled-event list is executed just before the first prompt is printed after the time when the command is scheduled. It is possible to miss the exact time when the command is to be run, but an overdue command will execute at the next prompt..."

10.5 Metacharacters

Metacharacters are special characters that are used to represent something other than themselves. As a rule of thumb, characters that are neither letters nor numbers may be metacharacters. The shell has its own set of metacharacters, often called *shell wildcards*. Shell metacharacters can be used to group commands together, to abbreviate filenames and pathnames, to redirect and pipe input/output, to place commands in the background, and so forth. Table 10.13 presents a partial list of shell metacharacters.

Table 10.13 Shell Metacharacters

Metacharacter	*Purpose*	*Example*	*Meaning*
$	Variable substitution	*set name=Tom echo $name Tom*	Sets the variable *name* to *Tom*; displays the value stored there.
!	History substitution	*!3*	Reexecutes the third event from the history list.
*	Filename substitution	*rm **	Removes all files.
?	Filename substitution	*ls ??*	Lists all two character files.
[ ]	Filename substitution	*cat f[123]*	Displays contents of *f1, f2, f3*.
;	Command separator	*ls;date;pwd*	Each command is executed in turn.
&	Background processing	*lp mbox&*	Printing is done in the background. Prompt returns immediately.
>	Redirection of output	*ls > file*	Redirects standard output to *file*.
<	Redirection of input	*ls < file*	Redirects standard input from *file*.
>&	Redirection of output and error	*ls >& file*	Redirects both output and errors to *file*.
>!	If *noclobber* is set, override it	*ls >! file*	If *file* exists, truncate and overwrite it, even if *noclobber* is set.
>>!	If *noclobber* is set, override it	*ls >>! file*	If *file* does not exist, create it, even if *noclobber* is set.
( )	Groups commands to be executed in a subshell	*(ls ; pwd) >tmp*	Executes commands and sends output to *tmp* file.
{ }	Groups commands to be executed in this shell	*{ cd /; echo $cwd }*	Changes to root directory and displays current working directory.

10.5.1 Filename Substitution

When evaluating the command line, the shell uses metacharacters to abbreviate filenames or pathnames that match a certain set of characters. The filename substitution metacharacters listed in Table 10.14 are expanded into an alphabetically listed set of filenames. The process of expanding a metacharacter into filenames is also called *globbing*. Unlike the other shells, when the C shell cannot substitute a filename for the metacharacter it is supposed to represent, the shell reports "*No match.*"

Table 10.14 Shell Metacharacters and Filename Substitution

Metacharacter	*Meaning*
*	Matches zero or more characters
?	Matches exactly one character
[abc]	Matches one character in the set: *a*, *b*, or *c*
[a-z]	Matches one character in the range *a* to *z*
[^abc]	Matches any character that is not *a*, *b*, or *c*
{a, ile, ax}	Matches for a character or set of characters
~	Substitutes the user's home directory for tilde
\	Escapes or disables the metacharacter

Expanding the Metacharacters. The shell performs filename substitution by evaluating its metacharacters and replacing them with the appropriate letters or digits in a filename.

The Asterisk. The asterisk matches zero or more characters in a filename.

EXAMPLE 10.44

```
1   > ls
    a.c b.c abc ab3 file1 file2 file3 file4 file5

2   > echo *
    a.c b.c abc ab3 file1 file2 file3 file4 file5

3   > ls  *.c
    a.c b.c

4   > ls ^*.c
    abc ab3 file1 file2 file3 file4 file5

5   > rm  z*p
    No match.
```

EXPLANATION

1 All the files in the current directory are listed.

2 The *echo* program prints all its arguments to the screen. The asterisk (also called a *splat*) is a wildcard that means "*match for zero or more of any characters found in a filename.*" All the files in the directory are matched and echoed to the screen.

3 Filenames ending in *.c* are listed.

4 All files **not** ending in *.c* are listed.

5 Because none of the files in the directory start with *z*, the shell reports "*No match.*"

The Question Mark. The question mark matches exactly one character in a filename.

EXAMPLE 10.45

```
1   > ls
    a.c b.c abc ab3 file1 file2 file3 file4 file5

2   > ls ???
    abc ab3

3   > echo How are you?
    No match.

4   > echo How are you\?
    How are you?
```

EXPLANATION

1 All the files in the current directory are listed.

2 The question mark matches for a single-character filename. Any filenames consisting of three characters are listed.

3 The shell looks for a filename spelled *y-o-u* followed by one character. There is not a file in the directory that matches these characters. The shell prints "*No match.*"

4 The backslash preceding the question mark is used to turn off the special meaning of the question mark. Now the shell treats the question mark as a literal character.

The Square Brackets. The square brackets match a filename for one character from a set or range of characters.

EXAMPLE 10.46

```
1  > ls
   a.c b.c abc ab3 file1 file2 file3 file4 file5 file10
   file11  file12

2  > ls file[123]
   file1 file2 file3

3  > ls file[^123]
   file4 file5

4  > ls [A-Za-z][a-z][1-5]
   ab3

5  > ls file1[0-2]
   file10 file11 file12
```

EXPLANATION

1 All the files in the current directory are listed.

2 Filenames ending in *file* followed by *1, 2,* or *3* are matched and listed.

3 Filenames ending in *file* followed by *1, 2,* or *3* are matched and listed.

4 Filenames starting with one capital letter, followed by one lowercase letter, and followed by one number are matched and listed.

5 Filenames starting with *file1* and followed by a *0, 1,* or *2* are listed.

The Curly Braces. The curly braces match for a character or string of characters in a filename that may or may not already exist.

EXAMPLE 10.47

```
1  > ls
   a.c b.c abc ab3 ab4 ab5 file1 file2 file3 file4 file5 foo
   faa fumble

2  > ls f{oo,aa,umble}
   foo faa fumble

3  > ls a{.c,c,b[3-5]}
   a.c ab3 ab4 ab5

4  > mkdir prog{1,2,3}

5  > echo tweedle{dee,dum}, {l,cl,m}ove{r}
   tweedledee tweedledum, lover clover mover
```

EXPLANATION

1 All the files in the current directory are listed.

2 Files starting with *f* and followed by the strings *oo*, *aa*, or *umble* are listed. Spaces inside the curly braces will cause the error message *Missing }*.

3 Files starting with *a* followed by *.c, c*, or *b3, b4*, or *b5* are listed. (The square brackets can be used inside the curly braces.)

4 Rather than typing *prog1, prog2,* and *prog3* and separate arguments to the *mkdir* command, you can use the braces to generate the new directory names.

5 Each of the words is expanded using the braced portions either as prefixes or suffixes. It is important that the words in braces contain no white space.

Escaping Metacharacters and *nonomatch*. The backslash is used to escape the special meaning of a single character. The escaped character will represent itself.

EXAMPLE 10.48

```
1   > got milk?
    got: No match.

2   > got milk\?
    got: Command not found.

3   > set nonomatch
    > got milk?
    got: Command not found.
```

EXPLANATION

1 The question mark is a file substitution metacharacter and evaluates to a single character. The shell looks for a file in the present working directory that contains the characters *m-i-l-k*, followed by a single character. If the shell cannot find the file, it reports *No match.* This shows you something about the order in which the shell parses the command line. The metacharacters are evaluated before the shell tries to locate the *got* command.

2 The backslash protects the metacharacter from interpretation, often called escaping the metacharacter. Now the shell does not complain about a *No match,* but searches the path for the *got* command, which is not found.

3 The built-in *nonomatch* variable, when set, turns off error reporting when a metacharacter is not matched. Instead of reporting *No match*, Linux reports that *got* is not a command.

Tilde Expansion. The tilde character by itself expands to the full pathname of the user's home directory. When the tilde is prepended to a username, it expands to the full pathname of that user's home directory. When prepended to a path, it expands to the home directory and the rest of the pathname.

EXAMPLE 10.49

```
1   > echo ~
    /home/jody/ellie

2   > cd ~/desktop/perlstuff
    > pwd
    /home/jody/ellie/desktop/perlstuff

3   > cd ~joe
    > pwd
    /home/bambi/joe
```

EXPLANATION

1 The tilde expands to the user's home directory.

2 The tilde followed by a pathname expands to the user's home directory, followed by */desktop/perlstuff*.

3 The tilde followed by a username expands to the home directory of the user. In this example, the directory is changed to that user's home directory.

Turning Off Metacharacters with *noglob*. If the *noglob* variable is set, filename substitution is turned off, meaning that all metacharacters represent themselves; they are not used as wildcards. This can be useful when searching for patterns in programs like *grep, sed*, or *awk*, which may contain metacharacters that the shell may try to expand.

EXAMPLE 10.50

```
1   > set noglob
2   > echo * ?? [] ~
    * ?? [] ~
```

EXPLANATION

1 The variable *noglob* is set. It turns off the special meaning of the wildcards.

2 The metacharacters are displayed as themselves without any interpretation.

10.6 Redirection and Pipes

Normally, standard output (*stdout*) from a command goes to the screen, standard input (*stdin*) comes from the keyboard, and error messages (*stderr*) go to the screen. The shell allows you to use the special redirection metacharacters to redirect the input/output to or from a file. The redirection operators (<, >, >>, >&) are followed by a filename. This file is opened by the shell before the command on the left-hand side is executed.

Pipes, represented by a vertical bar (|) symbol, allow the output of one command to be sent to the input of another command. The command on the left-hand side of the pipe is called the *writer* because it writes to the pipe. The command on the right-hand side of the pipe is the *reader* because it reads from the pipe. See Table 10.15 for a list of redirection and pipe metacharacters.

Table 10.15 Redirection Metacharacters

<table>
<tr><th>Metacharacter</th><th>Meaning</th></tr>
<tr><td>command < file</td><td>Redirects input from file to command.</td></tr>
<tr><td>command > file</td><td>Redirects output from command to file.</td></tr>
<tr><td>command >& file</td><td>Redirects output and errors to file.</td></tr>
<tr><td>command >> file</td><td>Redirects output of command and appends it to file.</td></tr>
<tr><td>command >>& file</td><td>Redirects and appends output and errors of command to file.</td></tr>
<tr><td>command << WORD</td><td>Redirects input from first WORD to terminating WORD to command.</td></tr>
<tr><td><input></td><td>User input goes here. It will be treated as a doubly quoted string of text.</td></tr>
<tr><td>WORD</td><td>WORD marks the termination of input to command.</td></tr>
<tr><td>command | command</td><td>Pipes output of first command to input of second command.</td></tr>
<tr><td>command |& command</td><td>Pipes output and errors of first command to input of second command.</td></tr>
<tr><td>command >! file</td><td>If the noclobber variable is set, overrides its effects for this command and either open or overwrite file.</td></tr>
<tr><td>command >>! file</td><td>Overrides noclobber variable; if file does not exist, it is created and output from command is appended to it.</td></tr>
<tr><td>command >>&! file</td><td>Overrides noclobber variable; if file does not exist, it is created and both output and errors are appended to it.</td></tr>
</table>

10.6.1 Redirecting Input

Instead of the input coming from the terminal keyboard, it can be redirected from a file. The shell will open the file on the right-hand side of the < symbol and the program on the left will read from the file. If the file does not exist, the error "*No such file or directory*" will be reported by the C shell.

FORMAT

```
command < file
```

EXAMPLE 10.51

```
mail bob < memo
```

EXPLANATION

The file *memo* is opened by the shell, and the input is redirected to the *mail* program. Simply, the user *bob* is sent a file called *memo* by the *mail* program.

10.6.2 The *Here* Document

The *here* document is another way to redirect input to a command in the form of a quoted block of text. It is used in shell scripts for creating menus and processing input from other programs. Normally, programs that accept input from the keyboard are terminated with Control-D (^D). The *here* document provides an alternate way of sending input to a program and terminating the input without typing ^D. The << symbol is followed by a user-defined word, often called a *terminator.* Input will be directed to the command on the left-hand side of the << symbol until the user-defined terminator is reached. The final terminator is on a line by itself, and *cannot* be surrounded by any spaces. Variable and command substitution are performed within the *here* document. Normally, *here* documents are used in shell scripts to create menus and provide input to commands such as *mail, bc, ex, ftp*, etc. See Example 11.34 on page 651.

FORMAT

```
command << MARK
        ... input ...
MARK
```

EXAMPLE 10.52

```
(Without the "Here" Document)

(The Command Line)
1   > cat
2   Hello There.
    How are you?
    I'm tired of this.
3   ^d

(The Output)
4   Hello There.
    How are you?
    I'm tired of this.
```

EXPLANATION

1 The *cat* program, without arguments, waits for keyboard input.

2 The user types input at the keyboard.

3 The user types ^D to terminate input to the *cat* program.

4 The *cat* program sends its output to the screen.

EXAMPLE 10.53

```
(With the "Here" Document)

(The Command Line)
1   > cat << DONE
2   ? Hello There.
    ? How are you?
    ? I'm tired of this.
3   ? DONE
4   Hello There.    <----The output from the here document
    How are you?
    I'm tired of this.
```

EXPLANATION

1 The *cat* program will receive input from the first *DONE* to the terminating *DONE.* The words are user-defined terminators.

EXPLANATION (CONTINUED)

2 The question mark (*?*) is the secondary prompt, *prompt2*. It will appear until the *here* document is terminated with the user-defined terminator, *DONE*. These lines are input. When the word *DONE* is reached, no more input is accepted.

3 The final terminator marks the end of input. There cannot be any spaces on either side of this word.

4 The text between the first word *DONE* and the final word *DONE* is the output of the *cat* command (from *here* to *here*) and is sent to the screen. The final *DONE* must be against the left margin with no space or other text to the right of it.

EXAMPLE 10.54

```
(The Command Line)
1   > set name = steve
2   > mail $name << EOF
3   ? Hello there, $name
4   ? The hour is now `date +%H`
5   ? EOF
6   >
```

EXPLANATION

1 The shell variable *name* is assigned the username *steve*. (Normally, this example would be included in a shell script.)

2 The variable *name* is expanded within the *here* document.

3 The question mark (*?*) is the secondary prompt, *prompt2*. It will appear until the *here* document is terminated with the user-defined terminator, *EOF*. The *mail* program will receive input until the terminator *EOF* is reached.

4 Command substitution is performed within the *here* document; that is, the command within the back quotes is executed and the output of the command is replaced within the string.

5 The terminator *EOF* is reached, and input to the *mail* program is stopped.

10.6.3 Redirecting Output

By default, the standard output of a command or commands normally goes to the terminal screen. To redirect standard output from the screen to a file, use the > symbol. The command is on the left-hand side of the > symbol, and a filename is on the right-hand side. The shell will open the file on the right-hand side of the > symbol. If the file does not exist, the shell will create it; if it does exist, the shell will open the file and truncate it. Often files are inadvertently removed when using redirection. (A special *tcsh* variable, called *noclobber*, can be set to prevent redirection from clobbering an existing file. See Table 10.16.)

FORMAT

```
command > file
```

EXAMPLE 10.55

```
cat file1 file2 > file3
```

EXPLANATION

The contents of *file1* and *file2* are concatenated and the output is sent to *file3*. Remember that the shell opens *file3* before it attempts to execute the *cat* command. If *file3* already exists and contains data, the data will be lost. If *file3* does not exist, it will be created.

Appending Output to an Existing File. To append output to an existing file, use the >> symbol. If the file on the right-hand side of the >> symbol does not exist, it is created; if it does exist, the file is opened and output is appended to the end of the file.

FORMAT

```
command >> file
```

EXAMPLE 10.56

```
date >> outfile
```

EXPLANATION

The standard output of the *date* command is redirected and appended to *outfile*.

Redirecting Output and Error. The >& symbol is used to redirect both standard output and standard error to a file. Normally, a command is either successful and sends its output to *stdout*, or fails and sends its error messages to *stderr*. Some recursive programs, such as *find* and *du*, send both standard output and errors to the screen as they move through the directory tree. When you use the >& symbol, both standard output and standard error can be saved in a file and examined. The C shell does not provide a symbol for redirection of only standard error, but it is possible to get just the standard error by executing the command in a subshell. See Figure 10.3.

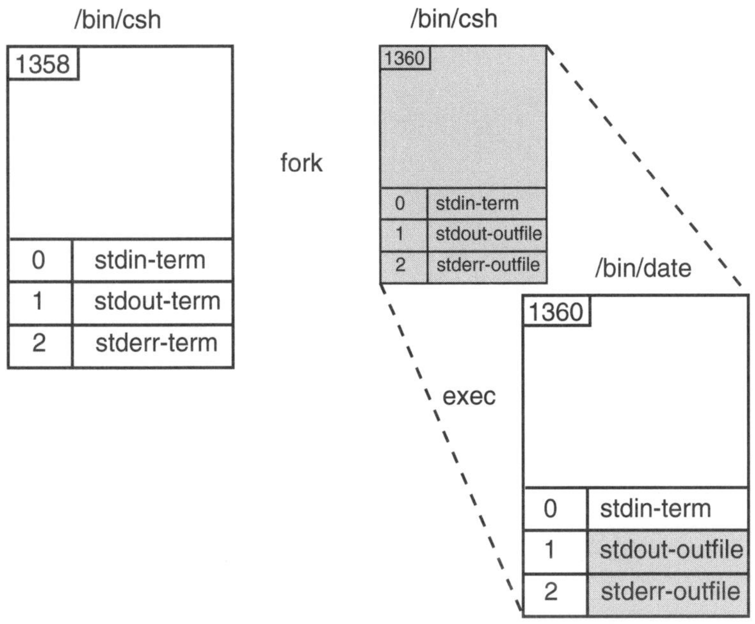

Figure 10.3 Redirecting *stdout* and *stderr*. See Example 10.57.

EXAMPLE 10.57

```
1   > date
    Tue Aug 3 10:31:56  PDT  2000
2   > date >& outfile
3   > cat outfile
     Tue Aug 3 10:31:56  PDT  2000
```

EXPLANATION

1 The output of the *date* command is sent to standard output, the screen.

2 The output and errors are sent to *outfile*.

3 Because there were no errors, the standard output is sent to *outfile* and the contents of the file are displayed.

EXAMPLE 10.58

```
1   > cp file1 file2
2   > cp file1
    cp: missing destination file
    Try 'cp --help' for more information
3   > cp file1 >& errorfile
4   > cat errorfile
    cp: missing destination file
    Try 'cp --help' for more information
```

EXPLANATION

1 To copy a file, the *cp* command requires both a source file and a destination file. The *cp* command makes a copy of *file1* and puts the copy in *file2*. Because the *cp* command is given the correct syntax, nothing is displayed to the screen. The copy was successful.

2 This time the destination file is missing and the *cp* command fails, sending an error to *stderr*, the terminal.

3 The *>&* symbol is used to send both *stdout* and *stderr* to *errorfile*. Because the only output from the command is the error message, that is what is saved in *errorfile*.

4 The contents of errorfile are displayed, showing that it contains the error message produced by the *cp* command.

Separating Output and Errors. Standard output and standard error can be separated by enclosing the command in parentheses. When a command is enclosed in parentheses, the C shell starts up a subshell, handles redirection from within the subshell, and then executes the command. By using the technique shown in Example 10.59, you can separate the standard output from the errors.

EXAMPLE 10.59

```
(The Command Line)
1   > find . -name '*.c' >& outputfile
2   > (find . -name '*.c' > goodstuff) >& badstuff
```

EXPLANATION

1 The *find* command will start at the current directory, searching for all files ending in *.c,* and will print the output to *outputfile*. If an error occurs, that will also go into *outputfile*.

EXPLANATION (CONTINUED)

2 The *find* command is enclosed within parentheses. The shell will create a subshell to handle the command. Before creating the subshell, the words outside the parentheses will be processed; that is, the *badstuff* file will be opened for both standard output and error. When the subshell is started, it inherits the standard input, output, and errors from its parent. The subshell then has standard input coming from the keyboard, and both standard output and standard error going to the *badstuff* file. Now the subshell will handle the > operator. The *stdout* will be assigned the file *goodstuff*. The output is going to *goodstuff*, and the errors are going to *badstuff*. See Figure 10.4.

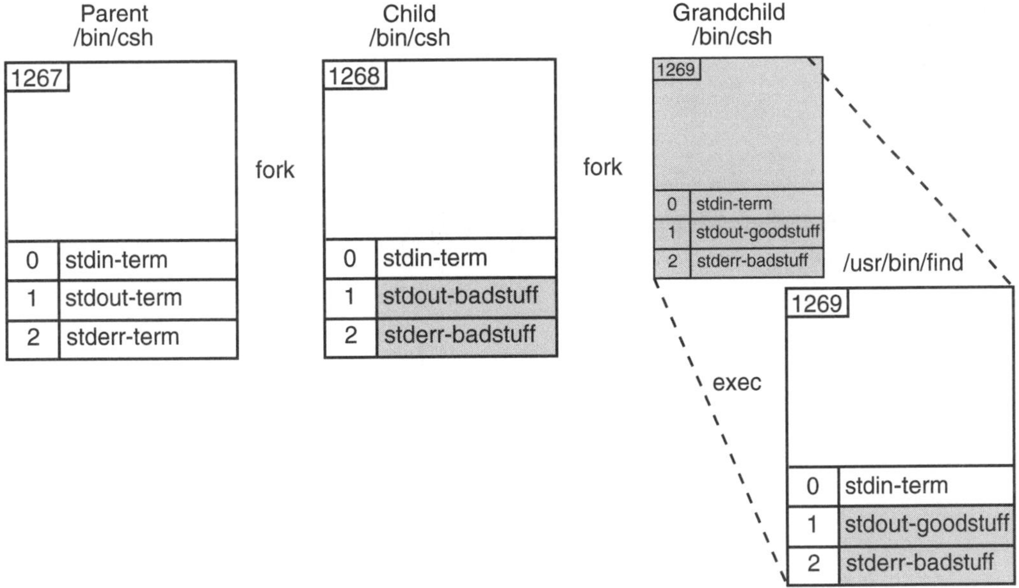

Figure 10.4 Separating *stdout* and *stderr*.

The *noclobber* Variable. The special C shell built-in variable *noclobber*, when set, protects you from clobbering files with redirection. See Table 10.16.

Table 10.16 The *noclobber* Variable

noclobber *Is Not Set*	***File Exists***	***File Does Not Exist***
command > *file*	*File* is overwritten.	*File* is created.
command >> *file*	*File* is appended to.	*File* is created.
noclobber *Is Set*		
command > *file*	Error message.	*File* is created.
command >> *file*	*File* is appended to.	Error message.
***Overwriting* noclobber**		
command >! *file*	If the *noclobber* variable is set, override its *effects* for this *command* and either open or truncate *file*, redirecting output of *command* to *file*.	
command >>! *file*	Override *noclobber* variable; if *file* does not exist, it is created and output from *command* is appended to it. (See Example 10.60.)	

EXAMPLE 10.60

```
1   > cat filex
    abc
    123

2   > date > filex
3   > cat filex
    Tue Mar 18 11:51:04  PST 2000

4   > set noclobber
5   > date > filex
    filex: File exists.

6   > ls >! filex      Override noclobber for this command only
    > cat filex
    abc
    ab1
    dir
    filex
    plan.c

7   > ls > filex
    filex:  File exists.

8   > date >> XXX
    XXX: No such file or directory.

9   > date >>! XXX         Override noclobber for this command only

10  > unset noclobber      Turn off noclobber permanently
```

EXPLANATION

1. The contents of *filex* are displayed on the screen.
2. The output of the *date* command is redirected to *filex*. The file is truncated and its original contents overwritten.
3. The contents of *filex* are displayed.
4. The *noclobber* variable is set.
5. Because *filex* already exists and *noclobber* is set, the shell reports that the file exists and will not allow it to be overwritten.
6. The output of *ls* is redirected to *filex* because the *>!* operator overrides the effects of *noclobber.*
7. The effects of the *>!* symbol were temporary. It does not turn off *noclobber.* It simply overrides *noclobber* for the command where it is implemented.
8. Attempting to redirect and append the output of the *date* command to a nonexistent file causes an error message when *noclobber* is set.
9. The *noclobber* variable is overridden with the exclamation mark attached to the >> redirection symbol.
10. The *noclobber* variable is unset.

10.7 Variables

Tcsh variables hold only strings or a set of strings. Some variables are built into the shell and can be set either by turning them on or off, such as the *noclobber* or *filec* variable. Others are assigned a string value, such as the *path* variable. You can create your own variables and assign them to strings or the output of commands. Variable names are case-sensitive and may contain up to 20 characters consisting of numbers, letters, and the underscore.

There are two types of variables: local and environment. The scope of a variable is its visibility. A local variable is visible to the shell where it is defined. The scope of environment variables is often called *global*. Their scope is for this shell and all processes spawned (started) from this shell. If a local variable is created with *set -r*, it will be *read-only* meaning that it cannot be changed or unset (*tcsh*).

The dollar sign (*$*) is a special metacharacter that, when preceding a variable name, tells the shell to extract the value of that variable. The *echo* command, when given the variable as an argument, will display the value of the variable after the shell has processed the command line and performed variable substitution.

The special notation *$?*, when prepended to the variable name, lets you know whether the variable has been set. If a one is returned, it means true, the variable has been set. If a zero is returned, it means false, the variable has not been set.

EXAMPLE 10.61

```
1   > set autologout
2   > set history = 50
3   > set name = George
4   > set machine = `uname -n`
5   > echo $?machine
     1
6    echo  $?blah
     0
```

EXPLANATION

1. Sets the *tcsh* built-in variable *autologout* variable to cause automatic logout after a specified time of inactivity has passed.
2. Sets the built-in variable *history* to *50* to control the number of events displayed.
3. Sets the user-defined variable *name* to *George*.
4. Sets the user-defined variable *machine* to the output of the UNIX command. The command is in back quotes, telling the shell to perform command substitution.
5. The *$?* is prepended to the variable name to test whether or not the variable has been set. Because the test yields a 1 (true), the variable has been set.
6. The *$?* yields 0 (false). The variable has not been set.

10.7.1 Printing the Values of Variables

The *echo* Command. The built-in *echo* command prints its arguments to standard output. The *echo* allows the use of numerous escape sequences which are interpreted and displayed as tabs, newlines, form feed, etc. Table 10.17 lists the *echo* options and escape sequences.

The TC shell uses the style of both BSD and SVR4, but allows you to modify the behavior of the *echo* command by using the built-in *echo_style* variable; e.g., *set echo_style=bsd.* See Table 10.18. See the manual page for *echo*.

Table 10.17 *echo* Options and Escape Sequences

Option	*Meaning*
-n	Suppresses newline at the end of a line of output
Escape Sequence	
\a	Alert (bell)
\b	Backspace
\c	Print the line without a newline
\f	Form feed
\n	Newline
\r	Return
\t	Tab
\v	Vertical tab
\\	Backslash
\nnn	The character whose ASCII code is *nnn* (octal)

Table 10.18 The *echo_style* Variable

bsd	If the first argument is *-n*, the newline is suppressed.
sysv	Expands escape sequences in echo strings.
both	Both *-n* and escape sequences are in effect (the default).
none	Recognizes neither *sysv* or *bsd*.

EXAMPLE 10.62

```
1   > echo The username is $LOGNAME.
    The username is ellie.

2   > echo "\t\tHello there\c"
                Hello there>

3   > echo -n "Hello there"
    Hello there$

4    > set echo_style=none

5    > echo   "\t\tHello there\c"
     -n \t\tHello there\c
```

EXPLANATION

1 The *echo* command prints its arguments to the screen. Variable substitution is performed by the shell before the *echo* command is executed.

2 The *echo* command by default, supports escape sequences similar to those of the C programming language and used in the SVR4 version of *echo*. The > is the shell prompt.

3 With the *-n* option, echo displays the string without the newline.

4 The *echo_style* variable is assigned the value *none*. Neither the BSD *-n* switch nor the SVR4 escape sequences are in effect.

5 With the new *echo* style, the string is displayed.

The *printf* Command. The Gnu version of *printf* can be used to format printed output. It prints the formatted string, in the same way as the C *printf* function. The format consists of a string that may contain formatting instructions to describe how the printed output will look. The formatting instructions are designated with a % followed by specifiers (*diouxXfeEgGcs*), where *%f* would represent a floating point number and *%d* would represent a whole (decimal) number.

To see a complete listing of *printf* specifiers and how to use them, type at the command line prompt: *printf --help.* To see what version of *printf* you are using, type *printf --version.* If using *bash 2.x*, the built-in *printf* command uses the same format as the executable version in */usr/bin.*

FORMAT

```
printf format [argument...]
```

EXAMPLE 10.63

```
printf "%10.2f%5d\n" 10.5  25
```

Table 10.19 Format Specifiers for the *printf* Command

Format Specifier	***Value***
\"	Double quote
0NNN	An octal character in which *NNN* represents 0 to 3 digits
\\\\	Backslash
a	Alert or beep
b	Backspace
c	Produce no further output
f	Form feed
n	Newline
r	Carriage return
t	Horizontal tab
v	Vertical tab
xNNN	Hexadecimal character in which *NNN* is 1 to 3 digits
%%	Single %
%b	ARGUMENT as a string with \ escapes interpreted

EXAMPLE 10.64

```
1   > printf --version
    printf (GNU sh-utils) 1.16

2   > printf "The number is %.2f\n" 100
    The number is 100.00

3   > printf "%-20s%-15s%10.2f\n" "Jody" "Savage" 28
    Jody                Savage              28.00

4   > printf "|%-20s|%-15s|%10.2f|\n" "Jody" "Savage" 28
    |Jody                |Savage         |     28.00|

5   > printf "%s's average was %.1f%%.\n" "Jody" $(( (80+70+90)/3 ))
    Jody's average was 80.0%.
```

EXPLANATION

1 The Gnu version of the *printf* command is printed. It is found in */usr/bin*.

2 The argument *100* is printed as a floating point number with only two places to the right of the decimal point printing, designated by the format specification *%.2f* in the format string. Note that unlike C, there are no commas separating the arguments.

3, 4 This time the format string specifies that three conversions will take place: the first one is *%-20s* (a left-justified, 20-character string), next is *%-15s* (a left-justified, 15-character string), and last *%10.2f* (a right-justified 10-character floating point number, one of those characters is the period and the last two characters are the two numbers to the right of the decimal point). Each argument is formatted in the order of the corresponding % signs, so that string *"Jody"* corresponds to first %, string *"Savage"* corresponds to the second %, and the number *28* to the last % sign. The vertical bars are used to demonstrate the width of the fields.

5 The *printf* command formats the string *Jody* and the result of the arithmetic expansion. (See "Arithmetic Expansion" on page 356.) Two percent (%%) signs are needed to print one percent sign (%).

Curly Braces and Variables. Curly braces insulate a variable from any characters that may follow it. They can be used to concatenate a string to the end of the variable.

EXAMPLE 10.65

```
1   > set var = net
    > echo $var
    net

2   > echo $varwork
    varwork: Undefined variable.

3   > echo ${var}work
    network
```

EXPLANATION

1. The curly braces surrounding the variable name insulate the variable from characters that follow it.
2. A variable called *varwork* has not been defined. The shell prints an error message.
3. The curly braces shield the variable from characters appended to it. *$var* is expanded and the string *work* is appended.

10.7.2 Local Variables (Visibility and Naming)

Local variables are known only in the shell where they were created. If a local variable is set in the *.cshrc* file, the variable will be reset every time a new C shell is started. By convention, local variables are named with lowercase letters.

Setting Local Variables. If the string being assigned contains more than one word, it must be quoted; otherwise, only the first word will be assigned to the variable. It does not matter if there are spaces around the equal sign, but if there is a space on one side of the equal sign, there must be one on the other side.

EXAMPLE 10.66

```
1   > set round = world
2   > set name = "Santa Claus"

3   > echo $round
     world

4   > echo $name
    Santa Claus

5   > tcsh              start a subshell
6   > echo $name
    name: Undefined variable.
```

EXPLANATION

1 The local variable *round* is assigned the value *world.*

2 The local variable *name* is assigned the value *Santa Claus*. The double quotes keep the shell from evaluating the white space between *Santa* and *Claus*.

3 The dollar sign prepended to the variable allows the shell to perform variable substitution, that is, to extract the value stored in the variable.

4 Variable substitution is performed.

5 A new C shell (called a subshell) process is started.

6 In the subshell, the variable *name* has not been defined. It was defined in the parent shell as a local variable.

Read-Only Variables. Read-only variables are local variables that, once set, cannot be changed or unset or an error message will result. Environment variables cannot be made read-only.

EXAMPLE 10.67

```
1   > set -r name = Tommy

2   > unset name
    unset: $name is read-only.

3   > set name = Danny
    set: $name is read-only
```

The *set* Command. The *set* command prints all local variables set for this shell.

EXAMPLE 10.68

```
(The Command Line)
> set
addsuffix
argv          ()
cwd           /home/jody/meta
dirstack      /home/ellie/meta
echo_style both
edit
```

EXAMPLE 10.68 (CONTINUED)

```
gid        501
group      ellie
history    500
home       /home/ellie
i          /etc/profile.d/mc.csh
owd        /home/ellie
noclobber
path    (/usr/sbin /sbin /usr/local/bin /bin  /usr/bin /usr/X11R6/bin )

prompt     [%n@%m  %c]#
prompt2    %R?
prompt3    CORRECT>%R  (y|n|e|a)?
savedirs
shell      /bin/tcsh
shlvl      2
status     0
tcsh       6.07.09
term       xterm
user       ellie
version tcsh 6.07.09 (Astron) 1998-07-07 (i386-intel-linux)
options 8b,nls,dl,al,rh,color
```

EXPLANATION

All of the local variables set for this shell are printed. Many of these variables, such as *history, dirstack,* and *noclobber*, are set in the *.tcshrc* file. Others, such as *argv, cwd, shell, term, user, version,* and *status* variables are preset, built-in variables.

Built-In Local Variables. The shell has a number of predefined variables with their own definitions. Some of the variables are either on or off. For example, if you set *noclobber*, the variable is on and effective, and when you unset *noclobber*, it is turned off. Some variables require a definition when set. Built-in variables are usually set in the *.tcshrc* file if they are to be effective for all interactive TC shells and *tcsh* scripts. Some of the built-in variables already discussed include *noclobber, cdpath, history, rmstar,* and *noglob*. For a complete list, see Table 10.24 on page 591.

10.7.3 Environment Variables

Environment variables are often called *global* variables. They are defined in the shell where they were created and inherited by all shells spawned from that shell. Although environment variables are inherited by subshells, those defined in subshells are not passed back to parent shells. Inheritance is from parent to child, not the other way around (like real life). By convention, environment variables are named with capital letters.

EXAMPLE 10.69

```
(The Command Line)
1  > setenv TERM wyse
2  > setenv PERSON "Joe Jr."
3  > echo $TERM
   wyse
4  > echo $PERSON
   Joe Jr.
5  > echo $$          $$ evaluates to the PID of the current shell
   206

6  > tcsh                        start a subshell
7  > echo $$
   211
8  > echo $PERSON
   Joe Jr.

9  > setenv PERSON "Nelly Nerd"
10 > echo $PERSON
   Nelly Nerd
11 > exit                        exit the subshell

12 > echo $$
   206
13 > echo $PERSON        back in parent shell
   Joe Jr.
```

EXPLANATION

1 The shell environment variable *TERM* is set to a *wyse* terminal.

2 The user-defined variable *PERSON* is set to *Joe Jr.* The quotes are used to protect the space.

3 The dollar sign (*$*) prepended to the variable name allows the shell to evaluate the contents of the variable, called variable substitution.

4 The value of the environment variable *PERSON* is printed.

5 The *$$* variable contains the PID of the current shell. The PID is *206.*

6 The *tcsh* command starts a new TC shell, called a subshell.

7 The PID of the current shell is printed. Because this is a new TC shell, it has a different PID number. The PID is *211.*

8 The environment variable *PERSON* was inherited by the new shell.

9 The *PERSON* variable is reset to "*Nelly Nerd.*" This variable will be inherited by any shells spawned from this shell.

EXPLANATION (CONTINUED)

10 The new value of the *PERSON* variable is printed.

11 This shell is exited.

12 The original shell is running; to attest to that, the PID *206* is printed. It is the same as it was before the subshell was started.

13 The *PERSON* variable contains its original value.

Displaying Environment Variables. The *printenv* (BSD) and *env* (SVR4) print all the environment variables set for this shell and its subshells. The *setenv* command prints variables and their values on both the UCB and SVR4 versions of C shell.

EXAMPLE 10.70

```
> env  or  printenv  or  setenv
USERNAME=root
COLORTERM=rxvt-xpm
HISTSIZE=1000
HOSTNAME=homebound
LOGNAME=ellie
HISTFILESIZE=1000
MAIL=/var/spool/mail/ellie
MACHTYPE=i386
COLORFGBG=0;default;15
TERM=xterm
HOSTTYPE=i386-linux
PATH=/usr/sbin:/sbin:/usr/local/bin:/bin:/usr/bin:/usr/X11R6/bin:/hom
e/ellie/bin;/root/bash-
2.03/:/usr/X11R6/bin:/home/ellie/bin;/root/bash-2.03/:/usr/X11R6/bin
HOME=/root
SHELL=/bin/bash
PS1=[\u@\h \W]\$
USER=ellie
VENDOR=intel
GROUP=ellie
HOSTDISPLAY=homebound:0.0
DISPLAY=:0.0
HOST=homebound
OSTYPE=linux
WINDOWID=37748738
PWD=/home/ellie
SHLVL=6
_=/usr/bin/env
```

EXPLANATION

The environment variables are set for this session and all processes that are started from this shell are displayed by using either one of the built-in commands: *env* or *printenv*. Many applications require the setting of environment variables. For example, the *mail* command has a *MAIL* variable set to the location of the user's mail spooler and the *xterm* program has a *DISPLAY* variable that determines which bit map display terminal to use. When any of these programs are executed, the values in their respective variables are passed on to them.

10.8 Arrays

10.8.1 What Is an Array?

In the TC shell, an array is simply a list of words, separated by spaces or tabs, and enclosed in parentheses. The elements of the array are numbered by subscripts starting at one. If there is not an array element for a subscript, the message "*Subscript out of range*" is displayed. Command substitution will also create an array. If the *$#* notation precedes an array name, the number of elements in the array is displayed.

EXAMPLE 10.71

```
1   > set fruit = ( apples pears peaches plums )
2   > echo $fruit
    apples pears peaches plums

3   > echo $fruit[1]      Subscripts start at 1
    apples

4   > echo $fruit[2-4]    Prints the 2nd, 3rd, and 4th elements
    pears peaches plums

5   > echo $fruit[6]
    Subscript out of range.

6   > echo $fruit[*]      Prints all elements of the array
    apples pears peaches plums

7   > echo $#fruit        Prints the number of elements
    4

8   > echo $%fruit        Prints the number of characters in the list
    23
```

EXAMPLE 10.71 (CONTINUED)

```
9    > echo $fruit[$#fruit]       Prints the last element
     plums

10   > set fruit[2] = bananas       Reassigns the second element
     > echo $fruit
     apples bananas peaches plums

11   > set path = ( ~ /usr/bin /usr /usr/local/bin . )
     > echo $path
     /home/jody/ellie /usr/bin /usr /usr/local/bin .

12   > echo $path[1]
     /home/jody/ellie
```

EXPLANATION

1 The wordlist is enclosed within parentheses. Each word is separated by white space. The array is called *fruit.*

2 The words in the *fruit* array are printed.

3 The first element of the *fruit* array is printed. The subscripts start at one.

4 The second, third, and fourth elements of the wordlist are printed. The dash allows you to specify a range.

5 The array does not have six elements. The subscript is out of range.

6 All elements of the *fruit* array are printed.

7 The *$#* preceding the array is used to obtain the number of elements in the array. There are four elements in the *fruit* array.

8 The *$%* preceding a variable or an array prints the number of characters in the word(s).

9 Because the subscript *$#fruit* evaluates to the total number of elements in the array, if that value is used as an index value of the array, i.e., [*$#fruit*], the last element of the *fruit* array is printed.

10 The second element of the array is assigned a new value. The array is printed with its replaced value, *bananas.*

11 The *path* variable is a special C shell array of directories used to search for commands. When you create an array, the individual elements of the path can be accessed or changed.

12 The first element of *path* is printed.

The *shift* Command and Arrays. If the built-in *shift* command takes an array name as its argument, it shifts off (to the left) the first element of the array. The length of the array is decreased by one. Without an argument, the *shift* command shifts off the first element of the built-in *argv* array.

Table 10.20 Variable Modifiers

Special Modifier	*Example*	*What It Means*
$?	*$?var*	Returns 1 if *var* is set; 0 if not.
$#	*$#var*	Returns the number of words in *var.*
$%	*$%var*	Returns the number of characters in *var.*

EXAMPLE 10.72

```
1   > set names = ( Mark Tom Liz Dan Jody )

2   > echo $names
    Mark Tom Liz Dan Jody

3   > echo $names[1]
    Mark

4   > shift  names

5   > echo $names
    Tom Liz Dan Jody

6   > echo $names[1]
    Tom

7   > set days = ( Monday Tuesday )

8   > shift days

9   > echo $days
    Tuesday

10  > shift days

11  > echo $days

12  > shift days
    shift: no more words.
```

EXPLANATION

1 The array is called *names*. It is assigned the list of words in parentheses. Each word is separated by white space.

2 The array is printed.

3 The first element of the array is printed.

4 The array is shifted to the left by one element. The word *Mark* is shifted off.

5 The array was decreased by one element after the *shift*.

6 The first element of the array, after the *shift*, is *Tom*.

7 An array, called *days*, is created. It has two elements, *Monday* and *Tuesday*.

8 The array, *days*, is shifted one to the left.

9 The array is printed. *Tuesday* is the only element left.

10 The array, *days*, is shifted again. The array is empty.

11 The *days* array is empty.

12 This time, attempting to shift causes the shell to send an error message indicating that it cannot shift elements from an empty array.

Creating an Array from a String. You may want to create a wordlist out of a quoted string. This is accomplished by placing the string variable within a set of parentheses.

EXAMPLE 10.73

```
1   > set name = "Thomas Ben Savage"
    > echo $name[1]
    Thomas Ben Savage

2   > echo $name[2]
    Subscript out of range.

3   > set name = ( $name )

4   > echo $name[1] $name[2] $name[3]
    Thomas Ben Savage
```

EXPLANATION

1 The variable *name* is assigned the string *"Thomas Ben Savage."*

2 When treated as an array, there is only one element, the entire string.

3 The variable is enclosed in parentheses, creating an array of words, called *name.*

4 The three elements of the new array are displayed.

10.9 Special Variables and Modifiers

Built into the TC shell are several variables consisting of one character. The *$* preceding the character allows variable interpretation. See Table 10.21.

Table 10.21 Variables and Their Meanings

Variable	*Example*	*Meaning*
$?var	*echo $?name*	Returns 1 if variable has been set, 0 if not.
$#var	*echo $#fruit*	Prints the number of elements in an array.
$%var	*echo $%name*	Prints number of characters in a variable or array.
$$	*echo $$*	Prints the PID of the current shell.
$<	*set name = $<*	Accepts a line of input from user up to newline.
$?	*echo $?*	Same as *$status*. Contains the exit status of the last command.
$!	*kill $!*	Contains the process id number of the last job put in the background.

EXAMPLE 10.74

```
1   > set num
    > echo $?num
    1

2   > echo $path
    /home/jody/ellie  /usr /bin  /usr/local/bin
    > echo $#path
    3

3   > echo $$
    245

    > tcsh   Start a subshell
    > echo $$
    248

4   > set name = $<
    Christy Campbell
    > echo $name
    Christy

5   > set name = "$<"
    Christy Campbell
    > echo $name
    Christy Campbell
```

EXPLANATION

1 The variable *num* is set to null. The *$?* preceding the variable evaluates to one if the variable has been set (either to null or some value), and to zero if the variable has not been set.

2 The *path* variable is printed. It is an array of three elements. The *$#* preceding the variable extracts and prints the number of elements in the array.

3 The *$$* is the PID of the current process, in this case, the C shell.

4 The *$<* variable accepts a word of input from the user up to the first space or newline, whichever comes first, and stores the word in the *name* variable. The value of the *name* variable is displayed.

5 The *$<* variable, when quoted (double quotes) accepts a line of input from the user up to, but not including, the newline, and stores the line in the *name* variable. The value of the *name* variable is displayed.

10.9.1 Pathname Variable Modifiers

If a pathname is assigned to a variable, it is possible to manipulate the pathname variable by appending special TC shell extensions to it. The pathname is divided into four parts: *head*, *tail*, *root*, and *extension*. See Table 10.22 for examples of pathname modifiers and what they do.

Table 10.22 Pathname Modifiers
`set pn = /home/ellie/prog/check.c`

Modifier	*Meaning*	*Example*	*Result*
:r	root	*echo $pn:r*	/home/ellie/prog/check
:h	head	*echo $pn:h*	/home/ellie/prog
:t	tail	*echo $pn:t*	check.c
:e	extension	*echo $pn:e*	c
:g	global	*echo $p:gt*	(See Example 10.75)

EXAMPLE 10.75

```
1   > set pathvar = /home/danny/program.c

2   > echo $pathvar:r
    /home/danny/program

3   > echo $pathvar:h
    /home/danny

4   > echo $pathvar:t
    program.c

5   > echo $pathvar:e
    c

6   > set pathvar = ( /home/* )
    echo $pathvar
    /home/jody /home/local /home/lost+found /home/perl /home/tmp

7   > echo $pathvar:gt
    jody  local  lost+found  perl tmp
```

EXPLANATION

1. The variable *pathvar* is set to */home/danny/program.c.*
2. When *:r* is appended to the variable, the extension is removed when displayed.
3. When *:h* is appended to the variable, the head of the path is displayed; that is, the last element of the path is removed.
4. When *:t* is appended to the variable, the tail end of the path (the last element) is displayed.
5. When *:e* is appended to the variable, the extension is displayed.
6. The variable is set to */home/**. The asterisk expands to all the pathnames in the current directory starting in */home/.*
7. When *:gt* is appended to the variable, the tail end of each (global) of the path elements is displayed.

10.9.2 Upper- and Lowercase Modifiers

A special history modifier can be used to change the case of letters in a variable.

Table 10.23 Case Modifiers (*tcsh*, not *csh*)

:u	uppercase the first lowercase letter in a word
:l	lowercase the first uppercase letter in a word
:g	apply a modifier once to each word
:a	apply a modifier as many times as possible to a single word

EXAMPLE 10.76

```
1   > set name = nicky
    > echo $name:u
    Nicky

2   > set name = ( nicky jake )
    > echo $name:gu
    Nicky Jake

3   > echo $name:agu
    NICKY JAKE
```

EXAMPLE 10.76 (CONTINUED)

```
4   > set name = ( TOMMY DANNY )
    > echo $name:agl
    tommy danny

5   > set name = "$name:agu"
    > echo $name
    TOMMY DANNY
```

EXPLANATION

1 When *:u* is appended to the variable, the first letter in its value is uppercased.

2 When *:gu* is appended to the variable, the first letter in each word in the list of values is uppercased.

3 When *:agu* is appended to the variable, all letters in its value are uppercased.

4 When *:agl* is appended to the variable, all letters in its value are lowercased.

5 The variable is reset with all letters in its list uppercased.

10.10 Command Substitution

10.10.1 Backquotes

A string or variable can be assigned the output of a Linux command by placing the command in back quotes. This is called *command substitution.* (On the keyboard, the back quotes are normally below the tilde character.) If the output of a command is assigned to a variable, it is stored as a wordlist or array. (See "Wordlists and Command Substitution" on page 581.)

EXAMPLE 10.77

```
1   > echo The name of my machine is `uname -n`.
    The name of my machine is stardust.

2   > echo The present working directory is `pwd`.
    The present working directory is /home/stardust/john.

3   > set d = `date`
    > echo $d
    Tue Mar 28 14:24:21 PDT 2000
```

EXPLANATION

1 The Linux command *uname -n* is enclosed in back quotes. When the shell encounters the back quotes, it will execute the enclosed command, *uname -n*, and substitute the output of the command, *stardust*, into the string. When the *echo* command prints its arguments to standard output, the name of the machine will be one of its arguments.

2 The Linux command *pwd* is executed by the shell and the output is substituted in place within the string.

3 The local variable *d* is assigned the output of the *date* command. The output is stored as a list of words (an array).

Wordlists and Command Substitution. When a command is enclosed in back quotes and assigned to a variable, the resulting value is an array (wordlist). Each element of the array can be accessed by appending a subscript to the array name. The subscripts start at one. If a subscript that is greater than the number of words in the array is used, the C shell prints "*Subscript out of range*." If the output of a command consists of more than one line, the newlines are stripped from each line and replaced with a single space.

After an array is created, the built-in *shift* command can be used to remove words starting at word number one. Once a word is shifted off, it cannot be retrieved. (See Example 10.79.)

EXAMPLE 10.78

```
1    > set d = `date`
     > echo $d
     Tue Mar 28 14:04:49 PST 2000

2    > echo $d[1-3]
     Tue Mar 28

3    > echo $d[6]
     2000

4    > echo $d[7]
     Subscript out of range.

5    > echo "The calendar for the month of March is `cal 3 2000`"
     The calendar for month of March is March 2000 S M Tu W
     Th F S 1 2 3 4 5 6 7 8 9 10 11 12 13 14 15 16 17 18 19 20 21
     22 23 24 25 26 27 28 29 30 31
```

EXPLANATION

1 The variable *d* is assigned the output of the Linux *date* command. The output is stored as an array. The value of the variable is displayed.

2 The first three elements of the array are displayed.

3 The sixth element of the array is displayed.

4 There are not seven elements in the array. The shell reports that the subscript is out of range.

5 The output spans more than one line. Each newline is replaced with a space. This may not be the output you expected.

EXAMPLE 10.79

```
1   > set machine = `rusers | awk '/tom/{print $1}'`

2   > echo $machine
    dumbo bambi dolphin

3   > echo $#machine
    3

4   > echo $machine[$#machine]
    dolphin

5   > echo $machine
    dumbo bambi dolphin

6   > shift $machine
    > echo $machine
    bambi dolphin

7   > echo $machine[1]
    bambi

8   > echo $#machine
    2
```

EXPLANATION

1 The output of the *rusers* command is piped to *awk*. If the regular expression *tom* is found, *awk* prints the first field. The first field, in this case, is the name of the machine(s) where user *tom* is logged on.

2 User *tom* is logged on three machines. The names of the machines are displayed.

EXPLANATION (CONTINUED)

3 The number of elements in the array is accessed by preceding the array name with *$#*. There are three elements in the array.

4 The last element of the array is displayed. The number of elements in the array (*$#machine*) is used as a subscript.

5 The array is displayed.

6 The *shift* command shifts the array to the left. The first element of the array is dropped and the subscripts are renumbered, starting at one.

7 The first element of the array after the *shift* is displayed.

8 After the *shift*, the length of the array has decreased by one.

10.11 Quoting

The TC shell has a whole set of metacharacters that have some special meaning. In fact, almost any character on your keyboard that is not a letter or a number has some special meaning for the shell. Here is a partial list:

```
* ? [ ] $ ~ ! ^ & { } ( ) > < | ; : %
```

The backslash and quotes are used to escape the interpretation of metacharacters by the shell. Whereas the backslash is used to escape a single character, the quotes can be used to protect a string of characters. There are some general rules for using quotes:

1. Quotes are paired and must be matched on a line. The backslash character can be used to escape a newline so that a quote can be matched on the next line.
2. Single quotes will protect double quotes, and double quotes will protect single quotes.
3. Single quotes protect all metacharacters from interpretation, with the exception of the history character (*!*).
4. Double quotes protect all metacharacters from interpretation, with the exception of the history character (*!*), the variable substitution character (*$*), and the back quotes (used for command substitution).

10.11.1 The Backslash

The backslash is used to quote a single character and is the only character that can be used to escape a history character sequence (such as *!!* or *!string* or *!5*). Often the backslash is used to escape the newline character. The special *tcsh* variable, *backslash_quote,* can be used for quoting quotes and backslashes, but will not work in *csh* scripts. (See Example 10.80.)

EXAMPLE 10.80

```
1    > echo Who are you?
     echo: No match.

2    > echo Who are you\?
     Who are you?

3    > echo This is a very,very long line and this is where\
     ? I break the line.
     This is a very, very long line and this is where I break the
     line.

4    > echo "\abc"
     \abc
     > echo '\abc'
     \abc
     > echo \\abc
     \abc

5    > echo 'I can\'t help it!'
     Unmatched '.

6    > set backslash_quote
     > echo 'I can't help it!'
      I can't help it!
```

EXPLANATION

1 The question mark is used for filename expansion. It matches for a single character. The shell is looking for a file in the current directory that is spelled *y-o-u*, followed by a single character. Because there is not a file by that name in the directory, the shell complains that it could not find a match with "*No match*."

2 The shell will not try to interpret the question mark, because it is escaped with the backslash.

3 The string is continued to the next line by escaping the newline with a backslash. (The *?* is the secondary prompt, *prompt2*).

4 If the backslash is enclosed in either single or double quotes, it is printed. When not enclosed in quotes, the backslash escapes itself.

5 When enclosed in single quotes the backslash is ignored as a quoting character; i.e., it will not protect the single apostrophe in *can't*. The shell sees three single quotes and reports an unmatched quote.

6 The *tcsh* variable *backslash_quote*, if set, causes backslashes to always quote backslashes, single quotes, and double quotes.

10.11.2 Single Quotes

Single quotes must be matched on the same line and will escape all metacharacters with the exception of the history (bang) character (*!*) which is not protected because the shell evaluates history before it does quotes, but not before backslashes.)

EXAMPLE 10.81

```
1  > echo 'I need $5.00'
   I need $5.00

2  > cp file1 file2
   > echo 'I need $500.00 now!!'
   echo 'I need $500.00 nowcp file1 file2'

3  > echo 'I need $500.00 now\!\!'
   I need $500.00 now!!

4  > echo 'This is going to be a long line so
   Unmatched '.

5  > echo 'This is going to be a long line so \
   ? I used the backslash to suppress the newline'
   This is going to be a long line so
   I used the backslash to suppress the newline
```

EXPLANATION

1. The string is enclosed in single quotes. All characters, except the history (bang) character (*!*), are protected from shell interpretation.
2. After you use the *cp* command, the *echo* program is executed. Because the *!!* was not protected from shell interpretation, by using the backslash character, the last command on the history list is reexecuted and the *cp* command becomes part of the string.
3. By quoting the history characters (*!!*) with backslashes, they are protected from history substitution.
4. The quotes must be matched on the same line, or the shell reports "*Unmatched.*"
5. If the line is to be continued, the backslash character is used to escape the newline character. The quote is matched at the end of the next line. Even though the shell ignored the newline, the *echo* command did not. (The *?* is the secondary prompt, *prompt2*.)

10.11.3 Double Quotes

Double quotes must be matched, will allow variable and command substitution, and hide everything else, except the history (bang (*!*)). The backslash will not escape the dollar sign when enclosed in double quotes.

EXAMPLE 10.82

```
1   > set name = Bob
    > echo "Hi $name"
    Hi Bob

2   > echo "I don't have time."
     I don't have time.

3   > echo "WOW!!"        Watch the history metacharacter!
    echo "Wowecho "Wow!!""

4   > echo "WOW\!\!"
    Wow!!

5   > echo "I need \$5.00"
    I need \.00
```

EXPLANATION

1. The local variable *name* is assigned the value *Bob.* The double quotes allow the dollar sign to be used for variable substitution.
2. The single quote is protected within double quotes.
3. Double or single quotes will not protect the exclamation point from shell interpretation. The built-in *history* command is looking for the last command that began with a double quote and that event was not found.
4. The backslash is used to protect the exclamation point.
5. The backslash does not escape the dollar sign when used within double quotes.

10.11.4 Combining Double and Single Quotes

As long as the quoting rules are adhered to, double quotes and single quotes can be used in a variety of combinations in a single command.

EXAMPLE 10.83

```
1    > set name = Tom

2    > echo "I can't give $name" ' $5.00\!\!'
     I can't give Tom $5.00!!

3    > echo She cried, \"Oh help me\!\!'" ', $name.
     She cried, "Oh help me!!", Tom.
```

EXPLANATION

1 The local variable *name* is assigned *Tom.*

2 The single quote in the word *can't* is protected when enclosed within double quotes. The shell would try to perform variable substitution if the dollar sign in *$5.00* were within double quotes. Therefore, the string *$5.00* is enclosed in single quotes so that the dollar sign will be a literal. The exclamation point is protected with a backslash because neither double nor single quotes can protect it from shell interpretation.

3 The first conversational quotes are protected by the backslash. The exclamation point is also protected with a backslash. The last conversational quotes are enclosed in a set of single quotes. Single quotes will protect double quotes.

10.11.5 Steps to Successful Quoting

In a more complex command, it is often difficult to match quotes properly unless you follow the steps listed here. (See Appendix C.)

1. Know the Linux command and its syntax. Before variable substitution, hard code the values into the command line, to see if you get the expected results.

```
> awk -F: '/^Zippy Pinhead/{print "Phone is  " $2}' datafile
Phone is 408-123-4563
```

2. If the Linux command worked correctly, then plug in the variables. At this point, do not remove or change any quotes. Simply put the variables in place of the words they represent. In this example, replace *Zippy Pinhead* with *$name.*

```
> set name = "Zippy Pinhead"
> awk -F: '/^$name/{print "Phone is " $2}' datafile
```

3. Play the quoting game as follows: Starting at the left-hand side with the first single quote, insert a matching single quote just before the dollar sign in *$name*. Now you have a set of matched quotes.

```
awk -F: '/^'$name/{print "Phone is " $2}' datafile
```

Now, right after the last letter, *e* in *$name*, place another single quote. (Believe me, this works.) This quote matches the quote after the closing curly brace.

```
> awk -F: '/^'$name'/{print "Phone is  " $2}' datafile
```

Count the number of single quotes, starting at the left-hand side. You have four, a nice even number. Everything within each set of single quotes is ignored by the shell. The quotes are matched as follows:

```
> nawk -F: '$1 ~ /'$name'/{print $2}' filename
```

4. Last step: Double quote the variables. Surround each variable very snugly within a set of double quotes. The double quotes protect the white space in the expanded variable; for example, the space in *Zippy Pinhead* is protected.

```
> nawk -F: '$1 ~ /'"$name"'/{print $2}' filename
```

10.11.6 Quoting Variables

The *:x* and *:q* modifiers are used when it's necessary to quote variables.

Quoting with the *:q* Modifier. The *:q* modifier is used to replace double quotes.

EXAMPLE 10.84

```
1    > set name = "Daniel Savage"

2    > grep $name:q database
         same as

3    > grep "$name" database

4    > set food = "apple pie"

5    > set dessert = ( $food "ice cream")

6    > echo $#dessert
     3

7    > echo $dessert[1]
     apple

8    > echo $dessert[2]
     pie
```

EXAMPLE 10.84 (CONTINUED)

```
9    > echo $dessert[3]
     ice cream

10   > set dessert = ($food:q "ice cream")

11   > echo $#dessert
     2

12   > echo $dessert[1]
     apple pie

13   > echo $dessert[2]
     ice cream
```

EXPLANATION

1. The variable is assigned the string "*Daniel Savage*."
2. When *:q* is appended to the variable, the variable is quoted. This is the same as enclosing the variable in double quotes.
3. The double quotes surrounding the variable *$name* allow variable substitution to take place, but protect any white space characters. Without the double quotes, the *grep* program will search for *Daniel* in a file called *Savage* and a file called *database*.
4. The variable *food* is assigned the string "*apple pie*".
5. The variable *dessert* is assigned an array (wordlist) consisting of "*apple pie*" and "*ice cream*."
6. The number of elements in the *dessert* array is three. When the *food* variable was expanded, the quotes were removed. There are three elements, *apple, pie*, and *ice cream*.
7. The first element of the array is printed. The variable expands to separated words if not quoted.
8. The second element of the array is printed.
9. Since "*ice cream*" is quoted, it is treated as one word.
10. The *dessert* array is assigned *apple pie* and *ice cream*. The *:q* can be used to quote the variable in the same way double quotes quote the variable; i.e., *$food:q* is the same as *"$food"*.
11. The array consists of two strings, *apple pie* and *ice cream*.
12. The first element of the array, *apple pie*, is printed.
13. The second element of the array, *ice cream*, is printed.

Quoting with the *:x* Modifier. If you are creating an array and any of the words in the list contain metacharacters, *:x* prevents the shell from interpreting the metacharacters when performing variable substitution.

EXAMPLE 10.85

```
1   > set  things = "*.c   a??   file[1-5]"
    > echo $#things
    1

2   > set newthings = ( $things )
    set: No match.

3   > set newthings = ( $things:x )

4   > echo $#newthings
    3

5   > echo "$newthings[1] $newthings[2] $newthings[3] "
    *.c  a??   file[1-5]

6   >  grep $newthings[2]:q filex
```

EXPLANATION

1. The variable *things* is assigned a string. Each string contains a wildcard. The number of elements in the variable is one, one string.
2. When attempting to create an array out of the string *things*, the C shell tries to expand the wildcard characters to perform filename substitution within *things* and produces a *No match*.
3. The *:x* extension prevents the shell from expanding the wildcards in the *things* variable.
4. The array *newthings* consists of three elements.
5. To print the elements of the array, they must be quoted or, again, the shell will try to expand the wildcards.
6. The *:q* quotes the variable just as though the variable were surrounded by double quotes. The *grep* program will print any lines containing the pattern *a??* in file *filex*.

10.12 Built-In Commands

Rather than residing on disk like Linux executable commands, built-in commands are part of the TC shell's internal code and are executed from within the shell. If a built-in command occurs as any component of a pipeline except the last, it is executed in a subshell. The *tcsh* command aptly called, *builtins,* lists all the built-in commands:

EXAMPLE 10.86

```
1  > builtins
:          @          alias      alloc     bg         bindkey    break
breaksw    builtins   case       cd        chdir      complete   continue
default    dirs       echo       echotc    else       end        endif
endsw      eval       exec       exit      fg         filetest   foreach
glob       goto       hashstat   history   hup        if         jobs
kill       limit      log        login     logout     ls-F       nice
nohup      notify     onintr     popd      printenv   pushd      rehash
repeat     sched      set        setenv    settc      setty      shift
source     stop       suspend    switch    telltc     time       umask
unalias    uncomplete unhash     unlimit   unset      unsetenv   wait
where      which      while
```

See Table 10.24 for a list of built-in commands.

Table 10.24 Built-In Commands and Their Meanings

Built-In Command	*Meaning*
:	Interprets null command, but performs no action.
alias [name [wordlist]]	A nickname for a command. Without arguments, prints all aliases; with a name, prints the name for the alias, and with a name and wordlist sets the alias.
alloc	Displays amount of dynamic memory acquired, broken down into used and free memory. Varies across systems.
bg [%job]	Runs the current or specified jobs in the background.
%job &	A synonym for the *bg* built-in command.

Table 10.24 Built-In Commands and Their Meanings (Continued)

Built-In Command	*Meaning*
bindkey [-l|-d|-e|-v|-u] (+) *bindkey [-a] [-b] [-k] [-r] [--] key* *bindkey [-a] [-b] [-k] [-c|-s] [--] key command*	Without options, the first form lists all bound keys and the editor command to which each is bound, the second form lists the editor command to which key is bound, and the third form binds the editor command command to key. Options include: *-l* Lists all editor commands and a short description of each. *-d* Binds all keys to the standard bindings for the default editor. *-e* Binds all keys to the standard Gnu *emacs*-like bindings. *-v* Binds all keys to the standard *vi*(1)-like bindings. *-a* Lists or changes key-bindings in the alternative key map. This is the key map used in *vi* command mode. (*tcsh* only) *-b* This key is interpreted as a control character written as ^character (e.g., ^*A*) or C-character (e.g., *C-A*), a meta-character written M-character (e.g., *M-A*), a function key written F-string (e.g., *F-string*), or an extended prefix key written X-character (e.g., *X-A*). (*tcsh* only) *-k* This key is interpreted as a symbolic arrow key name, which may be one of "down," "up," "left," or "right." (*tcsh* only) *-r* Removes key's binding. Be careful: *bindkey-r* does not bind key to self-insert-command (q.v.), it unbinds key completely. (*tcsh* only) *-c* This command is interpreted as a built-in or external command, instead of an editor command. (*tcsh* only) *-s* This command is taken as a literal string and treated as terminal input when key is typed. Bound keys in commands are themselves reinterpreted, and this continues for 10 levels of interpretation. (*tcsh* only) -- Forces a break from option processing, so the next word is taken as a key even if it begins with a hyphen (-). (*tcsh* only) *-u* (or any invalid option) Prints a usage message. This key may be a single character or a string. If a command is bound to a string, the first character of the string is bound to sequence-lead-in and the entire string is bound to the command. Control characters in key can be literal (they can be typed by preceding them with the editor command quoted-insert, normally bound to ^*V*) or written caret-character style, e.g., ^*A*. Delete is written ^*?* (caret-question mark). Key and command can contain backslashed escape sequences (in the style of System V echo(1)) as follows: *a* Bell *f* Form feed *t* Horizontal tab *b* Backspace *n* Newline *v* Vertical tab *e* Escape *r* Carriage return *nnn* The ASCII character corresponding to the octal number *nnn* \\ nullifies the special meaning of the following character, if it has any, notably backslash (\\) and caret (^).

Table 10.24 Built-In Commands and Their Meanings (Continued)

Built-In Command	*Meaning*
break	Breaks out of the innermost *foreach* or *while* loop.
breaksw	Breaks from a switch, resuming after the *endsw.*
builtins	Prints the names of all built-in commands. (*tcsh* only)
bye	A synonym for the logout built-in command. Available only if the shell was so compiled; see the version shell variable. (*tcsh* only)
case label:	A label in a switch statement.
cd [dir]	Changes the shell's working directory to *dir.* If no argument is given, changes to the home directory of the user.
cd [-p] [-l] [-n|-v] [name]	If a directory name is given, changes the shell's working directory to name. If not, changes to home. If *name* is "-" it is interpreted as the previous working directory. *-p*, prints the final directory stack, just like *dirs.* *-l*, *-n*, and *-v* flags have the same effect on cd as on dirs, and they imply *-p*. (*tcsh* only)
chdir	A synonym for the *cd* built-in command.
complete [command [word/pattern/list[:select]/[[suffix]/] ...]]	Without arguments, lists all completions. With command, lists completions for command. With command and word etc., defines completions. (See "Programming Completions" on page 528.) (*tcsh* only)
continue	Continues execution of the nearest enclosing *while* or *foreach.*
default:	Labels the *default* case in a switch statement. The *default* should come after all case labels.
dirs [-l] [-n|-v] *dirs -S|-L [filename]* *dirs -c*	The first form prints the directory stack. The top of the stack is at the left and the first directory in the stack is the current directory. *-l*, ~ or *~name* in the output is expanded explicitly to home or the pathname of the home directory for user name. (+) *-n*, entries are wrapped before they reach the edge of the screen. (+) *-v*, entries are printed one per line preceded by their stack postions. *-S*, the second form saves the directory stack to filename as a series of *cd* and *pushd* commands. (*tcsh* only) *-L*, the shell source's filename, which is presumably a directory stack file saved. (*tcsh* only) In either case *dirsfile* is used if filename is not given and *~/.cshdirs* is used if *dirsfile* is unset. With *-c*, form clears the directory stack. (*tcsh* only)

Table 10.24 Built-In Commands and Their Meanings (Continued)

Built-In Command	***Meaning***
echo [-n] list	Writes the words in *list* to the shell's standard output, separated by SPACE characters. The output is terminated with a NEWLINE unless the *-n* option is used.
echo [-n] word ...	Writes each word to the shell's standard output, separated by spaces and terminated with a newline. The *echo_style* shell variable may be set to emulate (or not) the flags and escape sequences of the BSD and/or System V versions of echo.
echotc [-sv] arg ...	Exercises the terminal capabilities (see term-cap(5)) in args. For example, *'echotc home'* sends the cursor to the home position. If arg is *'baud'*, *'cols'*, *'lines'*, *'meta'*, or *'tabs'*, prints the value of that capability. With *-s*, nonexistent capabilities return the empty string rather than causing an error. With *-v*, messages are verbose. (*tcsh* only)
else if (expr2) then	See "Flow Control and Conditional Constructs" on page 627.

else
end
endif
endsw
	See the description of the *foreach*, *if*, *switch*, and *while* statements below.

end	Executes the commands between the *while* and the matching *end* while *expr* evaluates nonzero. *while* and *end* must appear alone on their input lines. *break* and *continue* may be used to terminate or continue the loop prematurely. If the input is a terminal, the user is prompted the first time through the loop as with *foreach.*
eval arg ...	Treats the arguments as input to the shell and executes the resulting command(s) in the context of the current shell. This is usually used to execute commands generated as the result of command or variable substitution, since parsing occurs before these substitutions.
eval command	Runs *command* as standard input to the shell and executes the resulting commands. This is usually used to execute commands generated as the result of command or variable substitution, since parsing occurs before these substitutions (e.g., *eval 'tset -s options'*).
exec command	Executes *command* in place of the current shell, which terminates.
exit [(expr)]	Exits the shell, either with the value of the status variable or with the value specified by *expr.*
fg [% job] *%job*	Brings the current or specified *job* into the foreground. A synonym for the *fg* built-in command.

Table 10.24 Built-In Commands and Their Meanings (Continued)

Built-In Command	***Meaning***
filetest -op file ...	Applies *op* (which is a file inquiry operator) to each file and returns the results as a space-separated list. (*tcsh* only)
foreach name (wordlist) ... *end*	(See "Looping Commands" on page 655.)
foreach var (wordlist)	See "The foreach Loop" on page 650.
getspath	Prints the system execution path. (TCF only) (*tcsh* only)
getxvers	Prints the experimental version prefix. (TCF only) (*tcsh* only)
glob wordlist	Performs filename expansion on wordlist. Like *echo*, but no *escapes* (\) are recognized. Words are delimited by null characters in the output.
goto label	See "The goto" on page 638.
goto word	*word* is filename and command-substituted to yield a string of the form "label." The shell rewinds its input as much as possible, searches for a line of the form "label:", possibly preceded by blanks or tabs, and continues execution after that line.
hashstat	Prints a statistics line indicating how effective the internal hash table has been at locating commands (and avoiding *execs*). An *exec* is attempted for each component of the path where the hash function indicates a possible hit, and in each component that does not begin with a backslash.
history [-hTr] [n] *history -S|-L|-M [filename]* *history -c*	The first form prints the history event list. If *n* is given, only the *n* most recent events are printed or saved. With *-h*, the history list is printed without leading numbers. If *-T* is specified, timestamps are printed also in comment form. (This can be used to produce files suitable for loading with *'history -L'* or *'source -h'*. (*tcsh* only)) With *-r*, the order of printing is most recent first rather than oldest first. (See "History" on page 508.) With *-c*, clears the history list (*tcsh* only).
hup [command]	With command, runs command such that it will exit on a hangup signal and arranges for the shell to send it a hangup signal when the shell exits. Note that commands may set their own response to hangups, overriding *hup*. Without an argument (allowed only in a shell script), causes the shell to exit on a hangup for the remainder of the script. (*tcsh* only)

Table 10.24 Built-In Commands and Their Meanings (Continued)

Built-In Command	***Meaning***
if (expr) command	If *expr* evaluates true, then command is executed. Variable substitution on command happens early, at the same time it does for the rest of the *if* command. Command must be a simple command, not an alias, a pipeline, a command list or a parenthesized command list, but it may have arguments. Input/output redirection occurs even if *expr* is false and command is thus not executed; this is a bug.

if (expr) then
...
else if (expr2) then
...
else
...
endif
	If the specified *expr* is true then the commands to the first else are executed; otherwise if *expr2* is true then the commands to the second else are executed, etc. Any number of else-if pairs are possible; only one *endif* is needed. The else part is likewise optional. (The words *else* and *endif* must appear at the beginning of input lines; the *if* must appear alone on its input line or after an *else*.)

inlib shared-library ...	Adds each shared-library to the current environment. There is no way to remove a shared library. (Domain/OS only) (*tcsh* only)
jobs [-l]	Lists the active *jobs* under job control. With *-l*, lists IDs in addition to the normal information.
kill [-sig] [pid] [%job] ... *kill -l*	Sends the *TERM* (terminate) signal, by default or by the signal specified, to the specified ID, the job indicated, or the current job. Signals are given either by number or name. There is no default. Typing *kill* does not send a signal to the current job. If the signal being sent is *TERM* (terminate) or *HUP* (hangup), then the job or process is sent a *CONT* (continue) signal as well. With *-l* lists the signal names that can be sent.
limit [-h] [resource [max-use]]	Limits the consumption by the current process or any process it spawns, each not to exceed *max-use* on the specified *resource*. If *max-use* is omitted, print the current *limit*; if *resource* is omitted, display all *limits*. With *-h*, uses hard limits instead of the current limits. Hard limits impose a ceiling on the values of the current limits. Only the superuser may raise the hard limits. Resource is one of: *cputime,* maximum CPU seconds per process; *filesize*, largest single file allowed; *datasize*, maximum data size (including stack) for the process; *stacksize*, maximum stack size for the process; *coredump*, maximum size of a core dump; and *descriptors*, maximum value for a file descriptor.
log	Prints the *watch* shell variable and reports on each user indicated in watch who is logged in, regardless of when they last logged in. See also *watchlog*. (*tcsh* only)
login	Terminates a login shell, replacing it with an instance of */bin/login*.

Table 10.24 Built-In Commands and Their Meanings (Continued)

Built-In Command	*Meaning*
login [username|-p]	Terminates a *login* shell and invokes *login(1)*. The *.logout* file is not processed. If *username* is omitted, *login* prompts for the name of a user. With *-p*, preserves the current environment (variables).
logout	Terminates a login shell.
ls-F [-switch ...] [file ...]	Lists files like *ls -F*, but much faster (*tcsh* only). It identifies each type of special file in the listing with a special character: / Directory * Executable # Block device % Character device | Named pipe (systems with named pipes only) = Socket (systems with sockets only) @ Symbolic link (systems with symbolic links only) + Hidden directory (AIX only) or context-dependent (HP/UX only) : Network special (HP/UX only) If the listlinks shell variable is set, symbolic links are identified in more detail (only, of course, on systems which have them): @ Symbolic link to a nondirectory > Symbolic link to a directory & Symbolic link to nowhere The *ls-F* built-in can list files using different colors depending on the filetype or extension.
migrate [-site] pid|%jobid ... *migrate -site*	The first form migrates the process or job to the site specified or the default site determined by the system path (*tcsh* only). The second form is equivalent to *migrate -site $$* (*tcsh* only). It migrates the current process to the specified site. Migrating the shell itself can cause unexpected behavior, since the shell does not like to lose its *tty*. (TCF only)
@ *@ name = expr* *@ name[index] = expr* *@ name++|--* *@ name[index]++|--*	The first form prints the values of all shell variables. The second form assigns the value of *expr* to name. The third form assigns the value of *expr* to the index'th component of name; both name and its index'th component must already exist. The fourth and fifth forms increment (++) or decrement (--) name or its index'th component.
newgrp [-] group	Equivalent to *exec newgrp*; see newgrp(1). Available only if the shell was so compiled; see the version shell variable. (*tcsh* only)

Table 10.24 Built-In Commands and Their Meanings (Continued)

Built-In Command	***Meaning***
nice [+number] [command]	Sets the scheduling priority for the shell to number, or, without number, to 4. With command, runs command at the appropriate priority. The greater the number, the less CPU the process gets. The superuser may specify negative priority by using *nice -number ....* Command is always executed in a subshell, and the restrictions placed on commands in simple if statements apply.
nohup [command]	Runs *command* with *HUP*s (hangups) ignored. With no arguments, ignores *HUP*s throughout the remainder of a script.
notify [%job]	Notifies the user asynchronously when the status of the current or of a specified *job* changes.
onintr [- | label]	Controls the action of the shell on interrupts. With no arguments, *onintr* restores the default action of the shell on interrupts. (The shell terminates shell scripts and returns to the terminal command input level.) With the minus sign argument, the shell ignores all interrupts. With a *label* argument, the shell executes a *goto label* when an interrupt is received or a child process terminates because it was interrupted.
popd [+n]	Pops the directory stack and *cd* to the new top directory. The elements of the directory stack are numbered from zero, starting at the top. With *+n*, discard the *n*th entry in the stack.
printenv [name]	Prints the names and values of all environment variables or, with name, the value of the environment variable name. (*tcsh* only)
pushd [+n | dir]	Pushes a directory onto the directory stack. With no arguments, exchanges the top two elements. With *+n*, rotates the *n*th entry to the top of the stack and *cd* to it. With *dir*, pushes the current working directory onto the stack and changes to *dir*.
rehash	Recomputes the internal hash table of the contents of directories listed in the *path* variable to account for new commands added.
repeat count command	Repeats command *count* times.
rootnode //nodename	Changes the rootnode to *//nodename*, so that / will be interpreted as *//nodename*. (Domain/OS only) (*tcsh* only)
sched *sched [+]hh:mm command* *sched -n*	The first form prints the scheduled-event list (*tcsh* only). The *sched* shell variable may be set to define the format in which the scheduled-event list is printed. The second form adds command to the scheduled-event list. (*tcsh* only)

Table 10.24 Built-In Commands and Their Meanings (Continued)

Built-In Command	*Meaning*
set *set name ...* *set name=word ...* *set [-r] [-f|-l] name=(wordlist) ... (+)* *set name[index]=word ...* *set -r* *set -r name ...* *set -r name=word ...*	The first form of the command prints the value of all shell variables. Variables which contain more than a single word print as a parenthesized word list. The second form sets name to the null string. The third form sets name to the single word. The fourth form sets name to the list of words in wordlist. In all cases the value is command and filename expanded. If *-r* is specified, the value is set read-only. If *-f* or *-l* are specified, set only unique words keeping their order. *-f* prefers the first occurrence of a word, and *-l* the last occurrence of the word. The fifth form sets the index'th component of name to word; this component must already exist. The sixth form lists the names (only) of all shell variables which are read-only (*tcsh* only). The seventh form makes name read-only, whether or not it has a value (*tcsh* only). The eighth form is the same as the third form, but makes name read-only at the same time (*tcsh* only).
set [var [= value]]	See "Variables" on page 561.
setenv [VAR [word]]	See "Variables" on page 561. The most commonly used environment variables, *USER, TERM,* and *PATH*, are automatically imported to and exported from the *csh* variables, *user, term*, and *path*; there is no need to use *setenv* for these. In addition, the shell sets the *PWD* environment variable from the *csh* variable *cwd* whenever the latter changes.
setenv [name [value]]	Without arguments, prints the names and values of all environment variables. Given name, sets the environment variable name to value or, without value, to the null string.
setpath path	Equivalent to setpath(1). (Mach only) (*tcsh* only)
setspath LOCAL|site|cpu ...	Sets the system execution path. (TCF only) (*tcsh* only)
settc cap value	Tells the shell to believe that the terminal capability cap (as defined in termcap(5)) has the value *value*. No sanity checking is done. Concept terminal users may have to *settc xn no* to get proper wrapping at the rightmost column. (*tcsh* only)
setty [-d|-q|-x] [-a] [[+|-]mode]	Controls which tty modes the shell does not allow to change. *-d, -q,* or *-x* tells *setty* to act on the *edit, quote,* or *execute* set of *tty* modes, respectively; without *-d, -q,* or *-x, execute* is used. Without other arguments, *setty* lists the modes in the chosen set which are fixed on (*+mode*) or off (*-mode*). The available modes, and thus the display, vary from system to system. With *-a*, lists all tty modes in the chosen set whether or not they are fixed. With *+mode, -mode,* or *mode,* fixes mode on or off or removes control from mode in the chosen set. For example, *setty +echok echoe* fixes *echok* mode on and allows commands to turn *echoe* mode on or off, both when the shell is executing commands. (*tcsh* only)

Table 10.24 Built-In Commands and Their Meanings (Continued)

Built-In Command	***Meaning***
setxvers [string]	Sets the experimental version prefix to string, or removes it if string is omitted. (TCF only) (*tcsh* only)
shift [variable]	The components of *argv*, or *variable*, if supplied, are shifted to the left, discarding the first component. It is an error for *variable* not to be set, or to have a null value.
source [-h] name	Reads commands from *name. Source* commands may be nested, but if they are nested too deeply, the shell may run out of file descriptors. An error in a sourced file at any level terminates all nested *source* commands. Used commonly to reexecute the *.login* or *.cshrc* files to ensure variable settings are handled within the current shell, i.e., shell does not create a child shell (fork). With *-h*, places commands from the filename on the history list without executing them.
stop [%job] ...	Stops the current or specified background *job.*
suspend	Stops the shell in its tracks, much as if it had been sent a stop signal with ^Z. This is most often used to stop shells started by *su.*
switch (string)	See "The switch Command" on page 645.
telltc	Lists the values of all terminal capabilities (see termcap(5)). (*tcsh* only)
time [command]	With no argument, prints a summary of *time* used by this shell and its children. With an optional *command*, executes *command* and print a summary of the *time* it uses.
umask [value]	Displays the file creation mask. With *value*, sets the file creation mask. *Value*, given in octal, is XORed with the permissions of 666 for files and 777 for directories to arrive at the permissions for new files. Permissions cannot be added via *umask.*
unalias pattern	Removes all aliases whose names match pattern. *unalias* * thus removes all aliases. It is not an error for nothing to be unaliased.
uncomplete pattern	Removes all completions whose names match pattern. *uncomplete* * thus removes all completions. (*tcsh* only)
unhash	Disables the internal hash table.
universe universe	Sets the universe to universe. (Masscomp/RTU only) (*tcsh* only)
unlimit [-h] [resource]	Removes the limitation on resource or, if no resource is specified, all resource limitations. With *-h*, the corresponding hard limits are removed. Only the superuser may do this.

Table 10.24 Built-In Commands and Their Meanings (Continued)

Built-In Command	***Meaning***
unsetenv pattern	Removes all environment variables whose names match pattern. *unsetenv* * thus removes all environment variables; this is a bad idea. If there is no pattern to be *unsetenv*ed, no error will result from this built-in.
unsetenv variable	Removes *variable* from the environment. Pattern matching, as with *unset*, is not performed.
@ [var =expr] *@ [var[n] =expr]*	With no arguments, displays the values for all shell variables. With arguments, the variable *var*, or the *n*th word in the value of *var*, is set to the value that *expr* evaluates to.
ver [systype [command]]	Without arguments, prints SYSTYPE. With *systype*, sets SYSTYPE to *systype*. With *systype* and *command*, executes *command* under *systype*. *systype* may be *bsd4.3* or *sys5.3*. (Domain/OS only) (*tcsh* only)
wait	Waits for background jobs to finish (or for an interrupt) before prompting.
warp universe	Sets the universe to universe. (Convex/OS only) (*tcsh* only)
watchlog	An alternate name for the log built-in command (q.v.). Available only if the shell was so compiled; see the version shell variable. (*tcsh* only)
where command	Reports all known instances of command, including aliases, built-ins, and executables in path. (*tcsh* only)
which command	Displays the command that will be executed by the shell after substitutions, path searching, etc. The built-in command is just like which(1), but it correctly reports *tcsh* aliases and built-ins and is 10 to 100 times faster. (*tcsh* only)
while (expr)	See "Looping Commands" on page 655.

10.12.1 Special Aliases (*tcsh* Only)

If set, each of the TC shell aliases executes automatically at the indicated time. They are all initially undefined.

beepcmd	Runs when the shell wants to ring the terminal bell
cwdcmd	Runs after every change of working directory
periodic	Runs every *tperiod* minutes; e.g., > *set tperiod = 30* > *alias periodic date*
precmd	Runs just before each prompt is printed; e.g., *alias precmd date*

10.12.2 Special Built-In Shell Variables

The built-in shell variables have special meaning to the shell and are used to modify and control the way many of the shell commmands behave. They are local variables and therefore most of them are set in the *.tcshrc* file if they are to be passed on to and affect child TC shells.

When the shell starts up, it automatically sets the following variables: *addsuffix, argv, autologout, command, echo_style, edit, gid, group, home, loginsh, oid, path, prompt, prompt2, prompt3, shell, shlvl, tcsh, term, tty, uid, user,* and *version.* Unless the user decides to change them, these variables will remain fixed. The shell also keeps track of and changes special variables that may need period updates, such as, *cwd, dirstack, owd,* and *status*, and when the user logs out, the shell sets the *logout* variable.

Some of the local variables have a corresponding environment variable of the same name. If one of the environment or local variables are affected by a change in the user's environment, the shell will synchronize the local and environment variables[10] so that their values always match. Examples of cross-matched variables are: *afuser, group, home, path, shlvl, term,* and *user.* (Although *cwd* and *PWD* have the same meaning, they are not cross-matched. Even though the syntax is different for the path and PATH variables, they are automatically crossed-matched if either one is changed.)

10. This is true unless the variable is a read-only variable, and then there will be no synchronization.

Table 10.25 Special Shell Variables
(Descriptions taken from tcsh manual pages.)

addsufix	For filename completion, adds slashes at the end of directories and space to the end of normal files if they are matched. *(tcsh)* Set by default.
afsuser	If set, autologout's autolock feature uses its value instead of the local username for kerberos authentication. (*tcsh*)
ampm	If set, all times are shown in 12-hour AM/PM format. (*tcsh*)
argv	An array of command line arguments to the shell; also represented as $1, $2, etc.
autocorrect	Invokes the spell checker before each attempt at filename, command, or variable completion. (*tcsh*)
autoexpand	If set, the expand-history editor command is invoked automatically before each completion attempt. (*tcsh*)
autolist	If set, possibilities are listed after an ambiguous completion. If set to *ambiguous*, possibilities are listed only when no new characters are added by completion.
autologout	Its argument is the number of minutes of inactivity before automatic logout; the second optional argument is the number of minutes before automatic locking causes the screen to lock. (*tcsh*)
backslash_quote	If set, a backslash will always quote itself, a single quote, or a double quote. (*tcsh*)
cdpath	A list of directories in which *cd* should search for subdirectories if they aren't found in the current directory.
color	Enables color display for the built-in command, *ls-F* and passes *--color=auto* to *ls*. (*tcsh*)
complete	If set to *enhance*, completion ignores case, considers periods, hyphens and underscores to be word separators, and hyphens and underscores to be equivalent. (*tcsh*)
correct	If set to *cmd*, commands are automatically spelling-corrected. If set to *complete*, commands are automatically completed. If set to *all*, the entire command line is corrected. (*tcsh*)
cwd	The full path name of the current working directory.
dextract	If set, *pushd +n* extracts the *n*th directory from the directory stack rather than rotating it to the top. *(tcsh)*
dirsfile	The default location in which *dirs -S* and *dirs -L* look for a history file. If unset, *~/.cshdirs* is used.

Table 10.25 Special Shell Variables (Continued)
(Descriptions taken from tcsh manual pages.)

dirstack	A list of all directories on the directory stack. (*tcsh*)
dunique	Will not allow *pushd* to keep duplicate directory entries on the stack. (*tcsh*)
echo	If set, each command with its arguments is echoed just before it is executed. Set by the *-x* command line option.
echo-style	Sets the style for *echo*. If set to *bsd* will not echo a newline if the first argument is *-n*; if set to *sysv*, recognizes backslashed escape sequences in echo strings; if set to *both*, recognizes both the *-n* flag and backslashed escape sequences; the default, and if set to none, recognizes neither. (*tcsh*)
edit	Sets the command-line editor for interactive shells; set by default.
ellipsis	If set, the '%c'/'%.' and '%C' prompt sequences (see the "The Shell Prompts" on page 500) indicate skipped directories with an ellipsis (...) instead of /<*skipped*>. (*tcsh*)
fignore	Lists filename suffixes to be ignored by completion.
filec	In *tcsh*, completion is always used and this variable is ignored. If set in *csh*, filename completion is used.
gid	The user's read group id number. (*tcsh*)
group	The user's group name. (*tcsh*)
histchars	A string value determining the characters used in history substitution. The first character of its value is used as the history substitution character to replace the default character, *!*. The second character of its value replaces the character ^ in quick substitutions.
histdup	Controls handling of duplicate entries in the history list. Can be set to *all* (removes all duplicates), *prev* (removes the current command if it duplicates the previous command), or *erase* (inserts the current event for an older duplicate event). (*tcsh*)
histfile	The default location in which *history -S* and *history -L* look for a history file. If unset, *~/.history* is used.
histlit	Enters events on the history list literally; i.e., unexpanded by history substitution. (*tcsh*)
history	The first word indicates the number of history events to save. The optional second word (+) indicates the format in which history is printed.
home	The home directory of the user; same as ~.
ignoreeof	If logging out by pressing Control-D, prints *Use "exit"* to leave *tcsh*. Prevents inadvertently logging out.

Table 10.25 Special Shell Variables (Continued)
(Descriptions taken from tcsh manual pages.)

implicitcd	If set, the shell treats a directory name typed as a command as though it were a request to change to that directory and changes to it. (*tcsh*)
inputmode	If set to *insert* or *overwrite*, puts the editor into that input mode at the beginning of each line. (*tcsh*)
listflags	If set to *x*, *a*, or *A*, or any combination (e.g., *xA*), values are used as flags to *ls-F*, making it act like *ls -xF*, *ls -Fa*, *ls -FA*, or any combination of those flags. (*tcsh*)
listjobs	If set, all jobs are listed when a job is suspended. If set to *long*, the listing is in long format. *(tcsh)*
listlinks	If set, the *ls-F* built-in command shows the type of file to which each symbolic link points. (*tcsh*)
listmax	The maximum number of items which the *list-choices* editor command will list without asking first. (*tcsh*)
listmaxrows	The maximum number of rows of items which the *list-choices* editor command will list without asking first. (*tcsh*)
loginsh	Set by the shell if it is a login shell. Setting or unsetting it within a shell has no effect. See also *shlvl* later in this table. (*tcsh*)
logout	Set by the shell to *normal* before a normal logout, *automatic* before an automatic logout, and *hangup* if the shell was killed by a hangup signal. (*tcsh*)
mail	The names of the files or directories to check for incoming mail. After 10 minutes if new mail has come in, will print *"You have new mail"*.
matchbeep	If set to *never*, completion never beeps; if set to *nomatch*, completion beeps only when there is no match, and when set to *ambiguous*, beeps when there are multiple matches.
nobeep	Disables all beeping.
noclobber	Safeguards against the accidental removal of existing files when redirection is used; e.g., *ls > file*.
noglob	If set, inhibits filename and directory stack substitutions when using wildcards.
nokanji	If set and the shell supports Kanji (see the version shell variable), it is disabled so that the meta key can be used. (*tcsh*)
nonomatch	If set, a filename substitution or directory stack substitution which does not match any existing files is left untouched rather than causing an error. (*tcsh*)

Table 10.25 Special Shell Variables (Continued)
(Descriptions taken from tcsh manual pages.)

nostat	A list of directories (or glob-patterns which match directories); that should not be stat(2)ed during a completion operation. This is usually used to exclude directories which take too much time to stat(2). *(tcsh)*
notify	If set, the shell announces job completions asynchronously instead of waiting until just before the prompt appears.
oid	The user's real organization ID. (Domain/OS only) *(tcsh)*
owd	The old or previous working directory. *(tcsh)*
path	A list of directories in which to look for executable commands. *path* is set by the shell at startup from the *PATH* environment variable or, if *PATH* does not exist, to a system-dependent default something like (*/usr/local/bin /usr/bsd /bin /usr/bin*).
printexitvalue	If set and an interactive program exits with a nonzero status, the shell prints *Exit status.*
prompt	The string which is printed before reading each command from the terminal which may include special formatting sequences (See "The Shell Prompts" on page 500).
prompt2	The string with which to prompt in *while* and *foreach* loops and after lines ending in \. The same format sequences may be used as in *prompt*; note the variable meaning of *%R*. Set by default to *%R?* in interactive shells. *(tcsh)*
prompt3	The string with which to prompt when confirming automatic spelling correction. The same format sequences may be used as in prompt ; note the variable meaning of *%R*. Set by default to *CORRECT>%R (y|n|e|a)?* in interactive shells. *(tcsh)*
promptchars	If set (to a two-character string), the *%#* formatting sequence in the prompt shell variable is replaced with the first character for normal users and the second character for the superuser. *(tcsh)*
pushtohome	If set, *pushd* without arguments does *pushd ~*, like *cd. (tcsh)*
pushdsilent	If set, *pushd* and *popd* to not print the directory stack. *(tcsh)*
recexact	If set, completion completes on an exact match even if a longer match is possible. *(tcsh)*
recognize_only_ executables	If set, command listing displays only files in the path that are executable. *(tcsh)*
rmstar	If set, the user is prompted before *rm* * is executed. *(tcsh)*

Table 10.25 Special Shell Variables (Continued)
(Descriptions taken from tcsh manual pages.)

rprompt	The string to print on the right-hand side of the screen (after the command input) when the prompt is being displayed on the left. It recognises the same formatting characters as prompt. It will automatically disappear and reappear as necessary, to ensure that command input isn't obscured, and will only appear if the prompt, command input, and itself will fit together on the first line. If edit isn't set, then *rprompt* will be printed after the prompt and before the command input. (*tcsh*)
savedirs	If set, the shell does *dirs -S* before exiting. (*tcsh*)
savehist	If set, the shell does *history -S* before exiting. If the first word is set to a number, at most that many lines are saved. (The number must be less than or equal to history.) If the second word is set to *merge*, the history list is merged with the existing history file instead of replacing it (if there is one) and sorted by timestamp and the most recent events are retained. (*tcsh*)
sched	The format in which the *sched* built-in command prints scheduled events; if not given, *%h\t%T\t%R\n* is used. The format sequences are described above under prompt; note the variable meaning of *%R*. (*tcsh*)
shell	The file in which the shell resides. This is used in forking shells to interpret files which have execute bits set, but which are not executable by the system. (See the description of built-in and nonbuilt-in command execution.) Initialized to the (system-dependent) home of the shell.
shlvl	The number of nested shells. Reset to 1 in login shells. See also *loginsh*. (*tcsh*)
status	The status returned by the last command. If it terminated abnormally, then 0200 is added to the status. Built-in commands that fail return exit status 1, all other built-in commands return status 0.
symlinks	Can be set to several different values to control symbolic link (*symlink*) resolution. (See *tcsh* man page for examples.) (*tcsh*)
tcsh	The version number of the shell in the format *R.VV.PP*, where *R* is the major release number, *VV* the current version, and *PP* the patch level. (*tcsh*)
term	The terminal type. Usually set in *~/.login* as described under "Startup" on page 492.

Table 10.25 Special Shell Variables (Continued)
(Descriptions taken from tcsh manual pages.)

time	If set to a number, then the time built-in executes automatically after each command which takes more than that many CPU seconds. If there is a second word, it is used as a format string for the output of the time built-in. (u) The following sequences may be used in the format string: *%U* The time the process spent in user mode in CPU seconds. *%S* The time the process spent in kernel mode in CPU seconds. *%E* The elapsed (wall clock) time in seconds. *%P* The CPU percentage computed as (*%U* + *%S*) / *%E*. *%W* Number of times the process was swapped. *%X* The average amount in (shared) text space used in KB. *%D* The average amount in (unshared) data/stack space used in KB. *%K* The total space used (*%X* + *%D*) in KB. *%M* The maximum memory the process had in use at any time in KB. *%F* The number of major page faults (page needed to be brought from disk). *%R* The number of minor page faults. *%I* The number of input operations. *%O* The number of output operations. *%r* The number of socket messages received. *%s* The number of socket messages sent. *%k* The number of signals received. *%w* The number of voluntary context switches (waits). *%c* The number of involuntary context switches. Only the first four sequences are supported on systems without BSD resource limit functions. The default time format is *%Uu %Ss %E %P %X+%Dk %I+%Oio %Fpf+%Ww* for systems that support resource usage reporting and *%Uu %Ss %E %P* for systems that do not. Under Sequent's DYNIX/ptx, *%X*, *%D*, *%K*, *%r*, and *%s* are not available, but the following additional sequences are: *%Y* The number of system calls performed. *%Z* The number of pages which are zero-filled on demand. *%i* The number of times a process's resident set size was increased by the kernel. *%d* The number of times a process's resident set size was decreased by the kernel. *%l* The number of read system calls performed. *%m* The number of write system calls performed. *%p* The number of reads from raw disk devices. *%q* The number of writes to raw disk devices. The default time format is *%Uu %Ss $E %P %I+%Oio %Fpf+%Ww*. Note that the CPU percentage can be higher than 100 percent on multiprocessors.
tperiod	The period, in minutes, between executions of the *periodic* special alias. (*tcsh*)

Table 10.25 Special Shell Variables (Continued)
(Descriptions taken from tcsh manual pages.)

tty	The name of the *tty*, or empty if not attached to one. (*tcsh*)
uid	The user's real user ID. (*tcsh*)
user	The user's login name.
verbose	If set, causes the words of each command to be printed, after history substitution (if any). Set by the *-v* command line option.
version	The version ID stamp. It contains the shell's version number (see *tcsh*), origin, release date, vendor, operating system, etc.

Shell Command Line Switches. The TC shell can take a number of command line switches (also called flag arguments) to control or modify its behavior. The command line switches are listed in Table 10.26.

Table 10.26 Shell Command Line Switches

-	Specifies the shell is a login shell.
-b	Forces a "break" from option processing. Any shell arguments thereafter, will not be treated as options. The remaining arguments will not be interpreted as shell options. Must include this option if shell is set-user id.
-c	If a single argument follows the *-c*, commands are read from the argument (a filename). Remaining arguments are placed in the *argv* shell variable.
-d	The shell loads the directory stack from *~/.cshdirs*.
-Dname[=value]	Sets the environment variable name to value.
-e	The shell exits if any invoked command terminates abnormally or yields a nonzero exit status.
-f	Called the fast startup because the shell ignores *~/.tcshrc*, when starting a new TC shell.
-F	The shell uses fork(2) instead of vfork(2) to spawn processes. (Convex/OS only)
-i	The shell is interactive and prompts input, even if it appears to not be a terminal. This option isn't necessary if input and output are connected to a terminal.
-l	The shell is a login shell if *-l* is the only flag specified.
-m	The shell loads *~/.tcshrc* even if it does not belong to the effective user.

Table 10.26 Shell Command Line Switches (Continued)

-n	Used for debugging scripts. The shell parses commands but does not execute them.
-q	The shell accepts the SIGQUIT signal and behaves when it is used under a debugger. Job control is disabled. (u)
-s	Command input is taken from the standard input.
-t	The shell reads and executes a single line of input. A backslash (\) may be used to escape the newline at the end of this line and continue on to another line.
-v	Sets the verbose shell variable, so that command input is echoed after history substitution. Used to debug shell scripts.
-x	Sets the echo shell variable, so that command are echoed before execution and after history and variable substitution. Used to debug shell scripts.
-V	Sets the verbose shell variable before executing the *~/.tcshrc* file.
-X	Sets the echo shell variable before executing the *~/.tcshrc* file.

THE TC SHELL LAB EXERCISES

Lab 1—Getting Started

1. What does the *init* process do?

2. What is the function of the *login* process?

3. How do you know what shell you are using?

4. How can you change your login shell?

5. Explain the difference between the *.tcshrc, .cshrc,* and *.login* files. Which one is executed first?

6. Edit your *.tcshrc* file as follows:

    a. Create three of your own aliases.

    b. Reset your prompt with the host machine name, time, username.

    c. Set the following variables and put a comment after each variable explaining what it does.

EXAMPLE 10.87

```
noclobber # protects clobbering files
          # from redirection overwriting
history
ignoreeof
savehist
prompt2
```

7. Type the following:

   ```
   source .tcshrc
   ```

   What does the *source* command do?

8. Edit your *.login* file as follows.

   a. Welcome the user.

   b. Add your home directory to the path if it is not there.

   c. Source the *.login* file.

9. What is the difference between *path* and *PATH*?

Lab 2—History

1. In what file are history events stored when you log out? What variable controls the number of history events to be displayed? What is the purpose of the *savehist* variable?

2. Print your history list in reverse.

3. Print your history list without line numbers.

4. Type the following commands:

   a. ls -a

   b. date '+%T'

   c. cal 2000

   d. cat /etc/passwd

   e. cd

5. Type *history*. What is the output?

   a. How do you reexecute the last command?

   b. Now type: *echo a b c*

   Use the *history* command to reexecute the *echo* command with only its last argument, *c*.

6. Use history to print and execute the last command in your history list that started with the letter "d."

7. Execute the last command that started with "c."

8. Execute the *echo* command and the last argument from the previous command.

9. Use the history substitution command to replace the "T" in the *date* command to an "H."

10. How do you use the *bindkey* command to start the *vi* editor for command line editing?

11. How do you list the editor commands and what they do?

12. How do you see how the editing keys are actually bound?

13. Describe what the *fignore* variable does.

Lab 3—Shell Metacharacters

1. Type at the prompt:

   ```
   touch ab abc a1 a2 a3 all a12 ba ba.1 ba.2 filex filey AbC ABC
   ABc2 abc
   ```

2. Write and test the command that will:

   a. List all files starting with *a*.

   b. List all files ending in at least one digit.

   c. List all files not starting with an *a* or *A*.

   d. List all files ending in a period, followed by a digit.

   e. List all files containing just two alphas.

   f. List three character files where all letters are uppercase.

   g. List files ending in *11* or *12*.

   h. List files ending in *x* or *y*.

i. List all files ending in a digit, an uppercase letter, or a lowercase letter.

j. List all files containing a *b*.

k. Remove two character files starting with *a*.

Lab 4—Redirection

1. What are the names of the three file streams associated with your terminal?
2. What is a file descriptor?
3. What command would you use to:

   a. Redirect the output of the *ls* command to a file called *lsfile*?

   b. Redirect and append the output of the *date* command to *lsfile*?

   c. Redirect the output of the *who* command to *lsfile*? What happened?

   d. What happens when you type *cp* all by itself?

   e. How do you save the error message from the above example to a file?

   f. Use the *find* command to find all files, starting from the parent directory, and of type "directory." Save the standard output in a file called *found* and any errors in a file called *found.errs*.

   g. What is *noclobber*? How do you override it?

   h. Take the output of three commands and redirect the output to a file called *gottemall*.

   i. Use a pipe(s) with the *ps* and *wc* commands to find out how many processes you are currently running.

Lab 5—Variables and Arrays

1. What is the difference between a local variable and an environment variable?
2. How do you list all local variables? Environmental variables?
3. In what initialization file would you store local variables? Why?
4. Create an array called *fruit*. Put five kinds of fruit in the array.

   a. Print the array.

   b. Print the last element of the array.

c. Print the number of elements in the array.

d. Remove the first element from the array.

e. If you store an item that isn't fruit in the array, is it OK?

5. Describe the difference between a wordlist and a string.

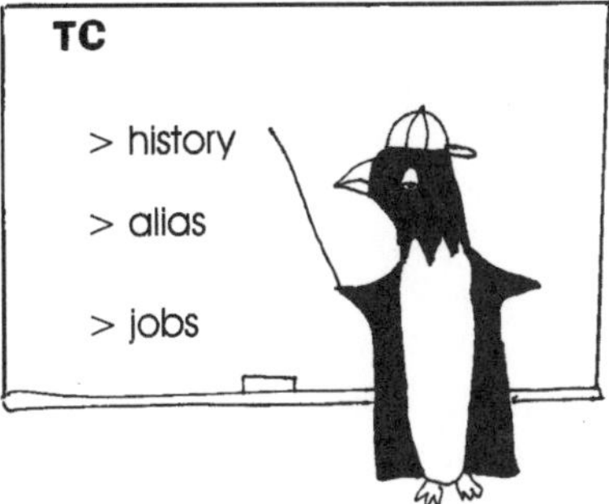

CHAPTER

11

PROGRAMMING WITH THE TC SHELL

11.1 Steps in Creating a Shell Script

A shell script is normally written in an editor and consists of commands interspersed with comments. Comments are preceded by a pound sign and consist of text used to document what is going on.

11.1.1 The First Line

At the top left corner, the line preceded by *#!* (often called "shbang") indicates the program that will be executing the lines in the script. This line is commonly:

```
#!/bin/tcsh
```

The *#!* is called a magic number and is used by the kernel to identify the program that should be interpreting the lines in the script. When a program is loaded into memory, the kernel will examine the first line. If the first line is binary data, the program will be executed as a compiled program; if the first line contains the *#!*, the kernel will look at the path following the *#!* and start that program as the interpreter. If the path is */bin/tcsh*, the TC shell will interpret the lines in the program. This line must be the top line of your script or the line will be treated as a comment line.

When the script starts, the *.tcshrc* file is read first and executed, so that anything set within that file will become part of your script. You can prevent the *.tcshrc* from being read by using the *-f* (fast) option to the TC shell program. The startup line is written as follows:

```
#!/bin/tcsh -f
```

11.1.2 Comments

Comments are lines preceded by a pound sign. They are used to document your script. It is sometimes difficult to understand what the script is supposed to do if it is not commented. Although comments are important, they are often too sparse or not even used at all. Try to get used to commenting what you are doing not only for someone else, but also for yourself. Two days from now you may not remember exactly what you were trying to do.

11.1.3 Making the Script Executable

When you create a file, it is not given execute permission. You need this permission to run your script. Use the *chmod* command to turn on execute permission.

EXAMPLE 11.1

```
1    > chmod +x myscript
2    > ls-F myscript
     -rwxr--xr--x    1  ellie   0 Jul   13:00 myscript*
```

EXPLANATION

1. The *chmod* command is used to turn on execute permission for the user, the group, and others.
2. The output of the *ls* command indicates that all users have execute permission on the *joker* file. The asterisk at the end of the filename (resulting from the *-F* option) also indicates that this is an executable program.

11.1.4 An Example Scripting Session

In the following example, the user will create the script in the editor. After saving the file, the execute permissions are turned on with the *chmod* command, and the script is executed. If there are errors in the program, the C shell will respond immediately.

EXAMPLE 11.2

```
(The Script - info)
   #!/bin/tcsh -f
   # This script is called info
1  echo Hello ${LOGNAME}!
2  echo The hour is `date +%H`
3  echo "This machine is `uname -n`"
4  echo The calendar for this month is
5  cal
6  echo The processes you are running are:
7  ps au | grep  "^ *$LOGNAME"
8  echo "Thanks for coming. See you soon\!\!"
```

EXAMPLE 11.2 (CONTINUED)

```
   (The Command Line)
9  > chmod +x info
10 > ./info
1  Hello ellie!
2  The hour is 09
3  This machine is jody
4  The calendar for this month is
5     January 2000
   S  M Tu  W Th  F  S
                     1
   2  3  4  5  6  7  8
   9 10 11 12 13 14 15
  16 17 18 19 20 21 22
  23 24 25 26 27 28 29
  30 31
7  The processes you are running are:
   < output of ps prints here >
8  Thanks for coming. See you soon!!
```

EXPLANATION

1 The user is greeted. The variable *LOGNAME* holds the user's name. On BSD systems, *USER* is used. The curly braces shield the variable from the exclamation point. The exclamation point does not need to be escaped because it will not be interpreted as a history character unless there is a character appended to it.

2 The *date* command is enclosed in back quotes. The shell will perform command substitution and the date's output, the current hour, will be substituted into the *echo* string.

3 The *uname -n* command displays the machine name.

4 The *cal* command is not enclosed in back quotes because when the shell performs command substitution, the newlines are all stripped from the output. This produces a strange-looking calendar. By putting the *cal* command on a line by itself, the formatting is preserved.

5 The calendar for this month is printed.

6, 7 The user's processes are printed.

8 The string is printed. Note that the two exclamation points are prepended with backslashes. This is necessary to prevent history substitution.

11.1.5 Variables (Review)

To write shell programs, you will use variables to hold information. The values will be assigned either directly to the variable in the script, or passed in from the command line, or retreived as user input. See "Variables" on page 561 and "Environment Variables" on page 569 for a complete description of local and environment variables.

EXAMPLE 11.3

```
set name = "Ellie"     # local variable assignment
setenv NAME "Tom"      # environment variable assignment
echo $name             # printing value of local variable
echo $NAME             # printing value of environment variable
```

11.2 Reading User Input

11.2.1 The *$<* Variable

To make a script interactive, a special TC shell variable is used to read standard input into a variable. The *$<* symbol reads a word from standard input up to the first white space but not including the newline, and assigns the word to a variable. By placing *$<* in double quotes (or parentheses)[1], a whole line is read, not including the newline.

EXAMPLE 11.4

```
(The Script - greeting)
    #!/bin/tcsh -f
    # The greeting script
1   echo -n  "What is your name? "
2   set name = "$<"
3   echo Greetings to you, $name.

(The Command Line)
    > chmod +x greeting
    > greeting
1   What is your name?  Dan Savage
3   Greetings to you, Dan Savage
```

EXPLANATION

1 The string is echoed to the screen. The *-n* option causes the *echo* command to suppress the newline at the end of the string. On some versions of *echo*, use a *\c* at the end of the string to suppress the newline; e.g., *echo "hello\c"*.

2 Whatever is typed at the terminal, up to the newline is stored as a string in the *name* variable.

3 The string is printed after variable substitution is performed.

---

1. The C shell does not require double quotes around the *$<* variable to read a whole line.

11.2.2 Creating a Wordlist from the Input String

Because the input from the *$<* variable is stored as a string, you may want to break the string into a wordlist. You can also use the Linux *head* command to read input from the user and store it as a wordlist. (See "Command Substitution" on page 580.)

EXAMPLE 11.5

```
1     > echo What is your full name\?
2     > set name = "$<"
       Daniel Leo Stachelin

3     > echo Hi $name[1]
      Hi Daniel Leo Stachelin

4     > echo $name[2]
      Subscript out of range.

5     > set name = ( $name )

6     > echo Hi $name[1]
      Hi Daniel

7     > echo $name[2] $name[3]
      Leo Stachelin

8     > echo Where do you live\?
9     > set city = `head -1`
       Chico, California

10    > echo "$city[1] is a college town, isn't it?"
```

EXPLANATION

1. The user is asked for input.
2. The special variable *$<* accepts input from the user in a string format.
3. Because the value *Daniel Leo Stachelin* is stored as a single string, the subscript *[1]* displays the whole string. Subscripts start at one.
4. The string consists of one word. There are not two words, so by using a subscript of *[2]*, the shell complains that the *Subscript is out of range*.
5. To create a wordlist, the string is enclosed in parentheses. An array is created. The string is broken up into a list of words and assigned to the variable *name*.
6. The first element of the array is printed.
7. The second and third elements of the array are printed.

EXPLANATION (CONTINUED)

8 The user is asked for input.

9 The Linux *head* command with a numeric option of 1 will take one line of input. (If -2 were given as an option, two lines of input would be read). The *head* command is in backquotes causing the shell to perform command substitution, i.e., return the output of the *head* command and assign it to the variable, *city*. The user's input will be returned. When command substitution is performed, the returned values are stored as a list or array of space-separated strings. The variable *city* is an array. *Chico* is the first element of the array.

10 The first element of the *city* array is printed.

11.3 Arithmetic

There is not really a need to do math problems in a shell script, but sometimes arithmetic is necessary, e.g., to increment or decrement a loop counter. The TC shell supports integer arithmetic only. The @ symbol is used to assign the results of calculations to numeric variables.

11.3.1 Arithmetic Operators

The following operators in Table 11.1 are used to perform integer arithmetic operations. They are the same operators found in the C programming language. See Table 11.6 on page 629 for operator precedence. Also borrowed from the C language are shortcut assignment operators, shown in Table 11.2.

Table 11.1 Operators

Function	*Operator*
Addition	+
Subtraction	–
Division	/
Multiplication	*
Modulus	%
Left shift	<<
Right shift	>>

Table 11.2 Shortcut Operations

Operator	*Example*	*Equivalent to*
+=	@ num += 2	@ num = $num + 2
–=	@ num –= 4	@ num = $num – 4
*=	@ num *= 3	@ num = $num * 3
/=	@ num /= 2	@ num = $num / 2
++	@ num++	@ num = $num + 1
--	@ num--	@ num = $num – 1

EXAMPLE 11.6

```
1   > @ sum = 4 + 6
    echo $sum
    10

2   > @ sum++
    echo $sum
    11

3   > @ sum += 3
    echo $sum
    14

4   > @ sum--
    echo $sum
    13

5   > @ n = 3+4
    @: Badly formed number
```

EXPLANATION

1. The variable *sum* is assigned the result of adding *4* and *6*. (The space after the @ is required.)
2. The variable *sum* is incremented by *1*.
3. The variable *sum* is incremented by *3*.
4. The variable *sum* is decremented by *1*.[a]
5. Spaces are required after the @ symbol and surrounding the operator.

a. Associativity is right-to-left in expressions where the precedence is equal. For example, in (*b* * *c*/*a*), division is done before multiplication. See "Precedence and Associativity" on page 628.

11.3.2 Floating Point Arithmetic

Because floating point arithmetic is not supported by this shell, if you should need more complex mathematical operations, you can use Linux utilities.

The *bc* and *nawk* utilities are useful if you need to perform complex calculations.

EXAMPLE 11.7

```
(The Command Line)
1   set n=`echo "scale=3; 13 / 2" | bc`
    echo $n
    6.500

2   set product=`awk -v x=2.45 -v y=3.124 \
       'BEGIN{printf "%.2f\n", x * y }'`

    > echo $product
    7.65
```

EXPLANATION

1 The output of the *echo* command is piped to the *bc* program. The scale is set to *3*; that is, the number of significant digits to the right of the decimal point that will be printed. The calculation is to divide *13* by *2*. The entire pipeline is enclosed in back quotes. Command substitution will be performed and the output assigned to the variable *n*.

2 The *awk* program gets its values from the argument list passed in at the command line. Each argument passed to *awk* is preceded by the *-v* switch; for example, *-v x=2.45* and *-v y=3.124*. After the numbers are multiplied, the *printf* function formats and prints the result with a precision of *2* places to the right of the decimal point. The output is assigned to the variable *product*.

11.4 Debugging Scripts

TC shell scripts often fail due to some simple syntax error or logic error. Options to the *tcsh* command are provided to help you debug your programs. See Table 11.3.

Table 11.3 *echo* (*-x*) and *verbose* (*-v*)

As options to tcsh	
tcsh -x scriptname	Display each line of script after variable substitution and before execution.
tcsh -v scriptname	Display each line of script before execution, just as you typed it.
tcsh -n scriptname	Interpret but do not execute commands.

Table 11.3 *echo* (*-x*) and *verbose* (*-v*) (Continued)

As arguments to the* set *command	
set echo	Display each line of script after variable substitution and before execution.
set verbose	Display each line of script before execution, just as you typed it.
As the first line in a script	
#!/bin/tcsh -xv	Turn on both echo and verbose. These options can be invoked separately or combined with other *csh* invocation arguments.

EXAMPLE 11.8

```
(The -v and -x Options)
1   > cat practice
    #!/bin/tcsh -f
    echo Hello $LOGNAME
    echo The date is 'date'
    echo Your home shell is $SHELL
    echo Good-bye $LOGNAME

2   > tcsh -v practice
    echo Hello $LOGNAME
    Hello ellie
    echo The date is 'date'
    The date is Mon May 24 12:26:07 PDT  2000
    echo Your login shell is $SHELL
    Your login shell is /bin/csh
    echo Good-bye $LOGNAME
    Good-bye ellie

3   > tcsh -x practice
    echo Hello ellie
    Hello ellie
    echo The date is 'date'
    date
    The date is Mon May 24 12:26:15 PDT 2000
    echo Your login shell is /bin/tcsh
    Your login shell is /bin/tcsh
    echo Good-bye ellie
    Good-bye ellie
```

EXPLANATION

1 The contents of the TC shell script are displayed. Variable and command substitution lines are included so that you can see how *echo* and *verbose* differ.

2 The *-v* option to the *tcsh* command causes the *verbose* feature to be enabled. Each line of the script is displayed as it was typed in the script, and then the line is executed.

3 The *-x* option to the *tcsh* command enables echoing. Each line of the script is displayed after variable and command substitution are performed, and then the line is executed. Because this feature allows you to examine what is being replaced as a result of command and variable substitution, it is used more often than the *verbose* option.

EXAMPLE 11.9

```
(Echo and Verbose)
1   > cat practice
    #!/bin/tcsh -f
    echo Hello $LOGNAME
    echo The date is 'date'
    set echo
    echo Your home shell is $SHELL
    unset echo
    echo Good-bye $LOGNAME

2   > chmod +x practice

3   > practice
    Hello ellie
    The date is Mon May 24 12:25:16 PDT 2000
--> echo Your login shell is /bin/tcsh
--> Your login shell is /bin/tcsh
--> unset echo
    Good-bye ellie
```

EXPLANATION

1 The *echo* option is set and unset within the script. This enables you to debug certain sections of your script where you have run into a bottleneck, rather than echoing each line of the entire script.

2 The execute permission is turned on with *chmod.*

3 The --> marks where the echoing was turned on. Each line is printed after variable and command substitution and then executed.

EXAMPLE 11.10

```
1   > cat practice
    #!/bin/tcsh -f
    echo Hello $LOGNAME
    echo The date is 'date'
    set verbose
    echo Your home shell is $SHELL
    unset verbose
    echo Good-bye $LOGNAME

2   > practice
    Hello ellie
    The date is Mon May 24 12:30:09 PDT 2000
--> echo Your login shell is $SHELL
--> Your login shell is /bin/csh
--> unset verbose
    Good-bye ellie
```

EXPLANATION

1. The *verbose* option is set and unset within the script.
2. The --> marks where *verbose* was turned on. The lines are printed just as they were typed in the script and then executed.

11.5 Command Line Arguments

Shell scripts can take command line arguments. Arguments are used to modify the behavior of the program in some way. The TC shell assigns command line arguments to positional parameters and enforces no specific limit on the number of arguments that can be assigned. (The Bourne shell sets a limit of nine positional parameters.) Positional parameters are number variables. The script name is assigned to *$0*, and any words following the script name are assigned to *$1, $2, $3 . . . ${10}, ${11}*, and so on. *$1* is the first command line argument. In addition to using positional parameters, the TC shell provides the *argv* built-in array.

11.5.1 Positional Parameters and *argv*

If you are using the *argv* array notation, a valid subscript must be provided to correspond to the argument being passed in from the command line or the error message "*Subscript out of range*" is sent by the TC shell. The *argv* array does not include the script name. The first argument is *$argv[1]*, and the number of arguments is represented by *$#argv*. (There is no other way to represent the number of arguments.) See Table 11.4 for a list of command line arguments.

Table 11.4 Command Line Arguments

Argument	*Meaning*
$0	The name of the script.
$1, $2, . . . ${10}...	The first and second positional parameters are referenced by the number preceded by a dollar sign. The curly braces shield the number *10* so that it does not print the first positional parameter followed by a zero.
*$**	All the positional parameters.
$argv[0]	Not valid; nothing is printed. C shell array subscripts start at 1.
$argv[1] $argv[2]...	The first argument, second argument, etc.
$argv[*]	All arguments.
$argv	All arguments.
$#argv	The number of arguments.
$argv[$#argv]	The last argument.

EXAMPLE 11.11

```
(The Script)
    #!/bin/tcsh -f
    # The greetings script
    # This script greets a user whose name is typed in at the
    # command line.

1   echo $0 to you $1 $2 $3
2   echo Welcome to this day `date | awk '{print $1, $2, $3}'`
3   echo Hope you have a nice day, $argv[1]\!
4   echo Good-bye $argv[1] $argv[2] $argv[3]

(The Command Line)
    > chmod +x greetings

    > greetings Guy Quigley
1   greetings to you Guy Quigley
2   Welcome to this day Fri Aug 28
3   Hope you have a nice day, Guy!
4   Subscript out of range
```

EXPLANATION

1 The name of the script and the first three positional parameters are to be displayed. Because there are only two positional parameters coming in from the command line, *Guy* and *Quigley*, *$1* becomes *Guy*, *$2* becomes *Quigley*, and *$3* is not defined.

2 The *awk* command is quoted with single quotes so that the shell does not confuse *awk*'s field numbers *$1, $2,* and *$3* with positional parameters. (Do not confuse *awk*'s field designators *$1, $2,* and *$3* with the shell's positional parameters.)

3 The *argv* array is assigned values coming in from the command line. *Guy* is assigned to *argv[1]* and its value is displayed. You can use the *argv* array to represent the command line arguments within your script, or you can use positional parameters. The difference is that positional parameters do not produce an error if you reference one that has no value, whereas an unassigned *argv* value causes the script to exit with the *Subscript out of range* error message.

4 The shell prints the error *Subscript out of range* because there is no value for *argv[3]*.

11.6 Flow Control and Conditional Constructs

When making decisions, the *if, if/else, if/else if/else*, and *switch* commands are used. These commands control the flow of the program by allowing decision-making based on whether an expression is true or false.

11.6.1 Testing Expressions

An expression consists of a set of operands separated by operators. Operators are listed in Tables 11.5 and 11.6. To test an expression, the expression is surrounded by parentheses. The TC shell evaluates the expression, resulting in either a zero or nonzero numeric value. If the result is *nonzero*, the expression is *true*; if the result is *zero*, the expression is *false*.

When evaluating an expression with the logical AND (*&&*), the shell evaluates from left to right. If the first expression (before the *&&*) is false, the shell assigns false as the result of the entire expression, never checking the remaining expressions. If the first expression is false, the whole expression is false when using the logical AND (*&&*) operator. Both expressions surrounding a logical *&&* operator must be true for the entire expression to evaluate to true.

When evaluating an expression with the logical OR (||), if the first expression to the left of the || is true, the shell assigns TRUE to the entire expression and never checks further. In a logical || expression, only one of the expressions must be true.

The logical NOT is a unary operator; that is, it evaluates one expression. If the expression to the right of the NOT operator is true, the expression becomes false. If it is false, the expression becomes true.

Table 11.5 Comparison and Logical Operators

Operator	*Meaning*	*Example*
==	Is equal to	*$x == $y*
!=	Is not equal to	*$x != $y*
>	Is greater than	*$x > $y*
>=	Is greater than or equal to	*$x >= $y*
<	Is less than	*$x < $y*
<=	Is less than or equal to	*$x <= $y*
=~	String matches	*$ans =~ [Yy]**
!~	String does not match	*$ans !~ [Yy]**
!	Logical NOT	*! $x*
||	Logical OR	*$x || $y*
&&	Logical AND	*$x && $y*

Precedence and Associativity. Like C, the TC shell uses precedence and associativity rules when testing expressions. If you have an expression with a mix of different operators, such as . . .

```
@  x = 5 + 3 * 2
echo $x
11
```

. . . the shell reads the operators in a certain order. *Precedence* refers to the order of importance of the operator. *Associativity* refers to whether the shell reads the expression from left to right or right to left when the precedence is equal. Other than in arithmetic expressions (which you will not readily need in shell scripts anyway), the order of associativity is from left to right if the precedence is equal. You can change the order by using parentheses (see Table 11.6):

```
@ x = ( 5 + 3 ) * 2
echo $x
16
```

Expressions can be numeric, relational, or logical. Numeric expressions use the following arithmetic operators:

```
+ - * /  ++ -- %
```

Relational expressions use the operators that yield either a true (nonzero) or false (zero) result:

```
>  <  >=  <=  ==  !=
```

Logical expressions use these operators:

```
!  &&  ||
```

Table 11.6 Operator Table of Precedence

<table>
<tr><th>Precedence</th><th>Operator</th><th>Meaning</th></tr>
<tr><td>High</td><td>( )</td><td>Change precedence; group</td></tr>
<tr><td>↑</td><td>~</td><td>Complement</td></tr>
<tr><td></td><td>!</td><td>Logical not, negation</td></tr>
<tr><td></td><td>* / %</td><td>Multiply, divide, modulo</td></tr>
<tr><td></td><td>+ -</td><td>Add, subtract</td></tr>
<tr><td></td><td><< >></td><td>Bitwise left and right shift</td></tr>
<tr><td></td><td>> >= < <=</td><td>Relational operators: greater than, less than</td></tr>
<tr><td></td><td>== !=</td><td>Equality: equal to, not equal to</td></tr>
<tr><td></td><td>=~ !~</td><td>Pattern matching: matches, does not match</td></tr>
<tr><td></td><td>&</td><td>Bitwise and</td></tr>
<tr><td></td><td>^</td><td>Bitwise exclusive or</td></tr>
<tr><td></td><td>|</td><td>Bitwise inclusive or</td></tr>
<tr><td>↓</td><td>&&</td><td>Logical and</td></tr>
<tr><td>Low</td><td>||</td><td>Logical or</td></tr>
</table>

11.6.2 The *if* Statement

The simplest form of conditional is the *if* statement. After the *if* is tested, and if the expression evaluates to true, the commands after the *then* keyword are executed until the *endif* is reached. The *endif* keyword terminates the block. The *if* statement may be nested as long as every single *if* statement is terminated with a matching *endif*. The *endif* goes with the nearest enclosing *if*.

FORMAT

```
if ( expression ) then
   command
   command
endif
```

EXAMPLE 11.12

```
(In the Script—Checking for Arguments)
1  if ( $#argv != 1 ) then
2     echo "$0 requires an argument"
3     exit 1
4  endif
```

EXPLANATION

1. This line reads: *If the number of arguments ($#argv) passed in from the command line is not equal to one, then...*
2. If the first line is true, this line and line 3 are executed.
3. The program exits with a value of one, meaning it failed.
4. Every *if* block is closed with an *endif* statement.

Testing and Unset or Null Variables. The *$?* special variable is used to test if a variable has been set. It will return true if the variable is set to null.

EXAMPLE 11.13

```
(From .tcshrc File)
   if ( $?prompt ) then
      set history = 32
   endif
```

EXPLANATION

The *.tcshrc* file is executed every time you start a new *tcsh* program. *$?* is used to check to see if a variable has been set. In this example, the shell checks to see if the prompt has been set. If the prompt is set, you are running an interactive shell, not a script. The prompt is only set for interactive use. Because the history mechanism is only useful when running interactively, the shell will not set history if you are running a script.

EXAMPLE 11.14

```
(The Script)
    echo -n "What is your name? "
1   set name = "$<"
2   if ( "$name" != "" ) then
        grep "$name" datafile
    endif
```

EXPLANATION

1 The user is asked for input. If the user just presses Enter, the variable *name* is set, but it is set to null.

2 The variable is quoted (double quotes) so that if the user enters more than one word in *name*, the expression will still be evaluated. If the quotes were removed and the user entered first and last name, the shell would exit the script with the error message *if: Expression syntax.* The empty double quotes represent a null string.

11.6.3 The *if/else* Statements

The *if/else* construct is a two-way branching control structure. If the expression after the *if* command is true, the block following it is executed; otherwise, the block after the *else* is executed. The *endif* matches the innermost *if* statement and terminates the statement.

FORMAT

```
if ( expression ) then
    command
else
    command
endif
```

EXAMPLE 11.15

```
1   if ( $answer =~ [Yy]* ) then
2       mail bob < message
3   else
4       mail john < datafile
5   endif
```

EXPLANATION

1 This line reads: *If the value of $answer matches a* Y *or a* y, *followed by zero or more characters, then go to line 2; otherwise, go to line 3.* (The * is a shell metacharacter.)

EXPLANATION (CONTINUED)

2 The user *bob* is mailed the contents of the file *datafile.*

3 The commands under the *else* are executed if line 1 is not true.

4 The user *john* is mailed the contents of the file *datafile.*

5 The *endif* block ends the *if* block.

11.6.4 Debugging Expressions

The *-x* option (called *echoing*) to the TC shell allows you to trace what is going on in your script as it executes. If you are unsure what is going on, this is a good way to debug your script.

EXAMPLE 11.16

```
(The Script—Using Logical Expressions and Checking Values)
    #!/bin/tcsh -f
    # Script name: logical
    set x = 1
    set y = 2
    set z = 3
1   if ( ( "$x" && "$y" ) ||  ! "$z" ) then
       # Note: grouping and parentheses
2      echo TRUE
    else
       echo FALSE
    endif

(The Output)
3   > tcsh -x logical
    set x = 1
    set y = 2
    set z = 3
    if ( ( 1 && 2 )  ||  !  3 )  then
    echo TRUE
    TRUE
    else
    >
```

EXPLANATION

1 The logical expression is being evaluated. The first expression is enclosed in parentheses (not necessary because *&&* is of higher precedence than ||). The parentheses do not require spaces when nested, but the negation operator (*!*) must have a space after it.

2 If the expression evaluates true, this line is executed.

3 The *tcsh* program is executed with the *-x* switch. This turns on echoing. Every line in your script is echoed back to you after variable substitution has been performed.

11.6.5 The *if* statement and a Single Command

If an expression is followed by a single command, the *then* and *endif* keywords are not necessary.

FORMAT

```
if ( expression ) single command
```

EXAMPLE 11.17

```
if ($#argv == 0) exit 1
```

EXPLANATION

The expression is tested. If the number of command line arguments, *$#argv*, is equal to zero, the program is exited with a status of one.

11.6.6 The *if/else if* Statements

The *if/else if* construct offers a multiway decision-making mechanism. A number of expressions can be tested, and when one of the expressions evaluated is true, the block of statements that follow is executed. If none of the expressions are true, the *else* block is executed.

FORMAT

```
if ( expression ) then
     command
     command
else if ( expression ) then
     command
     command
else
     command
endif
```

EXAMPLE 11.18

```
(The Script - grade)
    #!/bin/tcsh -f
    # This script is called grade
    echo  -n "What was your grade? "
    set grade = $<
1   if ( "$grade" < 0 || "$grade" > 100 ) then
        echo "Illegal grade!"
        exit 1
    endif
```

EXAMPLE 11.18 (CONTINUED)

```
2  if ( $grade >= 90 && $grade <= 100 ) then
      echo "You got an A\!"
3  else if ( $grade > 79 ) then
      echo "You got a B"
4  else if ( $grade > 69 ) then
      echo "You're average"
   else
5     echo "Better study"
6  endif
```

EXPLANATION

1. If *grade* is less than *0* OR *grade* is greater than *100*, the user has entered an illegal grade. Note the OR here. Only one of the expressions must evaluate to true for the whose expression to be true.
2. If *grade* is greater than or equal to *90* AND *grade* is less than or equal to *100*, then *echo "You got an A!" Both* expressions surrounding the *&&* must be true or program control will go to the *else if* on line 2.
3. If line 1 is false, test the expression (line 2), and if it is true, *echo "You got a B."*
4. If line 1 and 2 are both false, try this one. If this expression is true, then *echo "You're average."*
5. If all of the above expressions test false, the statements in the *else* block are executed.
6. The *endif* ends the entire *if* construct.

11.6.7 Exit Status and the Status Variable

Every Linux command returns an exit status. If the command was successful, it returns an exit status of zero. If the command failed, it returns a nonzero exit status. You can test to see whether the command succeeded or failed by looking at the value of one of the TC shell variables: *status* or *?*. The status variable contains the exit status of the last command executed.

EXAMPLE 11.19

```
1  > grep ellie /etc/passwd
   ellie:pHAZk66gA:9496:41:Ellie:/home/jody/ellie:/bin/csh
2  > echo $status   or $?
   0                    Zero shows that grep was a success

3  > grep joe /etc/passwd
4  > echo $status
   1                    Nonzero shows that grep failed
```

EXPLANATION

1. The *grep* program found *ellie* in the */etc/passwd* file.
2. The *grep* program, if it finds the pattern *ellie*, returns a zero status when it exits.
3. The *grep* program did not find *joe* in the */etc/passwd* file.
4. The *grep* program returns a nonzero status if the pattern is not found.

11.6.8 Exiting from a Shell Script

In your shell script, the *exit* command will take you back to the shell prompt. The *exit* command takes an integer value to indicate the type of exit. A nonzero argument indicates failure; zero indicates success. The number must be between 0 and 255.

EXAMPLE 11.20

```
(The checkon Shell Script)
     #!/bin/tcsh -f
1    if ( $#argv != 1 ) then
2            echo "$0 requires an argument"
3            exit 2
4    endif

     (At the command line)
5    > checkon
      checkon requires an argument
6    > echo $status
     2
```

EXPLANATION

1. If the number of arguments passed in from the command line (*$#argv*) is not equal to one, then go to line 2.
2. The *echo* prints the script name (*$0*) and the string "*requires an argument*".
3. The program exits back to the prompt with a value of 2. This value will be stored in the *status* variable of the parent shell.
4. The end of the conditional *if*.
5. At the command line, the program *checkon* is executed without an argument.
6. The program exits with a value of 2, which is stored in the *status* variable.

11.6.9 Using the Status Variable in a Script

The *status* variable can be used in a script to test the status of a command. The *status* variable is assigned the value of the last command that was executed.

EXAMPLE 11.21

```
(The Script)
        #!/bin/tcsh -f
1       ypmatch  $1  passwd >& /dev/null
2       if ( $status == 0 ) then
3           echo Found $1 in the NIS database
        endif
```

EXPLANATION

1. The *ypmatch* program checks the NIS database to see if the name of the user, passed in as the first argument, is in the database.
2. If the *status* returned from the last command is zero, the *then* block is executed.
3. This line is executed if the *if* test expression evaluated to be true.

11.6.10 Evaluating Commands within Conditionals

The TC shell evaluates *expressions* in conditionals. To evaluate *commands* in conditionals, curly braces must enclose the command. If the command is successful, that is, returns an exit status of zero, the curly braces tell the shell to evaluate the expression as true (1).[2] If the command fails, the exit status is nonzero, and the expression is evaluated as false (0).

It is important, when using a command in a conditional, to know the exit status of that command. For example, the *grep* program returns an exit status of zero when it finds the pattern it is searching for, one when it cannot find the pattern, and two when it cannot find the file. When *awk* or *sed* are searching for patterns, those programs return zero whether or not they are successful in the pattern search. The criteria for success with *awk* and *sed* is based on whether or not the syntax is right; that is, if you typed the command correctly, the exit status of *gawk* and *sed* is zero.

If the exclamation mark is placed before the expression, it *nots* the entire expression so that if true, it is now false, and vice versa. Make sure a space follows the exclamation mark, or the TC shell will invoke the history mechanism.

2. The command's exit status is inverted by the shell so that the expression yields a true or false result.

FORMAT

```
if  { ( command ) }  then
        command
        command
endif
```

EXAMPLE 11.22

```
    #!/bin/tcsh -f
1   if  { ( who | grep $1 >& /dev/null ) } then
2           echo $1 is logged on and running:
3           ps au | grep "^ *$1" # ps -ef for SVR4
4   endif
```

EXPLANATION

1. The *who* command is piped to the *grep* command. All of the output is sent to */dev/null*, the *Linux* "bit bucket." The output of the *who* command is sent to *grep*; *grep* searches for the name of the user stored in the *$1* variable (first command line argument). If *grep* is successful and finds the user, an exit status of zero is returned. The shell will then invert the exit status of the *grep* command to yield one, or true. If the shell evaluates the expression to be true, it executes the commands between the *then* and *endif*.
2. If the TC shell evaluates the expression in line 1 to be true, lines 2 and 3 are executed.
3. All the processes running and owned by *$1* are displayed.
4. The *endif* ends the *if* statements.

FORMAT

```
if ! { (command) } then
```

EXAMPLE 11.23

```
1   if  !  { ( ypmatch $user passwd >& /dev/null ) } then
2       echo $user is not a user here.
        exit 1
3   endif
```

EXPLANATION

1 The *ypmatch* command is used to search the NIS *passwd* file, if you are using a network. If the command succeeds in finding the user (*$user*) in the *passwd* file, the expression evaluates to be true. The exclamation point (*!*) preceding the expression *nots* or complements the expression; that is, makes it false if it is true, and vice versa.

2 If the expression is not true, the user is not found and this line is executed.

3 The *endif* ends this *if* block.

11.6.11 The *goto*

A *goto* allows you to jump to some label in the program and start execution at that point. Although the *goto* is frowned upon by many programmers, it is sometimes useful for breaking out of nested loops. A label is a user-defined word appended with a colon and placed on a line by itself.

EXAMPLE 11.24

```
(The Script)
    #!/bin/tcsh -f
    # Scriptname: grades2
1   startover:
2   echo -n "What was your grade? "

    set grade = $<
3   if ( "$grade" < 0 || "$grade" > 100 ) then
4           echo "Illegal grade"
5           goto startover
    endif
    if ( $grade >= 89 ) then
            echo "A for the genius\!"
    else if ( $grade >= 79 ) then
            .. < Program continues >
```

EXPLANATION

1 The label is a user-defined word with a colon appended. The label is called *startover*. During execution of the program, the label is ignored by the shell, unless the shell is explicitly directed to go to the label.

2 The user is asked for input.

3 If the expression is true, (the user entered a grade less than *0* or greater than *100*), the string "*Illegal grade*" is printed, and the *goto* starts execution at the named label, *startover*. The program continues to execute from that point.

4 The *if* expression tested false, so this line is printed.

5 The *goto* sends control to line 1 and execution starts after the label, *startover*.

11.6.12 File Testing

The TC shell has a built-in set of options for testing attributes of files, such as "*Is the file a directory, a plain file (not a directory), or a readable file,*" and so forth. The operators listed in Table 11.7 return 1 for true and 0 for false after testing an attribute of a file or directory in terms of the real user. The built-in options for file inquiry are listed in Table 11.7. The TC shell allows these operators to be bound together (the C shell does not). The form *-rwx* is the same as *-r && -w && -x*.

Table 11.7 File Testing

Test Flag	*(What It Tests) True If*
-b	File is a block special file.
-c	File is a character special file.
-d	File is a directory.
-e	File exists.
-f	File is a plain file.
-g	Set-group-ID bit is set.
-k	Sticky bit is set.
-l	File is a symbolic link.
-L	Applies subsequent operators in a multiple-operator list to a symbolic link rather than to the file to which it is linked.
-o	Current user owns the file.
-p	File is named pipe (fifo).
-r	Current user can read the file.
-s	File is nonzero size.
-S	File is a socket special file
-t file	(file must be a digit) is an open file descriptor for a terminal device.
-w	Current user can write to the file.
-x	Current user can execute the file.
-z	File is zero length.
-L	Applies subsequent operators in a multiple-operator test to a symbolic link rather than to the file to which the link points
-R	Has been migrated (convex only).
-S	File is a socket special file.

EXAMPLE 11.25

```
    #!/bin/tcsh -f
    # Scriptname: filetest1
1   if ( -e file ) then
       echo file exists
    endif

2   if ( -d file ) then
       echo file is a directory
    endif

3   if ( ! -z file ) then
       echo file is not of zero length
    endif

4   if ( -r file && -w file && -x file) then
       echo  file is readable and writable and executable.
    endif

5   if ( -rwx file ) then
       echo file is readable and writable and executable.
    endif
```

EXPLANATION

1. The statement reads, *if the file exists, then ...*
2. The statement reads, *if the file is a directory, then ...*
3. The statement reads, *if the file is not of zero length, then ...*
4. The statement reads, *if the file is readable and writeable, then ...* A single option precedes the filename (e.g., *-r file && -w file && -x file).*
5. The file testing flags can be stacked, as in *-rwx file* (new with *tcsh*).

EXAMPLE 11.26

```
    #!/bin/tcsh -f
    # Scriptname: filetest2
1   foreach file (`ls`)
2      if ( -rwf $file ) then
3         echo "${file}: readable/writeable/plain file"
       endif
    end
```

EXAMPLE 11.26 (CONTINUED)

```
(Output)
3  complete: readable/writeable/plain file
   dirstack: readable/writeable/plain file
   file.sc: readable/writeable/plain file
   filetest: readable/writeable/plain file
   glob: readable/writeable/plain file
   modifiers: readable/writeable/plain file
   env: readable/writeable/plain file
```

EXPLANATION

1. The *foreach* loop iterates through the list of files produced by the *Linux ls* program, one file at a file, assigning each filename to the variable *file*.
2. If the file is readable, writable, and a plain file (*-rwf*), line number 3 is executed. The stacking of these file testing options is legal in *tcsh*, but not in *csh*.
3. This line is executed if the filename being tested is readable, writable, and executable.

The *filetest* Built-In. The *tcsh* built-in, *filetest,* command applies one of the file inquiry operators to a file or list of files and returns a space-separated list of numbers; 1 for true and 0 for false.

EXAMPLE 11.27

```
1  > filetest -rwf dirstack file.sc xxx
   1 1 0

2  > filetest -b hdd
   1

3  > filetest -lrx /dev/fd
   1
```

EXPLANATION

1. Each of the files, *dirstack, file.c,* and *xxx*, are tested to see if they are readable, writable, plain files. For the first two files the test returns true (1 1), and for the last the test returns false (0).
2. The *filetest* command returns 1 if the file, *hdd*, is a block special device file. It is. Otherwise, 0 is returned.
3. The *filetest* command returns 1 if the file, *fd*, is a symbolic link and is readable and executable. It is. Otherwise, 0 is returned.

Additional *tcsh* File Testing Operators. There are an additional set of file testing operators (*tcsh* only) that return information about files. Because the returned values are not true/false values, a -1 indicates failure (except *F,* which returns a ":").

Table 11.8 Additional File Tests

-A	Last file access time, as the number of seconds since the epoch (*Jan. 1, 1970*).
-A:	Like *A*, but in timestamp format, e.g., *Fri. Aug. 27 16:36:10 1999.*
-M	Last file modification time.
-M:	Like *M*, but in timestamp format.
-C	Last inode modification time.
-C:	Like *C*, but in timestamp format.
-F	Composite file identifier, in the form *device:inode.*
-G	Numeric groupid.
-G:	Groupname or numeric groupid if the groupname is unknown.
-L	The name of the file pointed to by a symbolic link.
-N	Number of (hard) links.
-P	Permissions, in octal, without a leading zero.
-P:	Like *P,* with leading a zero.
-Pmode	Equivalent to *-P file & mode*; e.g., *-P22 file* returns *22* if file is writable by group and other, *20* if by group only, and *0* if by neither.
-Mode:	Like *PMode:*, with leading zero.
-U	Numeric userid.
-U:	Username, or the numeric userid if the username is unknown.
-Z	Size, in bytes.

EXAMPLE 11.28

```
1    > date
     Wed Jan 12 13:36:11 PST 2000

2    > filetest -A myfile
     934407771

3    > filetest -A: myfile
     Wed Jan 12 14:42:51 2000

4    > filetest -U myfile
     501

5    > filetest -P: myfile
     0600

     > filetest -P myfile
     600
```

EXPLANATION

1 Today's date is printed.

2 With the *-A* option, the *filetest* built-in prints the date (in epoch form) when *myfile* was last accessed.

3 With the *-A:* option, the *filetest* built-in prints the date in timestamp format.

4 With the *-U* option, the *filetest* built-in prints the numeric user id for the owner of *myfile.*

5 With the *-P:* option, the *filetest* built-in prints the octal permission mode with a leading 0. Without the colon, the leading zero is removed.

11.6.13 Nesting Conditionals

Conditional statements can be nested. Every *if* must have a corresponding *endif* (*else if* does not have an *endif*). It is a good idea to indent nested statements and line up the *if*s and *endif*s so that you can read and test the program more effectively.

EXAMPLE 11.29

```
(The Script)
     #!/bin/tcsh -f
     # Scriptname: filecheck
     # Usage: filecheck filename
1    alias Usage 'echo "    Usage: $0 filename\!*" ; exit 1'
2    alias Error 'echo "    Error: \!* "; exit 2'
3    set file=$1
4    if ( $#argv == 0 ) then
        Usage
     endif
5       if ( ! -e $file ) then
           Error "$file does not exist"
        endif
6    if ( -d $file ) then
        echo "$file is a directory"
7    else if (-f $file) then
8       if ( -rx $file ) then       # nested if construct
           echo "You have read and execute permission on $file"
9       endif
     else
        print "$file is neither a plain file nor a directory."
10   endif

(The Command Line)
     $ filecheck grade
     You have read and execute permission of file testing.
```

EXPLANATION

1 This is an alias called *Usage* that can be used to produce an error message and exit the program.

2 This is an alias called *Error* that will produce an error message followed by any arguments passed when called.

3 The variable *file* is set to the first argument passed in from the command line, *$1*.

4 If the number of arguments passed is 0, i.e., no arguments were provided, the alias *Usage* will print its message to the screen.

5 If *file* (after variable substitution) is a file that does not exist (note the *not* operator, *!*), the alias, *Error,* under the *then* keyword displays its message.

6 If the *file* is a directory, print "*testing is a directory.*"

7 If the *file* is not a directory, *else if* the *file* is a plain file, *then* ... the next statement is executed, another *if*.

EXPLANATION (CONTINUED)

8 This *if* is nested in the previous *if*. If *file* is readable and executable, *then* ... This *if* has its own *endif* and is lined up to indicate where it belongs.

9 The *endif* terminates the innermost *if* construct.

10 The *endif* terminates the outermost *if* construct.

11.6.14 The *switch* Command

The *switch* command is an alternative to using the *if–then–else if* construct. Sometimes the *switch* command makes a program clearer to read when handling multiple options. The value in the *switch* expression is matched against the expressions, called *labels*, following the *case* keyword. The *case* labels will accept constant expressions and wildcards. The label is terminated with a colon. The *default* label is optional, but its action is taken if none of the other cases match the *switch* expression. The *breaksw* is used to transfer execution to the *endsw*. If a *breaksw* is omitted and a label is matched, any statements below the matched label are executed until either a *breaksw* or *endsw* is reached.

FORMAT

```
switch (variable)
case constant:
        commands
        breaksw
case constant:
        commands
        breaksw
endsw
```

EXAMPLE 11.30

```
(The Script - colors)
   #!/bin/tcsh -f
   # This script is called colors
1  echo -n "Which color do you like? "
2  set color = $<
3  switch ("$color")
4  case bl*:
      echo I feel $color
      echo The sky is $color
5     breaksw
6  case red:           # Is is red or is it yellow?
7  case yellow:
8     echo The sun is sometimes $color.
9     breaksw
10 default:
```

EXAMPLE 11.30 (CONTINUED)

```
11     echo $color not one of the categories.
12     breaksw
13  endsw

(The Output)
1   Which color do you like? red
8   The sun is sometimes red.
1   Which color do you like? Doesn't matter
11  Doesn't matter is not one of the categories.
```

EXPLANATION

1 The user is asked for input.

2 The input is assigned to the *color* variable.

3 The *switch* statement evaluates the variable. The variable is enclosed in double quotes in case the user entered more than one word. The *switch* statement evaluates a single word or string of words if the string of words is held together with double quotes.

4 The *case* label is *bl**, meaning that the *switch* expression will be matched against any set of characters starting with *b*, followed by an *l*. If the user entered *blue, black, blah, blast*, and so forth, the commands under this *case* label would be executed.

5 The *breaksw* transfers program control to the *endsw* statement.

6 If the *switch* statement matches this label, *red*, the program starts executing statements until the *breaksw* on line 9 is reached. Line 8 will be executed. *"The sun is sometimes red"* is displayed.

7 If line 4 is not matched, cases *red* and *yellow* are tested.

8 If either label, *red* or *yellow*, is matched, this line is executed.

9 The *breaksw* transfers program control to the *endsw* statement.

10 The default label is reached if none of the case labels matches the *switch* expression. This is like the *if/else if/else* construct.

11 This line is printed if the user enters something not matched in any of the above cases.

12 This *breaksw* is optional because the switch will end here. It is recommended to leave the *breaksw* here so that if more cases are added later, it will not be overlooked.

13 The *endsw* terminates the *switch* statement.

Nesting Switches. Switches can be nested; i.e., a *switch* statement and its cases can be contained within another *switch* statement as one of its cases. There must be an *endsw* to terminate each *switch* statement. A *default* case is not required.

EXAMPLE 11.31

```
(The Script - systype)
     #!/bin/tcsh -f
     # This script is called systype
     # Program to determine the type of system you are on.
     #
     echo "Your system type is: "
1    set release = ('uname -r')
2    switch ('uname -s')
3    case SunOS:
4       switch ("$release")
5       case 4.*:
              echo "SunOS $release"
              breaksw
6       case [5-8].*:
              echo "Solaris $release"
              breaksw
7       endsw
        breaksw
     case HP*:
        echo HP-UX
        breaksw

     case Linux:
        echo Linux
        breaksw
8    endsw

(The Command Line)
     > systype
      Your system type:
      SunOS 5.5.1
```

EXPLANATION

1. The variable *release* is assigned the output of *uname -r*, the release number for the version of the operating system.
2. The *switch* command evaluates the output of *uname -s*, the name of the operating system.
3. If the system type is *SunOS*, the *case* command on line 3 is executed.
4. The value of the variable *release* is evaluated in each of the cases for a match.
5. The *case* for all release versions 4 are tested.
6. The *case* for all release versions 5 through 8 are tested.
7. The inner *switch* statement is terminated.
8. The outer *switch* statement is terminated.

11.6.15 The *Here* Document and Menus

The *here* document (discussed on page 553) is used in shell scripts to produce a menu. It is often used in conjunction with the *switch* statement. Once the user has seen the menu, he selects an item, and then his choice is matched in the *switch* statement to the *case* that corresponds to his choice. The *here* document reduces the number of *echo* statements that would, otherwise, be needed and makes the program easier to read.

EXAMPLE 11.32

```
   #! /bin/tcsh
1  echo "Select from the following menu:"
2  cat << EOF
      1) Red
      2) Green
      3) Blue
      4) Exit
3  EOF
4  set choice = $<
5  switch ("choice")
```

EXAMPLE 11.32 (CONTINUED)

```
    case 1:
            echo Red is stop.
            breaksw
    case 2:
            echo Green is go!
            breaksw
    case 3:
            echo Blue is a feeling...
            breaksw
    case 4:
            exit
            breaksw
    default:
            echo Not a choice\!\!
            endsw
            echo Good-bye

(The Output)
Select from the following menu:
    1) Red
    2) Green
    3) Blue
    4) Exit
2
Green is a go!
Good-bye
```

EXPLANATION

1 The user is asked to select from the menu.

2 The *here* document starts here. EOF is a user-defined word terminator. Until EOF is found on a line by itself (against the left-hand margin), the text after the first EOF will be sent as a quoted block to the *cat* program. The *cat* program will send the text to standard output, the user's terminal.

3 This EOF terminates the *here* document.

4 The user types his choice from the menu items displayed; i.e., 1, 2, 3, or 4.

5 The *switch* statement is used to evaluate the choice.

11.7 Loops

Looping constructs allow you to execute the same statements a number of times. The C shell supports two types of loops: the *foreach* loop and the *while* loop. The *foreach* loop is used when you need to execute commands on a list of items, one item at a time, such as a list of files or a list of usernames. The *while* loop is used when you want to keep executing a command until a certain condition is met.

11.7.1 The *foreach* Loop

The *foreach* command is followed by a variable and a wordlist enclosed in parentheses. The first time the loop is entered, the first word in the list is assigned to the variable. The list is shifted to the left by one and the body of the loop is entered. Each command in the loop body is executed until the *end* statement is reached. Control returns to the top of the loop. The next word on the list is assigned to the variable, the commands after the *foreach* line are executed, the end is reached, control returns to the top of the *foreach* loop, the next word in the wordlist is processed, and so on. When the wordlist is empty, the loop ends.

FORMAT

```
foreach variable (wordlist)
    commands
end
```

EXAMPLE 11.33

```
foreach person (bob sam sue fred)
     mail $person < letter
end
```

EXPLANATION

1 The *foreach* command is followed by a variable, *person*, and a wordlist enclosed in parentheses. The variable *person* will be assigned the value *bob* the first time the *foreach* loop is entered. Once *bob* has been assigned to *person*, *bob* is shifted off (to the left) and *sam* is at the beginning of the list. When the *end* statement is reached, control starts at the top of the loop, and *sam* is assigned to the variable *person*. This procedure continues until *fred* is shifted off, at which time the list is empty and the loop is over.

2 The user *bob* will be mailed the contents of the file *letter* the first time through the loop.

3 When the *end* statement is reached, loop control is returned to the *foreach*, and the next element in the list is assigned to the variable *person*.

EXAMPLE 11.34

```
(The Command Line)
    > cat maillist
    tom
    dick
    harry
    dan

(The Script - mailtomaillist)
    #!/bin/tcsh -f
    # This script is called mailtomaillist
1   foreach person (`cat maillist`)
        # Here Document follows
2       mail $person <<EOF
        Hi $person,
        How are you? I've missed you. Come on over
        to my place.
        Your pal,
              $LOGNAME@`uname -n`
    EOF

3   end
```

EXPLANATION

1 Command substitution is performed within the parentheses. The contents of the file *maillist* become the wordlist. Each name in the wordlist *(tom, dick, harry, dan)* is assigned, in turn, to the variable *person*. After the looping statements are executed and the *end* is reached, control returns to the *foreach*, a name is shifted off from the list, and assigned to the variable *person*. The next name in the list replaces the one that was just shifted off. The list therefore decreases in size by one. This process continues until all the names have been shifted off and the list is empty.

2 The *"here" document* is used. Input is sent to the *mail* program from the first *EOF* to the terminating *EOF*. (It is important that the last *EOF* is against the left-hand margin and has no surrounding white space.) Each person in the list will be sent the *mail* message.

3 The *end* statement for the *foreach* loop marks the end of the block of lines that is executed within this loop. Control returns to the top of the loop.

EXAMPLE 11.35

```
1   foreach file (*.c)
2      cc $file -o $file:r
    end
```

EXPLANATION

1 The wordlist for the *foreach* command is a list of files in the current directory ending in *.c* (i.e., all the C source files).

2 Each file in the list will be compiled. If, for example, the first file to be processed is *program.c*, the shell will expand the *cc* command line to:

```
cc program.c -o program
```

The *:r* causes the *.c* extension to be removed.

EXAMPLE 11.36

```
(The Command Line)
1   > runit f1 f2 f3 dir2 dir3

(The Script)
    #!/bin/tcsh -f
    # This script is called runit.
    # It loops through a list of files passed as
    # arguments

2   foreach arg ($*)
3       if ( -e $arg ) then
        ...         Program code continues here

        else
        ...         Program code continues here
        endif
4   end
5   echo "Program continues here"
```

EXPLANATION

1 The script name is *runit*; the command line arguments are *f1, f2, f3, dir2*, and *dir3*.

2 The *$** variable evaluates to a list of all the arguments (positional parameters) passed in at the command line. The *foreach* command processes, in turn, each of the words in the wordlist, *f1, f2, f3, dir2,* and *dir3*. Each time through the loop, the first word in the list is assigned to the variable *arg*. After a word is assigned, it is shifted off (to the left) and the next word is assigned to *arg*, until the list is empty.

3 The commands in this block are executed for each item in the list until the *end* statement is reached.

4 The *end* statement terminates the loop after the wordlist is empty.

5 After the loop ends, the program continues to run.

11.7.2 The *while* Loop

The *while* loop evaluates an expression, and as long as the expression is true (nonzero), the commands below the *while* command will be executed until the *end* statement is reached. Control will then return to the *while* expression, the expression will be evaluated, and if still true, the commands will be executed again, and so on. When the *while* expression is false, the loop ends and control starts after the *end* statement.

EXAMPLE 11.37

```
(The Script)
    #!/bin/tcsh -f
1   set num = 0
2   while ($num < 10)
3        echo $num
4        @ num++          (See arithmetic)
5   end
6   echo "Program continues here"
```

EXPLANATION

1 The variable *num* is set to an initial value of zero.

2 The *while* loop is entered and the expression is tested. If the value of *num* is less than *10*, the expression is true, and lines 3 and 4 are executed.

3 The value of *num* is displayed each time through the loop.

4 The value of the variable, *num*, is incremented. If this statement were omitted, the loop would continue forever.

5 The *end* statement terminates the block of executable statements. When this line is reached, control is returned to the top of the *while* loop and the expression is evaluated again. This continues until the *while* expression is false (i.e., when *$num* is *10*).

6 Program execution continues here after the loop terminates.

EXAMPLE 11.38

```
(The Script)
    #!/bin/tcsh -f
1   echo -n  "Who wrote \"War and Peace\"?"
2   set answer = "$<"
3   while ( "$answer" != "Tolstoy" )
         echo "Wrong,  try again\!"
4        set answer = "$<"
5   end
6   echo Yeah!
```

EXPLANATION

1 The user is asked for input.

2 The variable *answer* is assigned whatever the user inputs.

3 The *while* command evaluates the expression. If the value of *$answer* is not equal to the string *"Tolstoy"* exactly, the message *"Wrong, try again!"* is printed and the program waits for user input.

EXPLANATION (CONTINUED)

4 The variable *answer* is assigned the new input. This line is important. If the value of the variable *answer* never changes, the loop expression will never become false, thus causing the loop to spin infinitely.

5 The *end* statement terminates the block of code inside the *while* loop.

6 If the user enters *"Tolstoy,"* the loop expression tests false, and control goes to this line. *Yeah!* is printed.

11.7.3 The *repeat* Command

The *repeat* command takes two arguments, a number and a command. The *command* is executed *that* number of times.

EXAMPLE 11.39

```
> repeat 3 echo hello
hello
hello
hello
```

EXPLANATION

The *echo* command is executed three times.

11.7.4 Looping Commands

The *shift* Command. The *shift* command, without an array name as its argument, shifts the *argv* array by one word from the left, thereby decreasing the size of the *argv* array by one. Once shifted off, the array element is lost.

EXAMPLE 11.40

```
(The Script)
    #!/bin/tcsh -f
    # Script is called loop.args
    while ($#argv)
          echo $argv
          shift
    end
```

EXAMPLE 11.40 (CONTINUED)

```
(The Command Line)
5  > loop.args a b c d e
   a b c d e
   b c d e
   c d e
   d e
   e
```

EXPLANATION

1 *$#argv* evaluates to the number of command line arguments. If there are five command line arguments, *a, b, c, d,* and *e*, the value of *$#argv* is *5* the first time in the loop. The expression is tested and yields *5*, true.

2 The command line arguments are printed.

3 The *argv* array is shifted one to the left. There are only four arguments left, starting with *b.*

4 The end of the loop is reached, and control goes back to the top of the loop. The expression is reevaluated. This time, *$#argv* is *4*. The arguments are printed, and the array is shifted again. This goes on until all of the arguments are shifted off. At that time, when the expression is evaluated, it will be 0, which is false, and the loop exits.

5 The arguments *a, b, c, d,* and *e* are passed to the script via the *argv* array.

The *break* Command. The *break* command is used to break out of a loop so that control starts after the *end* statement. It breaks out of the innermost loop. Execution continues after the *end* statement of the loop. If multiple breaks are listed on the same line, it is possible to break out of multilevel loops.

EXAMPLE 11.41

```
   #!/bin/tcsh -f
   # This script is called baseball
1  echo -n "What baseball hero died in August, 1995? "
2  set answer = "$<"
3  while ("$answer" !~ [Mm]*)
4          echo "Wrong\! Try again."
           set answer = "$<"
5          if ( "$answer" =~  [Mm]* ) break
6  end
7  echo "You are a scholar."
```

EXPLANATION

1. The user is asked for input.
2. The input from the user is assigned to the variable *answer* (answer: Mickey Mantle).
3. The *while* expression reads: *While the value of answer does not begin with a big M or little m, followed by zero or more of any character, enter the loop.*
4. The user gets to try again. The variable is reset.
5. If the variable *answer* matches *M* or *m*, *break* out of the loop. Go to the *end* statement and start executing statements at line 7.
6. The *end* statement terminates this block of statements after the loop.
7. After the loop exits, control starts here and this line is executed.

EXAMPLE 11.42

```
     #!/bin/tcsh -f
     # This script is called database
1    while (1)
         echo "Select a menu item"
2        cat << EOF
         1) Append
         2) Delete
         3) Update
         4) Exit
     EOF
3        set choice = "$<"
4        switch ($choice)
         case 1:
              echo "Appending"
5             break           # Break out of loop; not a breaksw
         case 2:
              echo "Deleting"
              break
         case 3:
              echo "Updating"
              break
         case 4:
              exit 0
         default:
6             echo "Invalid choice. Try again."
         endsw
7    end
8    echo "Program continues here"
```

EXPLANATION

1. This is called an *infinite* loop. The expression always evaluates to one, which is true.
2. This is a *"here" document*. A menu is printed to the screen.
3. The user selects a menu item.
4. The *switch* command evaluates the variable.
5. If the user selects a valid choice, between 1 and 4, the command after the appropriate matching *case* label is executed. The *break* statement causes the program to break out of the loop and start execution on line 8. Don't confuse this with the *breaksw* statement, which merely exits the switch at *endsw.*
6. If the *default case* is matched, that is, none of the cases are matched, program control goes to the end of the loop and then starts again at the top of the *while*. Because the expression after the *while* always evaluates true, the body of the loop is entered and the menu is displayed again.
7. End of the *while* loop statements.
8. After the loop is exited, this line is executed.

Nested Loops and the *repeat* Command. Rather than a *goto*, the *repeat* command can be used to break out of nested loops. The *repeat* command will not do this with the *continue* command.

EXAMPLE 11.43

```
(Simple Script)
    #!/bin/tcsh -f
    # Script name: looper
1   while (1)
        echo "Hello, in 1st loop"
2       while (1)
                echo "In 2nd loop"
3               while (1)
                    echo "In 3rd loop"
4                   repeat 3 break
                end
        end
    end
5   echo "Out of all loops"

(The Output)
    Hello, in 1st loop
    In 2nd loop
    In 3rd loop
    Out of all loops
```

EXPLANATION

1 Start the first *while* loop.

2 Enter the second nested *while* loop.

3 Enter the third nested *while* loop.

4 The *repeat* command will cause *break* to be executed three times; it will break first out of the innermost loop, then the second loop, and last, the first loop. Control continues at line 5.

5 Program control starts here after loop terminates.

The *continue* Command. The *continue* statement starts execution at the top of the innermost loop.

EXAMPLE 11.44

```
1   set done = 0
2   while ( ! $done )
        echo "Are you finished yet?"
        set answer = "$<"
3       if ("$answer" =~ [Nn]*) continue
4       set done = 1
5   end
```

EXPLANATION

1 The variable *done* is assigned zero.

2 The expression is tested. It reads: *while (! 0). Not 0* is evaluated as true (logical NOT).

3 If the user entered *No, no,* or *nope* (anything starting with *N* or *n*), the expression is true and the *continue* statement returns control to the top of the loop where the expression is reevaluated.

4 If *answer* does not start with *N* or *n*, the variable *done* is reset to one. When the end of the loop is reached, control starts at the top of the loop and the expression is tested. It reads: *while (! 1). Not 1* is false. The loop exits.

5 This marks the end of the *while* loop.

EXAMPLE 11.45

```
(The Script)
   #!/bin/tcsh -f
1  if ( ! -e memo ) then
      echo  "memo file non existent"
      exit 1
   endif
2  foreach person ( anish bob don karl jaye)
3     if ("$person" =~ [Kk]arl) continue
4     mail -s "Party time"  $person < memo
   end
```

EXPLANATION

1. A file check is done. If the file *memo* does not exist, the user is sent an error message and the program exits with a status of 1.
2. The loop will assign each person in the list to the variable *person*, in turn, and then shift off the name in the list to process the next one.
3. If the person's name is *Karl* or *karl*, the *continue* statement starts execution at the top of the *foreach* loop (*Karl* is not sent the memo because his name was shifted off after being assigned to *person*). The next name in the list is assigned to *person*.
4. Everyone on the mailing list is sent the memo, except *karl*.

11.8 Interrupt Handling

If a script is interrupted with the Interrupt key, it terminates and control is returned to the TC shell, that is, you get your prompt back. The *onintr* command is used to process interrupts within a script. It allows you to ignore the interrupt (^C) or transfer control to another part of the program before exiting. Normally, the *interrupt* command is used with a label to "clean up" before exiting. The *onintr* command without arguments restores the default action.

EXAMPLE 11.46

```
(The Script)
onintr finish
   < Script continues here >
finish:
onintr -        # Disable further interrupts
echo Cleaning temp files
rm $$tmp* ; exit 1
```

EXPLANATION

1 The *onintr* command is followed by a label name. The label *finish* is a user-defined label; control will be transferred to the *finish* label if an interrupt occurs. Usually this line is at the beginning of the script. It is not in effect until it is executed in the script.

2 The rest of the script lines are executed unless ^C (Interrupt key) is pressed while the program is in execution, at which time, control is transferred to the label.

3 This is the label; when the interrupt comes in, the program will continue to run, executing the statements below the label.

4 To shield this part of the script from interrupts, the *onintr* – is used. If Control-C is entered now, it will be ignored.

5 This line is echoed to the screen.

6 All *tmp* files are removed. The *tmp* files are prefixed with the shell's PID (*$$*) number and suffixed with any number of characters. The program exits with a status of 1.

11.9 *setuid* Scripts

Whoever runs a *setuid* program temporarily (as long as he or she is running the *setuid* program) becomes the owner of that program and has the same permissions as the owner. The *passwd* program is a good example of a *setuid* program. When you change your password, you temporarily become *root*, but only during the execution of the *passwd* program. That is why you are able to change your password in the */etc/passwd* (or */etc/shadow*) file, which is off-limits to regular users.

Shell programs can be written as *setuid* programs. You might want to do this if you have a script that is accessing a file containing information that should not be accessible to regular users, such as salary or personal information. If the script is a *setuid* script, the person running the script can have access to the data, but it is still restricted from others. A *setuid* program requires the following steps:

1. In the script, the first line is:

```
#!/bin/tcsh -feb

The -feb options:
    -f    fast start up; don't execute .cshrc
    -e    abort immediately if interrupted
    -b    this is a setuid script
```

2. Next, change the permissions on the script so that it can run as a *setuid* program:

```
> chmod 4755 script_name
            or
> chmod +srx script_name
> ls -l
-rwsr-xr-x   2 ellie         512 Oct 10 17:18 script_name
```

11.10 Storing Scripts

After creating successful scripts, it is customary to collect them in a common script directory and change your path so that the scripts can be executed from any location.

EXAMPLE 11.47

```
1   > mkdir ~/bin
2   > mv myscript ~/bin
3   > vi .login

    In .login reset the path to add ~/bin.
4       set path = ( /usr/ucb /usr /usr/etc ~/bin . )

5   (At command line)
    > source .login
```

EXPLANATION

1 Make a directory under your home directory called *bin*, or any other name you choose.

2 Move any error-free scripts into the *bin* directory. Putting buggy scripts here will just cause problems.

3 Go into your *.login* file and reset the path.

4 The new path contains the directory *~/bin*, which is where the shell will look for executable programs. Because it is near the end of the path, a system program that may have the same name as one of your scripts will be executed first.

5 By sourcing the *.login*, the *path* changes are affected; it is not necessary to log out and back in again.

11.11 Built-In Commands

Rather than residing on disk like Linux executable commands, built-in commands are part of the TC shell's internal code and are executed from within the shell. If a built-in command occurs as any component of a pipeline except the last, it is executed in a subshell. The *tcsh* command aptly called, *builtins,* lists all the built-in commands (see Example 11.48 below). For a description of each built-in, see Table 10.24 on page 591.

EXAMPLE 11.48

```
1  > builtins
:          @          alias      alloc      bg         bindkey    break
breaksw    builtins   case       cd         chdir      complete   continue
default    dirs       echo       echotc     else       end        endif
endsw      eval       exec       exit       fg         filetest   foreach
glob       goto       hashstat   history    hup        if         jobs
kill       limit      log        login      logout     ls-F       nice
nohup      notify     onintr     popd       printenv   pushd      rehash
repeat     sched      set        setenv     settc      setty      shift
source     stop       suspend    switch     telltc     time       umask
unalias    uncomplete unhash     unlimit    unset      unsetenv   wait
where      which      while
```

11.11.1 Shell Command Line Switches

The TC shell can take a number of command line switches (also called flag arguments) to control or modify its behavior. The command line switches are listed in Table 11.9.

Table 11.9 Shell Command Line Switches

-	Specifies the shell is a login shell.
-b	Forces a "break" from option processing. Any shell arguments thereafter, will not be treated as options. The remaining arguments will not be interpreted as shell options. Must include this option if shell is set-user id.
-c	If a single argument follows the *-c*, commands are read from the argument (a filename). Remaining arguments are placed in the *argv* shell variable.
-d	The shell loads the directory stack from *~/.cshdirs*.
-Dname[=value]	Sets the environment variable name to value.

Table 11.9 Shell Command Line Switches (Continued)

-e	The shell exits if any invoked command terminates abnormally or yields a nonzero exit status.
-f	Called the fast startup because the shell ignores *~/.tcshrc*, when starting a new TC shell.
-F	The shell uses fork(2) instead of vfork(2) to spawn processes. (Convex/OS only)
-i	The shell is interactive and prompts input, even if it appears to not be a terminal. This option isn't necessary if input and output are connected to a terminal.
-l	The shell is a login shell if *-l* is the only flag specified.
-m	The shell loads *~/.tcshrc* even if it does not belong to the effective user.
-n	Used for debugging scripts. The shell parses commands but does not execute them.
-q	The shell accepts the SIGQUIT signal and behaves when it is used under a debugger. Job control is disabled.
-s	Command input is taken from the standard input.
-t	The shell reads and executes a single line of input. A backslash (\) may be used to escape the newline at the end of this line and continue on to another line.
-v	Sets the verbose shell variable, so that command input is echoed after history substitution. Used to debug shell scripts.
-x	Sets the echo shell variable, so that commands are echoed before execution and after history and variable substitution. Used to debug shell scripts.
-V	Sets the verbose shell variable before executing the *~/.tcshrc* file.
-X	Sets the echo shell variable before executing the *~/.tcshrc* file.

THE TC SHELL LAB EXERCISES

Lab 1—First Script

1. Write a script called *greetme* that will:

   a. Greet the user.

   b. Print the date and time.

   c. Print a calendar for this month.

   d. Print the name of your machine.

   e. Print a list of all files in your parent directory.

   f. Print all the processes you are running.

   g. Print the value of the TERM, PATH, and HOME variables.

   h. Print "*Please couldn't you loan me $50.00?*"

   i. Tell the user "*Good bye*" and the current hour. (See *man* pages for the *date* command.)

2. Make sure your script is executable.

   ```
   chmod +x greetme
   ```

3. What was the first line of your script?

Lab 2—Getting User Input

1. Write a script called *nosy* that will:

   a. Ask the user's full name—first, last, and middle name.

   b. Greet the user by his or her first name.

   c. Ask the user's year of birth and calculate the user's age.

   d. Ask the user's login name and print user's ID (*from /etc/passwd*).

   e. Tell the user his or her home directory.

   f. Show the user the processes he or she is running.

   g. Tell the user the day of the week, and the current time in nonmilitary time.

   The output should resemble:

   "The day of the week is Tuesday and the current time is 04:07:38 PM."

2. Create a text file called *datafile* (unless this file has already been provided for you.) Each entry consists of fields separated by colons. The fields are:

   a. First and last name

   b. Phone number

   c. Address

   d. Birthdate

   e. Salary

3. Create a script called *lookup* that will:

   a. Contain a comment section with the script name, your name, the date, and the reason for writing this script. The reason for writing this script is to display the *datafile* in sorted order.

   b. Sort the *datafile* by last names.

   c. Show the user the contents of the *datafile*.

   d. Tell the user the number of entries in the file.

4. Try the *echo* and *verbose* commands for debugging your script. How did you use these commands?

Lab 3—Command Line Arguments

1. Write a script called *rename* that will:

   a. Take two filenames as command line arguments, the first file is the old file and the second file is the new one.

   b. Rename the old filename with the new filename.

   c. List the files in the directory to show the change.

2. Write a script called *checking* that will:

   a. Take a command line argument, a user's login name.

   b. Test to see if a command line argument was provided.

   c. Check to see if the user is in the */etc/passwd* file. If so, will print:

   "Found <user> in the /etc/passwd file."

   Otherwise will print:

   "No such user on our system."

Lab 4—Conditionals and File Testing

1. In the *lookup* script, ask the user if he or she would like to add an entry to the *datafile*. If *yes* or *y*:

   a. Prompt the user for a new name, phone, address, birthday, and salary. Each item will be stored in a separate variable. You will provide the colons between the fields, and append the information to the *datafile*.

   b. Sort the file by last names. Tell the user you added the entry, and show the line preceded by the line number.

2. Rewrite *checking*.

   a. After checking whether the named user is in the */etc/passwd* file, the program will check to see if he or she is logged on. If so, the program will print all the processes that are running; otherwise it will tell the user:

   "<user> is not logged on."

3. The lookup script depends on the *datafile* in order to run. In the *lookup* script, check to see if the *datafile* exists and if it is readable and writeable.

4. Add a menu to the *lookup* script to resemble the following:

   [1] Add entry
   [2] Delete entry
   [3] View entry
   [4] Exit

5. You already have the *Add entry* part of the script written. The *Add entry* routine should now include code that will check to see if the name is already in the *datafile* and if it is, tell the user so. If the name is not there, add the new entry.

6. Now write the code for the *Delete entry*, *View entry*, and *Exit* functions.

7. The *Delete* part of the script should first check to see if the entry exists before trying to remove it. If the entry does not exist, notify the user; otherwise remove the entry and tell the user you removed it. On exit, make sure that you use a digit to represent the appropriate exit status.

8. How do you check the exit status from the command line?

Lab 5—The Switch Statement

1. Rewrite the following script using a switch statement.

```
#!/bin/tcsh -f
# Grades program

echo -n "What was your grade on the test? "
set score = $<
if ( $grade >= 90 && $grade <= 100 ) then
   echo You got an A\!
else if ( $grade >= 80 && $grade < 89 ) then
   echo You got a B.
else if ( $grade >= 79 && $grade < 79 ) then
   echo "You're average."
else if ( $grade >= 69 && $grade < 69 ) then
   echo Better study harder
else
   echo Better luck next time.
endif
```

2. Rewrite the lookup script using switch statements for each of the menu items.

Lab 6—Loops

1. Write a program called *picnic* that will mail a list of users, one at a time, an invitation to a picnic. The list of users will be in a file called *friends*. One of the users listed in the *friends* file will be Popeye.

   a. The invitation will be in another file, called *invite*.

   b. Use file testing to check that both files exist and are readable.

   c. A loop will be used to iterate through the list of users. When Popeye is reached, he will be skipped over (i.e., he does not get an invitation), and the next user on the list sent an invitation, and so forth.

   d. Keep a list with the names of each person who received an invitation. Do this by building an array. After everyone on the list has been sent mail, print the number of people who received mail and a list of their names.

Bonus: If you have time, you may want to customize your *invite* file so that each user receives a letter containing his or her name. For example, the message might start:

Dear John,
Hi John, I hope you can make it to our picnic....

To do this your *invite* file may be written:

Dear XXX,
Hi XXX, I hope you can make it to our picnic....

With *sed* or *awk,* you could then substitute *XXX* with the user name. (It might be tricky putting the capital letter in the user name, because user names are always lowercase.)

2. Add a new menu item to the *lookup* script to resemble the following:

```
[1] Add entry
[2] Delete entry
[3] Change entry
[4] View entry
[5] Exit
```

   After the user has selected a valid entry, when the function has completed, ask the user if he or she would like to see the menu again. If an invalid entry is entered, the program should print:

   Invalid entry, try again.

   The menu will be redisplayed.

3. Create a submenu under *View entry* in the *lookup* script. The user will be asked if he or she would like to view specific information for a selected individual:

   a) Phone
   b) Address
   c) Birthday
   d) Salary

4. Add the *onintr* command to your script using a label. When the program starts execution at the label, any temporary files will be removed, the user will be told *Good–bye*, and the program will exit.

APPENDIX

A USEFUL LINUX/UNIX UTILITIES FOR SHELL PROGRAMMERS

apropos—searches the what is database for strings

```
apropos keyword ...
```

apropos searches a set of database files (see directory */usr/man/whatis*) containing short descriptions of system commands for keywords and displays the result on the standard output. Same as *man -k.*

EXAMPLE A.1

```
1 $ apropos bash
  bash (1)                    - GNU Bourne-Again SHell

2 $ man -k tcsh
  tsh (1)                   - C shell with filename completionand
                              command line editing
```

EXPLANATION

1 *apropos* searches for the keyword *bash* and prints a short description of what it is.

2 *man -k* behaves the same as *apropos.*

arch—prints the machine architecture (see *uname -m*)

```
arch
```

On current Linux systems, *arch* prints things such as *i386*, *i486*, *i586*, *alpha*, *sparc*, *arm*, *m68k*, *mips*, or *ppc*.

EXAMPLE A.2

```
$ arch
i386
```

at—at, atq, atrmbatch—execute commands at a later time

```
at [-V] [-q queue] [-f file] [-mldbv] TIME
at -c job [job...]
atq [-V] [-q queue] [-v]
atrm [-V] job [job...]
batch [-V] [-q queue] [-f file] [-mv] [TIME]
```

at and *batch* read commands from standard input to be executed at a later time. *at* allows you to specify when the commands should be executed, while jobs queued with *batch* will execute when system load level permits. Executes commands read from *stdin* or a file at some later time. Unless redirected, the output is mailed to the user.

atq lists the user's pending jobs, unless the user is the superuser; in that case, everybody's jobs are listed. Same as at *-l*.

atrm deletes jobs. *atrm 3 4 5* same as at *-d*.

EXAMPLE A.3

```
1   $ at 6:30am Dec 12 < program
    warning: commands will be executed using /bin/sh
    job 2 at 1999-12-12 06:30
2   $ at teatime today < program
    warning: commands will be executed using /bin/sh
    job 4 at 1999-10-20 16:00
3   $ at 7:45 pm August 9 < program
    warning: commands will be executed using /bin/sh
    job 5 at 1999-08-09 19:45
4   $ at now + 3 hours < program
    warning: commands will be executed using /bin/sh
    job 9 at 1999-10-20 23:18
```

EXAMPLE A.3 (CONTINUED)

```
5  $ at 2am tomorrow
   at> man bash | lpr
   at> <EOT>
   warning: commands will be executed using /bin/sh
   job 7 at 1999-10-19 02:00
6  $ atq
   6       1999-10-19 12:00 a
   7       1999-10-19 02:00 a
7  $ at -f file 17:05 monday
   warning: commands will be executed using /bin/sh
   job 9 at 1999-10-18 17:05
```

EXPLANATION

1 At 6:30 in the morning on December 12th, start the job. The warning message appears after each command.

2 At 4:00 this afternoon, start the job.

3 At 7:45 in the evening on August 9th, start the job.

4 In three hours start the job.

5 At 2 am tomorrow morning, execute the following commands. *at>* is the at prompt. Use Control-D to exit.

6 *atq* lists users' jobs currently pending.

7 Following the *-f* option is a filename. This file contains the program that will be executed at 7:05 on Monday.

awk (gawk)—pattern scanning and processing language

```
gawk [ POSIX or Gnu style options ]  -f program-file [ - ] file...
```

awk scans each input filename for lines that match any of a set of patterns specified in *prog.* (See Chapter 5, "The *gawk* Utility: *gawk* as a Linux Tool.") In the following example, use *awk*, *nawk*, or *gawk*, depending on your version of *awk.*

EXAMPLE A.4

```
awk '{print $1, $2}' file
awk '/John/{print $3, $4}' file
awk -F: '{print $3}' /etc/passwd
date | awk '{print $6}'
```

EXPLANATION

1 Prints the first two fields of *file* where fields are separated by white space.

2 Prints fields 3 and 4 if the pattern *John* is found.

3 Using a colon as the field separator, prints the third field of the */etc/passwd* file.

4 Sends the output of the *date* command to *awk* and prints the sixth field.

banner—make posters

banner prints its arguments (each up to 10 characters long) in large letters on the standard output.

EXAMPLE A.5

```
banner Happy Birthday
```

EXPLANATION

Displays in banner format the string *Happy Birthday.*

basename—with a directory name delivers portions of the pathname

```
basename string [ suffix ]
dirname string
```

basename deletes any prefix ending in / (forward slash) and the suffix (if present in string) from string, and prints the result on the standard output.

EXAMPLE A.6

```
1  basename /usr/local/bin
2  scriptname="`basename $0`"
```

EXPLANATION

1 Strips off the prefix */usr/local/* and displays *bin.*

2 Assigns just the name of the script, *$0*, to the variable *scriptname.*

bash—Gnu Bourne Again Shell

```
bash [options] [file[arguments]]
sh [options] [file[arguments]]
```

Bash is Copyright © 1989, 1991 by the Free Software Foundation, Inc. Bash is an sh-compatible command language interpreter that executes commands read from the standard input or from a file. Bash also incorporates useful features from the Korn and C shells (*ksh* and *csh)*. (See Chapters 8 and 9.)

bc—processes precision arithmetic

```
bc [ -lwsqv ] [long-options] [  file ... ]
```

bc is an interactive processor for a language that resembles C but provides unlimited precision arithmetic. It takes input from any files given, then reads the standard input.

EXAMPLE A.7

```
1   bc << EOF
    scale=3
    4.5 + 5.6 / 3
    EOF
    Output : 6.366
    -----------------------------
2   bc
    ibase=2
    5
    101 (Output)
    20
    10100 (Output
    ^D
```

EXPLANATION

1 This is a *here* document. From the first EOF to the last EOF, input is given to the *bc* command. The scale specifies the number of digits to the right of the decimal point. The result of the calculation is displayed on the screen.

2 The number base is two. The number is converted to binary (ATT only).

biff [ny]—be notified if mail arrives and who it is from

n Disables notification.
y Enables notification.

cal—displays a calendar

```
cal   cal [-jy] [month [year]]
```

cal Prints a calendar for the specified year. If a month is also specified, a calendar just for that month is printed. If neither is specified, a calendar for the present month is printed.
-j Displays Julian dates (days one-based, numbered from January 1).
-y Displays a calendar for the current year.

EXAMPLE A.8

```
1 $ cal
    October 1999
Su Mo Tu We Th Fr Sa
                1  2
 3  4  5  6  7  8  9
10 11 12 13 14 15 16
17 18 19 20 21 22 23
24 25 26 27 28 29 30
31

2 $ cal -j
          October 1999
Sun Mon Tue Wed Thu Fri Sat
                    274 275
276 277 278 279 280 281 282
283 284 285 286 287 288 289
290 291 292 293 294 295 296
297 298 299 300 301 302 303
304
```

EXPLANATION

1 Prints the current month.

2 Prints month in Julian, starting with day 1 on January 1.

cat—concatenates and displays files

```
cat [-benstuvAET] [--number] [--number-nonblank]
    [--squeeze-blank] [--show-nonprinting] [--show-ends]
    [--show-tabs] [--show-all] [--help] [--version] [file...]
```

cat reads each filename in sequence and writes it on the standard output. If no input file is given, or if the "-" argument is encountered, *cat* reads from the standard input file. Use the *--help* option to see a short description of all of the options to the *cat* command.

EXAMPLE A.9

```
1   cat /etc/passwd
2   cat -n file1 file2 >> file3
3   cat -T datafile
4   cat -b datafile
```

EXPLANATION

1 Displays the contents of the */etc/passwd* file.

2 Concatenates *file1* and *file2* and appends output to *file3*. The *-n* switch causes each line to be numbered.

3 Displays tabs as ^I.

4 Numbers all nonblank lines.

chfn—change the finger information

```
chfn  [ -f full-name ] [ -o office ] [ -poffice-phone ]
      [ -h home-phone ] [ -u ] [ -v ] [ username ]
```

chfn is used to change your finger information. This information is stored in the */etc/passwd* file, and is displayed by the finger program. The Linux *finger* command will display four pieces of information that can be changed by *chfn*: your real name, your work room and phone, and your home phone.

chmod—change the permissions mode of a file

```
chmod [-Rcfv] [--recursive] [--changes] [--silent]
      [--quiet] [--verbose] [--help] [--version] mode file...
```

chmod changes or assigns the mode of a file. The mode of a file specifies its permissions and other attributes. The mode may be absolute or symbolic.

EXAMPLE A.10

```
1  chmod +x script.file
2  chmod u+x,g-x file
3  chmod 755 *
```

EXPLANATION

1. Turns on execute permission for user, group, and others on *script.file*.
2. Turns on execute permission for user, and removes it from group on *file*.
3. Turns on read, write, and execute for the user, read and execute for the group, and read and execute for others on all files in the current working directory. The value is octal (111 101 101), `rwxr-xr-x`.

chown—change the user and group ownership of files

```
chown [-Rcfv] [--recursive] [--changes] [--help] [--version]
      [--silent] [--quiet] [--verbose]  [user][:.][group] file...
```

chown (Gnu) changes the user and/or group ownership of each given file, according to its first nonoption argument, which is interpreted as follows. If only a user name (or numeric user ID) is given, that user is made the owner of each given file, and the files' group is not changed. If the user name is followed by a colon or dot and a group name (or numeric group ID), with no spaces between them, the group ownership of the files is changed as well. If a colon or dot but no group name follows the user name, that user is made the owner of the files and the group of the files is changed to that user's login group. If the colon or dot and group are given, but the user name is omitted, only the group of the files is changed; in this case, *chown* performs the same function as *chgrp*. Must be root to use *chown*.

EXAMPLE A.11

```
1   chown john filex
2   chown -R ellie ellie
```

EXPLANATION

1 Changes the user id of *filex* to *john*. Must be root to change ownership

2 Recursively changes the ownership to *ellie* for all files in *ellie* directory.

chsh—change your login shell

```
chsh [ -s shell ] [ -l ] [ -u ] [ -v ] [ username ]
```

chsh is used to change your login shell. If a shell is not given on the command line, *chsh* prompts for one. All valid shells are listed in the */etc/shells* file.

-s, --shell	Specifies your login shell.
-l, --list-shells	Prints the list of shells listed in */etc/shells* and exits.
-u, --help	Prints a usage message and exits.
-v, --version	Prints version information and exits.

EXAMPLE A.12

```
1 $ chsh -l
/bin/bash
/bin/sh
/bin/ash
/bin/bsh
/bin/tcsh
/bin/csh
/bin/ksh
/bin/zsh

2 $ chsh
Changing shell for ellie.
New shell [/bin/sh] tcsh
chsh: shell ust be a full path name.
```

EXPLANATION

1 Lists all available shells on this Linux system.

2 Asks the user to type in the full pathname for a new login shell. Fails unless a full pathname such as, */bin/tcsh*, is given.

clear—clears the terminal screen

cmp—compares two files

```
cmp [ -l ] [ -s ] filename1 filename2
```

The two files are compared. *cmp* makes no comment if the files are the same; if they differ, it announces the byte and line numbers at which the first difference occurred.

EXAMPLE A.13

```
cmp file.new file.old
```

EXPLANATION

If the files differ, the character number and the line number are displayed.

compress—compress, uncompress, zcat compress, uncompress files, or display expanded files

```
compress [ -f ] [ -v ] [ -c ] [ -V ] [ -r ] [ -b bits] [ name ...]
uncompress [ -f ] [ -v ] [ -c ] [ -V ] [ name ...  ]
zcat [ -V ] [ name ...  ]
```

compress reduces the size of the named files using adaptive Lempel-Ziv coding. Whenever possible, each file is replaced by one with a .Z extension. The ownership modes, access time, and modification time will stay the same. If no files are specified, the standard input is compressed to the standard output.

EXAMPLE A.14

```
1   compress -v book
    book:Compression:35.07% -- replaced with book.Z
2   ls
    book.Z
```

EXPLANATION

1 Compresses the book into a file called *book.Z* and displays the percentage that the file was compressed and its new name.

2 The listing displays the compressed Z file.

cp—copies files

```
cp [options] source dest
cp [options] source... directory
```

The *cp* command copies a filename to another target which is either a file or directory. The filename and target cannot have the same name. If the target is not a directory, only one file may be specified before it; if it is a directory, more than one file may be specified. If the target does not exist, *cp* creates a file named *target*. If the target exists and is not a directory, its contents are overwritten. If the target is a directory, the file(s) are copied to that directory.

EXAMPLE A.15

```
1   cp --help
2   cp chapter1 book
3   cp -r desktop /usr/bin/tester
```

EXPLANATION

1 Displays information about *cp* and its options, and exits.

2 Copies the contents of *file1* to *file2*.

3 Copies the contents of *chapter1* to the *book* directory. In the *book* directory *chapter1* has its original name. Recursively copies the entire *desktop* directory into */usr/bin/tester*.

cpio—copy file archives in and out

```
cpio -i [ bBcdfkmrsStuvV6 ] [ -C bufsize ] [ -E filename ]
  [ -H header ] [ -I filename [ -M message ] ] [ -R id ]
  [ pattern ... ]
cpio -o [ aABcLvV ] [ -C bufsize ] [ -H header ]
  [ -O filename [ -M message ] ]
cpio -p [ adlLmuvV ] [ -R id ] directory
```

Copies file archives according to the modifiers given, usually for backup to a tape or directory.

EXAMPLE A.16

```
find . -depth -print | cpio -pdmv /home/john/tmp
```

EXPLANATION

Starting at the current directory, *find* descends the directory hierarchy, printing each of the entries of the directory even if the directory does not have write permission, and sends the filenames to *cpio* to be copied into the *john/tmp* directory in the */home* partition.

cron—the clock daemon

cron executes commands at specified dates and times. Regularly scheduled jobs can be specified in the */etc/crontab* file. (Must have superuser privileges.)

crypt—encodes or decodes a file

```
crypt [ password ]
```

crypt encrypts and decrypts the contents of a file. The password is a key that selects a type of transformation.

cut—removes selected fields or characters from each line of a file

```
cut {-b byte-list, --bytes=byte-list} [-n][--help][--version] [file...]
cut {-c character-list, --characters=character-list}[--help] [--version]
    [file...]
cut {-f  field-list, --fields=field-list} [-d delim][-s][--delimiter=delim]
    [--only-delimited] [--help][--version] [file...]
```

The *cut* command cuts out columns or characters from a line of a file and if no files are given, uses standard input. The *-d* option specifies the field delimiter. The default delimiter is a tab.

EXAMPLE A.17

```
1   cut --help
2   cut -d: -f1,3 /etc/passwd
3   cut -d: -f1-5 /etc/passwd
4   cut -c1-3,8-12 /etc/passwd
5   date | cut -c1-3
```

EXPLANATION

1. The *help* option displays information about options and arguments to *cut*.
2. Using the colon as a field delimiter, displays fields 1 and 3 of the */etc/passwd* file.
3. Using the colon as a field separator, displays fields 1 through 5 of the *etc/passwd* file.
4. Cuts and displays characters 1 through 3 and 8 through 12 of each line from the */etc/passwd* file.
5. Sends the output of the *date* command as input to *cut*. The first three characters are printed.

date—displays the date and time or sets the date

```
date [-u] [-d datestr] [-s datestr] [--utc][--universal]
    [--date=datestr] [--set=datestr]  [--help][--version]
    [+FORMAT] [MMDDhhmm[[CC]YY][.ss]]
```

Without arguments, the *date* command displays the date and time. If the command line argument starts with a plus sign, the rest of the argument is used to format the output. If a percent sign is used, the next character is a formatting character to extract a particular part of the date, such as just the year or weekday. To set the date, the command line argument is expressed in digits representing the year, month, day, hours, and minutes.

EXAMPLE A.18

```
1   date +%T
2   date +20%y
3   date "+It is now %m/%d /%y"
4   date --help
```

EXPLANATION

1. Displays the time as *20:25:51.*
2. Displays *2096.*
3. Displays *It is now 10/25/99.*
4. Prints out all options and time formats for date.

dd—converts a file while copying it

```
dd [--help] [--version] [if=file] [of=file][ibs=bytes] [obs=bytes]
   [bs=bytes] [cbs=bytes] [skip=blocks] [seek=blocks] [count=blocks]
   [conv={ascii,ebcdic,ibm,block,unblock,lcase,ucase,swab,noerror,notrunc, sync}]
```

Copies a file from one place to another, most commonly to and from tape drives or from different operating systems.

EXAMPLE A.19

```
1   $ dd --help
2   $ dd if=inputfile of=outputfile conv=ucase
```

EXPLANATION

1. Prints all options and flags with a short description of each.
2. Converts all characters in *inputfile* to uppercase and sends output to *outputfile.*

diff—compares two files for differences

```
diff [-bitw] [-c | -Cn
```

Compares two files and displays the differences on a line-by-line basis. Also displays commands that you would use with the *ed* editor to make changes. (Note: may not be supported by your version of Linux.)

EXAMPLE A.20

```
diff file1 file2
1c1
< hello there
---
> Hello there.
2a3
> I'm fine.
```

EXPLANATION

Shows how each line of *file1* and *file2* differ. The first file is represented by the < symbol, and the second file by the > symbol. Each line is preceded by an *ed* command, indicating the editing command that would be used to make the files the same.

dos, xdos, dosexec, dosdebug—a Linux dos emulator that runs MS-DOS and MS-DOS programs under Linux

(See Linux man page for a complete description. It's long...)

df—summarizes free disk space

```
df [-aikPv] [-t  fstype] [-x fstype] [--all][--inodes][--type=fstype]
   [--exclude-type=fstype][--kilobytes] [--portability] [--print-type]
   [--help] [--version] [filename...]
```

The *df* command shows information about the file system on which each FILE resides, or all file systems by default.

EXAMPLE A.21

```
df
Filesystem          1024-blocks  Used Available Capacity
Mounted on
/dev/hda5             1787100 1115587   579141      66%   /
```

du—summarizes disk usage

```
du [-arskod] [name ...]
```

The *du* command reports the number of 512-byte blocks contained in all files and (recursively) directories within each directory and file specified.

EXAMPLE A.22

```
1  du --help
2  du -s /desktop
3  du -a
```

EXPLANATION

1 Displays arguments and options to *du*.

2 Displays a summary of the block usage for all the files in */desktop* and its subdirectories.

3 Displays block usage for each file in this directory and subdirectories.

echo—echoes arguments

```
echo [ argument ] ...
echo [ -n ] [ argument ]
```

echo writes its arguments separated by blanks and terminated by a newline on the standard output.

```
System V echo options:
\b      backspace
\c      suppress newline
\f      form feed
\n      new line
\r      carriage return
\t      tab
\v      vertical tab
\\      backslash
\0n     n is a 1, 2, or 3, octal value
```

egrep—searches a file for a pattern using full regular expressions

```
egrep [ -bchilnsv ] [ -e special-expression ][ -f filename ]
   [ strings ] [ filename ... ]
```

egrep (expression *grep*) searches files for a pattern of characters and prints all lines that contain that pattern. *egrep* uses full regular expressions (expressions that have string values that use the full set of alphanumeric and special characters) to match the patterns. (See Chapter 3 for *grep* and *grep -E*.)

EXAMPLE A.23

```
1   egrep 'Tom|John' datafile
2   egrep '^ [A-Z]+' file
```

EXPLANATION

1 Displays all lines in *datafile* containing the pattern either *Tom* or *John*.

2 Displays all lines starting with one or more uppercase letters.

expr—evaluates arguments as an expression

```
expr expression...
expr {--help,--version}
```

The arguments are taken as an expression. After evaluation, the result is written on the standard output. The terms of the expression must be separated by blanks. Characters special to the shell must be escaped. Used in Bourne shell scripts for performing simple arithmetic operations.

EXAMPLE A.24

```
1   expr 5 + 4
2   expr 5 \* 3
3   num=0
    num=`expr $num + 1`
```

EXPLANATION

1 Prints the sum of *5 + 4*.

2 Prints of result of *5 * 3*. The asterisk is protected from shell expansion.

3 After assigning 0 to variable *num*, the *expr* command adds 1 to *num* and the result is assigned to *num*.

fgrep—search a file for a character string

```
fgrep [ -bchilnsvx ] [ -e special string ]
[ -f filename ] [ strings ] [ filename ... ]
```

fgrep (fast *grep*) searches files for a character string and prints all lines that contain that string. *fgrep* is different from *grep(1)* and *egrep(1)* because it interprets regular expression metacharacters as literals. (See *grep* and *grep -F* in Chapter 3.)

EXAMPLE A.25

```
1   fgrep '***' *
2   fgrep '[ ] * ? $' filex
```

EXPLANATION

1 Displays any line containing three asterisks from each file in the present directory. All characters are treated as themselves; i.e., metacharacters are not special.

2 Displays any lines in *filex* containing the string enclosed in quotes.

file—determines the type of a file by looking at its contents

```
file [ -vbczL ] [ -f namefile ] [ -m magicfiles ] file ...
```

file performs a series of tests on each filename in an attempt to determine what it contains. If the contents of the file appear to be ASCII text, *file* examines the first 512 bytes and tries to guess its language.

EXAMPLE A.26

```
1   file bin/ls
    /bin/ls:sparc pure dynamically linked executable
2   file go
    go:      executable shell script
3   file junk
    junk:    English text
```

EXPLANATION

1 *ls* is binary file dynamically linked when executed.

2 *go* is a shell script.

3 *junk* is a file containing ASCII text.

find—finds files

```
find path-name-list expression
```

find recursively descends the directory hierarchy for each pathname in the pathname list (i.e., one or more pathnames) seeking files that match options. The first argument is the path where the search starts. The rest of the arguments specify some criteria by which to find the files, such as name, size, owner, permissions, etc. Check the UNIX manual pages for different syntax.

EXAMPLE A.27

```
1   find . -name \*.c -print
2   find .. -type f
3   find . -type d -print
4   find / -size 0 - exec rm "{}" \;
5   find ~ -perm 644 -print
6   find . -type f -size +500c -atime +21 -ok rm -f "{}" \;
7   find . -name core -print 2> /dev/null (Bash/Korn shells)
    ( find . -name core -print > /dev/tty ) >& /dev/null (C/TC shell)
8   find / -user ellie xdev -print
9   find ~ -atime +31 -exec mv {} /old/{} \; -print
```

EXPLANATION

1 Starting at the present working directory (dot), finds all files ending in dot *c* and prints the full pathname of the files.

2 Starting at the parent directory (dot dot), finds all files of type file; i.e., files that are not directories. With Linux, the *-print* option is no longer necessary.

3 Starting at the present directory (dot), finds all directory files.

4 Starting at the root directory, finds all files of size zero and removes them. The { } are used as a placeholder for the name of each file as it is found.

EXPLANATION (CONTINUED)

5 Starting at the user's home directory, finds all ~ files that have permissions 644 (read and write for the owner, and read permission for the group and others).

6 Starting at the present working directory, finds files that are over 500 bytes and have not been accessed in the past 21 days and asks if it is okay to remove them.

7 Starting at the present working directory, finds and displays all files named *core* and sends errors to */dev/null*, the UNIX bit bucket.

8 Prints all files on the *root* partition that belong to user *ellie*.

9 Moves files that are older than 31 days into the */old* directory, and prints the files as it moves them.

finger—displays information about local and remote users

```
finger [-lmsp] [user ...] [user@host ...]
```

By default, the *finger* command displays information about each logged-in user, including login name, full name, terminal name (prepended with a * if write permission is denied), idle time, login time, and location if known.

EXAMPLE A.28

```
% finger
Login     Name             Tty  Idle  Login Time    Office
Office Phone
ellie     Ellie Quigley    p0   1:06  Oct 19 11:41 (:0.0)
ellie     Ellie Quigley    p1         Oct 19 16:37 (:0.0)
ellie     Ellie Quigley    p2         Oct 19 16:45 (:0.0)
```

fmt—simple text formatters

```
fmt [ -c ] [ -s ] [ -w width | -width ] [ inputfile... ]
```

fmt is a simple text formatter that fills and joins lines to produce output lines of (up to) the number of characters specified in the *-w* width option. The default width is 72. *fmt* concatenates the input files listed as arguments. If none are given, *fmt* formats text from the standard input.

EXAMPLE A.29

```
fmt -c -w45 letter
```

EXPLANATION

Formats *letter.* The *-c* switch preserves the indentation of the first two lines within the paragraph and aligns the left margin of each subsequent line with that of the second line. The *-w* switch fills the output line with up to 45 columns.

fold—folds long lines

```
fold [-bs] [-w width] [--bytes] [--spaces][--width=width][--help]
   [--version] [file...]
```

Folds the contents of the specified filenames, or the standard input if no files are specified, breaking the lines to have maximum width. The default for width is 80. Width should be a multiple of eight if tabs are present, or the tabs should be expanded.

EXAMPLE A.30

```
% fold --help
Usage: fold [OPTION]... [FILE]...
Wrap input lines in each FILE (standard input by default),
writing to
standard output.

  -b, --bytes         count bytes rather than columns
  -s, --spaces        break at spaces
  -w, --width=WIDTH   use WIDTH columns instead of 80

Report bugs to textutils-bugs@gnu.ai.mit.edu
```

ftp—file transfer program

```
ftp [-v] [-d] [-i] [-n] [-g] [host]
```

The *ftp* command is the user interface to the Internet standard File Transfer Protocol (FTP). *ftp* transfers files to and from a remote network site. The file transfer program is not limited to UNIX machines.

EXAMPLE A.31

```
ftp ftp.uu.net
ftp -n 127.150.28.56
```

free—displays amount of free and used memory in the system

```
free [-b | -k | -m] [-o] [-s delay ] [-t] [-V]
```

free displays the total amount of free and used physical and swap memory in the system, as well as the shared memory and buffers used by the kernel.

EXAMPLE A.32

```
% free
             total       used       free     shared    buffers    cached
Mem:         64148      54528       9620      45632    3460       29056
-/+ buffers/cache:      22012      42136
Swap:        96352          0      96352
```

fuser—identifies processes using files or sockets

```
fuser [-a|-s] [-n space] [-signal] [-kmuv] name ...[-] [-n space]
   [-signal] [-kmuv] name ...
fuser -l
fuser -V
```

The *fuser* command displays the PIDs of processes using the specified file or file systems. In the default display mode, each filename is followed by a letter denoting the type of access.

EXAMPLE A.33

```
% fuser --help
usage: fuser [ -a | -q ] [ -n space ] [ -signal ] [ -kmuv ]
filename ... [ - ] [ -n space ] [ -signal ] [ -kmuv ] name
...
       fuser -l
       fuser -V
```

EXAMPLE A.33 (CONTINUED)

```
-a          display unused files too
-k          kill processes accessing that file
-l          list signal names
-m          mounted FS
-n          space  search in the specified name space
            (file, udp, or tcp)
-s          silent operation
-signal     send signal instead of SIGKILL
-u          display user ids
-v          verbose output
-V          display version information
-           reset options

udp/tcp names: [local_port][,[rmt_host][,[rmt_port]]]
```

gawk—pattern scanning and processing language

```
gawk [ POSIX or GNU style options ] -f program-file [-- ] file ...
gawk [ POSIX or GNU style options ] [ -- ]program-text file ...
```

gawk is the Gnu Project's implementation of the *awk* programming language. It conforms to the definition of the language in the POSIX 1003.2 Command Language And Utilities Standard. This version in turn is based on the description in *The AWK Programming Language*, by Aho, Kernighan, and Weinberger, with the additional features found in the System V Release 4 version of UNIX *awk*. *gawk* also provides more recent Bell Labs *awk* extensions, and some Gnu-specific extensions.

gcc, g++—Gnu project C and C++ Compiler (v2.7)

```
gcc [ option | filename ]...
g++ [ option | filename ]...
```

getopt(s)—parses command line options

The *getopts* command supercedes *getopt*. *getopts* is used to break up options in command lines for easy parsing by shell procedures and to check for legal options. (See *getopts*, in Chapter 9.)

grep—searches a file for a pattern (See Chapter 3)

```
grep  [-[AB] NUM] [-CEFGVbchiLlnqsvwxyUu] [-e PATTERN | -f FILE]
   [--extended-regexp] [--fixed-strings] [--basic-regexp]
   [--regexp=PATTERN] [--file=FILE] [--ignore-case] [--word-regexp]
   [--line-regexp] [--line-regexp] [--no-messages] [--revert-match]
   [--version] [--help] [--byte-offset] [--line-number]
   [--with-filename] [--no-filename] [--quiet] [--silent]
   [--files-without-match] [--files-with-matcces] [--count]
   [--before-context=NUM] [--after-context=NUM] [--context] [--binary]
   [--unix-byte-offsets] files...
```

grep searches the named input files (or standard input if no files are named, or the - filename is given) for lines containing a match to the given pattern. By default, *grep* prints the matching lines. There are three major variants of *grep*, controlled by the following options.

-G, --basic-regexp	Interpret pattern as a basic regular expression (see below). This is the default.
-E, --extended-regexp	Interpret pattern as an extended regular expression (see below).
-F, --fixed-strings	Interpret pattern as a list of fixed strings, separated by newlines, any of which is to be matched. In addition, two variant programs *egrep* and *fgrep* are available. *egrep* is similar (but not identical) to *grep -E*, and is compatible with the historical UNIX *egrep*. *fgrep* is the same as *grep -F*.

(See "rgrep" on page 713 for recursive *grep*.)

EXAMPLE A.34

```
1   grep Tom file1 file2 file3
2   grep -in '^tom savage' *
```

EXPLANATION

1 *grep* displays all lines in *file1*, *file2*, and *file3* that contain the pattern *Tom*.

2 *grep* displays all lines with line numbers from the files in the current working directory that contain *tom savage* if *tom savage* is at the beginning of the line, ignoring case.

groups—prints group membership of user

```
groups [ user... ]
```

The command *groups* prints on standard output the groups to which you or the optionally specified user belong.

gzip, gunzip, zcat—compresses or expands files

```
gzip [ -acdfhlLnNrtvV19 ] [-S suffix] [ name ... ]
gunzip [ -acfhlLnNrtvV ] [-S suffix] [ name ... ]
zcat [ -fhLV ] [ name ... ]
```

gzip reduces the size of the named files using Lempel-Ziv encoding (LZ77). Whenever possible, each file is replaced by one with the extension .GZ, while keeping the same ownership modes, access, and modification times.

head—outputs the first ten lines of a file(s)

```
head [-c N[bkm]] [-n N] [-qv] [--bytes=N[bkm]] [--lines=N] [--quiet]
   [--silent] [--verbose] [--help] [--version] [file...]
head [-Nbcklmqv] [file...]
```

head displays the first ten lines of each FILE to standard output. With more than one FILE, it precedes each file with a header giving the filename. With no FILE, or when FILE is -, reads from standard input.

host—prints information about specified hosts or zones in DNS

```
host [l]  [-v]  [-w]  [-r]  [-d]  [-t querytype]  [a]  host [server]
```

The *host* command prints information about specified Internet hosts. It gets its information from a set of interconnected servers spread across the country. By default, it converts between host names and IP addresses. With the *-a* or *-t* switch, all information is printed.

id—prints the username, user ID, group name, and group ID

```
id [-gnurG] [--group] [--name] [--real] [--user] [--group] [--help]
   [--version] [username]
```

id displays your user ID, username, group ID, and group name. If your real ID and your effective ID do not match, both are printed.

jsh—the standard, job control shell

```
jsh [ -acefhiknprstuvx ] [ argument...]
```

The command *jsh* is an interface to the standard Bourne shell. It provides all of the functionality of the Bourne shell and enables job control.

kill—sends a signal to terminate one or more processes

```
kill  [
```

kill sends a signal to terminate one or more process IDs.

killall—kills processes by name

less—opposite of more

```
less -?
less --help
less -V
less --version
less [-[+]aBcCdeEfgGiImMnNqQrsSuUVwX][-b bufs] [-h lines] [-j line]
   [-k keyfile][-{oO} logfile] [-p pattern] [-P prompt] [-t tag]
   [-T tagsfile] [-x tab] [-y lines] [-[z] lines] [+[+]cmd] [--]
   [filename]...
```

less is a program similar to *more*, but which allows backward movement in the file as well as forward movement. Also, *less* does not have to read the entire input file before starting, so with large input files it starts up faster than text editors like *vi*. *less* uses *termcal* (or *terminfo* on some systems), so it can run on a variety of terminals. There is even limited support for hardcopy terminals.

line—reads one line

line copies one line (up to a newline) from the standard input and writes it on the standard output. It returns an exit code of one on EOF and always prints at least a newline. It is often used within shell files to read from the user's terminal.

ln—creates hard links to files

```
ln [options] source [dest]
ln [options] source... directory
Options:
[-bdfinsvF] [-S  backup-suffix] [-V {numbered,existing,simple}]
[--version-control={numbered,existing,simple}] [--backup]
[--directory] [--force][--interactive] [--no-dereference] [--symbolic]
[--verbose] [--suffix=backup-suffix] [--help] [--version]
```

If the last argument names an existing directory, *ln* links each other given file into a file with the same name in that directory. If only one file is given, it links that file into the current directory. Otherwise, if only two files are given, it links the first onto the second. It is an error if the last argument is not a directory and more than two files are given. Symbolic links are used if crossing a partition.

OPTIONS:

-b, --backup	Makes backups of files that are about to be removed.
-d, -F, --directory	Allows the superuser to make hard links to directories.
-f, --force	Removes existing destination files.
i, --interactive	Prompts whether to remove existing destination files.
-n, --no-dereference	When the specified destination is a symbolic link to a directory, attempts to replace the symbolic link rather than dereferencing it to create a link in the directory to which it points. This option is most useful in conjunction with *--force*.
-s, --symbolic	Makes symbolic links instead of hard links.
-v, --verbose	Prints the name of each file before linking it.
--help	Prints a usage message on standard output and exits successfully.
--version	Prints version information on standard output then exits successfully.
-S, --suffix backup-suffix	The suffix used for making simple backup files can be set with the *SIMPLE_BACKUP_SUFFIX* environment variable, which can be overridden by this option. If neither of those is given, the default is ~, as it is in *emacs*.
-V, --version-control {numbered,existing,simple}	The type of backups made can be set with the *VERSION_CONTROL* environment variable.

EXAMPLE A.35

```
1   ls -l
    total 2
    drwxrwsr-x   2 ellie    root          1024 Jan 19 18:34 dir
    -rw-rw-r--   1 ellie    root            16 Jan 19 18:34 filex
2   % ln filex dir
3   % cd dir
4   % ls -l
    total 1
    -rw-rw-r--   2 ellie    root            16 Jan 19 18:34 filex
```

EXPLANATION

1 The output of the *ls* command displays a long listing for a directory called *dir* and a file called *filex*. The number of links on a directory is always at least two, one for the directory itself, and one for its parent. The number of links for a file is always at least one, one to link it to the directory where it was created. When you remove a file, its link count drops to zero.

2 The *ln* command creates a hard link. *fllex* is now linked to the directory, *dir*, as well as the current directory. A link does not create a new file. It simply gives an existing file an additional name or directory where it can be found. If you remove one of the links, you'll still have one left. Any changes made to one of the linked files, results in changes to the other, because they are the same file.

3 Change to the directory where *filex* was linked.

4 The link count for *filex* is 2. It is the same file but can now be accessed in this directory as well as the parent directory.

logname—gets the name of the user running the process

```
logname [--help]  [--version]
```

look—displays lines beginning with a given string

```
look [-dfa] [-t termchar] string [file]
```

look displays any lines in a file that contain a string as a prefix. As *look* performs a binary search, the lines in the file must be sorted. If a file is not specified, the file */usr/dict/words* is used, only alphanumeric characters are compared, and the case of alphabetic characters is ignored.

OPTIONS:

-d	Dictionary character set and order; i.e., only alphanumeric characters are compared.
-f	Ignores the case of alphabetic characters.
-a	Uses the alternate dictionary */usr/dict/web2.*
-t	Specifies a string termination character; i.e., only the characters in string up to and including the first occurrence of the termination character are compared.

The *look* utility exits 0 if one or more lines were found and displayed, 1 if no lines were found, and >1 if an error occurred.

EXAMPLE A.36

```
1  % look sunb
   sunbeam
   sunbeams
   Sunbelt
   sunbonnet
   sunburn
   sunburnt

2  % look karen sorted.datebook
3  % look Karen sorted.datebook
   Karen Evich:284-758-2857:23 Edgecliff Place, Lincoln, NB
   92086:7/25/53:85100
   Karen Evich:284-758-2867:23 Edgecliff Place, Lincoln, NB
   92743:11/3/35:58200
   Karen Evich:284-758-2867:23 Edgecliff Place, Lincoln, NB
   92743:11/3/35:58200
4  % look -f karen sorted.datebook
   Karen Evich:284-758-2857:23 Edgecliff Place, Lincoln, NB
   92086:7/25/53:85100
   Karen Evich:284-758-2867:23 Edgecliff Place, Lincoln, NB
   92743:11/3/35:58200
   Karen Evich:284-758-2867:23 Edgecliff Place, Lincoln, NB
   92743:11/3/35:58200
```

EXPLANATION

1. *look* displays all lines in */usr/dict/words* that start with the string *sunb*, assuming */usr/dict/words* is in the current directory.
2. *look* cannot find a line that starts with *karen* in a file called *sorted.datebook.* (The file must be sorted or *look* will not find anything.)
3. *look* displays all lines with lines starting with the string, *Karen*, in file, *sorted.datebook.*
4. The *-f* option folds upper and lowercase in the search string; i.e., turns off case-sensitivity.

lp (ATT, Linux)—sends output to a printer

```
lp [ -cmsw ] [ -ddest ] [ -number ] [ -ooption ] [ -ttitle ] filename ...
cancel [ ids ] [ printers ]
```

lp, cancel sends or cancels requests to a lineprinter.

EXAMPLE A.37

```
1  lp -n5 filea fileb
2  lp -dShakespeare filex
```

EXPLANATION

1 Send five copies of *filea* and *fileb* to the printer.

2 Specify *Shakespeare* as the printer where *filex* will be printed.

lpr (UCB, Linux)—sends output to a printer

```
lpr [ -Pprinter ] [ -#copies ] [ -Cclass ] [ -Jjob ] [ -Ttitle ]
   [ -i [ indent ] ] [ -1234font ] [ -wcols ] [ -r ] [ -m ] [ -h ]
   [ -s ] [ -filter-option ] [ filename ... ]
```

lpr creates a printer job in a spooling area for subsequent printing as facilities become available. Each printer job consists of a control job and one or more data files.

EXAMPLE A.38

```
1  lpr -#5 filea fileb
2  lpr -PShakespeare filex
```

EXPLANATION

1 Send five copies of *filea* and *fileb* to the printer.

2 Specify Shakespeare as the printer where *filex* will be printed.

lpstat (ATT)—prints information about the status of the LP print service

lpq (UCB, Linux)—prints information about the status of the printer

ls, dir, vdir—lists contents of directory

```
ls [-abcdfgiklmnpqrstuxABCFGLNQRSUX1] [-cols] [-T cols] [-I pattern]
   [--all] [--escape] [--directory] [--inode] [--kilobytes]
   [--numeric-uid-gid] [--no-group] [--hide-control-chars] [--reverse]
   [--size] [--width=cols] [--tab-size=cols] [--almost-all]
   [--ignore-backups] [--classify] [--file-type] [--full-time]
   [--ignore=pattern] [--dereference] [--literal] [--quote-name]
   [--recursive] [--sort={none,time,size,extension}]
   [--format={long,verbose,commas,across,vertical,single-column}]
   [--time={atime,access,use,ctime,status}][--help] [--vision]
   [--color[={yes,no,tty}]] [--colour[={yes,no,tty}]][name...]
```

For each directory argument, *ls* lists the contents of the directory; for each file argument, *ls* repeats its name and any other information requested. The output is sorted alphabetically by default. When no argument is given, the current directory is listed.

EXAMPLE A.39

```
1  ls -alF
2  ls -d a*
3  ls -i
```

EXPLANATION

1 The *-a* lists invisible files (those files beginning with a dot), the *-l* is a long listing showing attributes of the file, the *-F* puts a slash at the end of directory filenames, a * at the end of executable script names, and an @ symbol at the end of symbolically linked files.

2 If the argument to the *-d* switch is a directory, only the name of the directory is displayed, not its contents.

3 The *-i* switch causes each filename to be preceded by its inode number.

mail—mail, rmail—reads mail or send mail to users

```
Sending mail
   mail [ -tw ] [ -m message_type ] recipient...
   rmail [ -tw ] [ -m message_type ] recipient...
Reading mail
   mail [ -ehpPqr ] [ -f filename ]
Forwarding mail
   mail -F recipient...
Debugging
   mail [ -x debug_level ] [ other_mail_options ] recipient...
   mail [ -T mailsurr_file ] recipient...
```

A recipient is usually a username recognized by *login(1)*. When recipients are named, *mail* assumes a message is being sent. It reads from the standard input up to an end-of-file (Ctrl-D), or if reading from a terminal, until it reads a line consisting of just a period. When either of those indicators is received, *mail* adds the letter to the mailfile for each recipient.

mailx—interactive message processing system

```
mailx [ -deHiInNUvV ] [ -f [ filename|+folder ]] [ -T filename ]
   [ -u user ] [ recipient... ]
mailx [ -dFinUv ] [ -h number ] [ -r address ][ -s subject ]
    recipient...
```

The *mail* utilities listed above provide an interactive interface for sending, receiving, and manipulating mail messages. Basic networking utilities must be installed for some of the features to work. Incoming mail is stored in a file called *mailbox,* and after it is read, is sent to a file called *mbox.*

make—maintains, updates, and regenerates groups of related programs and files

```
make [ -f makefile ] ... [ -d ] [ -dd ] [ -D ]
   [ -DD ] [ -e ] [ -i ] [ -k ] [ -n ] [ -p ] [ -P ]
   [ -q ] [ -r ] [ -s ] [ -S ] [ -t ] [ target ... ]
   [ macro=value ... ]
```

make updates files according to commands listed in a description file, and if the target file is newer than the dependency file of the same name, *make* will update the target file.

man—formats and displays the online manual pages

```
man [-acdfhktwW] [-m system] [-p string] [-C config_file] [-M path]
    [-P pager] [-S section_list] [section] name...
```

manpath—determines user's search path for man pages

```
man [-acdfhkKtwW] [-m system] [-p string][-C config_file][-M path]
   [-P pager] [-S section_list][section] name  ...
```

man formats and displays the online manual pages. This version knows about the MANPATH and (MAN)PAGER environment variables, so you can have your own set(s) of personal man pages and choose whatever program you like to display the formatted pages. If section is specified, *man* only looks in that section of the manual.

mesg—permits or denies messages resulting from the write command

```
mesg [ -n ] [ -y ]
```

mesg with argument *-n* forbids messages via write(1) by revoking nonuser write permission on the user's terminal. *mesg* with argument *-y* reinstates permission. All by itself, *mesg* reports the current state without changing it.

mkdir—creates a directory

more—browses or pages through a text file

```
more [ -cdflrsuw ] [ -lines ] [ +linenumber ] [ +/pattern ]
   [ filename ... ]
page [ -cdflrsuw ] [ -lines ] [ +linenumber ] [ +/pattern ]
   [ filename ... ]
```

more is a filter that displays the contents of a text file on the terminal, one screenful at a time. It normally pauses after each screenful, and prints "*—More—*" at the bottom of the screen.

mtools—utilities to access DOS disks in UNIX

mtools is a public domain collection of tools to allow UNIX systems to manipulate MS-DOS files read, write, and move around files on an MS-DOS file system (typically a floppy disk). Where reasonable, each program attempts to emulate the MS-DOS equivalent command. However, unnecessary restrictions and oddities of DOS are not emulated. For instance, it is possible to move subdirectories from one subdirectory to another. *mtools* can be found at the following places (and their mirrors):

http://mtools.ltnb.lu/mtools-3.9.1.tar.gz

ftp://www.tux.org/pub/knaff/mtools/mtools-3.9.1.tar.gz

ftp://sunsite.unc.edu/pub/Linux/utils/disk-management/mtools-3.9.1.tar.gz

mv—moves or renames files

```
mv [options] source dest
mv [options] source... directory
Options:
[-bfiuv] [-S  backup-suffix] [-V {numbered,existing,simple}]
[--backup] [--force] [--interactive] [--update] [--verbose]
[--suffix=backup-suffix]
[--version-control={numbered,existing,simple}] [--help][--version]
```

The *mv* command moves a source filename to a target filename. The filename and the target may not have the same name. If target is not a directory, only one file may be specified before it; if it is a directory, more than one file may be specified. If target does not exist, *mv* creates a file named target. If target exists and is not a directory, its contents are overwritten. If target is a directory, the file(s) are moved to that directory.

EXAMPLE A.40

```
1   mv file1 newname
2   mv -i test1 test2 train
```

EXPLANATION

1. Renames *file1* to *newname*. If *newname* exists, its contents are overwritten.
2. Moves files *test1* and *test2* to the *train* directory. The *-i* switch is for interactive mode, meaning it asks first before moving the files.

nawk—pattern scanning and processing language

```
nawk [ -F re ] [ -v var=value ] [ 'prog' ] [ filename ... ]
nawk [ -F re ] [ -v var=value ] [ -f progfile ][ filename ... ]
```

nawk scans each input filename for lines that match any of a set of patterns. The command string must be enclosed in single quotes (') to protect it from the shell. *awk* programs consist of a set of pattern/action statements used to filter specific information from a file, pipe, or stdin. Linux uses *gawk*. (See "awk" on page 673.)

newgrp—logs in to a new group

```
newgrp [-] [ group ]
```

newgrp logs a user into a new group by changing a user's real and effective group ID. The user remains logged in and the current directory is unchanged. The execution of *newgrp* always replaces the current shell with a new shell, even if the command terminates with an error (unknown group).

news—prints news items

```
news [ -a ] [ -n ] [ -s ] [ items ]
```

news is used to keep the user informed of current events. By convention, these events are described by files in the directory */var/news*. When invoked without arguments, *news* prints the contents of all current files in */var/news*, most recent first, with each preceded by an appropriate header.

nice—runs a command at low priority

```
nice [ -increment ] command [ arguments ]
```

/usr/bin/nice executes a command with a lower CPU scheduling priority. The invoking process (generally the user's shell) must be in the time-sharing scheduling class. The command is executed in the time-sharing class. An increment of 10 is the default. The increment value must be in a range between 1 and 19, unless you are the superuser. *nice* is also, a *tc/csh* built-in.

nohup—makes commands immune to hangups and quits

```
/usr/bin/nohup command [ arguments ]
```

There are three distinct versions of *nohup*. *nohup* is built in to the C shell and is an executable program available in */usr/bin/nohup* when using the Bourne shell. The Bourne shell version of *nohup* executes commands such that it is immune to HUP (hangup) and TERM (terminate) signals. If the standard output is a terminal, it is redirected to the file *nohup.out*. The standard error is redirected to follow the standard output. The priority is incremented by five. *nohup* should be invoked from the shell with *&* in order to prevent it from responding to interrupts or input from the next user.

EXAMPLE A.41

```
nohup lookup &
```

EXPLANATION

The *lookup* program will run in the background and continue to run until it has completed, even if the user logs off. Any output generated goes to a file in the current directory called *nohup.out*.

od—dumps files in octal and other formats

```
oodd  [-abcdfhiloxv] [-s[bytes]] [-w[bytes]] [-A radix] [-j bytes]
   [-N  bytes] [-t  type] [--skip-bytes=bytes]
   [--address-radix=radix] [--read-bytes=bytes] [--format=type]
   [--output-duplicates] [--strings[=bytes]] [--width[=bytes]]
   [--traditional] [--help] [--version] [file...]
```

od displays filename in one or more formats, as selected by the first argument. If the first argument is missing, *-o* is default; e.g., the file can be displayed in bytes octal, ASCII, decimal, hex, etc.

pack—pack, pcat, unpack—compresses and expands files

```
pack [ - ] [ -f ] name ...
pcat name ...
unpack name ...
```

pack compresses files. Wherever possible (and useful), each input file *name* is replaced by a packed file *name.z* with the same access modes, access and modified dates, and owner as those of *name*. Typically, text files are reduced to 60–75% of their original size. *pcat* does for packed files what *cat(1)* does for ordinary files, except that *pcat* cannot be used as a filter. The specified files are unpacked and written to the standard output. Thus, to view a packed file named *name.z* use: *pcat name.z* or just *pcat name*. *unpack* expands files created by *pack*.

passwd—changes the login password and password attributes

```
passwd [ name ]
passwd [ -d | -l ] [ -f ] [ -n min ] [ -w warn ][ -x max ] name
passwd -s [ -a ]
passwd -s [ name ]
```

The *passwd* command changes the password or lists password attributes associated with the user's login name. Additionally, privileged users may use *passwd* to install or change passwords and attributes associated with any login name.

paste—merges same lines of several files or subsequent lines of one file

```
paste filename1 filename2...
paste -d list filename1 filename2...
paste -s [ -d list ] filename1 filename2...
```

paste concatenates corresponding lines of the given input files filename1, filename2, etc. It treats each file as a column or columns of a table and pastes them together horizontally (see “cut” on page 683).

EXAMPLE A.42

```
1   ls | paste - - -
2   paste -s -d"\t\n" testfile1 testfile2
3   paste file1 file2
```

EXPLANATION

1 Files are listed in three columns and glued together with a TAB.

2 Combines a pair of lines into a single line using a TAB and new line as the delimiter, i.e., the first pair of lines are glued with a TAB; the next pair are glued by a newline, the next pair by a TAB, etc. The *-s* switch causes subsequent lines from *testfile1* to be pasted first and then subsequent lines from *testfile2*.

3 A line from *file1* is pasted to a line from *file2*, glued together by a TAB so that the file lines appear as two columns.

pcat—(see "pack" on page 706)

pine—a Program for Internet News and E-mail

```
pine [ options ] [ address, address ]
pinef [ options ] [ address, address ]
```

pine is a screen-oriented message-handling tool. In its default configuration, *pine* offers an intentionally limited set of functions geared toward the novice user, but it also has a growing list of options and "power-user" and personal-preference features. *pinef* is a variant of *pine* that uses function keys rather than mnemonic single-letter commands. *pine*'s basic feature set includes: View, Save, Export, Delete, Print, Reply, and Forward messages.

pg—displays files a page at a time

```
pg [ -number ] [ -p string ] [ -cefnrs ] [ +linenumber ]
   [ +/pattern/ ] [ filename ... ]
```

The *pg* command is a filter that allows you to page through filenames one screenful at a time on a terminal. If no filename is specified or if it encounters the – filename, *pg* reads from standard input. Each screenful is followed by a prompt. If the user types a RETURN, another page is displayed. It allows you to back up and review something that has already passed. (See "more" on page 703.)

pr—prints files

```
pr [[-columns] [-wwidth] [-a]] [-eck] [-ick] [-drtfp]
    [+page] [-nck] [-ooffset] [-llength] [-sseparator]
    [-hheader] [-F] [filename ...]
pr [[-m] [-wwidth]] [-eck] [-ick] [-drtfp] [+page] [-nck]
    [-ooffset] [-llength] [-sseparator] [-hheader] [-F
    [filename1 filename2 ...]
```

The *pr* command formats and prints the contents of a file according to different format options. By default, the listing is sent to *stdout* and is separated into pages, each headed by the page number, the date and time that the file was last modified, and the name of the file. If no options are specified, the default file format is 66 lines with a 5-line header and 5-line trailer.

EXAMPLE A.43

```
pr -2dh "TITLE" file1 file2
```

EXPLANATION

Prints two columns double-sided, with header "TITLE" for *file1* and *file2*.

ping—reports if a remote system is reachable and alive

```
ping [-dfnqrvR] [-c count] [-i wait] [-l preload] [-p pattern]
   [-s packetsize]
```

ping sends ICMP ECHO_REQUEST packets to a host machine and waits for a response to tell you if the host or gateway is reachable and alive. It is used to track down network connectivity problems. If *ping* does not receive any reply packets at all it will exit with code 1. On error it exits with code 2. Otherwise it exits with code 0. This makes it possible to use the exit code to see if a host is alive or not.

This program is intended for use in network testing, measurement, and management. Because of the load it can impose on the network, it is unwise to use *ping* during normal operations or from automated scripts.

ps—reports process status

```
ps [ - ] [ lujsvmaxScewhrnu ] [ txx ] [ O[H-]k1[[+|-]k2...]]
```

ps prints information about active processes. Without options, *ps* prints information about processes associated with the controlling terminal. The output contains only the process ID, terminal identifier, cumulative execution time, and the command name. Otherwise, the information that is displayed is controlled by the options. The *ps* options are not the same for ATT and Berkeley type versions of UNIX.

EXAMPLE A.44

```
1 % ps l
  FLAGS   UID   PID  PPID PRI  NI   SIZE  RSS  WCHAN       STA TTY  TIME COMMAND
    100   501   496   495  12   0   1412  820  sigsuspend  S    p0  0:00 -tcsh
 100000   501  1165   496  13   0    952  492              R    p0  0:00 ps l
    100   501   506   505   0   0   1448  856  sigsuspend  S    p1  0:00 -tcsh
 100000   501   842   506   1   0   1300  848  do_select   S    p1  0:00 vi atfi

2 % ps -u
warning: '-' deprecated; use 'ps u', not 'ps -u'
USER     PID  %CPU  %MEM  SIZE  RSS  TTY  STAT  START  TIME  COMMAND
ellie    496  0.0   1.2   1416  824  p0   S     15:23  0:00  -tcsh
ellie    506  0.0   1.3   1448  856  p1   S     15:23  0:00  -tcsh
ellie    842  0.0   1.3   1300  848  p1   S     16:07  0:00  vi atfile
ellie   1166  0.0   0.7    856  492  p0   R     16:25  0:00  ps -u
%

3 % ps aux | grep '^linda'        ucb

4 % ps -ef | grep '^ *linda'    att
```

EXPLANATION

1. *ps* with the l option displays a long listing of information about each process. (Linux)
2. *ps* does not require a leading dash prepended to options; in fact, a warning is printed if you use a leading dash. The *u* option adds the username, time that the process was started, the percentage of CPU and memory used, etc. (Linux)
3. Prints all processes running and pipes the output to the *grep* program printing only those processes owned by user *linda,* where *linda* is at the beginning of each line. (Linux/*ucb* version)
4. Same as the first example, only the ATT version.

pstree—displays a tree of processes

```
pstree [-a] [-c] [-h] [-l] [-n] [-p] [-u] [-G|-U][pid|user]
pstree -V
```

pstree shows running processes as a tree. The tree is rooted at either *pid* or *init* if *pid* is omitted. If a username is specified, all process trees rooted at processes owned by that user are shown. *pstree* visually merges identical branches by putting them in square brackets and prefixing them with the repetition count, for example:

```
init-+-getty
     |-getty
     |-getty
     '-getty
```

becomes

```
init---4*[getty]
```

pwd—displays the present working directory name

quota—displays users' disk usage and limits

```
quota [ -guvv | q ]
quota [ -uvv | q ] user
quota [ -gvv | q ] group
```

quota displays users' disk usage and limits. By default, only the user quotas are printed.

- *-g* Prints group quotas for the group of which the user is a member.
- *-u* An optional flag, equivalent to the default.
- *-v* Displays quotas on file systems where no storage is allocated.
- *-q* Prints a more terse message, containing only information on file systems where usage is over quota.

rcp—remote file copy

```
rcp [-px] [-k realm] file1 file2
rcp [-px] [-r] [-k realm] file ... directory
```

The *rcp* command copies files between machines in the form:

remothostname:path
user@hostname:file
user@hostname.domainname:file

EXAMPLE A.45

```
1   rcp dolphin:filename /tmp/newfilename
2   rcp filename broncos:newfilename
```

EXPLANATION

1. Copy *filename* from remote machine *dolphin* to */tmp/newfilename* on this machine.
2. Copy *filename* from this machine to remote machine *broncos* and name it *newfilename*.

rdate—get the date and time via the network

```
rdate [-p] [-s] [host...]
```

rdate uses TCP to retrieve the current time of another machine using the protocol described in RFC 868. With the *-p* option, *rdate* prints the time retrieved from the remote machines. This is the default mode. With the *-s* option, *rdate* sets the local system time from the time retrieved from the remote machine. Only the superuser can reset the time. The time for each system is returned in ctime(3) format.

EXAMPLE A.46

```
1   rdate homebound atlantis
(Output)
 [homebound]   Tue Jan 18 20:35:41 2000
 [atlantis]    Tue Jan 18 20:36:19 2000
```

rgrep—a recursive, highlighting grep program

```
rgrep [ options] pattern [file] ......
```

rgrep, unlike *grep* and *egrep,* can recursively descend directories. The traditional way of performing this kind of search on UNIX systems utilizes the *find* command in conjunction with *grep*. Using *rgrep* results in much better performance. See also *xargs* command.

COMMAND LINE OPTIONS:

-?	Additional help (use *-?* to avoid shell expansion on some systems).
-c	Count matches.
-h	Highlight match (ANSI compatible terminal assumed).
-H	Output match instead of entire line containing match.
-i	Ignore case.
-l	List filename only.
-n	Print line number of match.
-F	Follow links.
-r	Recursively scan through directory tree.
-N	Do NOT perform a recursive search.
-R pat	Like *-r* except that only those files matching *pat* are checked.
-v	Print only lines that do NOT match the specified pattern.
-x ext	Check only files with extension given by *ext.*
-D	Print all directories that would be searched. This option is for debugging purposes only. No file is grepped with this option.
-W len	Lines are *len* characters long (not newline terminated).

SUPPORTED REGULAR EXPRESSIONS:

.	Matches any character except newline.
\d	Matches any digit.
\e	Matches ESC char.
*	Matches zero or more occurrences of previous RE.
+	Matches one or more occurrences of previous RE.
?	Matches zero or one occurrence of previous RE.
^	Matches beginning of line.
$	Matches end of line.
[...]	Matches any single character between brackets. For example, *[-02468]* matches "-" or any even digit, and *[-0-9a-z]* matches "-" and any digit between 0 and 9 as well as letters a through z.
\{ ...\}	Used for repetition; e.g., *x\{9\}* matches nine *x* characters.
\(...\)	Used for backreferencing. Pattern in \(...\) is tagged and saved. Starting at the left-hand side of the regular expression, allowed up to nine tags. To restore saved pattern, \1, \2 ... \9 are used.
\2 \1, =, ..., \9	Matches match specified by *n*th \(... \) expression. For example, *\([\t][a-zA-Z]+\)\1[\t]* matches any word repeated consecutively.

EXAMPLE A.47

```
1   rgrep -n -R '*.c' '^int'
2   rgrep -n -xc '^int'
```

EXPLANATION

1. Look in all files with a "c" extension in current directory and all its subdirectories looking for matches of "int" at the beginning of a line, printing the line containing the match with its line number.
2. Look in all files with a ".c" extension, printing the line beginning with "int" and preceded with its line number. (Same as above.)

rlogin—remote login

```
rlogin [ -L ] [ -8 ] [ -ec ] [ -l username ] hostname
```

rlogin establishes a remote login session from your terminal to the remote machine named *hostname*. Hostnames are listed in the host's database, which may be contained in the */etc/hosts* file, the Network Information Service (NIS) hosts map, the Internet domain name server, or a combination of these. Each host has one official name (the first name in the database entry), and optionally one or more nicknames. Either official hostnames or nicknames may be specified in *hostname*. A list of trusted hostnames can be stored in the machine's file */etc/hosts.equiv.*

rm—removes files from directories

```
rm [-f] [-i] filename...
rm -r [-f] [-i] dirname...[filename...]
```

rm removes the entries for one or more files from a directory if the file has write permission. If filename is a symbolic link, the link will be removed, but the file or directory to which it refers will not be deleted. User do not need write permission on a symbolic link to remove it, provided they have write permissions in the directory.

EXAMPLE A.48

```
1   rm file1 file2
2   rm -i *
3   rm -rf dir
```

EXPLANATION

1. Removes *file1* and *file2* from the directory.
2. Removes all files in the present working directory, but asks first if it is okay.
3. Recursively removes all files and directories below *dir* and ignores error messages.

rmdir—removes a directory

```
rmdir [-p] [-s] dirname...
```

Removes a directory if it is empty. With *-p,* parent directories are also removed.

rsh—starts a remote shell

```
rrsshh [--KKddnnxx] [--kk _r_e_a_l_m] [--ll _u_s_e_r_n_a_m_e] _h_o_s_t [command]
```

rsh connects to the specified hostname and executes the specified command. *rsh* copies its standard input to the remote command, the standard output of the remote command to its standard output, and the standard error of the remote command to its standard error. Interrupt, quit, and terminate signals are propagated to the remote command; *rsh* normally terminates when the remote command does. If a command is not given, then *rsh* logs you on to the remote host using *rlogin*.

EXAMPLE A.49

```
1   rsh bluebird ps -ef
2   rsh -l john owl ls; echo $PATH;cat .profile
```

EXPLANATION

1. Connect to machine *bluebird* and display all processes running on that machine.
2. Go to the remote machine owl as user *john* and execute all three commands.

ruptime—shows the host status of local machines

```
ruptime [ -alrtu ]
```

ruptime gives a status line like uptime for each machine on the local network; these are formed from packets broadcast by each host on the network once a minute. Machines for which no status report has been received for five minutes are shown as being down. Normally, the listing is sorted by hostname, but this order can be changed by specifying one of *ruptime*'s options.

rwho—who is logged in on local machines

```
rwho [ -a ]
```

The *rwho* command produces output similar to *who(1)*, but for all machines on your network. However, it does not work through gateways and host must have the directory */var/spool/rwho* as well as the *rwho* daemon running. If no report has been received from a machine for five minutes, *rwho* assumes the machine is down, and does not report users last known to be logged into that machine. If a user has not typed to the system for a minute or more, *rwho* reports this idle time. If a user has not typed to the system for an hour or more, the user is omitted from the output of *rwho,* unless the *–a* flag is given.

script—creates a typescript of a terminal session

```
script [ -a ] [ filename ]
```

script makes a typescript of everything printed on your terminal. The typescript is written to a filename. If no filename is given, the typescript is saved in the file called *typescript*. The script ends when the shell exits or when Ctrl-D is typed.

EXAMPLE A.50

```
1   script
2   script myfile
```

EXPLANATION

1 Starts up a script session in a new shell. Everything displayed on the terminal is stored in a file called *typescript*. Must press ^d or exit to end the session.

2 Starts up a script session in a new shell, storing everything displayed on the terminal in *myfile*. Must press ^d or exit to end the session.

sed—stream editor (see Chapter 4)

```
sed [-n] [-V] [--quiet] [--silent] [--version] [--help] [-e script]
    [--expresion=script] [-f script-file] [--file=script-file]
    [script-if-no-other-script] [file...]
```

sed copies the named filename (standard input default) to the standard output, edited according to a script of command. Does not change the original file. (Read about *sed* in Chapter 4.) *sed*'s ability to filter text in a pipeline distinguishes it from other editors.

EXAMPLE A.51

```
1   sed 's/Elizabeth/Lizzy/g' file
2   sed '/Dork/d' file
3   sed -n '15,20p' file
```

EXPLANATION

1 Substitutes all occurrences of *Elizabeth* with *Lizzy* in file and displays on the terminal screen.

2 Removes all lines containing *Dork* and prints the remaining lines on the screen.

3 Prints only lines 15 through 20.

size—prints section sizes in bytes of object files

```
size [ -f ] [ -F ] [ -n ] [ -o ] [ -V ] [ -x ] filename...
```

The *size* command produces segment or section size information in bytes for each loaded section in ELF or COFF object files. *size* prints out the size of the text, data, and *bss* (uninitialized data) segments (or sections) and their total.

sleep—suspends execution for some number of seconds

```
sleep time
```

sleep suspends execution for some number of seconds. It is used to execute a command after a certain amount of time.

EXAMPLE A.52

```
1   (sleep 105; command)&
2   (In Script)
       while true
       do
            command
            sleep 60
       done
```

EXPLANATION

1. After 105 seconds, command is executed. Prompt returns immediately.
2. Enters loop, executes command, and sleeps for a minute before entering the loop again.

sort—sort and/or merge files

```
sort  [-cmus] [-t separator] [-o output-file] [-T tempdir]
   [-bdfiMnr] [+POS1 [-POS2]] [-k POS1[,POS2]][file...]
sort {--help,--version}
```

The *sort* command sorts (ASCII) lines of all the named files together and writes the result on the standard output. Comparisons are based on one or more sort keys extracted from each line of input. By default, there is one sort key, the entire input line, and ordering is lexicographic by bytes in machine collating sequence.

EXAMPLE A.53

```
1   sort filename
2   sort -u filename
3   sort -r filename
4   sort +1 -2 filename
5   sort -2n filename
6   sort -t: +2n -3 filename
7   sort -f filename
8   sort -b +1 filename
```

EXPLANATION

1. Sorts the lines alphabetically.
2. Sorts out duplicate entries.
3. Sorts in reverse.
4. Sorts starting on field 1 (fields are separated by white space and start at field 0), stopping at field 2 rather than sorting to the end of the line.
5. Sorts the third field numerically.
6. Sorts numerically starting at field 3 and stopping at field 4, with the colon designated as the field separator (*-t:*).
7. Sorts folding in upper- and lowercase letters.
8. Sorts starting at field 2, removing leading blanks.

spell—finds spelling errors

```
spell [ -blvx ] [ -d hlist ] [ -s hstop ] [ +local_file ] [ filename]...
```

spell collects words from the named filenames and looks them up in a spelling list. Words that neither occur among nor are derivable from (by applying certain inflections, prefixes, and/or suffixes) words in the spelling list are printed on the standard output. If no filenames are named, words are collected from the standard input.

split—splits a file into pieces

```
split [ -n ] [ filename [ name ] ]
```

split reads *filename* and writes it in *n* line pieces into a set of output files. The first output file is named with *aa* appended, and so on lexicographically, up to *zz* (a maximum of 676 files). The maximum length of *name* is 2 characters less than the maximum filename length allowed by the filesystem. See *statvfs(2)*. If no output name is given, *x* is used as the default (output files will be called *xaa*, *xab*, and so forth).

EXAMPLE A.54

```
1   split -500 filea
2   split -1000 fileb out
```

EXPLANATION

1 Splits *filea* into 500 line files. Files are named *xaa*, *xab*, *xac*, etc.

2 Splits *fileb* into 1000 line files named *out.aa*, *out.ab*, etc.

strings—finds any printable strings in an object or binary file

```
strings [ -a|-|--all ] [-f|--print-file-name] [ -o ] [--help]
   [ -v|--version ] [-n min-len| min-len|--bytes=min-len]
   [-t  {o,x,d} [--target=bfdname] [--radix={o,x,d}|] filename... ]
```

The *strings* command looks for ASCII strings in a binary file. A string is any sequence of four or more printing characters ending with a newline or a null character. *strings* is useful for identifying random object files and many other things.

EXAMPLE A.55

```
strings /bin/nawk | head -2
```

EXPLANATION

Prints any ASCII text in the first two lines of the binary executable */bin/nawk*.

stty—sets the options for a terminal

```
stty  [ settings...]
stty { -a, --all, -g, --help, --save, --version} ] [ -g ] [ modes ]
```

stty sets certain terminal I/O options for the device that is the current standard input; without arguments, it reports the settings of certain options.

EXAMPLE A.56

```
1  stty erase <Press backspace key> or ^h
2  stty -echo; read secretword; stty echo
3  stty -a (ATT,Linux ) or stty -everything (BSD)
```

EXPLANATION

1 Sets the backspace key to erase.

2 Turns off echoing; waits for user input; turns echoing back on.

3 Lists all possible options to *stty*.

su—become superuser or another user

```
su [-flmp] [-c command]  [-s shell] [--login] [--fast]
   [--preserve-environment] [--command=command] [--shell=shell ]
   [ - ] [--help] [--version] [ username [ arg ... ] ]
```

su allows one to become another user without logging off. The default username is *root* (superuser). To use *su*, the appropriate password must be supplied (unless the invoker is already root). If the password is correct, *su* creates a new shell process that has the real and effective user ID, group IDs, and supplementary group list set to those of the specified username. The new shell will be the shell specified in the shell field of username's password file entry. If no shell is specified, *sh* (Bourne shell) is used. To return to normal user ID privileges, type Ctrl-D to exit the new shell. The – option specifies a complete login.

sum—calculates a checksum for a file

sync—updates the superblock and sends changed blocks to disk

tabs—sets tab stops on a terminal

tail—displays the tail end of a file

```
tail [-c [+]N[bkm]] [-n [+]N] [--bytes=[+]N[bkm]] [--lines=[+]N]
   [--follow] [--quiet] [--silent] [--verbose] [--help] [--version]
   [file...]]
```

When a plus sign precedes the number, *tail* displays blocks, characters, or lines counting from the beginning of the file. If a hyphen precedes the number, *tail* counts from the end of the file. Unlike the UNIX version, which uses a fixed size buffer, the Gnu version can output any amount of data.

EXAMPLE A.57

```
1   tail +50 filex
2   tail -20 filex
3   tail filex
```

EXPLANATION

1 Displays contents of *filex* starting at line 50.

2 Displays the last 20 lines of *filex*.

3 Displays the last 10 lines of *filex*.

talk—allows you to talk to another user

```
talk username [ ttyname ]
```

talk is a visual communications program which copies lines from your terminal to that of another user.

EXAMPLE A.58

```
talk joe@cowboys
```

EXPLANATION

Opens a request to talk to user *joe* on a machine called *cowboys*.

tar—stores and retrieves files from an archive file, normally a tape device

```
tar [ - ] c|r|t|u|x [ bBefFhilmopvwX0134778 ] [ tarfile ]
   [ blocksize ] [ exclude-file ] [ -I include-file ]
   filename1 filename2 … -C directory filenameN …
```

tar is an archiving program designed to store and extract files from an archive file, called a tarfile. The tarfile can be either a regular UNIX/Linux file or a tape device. Often used for saving files on a floppy disk. (See Linux man page for a complete list of options.)

EXAMPLE A.59

```
1   tar cvf /dev/diskette .
2   tar tvf /dev/fd0
3   tar xvf /dev/fd0
4   tar cvf mytarfile .
```

EXPLANATION

1. Sends all files under the present working directory (the dot directory) to a floppy on tape device */dev/diskette*, and prints the files as they are being sent.
2. Displays the table of contents of what is on the floppy at tape device */dev/fd0.*
3. Extracts files from the floppy on the device.
4. Creates a *tar* archive file called *myfile* consisting of everything from the current working directory down the tree

tee—replicates the standard output

```
tee [ -ai ] [--append] [--ignore-interrupts] [--help] [--version]
   [ filename... ]
```

tee copies the standard input to the standard output and one or more files, as in *ls|tee outfile.* Output goes to screen and to *outfile*.

EXAMPLE A.60

```
date | tee nowfile
```

EXPLANATION

The output of the *date* command is displayed on the screen and also stored in *nowfile*.

telnet—communicates with a remote host

EXAMPLE A.61

```
telnet necom.com
```

EXPLANATION

Opens a session with the remote host *necom.com*

test—evaluates an expression and check file types

```
test [expr]
test [--help, --version]
```

test evaluates an expression and returns an exit status indicating that the expression is either true (zero) or false (not zero). Now a built-in version is used primarily by Bourne, Bash, and Korn shells for string, numeric, and file testing. The C/TC shells have most of the tests built-in. (See the Bash built-in commands.)

EXAMPLE A.62

```
1   test 5 gt 6
2   echo $? (Bourne and Korn Shells)
    (Output is 1, meaning the result of the test is not true.)
```

EXPLANATION

1 The *test* command performs an integer test to see if 5 is greater than 6.

2 The *$?* variable contains the exit status of the last command. If a nonzero status is reported, the test results are not true; if the return status is zero, the test result is true.

time—displays a summary of time used by this shell and its children

timex—times a command; reports process data and system activity

```
timex [ -o ] [ -p [ -fhkmrt ] ] [ -s ] command
```

The given command is executed; the elapsed time, user time, and system time spent in execution are reported in seconds. Optionally, process accounting data for the command and all its children can be listed or summarized. Total system activity during the execution interval can also be reported. The output of *timex* is written on standard error.

top—displays top CPU processes

```
top [-] [d delay] [q] [c] [S] [s] [i]
```

top provides an ongoing look at the CPU's activity in real time and a listing of the most CPU-intensive tasks.

touch—updates access time and/or modification time of a file

```
touch [ -amc ] [ mmddhhmm [ yy ] ] filename...
```

touch causes the access and modification times of each argument to be updated. The filename is created if it does not exist. If no time is specified the current time is used.

EXAMPLE A.63

```
touch a b c
```

EXPLANATION

Three files, *a*, *b*, and *c* are created. If any of them already exist, the modification timestamp on the files is updated.

tput—initializes a terminal or queries the terminfo database

```
tput [ -Ttype ] capname [ parms...]
tput [ -Ttype ] init
tput [ -Ttype ] reset
tput [ -Ttype ] longname
tput -S <<
```

tput uses the *terminfo* database to make the values of terminal-dependent capabilities and information available to the shell, to initialize or reset the terminal, or return the long name of the requested terminal type.

EXAMPLE A.64

```
1   tput longname
2   bold=`tput smso`
    unbold=`tput rmso`
    echo "${bold}Enter your id: ${offbold}\c"
```

EXPLANATION

1 Displays a long name for the terminal from the *terminfo* database.

2 Sets the shell variable *bold* to turn on the highlighting of displayed text. Then sets the shell variable, *unbold*, to return to normal text display. The line *Enter your id:* is highlighted in black with white letters. Further text is displayed normally.

tr—translates characters

```
tr [ -cds ] [ string1 [ string2 ] ]
```

tr copies the standard input to the standard output with substitution or deletion of selected characters. Input characters found in string1 are mapped into the corresponding characters of string2. The forward slash can be used with an octal digit to represent the ASCII code. When string2 (with any repetitions of characters) contains fewer characters than string1, characters in string1 with no corresponding character in string2 are not translated. Octal values for characters may be used when preceded with a backslash:

```
\11     Tab
\12     New line
\042    Single quote
\047    Double quote
```

EXAMPLE A.65

```
tr 'A' 'B' < filex
tr '[A-Z]' '[a-z]' < filex
tr -d ' ' < filex
tr -s '\11' '\11' < filex
tr -s ':' ' ' < filex
tr '\047' '\042'
```

EXPLANATION

1 Translates *As* to *Bs* in *filex.*

2 Translates all uppercase letters to lowercase letters.

3 Deletes all spaces from *filex.*

4 Replaces (squeezes) multiple tabs with single tabs in *filex.*

5 Squeezes multiple colons into single spaces in *filex.*

6 Translates double quotes to single quotes in text coming from standard input.

true—provides successful exit status

true does nothing, successfully, meaning that it always returns a zero exit status, indicating success. Used in Bourne and Korn shell programs as a command to start an infinite loop.

```
while true
do
   command
done
```

tsort—topological sort

```
/usr/ccs/bin/tsort [filename]
```

The *tsort* command produces, on the standard output, a totally ordered list of items consistent with a partial ordering of items mentioned in the input filename. If no filename is specified, the standard input is understood. The input consists of pairs of items (nonempty strings) separated by blanks. Pairs of different items indicate ordering. Pairs of identical items indicate presence, but not ordering.

tty—gets the name of the terminal

```
tty [ -l ] [ -s ]
```

tty prints the pathname of the user's terminal.

umask—sets file-creation mode mask for permissions

```
umask [ ooo ]
```

The user file-creation mode mask is set to *000*. The three octal digits refer to read/write/execute permissions for owner, group, and other, respectively. The value of each specified digit is subtracted from the corresponding "digit" specified by the system for the creation of a file. For example, *umask 022* removes write permission for group and other (files normally created with mode 777 become mode 755; files created with mode 666 become mode 644). If *000* is omitted, the current value of the mask is printed. *umask* is recognized and executed by the shell.

EXAMPLE A.66

```
1   umask
2   umask 027
```

EXPLANATION

1. Displays the current file permission mask.
2. The directory permissions, 777, minus the *umask* 027 is 750. The file permissions, 666, minus the *umask* 027 is 640. When created, directories and files will be assigned the permissions created by *umask*.

uname—prints name of current machine

```
uname [ -amnprsv ]
uname [ -S system_name ]
```

uname prints information about the current system on the standard output. If no options are specified, *uname* prints the current operating system's name. The options print selected information returned by *uname(2)* and/or *sysinfo(2)*.

EXAMPLE A.67

```
1   uname -n
2   uname -a
```

EXPLANATION

1 Prints the name of the host machine.

2 Prints the machine hardware name, network nodename, operating system release number, the operating system name, and the operating system version—same as *-m*, *-n*, *-r*, *-s*, and *-v*.

uncompress—restores files to their original state after they have been compressed using the compress command

```
uncompress [ -cFv ] [ file . . . ]
```

EXAMPLE A.68

```
uncompress file.Z
```

EXPLANATION

Restore *file.Z* back to its original state; i.e., what it was before being compressed.

uniq—reports on duplicate lines in a file

```
uniq [ [ -u ] [ -d ] [ -c ] [ +n ] [ -n ] ] [ input [ output ] ]
```

uniq reads the input file, comparing adjacent lines. In the normal case, the second and succeeding copies of repeated lines are removed; the remainder is written on the output file. Input and output should always be different.

EXAMPLE A.69

```
1  uniq file1 file2
2  uniq -d -2 file3
```

EXPLANATION

1 Removes duplicate adjacent lines from *file1* and puts output in *file2*.

2 Displays the duplicate lines where the duplicate starts at third field.

units—converts quantities expressed in standard scales to other scales

units converts quantities expressed in various standard scales to their equivalents in other scales. It works interactively in this fashion:

```
You have: inch
You want: cm
   * 2.540000e+00
   / 3.937008e-01
```

unpack—expands files created by pack

unpack expands files created by pack. For each filename specified in the command, a search is made for a file called *name.z* (or just *name*, if *name* ends in *.z*). If this file appears to be a packed file, it is replaced by its expanded version. The new file has the *.z* suffix stripped from its name, and has the same access modes, access and modification dates, and owner as those of the packed file.

uucp—copies files to another system, UNIX-to-UNIX system copy

```
uucp [ -c | -C ] [ -d | -f ] [ -ggrade ] [ -j ] [ -m ] [ -nuser ]
   [ -r ] [ -sfile ] [ -xdebug_level ] source-file destination-file
```

uucp copies files named by the source-file arguments to the destination-file argument.

uuencode—uuencode, uudecode—encodes a binary file into ASCII text in order to send it through e-mail, or convert it back into its original form

```
uuencode [ source-file ] file-label
uudecode [ encoded-file ]
```

uuencode converts a binary file into an ASCII-encoded representation that can be sent using mail. The label argument specifies the output filename to use when decoding. If no file is given, *stdin* is encoded. *uudecode* reads an encoded file, strips off any leading and trailing lines added by mailer programs, and recreates the original binary data with the filename and the mode and owner specified in the header. The encoded file is an ordinary ASCII text file; it can be edited by any text editor. But it is best only to change the mode or file-label in the header to avoid corrupting the decoded binary.

EXAMPLE A.70

```
1  uuencode mybinfile decodedname > uumybinfile.tosend
2  uudecode uumybinfile.tosend
```

EXPLANATION

1. The first argument, *mybinfile,* is the existing file to be encoded. The second argument is the name to be used for the *uudecoded* file, after mailing the file, and *uumybinfile.tosend* is the file that is sent through the mail.
2. This decodes the *uuencoded* file and creates a filename which was given as the second argument to *uuencode.*

wc—counts lines, words, and characters

```
wc [ -lwc ] [ filename ... ]
```

wc counts lines, words, and characters in a file or in the standard input if no filename is given. A word is a string of characters delimited by a space, tab, or new line.

EXAMPLE A.71

```
1  wc filex
2  who | wc -l
3  wc -l filex
```

EXPLANATION

1. Prints the number of lines, words, and characters in *filex.*
2. The output of the *who* command is piped to *wc,* displaying the number of lines counted.
3. Prints the number of lines in *filex.*

what—extracts SCCS version information from a file by printing information found after the @(#) pattern

```
what [ -s] filename
```

what searches each filename for the occurrence of the pattern, @(#), that the SCCS *get* command substitutes for the *%Z%* keyword, and prints what follows up to a " >, newline, \, or null character.

which (UCB)—locates a command and displays its pathname or alias

```
which [ filename ]
```

which takes a list of names and looks for the files that would be executed had the names been given as commands. Each argument is expanded if it is aliased, and searched for along the user's path. Both aliases and path are taken from the user's *.cshrc* file. Only *.cshrc* file is used.

whereis (UCB)—locates the binary, source, and manual page files for a command

```
whereis [ -bmsu ] [ -BMS directory ... -f ] filename
```

who—displays who is logged on the system

write—writes a message to another user

```
write username [ ttyname ]
```

write copies lines from your terminal to another user's terminal.

xargs—constructs an argument list(s) and executes a command

```
xargs [ flags ] [ command [ initial-arguments ] ]
```

xargs allows you to transfer contents of files into a command line and dynamically build command lines. (See Linux man page for a long listing of all options.)

EXAMPLE A.72

```
1  ls $1 | xargs -i -t mv $1/{} $2/{}
2  ls | xargs -p -l rm -rf
3  find . -type f | xargs grep -l "ellie"
```

EXPLANATION

1 Moves all files from directory $1 to directory $2, and echos each *mv* command just before executing.

2 Prompts (*-p*) the user with files that are to be removed, one at a time, and removes each one.

3 The *find* command starts searching the current directory for plain files, and sends the list of files to *xargs*. *xargs* transfers the filenames to *grep*. Every file that contains the pattern *ellie* is printed. This is a way to make *grep* recursive.

zcat—uncompresses a compressed file to standard output. Same as *uncompress –c*

```
zcat [ file . . . ]
```

EXAMPLE A.73

```
zcat book.doc.Z | more
```

EXPLANATION

Uncompresses *book.doc.Z* and pipes the output to *more*.

zipinfo—lists detailed information about a ZIP archive

```
zipinfo [-12smlvhMtTz] file[.zip][file(s)...] [-x xfile(s) ...]
```

zipinfo lists technical information about files in a ZIP archive, most commonly found on MS-DOS systems. Such information includes file access permissions, encryption status, type of compression, version and operating system or file system of compressing program, and the like. The default behavior (with no options) is to list single-line entries for each file in the archive, with header and trailer lines providing summary information for the entire archive. The format is a cross between UNIX *ls -l* and *unzip -v* output.

zmore—file perusal filter for crt viewing of compressed text

```
zmore [ name ...  ]
```

zmore is a filter which allows examination of compressed or plain text files one screenful at a time on a soft-copy terminal. *zmore* works on files compressed with compress, pack, or gzip,and also on uncompressed files. If a file does not exist, *zmore* looks for a file of the same name with the addition of a .gz, .z, or .Z suffix. Behaves like the *more* command, printing a screenful at a time.

APPENDIX

B

COMPARISON OF THE SHELLS

Feature	*Bourne*	*C*	*TC*	*Korn*	*Bash*
Aliases	no	yes	yes	yes	yes
Advanced Pattern Matching	no	no	no	yes	yes
Command Line Editing	no	no	yes	yes*	yes
Directory Stacks (*pushd, popd*)	no	yes	yes	no	yes
Filename Completion	no	yes*	yes	yes	yes
Functions	yes	no	no	yes	yes
History	no	yes	yes	yes	yes
Job Control	no	yes	yes	yes	yes
Key Binding	no	no	yes	no	yes
Prompt Formatting	no	no	yes	no	yes
Spelling Correction	no	no	yes*	no	yes†

* not a default setting; must be set by the user

† *cdspell* is a *shopt* option set to correct minor spelling errors in directory names when *cd* is used.

B.1 *tcsh* versus *csh*

The TC shell (*tcsh*) is an enhanced version of the Berkeley C shell (*csh*). Listed here are some of the new features.

- An enhanced history mechanism
- A built-in command line editor (*emacs* or *vi*) for editing the command line
- Formatting the prompts
- A spelling correction facility and special prompts for spelling correction and looping
- Enhanced and programmed word completion for completing commands, filenames, variables, usernames, etc.
- Ability to create and modify key bindings
- Automatic, periodic, and timed events (scheduled events, special aliases, automatic logout, terminal locking, etc.)
- New built-in commands (*hup*, *ls -F*, *newgrp*, *printenv*, *which*, *where*, etc.
- New built-in variables (*gid*, *loginsh*, *oid*, *shlvl*, *tty*, *uid*, *version*, *HOST*, *REMOTEHOST*, *VENDOR*, *OSTYPE*, *MACHTYPE*)
- Read-only variables
- Better bug reporting facility

B.2 *bash* versus *sh*

The Bourne Again (*bash*) shell has the following features not found in the traditional Bourne shell (*sh*).

1. Formatting the prompts
2. History (*csh* style)
3. Aliases
4. A built-in command line editor (emacs or vi) for editing the command line
5. Directory manipulation with *pushd* and *popd*
6. *Csh* type job control to stop or run jobs in the background, bring them to the foreground, etc. with command such as *bg, fg,* Ctrl-Z, etc.
7. Tilde, brace, and parameter expansion
8. Key bindings to customize key sequences
9. Advanced pattern matching
10. Arrays
11. The select loop (from Korn shell)
12. Many new built-in commands

Feature	csh/tcsh	Bourne	Bash	Korn
Variables:				
Assigning values to local variables	`set x = 5`	`x=5`	`x=5`	`x=5`
Assigning variable attributes			`declare` *or* `typeset`	`typeset`
Assigning values to environment variables	`setenv NAME Bob`	`NAME='Bob'; export NAME`	`export NAME='Bob'`	`export NAME='Bob'`
Read-Only Variables:				

Accessing variables	`echo $NAME`
	`set var = net`
	`echo ${var}work`
	network
		`echo $NAME`
		`var=net`
		`echo ${var}work`
		network
			`echo $NAME`
			`var=net`
			`echo ${var}work`
			network
				`echo $NAME or print $NAME`
				`var=net`
				`print ${var}work`
				network

Number of characters	`echo $%var` (*tcsh* only)	N/A	`${#var}`	`${#var}`
Special Variables:				
PID of the process	`$$`	`$$`	`$$`	`$$`
Exit status	`$status, $?`	`$?`	`$?`	`$?`
Last background job	`$!` (*tcsh* only)	`$!`	`$!`	`$!`
Arrays:				

Assigning arrays	`set x = ( a b c )`	N/A	`y[0]='a'; y[2]='b';`
			`y[2]='c'`
			`fruit=(apples pears`
			`peaches plums)`
				`y[0]='a'; y[1]='b';`
				`y[2]='c'`
				`set -A fruit apples`
				`pears plums`

Accessing array elements	`echo $x[1] $x[2]`	N/A	`echo ${y[0]} ${y[1]}`	`print ${y[0]} ${y[1]}`
All elements	`echo $x or $x[*]`	N/A	`echo ${y[*]}, ${fruit[0]}`	`print ${y[*]}, ${fruit[0]}`
No. of elements	`echo $#x`	N/A	`echo $y{#[*]}`	`print ${#y[*]}`

Feature	*csh/tcsh*	*Bourne*	*Bash*	*Korn*
Command Substitution:				
Assigning output of command to variable	set d = \`date\`	d=\`date\`	d=$(date) or d=\`date\`	d=$(date) or d=\`date\`
Accessing values	echo $d echo $d[1], $d[2], ... echo $#d	echo $d	echo $d	print $d
Command Line Arguments (Positional Parameters):				
Accessing	$argv[1], $argv[2] or $1, $2 ...	$1, $2 ... $9	$1, $2, ... ${10} ...	$1, $2, ... ${10} ...
Setting positional parameters	N/A	set a b c set \`date\` echo $1 $2 ...	set a b c set \`date\` *or* set $(date) echo $1 $2 ...	set a b c set \`date\` *or* set $(date) print $1 $2 ...
No. of command line arguments	$#argv $# (*tcsh*)	$#	$#	$#
No. of characters in $arg[number]	$%1, $%2, (*tcsh*)	N/A	N/A	N/A
Metacharacters for Filename Expansion:				
Matches for:				
Single character	?	?	?	?
Zero or more characters	*	*	*	*
One character from a set	[abc]	[abc]	[abc]	[abc]
One character from a range of characters in a set	[a-c]	[a-c]	[a-c]	[a-c]

<table>
<tr><th>Feature</th><th>csh/tcsh</th><th>Bourne</th><th>Bash</th><th>Korn</th></tr>
<tr><td colspan="5">Metacharacters for Filename Expansion (continued):</td></tr>
<tr><td>One character not in the set</td><td><code>N/A</code> (csh)
<code>[^abc]</code> (tcsh)</td><td><code>[!abc]</code></td><td><code>[!abc]</code></td><td><code>[!abc]</code></td></tr>
<tr><td>? matches zero or one occurrences of any pattern in the parentheses. The vertical bar represents an OR condition; e.g., either 2 or 9. Matches abc21, abc91, or abc1. (see Table 8.16 for a complete list)</td><td></td><td></td><td><code>abc?(2|9)1</code></td><td><code>abc?(2|9)1</code></td></tr>
<tr><td>Filenames not matching a pattern</td><td><code>^pattern</code> (tcsh)</td><td></td><td></td><td></td></tr>
<tr><td colspan="5">I/O Redirection and Pipes:</td></tr>
<tr><td>Command output redirected to a file</td><td><code>cmd > file</code></td><td><code>cmd > file</code></td><td><code>cmd > file</code></td><td><code>cmd > file</code></td></tr>
<tr><td>Command output redirected and appended to a file</td><td><code>cmd >> file</code></td><td><code>cmd >> file</code></td><td><code>cmd >> file</code></td><td><code>cmd >> file</code></td></tr>
<tr><td>Command input redirected from a file</td><td><code>cmd < file</code></td><td><code>cmd < file</code></td><td><code>cmd < file</code></td><td><code>cmd < file</code></td></tr>
<tr><td>Command errors redirected to a file</td><td><code>(cmd > /dev/tty)>&errors</code></td><td><code>cmd 2>errors</code></td><td><code>cmd 2> file</code></td><td><code>cmd 2> errors</code></td></tr>
<tr><td>Output and errors redirected to a file</td><td><code>cmd >& file</code></td><td><code>cmd > file 2>&1</code></td><td><code>cmd >& file</code> or <code>cmd &> file</code>
or <code>cmd > file 2>&1</code></td><td><code>cmd > file 2>&1</code></td></tr>
</table>

<table>
<tr><th>Feature</th><th>csh/tcsh</th><th>Bourne</th><th>Bash</th><th>Korn</th></tr>
<tr><td colspan="5">I/O Redirection and Pipes (continued):</td></tr>
<tr><td>Assign output and ignore noclobber</td><td><code>cmd >| file</code></td><td>N/A</td><td><code>cmd >| file</code></td><td><code>cmd >| file</code></td></tr>
<tr><td>Here Document</td><td><code>cmd << EOF</code>
<code>input</code>
<code>EOF</code></td><td><code>cmd << EOF</code>
<code>input</code>
<code>EOF</code></td><td><code>cmd << EOF</code>
<code>input</code>
<code>EOF</code></td><td><code>cmd << EOF</code>
<code>input</code>
<code>EOF</code></td></tr>
<tr><td>Pipe output of one command to input of another command</td><td><code>cmd | cmd</code></td><td><code>cmd | cmd</code></td><td><code>cmd | cmd</code></td><td><code>cmd | cmd</code></td></tr>
<tr><td>Pipe output and error to a command</td><td><code>cmd |& cmd</code></td><td>N/A</td><td>N/A</td><td>(See coprocesses)</td></tr>
<tr><td>Coprocess</td><td>N/A</td><td>N/A</td><td>N/A</td><td><code>command |&</code></td></tr>
<tr><td>Conditional statement</td><td><code>cmd && cmd</code>
<code>cmd || cmd</code></td><td><code>cmd && cmd</code>
<code>cmd || cmd</code></td><td><code>cmd && cmd</code>
<code>cmd || cmd</code></td><td><code>cmd && cmd</code>
<code>cmd || cmd</code></td></tr>
<tr><td colspan="5">Reading from the Keyboard:</td></tr>
<tr><td>Read a line of input and store into variable(s)</td><td><code>set var = $<</code>
<code>set var = 'line'</code></td><td><code>read var</code>
<code>read var1 var2...</code></td><td><code>read var</code>
<code>read var1 var2...</code>
<code>read</code>
<code>read -p prompt</code>
<code>read -a arrayname</code></td><td><code>read var</code>
<code>read var1 var2...</code>
<code>read</code>
<code>read var?"Enter value"</code></td></tr>
<tr><td colspan="5">Arithmetic:</td></tr>
<tr><td>Perform calculation</td><td><code>@ var = 5 + 1</code></td><td><code>var=`expr 5 + 1`</code></td><td><code>((var = 5 + 1))</code>
<code>let var=5+1</code></td><td><code>((var = 5 + 1))</code>
<code>let var=5+1</code></td></tr>
</table>

Feature	*csh/tcsh*	*Bourne*	*Bash*	*Korn*
Tilde Expansion:				
Represent home directory of user	`~username`	N/A	`~username`	`~username`
Represent home directory	`~`	N/A	`~`	`~`
Represent present working directory	N/A	N/A	`~+`	`~+`
Represent previous working directory	N/A	N/A	`~-`	`~-`
Aliases:				
Create an alias	`alias m more`	N/A	`alias m=more`	`alias m=more`
List aliases	`alias`		`alias, alias -p`	`alias, alias -t`
Remove an alias	`unalias m`	N/A	`unalias m`	`unalias m`
History:				
Set history	`set history = 25`	N/A	`automatic or HISTSIZE=25`	`automatic or HISTSIZE=25`
Display numbered history list	`history`		`history, fc -l`	`history, fc -l`
Display portion of list selected by number	`history 5`		`history 5`	`history 5 10` `history -5`

Reexecute a command	`!! (last command)`
	`!5 (5th command)`
	`!v (last command starting with v)`
			`!! (last command)`
			`!5 (5th command)`
			`!v (last command starting with v)`
				`r (last command)`
				`r5 (5th command)`
				`r v (last command starting with v)`

Set interactive editor	N/A(csh) `bindkey -v` *or* `bindkey -e` (*tcsh*)	N/A	`set -o vi` `set -o emacs`	`set -o vi` `set -o emacs`

Feature	*csh/tcsh*	*Bourne*	*Bash*	*Korn*
Signals:				
Command	`onintr`	`trap`	`trap`	`trap`
Initialization Files:				
Executed at login	`.login`	`.profile`	`.bash_profile`	`.profile`
Executed every time the shell is invoked	`.cshrc`	N/A	`BASH_ENV=.bashrc` (or other filename) (bash 2.x) `ENV=.bashrc`	`ENV=.kshrc` (or other filename)
Functions:				
Define a function	N/A	`fun() { commands; }`	`function fun { commands; }`	`function fun { commands; }`
Call a function	N/A	`fun` `fun param1 param2 ...`	`fun` `fun param1 param2 ...`	`fun` `fun param1 param2 ...`
Programming Constructs:				

if conditional	`if ( expression ) then`
	`    commands`
	`endif`
	
	`if { ( command ) } then`
	`    commands`
	`endif`
		`if [ expression ]`
		`then`
		`    commands`
		`fi`
		
		`if command`
		`then`
		`    commands`
		`fi`
			`if [[ string expression ]]`
			`then`
			`    commands`
			`fi`
			
			`if (( numeric expression ))`
			`then`
			`    commands`
			`fi`
				`if [[ string expression ]]`
				`then`
				`    commands`
				`fi`
				
				`if (( numeric expression ))`
				`then`
				`    commands`
				`fi`

if/else conditional	`if ( expression ) then`
	`    commands`
	`else`
	`    commands`
	`endif`
		`if command`
		`then`
		`    commands`
		`else`
		`    ...`
		`fi`
			`if command`
			`then`
			`    commands`
			`else`
			`    ...`
			`fi`
				`if command`
				`then`
				`    commands`
				`else`
				`    ...`
				`fi`

Feature	*csh/tcsh*	*Bourne*	*Bash*	*Korn*
Programming Constructs (continued):				

if/else/elseif conditional	if (expression) then
	    commands
	else if (expression) then
	    commands
	else
	    commands
	endif
		if command
		then
		    commands
		elif command
		then
		    commands
		else
		    commands
		fi
			if command
			then
			    commands
			elif command
			then
			    commands
			else
			    commands
			fi
				if command
				then
				    commands
				elif command
				then
				    commands
				else
				    commands
				fi

goto	goto label ... label:	N/A	N/A	N/A

switch and *case*	switch ("$value")
	case pattern1:
	    commands
	    breaksw
	case pattern2:
	    commands
	    breaksw
	default:
	    commands
	    breaksw
	endsw
		case "$value" in
		pattern1) commands
		    ;;
		pattern2) commands
		    ;;
		*) commands
		    ;;
		esac
			case "$value" in
			pattern1) commands
			    ;;
			pattern2) commands
			    ;;
			*) commands
			    ;;
			esac
				case "$value" in
				pattern1) commands
				    ;;
				pattern2) commands
				    ;;
				*) commands
				    ;;
				esac

Loops:				

while loops	while (expression)
	    commands
	end
		while command
		do
		    command
		done
			while command
			do
			    command
			done
				while command
				do
				    commands
				done

for/foreach	foreach var (wordlist)
	    commands
	end
		for var in wordlist
		do
		    commands
		done
			for var in wordlist
			do
			    commands
			done
				for var in wordlist
				do
				    commands
				done

Feature	*csh/tcsh*	*Bourne*	*Bash*	*Korn*
Loops (continued):				

until		`until command`
		`do`
		`    commands`
		`done`
			`until command`
			`do`
			`    commands`
			`done`
				`until command`
				`do`
				`    commands`
				`done`

repeat	`repeat 3 "echo hello"` *`hello`* *`hello`* *`hello`*	N/A	N/A	N/A

select	N/A	N/A	`PS3="Please select a menu item"`
			`select var in wordlist`
			`do`
			`    commands`
			`done`
				`PS3="Please select a menu item"`
				`select var in wordlist`
				`do`
				`    commands`
				`done`

APPENDIX C

STEPS FOR USING QUOTING CORRECTLY

Backslash (see Table C.1):

1. Precedes a character and escapes that character
2. Same as putting single quotes around one character

Single Quotes (see Table C.1):

1. Must be matched
2. Protects all metacharacters from interpretation except:
   a. Itself
   b. Exclamation (`!`) point (*csh*)
   c. Backslash (`\`)

Double Quotes (see Table C.2):

1. Must be matched.
2. Protects all metacharacters from interpretation except:
   a. Itself
   b. Exclamation (`!`) point (*bash, csh*)
   c. `$` used for variable substitution
   d. Backquotes (`` ` ` ``) for command substitution

Table C.1 Using Single Quotes and Backslashes

C Shell	*Bourne Shell*	*Korn Shell*	*TC Shell*	*Bash Shell*
echo '$><%^&*'	echo '$*&!><?'	echo '$*&!><?'	echo '$><%^&*'	echo '$*&!><?'
echo 'I need $5.00\!'	echo 'I need $5.00!'	echo 'I need $5.00!'	echo 'I need $5.00!'	echo 'I need $5.00!'
echo 'She cried, "Help"'	echo 'She cried, "Help"'	echo 'She cried, "Help"'	echo 'She cried, "Help"'	echo 'She cried, "Help"'
echo '\\\\' \\\\	echo '\\\\' \\	print '\\\\' \\	echo '\\\\' \\	echo '\\\\'

Table C.2 Using Double Quotes

C Shell	*Bourne Shell*	*Korn Shell*	*TC Shell*	*Bash Shell*
echo "Hello $LOGNAME\!"	echo "Hello $LOGNAME!"	print "Hello $LOGNAME!"	echo "Hello $LOGNAME!"	echo "Hello $LOGNAME"\!
echo "I don't care"	echo "I don't care"	print "I don't care"	echo "I don't care"	echo "I don't care"
echo "The date is `date`"	echo "The date is `date`"	print "The date is $(date)"	echo "The date is `date`"	echo "The date is $(date)"
echo "\\\\" \\\\	echo "\\\\" \	print "\\\\" \	echo "\\\\" \\	echo "\\\\" \\

Combining Quotes:

The Goal:

The end result is to be able to embed the shell variable in the *awk* command line and have the shell expand the variable without interfering with *awk*'s field designators, $1 and $2.

Setting the Shell Variable:

```
name="Jacob Savage"      (sh, bash and ksh)
set name = "Jacob Savage"   (csh and tsh)
```

The Line from the Datafile:

```
Jacob Savage:408-298-7732:934 La Barbara Dr. , San Jose, CA:02/27/78:500000
```

The *awk* Command Line:

```
awk -F: '$1 ~ /^'"$name"'/{print $2}'  datafile
(Output)
408-298-7732
```

Step 1:

Test your knowledge of the Linux command at the command line before plugging in any shell variables.

```
awk -F: '$1 ~ /^Jacob Savage/{print $2}' filename
(Output)
408-298-7732
```

Step 2:

Plug in the shell variable without changing anything else. Leave all quotes as they were.

```
awk -F: '$1 ~ /^$name/{print $2}' datafile
```

Starting at the left-hand side of the *awk* command leave the first quote as is, and right before the shell dollar sign in *$name*, place another single quote. Now the first quote is matched and all text within these two quotes is protected from shell interference. The variable is exposed. Now put another single quote right after the *e* in *$name*. This starts another matched set of single quotes ending after *awk*'s closing curly brace. Everything within this set of quotes is also protected from shell interpretation.

```
awk -F: '$1 ~ /^'$name'/{print $2}' datafile
```

Step 3:

Enclose the shell variable in a set of double quotes. This allows the variable to be expanded but the value of the variable will be treated as a single string if it contains white space. The white space must be protected so that the command line is parsed properly.

```
awk -F: '$1 ~ /^'"$name"'/{print $2}'  datafile
```

Count the number of quotes. There should be an even number of single quotes and an even number of double quotes.

Example:

```
oldname="Ellie Main"
newname="Eleanor Quigley"
```

1. Make sure the command works.

```
awk -F: '/^Ellie Main/{$1="Eleanor Quigley"; print $0}' datafile
```

2. Plug in the variables.

```
awk -F: '/^$oldname/{$1="$newname"; print $0}' datafile
```

3. Play the quoting game. Starting at the first single quote at the left, move across the line until you come to the variable, *$oldname*, and place another single quote just before the dollar sign. Put another single quote right after the last letter in the variable name.

   Now move to the right and place another single quote right before the dollar sign in *$newname*. Put another single quote after the last character in *$newname*.

```
awk -F: '/^'$oldname'/{$1="'$newname'"; print $0}' datafile
```

4. Count the number of single quotes. If the number of single quotes is an even number, each quote has a matching quote. If not, you have forgotten a step.
5. Enclose each of the shell variables in double quotes. The double quotes are placed snugly around the shell variable.

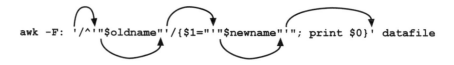

```
awk -F: '/^'"$oldname"'/{$1="'"$newname"'"; print $0}' datafile
```

INDEX

B

C

D

P

Q

T

U

V

ABOUT THE AUTHOR

Ellie Quigley is the author of *Perl by Example*, *UNIX Shells by Example*, and now *Linux Shells by Example*. She is also the creator of the world's number one interactive Perl course, *Perl Multimedia Cyber Classroom*. A leading instructor and trainer, her courses in Perl and UNIX shell programming at the University of California Santa Cruz Extension Program and at Sun Microsystems have become legendary throughout Silicon Valley.